Why are we here?

We are here because there is no refuge, finally, from ourselves. Until a person confronts himself in the eyes and hearts of others, he is running. Until he suffers them to share his secrets, he has no safety from them. Afraid to be known, he can know neither himself nor any other. He will be alone.

Where else but in our common ground can we find such a mirror? Here, at last, a person can appear clearly to himself, not as the giant of his dreams nor the dwarf of his fears, but as a man, part of a whole, with a share in its purpose.

In this ground, we can each take root and grow, not alone anymore as in death, but alive to ourselves and to others. - Richard Beauvais

From the author

This book almost didn't get written. The reason it almost didn't get written is, after getting about two-thirds of the way through my story, I thought, *who gives a shit about another addict's story? There are celebrities who have written stories about their addictions and their recovery. When you've read one story about addiction and recovery, you've read them all—right?* Wrong!

I read Mackenzie Phillips and Kristen Johnston's stories, then Shaka Senghor's *Writing My Wrongs*. After reading them, it occurred to me that my story is completely different from theirs, or anyone else's for that matter.

Each story brings its own twists and turns, characters, wisdom, insight—and yes—even endings. So instead of saying that I hope *No Refuge, Finally, From Ourselves* will bring you some completely different things to consider about addiction, recovery, and life—I will say that I know it will. Enjoy the journey. I did.

Note: Some of the names have been changed to protect the innocent...me! I had to change some people's names and some other identifying information to avoid frivolous lawsuits from paranoid nut jobs (you know who you are). One of those names is Amelia Hamilton. The name is fictitious, but our relationship, as described in this book, was not. In America we're supposed to have First Amendment rights of "free speech." Right. That's only if you can afford a really good team of lawyers!

Because of the nature of my story, I felt compelled to protect the anonymity of some, while others gave me permission to use their names. Then, there were those I chose to identify as a tribute to their memory because I know they would have wanted me to.

And now, for the cliché line that you could have seen coming from a mile away... *"If this book helps just one person and their family recover from the horrors of addiction then it was worth writing."* Nonsense! I want this book to help thousands of addicts and their loved ones. That's why I wrote the book. Hell, if I wanted to help an addict or two, I could do that without writing a 520-page book!

That brings me to my last point. The book is long, but you'll notice I didn't say it's "too long" because it's not. It is what it is. I felt I removed anything that was unnecessary and trimmed all the fat I could without compromising my story. The feedback I got from volunteers who read it was basically: "People who read it won't have a problem with the length, as long as it's good. Your book is good." The only people who had an issue with the length were publishers who make less money when there are more pages to print. I didn't write this for anyone's approval or to make anyone money, including myself.

They say that addiction is "cunning, baffling, and powerful." My goal is to put addiction and recovery under a microscope of sorts and make addiction less "cunning, baffling, and powerful" and make what it takes to recover, more understandable and attainable, especially for those of the hardcore, hopeless variety. My simple message to you is: We can *all* recover!

To view images related to this book, go to the website:

www.stevenfiorito.com

*** **WARNING:** *This book contains graphic descriptions of drug use. If you're in recovery, I suggest you have access to support if you experience being triggered.*

List of current/future books/materials

A Calming Daily Refuge: Daily Meditations for Handling Anger, and Emotions, and Enhancing Personal Growth

Heroin and Opioid Addiction and Recovery for Teens and Young Adults

Denial: The 7 Deadly Sins (Film)

Why Willpower Doesn't Work (Film)

Coming soon...

Junkie Wisdom: Daily Meditations in the Raw!

Rejecting Big Pharma: The Case for Drug-Free Recovery

Public UN-safety: The Bad "Marriage" Between Drug Treatment and the Criminal Justice System in Illinois

****

Dedicated to:
Paul, Warren, Billy, Leo, Ricky, Mark, Franko, Cal, Brian, Danny, John, David, and all addicts who still suffer.

There is hope.

Published by Street Light Publishing and Production Company Ltd.

Copyright © 2025
All rights reserved
Printed in United States of America

No part of this book may be reproduced without written permission.

ISBN: 978-0-9903546-4-2

No Refuge, Finally, From Ourselves: One Addict's Story

Steven Fiorito

CONTENTS

PART I: HITTING BOTTOM

LA 1984... 1

PART-II: A LIFE IN THIRTY SECONDS

It all started with Salerno Butter Cookies...4
JFK...7
It was a really big shoe...8
Pleasant Valley Sunday...9
First "highs" ...12
My secret...16
Juvenile delinquency takes hold... 18
198 miles to Colby Wisconsin - home of Colby Cheese...21
Junior High School - Preparing for the future?... 26

PART-III: THE FINAL INGREDIENTS IN THE RECIPE FOR DISASTER

Every journey begins with the first (mis)step...30
The 1970's (not to be confused with the 1960's) ... 31
Intro to the drug culture 101... 33
In search of the next high...36
Slipping deeper into the abyss... 38
Courage or chemically induced insanity? ...40
Tripping our way through school... 41
Da Dago Feast... 43
Choosing drugs over love... 44
You haven't got the stomach for it!...47
Discovering the greatest music ever made...48
The shack...49
High times at West Leyden "High" School...50
The early signs of trouble...57
Permit me to drive your car 58
In love: The first cut is the deepest...59
Home, home again...60
I fought the law... well, you know the rest...61
Under Gerhardt's wing (and thumb) ...62
A shot...and a save! ...64
Swing and a miss...65
Expanding my horizons (musical and otherwise) ...66
Dazed and confused...70
Frampton comes alive as Steve and Carol slowly die...72
Curse of the Grateful Dead...74
The eleventh-grade syndrome...75
Arsenic and Old Lace...77
School's out...79
Rejection: Adding insult to injury...81
Another crushing blow...82
Systems for Solar Control - A microcosm of race relations...84
The early casualties...89
Living is easy with eyes closed...91
No doze at Oddo's...93
I got those same old blues again...95
Falling in love again...97
West Side story...101
Franko: New friend or partner in crime? ...103
Trying to live a double life (and failing miserably) ...105
Mother's Day 1978...108
The first cracks in the wall appear...111
Pinball Wizard...113
Withdrawal leads to discovery...115
Unhappy Halloween...116
The frozen bean burrito that changed my life...117
Suburban Drugstore Cowboys...122
Hillbilly mafia...124
Trouble ahead, trouble behind...126
Noah's Ark was a Ford...130
Going to California with an achin' in my heart...131
The eye of the hurricane...134
Home of The Mother Lode...137
The gathering storm clouds on the horizon... 150
The second wall of the hurricane...152
The Steve & Laura merry-go-round...155
Desperado, why don't you come to your senses? ...157
Second attempt at a geographical cure...160
All it takes is a spark to start a fire...164
Is there a doctor in the house?... 164
S & L Quality Painting Services...167
"The best laid plans of mice and men" ...170
"Balloons" for Jessica's birthday... 171
The house of cards begins to collapse...172
The elaborate schemes of a desperate dope fiend...173

PART-IV: HITTING BOTTOM - CONTINUED

Thirty-one seconds and beyond...179
Escape from LA... 185
Committed to? ... 189
The charade must end...190
Stumbling blindly through The Maze...192

PART-V: HELP, A SHORT WORD BUT A LONG PROPOSITION

Kedzie House: Divine intervention...199
God sends the right man for the job... 213
Pain and discomfort: The best medicine...213
A new way to start the day—sober...216
My first shot of independence... 218
Ex-drug users look to future... 219
No refuge, finally, from ourselves... 220
The push I needed out of my comfort zone...224
Sober celebration and music deliver hope, not dope...229

Growth comes from unexpected places...231
Cook County Hospital: Where addicts go for gunshot wounds and more...235
Peeling a layer of the onion called denial...236
Happier Halloween...242
Birthday surprise... 245
When you come to the end of your rope tie a knot and hang on...249
Much more than a New Year's Eve dance...253
Is God a Bears fan?...257
Another name gets added to the guilt list... 260
Changes in values become changes in behavior...262
Once chased by police, becomes chief of police...264
A buried memory surfaces...268
Second Phase: Preparing to re-join the real world... 270
Fake it till you (don't) make it...277
Ain't but one way out...288
Johnny the drapery man puts his foot down...289
Groundhog Day (Same shit, different day) ...295
Third time's a charm...297
Eileen...297
Open Report...300
Silence is golden...303
Return to Kedzie House...306
A.A. stands for attitude adjustment...309
Fear begins to take its toll...313
Timely visit from an old friend...314
Déjà vu...316
Taking a stand for who I was becoming...316
Early gifts from God...319
Progress not perfection...321
Moving forward with flaws in tow...322
Second attempt at employment clean and sober...324
Doc—The right thing for the right reasons...327
A call from Oprah...328
A blast from the past...329
Drapery Cleaning Service...330

PART-VI: MIRACLES HAPPEN

Recognizing the signs from God...333
Moving on with an attitude of gratitude...335
Progress: A small bed to an even smaller couch...338
There but for the grace of God go I...340
Real recovery: The gift that keeps on giving...342
My second big test...347
A curse is lifted as creative energy is restored...349
You've got to give it away to keep it...350
Sticking my toe in the relationship pool...352
Katherine...355
A new path leads to new opportunities... 356
"We hate to see you go" ...359
There's nothing constant but change...359
Becoming a member of SA ...361
Lifeline...364
Freddy... 367
Little Miss Muffet... 368
Not so Sweetest Day...369
Navigating the ups and downs of early recovery...374
Christmas Fiorito style returns... 377
Amelia...379
The plot thickens...383
The comedy that made her cry...384
Meet the Hamiltons...386
Exploring the Chicago entertainment landscape ...389
Pressing onward while others around me fell...391
Lifeline to recovery or bedsheet to addiction? ...392
Northwest Youth Outreach ...396
Baptism by fire...397
Return to The Big Apple ...402
Chief Seattle's Reply...403
Hello old friend...406
Love letters from New York...410
Culture Shock! ...411
Go and tell your father about me...416
Visit from a *Ghost* brings about a spiritual epiphany... 420
Music takes center stage...422
Creative explosion at Big Stinky...427
The Fort...432
Sober in the recording studio...435
A different kind of men in blue...438
Wicker Park's groundbreaking Indie Rock scene...442
Sex...445
Northwest Youth Over-reach...447
"A three-hour tour, a three-hour tour" ...449
Urbis Orbis...450
It was the serenity prayer...452
Café Bustelo...455
Interventions...458
A poinsettia at Christmas time...464
1991-A Christmas story...466
No longer ruled by fear... 468
Promises kept...470
My addiction and recovery in a "nutshell" ...472
LA 1984 revisited...484

EPILOGUE... 488

Book Club Discussion Questions

Part I: Hitting Bottom

Breathe, breathe in the air. Don't be afraid to care.
— Pink Floyd

LA 1984

It was yet another beautiful, sunny Southern California day. The kind of day I had grown absolutely sick and tired of. I remember thinking, *can someone turn the damn sun off? Can we get a thunderstorm? Something?!* Actually, I don't remember what the weather was like that day, and I couldn't have cared less. All the things that fascinated me when I first came out West from the Chicago suburbs just a few short years before had all become meaningless. The warm sunshine, the smell of the ocean, the cactus flowers, the palm trees. I took them all for granted by then and paid them no attention. They became like background music that you're not really listening to. My reason for coming back to California at the urging of my older brother was to escape from my drug addiction. The plan had failed miserably.

It was November 29th, 1984. I had just turned 24 years old, and I was at the peak of my IV drug addiction. My drug of choice had again, recently switched from heroin back to cocaine. Big mistake. Heroin and other opiates became my maintenance drugs—drugs I did just to keep from getting sick and to feel semi-normal. Somehow, I had once again fallen madly in love with the rush from shooting cocaine—emphasis on the word *madly*. People think "heroin is the worst," but real dope fiends know that it's not. Shooting cocaine is worse, second only to crystal meth.

They say some addicts are just as addicted to the lifestyle as they are to the drugs. Not me. I would have had my drugs delivered like a pizza if I could have and never left the house. I just wanted that feeling.

The icy rush of cocaine would travel through the vein in my left arm, into my throat, my mouth, and then to my nose, creating the numbing blend of mint and rubbing alcohol-like taste and smell. Then, it would travel across the back of my skull in a wave of intense euphoria. My ears would ring followed by the rapid heartbeat, uncontrollable grinding of the jaw from side to side, leading to profuse sweating. Sometimes, I'd have to pace back and forth in a sort of "euphoric panic attack" so that my heart wouldn't give out.

The rush would last for about a minute or two, followed by intense euphoria that would last another several minutes, before the inevitable descent into physical discomfort, paranoia, hallucination, delusion, and ironically, intense craving to do more. This state of dysphoria could last for hours or until I did my next hit. I had to wait the right amount of time, or the next hit would be wasted and greatly reduce the euphoric effect. In the meantime, I would be pacing back and forth, peeking out windows, and thinking someone was watching me and either going to arrest me—or kill me.

With cocaine, the more you do, the more you want. You can never get enough, and stopping usually requires running out of coke and money, but even that wasn't necessarily going to get you released from the pit bull-like jaws of cocaine craving. When it happens, you start looking around for anything that's not nailed down that you can sell or barter to get more.

On your hands and knees, every crumb on the ground starts to look like a rock of cocaine. You can feel yourself deteriorating physically, mentally, and spiritually. Anyone who is still in your life sees it, but like with a horrific accident, they want to turn their heads away, but morbid curiosity has them spellbound as they witness the tragedy. While it's happening, you don't see it, and if you do, you don't care. You just want that next hit.

My current partner in crime was Todd. We had been on a cocaine binge for several days. We had run out of heroin the day before and shot our last balloon (often used for packaging heroin) from Jaime's connect. Jaime was the young, Mexican sidekick of our "friend" —and sometimes coke dealer—Tony.

While on our binge, Tony stopped by. He and my girlfriend, the mother of my kids, Laura, were apparently doing a lot of talking. Something that normally would have concerned me but that I barely noticed due to being totally preoccupied with cocaine.

Todd left in search of some opiates to deal with the impending withdrawal we would soon experience. That's when Laura pulled me into the bedroom. She informed me that because of her good luck with cards and dice Tony wanted to take her with him to Vegas. I, of course, said no. We argued, and she tried to assure me that it was only about the money, but I knew better. I had the "dope fiend sixth sense." I knew when game was being run on me, and it was. I started suspecting that Tony had a thing for Laura, but the steady flow of coke kept the truth at bay, and I chose to deny it.

"Fuck no! Absolutely not!" And I meant it. The trouble is, when you're an addict, it doesn't matter if you mean it or not; it doesn't mean you can stick to it. I loved Laura, but unfortunately, when you have a severe drug addiction, love only goes so far, and then addiction takes over.

Opiate withdrawal was kicking in, and combined with the crash from the coke I became as vulnerable as an addict gets. Laura made a second attempt and made me an offer I couldn't refuse—an eight-ball (eighth of an ounce) of coke. I caved almost immediately.

Tony didn't have the coke with him and had to go get it. In the meantime, he gave me approximately a half gram in folded blue paper from his "private stash." After Tony left, I went into the bathroom and reached for my works (drug shooting equipment), which I kept on top of the medicine cabinet. The fit (syringe) was on its last legs. Luckily, I had my backup. Todd and I nicknamed it the "harpoon." I stole it from a doctor's office. It was a big needle with a huge barrel about eight times the size of the diabetic 100-cc syringes we usually used.

I opened the odd-colored blue package Tony gave me and dumped about half of it into the spoon. I added the water from a cup on the sink. I stirred it up and watched the white powder become the desired clear liquid. I added the small ball of cotton through which I drew the hit into the syringe. I flicked the barrel a few times with my middle finger and pushed the plunger up in the barrel until the tiniest drop appeared at the tip of the needle. I tied myself off with my belt, putting the end of it in my mouth to keep it tight, and stuck the needle into the vein on my left forearm. I drew the plunger back and watched the blood cloud shoot into the clear liquid in the barrel.

I started to push the plunger in to inject the hit, but I immediately noticed something wasn't right, so I stopped. I noticed an unusual taste accompanied by my ears ringing. I pulled the needle from my arm, whispering, "Wait a minute." I set the syringe down on the sink, two-thirds of a bloody hit still in it. I got up and came out of the bathroom hoping to walk it off, as I sometimes had to do, but it wasn't working. The ringing in my ears became deafening, and I knew I was in trouble.

Laura was sitting on the couch, and my daughters Jessica and Melissa were playing on the other side of the room. I felt the cold, clammy sweat on my forehead. I took the deepest breaths I could, trying to get as much oxygen as possible out of each breath. I looked at Laura with what I'm sure was panic on my suddenly pale face. Her eyes got wide with shock. I made it to the dining room but I could no longer fight the tidal wave that was sweeping me away, and I surrendered to the feeling that was overtaking me.

Suddenly, I lost control of my body, and I was on the floor, flopping like a fish that had just been pulled out of the water. My ears were ringing so loudly that my hearing went out completely. I had zero control over my muscles. Oddly, I felt completely conscious and aware of my surroundings. As I flopped uncontrollably across the floor, I could see the legs of the dining room table and chairs as I flopped into the kitchen.

When I got to the kitchen, I was shocked to discover a figure sitting crouched between the stove and refrigerator where Laura and I always kept our garbage can. I noticed that this person (or whatever it was) was dressed in black from head to toe. I saw that it had three very distinct parts to its dress—a shroud, a hood, and a veil—that covered its entire face. I should mention that there was nothing ethereal about this being. I saw it as clearly as I would see you if you were sitting across from me right now. Again, nothing ethereal or ghostly about what I saw. I checked in with myself again and again as this unfolded. I felt completely conscious. Immediately upon looking into its eyes, I could feel my heart beating irregularly. Then, it stopped beating. I felt the blood withdrawing from my brain and my limbs, and I began to lose consciousness. At that moment, I was overwhelmed by fear because I knew I was dying. It's hard to explain, but you just know. I knew I would not make it out of this. My eyes were locked with this being's eyes, and I couldn't look away. Seconds seemed like eternity as time seemed to stand still.

There have been many reports over the years that when people have an NDE (near-death experience), their entire life often flashes before their eyes. This was certainly true for me. In the next 30 seconds, my entire life would replay in front of me. How did I get on this path? I was a good kid from a loving family. How did I come to this tragic end?

Part II: A Life In Thirty Seconds

It all started with Salerno Butter Cookies

I think it all started at the age of three when I became addicted to Salerno Butter Cookies. I quickly progressed from having one cookie on one finger and nibbling it into a ring of sorts, to having a cookie on every finger. My earliest memory was of my older brother Paul and sister Susan trying to appease my demand for the buttery treats by attempting to pass off saltines (crackers) for the cookies. I wasn't having it, and I remember throwing them down in my crib, which I was confined to, and aggressively stomping on them while having a temper tantrum. Being the chubby infant that I was (I wonder if all those cookies had anything to do with it?), this resulted in the bottom of the crib breaking and the mattress crashing to the floor. I was unharmed, and in fact, this wound up facilitating my escape from said confinement. I remember screaming through the large 1940s-style keyhole in our bathroom, "Maaaaaaaaaaaa! They're trying to give me crackers instead of cookies!"

I don't remember what the outcome was, but my tendency to *want what I want, when I wanted it,* had reared its ugly head early in my life. I was, after all, the baby of the family.

Or maybe it was the behavior problems I had early on at school. I recall getting sent out in the hall in kindergarten.

Then again, maybe the story actually begins as many people's stories do—before I was born. My grandfather on my father's side, Vincenzo Fiorito, came over from Italy at the turn of the century to the Port of New Orleans. He bought some land and made a lot of money on some crops but wound up losing it all when he chased my grandmother, Francesca Scandiffio, to New York City.

They wound up staying and raising their children in much less affluent circumstances there. My father was born in 1911 and was the middle child of 10. They moved to Chicago in 1919 when my father was eight years old.

Grandpa Fiorito was a musician and made harmonicas and squeezeboxes by hand for the kids. He also made his own wine. This, combined with exaggerations of his drinking, led me to believe that he was probably an alcoholic. Did I inherit more than just my grandpa's musical abilities?

Most stories I hear more recently imply that he probably wasn't. According to a reputable family source, he did not drink a half gallon of wine daily as I once heard, and as far as making his own wine, many who came from Italy did. This was out of necessity due to a lack of funds. My uncles Lawrence and Carl were drinkers. Were they alcoholic? No one will admit it, but my cousin Eddie once called my uncle Lawrence a drunk, ironically, while he was becoming one himself. More on that later.

Meanwhile, my grandfather on my mother's side did drink daily. Was he an alcoholic? The term wouldn't even exist for decades.

I was born on the West Side of Chicago in November of 1959 at Loretto Hospital. I was the youngest of four children born to John and Albina (Albie) Fiorito. The siblings I was raised with in order were Susan, Paul, and Mary Jo. My father had three kids from his previous marriage.

He owned North Oak Drapery Service, a small drapery cleaning and custom drapery business. We referred to it as "the shop."

Right before my arrival, it was time to move out of the city and into the suburbs. Back then, there was a smattering of houses sprinkled between farms, woods, and open space. They bought the house that they could afford in unincorporated Leyden Township, at 3103 Lee Street. The house was small, drafty, and covered with ugly dark green shingles. There was a creek just behind our backyard that separated us from railroad tracks and factories, specifically BF Goodrich, where they manufactured tires. The creek was clean and filled with fish and wildlife.

My backyard was a virtual fruit salad consisting of blackberry bushes, pear, apple, and crabapple trees. We were only a few miles from O'Hare International Airport. We were constantly interrupted, on the phone or in person, by the roar of planes taking off and landing. It became part of life, and we got used to it.

I can recall playing on dirt mounds made by a bulldozer. Seemingly out of nowhere, those mounds became rows of single-family, ranch-style homes with flat, square patches of grass in front, walkways, paved driveways, detached garages, and chain-link fences. Soon, a neighborhood would form. A big, happy family…well, more like a big dysfunctional family.

Mine was a warm, loving—and, of course, loud—Italian American family. My father, however, was a soft-spoken man who kept his feelings and thoughts to himself. Everybody loved "Johnny, the drapery man." He only got really mad about five times that I can recall, but when he did, you better run because years of bottled-up feelings were going to be unleashed. Not much of a drinker either. He would have a drink (Seagram's VO and 7 Up) when stopping at a bar occasionally and rarely drank at home.

Albie was even less inclined to drink; I can recall her drinking only on holidays. I'll never forget her singing at the top of her lungs while washing her nylons in the bathtub. I remember feeling good to hear my mom so happy. I think she puked and passed out later. The story was told for decades.

Susan was the oldest and was the babysitter and caretaker of her siblings, especially when our mother had to go to work to make ends meet. Sue was my second mom.

My older brother Paul was the rebel, though they say he was the sweetest little boy you'd ever want to meet. He took a turn for the worse when he was accused of slicing a boy's leather jacket with a razor blade at school. When he denied it, my mother didn't believe him. This seemed to be the turning point for Paul. I've heard it can be very damaging when you're not believed by your parents. Yeah, right. Anyway, he did it, as he later confessed to me. Paul and his friends were "greasers" with their hair slicked back, dark sunglasses, leather jackets, and cigarette packs rolled in their T-shirt sleeves. He constantly argued with our mother while "Johnny the drapery man" sat and read the newspaper, not saying a word.

Paul was an artist and had an unbelievable talent for drawing with ink or pencil. He and his best friend Frank and our cousin Larry (eldest son of Uncle Lawrence) created their own comic strips, which were quite good. Everybody hoped that, eventually, he would do something with the talent that earned him a scholarship to The Art Institute of Chicago. He never followed up. He couldn't get out of bed in the morning, a trait that many Fiorito men would be cursed with, including me. My father once told me that my Uncle Lawrence "could have been rich if he could only have gotten out of bed."

Next is Mary Jo. Being the middle child, she had typical "lost child" characteristics of being in her own world, as far back as I can remember. I had the "privilege" of doing dishes with her after dinner every night, so I was the target for whatever mean streak she had in her. Luckily, it wasn't much, although it would come out at times, likely due to the amount of time we were forced to spend together. She inherited me to look after when my eldest sister Susan left home. Mary Jo also had a very loving and caring side, of which I reaped many of the benefits. She read me stories, made me laugh, and sparked my imagination. She was artistic, creative, fun, and energetic as a child—just a little weird.

I should also mention that around age 11, I inherited an "adopted sister" named Barbara. Barb was really Mary Jo's best friend, who came from an abusive home, so in true Albie and John fashion, they took her in, just like they had with a few of Susan's friends, to rescue them from bad situations. She became like a sister to me. This situation would have an interesting twist in a few years.

Speaking of weird, finally, there's me. My mother said when she saw me for the first time, she knew I was special. Indeed, I was. I guess that could be interpreted in many ways.

I believe being "the baby" of the family had some negative effects on me though. It meant I was overprotected, underestimated, not allowed to, given too much attention, not given enough responsibility, heard "yes" when I needed to hear no, and heard "no" when I needed to hear yes. You get the picture—right? I was also very sensitive, comfortable, and safe in my warm, little Italian American family cocoon.

JFK

I can recall the first time my little "cocoon" was jostled. In fact, it was cracked wide open. It was my fourth birthday party, and all my relatives were coming over, as most did every Sunday. My birthday party was on Sunday, November 24th. I figured out by then that there would be cake and presents. Upon their arrival, I got a kiss and a "happy birthday" from everyone. Aunt Dorothy would pinch my cheek and call me a "cute little son of a bitch!" Uncle Frank, (or "Uncle friggin' Starvy," as he was called) was my dad's brother.

The mood was typical, with a lot of loud talking, but somehow, something felt different. I could sense that something was off, but at age four, I didn't know what. With the TV in the background, nothing seemed terribly unusual.

Then, suddenly, everything changed. The air was sucked out of the room, and the once-warm friendly chatterbox TV became a cold blue light. It was November 24, 1963. My family was somehow able to hide most of the feelings of loss after John F. Kennedy's assassination just two days earlier, but now, right in front of their eyes, on live TV, the man accused of killing the President of the United States, Lee Harvey Oswald, was gunned down by Jack Ruby. My family stood spellbound in front of the TV, and some began to cry. Suddenly, my birthday party became a funeral. My joy turned into fear and upset. I didn't understand what happened, but I understood on some level that maybe the world wasn't such a warm and loving place after all.

Many people believe that the world changed that weekend in 1963. I know mine did. My "pink cloud" of safety and security was blown away with JFK's brains. Fortunately, there was something on the horizon that would help us all heal from this terrible tragedy.

It was a really big "shoe"

I was very fortunate to grow up in a house with a wide, diverse selection of musical tastes. My father played the mandolin, and he and his brothers Lawrence and Sal fancied themselves a musical trio. They started their musical endeavors during the Great Depression in the 1930s, going around to speakeasies and singing barbershop-style harmonies.

Now, they were old wannabes who would get together occasionally and attempt a few tunes. Uncle Lawrence was on the organ. With Sal on guitar and my dad on mandolin, they would pluck and plink around with songs from the artists of their day.

If the kids were too loud or disruptive, my Uncle Sal would stop playing and yell, "Hey! I'm gonna send you back!" The adults would all laugh as we were all traumatized, wondering where "back" was. You just knew it was a horrible place that you didn't want to go.

Music was an important part of our lives. Everyone in my family seemed to have different musical tastes. I grew up hearing a musical smorgasbord that ranged from Frank Sinatra, Dean Martin, Judy Garland, and Jerry Vail to Elvis Presley, The Lettermen, The Righteous Brothers, The Beatles, The Kinks, The Animals, and The Rolling Stones. Later, Mary Jo would add The Monkees, James Taylor, Gordon Lightfoot, and Cat Stevens to the mix.

Paul was a wannabe musician too and plinked around on the guitar, but his real passion was the drums. Unfortunately, we couldn't afford them. So, he constructed a drum kit out of boxes, old pots, and coffee cans.

I was into Mary Poppins's... "Supercalifragilisticexpialidocious!"

There was always music in our house, but one night stands out and is forever etched in my psyche. It was February 9th, a Sunday evening in 1964. At 7 p.m., everyone got around the TV. My sisters were right in front of it. The fish of a man host stepped in front of the camera and mumbled his usual shtick: "Ladies and gentlemen, tonight we have a really big *shoe* for you." Then the audience started screaming, and my sisters started screaming as Ed Sullivan announced, "Ladies and gentlemen, THE BEATLES!"

> *Close your eyes and I'll kiss you, tomorrow I'll miss you,*
> *Remember, I'll always be true*
> *And then while I'm away, I'll write home every day*
> *And I'll send all my lovin' to you...*

I'd heard their music on the radio. I even had little figurines of them on my birthday cake, and now, there they were, playing that music on TV right in front of me, with Ringo's head bobbing from side-to-side! I was mesmerized as they sang and played their music and the emotion they evoked in my sisters and the people in the audience. It was electrifying! Even at five years old, I got it, and it planted a seed in me that has never gone away.

The Beatles' music was powerful medicine, resurrecting a nation that died a kind of moral death in November of 1963. Their music gave everyone a sense of fun, excitement, and, most importantly, hope for a brighter future.

Pleasant Valley Sunday

When I think about my childhood, I get a warm feeling inside. Reminiscing brings a smile to my face. The song "Pleasant Valley Sunday" by the band The Monkees comes to mind. The Monkees were my generation's version of The Beatles. Their Monday night TV show is part of my psyche, and the music (mostly written by great songwriters like Neil Diamond, Carole King, Tommy Boyce, and Bobby Hart) was an undeniable part of the soundtrack of my life…

Your local rock group down the street
Is trying hard to learn this song
To serenade the weekend squire
Just came out to mow his lawn.

Another Pleasant Valley Sunday
Charcoal burnin' everywhere
Rows of houses that are all the same
And no one seems to care…

As I close my eyes, I get a sense of how good the world seemed in those days. The two words that best describe my childhood are *rich* (though not financially) and *safe*. I took for granted the fact that I always felt safe and protected until later in my life when I discovered just how important it was, and how fortunate I was, to have had that sense of safety. As far as being rich goes, I had an abundance of great experiences that would ultimately outweigh any negatives there were.

I was a creative and imaginative child. Due to the age difference between my siblings and me, I had to play by myself a lot. I had my own version of *The Tonight Show with Johnny Carson*, where I'd interview various guests (mannequin heads with wigs on them at my mother's hairdressing table) in front of a live audience (the mirror) or cross-dress and wear wigs in an attempt to fool my siblings into believing I was a new girl on the block when they came home from school. Thank God my family didn't overreact and rush me off for sex change surgery! It was all about pretending (acting) and had nothing to do with gender.

My creativity was partly due to a lack of financing for my toy collection. At times, I got the neighborhood kid's hand-me-down bikes, toys, and even clothes, but for the most part, I had to use my imagination to create toys. There were wrapping paper-roll bazookas, vacuum-cleaner attachment swords, and bath towel capes.

At age three, I broke my collarbone, leaping off the couch with one of those capes while playing Superman. Apparently, I thought the towel cape would give me the ability to take flight. It didn't work. Cheap towels?

The neighborhood consisted of about a dozen kids who were close in age and lived within a three-block radius. Most of us came together for the annual neighborhood snowball fights, touch football games, and other sports. Many of our sports-related get-togethers were overseen and run by an older boy next door named Bruce.

Bruce truly was the "boy next door" in every sense, including actually living next door to us. He was short and stocky with an athletic build—a natural coach who loved taking the neighborhood kids under his wing. Sometimes, after our games, we would all pile into the back of his pickup truck for ice cream or a soda. I know some may be waiting for the perverted punchline, but there isn't one. In those days, there really were people like Bruce who didn't have any hidden agenda or ulterior motives. To us, he was just a nice guy who looked out for the neighborhood kids.

Each season brought its own colors and unique designs, from the fragrant lilac bushes of spring and the fresh-cut grass and charcoal grill smells of summer to the burning leaves of fall and the first freeze of the creek in winter. Winter made skates almost a permanent part of our feet. We'd skate until dark, or our feet were close to frostbitten.

Spring would bring a sudden explosion of color back into our world in the pink peony bushes, red tulips, white apple blossoms, and orange tiger lilies that bloomed annually in our yard. For the first 15 or so years of my life, the planet was still very robust and healthy. Spring also came with a strong sense that school was almost out, and summer was just around the corner. I would be completely carefree for three months! Well, except for things like cleaning my room, which I procrastinated most of the summer.

You see, under my bed was not a very good place, so I tried my best to avoid it like the plague—which quite possibly could have been lurking under there. It became a hiding place to put things to create the illusion of a clean room. Albie caught on, and I would eventually have to move the bed out and clean. Once, I found a half-eaten Pop-Tart under there. It could have been used like a Ninja death star to kill someone if I'd thrown it at them.

Then summer would finally arrive, bringing unlimited freedom and endless possibilities. From the minute school let out, we absorbed and relished every minute with nonstop activities: running, peddling, swimming, and exploring until the sun went down. We were on a mission to capture every bit of fun and adventure we possibly could, from sunup to sundown. I'd fight sleep like it was the enemy until I'd finally pass out from exhaustion.

Fall brought our favorite—Halloween. We waited all year and toiled about our costume until the day it arrived, and we'd realize that none of us could afford an elaborate costume. So, we'd dig up old clothes out of the back of our closets and dress as "bums." We would trick or treat well after. From the first day of October, we'd check the *TV Guide* daily until the film we waited for finally jump off the page—*The Wizard of Oz*!

Then, as November hit, we would rake the leaves into piles high enough to climb to the trees' upper branches and bellyflop into them. The smell of those leaves burning further etched the season into our psyches. The end of the season was always highlighted by my birthday.

Finally, winter, which never deterred our fun one bit. We simply morphed into winter kids. Winter brought picturesque landscapes, giant icicles, and abstract works of frost art on our windows. There were snowball fights, "king of the hill" contests, building snow forts and snowmen, ice skating, and hockey on the creek and ponds around the neighborhood.

At age 11, Chicago Blackhawks goalie "Tony O" Esposito was my hero. All my friends wanted to skate, stickhandle, and score goals. I was the only one that wanted to make the great saves I saw my hero Tony O make on WGN-TV. I fashioned my first set of goalie pads out of garbage-picked foam rubber, along with other makeshift equipment, and I became the neighborhood's first and only goalie.

Then, the holidays would arrive, accompanied by an indescribable spirit of joy and excitement. Particularly on Christmas Eve at our house, with numerous friends and family, who would pack the tiny house—much too small for the occasion. No one seemed to notice or care about the size of our house. The joy of the season made us oblivious to those things.

Our neighborhood was surrounded by factories and industry, which made for some unique ways to entertain ourselves. In the summers, we would spend the day behind the factories following the railroad tracks as far as we could while catching frogs, field mice, snakes, bees, and butterflies—or at our most daring—climbing the ladder onto the Franklin Park water tower.

We figured out how to create "summer toboggans" with giant pieces of cardboard by spraying the bottoms with Lemon Pledge. We'd slide down the big grass-covered hills on either side of I-294. Once we got the grass flattened, we were probably able to fly down those hills at what felt like 20 or 30 miles per hour! We were always getting cut, scraped, bruised, stung, bit, or attacked by something.

I remember running through sprinklers and playing games like Statue Maker, Kick the Can, Running Bases, Tag, and many more. If we were bored, we'd find any type of mischief we could get into, including raiding the neighbor's gardens. We walked around with saltshakers in our back pockets and feasted on tomatoes and cucumbers or fruit off fruit trees and bushes in our neighbors' backyards. We climbed every tree in the neighborhood, including the cherry trees in Mr. and Mrs. Butcher's yard. At summer's end, we'd get treats made of fresh honey from Mr. Butcher's beehives.

A few of my friends had pools, and we would swim until we were waterlogged, and our skin was as wrinkled as prunes. We'd spend the rest of our summer chasing down the ice cream man and "skitching" on the back of the truck as he pulled away by holding onto the back bumper with our father's old dress shoes on— "street-surfing," if you will. The man would catch us on occasion. Stopping the truck, he'd yell: "Get offa my truck, you crazy kids! You tryin' to kill yourselves?!"

The sight of my dad taking a nap on the couch on Sunday afternoons with the Chicago Cubs or White Sox game droning in the background gave me a sense that all was peaceful and right with the world.

Summer nights were spent catching lightning bugs, sneaking into neighbors' pools, or just sitting under the corner streetlight, laughing and joking under the watchful eye of a mother or two from their kitchen windows.

How lucky we were to grow up in a time before technology took over. Everything we did for entertainment and fun was real, not virtual. The only thing that was virtual was television, and that was limited mostly to times we absolutely had to be inside.

Looking back, I can't help but feel that, in some ways, my childhood was too good, too carefree. Maybe there was too much of a good thing, and there needed to be more balance instilled in me with responsibilities and discipline. But no one could have foreseen what it would lead to.

First "highs"

On the runs we would make, everyone who had some funds would pitch in. Everyone would stop talking and the radio would be shut off as the "boss" entered. They would dump all the money out in the middle of the table, small change to the right, the larger stuff to the left. The total would be announced. A list would be made of what everyone wanted, and several "mules" were selected to go on the run. Usually, at least one person went as "muscle" in case anyone messed with them on the way to score, or on the way back. They would go score while the rest of us sat and waited, nervously watching the clock.

When they finally returned with the goods, you could feel the excitement. The head mule would take out a lunch-sized brown paper bag from under their shirt, dump the stuff out, and the boss would start distributing it.

There were Hostess Snowballs, Tootsie Pops, Necco Wafers, Three Musketeers, M&Ms, Licorice Snaps, and Bazooka Joe bubble gum. Oh…I'm sorry…did you think I was talking about drugs? Nooooooo, silly! This was the summertime, almost daily run to the penny candy store. My sister Sue (the "boss") was the babysitter who ran the whole operation. That's right. We had a store in our neighborhood that sold mostly penny candy. It's only fitting that years later it would become a local bar and hangout.

Sugar is a minor mood-altering substance, and as you can see, there are a lot of correlations to harder drug use. I realized some years ago that one of my first addictions was sugar.

My mother had quite a sweet tooth of her own. One of her favorites was Fanny May Mint Meltaways. She would occasionally get a box and would surprise us and share a few with us after dinner. She soon realized that once Stevie, the little candy addict, knew they were in the house, she would be relentlessly pestered and hounded until she gave up the goods. Occasionally, she'd try a small fib, saying, "I ate them; they're all gone." I would then hunt for and usually find them. So, she started hiding them better.

One time, I was about eight years old, and I knew she had some. I looked everywhere in the house that a box of Fanny May Mint Meltaways could possibly fit with no luck. I was in her closet tearing it apart. Frustrated, I almost gave up. Then, I looked up. Up to a world that I barely knew existed. Up, to the top shelf in the closet. A place that, at my height, was not within my reach …unless…I stood on the hamper. I still couldn't quite make it, so I grabbed a box of stuff from the closet floor and put it on the hamper. Using the shelf to keep my balance, I got there.

The first thing I saw was…dust! Lots of it! I took the dusty cover off what appeared to be a hat box. Inside, what do you think I found? If you said a hat, you'd be correct, but also in that box was almost a full box of…FANNY MAY MINT MELTAWAYS! SCORE! I took two and rearranged the rest in the box. You could barely tell that any were missing. I got down and returned the box-turned-ladder back to its place on the floor and got out of there.

After consuming my spoils, I sat in my room, thinking: *Gee, that box was pretty full. I could easily get two more of those without her noticing.* So, I waited for the right moment (which usually was when Albie was talking on the phone) and made my move. I got a little greedy and grabbed three this time. I rearranged the rest of the box and thought to myself, *Still looks good,* though admittedly, not as good as it did before. So, while she was on the phone "chewing the fat" with her friend, I was chewing on some Mint Meltaways in my room.

Eventually, there were only four Mint Meltaways left in the box. At that point, I could no longer convince myself that she wouldn't notice. So instead, I said to myself the equivalent of "fuck it" (not using those words just yet). I would develop and perfect this technique in time. "Fuck it" would become my go-to ace in the hole. *I'm screwed anyway; I might as well eat the rest,* I thought.

"Addictive personality"? I had one. I was addicted to anything that I loved to do, while also becoming vehemently resistant to anything I didn't love to do. Bad combination. Later that week, she came out of the bedroom. "Steven, who ate my Fanny May?"

I replied in Vinnie Barbarino (*Welcome Back, Kotter*) style. "What…where…when?"

"I could have sworn I had a box and now I can't find them," she pressed.

Luckily, Albie got so good at hiding things that she would literally hide them from herself. Whew! I got away with one. And so, I found myself on the early road of gathering the "tools of the trade" of an addict—"Fuck it" and lying to avoid consequences.

My other early "addiction," as I've previously alluded to, was to play. Whether it was board games or outdoor stuff, once I started, it was hard for me to stop. I remember playing baseball or some other sport a few blocks from my house. We'd all hear my mother's unmistakable bellow echoing through the neighborhood: "STEEEEEVEEEEEEEEEN." One of my friends would say, "Steve, your mom's calling you." I'd respond with: "I know. Don't worry about it."

She would eventually send someone to find and retrieve me. But finding me didn't necessarily mean success. They still had to catch me. If it was Mary Jo and she caught me, she would pull my hair. On rare occasions, Albie sent my brother Paul. I usually didn't run from him but on one occasion, I did. He was apparently in no mood, so when he caught me, he dragged me over our gravel driveway all the way home from a neighbor's yard. I still have the scar on my right side to this day, a constant reminder of who I was early in my life.

Being "the baby" of the family, there were a lot of things I wasn't allowed to do, like crossing the busy street, Grand Avenue. So, in the fourth grade, when my new best buddy became Mark Mason, who lived in the forbidden zone, I had to sneak and lie to hang out at his house. We became friends because we were in the same class, but we also made each other laugh.

Laughter was one of the best feelings one could experience. It became another addiction and was right up there with eating candy and playing. I also learned that if you could make a person laugh, they would like and accept you.

We would sit in the corner of the playground at recess and recite the entire side two of the Bill Cosby album *To Russell, My Brother Whom I Slept With*, word for word. Then we progressed to improv! During our class's library time, we'd pick books to read at random. The only requirement for Mark and me was they had to have a lot of pictures. We'd find a secluded spot and read together with a slight variation from our teacher's instruction. We would make up our own words. Our imaginations conjured up terms like the "hairy toe" and "booger surprise sandwich." As you can imagine, there were a lot of stories that featured poop, farts, and tits.

If our laughter went too high above whisper level, we would get an occasional "Shhhhhhhhhhh" from the librarian, Mrs. Pikel, after which we would pretend to read until the heat was off. The characteristics of the class clown were taking shape.

In the fifth grade, my teacher was the cranky Mrs. Barca, whose bite was worse than her "Barca." She attempted to strong-arm me into good behavior, but when that didn't work, she tried the embarrassment method. I had a problem with chewing gum in class and she busted me yet again with a huge purple wad in my mouth. She paraded me from class to class with the wad on my nose. This, of course, got big laughs, so it backfired miserably on her.

By the sixth grade, I was a bona fide class clown. It was my ultimate claim to fame. The title was further cemented by being in class with…Roger Smith. I know you don't know Roger, or maybe you do? Well, you may know *a* Roger Smith. It's a common name, but doesn't the name itself ring of all-American, captain of the basketball team, straight-A student? I could not compete or ever measure up. So, I found my niche as the bad boy, class clown, who drew cool pictures. Usually cheap replicas, copied from my brother Paul.

I also had the dubious distinction of being one of three kids in the entire school whose parents gave permission to the school principal—Mr. Steven Mendik—to paddle our asses. He and my parents grew up in the same neighborhood, so they trusted him implicitly. The paddle was about 30 inches long, with four golf-ball-sized holes in it for aerodynamics. I was getting sent to the principal's office on a regular basis by then. I knew I was getting the paddle when he would call his secretary into the room and say the dreaded words "Can you come in here, Mrs. James?". Next, he'd give me his standard line: "Steven, this is going to hurt me more than it will you." I remember thinking, *hey, we're both named Steve, right? Can't I get a break?*

Then, with eyes closed tight…WHAP No. 1, then WHAP No. 2, and finally, WHAP No. 3 (the capitals are to emphasize the sound of the air going through the aerodynamic holes)! How many I got depended on the infraction. He'd then send me back to class. I remember feeling the heat radiating from my ass and wondering if it could actually melt snow like in the cartoons. Then, to rub salt in the wound, I'd return to my classmates smirking and snickering.

There I'd see the gold star system that my teacher had on huge posterboards hanging on the wall. Every day, I walked into class and staring me in the face was this huge reminder of what a loser I was. Roger Smith had 26 gold stars after his name; Steven Fiorito had...five. Great, if I were being rated as a restaurant or a hotel. I wasn't even in the same ballpark. But sadly, I was. I was a smart kid. The comments on the back of most of my report cards summed it up: *"Steven is a bright child that would do well if he'd just apply himself"* and *"Could be a good student but too much clowning around."*

Somewhere in my psyche, the words from an old song must have been deeply etched: "Be a clown. Be a clown. All the world loves a clown!" I just wanted to be loved or at least liked. Fear of rejection became an underlying driving force in my life, and luckily—or unluckily, as it turned out—I avoided it, most of the time.

At this time in my life, there were situations that magnified my fears and insecurities. When I wasn't clowning around or getting in trouble, I felt inadequate. I remember going to gym class and seeing four thick ropes that went to the ceiling. Our gym teacher, Mr. Marino, sat us in rows behind each rope and demonstrated while he explained the relay race that we were about to engage in. Each kid had to climb the rope to the ceiling, touch the ceiling, shimmy down the rope to the floor, run back, and touch the next person in line. I hid it but I was scared to death. I tried to find an excuse to get out of that line. Somehow, I did it but talk about traumatic—that's what it was for me.

Many of my friends were athletic when we were very young (some now have beer bellies down to their knees and can hardly walk). I was a late bloomer.

The recipe was starting to come together and laying the foundation for turning this sweet little boy into something I didn't want and never thought I'd be. The "bad recipe" still wasn't complete, though. There was still at least one or two key ingredients to add.

My secret

Another ingredient in the developing recipe for disaster was that I had a secret. Until I turned 12 years old, I wet the bed. Not only was this a source of secrecy and shame, but it also made my life very difficult. I had to hide it from not only my friends, but my own family, especially extended family like aunts, uncles, and cousins. Some knew and had to hide the fact that they knew from me. It meant that I couldn't sleep over at anyone's house, and if I did, I'd lay awake all night for fear that I would have an "accident." That's what my mother used to call them: accidents. I can't tell you how many times I turned down sleepovers and had to make up crazy excuses.

I'll never forget the family party at our house one Christmas Eve. My mother was explaining to my sister-in-law Rita (whom I secretly had the biggest crush on) why I couldn't have any more pop to drink. She slipped and said, "We don't want him to have an accident." I was embarrassed, but I tried to play it off like I was driving a car while responding, "Yeah, I might have an accident." Then I crashed into the wall and did a pratfall onto the floor. Rita cracked up with laughter. Whew! Saved by the class clown!

It also meant I had to get up early to clean up before school. I hated this ritual, especially in the winter in our cold, drafty, old house, getting scrubbed down with Ivory soap and a washcloth. Or if I was sick, Vick's VapoRub. To this day, I'm still not fond of either smell. Here is a little poem I wrote years later, to try to capture the Vicks experience…

Vick's

When I was a kid, and I was sick
My mom would cover my chest up with Vick's
She'd do this to me, right before bed
To loosen my chest, and clear up my head
I didn't mind because it helped me get well
It felt good going on, and I did love the smell
But there was one thing that would cause me dismay
A thing that would happen the very next day
She'd get me up early to wash the Vick's off
In our drafty, cold bathroom that gave me the cough
I'd shiver and scowl with sleep still in my eyes
The washrag grew cold, as the wintertime skies
When it finally was over, I'd think, "Why the fuss?"
Cause I still smelled like Vick's when I got on the bus

It's better to smell like Vicks than pee, I guess. My mother, God bless her, went to great lengths to help me deal with and keep my secret. She used to set an alarm for around 2 a.m. to wake me up to pee. It would work sometimes, but sometimes it didn't. She took me to the doctor, who informed her that I was just a heavy sleeper and couldn't wake myself up.

I can completely appreciate what my mother put up with now, but for the first 25 years of my life, I took everything she did for me for granted. So, an important ingredient in my bad recipe was shame. The fear of being found out and humiliated haunted me throughout my childhood.

Juvenile delinquency takes hold

At age 11 or 12, my behavior problems started to escalate. Good thing we could all run fast because it seemed we were always being chased by someone for something. Our neighbors got the brunt of our mischievous behavior. From raiding their gardens and fruit trees, to sneaking into their swimming pools or being in the line of fire of whatever sport we were playing.

Most neighbors were tolerant of our antics, but some were not. Especially if they had OCD about their lawns. Some suffered from OLD (obsessive lawn disorder). Their lawns were perfectly manicured, lush, green, and not a weed to be found anywhere. Mrs. Drexler would also delight in her flower beds every spring. And we would delight in blowing them up every 4th of July with firecrackers and cherry bombs.

The worst case of OLD was the Pegs, who had the misfortune of living smack dab in the middle of our playing zone on Lee Street. If our ball went onto their grass, we would have to run and get it before one of them got to it, or it would be confiscated, never to see the light of day again.

One day, our friend Mike Szady was showing us a contraption he learned to make. Mike was the most skilled and ingenious of us all. He's the one who came up with the idea to spray giant pieces of cardboard with Lemon Pledge to create our "summer toboggans." We were all standing in front of his house, which was directly across from the Pegs. The contraption was made of about six or eight of his dad's beer cans stuck together to form about a three-foot-long tube. The bottom can had a small hole in the side near the bottom. Did you know tennis balls fit perfectly snugly inside a beer can? Neither did I until that day. He pulled out a can of lighter fluid and squirted some into the small hole. He shook it to distribute the fluid and fumes throughout the tube, then dropped the ball in. He set the bottom on the ground and lit the small hole with a lighter while holding the tube straight up with his other hand. Suddenly, there was a loud FOOM sound, and the tennis ball flew about a half mile into the air! At that precise moment, Mrs. Peg came out of her back door to yell at us. Here comes the ball back into Earth's orbit. Can you guess where it landed? If you said on Mrs. Peg's grass you would be close; however, if you said square, dead center, in the middle of her head, you would be exactly right. THUMP! The sound literally echoed. It bounced about 20 feet in the air off the top of her head! We didn't know whether to laugh or cry. As I recall, we did both as we apologized profusely. She screamed, then continued to yell at us, now holding the top of her head. We went to our old standby—we scattered, and all ran in different directions. Oddly, nothing ever came of it that I can recall. She may have just chalked it up as a message from God for taking our balls for all those years.

It became obvious, who the more daring "troublemakers" were in our neighborhood, and we started to split off from the bigger group. We were the ones who would risk getting into trouble doing what we wanted to do. Our little subgroup would go on our Saturday morning run and hit several stores that offered a "five-finger discount." It was before the age of technology, so we were rarely caught, mostly stealing candy, so they would usually just give us a warning or ban us from the store for life. Of course, we'd be back within a few weeks.

Then there was the time we snuck under the fence of a construction company and started playing around on a crane that was parked facing a pickup truck. We noticed the keys were left in it, and we figured out how to operate the arm of the crane...well, sort of. Before we knew it, it hooked underneath the body of a pickup truck that was parked in front of it, flipping the truck over on its side. It all happened so fast. A few workers from the company came bolting out of the back door after us. We scattered and didn't get caught, but soon after, I was caught and arrested for vandalizing an abandoned tow truck in a field behind one of the factories and put on probation for criminal damage to property.

When my probation officer came for home visits, Albie would tell him that I was out of control and that she couldn't get me to do my homework or clean my room. She blamed it all on my association with my neighborhood partners in crime, Jim and Jeff Decino. The result was a "no contact order" on us, which we of course, completely ignored. My P.O. was a nice man, who was obviously displaced from his job as a shoe or insurance salesman and would try to sweet-talk me into "doing better." I would say whatever I thought he wanted to hear, but it wasn't working. Nothing was. Albie's wooden spoons had all been cracked or broken on various body parts by this time.

Where was my father through all this? Right there, reading the newspaper, not saying a word, as if nothing were happening. Two soft-boiled eggs, mixed with the smell of Old Spice aftershave, and cigarettes, was the smell of morning at our house. I think he may have thought if he ignored it, it would all just go away on its own. He was either in serious denial, or a very wise man. Only time would tell, but my mother wasn't happy with his methods.

That summer, at my mother's urging, he started taking me to work with him. Unfortunately, I would wait for the right moment to slip away and walk the 12 miles home. My legs became very strong that summer.

I would later write this song about growing up surrounded by industry, that was blue-collar Franklin Park, Illinois.

Behind The Factories

We were walkin', we were standing straight and proud
We were talkin', and I'm sure we were much too loud
And we didn't care what they thought of us, didn't care what they said,
Didn't care if we missed the bus; we'd stay home instead, stay home instead, go back to bed

We would follow the creek from my backyard
Couldn't swallow, all your schools, they were much too hard

And we didn't care what they thought of us, didn't care what they said,
Behind the factories, we were our own boss; we'd go where they fear to tread,
where they fear to tread, where they dare not tread

And we didn't care what the future would bring, never had any plans,
Our heroes wrote all the songs we would sing; they held our fate in their hands, they wrote all the plans

And now I know that these days of my lifetime can never be taken away
And though they're gone, I will never forget them and deep in my heart, they will stay
Cause I will always remember the streetlight and neighborhood games, we would play
We would follow the tracks from my backyard
Couldn't swallow all your rules, they were much too hard
And we didn't care what they thought of us, didn't care what they'd say
Behind the factories we could not foresee, the train that headed our way,
The train that rumbled our way, that runaway train

We were walkin',
We were walkin',

Follow the railroad tracks, out of the past, but look back
Follow the railroad tracks, out of the past, but look back

    To make this time even more interesting, Albie was also going through menopause, or "the change of life," as she called it. I remember her tantrums directed at my father, mostly due to his failure to intervene on my brother Paul and me. I recall the sound of spinning tires and stones flying and hitting the windows in the living room, as she backed out of our gravel driveway in anger. She even left him once or twice for a week or two, trying to get him to take action. He didn't and couldn't. Why couldn't he? I started to learn the answer to that question one day coming home from a job in the far north suburbs.

    As we were about to pass a cemetery, he suddenly pulled into the main entrance and said, "Do you want to meet your sister Alice?"

    "Who?" I replied.

    He proceeded to tell me the story of his first family. His second child died on October 13th (his birthday) shortly after being born. As if it couldn't get any worse, his wife Florence died of a blood clot while my dad was on the way to the hospital to bring her home. Unfortunately, tragedy apparently was not quite finished with him. He suddenly found himself a single father in the 1940s, raising a seven-year-old daughter. Six months later, on August 5, 1942, my sister Alice, whom I had never heard of until that day, was hit by a truck and killed. He lost his entire family within six months.

As we walked up and stood at their graves, he burst into tears. I remember being in shock and not knowing what to say or do. This was a man of few words, who never showed emotion. Car rides had long periods of silence, especially when he bailed me out of trouble and picked me up at the police station.

But at that moment, standing beside him while he let his guard down, and was actually crying, I was completely at a loss. I think I just asked him some questions about them to break my uncomfortable silence. I wouldn't connect the dots until years later, but I know this was a big reason for his disconnect from his kids—from me. Looking back, who could blame him?

As my behavior problems escalated, something had to give. I already needed a guardian angel. Maybe I had one. Maybe her name was…Alice? But here on earth, more practical angels intervened.

There was talk of me going to live with my sister Sue and brother-in-law Gary in their newly purchased house in Northlake, but Gary and his older brother Bud planned to buy a store left by their uncle Ted, who had just passed away. It was up north by Lake Superior. A town called Herbster, Wisconsin where we had vacationed. They were planning to move there and take me up for the summer to get me away from my friends, my mother, and the area for a while. Sounded cool, and it beat going to "juvey" detention, so I agreed.

198 miles to Colby Wisconsin - home of Colby Cheese

Gerhardt K. Glass was one of my role models. He was of Finnish descent, covered in freckles, with fiery red hair and a beard. He was my brother-in-law, married to my oldest sister Susan. Gary returned from Vietnam in March of 1968, after seeing approximately 10 months of heavy combat. He was hospitalized on one occasion with shrapnel wounds from a helicopter that was shelled while he was descending from it. He was one of the survivors.

I remember checking the mailbox daily, excitedly awaiting the standout, red, white, and blue striped military envelopes his letters came in. I remember reading the stories with his hand-drawn pictures of tanks and military vehicles he drove, including a flamethrower! His descriptions had a childlike, comic-book quality to them. I used to think to myself, *Cool!* He never let on about the hell that the war in Vietnam really was.

It was one of the things that I loved about Gary. He had this amazing, playful, childlike spirit. I'll never forget watching him and his friends play ice hockey at a local outdoor rink. They crashed and fell as the ice and snow chipped and sprayed from their blades. They drank beer and laughed through the whole game. Unfortunately, Gary came from a family history riddled with alcoholism. He had some other aspects of his personality that were not so fun, especially when he drank too much.

Sue and Gary conceived their first child out of wedlock, which hastened their marriage. Lil' Gary, as we called him, was born in 1967, followed by my niece Amy in 1969.

In the summer of 1971, Gary and I started on the 500-mile journey up to their new life in Herbster. The plan was to get things ready, before the arrival of my sister and the kids.

On the trip, we cracked jokes about the cultural oddities of Wisconsin. It seemed like every two miles, a sign read "200 miles to Colby, Wisconsin, Home of Colby Cheese," then "198 miles to Colby Wisconsin, Home of Colby Cheese." I looked up to and loved my brother-in-law Gary, and I feel we cemented our bond on that trip.

After driving for what seemed like all day, we neared our first destination of Cornucopia, or "Corny," as the locals call it. We pulled onto the dirt driveway that I recognized from our vacations, but the property looked different. It was unkept, cluttered, and dumpier than I remembered it, but I recognized the sauna—the main attraction of the property. To the right of the sauna was the not-so-attractive outhouse. Gary's mother, Elma owned and used to occupy the property when we came up for summer vacations but after Gary's father passed away, she remarried John Evanno, and they moved into "town."

Gary's brother Bud and his family now lived on the property. Bud (beer in hand) and wife Terry, son Butch, and daughter Gail came out to greet us and gave Gary a set of keys to the store. After a brief visit, we were off to our next stop. The store was about eight miles up Route 13, just a block from Lake Superior.

As Gary looked around and took a visual inventory of the place, something in the corner of my eye caught my attention. It was a brand-new Daisy BB gun. I asked to see it. Gary took it down and handed it to me. I asked Gary what I had to do to get it. He said, "If your sister says it's okay, you'll have to work for it."

I said, "Okay, what do you want me to do?"

Gary replied, "There's a lot to do, including cleaning this place up, but there's other things you're gonna do to earn money while you're up here."

I was ready and eager to work. I could already feel that something inside me had been awakened in the Northwoods. I wanted to grow up. It already started to occur to me that I was a "baby" for too long. Albie meant well, but was her love smothering me? Besides, I wanted that gun!

Our next stop was Gary's mother, and her new husband John's house in Herbster. Elma was a great lady. She was a schoolteacher, who taught briefly at my grade school, and in other nearby elementary schools in the Chicago suburbs. Elma's father and brother were casualties of the lake that Gordon

Lightfoot wrote about in his song "Wreck of the Edmund Fitzgerald." Like the song says, she "never gives up her dead." One of their bodies was never found.

Elma's new husband, John was a short, stocky man with dark hair and glasses of Russian and Austrian descent. He spoke with a heavy Northern Wisconsin/Canadian accent that turned words like about into "aboat." He was a good man—warm and genuine.

Elma made dinner and then dessert—fresh-picked wild strawberries on top of homemade ice cream, on cake rusks, with homemade berry sauce on top. We finished up and exchanged handshakes, hugs, and kisses, then made our way to our final destination for the night.

As dusk settled on the area, we arrived at Gary's sister Iva's and her husband Louie's. They had recently moved up there from the Chicago area. I remembered them from back home. Lou was a truly funny guy, with sharp, sarcastic wit, constantly cracking jokes and making everybody laugh. Beneath the surface, though, I sensed a dark side, that if disturbed, could result in great bodily harm. It's an Italian thing.

Morning came and we were on our way. We had some breakfast in town and drove up the road to the house that I would live in for the better part of the summer. The dirt road ran alongside Isaacson's Lumber Mill with a fence-lined pasture on the left. When the wildflowers mixed with fresh-cut lumber, the scent was like a unique perfume that was exclusive to the area.

The Isaacson's owned a lot of the land, livestock, businesses, and the log-cabin-style house that Sue and Gary rented. Across the road was a barn that was used mostly to store bales of hay. Directly behind it all, there were acres of pasture for cows and steers to graze upon, and miles of deep woods.

When we arrived, we went through each room. In the basement, Gary showed me an important switch—the switch to turn on just before dark to keep bears out! There was a three-quarter-inch steel cable that ran along the back of the property line about three feet off the ground and when that switch was flipped, it carried about 5,000 volts. If a bear came out of the woods at night, there was only going to be about 30 feet between you and it. I quickly got it etched into my brain that "we can NEVER forget to flip the switch at night."

"This is your first step toward earning that BB gun," Gary said as he pointed to the half-acre yard around the house. The grass was two and a half feet high. He handed me a sickle and a pair of gloves and said, "Get it down as far as you can, then I'll come behind you with this"—referring to a manual push mower. Somehow, we got that yard looking like a yard in the Chicago suburbs, despite our primitive tools.

My dad showed up with Sue, Lil' Gary, and Amy, just in time to see us finishing up my first day of hard work. Seeing me working for once may have given him a sense that there was hope for me after all.

The next day was painting day, and Gary taught me how to use a roller and a brush, foreshadowing a future vocation. I painted my first room ever.

For the first time, I took pride in the work I was doing. I felt good and felt more like a grownup than I ever had. It's interesting that from that day on, I never wet the bed again. Interesting.

Soon, I got my first job offer to paint the fence that enclosed Isaacson's pasture. I was going to get paid per section of the wooden fence. It ran alongside the dirt road and then around seemingly endless acres of pasture.

To add to my growing sense of responsibility, I walked the two-plus miles to work at the store a few times a week. One day, on my way to the store, I was walking past the lumberyard office, when a kid my age came out and introduced himself. "Hey, I'm Pauly Isaacson. What's your name?" I introduced myself. We hit it off right away and he showed me his Honda 50 minibike and gave me a ride to the store. He invited me to hang out with him and his friend Ricky (who had a matching Honda 50) the next day. I agreed.

When I got to the store, I did my usual duties, but this time, as I finished, Gary took the BB gun down from the display and handed it to me.

"I think you've earned this."

I felt like I just won the Heisman Trophy and the lottery at the same time!

I started out shooting at targets. Gary had a .22 rifle, and we would shoot at cans and targets in a clearing in the woods directly behind the house. He would let me shoot the .22 on occasion.

I had my first hunting experience in those woods, hunting quail. After that, I caught "hunting fever" and started hunting birds on my own. They became lifeless targets to me. I would get a thrill and feel a sense of triumph when I'd hit one and watched it fall to the ground. Most times, because of all the thick brush, I didn't see what I shot, so I would never see the result of what I was doing. I didn't know it then, but soon, it would be the last time I would senselessly take an animal's life.

I shot three birds that day. One off the phone wire, another off the roof of the barn. As usual, I didn't see either of them hit the ground after they fell, but the third bird was on the lower branch of a small tree, and I was much closer to it. I took aim and shot. Several feathers flew as it fell to the ground. This time, I was able to see the bird lying there.

I walked up to it and bent down to pick up the grey, lifeless bird. As I got closer, the first thing I noticed was its unusual light silver-grey feathers. I turned it over and saw all the intricacies of color woven into its tail feathers, and its beautiful bright yellow chest set against the silver-grey wing feathers. In the center of its chest was a single red drop of blood in the shape of a teardrop. The bird's eyes were now cold and lifeless. I stared at the bird as if I was seeing one for the first time in my life, and in some ways, I was. For the first time, I recognized the creature's unique and special beauty. From far away, it looked like just a grey blur, a moving target, but once I got close to it, I saw the reality of this creature for what it really was—a beautiful work of art, created by God to beautify and gladden the world. Then I realized that I took it away from the world, and for what? So that I could have something to do and experience the rush of the hunt and the cheap thrill of killing? I felt a knot in my gut, and I had a realization at that moment: I was not a killer.

I never shot or killed another living animal again. From that day on, I only shot at targets, bottles, and cans. I buried the bird along with my shame and guilt, but out of it, came the value; killing for survival is one thing, but killing for sport just wasn't for me.

For the remainder of the summer, I hung out with my new buddies Pauly and Ricky. We got into mischief, tried to impress a few local girls, and smoked cigarettes. The time flew as I started having fun with my new friends and before I knew it, it was time to go home.

The amount of fence that got painted by the time I went back home was embarrassing. It seems I had started to grow up a bit but then slipped right back into some old familiar behaviors. Once I started doing things I liked to do, I couldn't balance the two and sustain motivation and discipline to get it done.

I returned to the Chicago suburbs in August. My sister Susan returned in October. Apparently, I wasn't the only one who wasn't taking care of their responsibilities. Gary had started "hanging out" and drinking a bit too much and apparently forgot he had a wife and kids at home. My sister just didn't take to the Northwoods lifestyle.

Gary would follow in December after Bud ripped off the store and took everything that wasn't nailed down including the money and slipped away in the middle of the night. Lou and Iva stayed another four years but also moved back to the Chicago area. Our Northwoods adventure had come to an end. I took some good and some bad with me from the experience.

Upon my return, I learned we had to sell our house and were moving. This was because my father had not paid income taxes for years and owed the Internal Revenue Service thousands. I guess he thought if he read the paper and didn't say anything, the IRS wouldn't notice.

Junior High School - Preparing for the future?

Upon starting seventh grade, I started expanding my horizons and my social network beyond the three-block radius it had been for the first twelve years of my life. My new school was a merging of all the local grade schools. My brother and sisters all went to seventh and eighth grade at their grade schools, but I was fortunate enough to be part of the new, cutting-edge, high-tech thinking that the "powers that be" had "brainstormed" (I use the word brain loosely here) …the junior high school!

Instead of learning all your subjects from one teacher in one classroom, you would wander the halls from class to class to learn different subjects from different teachers. This would prepare us to wander the halls much better by the time we got to high school. Brilliant! It certainly did prepare me for the tremendous amount of aimless wandering of the halls I would do in high school.

In my English class, I had an annoying girl who sat directly behind me. She would mumble and whisper to herself, mainly about our teacher, Mrs. Heperly. "What a fucking bitch" was an oft repeated mantra of Pam's.

One day, I heard a loud THUD just behind my desk to my right. Pam had dropped a stack of books and folders on the floor purposely, where I could see them. I glanced down and saw in big, slightly psychotic bold letters "PAM & STEVE" scrawled on her folder. Hey, I was in no position to turn away admirers, even if they were a little bit nuts. We started talking after (and during) class, and I soon learned that there was more to this high-strung, ball of energy than met the eye. Pam was an awesome athlete who excelled at gymnastics. She was also right about Mrs. Heperly. The "fucking bitch" failed an assignment I did, right in front of the whole class, to purposely front me off.

It was an interpretation of the Don McClean song "American Pie" that was so good, she thought it was too good to be true. Okay, so I did get most of the information that I presented from my older brother and sisters, who had read an article in the newspaper about the symbolic history of Rock & Roll that was woven into the song. But I certainly didn't deserve public humiliation. Fucking bitch!

Pam wound up being my first date ever. We went to Amlings Haunted House in Melrose Park. Our romance was short-lived, mainly due to her friends—all guys (Pam was a bit of a tomboy), who would harass me every time I came to see her. Our friendship endured long after the romance fizzled.

Seventh grade was also the first place that my friend Calvin and I discovered …the hall pass. We became fast friends when he moved to the area the previous year in the middle of sixth grade. Cal was of French-Canadian descent and had dark curly hair, dark eyes, and one solid eyebrow. He was the only sixth grader who could have grown a full beard if he wanted to. We made each other laugh, so of course, we hit it off immediately.

We had several classes together, including health class, where they showed us a film that was hosted by an old, bald-headed fart with dark-rimmed glasses. He pointed at a screen with his pointer that showed a drawing of marijuana with an arrow pointing to pills, which had another arrow pointing to a syringe. The old guy proclaimed, "Marijuana will lead you to heroin." We looked at each other and covered our mouths to keep from laughing out loud. We were curious about marijuana by then, and this film was so corny and ridiculous, it was hard to take seriously. Maybe someone a bit younger than eighty-years-old telling us not to use drugs would have been more credible.

We also had math class together and we were lucky enough to have the most generous man with the hall pass in the whole school—Mr. Pucci. Once he realized that all Cal and I were going to be good for was to disrupt his class, he made good use of the hall pass by giving us one on most days, to the music room. This was apparently some kind of alternative to more serious punishment that the school came up with.

"Why don't you boys go down to the music room and learn how to play an instrument or something?" So, we did. Of course, we would stop in the bathroom along the way and have a quick smoke.

Once after class, Mr. Pucci offered us one of his Vantage non-menthols. Taking the pack from his front shirt pocket, he said, "Smoke?" Cal and I looked at each other, half shocked but also with a slight smirk, thinking *we've got the coolest teacher ever!* "No thanks, we've got our own." We headed out the door, bursting into laughter as soon as we got far enough down the hall.

While in the music room, we would pick up the guitar and try to play some chords and plink around with some riffs. Cal and I loved a lot of the same music, but he lost interest in playing pretty quickly. I, however, didn't, and I continued to play. I wasn't bad. I had a slight advantage because my father had just gotten a new Gibson ES-125 guitar, an amplifier, and a matching mandolin, as a bonus for a drapery job he did for a mobster. He was told the items "fell offa truck." After refusing the gifts several times, he was made an offer he couldn't refuse: "C'mon, Johnny. Don't be an asshole. Take the stuff!"

I came home from school one day and there "the stuff" was. I started plugging in and turning knobs right away. I found that I wasn't that into chords or song structure, and I mostly loved to play lead guitar and make up my own riffs. This got me some attention from peers, most of whom were further along than me but concentrated on playing chords. They thought it was cool that I could play my own riffs. I fell in love with the instrument, but I experienced a lot of frustration in my early days of playing. My fingers weren't doing what my brain wanted them to do.

Cal invited me over to hang out and listen to music, which, at the time, was mostly in the high-tech, new format…eight-track tapes. Cal lived with his parents, younger brother, and sister in the Crown Apartments, or "The Jungle," as we used to call it. It was the "ghetto" of the area just west of Mannheim Road—the main truck route that was lined with seedy hotels, bars, and truck stops and connected O'Hare International Airport travelers to the three major expressways.

I had a shortcut behind my house to Cal's apartment. Over the creek on the bridge that my next-door neighbor constructed, through a field and a few factories, and boom, I was there.

The first time at Cal's, I met his family. His father was in the kitchen drinking and eventually passed out at the table. His mother was in the living room listening to country music. Dan and Janice were his younger siblings.

In 1972, we would hang in Cal's room with the blacklight on. The walls were covered in blacklight posters that reflected and glorified the emerging drug culture. We'd listen to music, and of course, to Cheech and Chong, the comedy team that made all things marijuana, funny...

> "Who is it?"
> "It's me, Dave. Open up, I got the stuff!"
> ... "Dave's not here."

Cal and I used to read *The Fabulous Furry Freak Brothers* comics, one of several cartoony introductions to the drug culture. The culture started closing in on the 1970s like a swarm of locusts. The normalization of marijuana started popping up everywhere you looked. Like a cute girl winking at us from across the room, it was starting to pique our curiosity.

Surprisingly, I found out that I still had a healthy fear of marijuana when the first opportunity arose to try it. While riding our bikes on the trails behind McDonald's on Mannheim, Mark and I ran into two older friends on their bikes. One of them pulled out a joint and lit it. They passed it around. I was surprised to see Mark take a hit. He then passed it to me. I remember that healthy fear coming over me, *Man, that stuff smells strong and funny, and I don't know what that shit will do to me.* I also remember thinking; *I don't know these guys or what their bag is."* I passed, saying something like, "I can't right now." How long would I be able to fend off the growing peer pressure?

I started with a few beers that Cal stole from his dad. I hated the taste but played it off and choked about three-quarters of a beer down. I caught a buzz and felt dizzy. Beer would eventually become an acquired taste for me.

Within six months, Cal's mother would leave them, never to return. All she left was a note on the kitchen table. She apparently had had it with Roy's drinking and abandoned him and their three kids. Cal never talked about her or let on, but I know it affected him, and he was hurt and angry.

One Saturday afternoon while at Cal's, his friend Brian came over. Brian was a big, tall, blonde kid who came driving up on a minibike. The word *mini* had never seemed more appropriate because this thing looked really small with Brian's large frame riding it. It was almost comical.

Immediately, the two of them started talking about engines and how to "remove the governor," a trick that would make it go faster than it was supposed to. It was already going too fast for me and "engine speak" was like another language. Auto mechanics and I were like oil and water. Ironic, considering my oldest brother Joe, from my dad's second marriage, was a total grease monkey and a great mechanic. I had no interest and was lost when the two of them started talking about engines. This became an ongoing source of inferiority for me. Luckily, we all had other things in common. We liked girls, Rock & Roll music, we smoked cigarettes and drank beer.

Adjacent to Mannheim Junior High was a large piece of land that was part of someone's backyard. People started to congregate there in the morning about ten or fifteen minutes before school started. It quickly became apparent who was who, and what you were about when we started lighting up the cigs, and someone brought a pint of muscatel wine to pass around. All the "goody-goody" people disappeared. Gee, I wonder how much different this book would be if I had been one of them. Not much point wondering about that now.

My new circle of friends now consisted of Cal, Pam, Brian, Judy, and Danny Diaz. Danny and Pam had been friends in grade school. He was the undisputed toughest kid in the school, after a few fights he got in to prove himself. Danny was tough, but he was also a good guy with a big heart.

The only other memorable incidents from junior high were due to my defiance of authority. I got into three physical altercations with teachers. My rebellion against authority was fueled by the realization that no one could really stop me from doing whatever I wanted to do. Authority figures reacted by attempting to intervene and challenge me even more.

Once, I was out in the hall (hall pass?) having a whisper or two with a female student who was in class. I got caught by Mr. Kelly, a twerp of a man. He brought me into the class, where some words were exchanged. Because he was such a dork, we all suspected that the ties he wore were of the clip-on variety, which if proven, would cement his reputation as the dorkiest teacher in the school. As things escalated and he attempted to embarrass me, I impulsively grabbed and yanked his tie. Just as we had all suspected, it came off in my hand. After confirming the clippie-tie thing, the entire class burst into laughter. He responded with his best judo move and twisted my arm behind my back so badly that I really thought he was going to break it.

In another incident, I got thrown down the stairs of the school bleachers after disregarding several attempts to get me to stop talking during a school assembly. The gym teacher, Mr. Norgard, grabbed me by the arm and launched me from the top of the bleachers to the very bottom.

And finally, I got mouthy with one of my teachers, who was notorious for not putting up with any bullshit. As I started hanging out with tougher friends, I apparently started suffering from the delusion that it somehow made me tougher. I weighed about 115 pounds soaking wet at the time. Mr. Miradah was a tall, strong man. Some words were exchanged that eventually led to me *throwing down the gauntlet* and from my desk, I taunted, "What are you gonna do about it?"

You could see his face already getting beet red with frustration and me challenging him was the last straw. He lost it and flew across the room, grabbed me by the throat, pinned my head on the girl's desk behind me (the poor girl was probably in a state of shock), and yelled, "I'm going to beat the hell out of you!" My parents had to come to school resulting in a transfer out of his class.

These teachers were obviously unprepared for the unprecedented level of disrespect they encountered.

In retrospect, Mr. Pucci probably handled it the best; *Hey, if you want to screw up your life and not learn, here's a pass to go do it, and have one of my cigarettes while you're at it. With you out of the way, I can teach the kids who are trying to do something with themselves, while making my life a whole lot easier."* Looking back now, I can't say that I blame him.

PART III: THE FINAL INGREDIENT IN THE RECIPE FOR DISASTER

Every journey begins with the first (mis)step

It was 1972, I was 13 years old and working with my brother-in-law Gary for the summer. He worked for my father as a drapery installer since coming back from Herbster. We would drive all over Chicago and the suburbs installing draperies in homes and businesses. Gary knew I smoked cigarettes and allowed it. Hey, I was working and buying my own cigarettes—right?

While waiting for Gary in the van as he finished up with a customer, I noticed a few small, pink, hand-rolled stubs in the ashtray. Strawberry rolling papers were in back then. What remained of a joint was known as a "roach."

By now, I was being exposed to marijuana more frequently. Curiosity started overtaking fear, and Gary was the confirmation I needed to deem pot safe. After our last job was installed, Gary would light a joint. The smell grew on me, and I started to like it. One day we were talking, and out of the blue, he just handed it to me. He must have known that it was inevitable that I'd try it, so it might as well be with him. He instructed me, "Take a hit and hold it in."

Easy enough. I had seen him do it. I was getting stoned for the first time. "Don't tell your sister. She'll kill me," he said.

Then he cranked up the tunes. Gary always had the best sound equipment available. Songs like "Take it Easy" by the Eagles, "Listen to the Music" by the Doobie Brothers, and "Horse with No Name" by America had just hit the airwaves. I heard every note and every harmony as if for the first time. Music suddenly sounded great!

That bright sunny day became even brighter and sunnier, and I suddenly found myself in a world that was so much better than the one I was in just minutes before. The best way I can describe those days of smoking pot is like being in a cartoon or a movie. Marijuana is the "great reality enhancer." It can make the most boring, mundane things in life seem like a great adventure.

But I was about to discover the most appealing quality of pot beyond all others—laughter! I saw my reflection in Gary's mirror sunglasses and my nose looked huge. I started cracking up and I couldn't stop. I laughed the entire ride home. Gary had to pull over a block away from the house and just let me laugh myself out. It became like an outtake from a sitcom. The more I tried to stop, the more I laughed. He had trouble stopping his laughter too. "Okay, you ready to go in the house now?"

"Yeah, I'm ready," I replied and then I burst into laughter again. I finally got it under control after sitting there for God knows how long. He started the van, and we drove the block and pulled into the driveway.

We walked into the house and were greeted by both of my sisters, Susan and Mary Jo. I, of course, immediately burst into hysterical laughter. My sister Susan asked, "What's wrong with him?"

Gary answered nonchalantly, "It's just Steven; he's weird."

I guess that was a reasonable explanation for them because they walked away and went about their business.

The 1970s (not to be confused with the 1960s)

In the 1960s the "counterculture" was a movement that started a revolution in America. The young people of the 1960s rejected the status quo of the establishment, as they set out to change the country and the world for the better. The messages of peace and love were mixed with resistance and defiance of discrimination, oppression of minorities, the unequal treatment of women, and the Vietnam war—to name a few. Jim Morrison of The Doors personified this resistance and struggle in the song "Five to One." *They've got the guns, but we've got the numbers. Gonna win, yeah, we're takin' over. C'mon!*

In those days, men were burning draft cards and women were burning bras in protest. Well, okay, there may have been some men burning their bras, but most were still "in the closet" at that time. Young people had political awareness and were taking political stands on pertinent social issues.

By 1967, the Civil Rights Movement led by Dr. Martin Luther King Jr. was exploding throughout the country, especially in the Deep South. The Women's Liberation Movement ("women's lib," as it was known) was getting off the ground. Women were tired of being treated as second-class citizens and sex objects by men. They protested this by wearing something called the "miniskirt" and going braless? Yeah…I'm still confused about that.

Crosby, Stills, and Nash sang: *We can change the world, rearrange the world. It's dying. If you believe in justice, and if you believe in freedom, let a man live his own life. Rules and regulations—who needs them?*

Well, apparently, they did. The revolution was short-lived and got shot down, ironically, not by "The Man" or "the powers that be," but by the hippies and flower children themselves. They became victims of their own out-of-control desires and lust. They lost the handle on the whole thing. The 60s officially ended with the Charles Manson murders in August 1969 and the festival at Altamont Speedway near San Francisco in December. The fest of "peace and love" turned into murder, as a member of the Hell's Angels motorcycle group, hired as security (for $500 worth of beer?) by the Rolling Stones, stabbed an armed, unruly concertgoer to death.

The house of cards continued to crumble as "turning on" turned into addiction, "free love" turned into sexually transmitted diseases, and all those "groovy" acid trips turned into a trip to the looney bin alongside Sid Barrett, founding member of the band Pink Floyd. Were drugs ultimately behind the collapse of the counterculture? Some would say so, including me.

In the 1970s, we were exactly like those people in the 1960s, except for a few minor differences. We had no political views and no ideas for social change, took no stands, nor protested anything. We just wanted to GET HIGH! This was the residual culture that was the remnants of the 1960s. What profound cultural masterpiece best represents our era? The film *Saturday Night Fever*, about a paint store clerk who "dances really good!"

Another great movie representation of our era could be *Fast Times at Ridgemont High* (though technically released in 1982, it was pretty much about the 1970s). Jeff Spicoli (played by Sean Penn), though a caricature, was the poster child for the "stoners" of the 1970s, who floated aimlessly through life with no plans other than to get to the next party, and no goals other than to get to the next high. Spicoli having a pizza delivered to class because he had a really bad case of the munchies, personifies what most of my generation stood for: GETTING HIGH, anytime, anywhere we could.

People got high before, during, and after, school or work in the bathroom, auditorium, cars, or wherever. Even our football team got high. I suspect this may have had something to do with their 1-6 record. Hell, we even smoked weed in gym class while playing soccer outside on the field. Okay, so maybe we were nothing like the young people of the 1960s.

Decades later in 1993, the film *Dazed and Confused* would be released. The film title, compliments of Led Zeppelin, says it all. The film's soundtrack had some great songs from the era. Although a more accurate depiction, it still somehow fell short and failed to capture the true spirit of the times.

Later in 1998, *That 70s Show* would hit TVs across the country. This milquetoast series was, at best, a superficial depiction of the clothes, hairstyles, and maybe a catchphrase or two from the era, but not much beyond that.

Ironically, our biggest cultural contribution in the 1970s was music. The music of that decade was some of the best, most diverse music ever made, to this day. What set it apart from the music of today? It really was music! That's right, made with real instruments and real people who had real talent and really wrote and composed complex, original melodies, rhythms, and harmonies from their hearts and souls. Imagine that!

The music I hear today consists of incessant pounding, simple, repetitive, mechanical melodies a two-year-old could write on his Playschool toy. "Songs" laced with derogatory, vulgar, negative lyrics that are shouted or spoken more often than sung. Is it any wonder the world is in the shape it's in?

There were also some great films made in the 1970s, but ironically, most of the better ones were about the 1960s. Films such as *Easy Rider*, *Coming Home*, *The Deer Hunter*, and *Apocalypse Now*, were all groundbreaking movies. All were nominated or won multiple Academy Awards.

One of the nominees from that decade who did not bring home an Oscar was Amelia Hamilton. As a young man, I had a huge crush on Amelia's character in one of her films. I had no way of knowing at that time the important role she would someday play in my life.

Intro to the Drug Culture 101

After getting high with Gary, the preoccupation and obsession with getting high kicked in almost immediately. I couldn't wait until I got high again. It was like going on a date where you really hit it off. When the date is over, the first thing you think is, *when can I see you again?* Right?

After trying pot, I shared my experience with my neighborhood "homies" Jim, Jeff, Ricky, and Dave—all of whom were also curious and eager to try it. Within days, we pooled our money together and set out to find someone to buy some pot from. We thought someone somewhere had some pot and that they would sell some to a bunch of 13-year-olds? Are you kidding? Were we nuts!? Well, apparently not. We walked up to the McDonald's on Mannheim Road and asked a few people, "You know where we can get some pot?"

One guy just looked at us like we were crazy. We were about to leave when we saw a couple sitting in a black Corvette in the parking lot. It was my friend Pam's older sister Lori and her boyfriend Jeff.

"You ask her." "No, you ask her." "I'm not asking her." I finally did it. I don't know how. Lori was a hot blonde. After I asked, she turned to her guy.

"Jeff?" she said. "It's cool; he's Paul Fiorito's little brother."

Jeff hesitated for a second. "Sure, I can sell you a few joints

As we walked away, Lori cautioned, "Don't smoke too much; it's really good stuff."

Once we got far enough away, we could no longer contain our excitement and Jim said, in his overly dramatic voice: "Oh my God! We just bought some pot! We have pot!"

We all chimed in. Jeff insisted, "Let me see 'em."

I pulled the contraband out of my pocket and showed them to Jeff.

"Those are so skinny. There's hardly any pot in them."

Jim looked at them with concern. Ricky just looked confused about the sudden shift from excitement to aggravation and started biting his nails.

"They are," Jim said. "Look at that. They're all paper. That doesn't look like two dollars' worth. We got ripped off," Jim proclaimed.

We were complaining and whining that "we got burned" all the way back to the shack. The shack was our sanctuary, our hideout that we built on the bank of the creek along the railroad tracks. We needed a secret place to escape to, mostly to smoke cigarettes and evade the eyes of our parents and the adults in the neighborhood. Jim, Jeff, and I, were still forbidden to associate due to us being "bad influences" on each other.

The shack was a rectangular box that was built well enough to shield us from the elements. We also had a big hemp rope tied high up in a tree that straddled the creek banks, which doubled as a source of fun and emergency escape. We could swing across one at a time and then tie it up on the other bank.

The creek wasn't very deep by then and had become something you wanted to avoid immersing yourself in. The factories had been polluting it by dumping toxic chemicals in it for so long, it rarely froze in the winter anymore.

We arrived and huddled in the shack. We lit one and choked on about half a joint between the four of us. Our glazed red eyes and goofy smiles were immediately noticeable. Lori was right; it was good shit. I don't remember much of the details other than we acted goofy and laughed ourselves silly.

We went to Jim and Jeff's house where their mother, Carol, was seldom home. I was obviously not allowed in their house. We ate ourselves sick, including a whole bag of grapefruit, and every cookie in the house. We retreated to the basement to play ping-pong while we cranked music from the era. Black Sabbath's *Master of Reality* was a favorite back then. The opening track was the anthem to our newly discovered favorite pastime—smoking pot.

"*All right now, won't you listen? When I first met you, didn't realize. I can't forget you, or your surprise. You introduced me, to my mind, and left me wanting, you and your kind....*"

How prophetic would the lyrics to "Sweet Leaf" be?

This would become our standard ritual. We would time it, and I would leave right before their mother home from work. On occasion, she would come home early, or we would lose track of time. We would hear her pull into the driveway and proclaim: "Mom's home!" We would saturate the place with air freshener and hide cigarettes, beer, or whatever contraband we had. I'd have to sneak out the basement window. Sometimes we'd get bold, and they'd hide me in the crawlspace. She would come down to the basement to check-in.

"Are you guys burning that incense again?" she'd say. Then she'd yell at them for what they didn't get done all day, assign them some chores, and go upstairs.

That summer, between seventh and eighth grade, the second wave of the drug culture exploded all around us. It was not just about getting high, but a whole way of life. I'll never forget walking into the local "headshop," Rubber Soul Records, for the first time. These shops were popping up everywhere.

The combination of psychedelic lights and the enticing smell of patchouli incense would hit you the moment you walked in. Tracks played by artists like Traffic, Spooky Tooth, The Beatles, and The Rolling Stones, made us feel like we had crossed over into some other dimension. We sensed that we were discovering an exciting, new, taboo world that just a year ago was out of our reach. We peered through the glass counters at pipes and other apparatuses that looked more like artwork than drug paraphernalia. We thumbed through the album racks and marveled at some of the coolest album cover artwork ever printed, under the watchful eye of the owner George.

My brother was friends with George. Paul did a lot of the artwork for the store, including painting a giant wicked-faced sun that covered the entire ceiling. It was well done and cemented Paul as a local celebrity of the area.

George was an entrepreneur whose only goal was to make money. He was success-driven and impervious to the scene. But the drug culture was so alluring, it eventually even got to him, as it did many. Even "squares" who initially seemed immune to its allure started getting high. In time, George would eventually succumb to cocaine addiction and lose everything.

Soon, my friends and I were all completely immersed in this new culture. For some, it meant growing our hair, bellbottom jeans, combat boots ("stompers" as we called them), and army or jean jackets over flannel shirts. Many wore T-shirts with the Zig-Zag Man—a black and white design from the most popular rolling papers of the time. For others, it meant velvet blazers, big-collared button shirts with elaborate patterns, and platform shoes.

A few words about long hair—not everyone should have it. This was never more evident than in the 1970s. Just look in any yearbook from that era and you will inevitably see a whole lot of people who should not have worn their hair long. Let's just say some people's hair defied gravity and grew more sideways than it did down. The attempts to tame this "sideways hair" with water or whatever (or lack of any attempt in some cases), made for some really goofy photos.

We were always the kids who weren't satisfied and were always searching for excitement. Early on, it was illegal fireworks, catching snakes, hopping moving freight trains, and flying down a steep hill on homemade toboggans. Now, we had discovered the next level of excitement and adventure!

"We could not live and enjoy life as other people do. We had to have something different, and we thought we had found it in drugs" - Narcotics Anonymous, Basic Text.

In search of the next high

We were on the never-ending quest to find out who had pot. Cal said the Mexicans down the street always had it, and he was thinking about getting some.

"We should have a party. We can invite some girls and get some beer and some pot. There's a vacant apartment on the next block. We can break in and have it there," Cal said.

"Sounds cool," I replied.

The nonstop party had officially begun. Pot became easier to get. It suddenly seemed like almost everybody smoked. Cal and I bonded and had gotten closer now that marijuana was our primary muse. We were on a great adventure filled with nonstop laughter!

Once, at his older cousin Judy's, we had the munchies after smoking with her and her boyfriend. She found some cookies in the cabinet, and we all proceeded to dig in. While chewing the cookies, Cal and I slowly turned to look at each other as if in a well-timed comedy skit, as we almost choked to death on what turned out to be the dreaded…*Pecan Sandies*…the driest cookies ever made on the planet. At that moment with a deadly serious tone, I spoke the words that would go down in Steve and Cal folklore history: "Sand cookies!"

We sprayed cookie across the room as we laughed uncontrollably, which made us laugh even harder. We learned a harsh lesson that day—never eat *Pecan Sandies* if you have "cottonmouth"—a condition of dry mouth that would usually follow smoking some good pot.

This was an important incident in that it set a precedent that became a big part of the drug culture at least in our neck of the woods—creating "folklore"—funny stories of mishaps and adventures, pillage and plunder, which we would tell over and over. The good ones could last for years. "Hey, remember that time…" is how they would start.

It was as if you got social points just by being there too. "Were you there?" was often asked by the storyteller. "Yeah, man, I was there; we were so fucked up!"

Then, they would add their little side story and the legends grew. The crazier the story, the more "points" you got. And there were other ways to get points. Having a special skill or talent got you points too. I became one of the first who didn't need to use a rolling machine and rolled good joints by hand. "Let Steve roll it. He doesn't need a machine!"

So, just what were these "points" and how could you redeem them? They were peer acceptance. Those days were a time of constantly trying to "jockey for position" and establish some kind of social ranking. You had to have a niche—a place in the group where you fit. The "rules" were constantly pressuring you. The trouble was that they were all unwritten and unspoken. It was difficult to navigate and created a lot of social anxiety. "Luckily" (or unluckily, as it were), drugs and alcohol were a quick fix for that. They not only were a source of relief, but they were an automatic "in"—no skills or special talents needed. To be accepted in this group, you just had to get high.

If you were the one who told the story or were at least part of the story, you were "in" at least for a while. Being in didn't last forever, so you had to make sure that you kept up. This is why it sucked if you were grounded or sick. You would miss out on the latest adventures and thus, not be part of the story. You would then become less relevant and drop in "ranking" in the group. This was the social hierarchy that one had to navigate growing up in my neck of the woods. I imagine it was similar in most teenage peer groups.

I would soon experience this "drop" for the first time when I got strep throat and couldn't leave the house for over two weeks. During my absence, a guy we met in school named Warren started hanging out with Cal and kind of stole him from me. I liked Warren. We quickly hit it off in the lunchroom when we discovered we both had artistic talent and loved to draw (another source of points for me). He made me laugh when he went up to a kid and he introduced himself as "Lumpy." "Wanna know why they call me Lumpy?" he said.

"Why?" the kid asked.

Warren proceeded to headbutt the kid. We all cracked up as the kid rubbed his forehead with a shocked look on his face!

After my hiatus, Cal and I were never as close again, but because we hung with the same group of people, and I could still make him laugh, draw, and roll a good joint, I had enough "juice" to get me back "in." I was a little sore at first about Warren taking my place, but I got over it. Well, mostly.

It did take down my fragile self-esteem a few notches and created what I would later refer to as the "second best" syndrome—a demon that haunted me for years to come. I never felt good enough and settled for being "second best."

Soon, our stories got even crazier as we started experimenting with harder drugs.

Slipping deeper into the abyss

We started to lose all healthy fear of drugs, and we were on a quest, eager to experience the many different effects that different drugs would induce. In those days, the most available and popular drugs were barbiturate tranquilizers or sedative hypnotics— "downers" or "beans" as we called them. If someone was fucked up on beans, we deemed them "beaned out".

Despite the high-profile overdose deaths of movie stars like Marilyn Monroe and Judy Garland from these types of tranquilizers, they were still popular, widely used, and easily accessible.

On the other end of the spectrum were amphetamines ("speed"), which the girls seemed to prefer. Get high and lose weight simultaneously? Perfect!

In "The Jungle," there were many small-time dealers supplementing their low or no income by dealing drugs. In our area were Tuinal or "Tuies," and Seconal or "Reds." Then, there were the sedative-hypnotics; Quaaludes ('Ludes"), and ASers ("Soapers," a generic version of Quaaludes) and Benzodiazepine tranquilizers such as Valium ("V's") and Librium ("Yellow Jackets") were readily available.

These drugs were perfect for guys like me who didn't want to just lower teenage social anxiety but completely obliterate it. Downers made me carefree and lowered my inhibitions without the long, shitty-tasting process that had to be endured with alcohol, which I still hadn't quite acquired a taste for.

So, the party continued, but there was one problem: location. There just weren't a lot of places to party. We had to get creative, so we broke into an abandoned golf shack that used to be part of a pee-wee golf and driving range that went out of business. It still had electricity, so the lights and music were good, but it had no heat. We got the place looking pretty good and made a fire in a wood-burning stove we found stored in the back.

We had our second party, and I connected with a girl named Janice. I invited her through her sister Karen, who I had a class with at school. We connected and made out all night, only interrupted by me puking. I think she may have puked too. Your typical teenage romance: making out, feeling each other up, and puking! This went on all night until we both passed out.

We were awakened by the morning light, and the cold as the steam came from our breath. The fire had gone out due to the remaining partygoers also passing out. We were both hung over.

We had called our parents and lied about spending the night at some friend's house. Soon, it would not be unusual for me not to come home or call, and Albie's nights of being plagued with worry had officially begun.

Janice and I would have this relationship for about the next year or so. I think she loved me and wanted our relationship to be more than the occasional make-out, feel-up session that it was. Janice was great, but I just didn't have "that thing"—passion—for her. I would soon feel what it was like to be in Janice's shoes and have strong feelings for someone who didn't feel the same about me. The drama and pain of unrequited teenage love was about to begin, and it was confusing, and overwhelming. It was also normal and typical. In retrospect, I wish someone would have told me that then.

That summer, Cal met and introduced us to "Jimmy the Cocksucker." No, he wasn't gay. He just called everyone a "cocksucker." Every other sentence had the word cocksucker in it. "Hand me that wrench, you cocksucker," he would say. He owned a secondhand store in Maywood. His latest money maker was ten-speed bikes.

We all suddenly had a source of income stealing anything that wasn't nailed down for Jimmy the Cocksucker. We would steal bikes, lawnmowers, other yard and garden equipment, and car and home stereo equipment. Cal, Warren, Danny, Brian, I, and a few others became thieves and burglars. Overnight we had upped our game from stealing candy from grocery stores to stealing your snowblower out of your garage.

You can imagine the folklore that was generated by these endeavors. There was much folklore about being chased by bike owners and police. We got caught once by the Franklin Park police. When they asked where the bike was, I responded, "What bike?"

Warren relished the outlaw role and went as far as burglarizing a jewelry store. He came away with some expensive items. He barely got away from the Franklin Park cops in a foot chase through the snow. As good as he was at running in platform shoes, he had to ditch them and the bag of goods to get away. He came back the next day in broad daylight to look for and retrieve the bag of spoils and his shoes from someone's backyard.

I had one of the more unique folklore stories at that time after stealing a bike that was parked outside of a department store on a Saturday. That Monday, I went to school, and in my art class, I noticed the guy I always sat with, James Nelson, wasn't his usual jovial self. He and I would crack up constantly. When I asked him what was wrong, he said his bike got stolen over the weekend. "From where?" I asked.

"In front of Grant's," he replied.

"I have your bike," I whispered.

"What do you mean?"

"I took your bike. I'll give it back to you."

His chin about hit the floor. He didn't know whether to laugh or cry. So, I apologized, made the arrangements, and gave it back to him. What are the odds that you'd be sitting in art class with the guy who randomly stole your bike over the weekend?

Courage or chemically induced insanity?

I noticed that downers made me pretty bold when it came to stealing things. I would take chances when I was under the influence. Once, while walking home through The Jungle, fucked up on Ludes, I spotted an electric guitar and amplifier in someone's living room through their picture window. It was a warm night and most of the people who lived there couldn't afford air-conditioning, so the windows of the room on either side of the picture window were open. I walked back and forth several times to case the joint. I didn't see anybody, so I figured they were in the bedroom or bathroom in the back.

My Lude-induced boldness told me I could slip in, grab the guitar, and slip out quietly. I had to get through the screen, which I had to remove. I did so and I started to climb in. I got as far as my shoulders, when I felt someone grab me by the hair with one hand and pull me through. I also felt something on my throat, which turned out to be a very large butcher knife.

"Come on in, motherfucker" the bearded biker-type man said to the skinny 14-year-old. I realized that I had climbed through the wrong window. I was actually in the apartment next door. I explained this as he walked me across the room and pinned me up against the wall, the knife still to my throat.

"I see you're fucked up, but ya shouldn't be breaking into people's apartments. Stand there while I call the cops, and don't try anything!" he said.

He grabbed the phone off the wall and dialed 911.

He gave them his address and said he'd hold me until they got there.

I sobered up pretty quickly when I realized that I was about to get busted for breaking and entering and attempted burglary. I was already on probation for the second time. He was a long-haired cool-looking guy, so I decided to cop a plea. I told him about my record and that if I got arrested, I would probably go to juvey. It worked. He felt sorry for me. I'd be willing to bet that he had been to juvey at some point in his life. Out of nowhere, he said, "Get outta here and don't ever do any dumb shit like this again."

"Thanks man, I won't," I said, as I walked out his front door, and took off running all the way home. I must have been the luckiest guy alive. That guy could have slit my throat and would have been justified, and not only didn't he, but let me go before the cops arrived.

It's bad enough being young and dumb but adding "chemically emboldened" to the mix could have been lethal.

Tripping our way through school

In eighth grade, Cal and I would forego the bus most days and walk to school so we could smoke a joint. If we were late, we had to go to the office to get a hall pass. Being stoned at school was becoming a common occurrence. By then, a few of us had already started to experiment with hallucinogenic drugs like acid. Our friend Judy was one of the first from our little group.

One day, word got around that she dropped acid before school and was tripping. Mind you this was still real LSD like in the 1960s. I say that because people may not be aware that this got much more difficult to obtain, and within four or five years, it would be all but impossible once dealers figured out that they could substitute cheaper ingredients that produced similar effects.

Judy and I had English class together with the dreaded Mrs. Stearns. Stearns was exactly like the image that her name might invoke—an old woman with silver hair who was very strict and had a bit of a mean streak.

As we filed into the room, I noticed Judy was late. So was Stearns, so I took the opportunity to go around to the entire class and ask a little favor. "I'm playing a joke on my friend Judy," I explained as I gave them their instructions.

Judy arrived looking dazed and confused with a big grin on her face that she obviously had little control over. She looked at me and I shot her a few knowing smiles from across the room.

As Stearns wrapped up the day's lesson, the bell rang for the class to let out. To my surprise, the entire class followed my instructions and proceeded to grab their books and walk out of the classroom...backwards! Every nerd, bookworm, jock, freak, and yours truly, walked out of that class backwards. It was a sight to behold! Judy cringed and covered her face with her hands as she exited the classroom, now bursting into uncontrollable laughter. Even Mrs. Stearns smiled as she watched the creative exit from her class, though not knowing the true reason. "You okay?" I inquired.

"You fucker," she exclaimed, still grinning ear to ear.

Judy knew that I orchestrated the class's exit, and we cracked up before she said that she would kill me later and she probably could have. Judy was attractive in a tomboy sort of way, but she was a big girl, and she was tough.

By then, we had all become curious about acid. My brother Paul and brother-in-law Gary had tripped, along with several other people I knew. Most of the reviews were not only good, but made it sound like the coolest adventure ever. I found out that even Janice had tripped. She said it was really cool. She saw colors, and trails, and laughed a lot, but she only did about half of a hit.

My curiosity and sense of adventure about other drugs was now at a peak. Any healthy fear had vanished, and I viewed drugs as a safe, recreational activity, no different than board games, or sports. I told her I wanted to try it, so she agreed she would get some and we would do it after school.

The next day, we followed through on our plan. Her parents wouldn't be home for hours. When we got to her house, she pulled out a little baggie, and in the very corner was a tiny, brownish-tinted square about one-eighth inch in size. It looked like a piece of Kodak film, only slightly lighter in color. We went into the bathroom, got a razor blade, and cut about one-third of it off in the bathtub. Good thing, too, because it went flying and if we hadn't done it in the tub, we would never have found it. I looked at the tiny object, barely visible on the tip of Janice's finger, and said, "Are you sure that's going to be enough? I can't believe that little thing will do anything to me."

"It'll be enough," she said with a knowing smirk on her face.

"Put it under your tongue and let it dissolve."

We made out on the couch for about twenty minutes or so. Janice was getting giggly, and it was obvious she was "getting off" on the acid. I, however, was not. I proclaimed, "I'm not feeling anything."

"Oh, you will," Janice said with that same smirk on her face. I realized that our make-out session had made a mess of my hair, so I went to the bathroom to brush it. My hair was shoulder-length and parted in the middle.

In the bathroom, as I looked at myself in the mirror, my stomach started feeling funny. I stood there staring at my face, I took the brush and fluffed one side of my hair. It stood straight out, while the other side was perfectly combed. At that precise moment, I got off on the acid! I started laughing at myself and I thought, *I have to show Janice*. I came out of the bathroom pointing at my head, laughing hysterically. Janice joined me and we couldn't stop.

Then I noticed the sun pouring into the house from all directions and I not only could feel it, but I also understood on a deeper level the positive energy of it. Each beam of sunlight had intricate patterns running through it.

In the background, Edgar Winter's "Free Ride" was playing and suddenly I was "in the song" and I was living and breathing it! Yeah, I can't really explain what that means. I just knew it was true. I sat down in the living room, awed by the colors and patterns I saw, waving my hand back and forth and watching it leave multicolored trails behind each movement. I was describing it all to Janice and asking her, "Do you see that!?"

The drapes started breathing in unison with my breath. I couldn't stand to look at them anymore, so I looked at the floor. That provided no relief and was even more intense. The carpet in that room was purple with some intricate 1970's pattern repeated. The song "Magic Carpet Ride" comes to mind. I was on one! The floor started breathing as the music and the floor were pulsating in rhythm with each other. Janice continued to laugh at the look of awe and wonder on my face.

Time was distorted and almost inconceivable. It felt like we had lived our whole life together in one minute, yet hours felt like seconds. After about an hour and a half, I "peaked" and finally started to feel the "merry-go-round" slowing down. We were eventually able to discern what time it really was and realized that I had to go. Janice's mom would be home soon and would not have been happy to meet the boyfriend tripping on acid.

Most of our parents were like the parents in the *Peanuts* cartoons. All we usually saw of them was their legs and occasionally we would hear, "wah wah wah" out of their mouths. Others were virtually nonexistent. I think, in all the time we were together; I may have met her mother and her father once. Her dad met me when he caught us making out in their garage. "Hi there! I'm Steve. The guy who's corrupting your daughter and turning her into a juvenile delinquent!" I'm pretty sure he wanted to kill me.

I was still tripping on my way home from Janice's and felt the world was a sort of fairyland. I headed for Jim and Jeff's to share my experience with them. On my way, I suddenly noticed the intricacies of everything. I felt like I was seeing things for the first time. I was noticing aspects of the world that I had never noticed before and everything looked special and unique. First, I found a really cool rock. I picked it up and put it in my front pocket. Then I found some really cool, sparkly purple sand on the ground. I put a handful of that in my shirt pocket.

When I arrived, I checked, as I always did, to make sure Carol's car wasn't in the driveway, fearing that it was close to her time to come home from work. I knocked and they both came to the door. "What are you doing here? My mom's gonna be home any minute," Jim said.

"I'm tripping! Oh my God! It's sooo cool!"

"Really?!" Jim exclaimed. You could see them getting excited.

"Look what I found." I proceeded to show them what I'd collected in my shirt pockets. They both laughed at me. They didn't get it and couldn't see what I perceived about the objects.

Jim proclaimed: "We're going to get some. Let's plan it tomorrow." Just then, we saw Carol's car go past, which meant she'd be in the driveway in two seconds, and in the house in about 37 seconds (we had the timing down to a science). I left and went home. I couldn't wait to drop acid with my buddies!

Da Dago Feast

Warren, Cal, Brian, Danny, Pam, Judy, and the rest of us started spending a lot more time together. We solidified our bond that summer by going to the infamous Italian Fest in Melrose Park—better known as "Da Dago Feast" We experienced the sights, sounds, and smells of the fest, including the music, food, games, rides and the banter of Melrose Park dagos filled the air.

"Yo, Vinnie. Get Ma some lupini beans–will ya?"

"Where da fuck is she?"

"How da fuck do I know? Just get 'er some fuckin lupinis!!"

Ahhhh, Italian American conversations are like muzak to da ears! Warren and I unexpectedly bonded for the first time when we decided to go on a ride called The Zipper together. The whole ride spins while the individual cars also spin at a pretty good clip. We got a clue about what we were in for when we saw the deep hand imprints in the foam-rubber hand grips from previous riders holding on for dear life. Once the ride started, we both realized how terribly unprepared we were and started screaming like little girls! Of course, in an attempt to maintain our masculinity, we interjected words like "Shhiiiiiiiiit!" and "What the fuuuuuuck?!" Then, to make matters worse, both of our pockets, which were full of change, were unloaded into the car. It suddenly became a torture chamber of deadly coins flying all over the car at a high rate of speed! We were defenseless while getting pelted from every direction with pennies, nickels, dimes, and quarters (the quarters really hurt)!

When we got off the ride, we felt like we had just survived the Titanic! We bonded over our mutual PTZD (Post-traumatic zipper disorder) from the experience. The folklore was good for about nine months. "Remember when Steve and I went on the Zipper and almost got killed by the change in our pockets? We were sooo fucked up!"

Choosing drugs over love

My two groups of friends had one thing in common in those early days; we were always looking for places to party and hang out. They were still somewhat scarce, especially in the colder months. With my neighborhood homies, it was The Jungle basements. Jim, Jeff, Ricky, Dave, Dennis, and I would literally walk backwards for the entire one-mile trek in the teeth of 30-mph winds, snow, and frigid cold.

Dennis was a new addition to our little group. Like a "good Christian", his adopted mother kicked him out and disowned him, due to his drug use.

Once there, we'd get high, smoke cigarettes, laugh, then torture and punch each other in the arm. You know—guy stuff. After a few hours, we'd bundle up and prepare for the frigid but slightly more bearable walk home.

Warren lived a few blocks from Mary Dewitt, a female friend who he went to grade school with. I remember that we all started hanging out in Mary's basement. Her mother was one of the *Peanuts* cartoon parents I referred to earlier, and mostly left us alone, occasionally yelling the parent question of the times: "Are you burning that incense again?" Mary would acknowledge "yes" at times and other times would blame it on Pam's cigarette smoking. We finally had a comfortable place to hang out, listen to music, and party.

As we entered her basement, the smell of incense would hit us and the warmth would rush up from the basement and surround us after that long, cold, snowy walk outside. We would descend the basement stairs to songs like "You're So Vain" by Carly Simon. The song would forever remind me of Mary and have a bittersweet meaning for years to come.

I can't remember exactly when, but one day I found myself looking at Mary and I couldn't stop. I started noticing that she moved like a cat. Her eyes sparkled and penetrated you when she looked into yours. Her lips and smile were beautiful. Her voice and her laugh made my heart race.

Mary was the first girl I was ever in love with. Can I explain being in love with someone that I'd never kissed or even touched? I can't. She was graceful, gentle, pretty, intelligent, funny—and unfortunately—she was Cal's.

Cal was the undisputed leader of our little "gang." Once again, the "second best" role jumped me and clung to me like a cheap suit. It was like Roger Smith in sixth grade all over again, only this time it was socially, not academically. I couldn't compete. The more I was around her, the deeper I fell. The deeper I fell, the harder it was not to get tongue-tied. Then I'd fall into that "don't say anything stupid" mode, and of course, that was pretty much a guarantee that I would. Everybody knew it, too. I mean, it was impossible to hide. People had eyes and could see the way I looked at her. She had eyes too, and she knew. So, I've got some good news and some bad news: The good news…she and Cal were on and off, so I had my chances.

Once was at a party in Pam's basement. When Pam, Mary, and Janice came to my house and knocked on the door, they were greeted by my mother, who answered the door with an attitude and a huge butcher knife in her hand.

"Is Steve home?" Pam said in a quivery whisper, like the cowardly lion when he asked the wizard for some courage.

"No, I'm sorry, ladies; he can't go out. He's grounded." I was grounded because, while at the dinner table the previous day, beaned out on downers, I attempted to pour myself a glass of milk and completely missed the glass. My brother Paul's eyes almost popped out of his head as he witnessed the spectacle.

I had been begging her to reconsider so I could go to this party. She was unmoved by my constant badgering and wasn't budging. I needed to get out of there because I had taken more Quaaludes that day in anticipation of the party, and the drugs were starting to kick in. After they left, I decided to make a run for it and ran for the front door.

Albie screamed, "Don't you go out that door, you son of a bitch." She called me this a lot and apparently never realized that she was talking about herself! As I pulled the door open, I felt something nail me in the back of the head. It was the giant spaghetti spoon she'd been stirring a pot of sauce with! Albie couldn't have made that throw again if her life depended on it. The girls were waiting for me about a half block down. They laughed when they saw the spaghetti sauce in my hair, and we ran to the shortcut that allowed us to cross the creek and disappear behind the factories on our way to Pam's.

I had made up my mind. This was the day I was going to make my move on Mary. I had enough chemical courage in me. Oops, well, maybe a bit too much, as I tripped and fell UP the stairs in Pam's basement. No matter. I would not be deterred! I was finally going to kiss her.

As the house got filled with more people, I lost track of Mary. I was ready to make my move. I asked several people if they had seen her. Someone said she was outside in the backyard. I came out of the back door and noticed it had gotten dark. I made my way through the gangway, and I saw two figures in the dark standing close together. It was Mary and Danny. They were kissing. I was devastated. I went back inside and took another pill, shoved it in my mouth, and downed it with beer. I don't remember anything else about that night.

The next day, I woke up hungover. After searching my pockets and finding an empty baggie, I realized I had taken my entire stash of drugs. Looking back, I can't help but think of how easy it would have been to unwittingly cross that thin line between life and death and quietly slip into oblivion in my sleep, never to return. Unfortunately, this episode would be only one of many where I came dangerously close to crossing that line.

My survival would yield yet another chance with Mary a few months later. We were all in Mary's basement partying and we ran out of beer. This was a typical occurrence and usually, two of us (one with a fake ID and another for company) would volunteer to go on a beer run. There were some strong vibes in the air and there had been some heavy flirting going on between her and me. I'm sure everybody felt the vibes between us and knew that, at least for now, Cal was somewhat out of the picture. This was my chance, and I felt that everybody knew it and they were secretly rooting for me.

Suddenly, Pam, always the instigator, jumps up with a sly grin on her face and says, "I'm going with you," to whoever volunteered to go. She continued, "I think we should all go," referring to everyone but Mary and me. So, five people went to get beer, leaving Mary and me alone in her basement.

I was ready. I had enough liquid courage in me but not too much this time. Mary sat down next to me on the couch. She smiled that beautiful smile that I had come to love, and I dared to look right into those beautiful, mesmerizing eyes. Then…fate happened…she pulled out about a third of a joint and said, "Look what I found." She lit it, took a hit, and held it in. Then she blew the smoke in my face, as she often did when she was flirting. It was her signal to me that she knew how I felt about her. She smiled and her eyes sparkled as she handed it to me. Little did I know that the internal battle that ensued would be a sign of the journey I would embark on, and the fate that was in store for me. Simply put, would I choose love or drugs?

A voice in the back of my mind shouted in a quiet, desperate, whisper: *Noooooo! Don't do it!* I knew getting stoned meant I would soon feel goofy, and self-conscious. Not exactly the way I needed to feel to follow through with finally kissing the love of my life. But I couldn't say no, so I grabbed the joint from her and took a big hit. We smoked the rest, talked, and had a few laughs and that was it. My big chance went…up in smoke (pardon the pun), ironically, the title of Cheech and Chong's first movie. In other words, nothing happened.

So, the bad news is…I blew it.

Everybody returned from the longest beer run ever (over an hour). Pam came in looking at me, then at Mary with that same grin on her face and question marks in her eyes. The actual question was probably asked in whispers later. Jim and Jeff were there, and they immediately asked on the walk home: "Did you do anything? Did you at least kiss her? What happened?"

"Nothing, we got stoned and I lost my nerve," I said.

"You asshole!" Jim proclaimed.

This was the first time I had ever consciously chosen drugs over something (someone), who was really important to me. I couldn't turn down getting high. By then, I loved it just a little too much. My self-esteem was already pretty fragile, and now it was in the toilet.

You haven't got the stomach for it!

The summer before high school was one big party. One look at my yearbook picture for freshman year (taken at the end of that summer) was proof. As drugs started to take over my life, they interfered more and more with my ability to function as a normal person would.

"Our whole life and thinking was centered in drugs in one form or another—the getting and using and finding ways and means to get more. We lived to use and used to live. Very simply, an addict is a man or woman whose life is controlled by drugs." ... Narcotics Anonymous, Basic Text

My dad continued to try to pull me into normalcy by taking me to work most days. Some days, I was so out of it from being up partying the night before, I couldn't get out of bed.

One incident would haunt me for years. He needed me to help him with a big job. He made five or six attempts to get me out of bed but couldn't do it. On the last attempt, he went off on me. Being a man who rarely showed emotion, it was one of only a handful of times in my life that he did...

"Hey, I gotta go. Are you gonna get up!? No, you're not getting up—are you?!"

Then, he said the words that would ring in my head and create a knot in my gut for years to come: "You'll never be able to get up and go to work every day. YOU HAVEN'T GOT THE STOMACH FOR IT!!"

He slammed the door and left. My father couldn't hide it anymore—he was disgusted that his son was so weak. Deep down, I knew he was right, and I hated it. Though I couldn't admit it at the time, I was starting to hate myself.

Discovering the greatest music ever made

On the days, my father got me to go to the shop, I'd often look for a chance to slip away. If I had any money, I'd take the bus to the end of the line and walk the rest of the way home. I'd find my neighborhood pals and we'd hang at Jim and Jeff's, my house, or the shack. We were often treated to my brother turning the sound off on old Westerns and making up his own words...

"Please, Ben, don't go. Stay home and fuck the shit outta me."

"I must go, Helen. Now let go of me, you silly bitch before I have to slap the shit outta you!"

We would be rolling on the floor! We'd chime in and try, but no one was as good at it as Paul. Or we were treated to his eclectic tastes in music and listened to the finest Rock & Roll on the planet. Paul was a true Rock connoisseur. In his huge album collection were bootlegs, European imports, and everything you could imagine. He would occasionally let me pick an album from his collection to check out and listen to. I saw an album called *Beginnings* by The Allman Brothers Band. I was familiar with and loved their second album, *Idlewild South*. Cal and I would try to sing along in his room. "No, I'm not gonna let 'em catch me, no; not gonna let 'em catch the midnight rider."

Prophetic lyrics that were subliminally writing the scripts for our lives. I listened to their debut album and as a rookie guitarist, I was totally impressed. The album starts with a guitar explosion called "Don't Want You No More," then into the soulful "It's Not My Cross to Bear." But what stood out to me was the slide guitar in "Don't Keep Me Wonderin'" and "Trouble No More."

My brother's response to the praise was, "You liked that, huh? I want you to hear something, but let's smoke this first."

So, he lit a joint and we smoked it. "Okay, sit down here," grabbing a dining room chair and positioning me in the perfect place in the room to get a nice balance of all four kick-ass speakers he had. He cranked it up and out of the speaker came… "Okay, The Allman Brothers Band."

Suddenly, Duane Allman's slide guitar is ripping through my chest to my soul, while Berry Oakley's bass is thumping me in the gut. Then, Gregg with that soulful rock vocal, "Wake up, momma, turn your lamp down low!"

I was mesmerized! I could not move from that spot until all four sides of the double live album, *At Fillmore East,* had been played. Then Paul shared the bad news that both Duane and Berry had been killed in separate motorcycle accidents almost a year to the day apart in 1971 and 1972. I was saddened but intrigued and my interest in the band was born. I would later idolize the band's surviving guitarist, Dickey Betts for shouldering the load left by Duane's death.

With the explosion of Southern Rock, I would emulate the likes of Betts, Ronnie Van Zandt, and all those "good ole' boys." I wore cowboy boots and blue jeans almost every day of my life from that day on.

Music helped salvage my sinking self-esteem not only as a wannabe musician, but as a fan who was blessed by listening to inspired, meaningful lyrics and music. I was lucky to grow up in a musical era where both were in abundance. My hero, Gregg Allman, gave me a standard to strive for. From "Midnight Rider" to "Whipping Post," and the instrumentals in between, the Allman Brothers' music spoke to my heart and soul. Someday, I wanted my music to have that kind of sound and feel. But for now, I mostly just threw my guitar down on the bed in frustration.

In our forays to the music room, Cal and I met a guy named Juan Garcia, a short Mexican American, with a thick Mexican accent. He wore platform shoes, to compensate for being short. He mastered running from school security and police in them. Only Warren could do it better.

Juan was decent on the guitar, so we started jamming together. He lived in an apartment above an auto body shop with his mother, younger brother, and younger sister. Mom worked long hours and was rarely home, so that apartment became the site for many parties.

Juan had a cousin named Sylvia, who Cal started seeing on and off between seeing Mary. This was fine with me as I had not given up hope of being with Mary. Sylvia was great. She was funny and fun, especially when she was stoned, but she had these round spectacles and wild, frizzy black hair, and didn't hold a candle to Mary in the looks department. In any case, Juan and Sylvia were great additions to our little group.

The shack

As the summer of 1974 was ending, my neighborhood pals and I decided our shack needed to expand and be able to accommodate not only more people but also being upright. We preferred standing to crouching. So, we built our addition. When it was finished, we planned a party. We decided we would make it an acid party and get as many people tripping as we could.

It was a Sunday, and a lot of people showed up. There was a parking lot for a company called Turn Style just on the other side of the tracks. Adjacent to the parking lot was the BF Goodrich tire factory. Along the walls, they would stack tires that had flaws or defects to be recycled. Someone had the idea: "Wouldn't it be cool if we filled the whole parking lot with tires? Can you picture the looks on their faces when they come to work on Monday morning?"

It was a big company, and the lot would have over 100 cars or more in it on a Monday morning. I can't remember who started it, but one of us grabbed a tire and rolled it to the other end of the lot. Next thing you know, there were 10 or 12 teenagers, tripping on acid, rolling tires into the parking lot, laughing hysterically in a mad frenzy! We filled the entire thing with tires. Da Vinci had nothing on us. We stood there marveling at our masterpiece with an occasional giggle erupting from time to time (probably Janice, who giggled to herself often). Then, we all went back to the area by the shack and continued to party.

As the sun began to set, someone had an idea that we needed to build a fire. All was well until some asshole decided it would be cool if he set one of the tires on fire. Soon, a big plume of black smoke was billowing through the air. Of course, someone called the cops.

They arrived but couldn't get to us through the Turn Style parking lot due to the tires, so they parked at the other end of the building and walked down the tracks to get to us. This gave us time to hide any contraband before they got to us. We apologized and told them that the tire fire was an accident. One of them turned to us and asked, "Who put all those tires in the parking lot?"

We looked at each other, puzzled, as if the officer had just spoken Chinese to us. We collectively answered, "Uh, we don't know. Um, I think it was some guys that were here earlier, but they left."

"Okay, well, somebody get some water and let's put that tire out."

I volunteered and said I knew where a bucket was. I volunteered Pam too. "All right, go on, you two. What are you waiting for?" the cop ordered.

So, Pam and I went and grabbed a bucket that was next to the shack. On our way to get the water I started thinking, *the last thing I wanted to do was be tripping in the Franklin Park police station,* realizing I was likely headed for it, especially being on probation, which I usually was. So, once we were out of the cop's sight, I put the bucket down and took off running across the creek after discovering that the rope was tied on the other bank. Halfway across, I turned to Pam and said, "C'mon, let's go!" She whispered back, "I can't. I have my bike here." At that moment, I knew I was out of time and the cops were going to start wondering about us, so I said, "Okay, see ya." And I took off. I was the only one who got away. They all got hauled down to the station.

The only other significant event that summer was when Cal's father moved them back to Norridge, the Chicago suburb where they had lived before moving to the area. The move made for some interesting future adventures.

High times at West Leyden "High" School

All of us went to West Leyden High School in Northlake with the exception of Cal and Danny. Danny went to East Leyden due to living out of the district. Cal dropped out and went to work after moving back to Norridge, which ultimately led to a lot of train-hopping and hitchhiking to hang out with Danny and Cal on the weekends. To get to Danny's, we would ride our bikes across multiple tracks that all led to the Franklin Park train yards. Trains were going slow after picking up freight from nearby factories, so we'd throw our bikes onto a flat car, run and jump on, throw our bikes off, and jump off. We were again, risking our lives at times, but we never thought of it that way.

A particularly risky endeavor would occur when Warren and I would hitchhike to Cal's on the weekends, sometimes together, sometimes separately. In those days, hitchhiking was still fairly common and relatively safe. One thing that made hitchhiking to Norridge and back potentially deadly, and we weren't even aware of it at the time, was John Wayne Gacy.

We didn't know it then, but Cal lived less than a few miles south of the serial killer, and at the height of his killing spree. Any of those times hitchhiking up and down Irving Park Road, through the heart of his stomping grounds, could have ended in tragedy. What made it even riskier was being 15, weighing 118 pounds, and thinking you're tough. Thank God I never had to find out the hard way that I wasn't as tough as I thought, like some of those boys did who wound up buried in his crawlspace. Another Gacy "fun fact" that I found out later, was that my older sister Sissy dated him briefly. The man was actually in my driveway several times when I was about 10 years old. Was I lucky or was I blessed? I had no concept of either in those days.

As I mentioned previously, I was well prepared for my first day of high school after learning how to wander the halls aimlessly in junior high. These skills were put to the test immediately. I was having a normal amount of difficulty finding my classes, so I figured I'd just play that card if anyone stopped me. I got directions from the faculty, but everyone was lenient due to it being the first day, so I took the opportunity to get familiar with the premises.

Warren and I were already scoping out where we could take a nap without being disturbed. The staircase that led up to the balcony of the auditorium looked promising. It was cordoned off and was pretty isolated.

When I finally started going to classes the next day, I was in for a pleasant surprise. My first class was history, taught by Mr. Curry, who was also the coach of the football team. He used to design plays for the team. The whole class was films with brief worksheets at the end. I sat in the front of the classroom (for once) because his desk was in the back. As soon as the lights went off, my head hit the desk, and I was off to dreamland. The plan I devised was to enlist the assistance of a fellow student who would wake me up if…

A) Curry got up from his desk and got too close.

B) The film ended.

Or…

C) Five minutes were left of the class.

I would then copy off said student's worksheet and turn it in. Miraculously, I got a B in that class literally in my sleep. It may have been one of my highest grades and best subjects that year.

Next, there was art class, where Mrs. Schuller quickly learned that the only way to keep me engaged was to allow me to do art on my own terms. So, no matter what the assignment was for the rest of the class, papier mâché´, pointillism, acrylic painting, impressionism—you name it—all I had to do was turn in a drawing and I got a grade. I still can't decide if this was a good or a bad thing for her to do. It was enabling, but it was a creative way to keep me engaged. I was artistic, but pencil was the only motif I was comfortable with.

Another thing I really loved about the class was that Mary Almetta was in it. Mary wore the most revealing hippie tops that existed at the time—braless! I can tell you that if you were not a big fan of a great set of tits, you would be quickly converted upon feasting your eyes upon those babies!

For English, I had Mr. Swetin, a short, round, beetle of a man, who fancied himself a "hipster," progressive, but from my view, was a bit full of himself and an asshole. My sister Mary Jo was his pet. I'm sure he had high hopes for me, which were very quickly dashed upon finding out that not only was I not my sister Mary Jo, but I was nothing like her. Instead, he got an irreverent, disrespectful stoner, who loved to draw in his sketchpad during class. Quite the contrast from my sister.

The battle of wills ensued almost immediately. Not long into the semester, a big showdown occurred when, in front of the entire class, he threatened to rip up my sketchpad if I didn't "close it right now!" I promptly replied, "If you rip up my sketchpad, I'll rip up every book on your desk." He walked to my desk and picked up the sketchpad. I then walked to his desk and picking up his English Lit. text. We glared at each other while the class looked on in horror. Well, some in horror, others secretly rooting for me to do it. At that point, he backed down and went to his "ace in the hole" and sent me down to the dean's office. Needless to say, I didn't do well in English that semester.

The adventures of Mr. Swetin and I culminated after the school year that summer. While walking to Warren's one day, I spotted Swetin in his unmistakable little Volkswagen Beetle. He sees that it's me and I see him clearly through the windshield. At that precise moment, we simultaneously, and I do mean simultaneously (as in we couldn't have timed it better with hours of practice), gave each other the universal "salute"— flipping each other off! I think it was very satisfying and even somewhat therapeutic for both of us to express our true feelings for each other without the constraints of school.

I had a few more classes, that I can't remember, but my favorite class was lunch. I was good at it! So much so that I had Lunch-I and advanced Lunch-II. I loved making my entrance with the jukebox playing…

> *Say, Candy and Ronnie, have you seen them yet? Oh, but they're so spaced out. B-B-B-Bennie and the Jets. Oh, but they're weird and they're wonderful. Oh, Bennie, she's really keen. She's got electric boots, a mohair suit. You know I read it in a magazine, ohh ho. B-B-B-Bennie and the Jets,"*

Did we know what Elton was talking about? Hell no, and we didn't care! I always thought he said, *she's got electric boobs; she's so hirsute* (hairy). Whatever! It sounded good, and we were usually high anyway.

I wish I could tell you more about my classes in freshman year, but by this time, I was high every day. I was already losing interest in school except for getting my driver's license, which I couldn't do until my sophomore year. At the rate I was going, there was a good chance I wouldn't make it.

To make matters worse, I got into a physical altercation with one of the driver's ed. teachers, Mr. Lucas, who caught me aimlessly wandering the halls. He asked me my name, and I refused to give it to him. He wound up grabbing me by the shirt, and we wrestled to the ground. Another teacher passing by broke it up. I had my second of many trips to Dean Paske's office, though oddly, no one brought up the physical altercation.

I still had the inherited Fiorito trait of trouble waking up in the morning. It was magnified by drug use and staying up late. Some mornings, I would fall asleep under a tree by the bus stop. I would wait until my parents left, sneak back into the house, and go back to bed. When I woke up, I'd walk to school and make some of my classes. Even when I was there, I started cutting class and getting high in the adjacent cemetery. It was very accommodating for hiding from school security behind its trees, bushes, and memorial walls.

School security consisted mainly of four people. Outside security officer, Dave Cirqua was obviously a wannabe cop, with mirrored sunglasses, tinted car windows, and mounted searchlight. Inside security was Clay Krekelberg, a big, tall, German Gestapo-looking guy, complete with a military crew cut. Irv Bedard was a physical education teacher who presided over fitness training for all athletes and doubled as a "secret" security agent. He was part of a famous family of trapeze artists known as The Flying Bedards. The binoculars were a dead giveaway that he took his security role very seriously.

Finally, the brains of the outfit—dean of students—Herb Paske, who due to being quite portly, rarely came out from behind his desk. He always stayed in contact with his team via walkie-talkie. They were a sort of *Charlie's Angels* of West Leyden High.

Soon, it became a kind of competitive game for us. They would try to catch us, and we would run. If you've ever seen the TV show *The Monkees* and watched one of the high-speed chase scenes, you would have an idea of what it was like for us, running through the halls, up and downstairs to escape them. Remember, this was before the days of security cameras everywhere.

In one incident, we were tripping and being chased. Visual and audio distortions amplified the intrigue and fear we experienced. We thought we got away, but here comes Krekelberg, walkie-talkie in hand, reporting his position. We felt like TV show villains, being chased by the cops. I'm glad we didn't have to jump from rooftop to rooftop because none of us had stunt doubles. We ran but here comes Bedard, walking even faster, walkie-talkie in hand. We shot up some stairs and there's Dave Cirqua, who made a special trip inside on his walkie-talkie. We started to panic. Panting and sweaty, with occasional bursts of maniacal laughter, we doubled back, then down a flight of stairs. As soon as we turned the corner, there was Paske in a rare appearance from behind his desk, also with a walkie-talkie in hand, reporting that he had us and his position. We realized that it was over. We were cornered. They had us and they converged on us from all directions. Right before they got to us, Warren's eyes widened with panic on his face, as he pointed at my waste. I looked down and saw that due to all the running, the rolled-up bag of pot I had stashed in the elastic of my underwear was hanging out in plain sight! I quickly tucked it in just before they got to us. Bedard knew Warren and me because we had him for P.E. class. "Well, Mr. Erhedt, Mr. Fiorito, why are you guys running from us?"

"Because you were chasing us," Warren said, smartass that he was.

We felt that Bedard had it in for us and made it one of his goals to bust us out. They got the rest of our names and hauled us down to Paske's office.

Tripping in school could be fun at times, but other times, it wasn't, especially if we did too much acid or got an unusually strong dose.

Once, while tripping in math class, my pencil started melting and the numbers jumped off the page of my book and started dancing on my desk. I remember walking to the pencil sharpener to sharpen my pencil a few times, trying to snap myself back into reality, but the hallucinations became overwhelming. Upon seeing the teacher's head melt, I grabbed my books, got up, and without saying a word, just walked out of class, and out of the building. It was the first time I had "freaked out" and had a bad experience with acid.

So even though getting chased around the school while high on one drug or another gave things a certain sense of adventure, it was starting to happen too often and was getting too risky. As a result, we started cutting school more and hanging out in Warren's basement. He had decorated the place in psychedelia complete with curtains, black light, and black-light posters.

We also started experimenting with other drugs like angel dust. We bought some "dust" from one of the seniors who warned us not to do too much, or we might "forget how to breathe." Now, there's a great thing to have in your head right before you try a drug for the first time. Talk about the power of suggestion. We snorted a small line of the light brownish-white powder. Our heads and eyelids got super heavy and numb. Next, we felt like we were floating and couldn't feel ourselves. Then, of course…we forgot how to breathe! Luckily, we were able to tell each other how to do it.

"Just breathe through your mouth…yeah, like that. Just inhale, then exhale. Keep doing that!"

We also had no depth perception and little perception of movement, meaning you couldn't tell if you were moving or not, and if you could, you couldn't determine at what rate of speed. If you were driving, forget it. You could be going 90 mph, but it felt like you were going 10 mph.

During this time, Warren and I became closer, likely due to Cal's absence from day-to-day life during the week while school was in session. We met at his house one morning before school to trip. The plan was to peak early and then go to school and make it to some of our classes. The problem with that plan was the drug we took was blotter acid and was a little more potent than we had been used to. We were listening to the Emerson, Lake and Palmer album (ironically titled) *Brain Salad Surgery* in Warren's basement.

At one point, there is a song called "Toccata," which turned out to be the musical equivalent of a panic attack! We were both holding onto the arms of our chairs as if we were being hurled through space at a high rate of speed and our heads would explode. We had to get up and walk...right then, or we would not survive! We knew all this just by looking at each other.

This was the first time that Warren and I would experience the ability to read each other's minds while tripping. We would look at each other and know exactly what we were thinking. If you've ever looked at someone and thought you knew what they were thinking just by the expression on their face, you would have a small glimpse of what we experienced. Acid tapped into clairvoyance and intuition that was otherwise unattainable.

We left his house, went to The Jungle basements, and sat there for an undetermined amount of time. As we peaked on the drug, we began freaking out because we were finishing each other's sentences. We walked to Juan's house. Every time the wind blew, Warren's head would melt, and pieces would break off into the atmosphere. If you've ever looked into one of those concave mirrors at an amusement park, you would be close to what I saw. Warren was completely distorted. His head was huge, but his legs were short and small. Somehow, I knew I looked the same to him. We couldn't look at each other.

Every time the sun went behind the clouds, the whole mood would shift. We were both having a bad trip and we knew what the goal was—wait it out until we came down. We made it to Juan's, but he wasn't home, so we just sat in one of the old cars that they used for parts at the body shop and waited it out. We finally came down after sitting there for hours.

That day, I learned that Warren liked freaking out on acid. He was like a little kid who wanted to go on the scary ride again. His strange obsession with this would eventually be very costly.

The "party" continued in the summer between freshman and sophomore year. I was supposed to attend summer school but like anything else I didn't want to do, I just never showed up. We discovered the local forest preserve to hang at all day. Frisbee, softball, motorcycles, vans, Volkswagen busses, drinking, smoking pot, and any other drug were plentiful. We'd hitchhike, ride our bikes, or get rides from anyone with a car.

In the evenings, we would go to someone's shack and party. By this time, everyone had a basement, a shack, or a garage to party in. There was our shack, Brian's, and Jeff McElory's. We would go to people's houses whose parents didn't care or weren't home and throw parties. It became non-stop.

Cal lived just up the road from Schiller Woods, so we started spending more time at his house. He lived behind Rolling Stone Records, one of the biggest and most well-known record stores in the Midwest. We would spend hours perusing the rows of Albums, eight tracks, and the new cassette tape format. Half a block away was Harlem-Irving Plaza, one of the few outdoor malls at the time. The shopping mall concept was just starting to grow.

One evening, we had a big party at Cal's. All of us were there: Warren, Danny, Juan, Brian, Pam, Mary, Sylvia, Judy, and me. We got really fucked up and took a walk to the mall. While there, Warren threw a big rock through the window of a clothes store. He went in and burglarized the place with the alarm going off, while the rest of us ran back to Cal's. Warren went back and noticed that the alarm had faded, and no cops came.

So, we all crept back to the store. Cautious at first, we all started going through the racks with a flashlight, looking for our sizes. We were running out of the place with stacks of clothes. It was both exciting and scary. I think we were all a little paranoid the rest of the night and we all crashed at Cal's house.

My relationships with my new friends also started taking me away from my neighborhood friends more and more. The final separator took place at a party at Brian's shack. We were all really drunk and stoned, and Jim was starting to chase Judy around a bit, which had started at earlier get-togethers. Danny was there and didn't like Jim or Jeff for some reason. Danny was tough but usually well-restrained, however, he didn't do so well at restraining himself when he was drunk, and the rarely seen bully in him reared its ugly head. He walked up to Jim, removed his glasses, and punched him in the face. Jim responded by saying: "What the fuck! What did you do that for?"

Danny quipped back, "Why? What are you going to do about it?"

This was an awkward moment for me, especially because Cal and Warren thought it was funny. Brian did, too, but Brian was a little more of a peacemaker and a caretaker. Putting his arm around Danny and pulling him away, he asked, "Hey, Dan, what'd you do that for?"

I was torn; it was like I was being forced to choose. Looking back, I wish I had stood up for my friend, but at that time, I didn't. I just followed Jim outside, made sure he was okay, and told him, "You'd better go."

Jim's pride was hurt more than anything, so he and Jeff left. Judy was pissed off and yelled at Danny. Danny apologized but laughed it off, knowing he had likely scored some "folklore points." "Remember that time you punched Jim Decino in the face? You were soooo fucked up!!"

I never brought anyone from my neighborhood with me again. I officially had two distinctly separate sets of friends. My neighborhood friends were the ones who I could be myself, feel totally comfortable with, and who accepted me unconditionally. My school friends were tough, cool, feared, and respected, but required constant effort to prove myself and fit in with them. At that time in my life, I caved into the pressure of wanting to be tough and cool.

The early signs of trouble

The rest of the summer there would be frequent parties and acid trips. You can only do so much LSD until burnout starts setting in, which is what happened. I remember a party at Jeff McElory's shack. We were all tripping and laughing our asses off, but by the end of the evening, we were all sitting in a circle, in a depressed haze and uncomfortable silence. I'm sure we would all be diagnosed with some kind of "depression disorder" today, but back then, we just called it "coming down from acid." I called it the "unrequited love circle." Our faces were partially hidden due to the only light being candlelight, but the truth could still be seen on our faces. Janice was staring longingly at me, I was staring longingly at Mary, Mary was staring longingly at Cal, Cal was staring longingly at Sylvia, and Sylvia was staring longingly at Judy. I started to suspect that Sylvia was gay, despite her being with Cal at one time.

Nobody had what (who) they wanted. Despite all the great drugs that we took, nobody was happy, and for that moment, coming down from acid made us all painfully aware of it.

Along with this painful reality check and subsequent acid-induced-depression, came the actual brain damage that accompanied the psychological. I started noticing that even when I was not under the influence of acid, I was still seeing trails and mild hallucinations. This would linger for some time. I would eventually just get used to it. I decided to lay off acid for a while.

The bigger concern (if you can believe that there was one) was Warren. Something in his personality changed. It was difficult to put my finger on then, but he developed what could best be described as an "I don't care attitude." He started living on the edge, constantly flirting with physical danger. He never wanted to just get high anymore. He always sought total oblivion. Ironically, instead of us being concerned, he just earned extra "folklore points" from the group for his risky behaviors. It was simply normalized by the culture we found ourselves immersed in. A culture that at first was exciting and freeing. But it eventually changed, and a darker, more ominous side started to emerge.

I responded by somewhat retreating to the neighborhood and the safety of hanging with my homies in Jim and Jeff's basement. We would be getting high, listening to music, and playing cards, ping-pong, or hockey.

Playing hockey in their basement was an interesting endeavor. The basement was unfinished, so we had red duct tape as nets at either end of the concrete foundation. This made for some interesting arguments: "That was in!"

"No, it wasn't! It hit right here (pointing with my stick)."

"How is that a goal?!"

We'd play three on three, plus goalies, depending on how many people we had. The puck was made of a softer but thick hollow plastic. It had a bit more weight than your standard floor hockey puck, so if you got hit with a good shot, it was going to hurt and leave a mark. "Look at this slapper I took from Mike Szady!" They were like badges of honor. It's a hockey thing.

Permit me to drive your car

I got my driving permit at age 15. Once I got it, I figured, "Hey, close enough," and drove every chance I got. I would steal my dad's and brother Paul's cars when they were sleeping and drive around the neighborhood.

Once, we were really fucked up on Valium (likely stolen from Albie's purse), and Jim, Jeff, and I went for a spin (literally) in my brother's car. Jeff talked me into letting him drive. Next thing you know, he's driving like Mario Andretti and floors it (it's always the quiet ones) as we're coming to a T at the end of a neighborhood street. He's going too fast to make the turn and spins out into someone's front yard, tearing up their front lawn due to heavy rain the day before. Now stuck, he spins the tires, shooting mud all over the people's house. He finally gets out, and we get away. I took over driving and dropped them off. They jumped a fence to get home, narrowly missing the next part of the adventure. Right after making the turn onto my street from Belmont Avenue, I was pulled over by the police, who had obviously been called by the people with damage to their front yard. I was less than a block from my house. I got cuffed and taken to the station in a benzo-induced blackout.

My brother came and was trying to get me released, but I was being too rude and belligerent to the cops and they wanted me to stay in my cell until I settled down. They asked if he wanted to press charges. Paul, of course, declined and left, but later, my sister Sue came and bailed me out.

She told me how grounded I was going to be as she drove me home. I, still being fucked up and belligerent, thought, *"Oh no, I'm not. I've got shit to do tonight!"* I saw this movie on some TV cop show, and with me having drug-induced "superhuman strength" and all, I got ready to make my move. The car was only doing about 20 mph on a side street, so I probably wouldn't have died but I would no doubt have been seriously injured. Luckily, Sue saw me out of the corner of her eye, getting ready to jump out of the moving vehicle, so just as I opened the door and started propelling myself out of the car, she reached over and grabbed me by the hair, pulling me back into the car. She pulled over and screamed at me: "Are you crazy? Are you out of your mind?!" Amazingly, everything was dropped, and nothing came of the incident. And yes, Sue, I was.

In love: The first cut is the deepest

One Saturday, I went over to Jim and Jeff's just in time to see the unusual sight of three girls leaving. When I arrived, I asked who they were. Jim explained that Dave, Jeff, and Dennis had met them and that they took them to The Jungle basements, smoked a joint, and "made out" with them. Dave and Jeff confirmed this and that they were all a year behind us. They would be attending West Leyden that fall. I commented that the blonde was cute. Dave bragged: "That's the one I was with. Her name is Carol. You can have her; she's a terrible kisser." He explained that she "kissed like a pop bottle" and made an O shape with his mouth to demonstrate. We all laughed.

Jim informed me that their mom was going to Florida next week to visit her sister, and we were going to have a party there next Saturday night. They invited the girls and told them to bring some friends.

On Saturday, the girls showed up with a friend. The party was relatively small, but everyone was having a good time and listening to music. As we all stood around in a circle in the kitchen, I recall telling stories about how Jim was always booby-trapping us and the various methods he employed. The one that cracked everyone up was when Jim spiked a tub of chocolate pudding with plastic fork tips to sabotage us from eating it while he was gone.

We were all standing there laughing at the story when out of nowhere, I felt something brush against my ass. I dismissed it, but when I felt it a second time, and looked out of the corner of my eye. There was Carol's hand playing with my ass! I looked at her and she smiled this devilishly cute smile. I immediately took her by the hand and took her down to the basement.

We started kissing and fell onto the couch like the crumpled heap of human flesh we had suddenly become. Oh, and that "pop bottle" shit—that lasted about five seconds. I showed her how to kiss properly. She was an excellent student! It was a hot session that lasted the rest of the night. We did all we could to keep our clothes on. We fell hard for each other that night and before she left, we exchanged numbers and made a date for early the next week.

Our first date would be an interesting early test of our feelings due to me taking a slapshot in the mouth a few hours before we met. My upper lip had swollen like a balloon. I don't remember much about the date, but I remember that she was impressed that I showed up in that condition. She gently kissed my fat lip at the end of the date to show that her feelings for me hadn't changed. Neither had mine. We were officially "going out," as we used to say.

Home, home again

I remember being in Jim and Jeff's basement after partying all weekend with my other friends and being with Carol. This had become a rare appearance as I continued drifting away from the neighborhood. I remember coming down from acid, a drug I still did, though less frequently.

As I sank into the couch observing the antics of my childhood friends, I also sank into this kind of melancholy mood that by then, almost always accompanied "coming down" from acid. I remember Jim and Dave playing ping-pong and arguing. Jeff and Dennis were chiming in, arguing about who they thought was right and laughing at the intensity of their argument (Dennis laughed at everything). Ricky was biting his nails with a worried look on his face as he did whenever there was an argument. In the background, Pink Floyd's *The Dark Side of the Moon* album was playing...

"Home, home again. I like to be here when I can. And when I come home cold and tired, it's good to warm my bones beside the fire."

Maybe it was all the acid I did, but those words etched into my soul, and I remember feeling that this was where I belonged. These were the people who knew the real me and accepted me unconditionally. I got in touch with the sentimental feelings about the neighborhood that were likely magnified by the acid.

When I would come home from my forays into the world, they were "the fire" that warmed my bones. A slight smile came across my face, then, a deep sadness, sensing the inevitable, that it couldn't last. I didn't know at that moment just how right I was. Even through all the drugs, the true angst, growing pains, and the feelings of a teenager made their way, however briefly, to the surface. Some drastic changes were right around the corner.

As I said earlier, most of our parents were like the parents in the *Peanuts* cartoons. They were mostly non-existent and pretty much left us alone. In their defense, they really didn't have much choice. Our society has a lot of financial pressures that often require both parents to work. These, and other pressures, led some of our parents to divorce.

Being a single parent, of course, made this even more difficult with kids like us. Parenting teenagers under these conditions is inherently difficult, so they were in the dark about what we were up to. Even when they had a clue about what we were doing, they didn't know what to do about it. There wasn't a handbook in the 1970s that I'm aware of, that taught parents how to deal with delinquent substance-abusing kids. So, they were pioneers of sorts.

There were at least two parents, who deserve a lot of credit for taking bold, decisive action that likely saved their kids from destruction. The moves they made were not well received, but it goes to show why parents must do their job, even if their kids dislike or disagree with their decisions. It is usually in their kid's best interest, which, kids usually don't realize for years. It's one of the reasons kids need parents, not "buddies" like Cal's parent's were.

Mary's mother saw where she was headed and promptly yanked her out of West Leyden and sent her to an all-girls Catholic high school. If we thought that was drastic, it paled in comparison to what divorced, single mom Carol Decino did. That trip to Florida wasn't just to visit her sister. It was to lay the groundwork and plan to intervene and save her kids by moving there.

I vaguely remember Jim announcing that they were moving to Florida, probably because by then, I was in a drug-induced haze most of the time. By the time Jim and Jeff were close to leaving, there was already a cold apathy that had set in on both sides. I don't think I ever even said goodbye to Jeff.

I remember my biggest concern was getting my albums back that Jim borrowed over the course of time. I remember meeting him on the corner of Fletcher and Lee Street and getting my albums the day before they left. I don't remember exactly what words were exchanged, but I remember it was brief and barely cordial. I guess we needed to be mad at each other to "break up." I had already become numb about them leaving, at least on the surface. I was more concerned with where the next party and my next high was. But deep inside, I was wounded and grieving. Because of my drug use, I never allowed myself to feel my true feelings and grieve the loss of my lifelong friends.

I fought the law...well, you know the rest

My failure to appear at summer school hadn't gone unnoticed. As a result, a probation violation was filed, and I was brought back before the judge. It had been established that my parents couldn't handle me. To keep me from going to "juvey jail," my sister Sue and brother-in-law Gary offered to take me in. The judge gave me the option of going to the Juvenile Department of Corrections or going to live with my sister Sue and brother-in-law Gary and return to school. Obviously, I chose the latter.

When I moved in, their garage was used for storage, and it was a mess. I was going to need a place to play my guitar, so Gary and I installed a curtain ceiling to the floor, creating a cool little hangout space for me and my friends.

Soon after getting settled, I started jamming with a local guy I met. Bob L. played bass, and I played guitar. We met at the lunch table at school. We were both assigned to the "lame" lunch period and were the only "cool" guys who ate lunch at that time, so we sat at a table of all girls.

Bob would come over to my garage and hang out, and we would play covers of artists like Cream, Led Zeppelin, and Ten Years After.

Bob and I pitched in for some pot called Acapulco Gold. We had only heard about it through the likes of Cheech and Chong and a few other media sources. I recall us both remarking, "It better be good for what it cost."

We rolled a "toothpick" (a skinny joint), I lit it and took a hit. It expanded in my lungs, and I immediately choked it out. Bob did the same and after about two or three hits each, we put it out. We were stoned on our asses!

Out of the blue, Juan Garcia stopped by to jam with us. We excitedly told him about the pot we had. Juan fancied himself a "pot elitist" and connoisseur, due to his Mexican heritage. He bought a few skinny joints, and I charged him double the going rate for a normal-sized joint. He got an attitude and complained: "Oh, c'mon it's just pot; it's not *that* good."

We dared him to smoke a whole joint. He replied with a cocky tone in his voice: "Do you know who you're talking to? I could smoke both of these."

"Go ahead, if you can. I'll roll you two more," I said.

"Okay," Juan said with a cocky look to match his cocky tone.

He lit one and took a hit. He tried to hold it in but choked his ass off! Bob and I laughed. "Okay, that's one hit; keep going." Juan took a second hit and choked it out. His eyes were bloodshot, and tears were running down his face. With a big dopey grin on his face, he slowly reached for the ashtray and reluctantly conceded, "I think I'll…save it for later."

We cracked up! He couldn't play a lick of guitar and wound up going home. That story had folklore written all over it. Whenever Bob and I smoked a joint from that day on, we'd turn to each other and in our best Mexican accent, we'd say, "I think I'll…save it for later." Then, we'd burst into laughter.

Under Gerhardt's wing (and thumb)

My sophomore year of high school would be an adventure that would be full of ups and downs. Sue and Gary had a plan laid out for me that included a crash course in discipline, but also plenty of ways to earn privileges. Gary sat me down and basically laid down the law. The days of John reading the newspaper and not saying a word were over. Gary's law was simple: "Follow the rules or get your ass beat." That's the way it was in those days. There was none of this calling the police or the Department of Children and Family Services (DCFS), unless, of course, it went far enough beyond discipline.

The rules consisted of household chores, curfew, and going to school. Outside of that, he really didn't care what I did, including getting high. I guess that would have been hypocritical since he was getting high almost daily, too. It was the 1970s; everyone was getting high. Gary's motto was "You can do whatever you want, as long as you take care of your responsibilities." I did start to become more responsible, which included returning to somewhat regular attendance at school, though I still wasn't really doing much beyond that.

Sunday nights became another bonding experience for Gary and me. After Sue and the kids went to bed, we would turn the lights down low, get stoned, and listen to WXRT-FM's' radio simulcast of J.R.R. Tolkien's *The Hobbit* from the British Broadcasting Corporation (BBC).

"What does it gots in its pocket, my precious?"

We were both riveted to the story, and Nicole Williamson's character voices and awesome narration allowed our imaginations to visualize "Middle Earth" and its hobbits, elves, goblins, and other inhabitants.

Then, when Pink Floyd's long-awaited follow-up to *The Dark Side of the Moon* premiered on WXRT, we waited in anticipation for the broadcast. We surmised how there was no way they could touch *Dark Side*, so we really thought the album had a good possibility of "riding the gravy train" (no pun intended, a line from one of the tracks, "Have a Cigar"). It could have been a rushed spin-off of their hugely successful *The Dark Side of the Moon* LP.

The new album, *Wish You Were Here,* started playing and we heard the gentle synthesizer intro that builds to the first guitar notes of "Shine on You Crazy Diamond." In a classic Steven and Gerhardt moment that I shall never forget, we both slowly turned and looked at each other, our eyes bulging wide and big grins on our faces. We shook our heads "yes" in unison, followed by the exclamation of "Wow!" by the tongue-tied Gerhardt. We knew immediately that the album was going to be kick-ass from that moment on, and it was.

Working together, our adventures living in the Northwoods, teaching me how to play chess, and many other bonding moments, were key in establishing Gary as an important role model and mentor in my life, albeit somewhat tainted by substance abuse (both his and mine). Through his direction, he'd help me take one of my passions to the next level.

A shot... and a save!

Now that I had my permit, Gary taught me how to drive in his Dodge Ram van. He and my sister felt I needed to get involved in some positive activities, so they looked into local hockey leagues and signed me up for the fall league in Hoffman Estates. This was an exciting time because as a goalie in an organized league, I would finally get some real goalie gear. This meant a trip to Gunzo's, where the Chicago Blackhawks got their gear from.

I remember my excitement walking into the store and getting hit with that new hockey gear smell. I was like a kid in a candy store! I tried on pads until I found the ones that fit (no more foam rubber tied with drapery cord and old belts), then a glove (no more baseball mitt), blocker, stick, cup (no more stuffing a dish towel down my crotch), and the rest. My mask was the coolest. It was a new design more sophisticated than the old "Jason" masks (The film *Friday the 13th* had not come out yet, so the Jason reference hadn't been made yet) like my hero Tony O wore. It was built more like a catcher's mask.

The cost of everything was over $400.00, a lot of money in 1975. My parents split the cost with Sue and Gary. I loved goaltending and had some natural abilities, but I did not love practice. In full gear, I had to do the same drills as the rest of the team. It was grueling due to my frequent drug use.

Another thing that didn't occur to me at the time, but would bother me in the future, was that I never received any formal coaching on goaltending. The coaches would work on passing, shooting, stickhandling drills and techniques with the rest of the team but just stuck me in the net. I guess they assumed that because I had the gear, I knew how to play the position. The closest I came to getting any formal coaching was a referee who would warm up the goalies before games. He was a young guy in his early 20s. I remember he used to coach me for those three or four minutes. He would take shots at me while giving me tips on my stance, playing angles, and the like.

Carol would come to my games, and she overheard the coaches talking about me and passed on the compliment about my playing well despite my size.

Another unexpected compliment was when, for the first time in my life, my father came to a game and watched me play. This included when I played little league baseball for one season around age 12. He never came to one game.

The "emotionally unavailable, silent man" sat in the stands, not knowing what to expect. He barely knew that I played. He was genuinely surprised when he saw me in full gear. I could see that his eyes shined with excitement. It turned out to be one of the most exciting games of my life.

We were up 3-2 in the third period. If we won, we would advance to the playoffs. With just under two minutes left, a player for the other team sent a long pass up the ice that landed on the stick of their star player. He had a breakaway on me! I felt fear when I saw him coming at me. As he stickhandled toward me, I remembered a move that my hero Tony O made on a guy with a breakaway once. Suddenly, I felt fearless and inspired! Without warning, I shot out of the net straight at him. I stretched out my pads as if sliding into home plate. I knocked the puck off his stick and took his skates out from under him, knocking him on his ass! All perfectly legal. He was caught completely off guard and never got a shot off. I heard the crowd cheer and because of the way I had slid, I was facing the stands as the play unfolded. I saw my father leap to his feet, cheering with excitement on his face that I don't think I ever saw before or after that game. We were able to run out the clock and won the game!

My teammates skated to me, and they all gave me extra headbutts and whacks with their sticks. And I heard a lot of "nice save" even from the ref, who had a big grin on his face when he skated over to me and said, "Way not to give him any net to shoot at, Steve." Talk about a natural high? I had one!

Unfortunately, I was brought back down to earth when we got knocked out of the playoffs in the first round, but I had a nice little taste of hockey glory. It brings a question to mind: Why wasn't it enough to pull me off the path I was on? I'm sure many parents have asked that about all the kids who wasted their potential—zapped away by drugs and alcohol. My father's disappointment with my brother and me must have been unbearable at times.

Swing and a miss

There would be a few other notable attempts to intervene on me that year. At school, I was obviously on a list of high-risk students. As a result, I was invited to an event by a local counseling agency, Northwest Youth Outreach, whose team roamed the halls of West Leyden to engage students who might need their services. They were all relatively young and cool looking.

One of the lead outreach workers, Rick, had long black hair to the middle of his back, a full beard, and sandals. He could have passed for one of the Manson family or possibly Jesus. He commandeered me in the hall and struck up a conversation. "Hey Steve, we're having a get-together this Friday after school at the church next door. We're gonna hang out and have a rap session: there'll be some food and stuff. We'd really like it if you could come."

"Okay, sounds cool. I'll come," I replied. Being a sucker for free food, I decided to go.

After arriving at the church, some faces were vaguely familiar, but nobody I really knew. I gues no one at my level of "free-spiritedness" had shown up, which created some uneasiness from the start. After I grabbed some food and a can of pop, I was greeted by Rick. Then, he saw a fellow outreach worker who had just arrived and excused himself to talk to her.

I made my way to some chairs against the wall, sat down, and ate. I observed Rick and some of the staff sitting with several small groups of teens talking, while others sat and ate. One of the outreach workers asked me how I was doing, and we talked for a minute. I may have struck up a conversation with one or two of the other lone stragglers. Outside of that, I can't remember much, except feeling awkward, which never really went away. I left fairly early.

In all honesty, looking back, I would be one of "the ones that got away." They managed to get me there; unfortunately, they didn't know what to do with me once I got there. In their defense, it was 1975, and there weren't any research-driven treatment approaches back then. They were winging it. If they were playing baseball, I'd describe it as a "swing and a miss." It was a big "whiff" with me. I never went to another one of their events.

In another intervention, Dean Paske started a T.A. (Transactional Analysis) group for troubled students based on the book *I'm OK—You're OK* by Dr. Thomas Harris. I was required to attend three group sessions, after which my participation would be voluntary. I remember seeing another side of Paske in those groups that I didn't know about. He wasn't just the smug disciplinarian I had come to know. He was funny (though still stoic) and showed that he genuinely cared. He would read from the book and then lead a discussion. I remember attending my required sessions and participating in some lively discussions. Unfortunately, once it became voluntary, my attendance abruptly stopped. As a result, these events had no effect on me.

Expanding my horizons (musical and otherwise)

I started playing my guitar daily and as a result, my playing continued to improve. This got me into several social circles from which I developed relationships with a few "jamming buddies." We were all "wannabes," though some of us were more advanced and showed more promise than others.

One new musical connection I made was with my friend Diego. Though he was of Spanish descent, he was as American as apple pie, with skin as white as a ghost. Diego was high-functioning, clever, and quick-witted. He could be a bit intimidating if you couldn't "keep up" with his sharp wit. At times he could seem cocky, but he was also a good guy with a big heart. Diego played acoustic guitar (both nylon and steel string) and had a unique flamenco-like, pick-less style, with Latin and jazz influences.

We would get high and jam for hours at his house. We didn't know many cover songs, so we just played stream of consciousness, making up our own stuff, with me mostly on electric guitar. I used to say we wrote "pieces of songs" but lacked the ability to complete a composition. It was uncharted territory and a challenge for my blues-rock style, but a challenge that I enjoyed. It pushed me beyond my musical comfort zone. In my frantic search to find the notes that aligned with his Latin jazz style, we would occasionally find "the zone" and "flashes of brilliance" were the result. We started getting familiar with each other's "musical minds" and began developing our own style.

One of our shared guitar heroes was Carlos Santana. My brother and his friend took my friend Bob and me to see Eric Clapton. It was my first *real* concert, and Santana was the opening act. Santana's guitar sound was mesmerizing! It cut through your entire being, was clear as a bell, super loud, but smooth as silk. It was an awesome show! I went to that concert a Clapton fan and left a Santana fan. I found out later that Diego was at that show, too.

We loved to play, but I don't think we realized how much we relied on smoking pot for our "musical magic" until one day when it became painfully clear. We both set up our equipment, plugged into our amps, and were ready to play. We looked at each other with the expectation that one of us would light a joint and we'd take a few hits or so before we started. We both froze, staring at each other for a few seconds... "You got some pot—right?" I finally asked.

"No, I thought you had some," Diego replied.

At that moment, we both simultaneously turned our amps off, put our guitars back in the cases, and walked out the door and across the street to our friend Matt's. No one had any pot there, so we drove around all over until we discovered that there was a pot shortage in the area. We finally found some, albeit low-grade quality. We went back to his house, took a few hits off a joint, and jammed. We both got a headache, which is why we later dubbed it "Homegrown Headache Weed." We got it from our mutual friend Rick.

Rick was an interesting character, who grew up in the area and was an unusual combination of gearhead and stoner. He drove a souped-up Camaro and would explain the latest upgrade he installed in his vehicle whether you were interested or not. He would do this while driving at a high rate of speed while demonstrating just what his car was now capable of as a result. All while smoking pot and talking over his cranked stereo system. "Take the Highway" by Marshall Tucker Band would appropriately be blaring through the speakers as we "took the highway." Most of the time I feared for my life driving with Rick. Going 110 mph down the highway, stoned on our asses, seemed a bit risky, but somehow, we always arrived at our destination unscathed.

Rick, Diego, and Matt were part of a new circle of friends I connected with. We mostly hung out at Matt's who I knew from freshman-year gym class.

Matt's house was a big, old, rundown, two-story, Southern-style house, complete with pillars and a front porch. It was a "beautiful mess." It wasn't well maintained and reminded me of an old farmhouse. However, the people inside were, for the most part, beautiful. It was the closest thing to a hippie commune that you were going to find in the Chicago suburbs.

Matt's father was an alcoholic and was passed out most of the time, occasionally making an appearance, reaching for walls, and stumbling from room to room. The few strands of hair on his mostly bald head would stick straight up. His clothes were old, dirty, and wrinkled. Frank was a sad man.

Matt had a resentment for his father that bordered on hatred, and it ate at him. When Matt wasn't depressed or angry, he was a loving, caring, funny, loyal friend, who would literally give you the shirt off his back if he felt you needed it. His mother, Elsey was a quiet, sweet woman of few words, who would give you her last dollar, and unconditionally loved us all. She allowed us to come and go as we pleased and treated us like family. Matt was the only friend whose house was always open, with no need to knock on the door.

All were interesting characters (both male and female) whom I would refer to as my "hippie, intellectual, stoner friends." They were eclectic and read books because they actually wanted to! Most were of a metaphysical nature and focused on subjects like alternate realities and spiritual enlightenment. We explored the concept of a reality that was beyond the tangible daily drudge.

At Matt's, we listened to a wide range of music, some that were on the fringes of the Rock & Roll genre, including progressive jazz-rock performers: John McLaughlin, Al Di Meola, Jean Luc Ponty, Jeff Beck, and Jan Hammer--but also artists like Bob Dylan, Arlo Guthrie, and everything in between.

Matt and company were also big Frank Zappa fans and listened to albums by the comedy troupe Firesign Theater, what I'd refer to as "intellectual, stoner comedy." Two of their albums that were played at Matt's were, *Everything You Know Is Wrong* and *We're All Bozos on This Bus*. I had no way of knowing at that time what the relevance of those two albums would be in the future. Back then, they were just clever, funny, drug culture humor that sought to take the dumb out of the culture that Cheech and Chong represented and bring comedy to a higher, more cerebral level.

It seemed to be an underlying theme for many of the people who hung out at Matt's—to prove that you could get stoned daily and still be intelligent. I must admit that they did a pretty good job of it, too. Everybody played chess, and some people were dead serious about it and had ratings in chess magazines.

They were just as serious about getting stoned and actually knew someone with an airplane, who flew to Jamaica during the pot drought the area was experiencing and brought back some really good shit.

I learned to play chess by getting my ass kicked on a regular basis by Gerhardt, and now, these guys. On the weekends, we'd get stoned and play chess all day and night. Then, we'd all show up at Matt's religiously every Sunday evening, get stoned, and watch *Monty Python's Flying Circus*.

My brother-in-law Gary also hosted his own "stoner chess night" at our house on Friday nights, so I played often back then. It was weird walking in the door and seeing Gary and his friends drinking, and smoking pot, while engaged in a chess tournament with albums like Robin Trower's *Bridge of Sighs* cranked and blasting. No wonder it took those guys 20 minutes to make one move.

So, I added some new friends, and some new drugs to my repertoire. Being the hippies that they were (albeit the 1970s version), they did a lot of natural drugs at Matt's, like peyote and psilocybin mushrooms, which I indulged in. I did pass on the morning glory seeds though. One day, Matt looked like a mad scientist sitting cross-legged on the floor while staring intently at a tray of something or other. It turned out he was de-shelling morning glory seeds. Matt explained that when taken in large quantities, the seeds had hallucinogenic properties. You had to eat some ungodly amount though.

That November, on my sixteenth birthday, my parents would give me one of the best gifts I would ever receive. A gold chain and custom medallion engraved "Happy 16th Love Mom and Dad." Welded onto the front, overlapping each other, were the legendary, elusive, christening rings that I had asked about every year since seeing a photo of them around my neck as an infant. After age 12, I lost interest and forgot about them. What a great surprise! It was original. I loved that there wasn't another one like it in the world and I wore it every day from that day on.

Also, that year, my goal of obtaining my driver's license became a reality. I had achieved at least one of the goals that was keeping me in school.

Turning 16 also meant I was officially employable. My family knew some people who owned Bino's Italian Restaurant in Franklin Park. They begged the owner, "Please give him a job, so he can do something productive!"

The next thing I knew, I had my first job as a dishwasher. My favorite part of the job (besides getting paid) was getting to eat anything on the menu (except for steak and lobster) for free. My least favorite part of the job was the greasy Italian restaurant smell that permeated my entire being after every shift. But it served its purpose. I was able to have money (unfortunately, mostly for drugs) and with Christmas coming, I was able to buy Carol a present. I had strong feelings for her like I once had for Mary. The difference was that this time she had them for me too. It was as scary as hell, but exciting too.

So, I got her a nice necklace on sale. Hey, it was in a very nice, decorative box. I wrapped it myself and brought it to her on Christmas morning. I think her mother and sisters were genuinely impressed that I came by. She opened it up and her eyes got really big, you know, that fake kind of big. Then she said, "Thank you," you know, that "trying to be polite," kind of thank you. She slid over a kissed me. "Thank you, it's beautiful".

I replied, "I'm glad you like it, but what's that?"

"What?" she said with a puzzled look on her face.

"That."

I pointed to the edge of something that was sticking out slightly from beneath the velvet-covered cardboard that was holding the necklace. She pulled on the edges of what turned out to be two tickets to see Led Zeppelin at the Chicago Stadium. She almost jumped out of her pajamas and ran to show her sisters. I told her the story of how long Cal, Warren, Brian, and I stood in line and got the last eight seats in a row. Now her eyes got big for real and the hug and kiss I got was quite a bit more enthusiastic! We had tickets to see one of the biggest bands in Rock & Roll history!

Dazed and confused

The show was awesome, especially the new material from their upcoming release, *Physical Graffiti*. The light show was phenomenal, particularly during the drum solo in "Moby Dick." John Bonham looked like a bronze statue as his platform was slowly raised high into the air throughout the song. Jimmy Page did his not-quite-famous-yet bow thing in the bridge of "Dazed and Confused."

My feelings for Carol were a mixed bag of fear and excitement. The fear first started overtaking the excitement at a party that her best friend Marie and brother Mike had at their house.

Marie's older brother Mike was one of my friends and a regular at Matt's house. Like Diego, Mike was quick-witted. He wanted to prove that not only could you be intelligent and use drugs regularly, but you could also be in great shape and physically healthy. He was the first health-conscious person I'd ever met. He fasted, detoxed, and took herbs and supplements. He drank healthy concoctions with stuff like brewer's yeast in it that he would make himself.

At the party, there wasn't any brewer's yeast, but there was plenty of pot and alcohol. Carol and I had been hanging all over each other, as usual, from the moment I arrived. Everyone knew we were crazy about each other.

Wayne was an older guy in his junior year, who was a kind of muscle-head Jock. He walked up, beer in hand, introduced himself to us, and made some small talk. I had to leave due to hockey practice and didn't think I'd be back, so I left Carol at the party.

For reasons that I don't recall, practice was cancelled, so about 40 minutes later, I returned to the party. When I walked in, I immediately saw Wayne all over Carol, putting the moves on her. He saw me and recoiled trying to play it off, "Hey Steve, glad you made it back." Carol saw me and had a big "Uh oh, I'm in trouble" look on her face. I pointed her to a bedroom that nobody was occupying. Upon entering, I asked, "What's going on?"

"Nothing, we were just talking."

"Talking? Any closer and he would have had his tongue in your ear!"

"He's drunk. Maybe he was flirting a little, but I wasn't flirting back."

It escalated and she started crying. I stormed out, slamming the door and leaving the party. This was my earliest memory of my controlling, possessive jealousy. She tried to call me several times that weekend, but I didn't take her calls. I was hurt and angry and didn't know how to deal with it.

That Monday in school, as the music started playing, indicating the end of class (West Leyden had a custom soundtrack in place of a bell system), we all made our way to the hall. I was on my way to my next class when I saw Carol coming toward me on the other side of the hall. We hadn't spoken since the incident. I pretended not to see her and ignored her. As she got closer, she studied my face for some kind of sign. I gave her nothing until we were almost parallel with each other. At that point, not being a rude person, I said hi. She said hi back and smiled. My heart was aching. I glanced at her out of the corner of my eye as we passed and saw her start to physically shake. We both stopped and looked at each other. I felt the intensity of our feelings for each other. It was a very powerful feeling that I had never felt before. She started crying and ran across the crowded hall into my arms. Everyone in the hall started applauding. It was straight out of a movie! I held her and then pulled her into the doorway of an empty classroom, and we kissed passionately. She apologized and told me she loved me. I told her that I loved her too. We couldn't walk past each other. We were officially in love!

Sue and Gary took full advantage of it when I lived with them by making us their built-in babysitters. It was mutually beneficial. They had free childcare, and we had a comfortable place to be alone. Once my niece and nephews were in bed, and we knew they were sleeping, we would start out on the couch watching TV and making out, then wind up on the living room floor.

One Saturday night, things got really heated and we slipped into Sue and Gary's bedroom. We had always stopped short of intercourse, but that night we lost control. Overtaken by sexual passion, I couldn't even pull out. We were nervous for weeks and, as it turned out, for good reason. Our worst fear came true…she was pregnant.

I guess the good news was I had some really healthy sperm. The bad news? There was no way she could have that baby. Her mother and stepfather would have killed us both. I was 17, she was 16, but I didn't care. I loved her and I wanted her to have the baby, even though I knew she couldn't, so we made the difficult decision to get an abortion. I borrowed $350.00 from my buddy Rick's older brother, Dave. He was a nice guy who always treated me like his little brother. When he heard about our dilemma through Rick, he offered me the money. I didn't even have to ask.

On the day that we drove to the Chicago clinic, I remember being in the waiting room during the procedure. I paced with worry and the minutes felt like hours. My mind kept going to the worst-case scenario of her bleeding to death or something else going wrong, but mostly, I felt guilt and remorse for taking our baby's life. I vowed that I would never be a party to an abortion ever again. Carol came out of it fine, but I'm not so sure our relationship did.

Our friends knew we were in love and were rooting for us, but not everyone was a fan of our love. Especially one of my classmates, Penny Apoulosis. She had a thing for me and wanted me for herself. Penny had a healthy mane of long brown hair, sultry dark eyes, and a curvy, beautiful body. But I was in love with Carol.

Penny would constantly flirt with me in class and afterward in the halls. She would hint and make sexual innuendo but then play it off with "Just kidding." She had become a regular at Matt's, too. She was very respectful when Carol was around and nice to her, so much so that they kind of became fast friends. This led to an invitation to hang out, sort of a girl's night out thing. That was nice of her—wasn't it?

That summer, Hawthorne Racetrack in Cicero would host one of the biggest Rock & Roll events ever. I scored four tickets. The list of headliners was difficult to conceive of being on the same bill. The list was Peter Frampton, Yes, Lynyrd Skynyrd, and Gary Wright. Frampton had exploded onto the scene that year with the release of the live album *Frampton Comes Alive*.

I discovered Frampton much the same way I discovered the Allman Brothers Band. Rick's older brother Dave had just bought a shiny, new, Pontiac Trans-Am, and pulled into Schiller Woods with it.

"Hey, Free Bird, wanna go for a spin in my new ride?"

"Free Bird" was my new nickname, bestowed upon me by our mutual friend Frank Alagna. The Lynyrd Skynyrd song title seemed to accurately represent the irreverent, authority-resistant, free-spirited gypsy that I was.

I got in and as Dave took off, he said, "I want you to hear this. I want to see what you think. But let's smoke this first." Music always sounded better after smoking a joint. He cranked the cassette tape, *Frampton Comes Alive*. I loved everything about it. It was appropriately named too, since the material had all been recorded on previous studio albums with little to no success.

So, I bought tickets. I was mostly interested in seeing Frampton and Skynyrd. Warren and Pam were big fans of Yes. I was not. Gary Wright was unknown to me outside of his current hit song at the time, "Dream Weaver."

I should mention here that within one week; Dave crashed and totaled his new car while driving fucked up on downers. He was unhurt, and the car was covered by insurance. We were lucky that most of us escaped our tranquilizer and sedative phase with our lives, and without killing anyone else.

Frampton comes alive as Steve and Carol slowly die

August 15, 1976, the day of the show, finally arrived. The Chicago-area weather had a freak moment of cooperation, and it was a perfect, sunny day. I picked up my friend Ricky, the only person available for the fourth ticket, and I called Carol. Her sister Jeannette answered and informed me that she spent the night at Marie's down the street. That made sense since the plan was to pick Carol and Marie up there.

By this time, I was no longer welcome at Carol's house because I "made her cry too much." Her mother observed that almost every time she got off the phone with me, she'd be crying. Though this was an exaggeration, there was some truth to it. It was another sign of me being ill-equipped to handle the strong feelings I had for her. Her mother's perception of me started to change, and I became the bad boy, which to some extent, was not far from the truth.

I called Marie's house and let her know that we were on our way. She said that they overslept but would be getting in the shower soon. She suggested I should call from the pay phone at Vic's corner store when we got into the area, and they would walk over there. I thought; *That's odd, but okay.*

When Ricky and I arrived, we followed the instructions. I called and again, Marie answered, informing me that Carol was blow-drying her hair and couldn't come to the phone, but they'd be ready soon. I asked her to hurry because we were already running late. She apologized and agreed to hurry.

Fifteen minutes went by and still no sign of the girls. I became anxious and drove to Marie's. Upon arriving, Marie came out and up to my car and said, "Umm, okay, I have to be honest with you…I don't know where Carol is."

"What do you mean you don't know where she is?"

"She went out with Penny last night and they didn't come home."

"Really? Okay, well, I'm going to drive to Penny's and get her!"

"Okay, I'll wait here," Marie said.

I was pissed! I put the car in gear and took off as Ricky bit his nails.

"I'm going to fucking kill her!"

"Carol?" Ricky asked.

"No, Penny!" I replied.

I started driving toward Penny's when I spotted Carol walking toward us. She saw me and had that "tail between the legs" demeanor as I pulled up. On top of that, she looked hung over. "Get in," I said, and she opened the back door and climbed in. She said hi to Ricky, apologized, and rattled off her story for the whole mishap which, to be honest, I have little recollection of. Something about her and Penny running out of gas and having to crash at Penny's. Blah, blah, blah. I was not thrilled.

We picked up Marie and headed to the concert. I was able to shake off my anger because as we neared the venue, the excitement of seeing Frampton and Skynyrd began to take hold again.

It was general admission and because we were late, it was packed. It took us 30 minutes to worm our way up as close as we could. Gary Wright ended his set with his hit "Dream Weaver." Carol and Marie had to use the bathroom, so they started the trek immediately after he finished.

Lynyrd Skynyrd was next and hopefully, the girls would make it back before they started. They never made it back. Between Skynyrd and Frampton, Ricky and I tried to find them, but they were nowhere to be found. Later we learned that they "got lost?" Hmmm.

As the last band (Yes) played their set, we made our last effort to find them before making our way back to the car to wait for the girls. They found their way back to the car and said that the crowd had gotten too thick, and they couldn't remember where we were, so they gave up.

It was a great concert, but it would be forever tainted by the mishaps that occurred that day. Were they mishaps, or was Penny working her "black magic" to try to break Carol and me up?

Curse of the Grateful Dead

As I was leaving Matt's one night, there was an announcement on the radio that the Grateful Dead was coming to a local venue. The Dead's concerts were famous for being a traveling hippie commune, complete with every drug under the sun. I told Matt that I always wanted to see the Dead and that I was going to get tickets. He looked at me and smiled. "Yeah, that will be cool."

One year later, we would repeat the same exact scene. Matt pointed out to me, "Didn't you say that last year?"

"This year, I'm getting tickets and I'm taking Carol," I promised.

About two weeks later, I came over for our Sunday ritual of getting stoned and watching Monty Python's Flying Circus. The Dead was playing on the radio, reminding me to get tickets, which I exclaimed to Matt. He turned to me and said, "Well, you better hurry, because that's them playing right now at the Auditorium. It's being simulcast live on WXRT." Shit! I missed them again!

My third attempt to see the Grateful Dead occurred the following year with one of my friends—Matt's house regular—Al. At that time, the merging of a chain of theaters under one umbrella had started in our area. They became known as Plitt Theaters. This was a completely new concept. Al acquired two free promotional tickets good for any Plitt Theater anywhere in the country. We found out that the Grateful Dead was coming to one of them. I believe the venue was in southern Illinois.

On the day, of the show, we had our route all mapped out and some extremely good Hawaiian pot. I was finally going to see the Grateful Dead! We got slightly lost on the way there (we were very stoned) but gave ourselves plenty of time and it was daylight, so we found our way. We arrived, stood in line, tickets in hand, and finally got to the gate. When we handed the man our tickets, he looked at us like we were crazy and laughed.

It turned out that this was a concert venue that had an adjacent movie theater. The tickets were only good for the theater. To make matters worse, we got lost on the way back, and two stoned, hippie, white boys were about to run out of gas in a bad neighborhood on the South Side of Chicago, at night. We had to trade a good chunk of the Hawaiian pot for gas to get back.

The black attendant almost didn't do it because he had never seen weed like that and didn't trust us. We explained to him that it was really good shit. He finally took our word for it and gave us the gas. It was official, my attempts to see the Grateful Dead were cursed!

The eleventh-grade syndrome

The threat of getting my ass beat had gotten me back in school, taking the garbage out, and adhering to curfew, but unfortunately, being in and around the building did not guarantee scholastic success. Especially since, by junior year, we had all slid back into some of our old ways: getting high, at times in the building. We were, once again, cutting classes, and wandering aimlessly through the halls. I have to admit that it wasn't as fun as it once was. Teachers would see me in the hall and just ignore me. They started to give up on me.

My "hideout" was on the lower level. There was sort of an emergency exit and outdoor stairwell that was only used by maintenance on occasion. This was a great place to hide out and smoke a cigarette until the passing music played, again filling the halls with students going to their next class.

One day, while hiding out, I peeked into a classroom next to the exit. There was Matt sitting in the back row. So, of course, I was now on a mission to get his attention, torment him through the window, and make him laugh. I achieved my goal, but I also inadvertently got the attention of the teacher, Mr. DeYoung. He wasn't laughing when he came out into the hall and busted me.

Ron DeYoung wasn't just a guy who had a degree and wanted to get paid; he was a true teacher, meaning, he had natural teaching instincts that can't be taught. These instincts kicked in when he came upon me in the hall that day, and rather than sending me down to Dean Paske's office, he invited me into his class. He asked my name, introduced himself, and informed me that the class was called "Theater in Action." He invited me to have a seat and introduced me. "Class, this is Mr. Fiorito. I'm sure you won't mind if he joins us." Half of the class snickered and most already knew me or knew of me.

He went on with class reading briefly from a textbook about the history of improvisation. He put the book down and elaborated, occasionally drawing students into the conversation. He walked to the back of the classroom, where there was a big cardboard box, about 4 feet by 4 feet, and about 3 feet high. He had us all gather around the box. Inside, there were a bunch of odds and ends that looked like rejects from a Goodwill store. He explained that students would be challenged with different improvisational exercises using these objects.

The class was scheduled during my study hall time, so instead of going there, I started attending his class regularly, when I didn't have a detention to serve. How ironic—I couldn't make it to classes that I was supposed to attend, but I regularly attended a class that wasn't even on my schedule.

DeYoung would have us act out scenes from classic plays and various other exercises. One day, after discussing several theater techniques—alterego, aside, flashback, and a few others—he announced that we would be doing what he called "speed improv." You and a partner were given two randomly selected props from the box to improvise a scene and use one of the techniques he had discussed. We had three minutes out in the hall to come up with a five-minute scene using the props he chose, and your selected theatrical technique.

Matt was my partner, and it was our turn. We waited nervously in the hall. DeYoung came out with a chessboard and an empty whiskey bottle and handed them to us. "Here's your props, choose your technique, and you have three minutes to come up with a scene. Good luck!"

We were very familiar with both of our props, so obviously, our scene was going to focus on two men playing chess. We had, on a few occasions, played chess for shots. For every piece you took of your opponent's, you had to do a shot. Naaah, that was too obvious. We had our basic premise of drinking while playing chess, but it was the theatrical technique we chose that really made things interesting. We chose "aside," a technique whereby what the character is saying or doing isn't necessarily what they are thinking or feeling.

This technique required one to step outside of the scene to reveal the character's true motives, thoughts, and feelings. To enhance the effect and project this to the audience, the other character(s) would freeze while the person is performing their "aside" to the audience. We were required to set up the scene by giving a brief statement about the situation or background.

We explained that the scene was about two friends who had been playing chess together for years. My character had been beating Matt's character for the past few years. What we didn't tell them was that throughout the game both men would be drinking whiskey. Matt's character would be drinking more because he was frustrated with losing all the time and was about to snap while maintaining the facade on the surface that it didn't bother him.

I was polite as I whooped him at chess yet again, but I would share my harsh criticism of his play and his drinking in my asides. As the scene went on, Matt's character literally escalated into a mad, drunken rage. This would lead to the end of the scene with Matt's character losing it, picking up the bottle, and killing his friend by hitting him in the head with it…get this …in slow motion.

Matt was brilliant at portraying his calm facade that you could see was cracking as the game went on. His asides became more chilling as he went mad right in front of the class until I looked him in the eye, and with an arrogant smirk on my face, I announced, "Checkmate." He stared at me, and slowly went into uncontrollable shaking and twitching, (great effect, Matt!) until he picked up the bottle and just as we had planned, swung it, hitting me in the head in slow motion. My head moved in perfect rhythm to the blow, followed by a slow-motion fall off my chair to the ground, which to this day, I don't know how I did without losing my balance. Matt stood over me, bottle in hand, with an insane look on his face and saying the final line of the skit, "Checkmate!"

You could hear a pin drop in the room. Then, suddenly, mad applause! We were the only partners who got a standing ovation from the entire class, including Mr. DeYoung. I was hooked. I was officially bitten by the acting bug and so was Matt. He auditioned and got a part in the upcoming fall production of *Arsenic and Old Lace*.

A few weeks later, Mr. DeYoung asked if he could talk to me after class.

"Steve, I'm in a jam and I need your help. One of the guys was supposed to play two parts, but he's overwhelmed and can't handle both parts. I want you to play the other part. We only have two weeks before this show opens. I've seen what you're capable of, and I know you can handle it. It's not a big part but it's an important one that happens near the end of the play."

"What's the part?" I asked.

"You're a cop, a detective, Lieutenant Rooney. You'll be playing your friends Matt and Mike's supervisor."

"Okay, I'll do it," I said.

"Cool. Thanks! You'll be great. Here's the rehearsal schedule," he said, handing it to me.

"What about my hair?" I asked (which was down to my shoulders).

"Don't worry. We'll tuck it under your hat," and he pulled out a fedora. He put it on my head and tucked my hair inside it. I looked in the mirror and saw a face I hadn't seen since grade school. I looked like a square and was already getting a feel for the character.

Arsenic and Old Lace

Arsenic and Old Lace is a classic story that has stood the test of time and has graced many a theater stage all over the world since 1939. The play is about two old spinster sisters, who invite lonely elderly gentlemen over for a glass of elderberry wine (spiked with poison) with the intention of mercy killing them, to put them out of their "misery." They dispose of the bodies by having their nephew Teddy, a crazy who thinks he is President Theodore Roosevelt, bury them in their cellar, convincing him that they are yellow fever victims.

It turns out that they are not the only crazies in the family, and the plot thickens when their long-lost nephew Jonathan and his partner in crime (literally) Dr. Einstein, show up with their own twisted agenda. The only sane nephew (at least initially) Mortimer shows up with his fiancé Elaine to announce their engagement, and we have the makings for all kinds of overlapping plots full of comedy and suspense.

I showed up for my first rehearsal, script in hand, a bit nervous, but in a good way. I guess most define that as "excited." The cast was welcoming and made me feel at ease. I learned my cues, my blocking, my marks, and my lines––and caught on quickly. The story was set in Brooklyn with a lot of New York references, which director Ron DeYoung had us replace with local references.

The play was well cast. Everybody fit their role perfectly with the exception (if I'm being honest) of the guy who I replaced as Lieutenant Rooney. He now remained in only one role as Mr. Witherspoon, the director of the Happy Dale Sanitarium, where all the crazies would be heading to at the end of the play. He was stoic, stiff, and a bad actor. Hey, it's a high school production--right? As for the rest of the cast, the talent was off the charts. Our lead actor, Chris Bruzzini, was perfect, bringing the high level of nervous energy needed to pull off the role of Mortimer Brewster. Cary Grant played the role magnificently in the 1944 film. It was a difficult part with a lot of lines, and to keep that nervous energy high and believable took some real acting skills. I enjoyed watching the performances when I wasn't on stage, which was most of the play. I only came in at the end to bust everybody! Ironic.

I was taken backstage to the dressing rooms to try on my costume, consisting of a suit and tie, a trench coat, and a fedora hat. Mr. DeYoung came back to have a look at me once they got my hair under the fedora. "Perfect!" he exclaimed. Then he suggested that I might have some kind of gimmick or trademark. At the time, the series *Kojak* was a popular TV cop show. He had his signature Tootsie Pop that he often had in his mouth. I suggested gum.

"What if Rooney's thing is chewing some gum obnoxiously, like this?"

I demonstrated and said a few lines in character.

"Yes, that's it," he exclaimed!

On opening night, I realized that I loved everything about the theater. The electricity and excitement were palpable in the dressing room. There is almost nothing like watching a show come together from the ground up, even at that level. The comradery with your fellow actors and techs, the excitement of opening night, the makeup and costumes, the development of a character, and yes, the applause—but most of all, for me, the laughs!

I'll never forget that first performance. I watched the entire play from backstage. As my entrance got closer and closer, the butterflies in my stomach started. I stood stage right at my point of entry and waited until I saw the big stage fight happen and Officer Klein (Matt) hit Jonathan with his Billy club, knocking him unconscious. I noticed my left leg was shaking uncontrollably and then, my cue... "Well, what do you know about that?"

I twisted the doorknob and stepped out into the lights, hands on my hips, chomping on my gum. "What happened here?"

I was completely at home and at ease. No leg shaking, no butterflies. As soon as I hit that stage, it all went away. Then I heard and felt the eruption of laughter from the audience, including the heckles of a few close friends, who had come to see me in a play with their own eyes, and I knew I had them. And I played it!

We got standing ovations all three nights. I know it was only high school theater, but a standing ovation is a standing ovation, nonetheless. One of the most exhilarating feelings in my life at the time! Did it compare to taking drugs? Was it exhilarating enough? No, unfortunately it wasn't. Why not!? Why the hell not!? WHAT THE HELL WAS WRONG WITH ME!? What indeed.

School's out

By the spring of 1976, near the end of my junior year, things started to unravel, and not just for me. Gary, preoccupied with his own escalating addiction to alcohol, drugs, and as I later learned, domestic abuse of my sister, had backed off me by then. He had also been caught up in some counterfeiting ring and was under investigation by the FBI. I was off probation, so there was no more court leverage. Not putting the work into my classes the past two years, outside of eating lunch, finally caught up with me. You needed something like 16 credits to graduate, and I had some ridiculous number like six. I don't know what the actual numbers are, but I would say this is why most substance abusers drop out in the eleventh grade. Once you get to junior year and you know you're not likely to graduate with your class, you figure there's no point.

I continued getting high on various drugs on a regular basis. Luckily, I had slowed down on the acid considerably but was still indulging in natural hallucinogens, psilocybin, and peyote. I was also still doing a lot of downers, now adding Placidyl to my repertoire. This drug was good for nothing but getting you fucked up and was appropriately nicknamed "green monsters."

I made the mistake of taking one too many at school one day. I was so fucked up that I was sent to the nurse's office. They took my vitals and left me sitting in the examination room. I overheard the nurse call Paske's office.

"He's on something. He's incoherent. You'd better come over here."

I knew I would be screwed if Paske got to me, so I saw my opportunity and made a break for it, that is if you call stumbling through the hall while bouncing off the walls "a break for it." Somehow, I was able to find and slip out the back door. All they could prove was that I left school without permission, so I dodged another bullet, but my "luck" was about to run out.

About six weeks later, I wasn't so lucky. My friend Juan was starting to sell pot. I got him to bring me a "lid" (an ounce of weed) to school. We arranged to meet in the backstairs hallway after first-period homeroom to make the transaction. We were always cocky and reckless about drugs, but we never got caught or challenged, so it was understandable. Eventually, your luck runs out. We slipped under the stairwell to make the exchange. I took the $35 out and handed it to Juan. He took the baggie of pot out and handed it to me. I opened it and took a big whiff. A little green smelling, but not bad. Krekelberg timed it perfectly and stuck his head under the stairs. I quickly stuffed the bag into my pants pocket. "What are you guys doing under there?" Kreck asked.

"Just talking," Juan and I replied.

"We didn't even notice that the passing music had stopped."

"Well, you're late for class. You'd better get there quick."

So, we scurried off to our classes.

On my way to class, I wondered if he saw it. I went back and forth in my mind. *I think he saw it.* Then, I thought, *if he did, he would have busted us right there—wouldn't he?* I went to class and because Krek escorted me, I didn't have an opportunity to transfer the bag from my pocket to "the safety zone" in my underwear. Within 15 minutes, someone got me out of class. I still had hope because this was a common occurrence. Someone was always yanking me out of class and taking me to Paske's office for some infraction.

Upon entering Paske's outer office, any hope I had that this was just a "routine traffic stop" faded. I saw Juan sitting there waiting on the bench. He mouthed, "Say we found it," as I passed him. Krekelberg guarded the door, almost daring me to try to run. I was trapped with a big ounce of weed bulging (is that an ounce of weed or are you just happy to see me?) in my pocket.

Upon entering Paske's office, he cut right to the chase and asked me if I had any drugs on me. I, of course, replied: "No, I don't."

He asked me to empty out my pockets onto his desk. My reaction to this request was again inspired by the character Vinnie Barbarino on the TV series *Welcome Back Kotter*. With a glazed-over look on my face, I said something to the effect of: "What?" "Where?" "When?" "Why?" I stalled for as long as I could, which led to his final offer. "You can empty out your pockets, or we can call the police and have them come and do it for you—your choice."

At that moment, I knew there was no way out, so I pulled the weed out of my pocket and put it on his desk.

"Oh, I found this under the stairs," I said as nonchalantly as I could. I then emptied my other pocket, which contained rolling papers and a roach clip.

"I suppose you found the papers and the roach clip under there too, huh?" he said sarcastically.

"Yes, I did," I answered in a serious, polite tone.

"You sure you didn't get it from your friend Juan?" Paske pressed.

"No, I didn't. I really found it under the stairs." Being the master of the quick lie that I was, I added, "I called Juan to come under there and look to see if he thought it was real or fake."

"Okay, well, have a seat."

I did, as he called the Northlake police. He informed me that I was suspended indefinitely. They would review my case at the end of the week and I should call him at that time.

Upon their arrival, the two cops got the scoop from Paske. They cuffed me, read me my rights, and walked me out the back door to a waiting squad car. I appreciated that they didn't parade me through the office and the halls with a big purple wad of gum on my nose as Mrs. Barca did in the fifth grade. I'm pretty sure I wouldn't have gotten any laughs this time.

Down at the station, they questioned me, and I just stuck to my story with a few minor improvements. I told them that I was going to turn it in, but I got scared and was made to go to class. I said, I planned on turning it in after class, but that I never got the chance. They believed me. I was let go without any charges. An award-winning performance helped me to at least avoid getting locked up, or more likely, getting put back on probation.

I called Paske about two weeks later. My recollection of the conversation is vague, but the negotiations broke down and fell through. I think we figured out mathematically that it would have taken me too long to catch up and graduate and that a GED (General Educational Development) was a viable option. A shortcut to getting a high school diploma sounded like a good option to me, so I never went back. As Alice Cooper sang, "School's out, forever."

Warren had already dropped out and started working. I didn't want to be a student anymore. I just couldn't make it work. Brian was one of the few of us who graduated high school but partied every bit as hard as we did. Years later, I asked how he did it. He explained, "I knocked out my homework as soon as I got home before we went out." Duh!

Rejection: Adding insult to injury

After my school failure, some feelings of missing my friends Jim and Jeff started to surface. Their mother, Carol maintained a friendship with Ricky's mother, Phyllis. I got their phone number from Ricky, who was also still in touch with them and talked to them occasionally. I decided to give them a call one Sunday afternoon. I was nervous but excited to talk to my lifelong friends. Despite our estrangement, I still felt we were like brothers.

Their older brother John answered the phone. John was my sister Mary Jo's age and had his own problems, including shooting himself several years earlier while playing "Russian Roulette." I don't remember the details, but he was no angel. He never completely recovered. John described life in Florida, and he asked how I was doing. He said goodbye and went to get Jim. I could hear him in the background in an angry whisper, "Get on this phone, Jimmy! He's your friend!" Jim obviously didn't want to talk to me but reluctantly got on the phone. I played it off and pretended not to hear the exchange.

"Hey, Florida boy. How's it going?"

In an unenthusiastic monotone, he proceeded to tell me how good he and Jeff were doing. He said that they had enrolled in some type of religious behavior modification program and that they no longer smoked, drank, or did drugs—and that they were getting all As in school. I promptly responded by lying my ass off about how "good" I was doing, and that I had stopped all of that too, except for cigarettes. Hey, I had to make it somewhat realistic. He then put Jeff on the phone who always had the communication skills of a deaf-mute. That "conversation" had a lot of dead air in it and went down like a lead balloon. We said goodbye and that was it. I would never see or speak to them again.

After the call, I felt even more inferior, which put another dent in my already very low self-esteem. I walked out the door with a knot in my gut that I quickly covered up with sarcastic humor, mumbling to myself about the "goody, goody pussies" they'd become. I snickered, but deep inside I had a nagging feeling that the joke was really on me.

Another crushing blow

Not long after that jolt, I would have to endure the most crushing blow of my young life. Carol, my high school sweetheart, and first love of my life, broke up with me. Our demise was somewhat slow and painful. By then, I had moved out of Sue and Gary's and had become like a gypsy, living here and there. Carol's parents had officially forbidden her from seeing me by then. She ran away from home in protest in an attempt to save our relationship and we lived at my friend Rick's together for about three or four days but the "walls were closing in" on our relationship.

Her parents' rejection took its toll, but an even bigger factor was that Carol began to outgrow me. She wanted to go places and do things with her life. Aside from some ambiguous, undefined musical aspirations, I just wanted to get high, draw, and have sex. I was a "Spicoli-like" hippie-gypsy, with no goals except to find the next party and the next high. This may have been fun for her for a while, but I was going nowhere, and she saw it. I don't remember a lot of the details. I'm sure I drowned them out with drugs and alcohol, but I do remember the last few times we were together.

We were babysitting at Sue and Gary's one Saturday night. We went through our usual routine, starting out on the couch and ending up on the floor, but something felt different. I could feel that she was just going through the motions. When our love was on fire, we would both almost lose consciousness and be swept away by our feelings. I could feel that she was very conscious and in control and that no matter how I tried to get her to that place, I couldn't.

It happened again when she came to see me for the last time at one of the interim apartments that my parents had rented on the outskirts of Chicago. After selling our house, they would move several times. They would never live in their own home again.

While walking through the woods across the street, she started to cry. I don't remember the exact words, but in essence, she told me it was over. I was in denial and clung to some thread of hope that she left me with, saying something like; "Maybe in the future, blah, blah, blah…"

When the initial sting wore off, it was replaced by a deep hurt that would intensify and linger like a wound that wouldn't heal. I would spend the next several years of my life brokenhearted, wounded, and lost. Knocking at the door of age 18, with no real coping skills other than drugs, I couldn't handle the fact that someone, who once loved me passionately, now didn't. I didn't realize it at the time, but this was not only devastating to my heart, but also to my already badly damaged self-esteem, which was now hanging by a thread.

Looking back, it was an ideal time for me to focus on something that I was passionate about, and relatively good at, like hockey, but I had become lazy due to my drug use. The thought of drills and practice became a major barrier to me getting back into the sport. I was relegated to occasional rat hockey games at 2 a.m. with beer league outcasts. I *did* turn more to music, but the people I was playing with were all getting high just like me, so although it was a soothing distraction at times, it was not the answer, and in some ways, made my drug problem worse.

To rub salt in the wound, I was walking through the neighborhood and saw Carol in the passenger seat of a souped-up Z-28 Camaro next to her new boyfriend, Duane. I was devastated. One of the few forms of relief was sitting in my room listening to the hopeful messages in songs like "Try to Love Again," and "Already Gone" by the Eagles, and "Bell Bottom Blues" (which was our song) by Derek and The Dominos. Drugs and music were probably the only things standing between me and stepping in front of a freight train at that time. Getting high was the only thing that gave me any relief from my pain.

As a man, you weren't supposed to cry, but I remember pulling up in front of my sister Sue's house at about 11 p.m. after being at a party and pulling out a fifth of Southern Comfort (my drink of choice) from under the seat. My intention was to have a swig or two before going into the house. Then that familiar guitar intro came on the radio, and then the words…

Bell bottom blues, you make me cry. I don't want to lose this feeling. And if I could choose a place to die, it would be in your arms.
Do you want to see me crawl across the floor to you? Do you want to hear me beg you to take me back? I'd gladly do it because I don't want to fade away. Give me one more day, please. I don't want to fade away. In your heart, I want to stay.

Before I knew it, I drank half the bottle. I was sitting in the front seat of my car at midnight, crying like a baby until I passed out. I woke up the next morning sprawled across the front seat of the car, mouth dry, head pounding, and hung over as shit. Just a small sample of how costly the quest for killing emotional pain would be. A quest that I was now officially on.

Systems for Solar Control-A microcosm of race relations

After dropping out of school, impulsively quitting my job at Bino's (I didn't want to smell like an Italian restaurant anymore), and moving back in with my parents, I needed a job. My father promptly pointed to a drapery business acquaintance of his, who was looking for help in their warehouse. It was owned and operated by two friends—Paul and Marvin (No, they weren't a gay couple). My dad drove me to the interview in the heart of Uptown, near Lawrence Avenue on Clark Street.

I was interviewed by Marvin, who was a chubby Jew with pasty skin, curly black hair, and thick black-rim glasses. Marvin was the brains of the outfit. Paul was a skinny Jew who spoke with a slight New York accent and always had an out-of-season tan. Marvin showed me around and introduced me to the ladies in the workroom and their supervisor George, an older, slightly flamboyant, gay man in his 60s. "Nice to meet you, Stevie honey," he said while smoking his Virginia Slim extra-long cigarette in the break room.

The workroom where they made the drapes was huge. I was familiar with the drapery business, but this was on a grander scale than what I had experienced at my dad's shop. Systems for Solar Control was the name of the company, and they did mostly big commercial jobs like offices and high-rises downtown. They also did vertical and horizontal blinds. If a company moved to a new location, buying new window treatments could be a pricey endeavor. Some windows in these buildings were 15 feet high and eight feet wide. Often, they could refit the blinds and drapes to fit their new windows. This is one of the duties the position required.

We continued through the second floor, and I was introduced to the bookkeeper, Hasson—a short bald man with a Middle Eastern accent, of Lebanese descent. He chain-smoked and wasn't very friendly. He tried to cover up with a fake smile, what would later be revealed as his disdain for Americans. I had no idea at the time that anyone hated Americans. He seemed put out and perturbed by the fact that his work was interrupted by having to greet me.

We continued the tour to the lower level, where he showed me bins that went to the ceiling full of bolts of drapery material and every conceivable kind of hardware you could imagine. On the other side were bins where blinds, hardware, and draperies were staged and ready by the loading dock. The installers would come in the morning and load jobs into their vehicles.

Marvin introduced me to two black men—Johnny and Robert Johnson—brothers, both in their thirties. Johnny was the warehouse supervisor and the older brother. He was tall and dressed a bit funky with a black velvet suit, a colorful button shirt, suede boots, and a good-sized Afro. He had some gold chains and an earring in one ear. Johnny was the epitome of cool.

Robert ("Boo" as he was called) on the other hand, dressed like a railroad worker, with short hair, white Dago-T, work gloves, jeans, and work boots. Boo was a big, strong man. In a deep voice, he asked, "How you doin' young man?" They both seemed cool—as their big, genuine smiles conveyed.

"Boo, you better look busy; here comes Marvin," Johnny joked as Marvin and I got off the elevator and approached.

As it turned out, they never had to "look busy" because they always were. They demonstrated some of the duties I would have, including cutting down blinds, making custom drapery rods, and even electric ceiling track.

Just then, another man came in through the back door by the loading dock. His name was George. He was black, in his late twenties, and was a good-looking man with an infectious, genuine smile. He was part-time in the warehouse and a part-time installer in training.

Marvin walked me back upstairs, where my father was "chewing the fat" with Paul and a few ladies from the workroom.

"The job's yours if you want it, Steven," Marvin said.

I thanked him and accepted the job.

I was very excited about working there. It was full-time, a nice bump in pay, and in the heart of Chicago, which up to that point in my life, I had only experienced through a car window with my dad or brother-in-law Gary. Lastly, I felt comfortable around the guys I was going to be working with.

I can say, looking back, that I honestly was colorblind, even at that age. Aside from noting the differences in skin color and hair texture, my true feelings about it went no further than that. With me, you were either cool or you were an asshole, and these guys were obviously *way* cool.

Johnny, Boo, George, and I became fast friends. We would laugh, joke, and talk about women and music throughout the day. They nicknamed me "Stevie Wonder," also given to me as a kid by my gym teacher, Mr. Marino. They knew I was going through a difficult breakup and would try to encourage me that I was going to find somebody better. They would even try to match-make a bit. "Hey Stevie, what about her?" referring to one of the young Cuban girls in the workroom next door.

We shared a space with a clothes manufacturing company that was owned and operated by an older Cuban man. He hired many Cuban refugees, most of whom were women. The girl's name was Cecelia or Ce Ce, as everyone called her. We would catch each other looking at one another occasionally and I'd get a smile. She was cute, with a hot, petite figure. Unfortunately, she could barely speak English as I found out when I finally tried to talk to her. It was still a welcome occasional distraction from my broken heart.

It wasn't long before the subject came up at break time. "You smoke anything else besides cigarettes?" Johnny asked. "Sure do," I replied. "C'mon," he said, as the three of them started walking toward the loading dock. Johnny pulled out a joint and lit it, and the four of us passed it around.

They learned that I was saving for a new guitar—an Ibanez Les Paul copy that I had my eye on. It became a running joke that they knew an easy way for me to get it. Johnny would say, "I'm sure George upstairs would buy you that guitar if you went over his house…" followed by laughter.

The phone rang in the warehouse, snapping us back into reality and Johnny struggled to run in his Superfly black suede boots to answer it. It was for Boo. We could hear him talking in a serious tone. It turned out that one of his kids had an accident at school and may have broken her leg. Her mother called to get Boo's advice on whether to take her to the hospital, or not.

"I gotta go," Boo said after hanging up the phone. He instructed Johnny on what he was working on, put on his hat and coat, and left. He explained that Boo was a good father to his nine kids! Most of them had different mothers. I think five in all. I could hear the respect in his voice as he explained that Boo is always there for his kids and their mothers, no matter what.

He told me about growing up in a big family and the neighborhood they lived in. He confided that Boo was respected by all and that though he was the youngest, he was the toughest.

"Growing up, if we had a beef or someone was giving us trouble, we'd go get our little brother." I was impressed and I could see that not only was Boo physically strong, but he also had a big heart and was emotionally strong. He never shirked his responsibilities.

Johnny, being the warehouse manager, operated the radio. He recognized the need to give me some time to listen to rock stations, so he instituted a schedule. I remember being exposed to the popular black artists of the time: Marvin Gaye, Al Green, Barry White, P-Funk, The Isley Brothers, and Lou Rawls, who had a smash hit at the time, "You'll Never Find Another Love Like Mine," which was played often on every pop radio station.

The real Stevie Wonder had recently put out a great new album—*Songs in the Key of Life*. A few songs, such as "Sir Duke" and "Isn't She Lovely?" got a lot of airplay. Though not my usual Rock & Roll "cup of tea," the greatness of these artists and their songs was not wasted on me, and I developed a strong appreciation for the music.

One day, George and I were talking about music, and I was impressed to hear that he was familiar with and liked some of the music I grew up listening to. He especially liked Led Zeppelin, Credence Clearwater Revival, Deep Purple, and a few others. Headphones were a popular way to listen to music in the 1960s and '70s. Also, to this day, there has been no match for the sound quality of vinyl records, especially through a pair of quality headphones.

We talked about records that had the best fidelity and were best to listen to on headphones.

George proposed a little challenge since it was payday. "You pick the best album for headphones to buy and listen to for me, and I'll do the same for you. We'll come in on Monday and compare notes."

"Okay, you got a deal," I replied.

"Okay, my pick for you is *Songs in the Key of Life* by Stevie Wonder," George said.

Then it was my turn. "Okay, I got the ultimate album for you, but you have to promise that you'll smoke a joint before you listen to it," I said.

"You know I will, brother; that's a given," George assured me. "Okay, my pick for you is *The Dark Side of the Moon* by Pink Floyd."

"Okay, deal, and same for you before listening to Stevie's new album."

"Of course," I replied.

On Monday morning, we both walked up to each other with big grins on our faces, having followed each other's instructions. Johnny and Boo stood there with smiles on their faces, thoroughly enjoying the exchange between George and me, as we "high-fived".

I reported a great experience with *Songs in the Key of Life* and that I discovered what I thought were the real gems on the album that got almost no airplay at that time: "As" and "I Wish."

"Man, you are so right. Those are some bad-ass cuts!" George agreed.

Then, George exclaimed enthusiastically about *Dark Side of the Moon*. "Wow! I was blown away! I'm not shittin' you; that has to be the best album I've ever heard on headphones!" We both continued going back and forth, critiquing the two masterpieces.

Johnny chimed in, "Okay, you two, break up the love fest; we got some big jobs to get out today." "Oh, also, I need to inform you we're having a party at the crib this weekend and you guys are invited." Johnny wrote down the address and directions for me.

The party was at Johnny's house on the South Side at 79th and Sangamon Street. The fact that it was an all-black neighborhood in the heart of the South Side on a Friday night never even occurred to me. Maybe I was a bit naive, but I just didn't think like that back then.

When I arrived, Johnny, Boo, and George were there; Johnny took me around and introduced me to everybody. I was greeted warmly. I *did* overhear Johnny a while later say to someone, "Stevie, cool; he's the real deal."

I was the only white person at the party. We were drinking, smoking pot, shooting craps, rolling dice, playing cards, and having a good time. Johnny and Boo didn't let me out of their sight the whole night though, even when I was hit on by a pretty, curvy, young girl. They were like older brothers chaperoning me. Later, Johnny gave me directions back to the expressway and

I left around 1 a.m. Maybe I was naive and even a bit lucky, but I suspect everything went smoothly because the 1970s were a different time.

At work, we all reminisced about the party.

"Did you see Stevie rollin' sevens with those dice and cleaning up!?" Johnny said, laughing.

Then, the back door buzzer interrupted our little recap session.

"I'll get it," I said, heading for the loading dock.

At the door was a tall, light-skinned ("high-yellow," a term I'd later learn) black man, with his truck backed up to the loading dock. His greeting was far from warm: "Who the fuck is you. Where's Johnny?" His face was scrunched and wrinkled.

"I work here. Johnny's up front working. What do you need?"

"I need to pick up this job, and I don't need your honkey-ass getting smart with me," he barked, shoving the ticket for the job into my hand.

The company he worked for occasionally subcontracted work through our workroom. Still shocked at how rude this guy was, I opened the loading dock door and started to get the job together. Then I did something else he didn't like that I don't recall but he yelled at me, and I endured a few more racial slurs: "white ass" and "motherfucking cracker" were two that come to mind. Boo heard the tone of things and came back to investigate. Outside with the guy I overheard Boo say, "Don't come up in here starting no shit."

Johnny soon followed and had a similar talk with him as he did with one of the guys at the party the other night. "Stevie cool," Johnny said. "Man, Stevie's white," the man shot back.

I was angry but more hurt and in shock than anything. I didn't get it. It was the first time in my life; I felt hated for the color of my skin. The guy didn't even know me. I remember thinking, *how can you hate someone you never met?*

That day, I got a taste of what it was like to be black in this country at that time. Boo and Johnny basically explained racism to me. "There are people out there like that, Stevie. They just hate people because of their race or the color of their skin. They're assholes. You can't talk to them."

Soon after, I would get my second dose of racism after discovering an error on my paycheck. Johnny instructed me to go upstairs and talk to Hasson. Upon entering his smoke-filled office, he glanced up at me from his "adding machine" several times, purposely ignoring me.

"Um, excuse me, Hasson. Can I talk to you for a minute?"
"What is it?" he snapped without looking up from what he was doing.

I don't recall the details or how it was resolved but I remember the conversation that ensued. It included statements from him like, "You are a spoiled American teenager" and "Americans are terrible people." I asked him why he was here since he seemed to hate America and its people so much. His response: "There is no work. I can't make this kind of money in Lebanon."

How convenient. You love our capitalist system that allows you to make good money and support your family, but you hate the people who created and allowed you to engage in such a society? I suggested he "go the fuck back to Lebanon" if he didn't like it here and walked out of his office.

Again, I had that knot in my gut from feeling hated by someone who didn't know me or my character. It felt very unfair to me. It's a feeling of being completely helpless, too. You can't change someone's heart who has built-in hatred for you that has nothing to do with who you are as a person.

I worked at Systems for about nine months but had to quit abruptly due to my parents moving again. As a result, I no longer had quick access to the Chicago Transit Authority (CTA) bus lines.

It was a great experience. It unexpectedly showed me the possibilities of what race relations could be, but unfortunately, it also awakened me to some of the harsh realities of what they were. I was able to achieve one of my major goals at that time—I bought that new Ibanez Les Paul copy I had my eye on. I got it without any help from gay George.

Although I was still "the walking wounded" and broken-hearted, I moved forward into the next chapter of my life.

The early casualties

The casualties of the lifestyle had already started to mount by the end of 1977. They occurred throughout my drug use, but for obvious reasons, they increased as the years went by. We were all just trying to navigate our way out of the maze called adolescence and young adulthood. Some of us didn't make it.

The earliest I can remember was Larry Wrath, who was found hanging in his garage. He was a guitar player, and the guitar that Juan Garcia played used to be his. Larry was said to have been found with women's clothing on. A lot of suicides at that age (around 14 or 15) seem to be related to kids not being able to accept their sexuality.

Next was Danny's older brother Ray, who drowned after drinking too much and falling asleep on an inner tube while swimming at a local quarry.

Another friend, Scott, fell to his death at Starved Rock State Park after smoking a little too much pot while hiking. There were also a few overdoses.

Then there was the "tragic love triangle" losses that occurred when an acquaintance, Marty, was seeing two girls I knew. Both reported that they were pregnant. The pressure of getting two girls pregnant was too much for him and apparently led to his suicide. Unbeknownst to him, only one girl actually was pregnant; the other, Loretta, lied in a desperate attempt not to lose him. She also lied to another friend about being pregnant. I'd say this backfired on her when both young men committed suicide. After Marty and Dave killed themselves over her lies, Loretta couldn't live with the guilt and shot and killed herself.

But, of all these tragedies, the closest to us was Sylvia. She was found hanging in her garage shortly after Loretta shot herself. Loretta was Sylvia's best friend, and she apparently couldn't handle the grief.

One of the strangest of the early tragedies, though, was the death of our friend Tommy, who was killed, ironically by my buddy Cal, in a tragic motorcycle accident while on the way to the woods. Tommy stopped to get his hat that blew off on a blind curve in the road. Cal came flying around the corner on his bike at the wrong time and struck and killed him. Everyone knew it was just a freak accident, but I know Cal never totally got over it.

The "partying" lifestyle started to take its toll in other ways too. Not everyone died. Some were severely damaged. Our neighborhood friend Dennis just wasn't all there anymore after too many acid trips. The kid, who used to laugh at everything, became sort of a drugged zombie.

Wayne, the once cocky jock, who hit on Carol at that party, became almost derelict after getting into a bad motorcycle accident while high and drunk. Tragically, around the same time, his friend (also named Wayne) had the exact same thing happen. In fact, I believe they spent time rehabbing in the same hospital together. Both had to learn to walk and talk again. Both were athletes who developed severe alcohol problems after their accidents.

Then there was Diego. One week that summer, our friend Bob's parents went on vacation, and Bob threw a nonstop party that went on for four or five days straight. We were drinking, smoking pot, and using a variety of drugs the entire time. I remember his girlfriend Holly and some other friends bringing him into the house and him lying down on the couch in the other room. I went in to see if he was okay, and it was obvious that he wasn't. He was pale (even more than usual) sweating and had a splitting headache. I think we finally agreed that he needed to go to the hospital, so they called an ambulance, which transported him with Holly by his side. It turned out that he had kidney failure and wound up on dialysis with his name on a list for a kidney transplant.

Were they all drug-related? I'd say yes, whether directly in obvious ways, or indirectly in less obvious ways. Being overwhelmed and unable to cope with negative feelings is already hard enough to do at that age; throw drugs and alcohol into the mix and you have a disaster waiting to happen.

In Diego's case, they identified a birth defect that led to the failure of his kidneys, but drugs and alcohol was likely a contributing factor.

Then there were the relationship casualties. Most notably and closest to home, besides Carol and I, were my brother Paul and his first wife and high school sweetheart Diane. Then, the divorce of my sister Sue and brother-in-law Gary. Drug and alcohol abuse was a major factor in all of these.

I'll never forget, early one morning, in January of 1978. Gary left, leaving us something to remember him by—he methodically took out the right corner of the garage with his van. One of the biggest mentors in my life was gone. I was, once again, devastated as was my entire family, especially my brother Paul, who had gotten very close to him. Gary was important to us all; despite how fucked up he had become; he was still a special and unique person who brought a lot to the table. Talk about no closure. We were never going to see him again and we never even said goodbye.

The "nonstop party" was slowly turning into something it wasn't intended to be—a funeral. The "partying" lifestyle began to show another side that wasn't so fun and exciting anymore. Unfortunately, I had no other way to cope with these types of life failures. By the time the darker reality of the lifestyle started to emerge, it was all I knew.

Living is easy with eyes closed

Now that we were all out of school, working, and had money, it was kind of ironic that the "party" was somewhat over. Shouldn't that be where it begins? The thrill was mostly gone, and it started to become just the way I lived. This way of life was all about taking something that at first was like a "special occasion," trying to recapture it again and again, (watching *The Wizard of Oz* every day gets boring) and thus inadvertently turning it into something ordinary and mundane. So, it only stands to reason that I would seek out more intense highs. It eventually was not unusual to find me passed out somewhere.

I recall one time that I drank too much and did too much tetrahydrocannabinol (THC, pronounced *tick*). The drug was originally a powder extracted from cannabis but was slowly replaced by a cheaper chemical— phencyclidine (PCP)—a type of animal tranquilizer.

Once, I passed out on the corner of North Avenue and 25th Street around midnight. Some stranger woke me up and asked if I wanted him to call an ambulance. I declined and walked across the street to an all-night diner, where I proceeded to pass out into a cup of coffee. All I remember is the owner yelling, "Hey buddy. Wake up!" and seeing coffee dripping from my nose back into the cup as I lifted my head. I got up and staggered home.

On another occasion, at Schiller Woods, my cousin Danny and some friends just happened to walk by as I lay passed out in the grass. He exclaimed to his friends, "Hey, I think that's my cousin!" He woke me up, asking if I was okay.

These were the times that I remember. There were plenty of others that I can't recall. Then there are the times that I don't remember anything until suddenly coming out of a blackout.

One of these times involved a new drug, that came around for a while, that we dubbed "Mexican Quaaludes." These pills had some of the strangest effects that I had ever experienced. They would make you horny, but you would almost be guaranteed to go into a blackout at some point, and their effects would last for days. I remember taking some and waking up at my sister's house the next morning. When I picked my head up, I saw blood all over the pillowcase. In the mirror, I saw dry blood and cuts all over my face. I had obviously been in a fight but didn't remember it. I cleaned up, went to the backyard, and turned the radio on when the Eagles song "Desperado" came on.

Desperado, why don't you come to your senses? You've been out ridin' fences, for so long now. Oh, you're a hard one, but I know that you've got your reasons. These things that are pleasin' you can hurt you somehow.

I knew the song was about me, but I quickly pushed it out of my mind. I was in a haze, trying to snap out of the effects of the drug, when one of Carol's girlfriends stopped by. We still hung out on occasion. We smoked a joint and had a few beers, and the next thing I knew, I was fucked up all over again on these things. I went into another blackout until about 10 hours later.

When I came out of it, I found myself in bed with her. I literally came out of a blackout in the middle of fucking my ex-girlfriend's friend. It was dark in the room, so I had to strain to see her face so that I knew who it was. We came out of the bedroom into the middle of a party. It was great except for one thing—we didn't know one person there. We didn't know where we were, or how we got there. It was dark outside when we left. We were looking at street signs for something familiar until we got to Belmont Avenue and finally figured out where we were. We went our separate ways and went home.

Somehow, I made it to work the next day, but by then, my performance and attendance had started to decline. I had rediscovered all the factories in Franklin Park and had gotten a job as a spot welder. I didn't remember signing up for adulthood and wanted no part of it. Yet there I was, in it, however reluctantly.

I remember my first factory job at Leslie Locke Mfg. where a bathroom stall became a place to catch a few winks of sleep. We had a pact that if more than 10 minutes went by and you weren't seen, someone would go into the bathroom and wake you up, usually by pounding on the stall door. In other words, I could barely stay awake at work.

I didn't realize it then, but the constant seeking of chemical pleasure was conditioning me. An unintended effect was not being able to cope with responsibility, not only physically, but emotionally. I developed an intolerance for work that began to fester and grow. I watched the clock all day, knowing this would make the day drag, but because I had no impulse control, I would do it anyway. I was able to present myself well and was always able to get hired, but my ability to function and sustain employment continued to deteriorate.

No doze at Oddo's

It wasn't long before we discovered a neighborhood dive called Oddo's Lounge on the corner of Mannheim Road and Fullerton Avenue. We would walk through the back door, where there were two pool tables, tables, chairs, and benches along the walls. At the end of the pool table area there were several steps leading down to the bar. To the left was a bowling machine, the jukebox, the bathrooms and more tables and chairs. To the right, there was the bar. On the other side of the bar was the front door, which was usually only used by the old-timers or anyone who didn't want to walk past a bunch of young rowdies shooting pool and drinking. The place was mostly windowless, with dark-brown wood paneling, so it was pretty dark and dingy.

Several of us would meet after work for a few beers. Most weekdays, only the old-timers and alkies at the bar would be in there. We'd be upstairs shooting pool. The place was dead during the week but on the weekends, it became the place to be and was packed.

We didn't care what it looked like; it was ours. The legal drinking age had been lowered to 19 for beer and wine in 1973, but I had already been drinking at Oddo's for a year when I turned 19. I never got carded.

The bartender Gladys was in her early 50s. She was a throwback from the 1950s, complete with beehive hairdo, Bobby socks, tennis shoes, and pink lipstick. She was easygoing, cool, and liked by all.

Oddo's had the best jukebox in the world. To this day, I've never heard a jukebox that compared. Everything from Zeppelin's "Immigrant Song" to Lynyrd Skynyrd's "I Know a Little" and "Call Me the Breeze" to Sinatra's "Summer Wind" and "New York, New York." No matter what we were doing, when "New York, New York" came on, we'd do our best Sinatra imitation and start singing, though we'd make up our own words.

Throughout my "bar fly" days, I was usually trying to get laid. In all the time I spent in bars, I can count on less than one hand how many times it actually happened. I was just never one of those "smooth pick-up line" kind of guys. I felt it was forced and pushy to hit on a girl, so I just could never bring myself to do it. I tended to prefer girls to hit on me. Good thing I wasn't holding my breath, or my face would have been as blue as my balls and my heart was.

The song "The Boys Are Back in Town" by the band Thin Lizzy, in some ways, accurately portrayed the feel of those times. Though all the words didn't necessarily match up with our experiences, the line "and if the boys want to fight, you'd better let 'em" did, at least at times. Anytime there's alcohol and pool games for money, there's going to be fights. This was especially true when strangers came into the place thinking they were hot shit. Warren and the rest of us could hold our own, but Cal, Brian, and Danny were the real fighters.

They once got into a fight with a group of guys in the parking lot. Brian picked up an empty 55-gallon drum, threw it at a guy, and nailed him. Though outnumbered, they whooped those guys badly.

Too bad they weren't there when Frankie Appa, Pat Mac, and I got into it with some guys from a neighboring town. It was over a pool game for money.

I won the game with a great full-table-length bank shot. One of the guys we were playing against said, "I didn't call" the shot I made. I clearly did; he just didn't want to pay up. We were standing toe to toe arguing when he took a swing at me. He hit me with a glancing blow, but it wasn't enough to do any damage. I proceeded to go gonzo on his face, and I was kicking his ass. Next thing I know, I'm on the floor thinking, *How the hell did I get here? I was just kicking this guy's ass!* It turned out that one of his friends saw that I was beating his buddy up, so he came up behind me and cracked me in the back of the head with a full twelve-ounce long neck of Old Style. I think he may have watched too many Westerns and thought the bottle was going to shatter when it hit my head. In real life, it's the opposite—the bottle stays intact; it's your skull that shatters. Before you know it, Pat and Frankie are fighting the other guys, and Pat, who weighed about 300 pounds, is getting the better of one of them.

I got up and chased another outside. One of them picked up a pool cue and hit Pat in the head, knocking him out cold. I heard the scuffle from outside, so I came back in like *Kung Fu* and kicked the back door open, ready to do battle. The trouble was, I didn't know that Pat was unconscious on the floor on the other side of that door. I hit him with the door, hard! Gladys called the cops at that point when she saw that these guys were using weapons instead of fists.

I felt something running down my back, and Frankie informed me that I was bleeding like a stuck pig from the back of my head. I took my shirt off and put it on the back of my head. I knew I was in trouble when I could feel the blood pulsating right through my balled-up shirt. It was like that scene from the movie *Monty Python and the Holy Grail* where the Black Knight is spurting blood from every limb! Gladys took one look at my head and called an ambulance. Those guys never got out of the parking lot. They were arrested.

After hearing what happened from Gladys, the cops came to the ambulance and asked me if I wanted to press charges. I did because I was still pissed off that I was winning this fight until I got unfairly hit from behind. Something good did come of it, though. The girl I had been hitting on that night felt sorry for me and told the ambulance driver that she was my girlfriend and rode with me to the hospital. I got 43 stitches. She took me home and "took care of me". I thought to myself, *is this what it takes for me to get laid?*

Oddo's closed at 4 a.m., which was too early for true partiers like us to go home, so we would all head up Mannheim Road to the infamous, corrupt, speed-trap town of Stone Park. There was a dance club appropriately named Stay Out All Night or "Stay Out," as we called it. Right next door was a honky-tonk dive that was more my style called The Roadhouse.

The Roadhouse was the first place I ever played guitar in front of a live audience. One of my guitar buddies invited me to bring my "axe" on a Friday night. He said, there was a spot in the entertainment lineup where they would have an open jam session and invite any musicians in the audience up on stage. I brought my Ibanez and the next thing you know, I'm on stage plugging into an amp and playing "Ramblin' Man" by The Allman Brothers Band. I just found the key and tried to stay in it while soloing. It was very exciting!

Again, I had some natural ability, but I was too lazy and preoccupied with drugs to get any formal musical training. Other friends and acquaintances were doing just that and began putting bands together, while I remained relegated to the "basement jamming partner" or two.

I got those same old blues again

No matter where I went, or what I did, I brought my broken heart and my wounded soul with me. While constantly medicating them, I had one eye out for Carol, hoping I'd run into her, while the other eye was looking for any woman who would give me the time of day. There were far too many of these nights to recall, but one that stands out was at a Chicago Club called Biddy Mulligan's. Biddy's was a club that became well-known in the 1970s for great blues acts. I went to see one of mine and my brother Paul's favorite British blues bands—Savoy Brown. Oddly, what they were best known for had nothing to do with the band, but rather, the spinoff band that emerged from it—Foghat.

Foghat was headed by lead singer "Lonesome Dave" Peverette. Savoy Brown had two other lead singers that appeared on different albums—Chris Youlden, and Dave Walker. My favorite was Dave Walker, who influenced my style and was the singer on my favorite album by the band, *Lion's Share*.

I got to the club early, and stood in front, dead center stage. I couldn't help but notice someone, who like me, had the same idea about getting right in front of the stage early to see the show. I don't remember her name, but I do remember that she was beautiful. We struck up a conversation and I learned that she was of Native American descent. She had long dark brown hair down to her (extremely nice) butt, in some just-tight-enough blue jeans. She had a great smile and beautiful big brown eyes.

We started talking about our love of the band, and as it turned out, Dave Walker was her favorite, too. We completely hit it off.

By the time the band took the stage, the place was packed. They opened the show with one of my all-time favorites, "Shot in the Head." One of my guitar heroes, Kim Simmonds, was so close I could have touched him. Then Dave Walker came out and sang the words that I related to so well at that time in my life...

Hard case, musician me, hey, hey, hey.
It's kinda sad, but that's what I'll be, hey, hey hey.
I don't have nothin' but the clothes on my back, hey, hey, hey.
Do my sleepin' in an old brown sack, hey, hey, hey.

Dave was surprisingly scraggly looking, although in a ruggedly handsome sort of way. Not your typical blues/rock frontman, wearing jeans and a white T-shirt. He could have passed for a "carney" but for having all of his teeth. Throughout their set, he pounded 12-ounce plastic cups of beer, and after he finished one, he'd kick the empty cup into a space between the amplifiers behind him. By the end of their show, there was quite a pile of plastic cups. I remember thinking, *Wow Dave, got a little drinking problem, or what?*

But I was still dazzled by that voice, and him standing right in front of me, live. I also noticed that throughout the show, he kept making eye contact with, pointing at, and singing to my new friend.

After the show, we both talked about his apparent flirting as a way of possibly getting backstage to meet the band and get some autographs. That's exactly what we did. Backstage, I was talking to Kim telling him what a huge fan of his I was, while my new friend talked to Dave. I asked if I could get an autograph from the band, so Kim grabbed a small notepad, tore a piece out, signed it, then passed it to the rest of the band until it made it to Dave, who signed it last. He handed it to me as he continued talking to "my girl."

Suddenly, a limo pulls up at the back door for the band, so Dave gets up and says to her, "Hey, why don't you come for a ride?"

"Okay," she says as he takes her by the hand and walks her toward the limo. She looks back at me, smiles, shrugs her shoulders, and disappears into the night with Dave and a few other members of the band's entourage.

Then, a second limo pulls up and scoops up the remaining band members.

It all happened so fast. I just stood there dumbfounded. My father's old saying, "I didn't know whether to shit or go blind," comes to mind.

Talk about mixed emotions!? I had them, and they would linger for years, anytime I heard a song from that album. I just met and talked with members of one of my favorite bands in the world, and one of my favorite singers just stole my girl! I looked down and read the autographs, including Dave's, which said, "To Steve, Thanks, Dave Walker."

You're welcome, Dave...asshole!

Falling in love again

I was 18 years old, and I was a "garbage can"—a term I'd later use to describe my drug use. I would use just about any drug that would get me high. These ranged from amphetamines to my old staples of pot and alcohol and included PCP, acid, quaaludes, and benzos. My primary quest at this time in my life was to kill emotional pain. The trouble was these drugs dulled it but had ceased to kill the emotional pain I experienced almost daily. I was stuck in what I'd later refer to as "The Traumatic Trifecta" of pain. The combination of Carol and Jim and Jeff rejecting me, and my mentor and role model Gary leaving, had me completely overwhelmed. All I knew to do about it was more drugs. I felt hurt, depressed, abandoned, insecure, and fearful when I wasn't high, which was hardly ever. But, somehow, I still managed to have some fun too.

It was then that I discovered that my brother Paul had started using heroin. Warren and Cal had expressed curiosity and desire to try it. If you think about it, it was the next logical step in the progression of our drug use. Warren had lost almost all healthy fear of anything by then and just like with acid, had to push everything to the limit.

After Paul and Diane's marriage ended, Paul moved out and rented a house in Melrose Park, while Diane and one-year-old son Peter continued living with us at my parent's house. I started going over to my brother Paul's apartment in an attempt to...I don't know what... seeking any form of comfort I could find.

Paul and his friends would sit around the kitchen table and shoot heroin. I knew Paul was shooting it but never witnessed it until then. I'd be in the adjacent living room listening to music, smoking pot and drinking, sometimes doing some Valium too. Occasionally, someone would call out from the kitchen: "Hey Stevie, wanna try some? We'll save you a cotton."

"No thanks. I'm cool with my pot and Vs," I would say. But it was only a matter of time.

One day, after everyone had left, and it was just Paul and me alone, curiosity, combined with the fact that my usual drugs weren't really doing the trick anymore, led me to finally give in and say six simple words that would change the course of my life forever: "Let me try some of that."

It was the worst decision I made to that point in my life. Once again, any healthy fear I once had slowly eroded, and my curiosity overtook it. I find it somewhat ironic that as a kid, I had to literally be dragged to the doctor if I thought there was a possibility of getting a shot. They had to practically hold me down and promise me the world to get near me with a needle. But I guess that's how it goes. No matter how much you tell yourself, "I'll never do that," if you're constantly around it, you will eventually normalize whatever "it" is.

Paul shot me up for the first time. You might think, *what a terrible thing for a big brother to do*, but it was like the blind leading the blind. Neither one of us had any idea what we were getting ourselves into. We were immersed in the drug culture, and any rules that may have existed were slowly eroding and disappearing. Besides, if not Paul, it would have just been someone else.

He poured the light brown powder out of the folded tinfoil into a teaspoon. Then, he drew about a third of a diabetic syringe from a glass of water. He squirted it into the spoon, covering the powder until it started to dissolve. The light-brown powder turned into a dark-brown, coffee-colored liquid. He stirred the liquid, then heated it with a lighter, until it barely started to boil. It emitted a slight odor, that was unique. He ripped a small piece of cotton from a cigarette filter, rolled it into a tiny ball, and dropped it into the spoon. Pulling the plunger back, he drew the brown liquid into the fit through the cotton. It made a sucking sound as the needle sucked every bit of liquid through the cotton until it was dry. He then held the fit, directly in front of his face. Looking at it intently, he pushed the plunger up until all the air was gone and a little drip came to the tip of the needle. He flicked the syringe twice with his middle finger and tied me off using his belt around my bicep. He placed the needle in position to pierce the now-bulging vein. He blew on my arm as he pushed the needle in to lessen any pain of the needle as it penetrated.

I felt a nervous excitement—like when you're about to get onto a ride at an amusement park. The difference is rides at amusement parks only last a few minutes. This ride would last much longer. He drew the plunger back, and the blood cloud exploded into the syringe. I turned my head and looked away.

He warned me that because it was "some pretty good shit," I may get an upset stomach and feel like puking, but that this was normal; it would go away quickly, and I'd feel great after that. He slowly pushed the plunger in and told me to loosen the belt. I felt the drug's warmth crawl up my arm to my head. When it hit my brain, that warmth spread to my whole brain and body. The euphoric rush, which was nicknamed the "kick in the chest," took my breath away. Then, that unmistakable smell fills your nostrils. It's similar to the smell if you've been punched in the nose. The next feeling was being sick to my stomach, just as Paul said. If you can imagine that feeling, mixed with intense euphoria, it's quite different from feeling truly ill.

I immediately made my way to the bathroom and puked, but just as Paul said, after that, I felt great! The intense euphoria was heightened by an unexpected gift—magically, all the pain was gone! Not just dulled or covered up but completely gone! "Gary, who?" "Jim and Jeff, who?" I would eventually describe the experience with this statement: "Carol could have been fucking the whole football team, and I couldn't have cared less."

I had found my utopia, my salvation! I felt truly happy for the first time since I was a kid. Think of how powerful a drug is that makes you "feel" happy, even when you're not. I felt the weight of the world come off my shoulders and I was set free!

I immediately started itching and scratching, especially my arms, legs, and face. It's not an irritating sort of itch, but more of a euphoric itch. I also noticed that my voice had gotten deeper and scratchy or gravelly. For the next ten minutes, I felt I could take on the world.

After the initial rush subsided, then came the nod. The best way I can describe nodding on heroin or opiates is that it's similar to that stage of total relaxation one experiences right before drifting off to sleep with the euphoric aspect of it magnified 10 times. Not only are you in a total state of relaxation, but you're feeling the type of good that ordinary life seldom can produce.

The opiate nod is like a bad case of narcolepsy; you fall asleep no matter where you are or what you're doing. Leaning slowly to one side, drooling, and even falling off your chair are not uncommon. The effects usually lasted about five hours. This is why they say don't ever try heroin, not even once. Because you could become psychologically addicted just like that. Once you've experienced it, you can't help but want to experience it again and again. And that's exactly what happened to me. I pursued experiencing that complete relief, and sense of well-being, again and again, from that day on.

As if I needed any other justification, it was also normalized by my older brother and his friends, and even my musical heroes Gregg Allman, Eric Clapton, and John Lennon. They all did heroin, and now some of my best friends were doing it. Apparently, right around the same time I was having my first experiences with injecting heroin, Warren and Cal were, too.

We weren't ashamed either. It made us feel that we were the elite of the drug world. We were clever, irreverent, strong, tough, and cool—and could handle any drug—there was no drug that we couldn't handle. People who couldn't handle drugs were weak, stupid, and pussies. That's how we saw it.

My brother Paul copped primarily from the Puerto Ricans in Logan Square in the heart of Chicago. I remember driving to the city with him and a female friend of his.

Paul copped dope from a guy named Wolf (short for Wilfredo). We pulled up and Paul got out and rang the bell of the run-down, four-story building. Wolf came down and let us into the foyer area at the foot of the stairs. He got our money and ran up the stairs while we waited. He was obviously a middleman and wasn't the dealer. I felt nervous excitement as we stood in the dark, dingy hall with gang graffiti all over the walls.

The distinctive smell of Latino food wafted through the halls as did the Latino music mixed with a baby crying that seeped out under several apartment doors. We could hear the creaking stairs with each footstep as Wolf returned minutes later, tinfoil bags in hand. My brother asked him if we could "get off" anywhere in the building since he didn't want the three of us getting off in the car due to the neighborhood being pretty hot. He instructed us to go around through the alley to the back door and we would be able to do our business.

We did, and stood there nervously, waiting for him to open the back door for what seemed like forever. You start wondering who is watching you and might call the police or see you as a victim to rob you. Finally, the door opened, and we entered an even dingier back hall.

Wolf had a glass of water in his hand and asked if we had our own works. Paul had everything we needed. Wolf whispered, "Come on up here," referring to a back stairway. "Okay, right here," he said, and we each sat on a stair about halfway up the staircase. Paul and Wolf pulled out their respective works as Paul's friend and I anxiously looked on. They each put their bags into three spoons and cooked up the dope and the three of them got off. Then Paul cooked up a small hit and got me off. The initial "kick in the chest" took my breath away, and then that smell entered my nose again. I already loved that smell. After the initial rush, all was right with the world. The feelings of relief, well-being, and euphoria once again enveloped me.

The four of us were sitting in a back stairwell in Logan Square, scratching and nodding. I went into a deep, euphoric nod when suddenly, the old bald-headed fart with glasses was standing over me with the pointer in hand and pointing at me. "Marijuana will lead you to heroin," he scowled. The film Cal and I saw in seventh grade briefly flashed into my mind and snapped me out of a good nod. Here I was five years later, doing exactly what the old fart in that film warned us about.

West Side story

While Cal and Warren had also been pursuing their use of heroin, they discovered a connection on the West Side of Chicago. It was in the heart of a black neighborhood at 15th Street and Christiana Avenue. We compared notes and found that the dope was as good, and the bags were only $10 for the same amount of dope we were getting from the Ricans in Logan Square for $25.

We agreed to meet after work on Friday, and drive to the spot to cop. It was a 15-mile straight shot down the Eisenhower Expressway, but in Friday rush-hour traffic, it might as well have been 50 miles. As we came to our exit—Independence Boulevard—the butterflies started in the pit of my stomach. You could tell Warren and Cal were nervous too by the stupid jokes they'd start cracking and our nervous laughter in response. After exiting the expressway, we drove a mile or so to the dope spot.

It became apparent that this was not a good neighborhood for young white guys from the suburbs to be in. Not a white person in sight and rows of dilapidated, rundown houses, abandoned buildings, and vacant lots that made the landscape look like missing teeth, that rotted out of its head. Garbage and litter were everywhere. The gas station we passed had thick, bullet-proof glass in the attendant's booth. To say that this area was depressed would be an understatement. But a currency exchange or a liquor store was on every corner.

As we neared our destination, the car got still with silence, eventually broken by Cal, who was driving. "Give me your money." We ponied up our money, which was already out, and in our hands—mine, damp with sweat. "Okay, we want twelve bags all together—right?" Warren said.

I thought this sounded like too much, so I reiterated, "I only want two." Cal explained to me that they were copping for two other people, too and that their dope was free because the guys they were copping for thought the bags were $20 each. "You sly fuckers," I said. They laughed and Cal said, "We don't pay for our dope, Stevie." I got my first taste of the advantages of being the middleman, copping dope for other people.

As we turned onto the one-way street, Christiana, I saw guys on either side of the street were…washing their cars. Cal explained to me that it was how the operation worked, at least during the warm months. There was a car ahead of us, and one behind us. It was a "drive-thru dope stand" like a McDonald's. We pulled up and stopped. One of the guys came up to the driver's side.

"What do you need my man?"

"We need twelve."

"Boy or girl?" the man asked.

"Boy," Cal said.

"You sure you don't want any of that girl? It's primo," the man said, trying to upsell us some cocaine ("Would you like fries with that?").

"Not today; just the boy," Cal replied as he handed him the money.

The man counted it, then walked into the gangway, looking to make sure no one was following him. On the side of the house, he picked up a small milk carton, tipped it over, and counted out twelve small tinfoil packages. He came back and leaned inside the car window handing Cal the dope and advised us, "Don't get off anywhere around here; this area is hot as shit."

"Okay, we won't. Thanks, my man."

As we made our way back to the expressway, a squad car drove within sight of us. My heart sank into my stomach. Cal made sure he came to a complete stop at the stop sign.

Please understand, you didn't have to do anything wrong to get stopped in that hood. Just being white would be enough probable cause. This was the Chicago police in the 1970s. If they didn't have probable cause, they made one up. We were always tense until we made it to the expressway. Once there, the sigh of relief was palpable, and the jovial mood returned to the car.

We'd make our way to Oddo's where we would spend most of our Friday nights drinking beer, shooting pool, and carrying on with the rest of our friends. Most friends didn't use heroin, so we did a pretty good job of hiding it. It's not like we were a bunch of nodding, drooling, zombies on Friday nights while the rest of our friends partied around us. However, a nod could come on unexpectedly and catch you off guard. Heroin was frowned upon by most.

One such incident occurred at Matt's house. I was still spending time with Diego and the gang at Matt's, though this had decreased significantly once I started using heroin. This was not only due to my new love affair with the drug but was also one of the effects of Diego fighting for his life and being on dialysis due to his kidneys failing. He just wasn't as available, and his priorities started to shift as he fought to survive his ordeal.

I was jamming with Diego while all the regulars were around us in a circle. Matt was playing some bongos, and others played hand percussion. I was high on heroin, which no one at Matt's knew I was doing. Suddenly, out of nowhere, in the middle of a song, I stopped playing and went into this huge, long nod. I think I even drooled on myself as my head slowly went toward the floor. Everyone stopped playing and when I snapped out of it, they were staring at me with looks of concern on their faces. I made up some excuse and we continued to play, but you could tell that some people weren't buying it. Matt's older brother John had gotten into heroin some years earlier, and they were all totally against it. It was one of the last times I remember hanging out at Matt's. Having to hide my use from my other friends became too difficult.

Copping on the West Side became our payday ritual. It was every other week at first. It soon became every Friday and then, started spilling over into Saturday. Before we knew it, it was the whole weekend. A larger and larger chunk of the paycheck was spent on dope.

Also, our other operations on the side, such as stealing, hadn't ceased. We weren't making the daily effort we were a year or so before, but God forbid you left your garage door open. You'd be missing any expensive equipment.

I thought about Cal and Warren's little scam and pondered who I could get to buy dope for $20 a bag. It hit me immediately, Franko and Billy! Both had expressed an interest in trying heroin.

Franko: New friend or partner in crime?

I can't remember exactly when or how, but like most other friendships I had, Franko and I met at a few neighborhood parties. I remember being at a party with Frank in his neighborhood with Queen's prophetic "Keep Yourself Alive" blasting. Our early connection was also drug-related, as Frank had some good weed that I bought from him.

Frank was a bit of a "pseudo-dealer," but nothing heavy. I think it was more of a way for him to gain peer acceptance than anything else. It also helped to finance driving around the neighborhood in his mint 1970 GTO. Frank and I both played guitar and we just hit it off, which I'm sure was also due to making each other laugh. As you know by now, if you made me laugh, you were in.

Frank was a character with his own made-up lingo that was ever-changing and evolving and would crack us all up. It was a mixture of real and contrived words, that would often morph into new words, get words tacked on, or be replaced with new words. We deemed it "The Franko Language".

For example, everyone was called "Kid," which then morphed into a two-syllable word, "Ki-hid,", which later morphed into "Kee-hee." Apparently, it felt right to Frank to eliminate the D at the end. It was contagious and if you were around him enough, you would find yourself talking in "Franko speak." He had everyone doing it. Even my brother Paul, who found it a bit juvenile, would find himself engaged in Franko language occasionally.

A typical statement might go something like this: "Kee-hee, this try-hard thinks he's heat-sinking but he's tryin' low." Translation: "Steve, this fool thinks he's cool but he's really an idiot." The following is a list of some other "Frankoisms" in alphabetical order.

Heat-sinking: Doing something well.
Hingin or Hing-hoyng: A verb. This could be used in a variety of ways depending on the context.
Pinner: A person who doesn't measure up. An unattractive female.
Pinny: Feeling shitty.
Rippin: Stealing, lying, or trying to get over in some way.
Sho-wert or Wert: Taking a shower.
Try-hard or Hard-trier: A loser who is in denial about it.
Wertless Bum: In need of a shower.

There were, of course, many more, but these are the ones that come to mind.

Billy Kuhn was Frank's sidekick at the time. Billy was just a nice kid who liked to get high. His older sister Cathy likely got him started, which is pretty typical. I don't remember the details, but Franko and Billy knew I was doing heroin, and I told them about our forays to the West Side. They both proclaimed that they wanted to try it, so I told them that I would pick them up a few bags, when we went to the city on Friday. They agreed.

I stopped by and got their money. They each gave me $40. Of course, this was money for eight bags not four. I won't waste time on a lot of unnecessary details, but they went from snorting it to shooting it pretty quickly.

One particular trip to the West Side that stands out happened on one of those Fridays. We were going through our usual copping ritual, when the spot got taken down by a sting. Out of nowhere, we were surrounded by cops with their guns drawn and pointing at us. Through their car intercom, we heard: "All of you exit the vehicle with your hands up."

Cal, Warren, and I followed their command. They instructed us to bend over slightly with our hands on the squad car and spread our legs. If your legs weren't spread enough to their liking, they'd assist you by kicking them farther apart. They finally holstered their weapons and began to frisk us.

"You boys got anything on you we should know about? Any drugs or weapons?"

"No sir," we all said.

"Anything that's going to stab us, like needles or anything like that?"

Again responding, "No sir."

After frisking us, one of them ordered: "Okay, get in the squad, please." Cal and Warren did so, but I made the mistake of asking, "What for?"

Next thing you know—crack! I was seeing stars after getting whacked in the back of the head with his billy club. I guess I must have left my "white privilege" card at home that day!

They searched the car, which came up empty. Luckily, we had left all our works in Warren's truck back at Oddo's parking lot.

"What are you guys doing here?" one of the cops asked.

Quick liar that I was, I responded, "We got lost and got off at the wrong exit."

They ran our names for warrants, but nothing came up, so they let us go. Then, they warned us: "We find guys like you cut into pieces in dumpsters in the alley all the time around here. I wouldn't come back here again."

With that, they gave us our IDs, we piled back into our car and headed for home, never to return…well…at least not until the following Friday night.

Trying to live a double life (and failing miserably)

As we were unwittingly becoming "junkies" (a term that we, of course, never used to refer to ourselves), we were all living double lives as sons, brothers, cousins, employees, husbands, and soon, even fathers.

While hanging out at Warren's, I got fairly close to his older brother, Steve, younger brother Jeff, and younger sister, Chris. I never met his father, who I believe was estranged after he and Warren's mother divorced years earlier. His mother was one of the "Peanuts parents" and wasn't around very much. Though I knew her, I never so much as had a conversation with her. I never got close to any of my friends' parents. I think I oozed guilt, and I could sense that they knew it. Franko's parents would eventually become an exception to this. Maybe because they were Italian, I felt some kind of connection that I never felt with other parents.

Warren was the first of us to become a husband. He married his fiancée Julie at a local country club. I can't recall, but I think I was in the wedding party. Soon after, they had a son. By age 19, it was time for Warren to get out on his own. They rented an apartment in Melrose Park.

Warren went to work for Julie's father as a printer and was being groomed to eventually take over the small, but successful, print shop. He was making pretty good money, but due to his immaturity, he spent it frivolously and found himself deep in debt.

He bought a new pickup truck and had his first car payment, paid rent, and the expenses of a new baby. Being young, he also had some unnecessary, extravagant expenses, like a brand-new custom bar that he had built in their apartment. All of this, while shooting heroin every weekend.

There are three words that I can use to sum up Warren at this time in his life: stressed, overwhelmed, and inexperienced. Oh, let me just throw in another one that I almost forgot: reckless—a personality trait that I felt came about because of him doing too much acid. As I said earlier, he liked to push the envelope. He had to get fucked up and experience oblivion every time. This created a vicious cycle that he found himself in. The more stressed and overwhelmed he got, the more he used and drank. It also created a lot of conflict with his wife Julie, who saw that Warren was not living up to his role as a husband or a father. I'm sure this wasn't how she pictured their marriage going.

She and their son soon moved out and moved back home with her parents. I can certainly understand why she did, and couldn't blame her, but as it turned out, it made matters worse. Now, there was no one to answer to, and from that point on, we would often wind up at Warren's shooting dope.

I remember dreading driving with Warren while he was fucked up on drugs or alcohol. He would nod and I'd have to be ready to grab the steering wheel. I'm sure I helped avoid two or three head-on collisions back then. Ironically, Lynyrd Skynyrd's "That Smell" would be blaring through the speakers, and it seemed that Ronnie Van Zant was speaking directly to us:

Angel of darkness is upon you,
Stuck a needle in your arm,

*So take another toke, have a blow for your nose,
One more drink fool, would drown you.*

*Oo Oo, that smell
Can't you smell that smell?
Oo Oo, that smell
The smell of death surrounds you.*

"That smell," which meant relief, freedom, and euphoria was beginning to smell like something else—as Ronnie so bluntly put it—death.

I saw Warren start to spiral out of control. His antics used to be funny and the subject of much folklore, but now he was getting downright reckless and dangerous. When he was sober, which wasn't often, he would confide in me that he needed to cool it. I tried to be as supportive as I could and encouraged him to get it together, but unfortunately, I was limited by my own spiraling drug problem. I even suggested that he take Julie and his son and move.

Once, while we were beaned out (which at times acted as a sort of truth serum), Warren got honest about his need for help. I suggested that we go to his mother's and ask her for help. The memory is vague, but I remember that Warren's mother somehow thought his cry for help was just him wanting to come and live with her to ease his financial problems. She rejected him, likely, at least in part, because of the state we were in—being fucked up on downers.

At the time, a mutual friend of ours—Arnie—started selling Valium. Warren started buying them in an attempt to lay off heroin for a while. It seemed like a good idea and was the lesser of two evils. Wasn't it?

Payday was coming on Friday and in a phone conversation, he told me that he had some bills due, and he couldn't cop that week. I was supportive and I made him promise that he wouldn't and confessed I needed to cool it too. I reminded him that Arnie invited us to a party on Saturday night at his band's rehearsal space on Mannheim Road. "It should be cool to party with those guys and listen to the band." We would have some beers and maybe pop a few Vs like "the old days." He agreed. That was the plan.

What happened that Friday is sketchy, but I believe we just hung out at Oddo's shooting pool and drinking. I do remember feeling a sense of relief that Warren stuck to his promise and didn't go to the city and cop. I, on the other hand, did not stick to mine and I did, although I lied to Warren about it.

The following night we planned to meet at Oddo's, then head the mile south on Mannheim Road to the party at the band's rehearsal studio. I can't remember, who I was with in the early part of the evening, but I remember being at Oddo's shooting pool. The door would open and one familiar face after another would come in. With each person or small group, I would look for

Warren, but he wasn't with any of them. I got on the pay phone and called his house. No answer. So, I figured he went straight to the party at Arnie's.

I had my sister's car. I had to beg to borrow it. I jumped in it and went to the studio. I saw more familiar faces at the party and was greeted by several people. I screamed over the music in someone's ear, "You seen Warren?"

"No, haven't seen him!" the faceless person screamed back.

So, I grabbed a beer, grabbed a chair, and watched the band. They were tight, but their material wasn't my "cup of tea." Warren, on the other hand, loved this kind of stuff. I sat back and admired their musicianship. You could tell that they worked hard at their craft to be as good as they were. That was something I could never motivate myself to do but always felt that if I did, I'd be as good or better than any of those guys. After their set, I approached Arnie.

"You guys sound great. Where's Warren?"

"I don't know. I haven't seen him. I sold him some Vs the other day and he said you guys were coming."

I hung around until about 1 a.m. or so and people started heading over to Oddo's, so I decided to head back there, too. I figured he decided "screw the party" and just went to Oddo's. As I got into my car, it hit me; *I'll bet that asshole went to the city and copped!*

I turned the car around and headed to his apartment.

When I arrived, I immediately saw his truck parked out front, sort of haphazardly. I noticed the lights were on in the apartment. That's when I knew I was probably right about him copping and he was likely up there getting high. I rang the bell several times, but no one answered. I walked around to the front of the building to see if I could see or hear anything coming from the second-floor apartment. It was a beautiful spring night, and he had his windows open on either side of the picture window. I yelled, "Hey, Warren! You there?" Nothing. I thought, *Good, he's with someone and was smart enough to leave his truck and let them drive.* Other people had some of the same experiences I had with him driving, so they were probably relieved to get him out of the driver's seat. I thought, *He's probably with Cal. They'll eventually show up at Oddo's.* So, I headed back there.

While back at Oddo's, I hung out and shot some pool. I called his house again from the payphone at about 2:30 a.m. or so. No answer.

Oddo's closed at the usual 4 a.m. and we all headed to Mock's—the bar that stayed open until 6:00 a.m. on North Avenue. The owner, Tommy Mock, was a big, burly guy who survived getting shot six times. Long story.

Still no Warren. My concern grew, and I decided to go back to his apartment. It was starting to get light outside as I got back into my sister's car.

While driving, my concern continued to grow until finally, the worst-case scenario could no longer be ignored and I thought to myself, *if his truck is still there and the lights are still on, I'm going to try to get into that apartment.*

When I arrived, that's exactly what I found. I rang the bell and looked for a way to get the downstairs door open, but there wasn't one. Then, I looked for a way to get up to the window. I surmised there was no way without an extension ladder. I was starting to run out of energy and get sleepy.

I figured that he may have come home while I was back at Oddo's and passed out—something that was not unusual. We were always telling stories about one of us passing out. I knew I had to get home. My sister was already going to kill me for having her car way past her deadline. So, I left and figured I'd call him when I woke up.

Saturday night had slipped into Sunday morning with the sun starting to peek over the horizon. That Sunday was Mother's Day, and my parents and family were coming over. Mothers deserved to be honored, especially ours, for all the changes we put them through.

Mother's Day 1978

I went home and slept until about noon. I got up and came downstairs to find my sister Sue in the kitchen getting things ready for my mother. She gave me the silent treatment, something Sue often did when she was pissed off. I picked up the phone and called Warren's. No one answered. Finally, she broke the silence. "What time did you get home last night?"

"I don't know about two or so." By now, lies would just roll off my tongue without so much as a thought.

"Hahaha! Try about six or so!" she scowled.

I turned to her with obvious worry on my face. "Okay, I'm sorry, but I'm really worried about Warren."

I explained the story to her while leaving out the details about the particular drugs involved.

"Can I please use your car to go over there? I promise I'll come right back. I'm really worried about him."

I had every intention of ringing every bell until someone let me in that security entrance and then I planned on breaking down his door if I had to.

I knew that Warren had gotten close to at least one of his neighbors in the building named Butch and I thought maybe he'd help.

Sue's response: "Absolutely not! It's Mother's Day. Mom is coming here in less than an hour. I'm sure Warren's fine."

I tried one more time. "Please, Sue I'm not kidding. I'm worried."

"No! That's it. Forget it!" she barked back.

I knew I had it coming. By this time, my brother and I were both notorious for taking three hours or more to go out for cigarettes. I was "the boy who cried wolf" on too many occasions. There was no way she was going to take a chance on me disappearing for hours on Mother's Day.

The next day, Monday, May 15th, I called his apartment again from home, then from work. Still no answer. I feared the worst. It was time to find out what was really going on, so I made the decision to pull out my "ace in the hole" and called his mother's house. She answered the phone with a sound in her voice that let me know immediately that my worst fear was about to be realized, followed by the actual words…

"Warren's dead, Steve."

I'd like to be able to tell you the rest of what she said, and what I said to her, but I froze, and everything just stopped after hearing those words. I couldn't move or speak. A feeling of helplessness enveloped me. Near the end, it was like one of those nightmares where you're watching someone you care about heading for a cliff. You try to cry out to warn them, but you find that your voice is gone, and nothing is coming out of your mouth.

I hung up the phone and just stood there in shock. Then, I felt a single tear run down my cheek as a kaleidoscope of memories of our adventures flashed through my mind—from the change bouncing around in The Zipper ride at the Dago Feast, to tripping at school. The image of that smirk on his face, running from Bedard through the halls, laughing our asses off. His laughter, now echoing through the halls and fading in my mind, as I snapped back into reality of the sounds of the punch presses and other machines at work.

I had a knot in my gut and tears rolled off my chin as I walked up to my supervisor and told him that I just found out that my best friend died and that I wanted to be excused for the day. He saw that I was genuinely distraught.

"Go home, Steve. Punch out and take as much time as you need."

One little problem that confronts you
Got a monkey on your back
Just one more fix, Lord, might do the trick
One hell of a price for you to get your kicks

Oo Oo, that smell
Can't you smell that smell?
Oo Oo, that smell
The smell of death surrounds you

By the time he was waked, the stories had already started circulating. Two aspects that were particularly disturbing were that he was supposedly found by Julie and his little sister, Chris. Fortunately, I learned that this wasn't the case, and he was actually found by his mother's husband, Hal. Julie would have been the one to find him because she had the keys but waited for Hal and his mother to arrive because she was afraid to go in.

The scene was bad. He had apparently fixed, and upon overdosing, fell forward from the chair he was sitting in. His head was on the ground while his torso was still in the chair. It was said that this caused a lot of blood to rush to his head and when they found him, his face was black. The needle was still in his arm. This is what I was told, but of course, I couldn't verify it.

Back in those days, I doubt an autopsy was done. I mean, it was pretty obvious what happened, but if they had, I'm sure that they would have found Benzodiazepine in his system along with opiates. Soon, it would become apparent that Benzodiazepine, a class of tranquilizer, was a stealth killer.

Franko and I went to the wake together, and of course, we were high on heroin. This was significant because it showed the moral decline that was already underway. I couldn't face this scene without injecting some courage.

When we stepped into the funeral home, everyone was there in the lobby: Brian, Danny, Cal, Pam, Judy, and a bunch of other friends that I can't recall. Cal was pretty torn up, but I could tell he was high, too. Mary wasn't there due to being away at college. She likely took it the hardest. She was his oldest friend out of all of us. Juan wasn't there and took off for his second home in Mexico. I never saw him again. He cut ties with us after Warren's death.

Frank and I were directed to sign in and then approached the casket to pay our respects. As I entered the parlor, I saw Warren's family in the first pew, and the reality of Warren being gone set in upon seeing his little sister Chris with tears in her eyes. It broke my heart. I was still in shock, not knowing what to say or do. I went up to each of them and mouthed some words that I thought were appropriate like, "I'm so sorry for your loss."

We went up to the casket. I kneeled and tried to pray but I couldn't quiet my mind. It was all so surreal. He was just alive, laughing and talking last week and now, here he was, lying there in a casket with his hands folded and a rosary draped over them. I got my first real look at my friend. It barely looked like him. They did what they could with makeup, but his face was bloated, and fake-looking. I just wanted to get out of there. I couldn't handle it. I made the sign of the cross, got up from the kneeler, and bolted for the outer area.

Warren's close friends stood around in a circle out there, and we talked in almost a whisper. The girls asked what happened. I mean, they knew what happened, but they were looking for details. I don't recall my response, but I'm pretty sure I didn't give them any.

Suddenly, his mother came out of the chapel, and walked straight toward us, as she scolded: "You see him? Take a good look guys! That's going to be you if you don't quit this bullshit you're doing!" Her words were directed at Cal, then me. She abruptly turned and walked back into the chapel.

We all just stood there somewhat in shock. Cal and I hung our heads in shame. That was it for me. I couldn't handle it anymore. I said goodbye to the friends who were there, and Frank and I made our way to the exit.

Warren died and was found on Mother's Day, May 14, 1978. People would sometimes ask in the years that followed why he didn't get help. Help? What was that? It was 1978; there was no help. Or if there was, we sure as hell didn't know about it.

You would have thought that this event would have snapped us out of it like Warren's mother warned, but that's a misconception that people who don't understand addiction have. It actually snapped us deeper into it. I drove away from the funeral home that day in the passenger seat of Frank's GTO with more pain to kill, and more guilt to cover up.

The first cracks in the wall appear

One big change that occurred after Warren's death was that Franko became my new running buddy. Billy tagged along making an odd "threesome" at times, but as Frank and I started playing guitar more and more, Billy, who didn't play, started coming around less and less. Things were already heading that way anyway. Franko and I had already started hanging out more, because of how stressful and dangerous being around Warren had become.

Another change was that Cal, Danny, and the rest of us drifted further apart and saw each other much less. Warren's death had continued the separation that started when Cal moved back to Norridge, so it was mostly a matter of logistics. Cal and I continued to hang out on occasion with our heroin use now being our common bond. Sometimes, we'd run into each other on a Friday or Saturday night, but we were never as close again.

I believe Brian, Cal, and Danny got closer after Warren's death. Brian wound up playing nursemaid in a sense, trying to help Cal kick heroin. They would go up to Michigan where Cal had family, and he'd "dry out" on occasion. But, upon his return to the area, he'd soon be back at it, shooting dope again.

The merry-go-round of opiate addiction was in full swing. I continued to cop from the West Side for Franko, Billy, and myself, but we also discovered other connections. One connection was known as "The Hillbilly Mafia," a... shall we say, "interesting" group of people. More on them later.

By this time, weekend use spilled over into Mondays, then into Tuesdays. Only Wednesday and Thursday remained opiate-free and were gotten through with pot, alcohol, and pills. Though there was no serious withdrawal yet, I do remember feeling crappy when I didn't have dope in me.

Even after Warren's death, it never occurred to me that I had a serious problem, that is, until one day, late in August 1978. An important milestone in my drug use occurred while driving down the Eisenhower expressway to the West Side on a Friday evening in rush-hour traffic.

The bumper-to-bumper traffic was worse than usual. There must have been an accident. To make matters worse, it was like 98 degrees outside, with about 100 percent humidity—one of those super-hot and muggy Chicago days. My air conditioning was broken in my beater car, and despite having all the windows rolled down, I was sweating profusely all over myself.

I was inching up the Ike, nowhere near my destination on Independence Boulevard. Suddenly, out of nowhere, the real Steve broke through, like he had been bound and gagged all this time and had finally broken free! I remember saying to myself, "Are you crazy? What are you doing!? Get to the next exit, get off this Godforsaken expressway, and go home!!" And I really wanted to, but...I couldn't. A voice, much more like a whisper, in another part of my mind said, *Shut up, Steve. You know you're not getting off and going anywhere until you get that dope, so don't even try to fool yourself.*"

It was official. I was using against my will, and I knew it. It was at that moment I admitted to myself for the first time that I had a drug problem. I had my first moment of clarity, however, fleeting it may have been. I reached my destination, got my dope, and promptly snapped back into my malaise of denial.

I got tired of driving to the West Side by myself and eventually gave in to Franko and Billy's pressure to let them come with me to cop. To do this, I had to let them in on the secret, the bags were really $10 and not $20. I had to come up with some justification, which didn't take long. I blamed it on Cal and Warren.

"I'm sorry. I couldn't tell you. They made me promise not to tell anyone. What could I do?"

They expressed some anger for about 20 seconds, then all was forgiven and forgotten pretty quickly. That's how the dope game is—when you have dope in the spoon in front of you, it's a good time to confess any wrongs you may have committed. Having dope made everything tolerable and forgivable.

Unfortunately, my home life wasn't quite as tolerable and forgiving. Tensions mounted as my parents and I once again moved in with my sister Sue, my niece Amy, and nephews Gary and Jamie. It all came to a head one day as I was getting ready to go out.

I got into it with my 13-year-old nephew Gary. He was a sharp kid and began putting 2 + 2 together about what was wrong with some of the men in his life. I don't remember what started it, but it culminated in him calling me "a junkie." He obviously hit a nerve, so I went off on him and started yelling, calling him a little punk, telling him to mind his own business, and he didn't know what he was talking about.

Albie heard the commotion, came out of the bedroom, and started yelling at me. My dad had his face in the newspaper and proceeded to ignore the entire fiasco, until I told Albie to "shut the fuck up" and called her a "fucking bitch." This inspired a rare appearance from behind the newspaper. He put the paper down, jumped up out of his chair, and punched me square in the face! He yelled, "Don't you ever talk to your mother like that!"

I shot back, "Don't you ever hit me again, you son of a bitch! It's too late for that now. You should have done that a long time ago!"

And with that, I bolted out the front door and headed to Diego's house. I remember thinking, *Wow! Where did that come from?"* I didn't have the word in my vocabulary at the time, I would later realize that I had a hidden resentment for my father. It took a punch in the face to bring it to the surface. Deep inside was the truth. I felt his lack of ability to discipline me was a contributing factor in how things were turning out in my life. "Johnny, the drapery man", was *such* a nice guy, but was he responsible for the problems I was having?

Pinball Wizard

I had been working at a few different factories in Franklin Park as a spot welder. My brother pointed out that I was getting bowlegged and starting to walk like movie legend John Wayne. This was from stepping on the pedal of that machine for eight to ten hours a day, so my being fired was probably a blessing in disguise, but I needed a job.

My mother worked at a place in the area called Bally Manufacturing. They made pinball and game machines. They were the Xbox of the 1970s and '80s. People would drop pockets full of quarters addictively playing Space Invaders, Pac-Man, or pinball at bars and other public establishments. Albie encouraged me to apply because they paid well and had good benefits.

After putting in an application, I bugged the shit out of those people on a regular basis until they finally hired me. I would always say that I pestered my way into that job whenever I told the story.

Bally was the biggest, most fun place I had ever worked. It was like being in high school again. There were a lot of interesting characters and pretty girls. I was on an assembly line that was mostly all young people. You had to be because the line moved at top speed; If you were slow, you wouldn't last.

Our line made cables for pinball and other game machines. Each person on the line (mostly girls) wrapped their colored wires onto nails that were strategically placed at different points on the production board. The boards were on wheels on a track and would be pushed down to the next person on the line.

I was a "zip-tie gunner." Once all the wires were in place, my job was to wrap the cable and connect wire branches in specific spots, so that the cable would stay intact and could be cut from the board. I shot plastic zip-ties through a gun that was powered by an air compressor. I would pass the board down to be cut off and dumped it into a bin. The bin of cables would then be brought over to the soldering department to be prepped and soldered to the game board.

At lunch and break, people would go out to their cars and get high. We would get food from the "roach coach" and sit in the cafeteria laughing and joking around. You could get any drug you wanted; someone likely had it.

Speed was popular with the girls, usually "white cross," which came in handy if you were out too late the night before or were hungover. Like I said, it was like high school all over again.

At lunch, I hit it off right away with a coworker named Leo. Of course, we cracked each other up. Leo was a charismatic, sarcastic, funny guy, who everyone liked even though he made fun of everyone. We soon discovered that we had some things in common. We were both big fans of Frank Zappa and our older brothers were friends, so Leo knew of my brother Paul and knew who I was. But the biggest thing we had in common? We both shot heroin. What were the odds of that? We became fast friends, and he soon started hanging out with Franko, Billy, and me after work. We started finding more local places to cop dope and Franko found a connection for morphine tablets.

Within months of starting to shoot dope, Frank found himself in a bit of a pickle. He was driving through the hood when suddenly he was surrounded by marked and unmarked detectives. When he pulled over, they got out of their vehicles with guns drawn and told him to exit his vehicle with his hands where they could see them. He was cuffed and taken into custody. As it turned out, Frank was an accomplice in a string of aggravated armed robberies. Apparently, he had been keeping a little secret about where some of his money was coming from. He was the driver for the perpetrator of these crimes—Mike Lanfore.

Lanfore was captain of the football team, Mr. "most likely to succeed," all-American, star-athlete, on the outside. On the inside? A real, live, sociopathic, armed robber creep! He even pistol-whipped some of his victims. So, to avoid doing time, Frank had to "roll over" and spill the beans on Lanfore. I'm sure he was not too thrilled with Franko. The good news was it would be a long time before he'd see the light of day. Wouldn't it?

Withdrawal leads to discovery

Everyone's opiate use increased. As our tolerance grew, we were using more frequently and in greater amounts. This is when I first realized that I had "a habit". I remember going to bed one night and being restless and unable to sleep. This was something I had never experienced in my entire life. Remember, I had the "Fiorito curse." I could sleep anywhere, anytime, and it was difficult for me to wake up. Suddenly, I'm restless, I can't sleep, my eyes and nose are running, I have the chills, and my skin is crawling. I hadn't used in a few days. I realized I was experiencing withdrawal, I was "dope sick".

From that night on, things seemed to change. When withdrawal entered into the equation, it added a whole new twist to the dope game. The goal of using was always to get high, but now that was becoming more of a secondary goal. The primary goal started to become avoiding withdrawal. This created the need for and opened the door to a slew of other opiate drugs that were less expensive, more accessible, and easily obtainable. We had already discovered other opiates like Morphine Sulfate and Dilaudid. Our options now included pills like Percocet, Percodan, Darvon, Darvocet, Tylenol with Codeine, and others. It also included opiate cough syrups, Hycodan, Hycomine, and eventually what we would deem "the Cadillac of Cough Syrups"—Tussionex.

I can't remember who discovered Tussionex, but once we did, the chase was on. This stuff was like drinking liquid morphine and you only needed an ounce or two, well, at least in the early days.

Then there was the opiate replacement drug—Methadone, which was dispensed around the country to help addicts get off heroin. It was dispensed only by licensed clinics, usually in liquid form, but if you had a good connection, you could get the big orange wafers.

My brother Paul did a short stint in the army until he was discharged for medical reasons. He had terrible earaches all his life. Paul's medical discharge earned him veteran's benefits for life. This would eventually prove to be more of a curse than a blessing. He was eligible for Hines Veterans Hospital's Methadone maintenance program, which he took advantage of.

Franko and I also had a connection in the Belmont and Western area in the city for Methadone— a sweet young girl who would sell her bottles on certain days to supplement her income and feed her kids.

The way most Methadone clinics worked was, if you had so many clean urine tests, you would earn pick-ups or take-home bottles. If you continued to test negative, you would eventually only have to come to the clinic once per week. The max allowed was six take-homes. Frank and I would buy a 65-milligram bottle from her for $30 and split it.

Methadone was a strong, reliable, long-lasting high that induced a deep nod. The result was many cigarette burns, including fingers, car seats, pant legs, coffee tables—you name it—we branded it with cigarette burns. Long ashes would form at the end of cigarettes as you drooled, and your head bobbed. While most addicts would buy an occasional bottle, usually to avoid withdrawal, I actually preferred it to street dope. What it lacked in rush, it made up for in the aforementioned effects. God knows how many fires have been started by way of the Methadone nod. I'm lucky I never burned the house down.

Unhappy Halloween

As we headed toward the end of the month in October of 1978, Bally announced to their employees that there would be a Halloween party the following Thursday, October 31st. We were encouraged to wear a costume and bring a dish to pass. Leo and I started planning our costumes and we had a couple of "partners in crime."

Mary Beth and Nancy were two cuties who we started flirting with at work. After work, we would go to a bar called Carmie's (the old penny candy store that my sister Sue used to send us to when I was a kid) and hang out. Leo and Mary Beth hit it off and started dating. Nancy was okay, and we were friends, but she wasn't really my type. Leo was going to be a pimp, and Marybeth, a hooker. Nancy would be my pimp, and I would be the hooker in a little role reversal. The girls started helping us with our costumes. Mary Beth started sewing some things for Leo's costume and Nancy brought some slutty clothes for mine.

About a week before Halloween, I came to work, punched in, and went up to the break room, where a few of us would usually gather to have a quick smoke before going down to the floor and starting our shifts. You could see the time clock from there, so I kept an eye out for Leo to come through the door and punch in. It struck me as odd when he didn't, but I figured he was either late or called in sick.

As the day went on, and we made it to lunch, I called his house to confirm some things for the party, but no one answered, which in my mind proved he was faking and wasn't really sick.

I went back to my line to work. After about an hour, I started thinking about how I'd give Leo shit about calling in. Then, out of nowhere, one of the supervisors called me off the line and brought me to his office.

Upon entering, I saw Mary Beth sitting there crying. The supervisor then informed me that Leo was dead. He died in his sleep in the middle of the night. That's all they knew. They gave us both the rest of the day off. Nancy and several other friends who were close to us walked Mary Beth and me to the door, eyes wide with shock and frowns of sadness on our faces. I walked Mary Beth to her car, then got in mine. I don't remember anything after that.

Weeks later, I got the report from my brother Paul, who knew the family and was friends with his older brother Joe. The toxicology test showed that he overdosed on two things: Methadone and, if you guessed the stealth killer, benzodiazepine (Valium), you would be correct. I now had two friends who died mixing benzos with opiates, though in Warren's case, it was never confirmed. Leo went to sleep and never woke up and I lost another good friend.

I did go to the Halloween party as a hooker, and can you believe I got sent home to change because I was in violation of Bally's dress code!? My skirt was too short. The trouble was I got dropped off that day and didn't have a car. I remember walking almost two miles home in heels and a skirt in some crappy, cold weather. I even got honked at a few times.

I was overwhelmed by the sadness of Leo's death and about having to walk home in crappy weather dressed as a woman. Then, out of nowhere, I could hear Leo laughing his ass off somewhere in the universe at my plight. It brought a smile to my face, and I eventually laughed out loud in honor of my friend's irreverent sense of humor.

The frozen bean burrito that changed my life

At lunchtime, I usually preferred the food truck ("the roach coach") that would come by. Unfortunately, I'd often get there late and didn't like what they had left (the frozen bean burritos were just barely edible), so occasionally, I would go out for lunch. It wasn't my first choice though. By the time you got to a place, stood in line, and got your food, your lunch time was almost over.

While driving in the area on my day off, I discovered a little RV trailer that had been converted into a fast-food stand called The Beefer. It was close to my job, so I decided I would check it out next week.

The first time I went there, the place was packed. This concerned me and I almost turned around and walked out. How different might my life have been had I made that simple move? Sometimes, the things that you think are insignificant can make a huge difference in your life. Maybe I should have just choked down the bean burrito. However, I noticed that they were fast, and the line moved pretty quickly. They also had some good music playing that cemented my decision to stay. A local rock station played what should have been my theme song—Bob Seger's "Beautiful Loser" —as I stood in line.

He wants to dream like a young man, with the wisdom of an old man
He wants his home and security; he wants to live like a sailor at sea
Beautiful loser, where you gonna fall, when you realize, you just can't have it all?
He's your oldest and your best friend, if you need him, he'll be there again
He's always willing to be second best, a perfect lodger, a perfect guest
Beautiful loser, read it on the wall, and realize, you just don't need it all
You just don't need it all.

Don't need it all? Shit, I didn't think I'd get half of what I wanted, whatever that was. I was pretty sure I wanted to be a rock star like Bob, though.

Through the maze of mostly factory workers, this pretty, young blonde behind the counter caught my eye. She had the most beautiful eyes. Being a sucker for blondes with pretty eyes, I adjusted my position to get a better look. She had a nice petite figure in blue jeans, a jean jacket, and a turtleneck because it was as cold as shit in there. Those eyes looked directly into mine and she smiled. She handed some guy his order and smiled at him, but not like she smiled at me. I saw her talk to someone, and she smiled again, but still, not like she smiled at me. As I picked up my order, she did it again! You know the difference between someone just smiling, and someone sending you a signal. I smiled back and so did she, as her eyes and her smile followed me all the way to the door. In my car, while eating my beef sandwich, I thought to myself, "Hmmm." This went on for three days until I finally struck up a conversation.

"Hi, I'm Steve and you are?"

"Laura," with those eyes sparkling at me and smiling that smile.

"Hi, Laura."

Not being one for small talk, I just came out with it: "Do you have a phone number?"

"Yep," she teased.

"Can I get it?" I said, playing along.

"Yeah, you can," she said, finally putting me out of my misery of shyness. She pulled a pen out of her jacket pocket and wrote it on the back of a food order ticket.

"What time do you get off?" I asked.

"Four," she replied.

"I'll call you. I gotta get back to work," I said as I walked toward the door.

"Call me," she said and gave me one more of those pretty smiles to take back to work with me. Didn't Bonnie and Clyde meet in a similar way? Yeah…never mind.

In our first phone conversation, we discovered that we had a lot in common. For instance, we shared a sister. That's what I said, a sister, who ironically, actually wasn't either one of our sisters. Remember my "adopted sister" Barbara? She was Laura's older "sister", but actually, she was her cousin who moved in with them before Laura was born after Barb's mother wound up in a mental institution. Her father couldn't handle raising her. So, she was taken in by Laura's parents and Laura grew up as Barbara's sister.

My parents unofficially adopted Barb due to Laura's parents reportedly trying to screw Barb out of Social Security money, which became hers when she turned 18. She moved in, became like family, and was like a sister to me.

I was also casual friends with her older brother Mark, and the one time I was at his house, I remember Laura as a little girl, riding her tricycle up and down their driveway.

I exclaimed, "I can't believe you're that little girl that was playing in the driveway not long ago!" And, as it turned out, it wasn't that long ago. Laura was sixteen and I was nineteen when we met, though you wouldn't have known it to look at her.

Our relationship took off like a rocket. After going over to her family's rented house on the corner of Grand Avenue and Wolf Road, it became apparent that there weren't going to be a lot of rules to follow or objections to our relationship. I met most of her immediate family, who all lived in the house at the time, except for her oldest sister, who was married.

Sister Linda and her two kids, Janice and Lea, lived in the room across from Laura's. Linda and I got acquainted when she invited Mark, Laura, and me into their room to smoke a joint.

Then there was little brother Leon, a young entrepreneur (or extortionist, depending on how you look at it). He charged a quarter for anything you asked of him, and I mean anything. "Can you hand me a napkin?"

"For a quarter," was his standard reply.

Finally, there was her older brother Freddy, who, when I first met him, was sticking his head under a faucet, inhaling water from it, and choking. When I asked Laura about it, she explained that he was "cleaning out his lungs" and that "Freddy's a little nuts." It turned out that he did too much acid in the 1960s and had a touch of paranoid schizophrenia as a result.

Laura's father died several years earlier, so they sold their house and rented this one. The house was old, pretty beat, and adjacent to a gas station, so depending on which way the wind was blowing, the smell of gasoline would permeate the entire house.

I remember being in Laura's room for the first time. When I noticed it was getting dark outside, I said, "I should probably head home before your mother throws me out."

Laura assured me: "You can spend the night if you want. She never comes up here and she won't even know you're here."

Rhoda was pretty laid back. Some would even say "loose," so even after she knew I was spending the night, she didn't care. In those days no one made a big deal about our ages. Today, I'd be arrested for statutory rape and probably have to register as a sex offender for the rest of my life.

Laura quit school in her freshman year to pursue her "entrepreneurial spirit." She would buy an ounce of pot and roll the whole thing into joints. She would then sell them, mostly to the high school kids from West Leyden, which was literally two blocks away. She would triple her money.

Laura had an accountant's brain and was good with numbers. When it came to playing just about any game, she had that "horseshoe up her ass." Laura was great to have as a poker partner.

We were a perfect match, though my family didn't think so. They were always polite and treated her well, but they sensed that we were together for the wrong reasons. Hearing Barb's negative reports about her family and her home life didn't help either.

We were both "beautiful losers," full of hidden talents and untapped skills and abilities. All were sabotaged by impulsiveness, poor decision-making, lack of life skills, and most of all, substance abuse. I found out that Laura's drug of choice was THC ("tick"), but as I said earlier, by this time, it was actually PCP, an animal tranquilizer. I told her that my drug of choice was heroin. Her response to this displayed one of her key weaknesses. Laura knew right from wrong and would say the right things but could never follow through.

After I disclosed my heroin use to her, she sat me down and said, "I don't think we can continue to see each other if you keep doing that."

I responded defiantly, "Well then, we're going to stop seeing each other because that's what I like to do, and I'm not stopping for you."

That was it. Nothing else was ever said about it that I can remember, and we continued our relationship.

In January, the snowstorm of 1979 cemented our relationship when I got snowed in and I slept over every night. I was fired from Bally as a result.

One night, early in our relationship, we had both just fallen asleep when I was awakened by something hitting the window right above my head. I peeked out the window and saw someone who was obviously drunk. He was someone I sometimes hung out with and saw at parties. His name was Dave, but we all called him Willie. Laura woke up and opened the window.

"I'm sleeping."

"Come downstairs and let me in," he whispered.

"I have company; go home," Laura replied.

"Oh, okay; —sorry," he said, and he staggered away.

Willie had a bit of an alcohol problem. I remembered having to carry him around and load his passed-out ass into a car after a party. Laura apologized and explained that she went out with him a few times and now he would show up on her doorstep drunk. I shrugged it off and we went back to sleep.

About a month later, I was blindsided when Laura's period failed to arrive. Two months later, Laura developed this bump in her abdomen. She was pregnant. We thought it was mine, but when we went to the doctor to confirm it, we discovered that the timeline just didn't work out and it was likely her ex-boyfriend Russell's. No matter, I loved her, and I was going to be there for her.

I realized years later that it was exactly what I needed. It reconnected me with life and the normalcy that was on the verge of slipping away and sending me to the same fate that Warren and Leo had met. I had a reason to focus my attention on something other than getting high. This child, yet to be born, became a catalyst for me, at least somewhat, to get my shit together.

The next nine months were spent going to garage sales, buying onesies and other baby stuff, doctor visits, and preparing for the baby's arrival. It also included a lot of Sweet Tarts, lemons, and green apples. The strange pregnancy craving was apparently for anything sour.

Leon made a killing charging a quarter for all the new shit we needed him to do. I think we easily could have put him through his first year of college. Freddy began work on a spacesuit in case the aliens landed. Rhoda ate a lot of sweet rolls, drank a lot of coffee, and gained more weight than Laura. I became part of this dysfunctional family, that made mine look like *The Brady Bunch*.

Laura was amazing throughout her pregnancy and gave up everything. I think she may have smoked cigarettes but cut down and stopped everything else except for a few hits off a joint once or twice for the entire pregnancy.

I eventually got a call at work that Laura went to the hospital in labor. I got in my car and raced there but I was too late, and by the time I got scrubbed and dressed, she'd have already delivered.

On July 28th, 1979, my beautiful daughter Jessica Lynn was born. Okay, so she looked like a little old man when she first came out of the womb, but within days, she was already my beautiful little girl. I named her after Dickey Betts' instrumental composition on The Allman Brothers' album *Brothers and Sisters*. I claimed her as mine the day she claimed my heart. Every day that went by, Jessica stole my heart more and more. I couldn't have loved her more if she was my natural daughter. I was her dad and from that day on, I never felt any other way about it, and neither did anyone else that I'm aware of. Everyone seemed to understand the "heart bond" I had with that little girl that ran deeper than blood. Unfortunately, I continued my double life, walking a tightrope between being a daddy and being a drug addict.

After Jess was born, I was back on my rollercoaster of collecting unemployment benefits. I would try to sell drugs, but the only drug I found that I could sell without doing all the profit, was acid. Unfortunately, you really couldn't make a lot of money selling acid. The only other thing I did was "boosting" Merchandise from stores.

Boosting was stealing from stores with the intent of returning the merchandise for money without a receipt. Most big stores didn't care about a receipt back then, provided they knew it was their merch, and it was unopened.

I met Laura's friends which included my old best buddy from fourth grade, Mark Mason. He and our buddy Dave Ackerman were also aspiring guitarists, and we started jamming and hanging together frequently. I needed a job, and Mark got me hired to work with him for a company called Petrol Services that power washed anything that needed it.

Jimmy Carter was in the White House and jobs were getting scarce, along with gasoline. You haven't lived until you've waited in line for over an hour for gas.

Suburban Drugstore Cowboys

The cough syrup Tussionex became one of our most sought-after drugs. There was something about the high that took opiate euphoria to the next level. We started "cracking scripts" at local pharmacies. The problem was, to get it, you pretty much had three options: Go to a doctor's office or the emergency room and fake sick, steal a pad of scripts from a doctor's office and write your own, or find a crooked doctor. I could only manage option number one.

I would go to an ER and cough my ass off. I'd tell the doctor I had bronchitis, which I was diagnosed with. What a crock of shit that diagnosis is. Bronchitis is chronic inflammation and irritation of the lungs. Imagine that—a chronic cigarette smoker from age 13 with chronic inflammation and irritation of the lungs. I guess another term for bronchitis would be… cigarette smoker!

The doc would order a chest X-ray, which would show nothing, but just as the doctor would get ready to start writing me some namby-pamby script for Robitussin or some other wimpy crap, I'd inform him or her, "Oh, I've had that before and it really (cough, cough) didn't work at all."

The reply would usually be, "Well, what has worked for you?"

This is where my acting skills would come in handy and I would mispronounce and stumble ever so slightly over the word *Tussionex*: "Tussy, um, Tusssex, something like that. I can't remember."

Sometimes, they'd have to look it up in their PDR (Physician's Desk Reference), "Do you mean Tussionex?"

"Yes! Yes, that's it!"

This endeavor required a lot of chest X-rays. I remember thinking that my chest would probably be ravaged by radiation before I hit age 40. But when you're an addict, you're just not good at using future consequences to deter you from getting high today.

As far as the blank scripts go, we would steal a few here and there, but it wasn't our preferred method for several reasons, including you had to know how to write a script and make it look like a doctor wrote it. You also had to know the doctor's DEA (Drug Enforcement Administration) number, or the pharmacist would recognize that it was bogus.

Franko found a crooked doctor in Bellwood we nicknamed "Kuch". Kuch drove around in a Mercedes with a pager and catered to the whims of addicts just enough to keep his customers happy, while not losing his medical license. But, as the old saying goes, "All good things must come to an end" and so it was with the cough syrup game. We pressed our luck a little too much until we burned out local pharmacies. They started calling doctors to verify scripts and some even started calling the police.

If we saw them get on the phone, we would listen closely, and if they got a hold of the doctor, we'd calmly turn and walk out of the store. If it was the cops, we'd run!

We also pulled a few drugstore heists, which I won't go into detail about (don't want to give any young aspiring addicts a blueprint for wrongdoing). But they were few and far between. If you've ever seen the film *Drugstore Cowboy,* it wasn't quite that bad. We were more like "drugstore cowards" than cowboys and would only do what was easy.

Soon after our pursuit of the syrup started in earnest, Frank and I found out that a friend of his worked at a pharmacy chain—Osco Drugs, in the warehouse. Jackpot! He figured out how to beat the security camera system and would stick drugs in his socks. This included quart bottles of Tussionex!

The first time he sold us a bottle, it was cheap. He had no idea what it was worth. We were both "Jonesin" when we made the purchase, so we promptly cracked open the bottle and guzzled about three ounces each, right in front of him. It never dawned on us that he would do the same at home with another bottle he had. Not having any tolerance, he almost took himself out! He wound up violently ill and in bed for three days.

With Jessica's arrival, it was time to look for a more suitable place to live. I was concerned about gasoline fumes. I knew it wasn't good for an infant. Rhoda somehow found a good deal on a used mobile home in the Oasis Mobile Home Park in Des Plaines. We all moved there except for Linda, her daughters, and Mark. Leon made enough quarters in the move to put himself through the remainder of college. Linda had saved enough money to move out and get her own apartment. Mark went with her for rent support.

I recall one Monday after work, going over to Linda's. Laura and Jess had spent the better part of the day there. Shortly after I arrived, the phone rang and Linda answered, "Yes, he's here. I'll get him." Her eyes got big as she handed me the phone and whispered, "Steve, it's for you. It's your mother."

We were all shocked and puzzled because my mother had never called me the entire time Laura and I had been together. I took the phone and Albie said, "Steven, I've got some bad news…your friend Billy died last night. They don't know what happened. They couldn't wake him up; they think it may have been drugs. I hope you're not doing any of that stuff."

"I'm not, Ma," I lied to reassure her.

I hung up the phone, and still in shock, I told them what happened.

Another overdose identical to Warren and Leo's. Opiates (synthetic or otherwise) and benzos were turning out to be quite a lethal combination.

Billy died on September 23rd, 1979. I went to my third funeral in less than two years, this time as a pallbearer. The casualties were mounting.

Hillbilly Mafia

The Film *Rush* was made in 1991. It was about two undercover cops in the 1970s who infiltrated an elusive drug dealer's circle. The part of the dealer, Will Gaines, was played perfectly by one of my musical heroes, the late Gregg Allman. People like the character he played really existed in the Chicago area. We referred to them as the "Hillbilly Mafia." They all had thick Southern accents that made them stand out like sore thumbs in the Chicago suburbs.

My brother Paul established the first connection with the hard-to-get-next-to organization. He started copping dope from a guy named Sherman, and from there, was introduced to Sherman's mother, Hazel.

Hazel was in her early sixties. Can you imagine selling heroin to young guys and girls in your sixties? They were all just a little crazy, and some of them were downright scary. I was introduced to Hazel, while Franko somehow made a connection with another one of them, whom he referred to as "Bill the hill-bill."

One night Paul and I were both sick and couldn't find any dope in the area. I think Sherman, Hazel, and company went down South for a reunion and some of our other connects were either nowhere to be found or were out of dope. So, we went to the West Side, a place we hadn't been going to for a while. For me, it was somewhat out of respect for Warren. Besides, we now had closer connects that were just as good.

When we got there, it was after midnight. It looked like the boys had packed it in for the night but there was one guy walking down the street. We were desperate so we asked if he could cop. He spoke the lingo, so we handed him a hundred dollars and watched him disappear into the alley with our fingers crossed that he would return. We sat and waited and waited...and waited...and waited some more. We finally uncrossed our fingers and admitted that we'd been burned. When you're sick and waiting for dope, guess what happens? You get sicker, faster. Paul, who had a bit of an anger problem, took it really hard and banged on the steering wheel and yelled "motherfucker!" at the top of his lungs.

As we headed back toward the expressway, we noticed a group of about eight or nine black guys standing on the street corner, drinking. Paul pulled up to them, took his axe hammer out from under his seat, rolled down the window, and yelled at the top of his lungs, "Niggers suck!" You could hear it echo through the whole neighborhood.

I sank down into the passenger seat, sure I was going to have to duck bullets any second, but they just froze and stared at him in total shock. I guess they didn't expect a white guy yelling a racial slur at 1 a.m. I know I didn't.

Sounds like my brother Paul was a racist, and on the surface, at times, it looked that way. But racism is more complicated than most make it seem. My brother Paul was what I would later refer to as a "pseudo-racist." He acted and talked like a racist at times, but it was mostly all learned behavior that was passed down to him. It was an act. He didn't really hate black people. Real racists truly hate other races. In fact, when he was around black people, he started talking in Ebonics and got along famously with them. They loved Paul too, as most people did. This is what people need to understand about "racism." There are actually very few true racists whom I've ever encountered, though I've met a lot of people who were pseudo-racists. They acted and mimicked racist-like behaviors because they were taught to. Also, of the true racists I've encountered, they were pretty evenly split between black and white.

I mostly copped from Hazel who lived in The Jungle at the time. When I would cop, her younger boyfriend Mark would always be there bagging up dope, counting money, or something related to the "family business."

One night, I stopped by to cop, and Mark wasn't there. She asked how many I needed. I responded with the number, but instead of going to the backroom, and bringing them to where I was, she said: "Come on in I want to show you something." I stepped towards her. She proceeded to lift her shirt and show me her new tits!

"Did you ever see tits like these on an older woman?"

She apparently just had a boob job with some of the profits from selling drugs and those tits looked like they belonged on a twenty-year-old. "You like em? Wanna come check em out?"

"Umm, no, I can't…I've got someone waiting in the car."

Seeing that I wasn't interested, she backed off and never made a pass at me again. Thank God.

By far, the worst of the Hillbilly Mafia was her youngest son, Bobby Lee. If his name invokes the image of a big, dumb-ass, confederate-flag-waving, violent, redneck, jerk, in your mind—you'd be absolutely correct.

One day, I was coming out of a local honky-tonk appropriately called Texas Ranch, just as Bobby Lee was on his way in with a friend. He was obviously drunk. I said, "Hey, Bobby Lee." He spun around, yelled, "fuck you," pulled a pistol out of his pocket, and pointed it at me. I turned and ran toward Mannheim Road waiting to hear the shot ring out and hoping he'd miss. Luckily, it never came. His friend, who was a little more sober, stopped him.

Lastly was Roy. He was my main connect. I would cop from him at a local dive called Abner's on Mannheim Road. Roy was my preferred dealer and was a nice guy. He wasn't really cut out for the dope-dealing game but did it for the money. It subsidized his sky-blue, mint condition, 1964 Chevy Impala, complete with fuzzy dice hanging from the rearview mirror and white leather bucket seats. Roy had a soft spot in his heart that you really shouldn't have when you're dealing with addicts, which I admit, I took advantage of at times.

Once, I bought dope from him and I was so sick that I had to shoot it as soon as I got out the door. I went between the garbage dumpsters outside because I didn't have a car at the time. My hands were shaking so badly that I spilled the dope. I came back in and told him what had happened. I asked him to spot me replacement bags and I'd get him the money by Friday.

"Don't worry about it; this one's on me," he said as he handed me three bags of dope.

As the dope game continued to escalate, I found myself experiencing withdrawal more, and using to avoid it became a much bigger part of the game. My symptoms intensified including runny nose, insomnia, hot and cold sweats, diarrhea, stomach cramps, muscle spasms, and crawling skin. I was on the full-time merry-go-round of using to avoid withdrawal.

Trouble ahead, trouble behind

The Grateful Dead classic "Casey Jones" pretty much sums up the next chapter of my life.

Drivin' that train, high on cocaine,
Casey Jones, you better watch your speed,
Trouble ahead, trouble behind,
And you know that notion just crossed my mind.

The line about watching "your speed" appeared to refer to the stimulant "speed" and not velocity. Dealers cut cocaine with speed. No doubt this was the case when I tried shooting cocaine for the first time.

It was at one of my endless band rehearsals that never led to anything, well, except more rehearsals. We could never seem to make it out of the garage or the basement. Gee, I wonder why.

I took speed on occasion to get through work when hung over, or to combat low energy or sleepiness that I struggled with at times. I could add withdrawal-induced insomnia to the list. Other than that, it was never my thing.

Someone at the band rehearsal was selling coke, so a friend and I bought some. I had heard about the euphoria that people experienced shooting cocaine. Euphoria? It made me feel jittery and speedy. I remember thinking to myself, *I don't get what people like about this shit* and vowed never to do it again. How different things may have been had I stuck to that vow.

Franko's parents had planned a long trip to Italy that summer for almost two months. Frank's younger brother Max, the budding entrepreneur, saw this as a business opportunity to make money for college. Max sold pot occasionally and got high, though never with a needle and at that point, didn't know about Frank and me shooting dope. Max was disciplined and always knew not only where the line was but was always able to stay just on the right side of it. He had a connect for cocaine and his plan was to sell it while his parents were in Italy. Being the shrewd businessman that he was, he put his plan into motion the minute his parents left. To develop clientele and get business going, he decided not to step on the coke at all and get customers coming back for more. It worked like a charm. My brother Paul was one of his early customers.

I recall going to Paul's apartment and him raving about the coke that he copped from Max. He offered me some, but I told him that I wasn't interested. I described my previous experience with cocaine. He responded: "Sounds like you had some shitty, stepped-on coke. This shit is nothing like that. It's got a great rush and no speedy feeling afterwards. This piqued my curiosity so, I thought, *okay, I'll try it.* This would prove to be the biggest mistake of my life. Even bigger than my decision to try heroin.

I dumped an amount that Paul suggested into the spoon. The first difference I noticed was the fluffy rather than powdery consistency. Upon adding water from my outfit, it disappeared into a clear liquid immediately, as the "doctor's office smell" reached my nostrils. Paul informed me, "You don't have to cook this stuff. Just add water, stir it a few times, and it's ready to go."

The other coke still had undissolved particles in it even after I stirred it. This dissolved immediately into a clear liquid. I drew it through the cotton, into the fit, tied myself off, and shot it.

Whoa!! The euphoria that I experienced that first time is difficult to describe, except to say that it was intense and came in waves. In some ways, it was better than the rush from heroin. When it wore off, I experienced no negative side effects at all, that is, except, intense craving—I wanted more. As I learned that day from Paul, to experience a good rush, you had to wait long enough between hits. This was hard to do when you were experiencing intense craving, and you had more right in front of you. It's also hard when you run out. You still want more. We called Max and immediately scored more coke.

For the next two months, Paul and I shot high-quality cocaine. We all got a bit spoiled. I even brought some home and Laura and I snorted it. We both liked it and became "Chatty Cathys" and talked our asses off until 2 a.m.

Then came the day we all knew would eventually come. Their parents returned from Italy and just as he said he would, Max abruptly stopped dealing coke. Talk about being left hanging. What were we supposed to do now? We were all strung out on this high-quality cocaine.

As fate would have it, Max turned a few friends on to his connect and they started dealing it. Unfortunately, they were greedier and more heartless than Max and started cutting and stepping all over it. This did not deter us, and we continued the search for that elusive, high-quality rush, which of course, we rarely, if ever, experienced again.

Next, I discovered the "speedball"—a mixture of heroin and cocaine together. The heroin took any edge there may have been off the coke and reduced the cravings that would follow upon running out. It was also a potent mixture of the two types of rushes. There is no chemical euphoria quite like it. Speedball became my thing. Talk about champagne tastes on a beer budget.

Franko didn't get into the coke as much as Paul and I did. He still preferred opiates. Opiates became his method of treating chronic back pain due to a work injury, as well as getting high.

It was 1980 and loss of control over our use continued to progress. We found ourselves in desperation mode more and more. Once, Frank and I copped on the West Side on the Puerto Rican side of Wicker Park neighborhood. For some reason, we had no works and had to get an outfit from someone selling them where we bought the dope. We had no cooker or water either. We drove to a White Castle parking lot on Armitage and Western Avenues to fix. The place was crawling with gangbangers. We wound up stealing the metal saltshaker off the counter and using it for a cooker. We drew water from a puddle alongside the car from the heavy rain that happened the night before.

At times, our desperation had us going through our hiding spots to find old spoons with hardened cottons in them. We'd add water, cook them up, and get a hit. Sometimes, this would result in a case of "cotton fever"—a bacterial infection from shooting some bad bacteria or germs. It would often lead to fever, chills, sweats, headache, muscle aches, and sometimes diarrhea.

We were growing tired of the merry-go-round we were on and couldn't get off of. This was usually followed by moments of clarity and the realization that we needed to stop. We realized that most of the time, we were using dope just to avoid withdrawal.

One day Frank turned to me with a rare, serious look on his face, and announced: "Kid, we need to quit this shit."

"I know," I replied with equal sincerity and earnestness.

Max had a plan to check out a local college and I think Frank started to feel the pressure of the sibling rivalry. We were wasting our lives, and we knew it. Frank pulled over next to an empty field and took his dope kit out from under his seat. He looked at me. "C'mon kid. We gotta do it."

I took my fit and my spoon out from under the passenger seat and handed them to Frank. He tossed them all out the window into some tall grass, and we drove away. We went back to his house, and as we often did, jammed on our guitars in his room.

Frank's mother invited me to stay for dinner, and I accepted. She was the typical, nurturing Italian mother, trying to feed you too much food. She was a great cook. Frank's little sister and brother Max joined us. His father spoke with a thick Italian accent. He obviously preferred to speak Italian and spoke English only out of necessity. He could put away the red wine too, and of course, he made his own, just like my grandfather used to. They were good people, and one of the few families of my friends who made me feel welcome and comfortable.

Frank suggested that we go with Max to check out some classes at Triton Community College. The next day, the three of us went, though we didn't have a clue as to what we wanted to do, or what classes we wanted to take. Frank and I just wanted something to magically get us out of the life we were living and give us a chance to be successful. We were starting to look for an escape hatch, a way out, and college seemed like a possibility.

As we were looking through the Triton catalogue, Max read "computer programming" out loud. Computers were the latest trend, and there was mounting evidence that they were going to be the future. Frank suggested that Max take the class because he knew a guy who programmed computers. He was always dressed in sharp suits and was apparently making good money. Meanwhile, Frank and I decided on "Class Piano, Intro to Computers, Floor Hockey, and Music Theory." I also took GED classes because I would not get college credit until I took and passed the high school equivalency exam.

By the time we got out of there, whatever drugs we had left in our systems started to wear off. Soon, we were sick as dogs. Being the big babies that we were, we didn't last long. We quickly caved and copped some dope, but first, we swung by the field where we threw our works away. We desperately searched the tall grass and found them still intact.

This attempt at quitting by throwing our works out the window would happen on more than one occasion. Eventually we started to break the needles off the syringes. But we would just get new syringes when we caved.

As Max embarked on a new career as a computer programmer, Frank and I continued to chase dope around while regularly talking about quitting. As a result, we missed (or were late for) many of our classes. I did manage to get an A in Floor Hockey, but unfortunately, my other classes…not so good.

Noah's Ark was a Ford

Not long after our attempt at higher education, the "perfect storm" would come together, facilitating one of the greatest adventures of our young lives. First, were our numerous failed attempts at quitting drugs. It was getting frustrating and discouraging, especially as we watched many of our friends and acquaintances move their lives forward while we continued to spin our wheels.

Next was me getting a job at a plastics injection molding company. I was desperate due to the tanking economy of the early 80s (Carter was still in office) and had begrudgingly taken the low-paying job that started too early (6 a.m., Ugh!) for me. I had to wear a shit-breather mask and protective clothing due to the toxic nature of the materials I worked with. I hated it, especially with my addiction progressing. It was hard enough for me to work any job, let alone a really shitty one. I immediately started plotting how I could get out of there and get some free money.

I decided I would "fall" from the platform that I worked on. To do this, I simply laid on the floor at the bottom of the stairs and cried for help until someone came along. They called an ambulance and soon, I was filing a workman's comp claim. I can't help but think how many of my scams would not have worked in these current days of video surveillance everywhere.

These things, combined with Frank getting an invitation for a fresh start from a high school friend who had moved to Northern California, made the decision easy. We needed a change of scenery or, as we referred to it, we needed to "get the hell outta Dodge!"

Frank's friend Tom was three or four years older than Frank and me. I don't even know how Frank knew him, and I never asked. Tom made the move a few years earlier and started his own chiropractic practice in a town called Sonora, in Northern California. In a phone conversation, he invited Frank and I to come out there. Tom said he would put us up in a vacant basement apartment of the building he owned until we got on our feet. I believe one of the reasons for the offer was that Tom saw dollar signs when Frank told him about my pending workman's comp claim. He would give me regular adjustments free of charge and bill my insurance.

The final piece of the puzzle for me was Laura and I breaking up. Her flirting, and my possessive jealousy, along with our drug use, was a bad combination that led to constant conflict and arguments.

But all those reasons aside, I would not find out about the major deciding factor for Frank for over a year. As it turned out, Frank apparently caught wind of Mike Lanfore's soon-to-be early release from prison. He vowed to pay Frank a visit upon his release, and judging by his previous sociopathic behavior, Frank had good reason to be concerned. We had to do something. It was decided that we would stop using heroin (and, for me, cocaine) and try to start our lives over, in the gold-rush country of Northern California.

Frank acquired a Ford van in pretty good condition for our trek. The green van would be our "Noah's Ark" in more ways than one. It would not only carry us from our miserable existence to a brand-new life, but it would also double as a hotel room on our 2000-mile journey across the country. We certainly couldn't afford to stay in real hotels.

Our adventure began before we even left Frank's driveway, as we customized the entire van, including building the equivalent of a queen-sized bed in the back; the bed opened on hinges to accommodate storage. We covered the entire interior with plywood and lime-green shag carpeting for extra insulation. We installed a curtain that divided the front cab from the rear of the vehicle and curtains on all the windows. We added quad speakers for great sound quality to accommodate the many tunes we'd be cranking on our journey.

The money I got from the Oddo's bar fight settlement was my ticket out. I had called one of the perpetrators on the phone and made a deal with him; they would pay me $1,500 to drop the charges against them, $800 before our case was called, and $700 after I dropped the charges. They kept their word and so did I. I had the funds I needed for the trip across the country and to sustain me for at least a little while, until we got settled 2000 miles from home.

Going to California with an achin' in my heart

We were delayed by one of the worst and longest Chicago winters in recent history. In March of 1982, the weather finally started to break. We put the finishing touches on the van and were ready to begin our journey. We packed all our essential belongings, clothes, food, music collection, and guitars. We said our goodbyes to friends and family and set out on the road.

Although we had gotten through the brunt of it before leaving, we were not completely through withdrawal. We had to endure the tail end of it when we left in early April. We bought a bag of some pretty good pot and had a case of beer to ease whatever withdrawal symptoms remained. Tired of winter, we set our sights on our destination, Sonora, California.

As we hit Interstate 80, a palpable mix of relief, fear, hope, and heartache, hung in the air as everything we had ever known faded from the rearview mirror. Frank played the appropriate tape, *Led Zeppelin IV*, and everything got quiet and a little sad as the intro to the song led into Robert Plant's appropriate lyrics for the occasion.

Spent my days with a woman unkind
Smoked my stuff and drank all my wine
Made up my mind to make a new start
Going to California with an achin' in my heart...

The "achin'" had already started for Laura and Jessica, but deep down, I knew this was something that had to happen. Besides, we were on the road and there was no turning back now.

We could almost smell spring in the air as we traveled westbound on I-80 into Iowa. About midway through the state, the last remnants of winter began to hit our windshield. We figured that as we headed further west into Nebraska, the temperature would begin to rise, and we'd be through it. Wrong! It got worse—much worse!

We suddenly found ourselves driving into the teeth of a strong winter storm. You'd think we would have listened to a weather report or something, but we were too busy cranking the tunes through the new quad speakers. Our visibility became worse, as did the road. We could only do about 5 to 10 mph on the snowy, icy highway. It was late afternoon when we started talking about getting off the road and getting into a hotel room before dark, but we started to get the idea from the reports on the radio that if we did, we could be stuck for days. Who wanted to be stuck in the armpit they call Nebraska? Sorry if you're a Cornhusker, but there's nothing but flat as far as the eye can see in any direction. Getting stuck there would put a pretty good dent in our plan and our funds. Our adventure may have been over before it began.

We pulled over and looked at the map. We were coming up on I-25, which could take us south into Colorado and then into New Mexico. We wanted to check out San Diego anyway. Now it made sense to do it sooner than later. We had no choice; we had to escape that storm. We would go the Southern route and drive up the entire coast of California to our destination. Cool!

We continued south on I-25 until the snow finally started to diminish. We made it somewhere near Colorado Springs as darkness fell. We were exhausted from the stress, the long day, not to mention the amount of booze and pot we consumed.

We got off the interstate and parked in the lot behind a small business. We did it! We had avoided getting stuck in a blizzard. We shut the van off and got into bed. It got cold in there fast. Luckily, we were covered in sleeping bags and a ton of blankets. We cracked jokes for a few minutes, like two kids camping, but we both passed out pretty quickly and slept like rocks.

The next morning, we were awakened by the sun sneaking in through some cracks in the drapes that didn't cover parts of the windows. We came out from under our cocoon of blankets and saw the long trail of steam coming from our breath. Frank braved the temps in his long johns and went up to the cab, started the van, and blasted the heat. He looked out the windshield and exclaimed, "Oh man, Ki-hid!"

"What?" I replied.

"Look out the window," he said nervously.

I moved the drape from the back window and wiped away the condensation with my hand. There was about eight inches of snow covering the ground and the van. We wondered if we were stuck and got out to assess the situation. We were stuck, but luckily, not too badly. Nothing that two guys that grew up in the Midwest couldn't handle.

We got on the road and back onto I-25, headed toward New Mexico. As we crossed the state line headed toward Albuquerque, the weather started getting into the 50s, then the 60s. Finally, we could really celebrate. "We did it!" Our plan worked. We were finally clear of the weather that could have ended our trip. We would later learn that Illinois got hit with 10 to 13 inches of snow and ice from that storm.

As we merged onto I-40 near Albuquerque, we started our ascent into the mountains. Our ears popped as we climbed in altitude. We had just finished celebrating our victory over the storm, when, out of nowhere, the windshield was suddenly being pelted with snow again, and this time with snowflakes on steroids! They were the size of our hands! The wipers could barely handle these things; they were so big. We both yelled, "What the fuck!?" Then, just as quickly as it started, it was over. We looked at each other and cracked up.

"What the hell was that? The gods playing some cruel joke on us!?" I exclaimed. We had never experienced anything like that. It was in the 60s one minute, and we were being pelted with giant snowflakes the next. We found out later that in the mountains, at that time of year, those kinds of brief but intense flurries were fairly common.

From then on, everything was a new experience. Sorry to beat this analogy to death, but it felt like being in *The Wizard of Oz*. We had left the droll, black-and-white landscape of the Midwest and suddenly found ourselves in a land of "technicolor." There were cactuses like we had only seen in Western movies, the soil was red, with giant red and orange rocks and cliffs protruding from the ground and filling the horizon. There were American Indian teepees. I immediately rolled down the window to take pictures with my shitty little camera that, unbeknownst to me at the time, could never begin to capture the true beauty of that landscape.

The long-awaited spring didn't come to us—we came to it—and it was heightened and accentuated by these awesome new visuals. Any withdrawal symptoms that may have been lingering were eradicated by adrenaline and the exhilaration we were experiencing. It was the exclamation point on a new start on life for Frank and me. We drove through Arizona until, finally, we could see our hope on the horizon written on the sign; "Welcome to California.".

The eye of the hurricane

We embarked on a tour of the California coast on Freeway 101— "The 101" —as the natives call it. Our first stop was San Diego, where we drove past the bay, home of many big U.S. Navy ships. The huge, grey monstrosities loomed large on the horizon.

Most people in the area were "jarheads"—enlisted Navy personnel. I recalled the term from the book I just finished: *No One Here Gets Out Alive*, a biography about Jim Morrison and The Doors. It was one of the few books I had ever read cover to cover. Jim Morrison's father was an admiral, and his parents still lived in the area.

I had always loved The Doors' music and Jim Morrison's lyrics and vocals, but had recently become intrigued by their story, and particularly Morrison, who I found a fascinating, prophetic, and almost mythical character. Frank was slightly less intrigued, but he became interested through me. So, the tour we were embarking on doubled as a tour of Doors landmarks mentioned in the book. Our drive up the coast led to our next major stop — L.A.

Well, I just got into town about an hour ago
Took a look around, see which way the wind blow
Where the little girls, in their Hollywood bungalows
Are you a lucky little lady in a city of light?
Or just another lost angel?
City of night, city of night
L.A. woman, L.A. woman,
L.A. woman Sunday afternoon
Drive through your suburbs, into your blues…

After arriving in Los Angeles, our first stop was Venice Beach. Whoa! Can you imagine two Midwestern boys seeing that freak show for the first time? Frank and I got stoned before we departed from the van. The smell of pot was everywhere as the first sight to behold entered our view. It was an old black man with long, purple hair; a long, flowing, white beard; and flowing white robes, that made him look biblical or even heavenly. He whizzed by us on roller skates! Frank looked at me with his eyes wide and bulging and commented, "He's heat-sinking." I appropriately replied, "What's he trying hard about?"

The amount of scantily clad, hot women on roller skates could not be counted. I'm sure this was what inspired the Dire Straits song "*Skateaway.*"

Hallelujah, here she comes, Queen Rollerball
In an Enchante, what can I say, don't care at all

You know she used to have to wait around
She used to be the lonely one
But now that she can skate around town
She's the only, only one

No fear, alone at night
She's sailing through the crowd
In her ears the phones are tight
And the music's playing loud

We spent the rest of the day on the beach, jamming on our guitars, soaking up the sun and the strong ocean breeze, and taking in the sights (girls!). We watched the waves crashing, as we drank beer and got stoned. I took my first swim in the ocean, and hence, swallowed my first (and last) mouthful of saltwater. I was inspired and wrote an instrumental on my guitar that I appropriately titled "On the Coast."

We attracted a small crowd. One of our new acquaintances showed us the exact spot where Ray Manzarek and Jim Morrison first met, talked about starting The Doors, and Morrison sang Ray the lyrics to the song "Moonlight Drive." We were awestruck not only with the sights and sounds but also experiencing the places that had been part of mythical stories we had always heard. We were trudging through the same sand that Morrison and the Doors trudged through in the mid-1960s.

Withdrawal now behind us, we felt like we were in paradise…and as it turned out…we were! As the "red rubber ball" began to sink into the Pacific, we left the beach and headed to our next destination—Sunset Strip. We were without a shower for a few days, so we decided to break down and get a room. Of course, we cheaped out and rented a room at "The Fleabag Motel" but, I must say: a lumpy twin bed and a lukewarm shower never felt so good.

The next morning, we toured Sunset Strip, ending at our second L.A. destination, the Whiskey a Go Go. Some local bands were on the marquee outside and even though it was early, to our surprise, it was open. We stepped inside and saw the walls lined with tributes to all the great bands that had graced that stage. I got up my nerve to get up on the stage and imagined how it must've felt to be Jim Morrison singing "The End," to a packed standing room only crowd. I could almost feel what it was like to have been there.

Our next stop on The Doors tour was West Hollywood at the intersection of Santa Monica and La Cienega boulevards. This was the main stomping grounds of the band. First, we saw the small dive, Tropicana Motel, where Jim Morrison lived for years. Next, we walked up the street to 8512 Santa Monica Blvd.—The Doors headquarters. This is where they recorded my favorite Doors album, *L.A. Woman*. The building was in the process of being renovated at the time, so it was open. It was the weekend, so no one was on the site working. You got the feeling that soon it would never again be as it was when The Doors were there. As we entered and went through the rooms, we came across a small bathroom. I poked my head in and immediately looked up at the ceiling. There it was, the unusually high ceiling, just like I had read about in the stories of recording the song "Riders on the Storm." I immediately started singing…

Riders on the storm, riders on the storm
Into this house we're born, into this world we're thrown
Like a dog without a bone, an actor out on lone
Riders on the storm, yeeeaaaaaaah!

I could hear the strange echo of my voice as it bounced oddly off the ceiling and the walls, like the whisper of a ghost. It was said that this was the reason he recorded the vocals in that bathroom. Frank laughed in acknowledgement that we had both just been privy to something special that all our friends back home would never experience.

We stayed on Sunset Strip one more night and went to our first strip club. We drank too much, which was starting to occur more frequently by then. Replacing heroin with alcohol didn't seem like such a bad idea at the time.

The next morning, we continued our journey north on the 101. We were listening to the radio and we heard an ad for the Grateful Dead. I looked at Frank and said, "You know I've been trying to see them for years—right?"

"Let's go see 'em. They're playing tomorrow night, at Davis Hall." Frank said.

We stopped and asked someone if they had ever heard of it.

"You're about 250 miles away. It's actually called Davies Hall. It's in the Dead's stomping ground, San Francisco. Just keep going on the freeway and when you get to the Bay Area, you'll see the signs."

We were on a mission to finally see the Dead! We got to San Francisco in the early evening and did some sight-seeing. We got to the area near Davies Hall and grabbed some food. Someone pointed out a store that sold concert tickets and told us we could get tickets there. Unfortunately, when we got there, it had just closed. We saw the Ticketmaster sign in the window, so we knew we were in the right place. With nothing left to do, we decided to turn in early in their parking lot and make sure we got tickets as soon as they opened. I was finally going to my first Dead concert!

The next morning, we woke up bright and early. The streets started getting populated as the city awoke to another typical day. We looked out the window and immediately noticed something not so typical. Walking on the sidewalk was a black man with long hair and a beard. Nothing unusual about that, right? Yeah, except he was wearing a short, tight skirt and high heels and carrying a purse. We started noticing similar people going into the store, which had just opened, and men walking and holding hands. We had never seen anything like it in our lives. I remarked, "Well, whatever; let's go."

Frank looked at me like a dear in the headlights. "Kee-hee, you sure we should go out there?"

"Yeah, why not?" I replied.

"They're gonna think we're gay," Frank said, almost whispering.

"Who gives a fuck!? They're all gay!"

We emerged from the van and walked into the store. We walked up to the counter and asked, "Can we get two general admission tickets for Grateful Dead at Davies Hall?"

"Sure can. That'll be seventy-four doll…um, did you say Davies Hall?"

"Yes, two tickets," I replied.

"Sorry, but they're not playing at Davies Hall. They're playing at U.C. Davis Hall in Sacramento."

Frank and I froze and stared at the man as if he just told us our dog died. The curse of the Grateful Dead remained unbroken. I decided then and there, I would never try to see the band again.

Home of The Mother Lode

After the disappointment of the Grateful Dead debacle, there was nothing left to do but head for our final destination—Sonora, California. We continued drinking and smoking pot daily. Once we got to the scenic Route 4, we were struck by the beauty of the rolling hills and picturesque surroundings. When we got into town, we noticed we were through it in the blink of an eye. We suddenly found ourselves surrounded by huge pine trees, and heading into the foothills of the Sierra Nevada Mountains. We literally watched the weather go from sunny to rain, to sleet, and finally, to snow, in less than half an hour.

We saw all the quaint shops, saloons, and hotels—the biggest being the Sonora Inn. There were signs sprinkled throughout the town depicting its famous history as one of the huge gold rush towns of 1849— "Home of The Mother Lode". There was even a precious metals store that paid for mined gold, silver, and the like. There were still prospectors who mined and panned for gold in the area, though all the big hauls had been ripped out of the earth and streams long ago. You could literally drink from the local streams; they were so crystal clear. It was the best tasting water we'd ever drank.

We recognized our destination on Washington Street and could see Tom's sign outside the two-story building. Frank ran in to announce our arrival to Tom. He returned with keys, and we went around the back, where Tom met us at the walk-in entrance to the basement apartment.

Tom was a tall, good-looking guy who dressed in typical golfer, doctor, Rat Pack-wannabe clothes. He had hair that was slightly longer than it should have been, typical of the times. Tom was a partier, at times, heavy on booze and cocaine, but he took his work seriously and never mixed business with pleasure. Apparently, it may have contributed to his being "mostly divorced" when we arrived. Before we could finish moving in, he showed me to the chiropractic table and did his first adjustment on me.

After we got moved in, we were invited up to Tom's office, where he had me fill out a workman's comp claim. He told us all about how cool the town and the area was, and where everything was located. This included the unemployment office, welfare office, and Western Union, which we planned on visiting in the morning.

The phone rang, and Tom got up to answer it in the other room. As Frank and I continued to talk, Tom came back and said, "Steve, it's for you." I looked at him in shock, thinking to myself, *every time I get a phone call out of the blue, somebody's dead.* "It's for me?"

"Yeah, it's your cousin Ed. He says he walked here from Chicago."

"That sounds like something Ed would do," I replied.

So, I went into the other room and got on the phone. As it turned out, he didn't walk all the way from Chicago, just most of the way. I guess he had trouble hitchhiking rides. He said he was at our cousin Kiki's house near L.A., and he was on his way to us and wanted the address. I gave it to him, and he said he'd see me in a few days. I came back into the room, and we all had a good laugh at the absurdity of Ed's story.

Frank and I went to the welfare office the next day. We walked out of the place with two books of food stamps in our hands and a check in the mail. We were shocked at how easy it was to get benefits in California.

We started hanging out at the two local saloons and shooting pool, playing pinball, darts, and bar games daily. Eventually, it got old, and we started getting bored. So much so, that Frank decided to turn in extremely early on one Friday night after shooting pool and drinking all day in the saloon. I was wide awake and bored with nothing to do while Frank snored away, so I decided to do a little exploring on my own.

I found myself walking past the Sonora Inn, where the faint sound of live music coming from inside caught my attention. I went in and to my surprise, I saw a decent-sized crowd. The sound got clearer as I got closer to the large banquet room, and I was finally able to make out the song "Evil Ways" by Santana. I opened the door and there was a small crowd watching the band.

They sounded pretty good. I remember being impressed that a band in that area would be doing a Santana song, albeit an older one. I was also pleasantly surprised to see an attractive, black-haired woman playing shakers during the guitar solo, then making her way back to the mic at the center of the stage…

When I come home, baby, my house is dark, and my pots are cold. You hangin' round, baby, with Jean and Joan and who knows who.

She had a great voice! It was strong, and dead-on key on every note. She had just enough of a sweet quality to remind you that she was a woman, sort of like Bonnie Raitt, who, it turned out, was one of her musical heroes before most people had ever heard of her.

I grabbed a beer at the bar and a chair near the stage. I watched them and immediately went into critique mode. My ears always listened for the subtleties that made a band good, or not so good. I always got anxious to play when I saw a band that played the kind of stuff I liked. She smiled at me and that's when I made the decision—when they took a break, I'd ask her if I could get up and play a song with them. Hey, I figured all she could do is say no.

When they took their break, I somehow got the nerve and walked up to her. "Hey, you guys sound really good!"

"Thanks," she replied with a smile. "I'm Dusty."

"I'm Steve, from Chicago."

"Nice to meet you, Steve, from Chicago."

"Hey, I wanted to ask you: my friend and I just moved here and we're both musicians…Anyway, do you think I could get up there and play a song with you guys when you go back on?"

"Where's your friend?" she asked.

"We were bored, and he went to sleep back at our apartment," I explained.

"What do you play, Steve from Chicago?"

"Guitar and vocal."

"What kind of stuff?"

"Allman Brothers, Clapton, Skynyrd, Zeppelin, Doors—ya know, that kind of thing."

"We love all of those. We know "Roadhouse Blues" and "Call Me the Breeze," but no one knows the words."

"I know the words to both," I said, starting to get excited.

"Okay, Steve from Chicago, you got a deal. I'll call you up in the middle of the second set."

"I'm going to get my guitar; it will only take me a few minutes," I said.

"Cool," Dusty replied. "Guys, this is Steve from Chicago. He's going to join us in the second set for a few songs. He knows the words "Roadhouse" and "Call Me the Breeze."

"Cool," a few of them responded.

When I got back to the apartment, I woke Frank up and told him what was happening. I grabbed my Ibanez and threw it in the case. Frank got dressed and grabbed the camera and we were off.

We grabbed a beer and a seat, then, about halfway through their set, as promised, she walked up to the mic and said: "We'd like to invite a special guest to join us now. All the way from Chicago, Illinois, put your hands together for Chicago, Steve!"

I took the stage to surprising applause. They showed me to an amp on stage that I could plug into and as we got my guitar up to speed, Dusty grabbed a tambourine and surrendered the center stage mic. Before I knew it, the pounding guitar intro started, and the keyboard player pulled a harp out of his pocket and chimed in. I stepped up to the mic and my skinny ass belted out...

Ah, keep your eyes on the road, your hands upon the wheel
Keep your eyes on the road, your hands upon the wheel
Yeah, we're goin' to the roadhouse, gonna have a real... good time!

When I opened my eyes, I couldn't believe what I was seeing and hearing. Everyone was standing and cheering. The next thing I know, people are coming into the banquet room from the main bar, standing and cheering. It's like the whole place suddenly came to life! The energy from the audience inspired my performance, and now, I was really about to get 'em...
Their lead guitarist and I traded off licks on the solo and then...

You gotta roll, roll, roll, you gotta thrill my soul, all right
Roll, roll, roll, gotta thrill my soul
You gotta, chonk a chew chon chonk a tonk a te tonk
Bop bop ba bip bop alula con ca che no no ...

The band all had smiles from ear to ear when I went into my Morrisonesque improvisation. After "Roadhouse," we went right into "Call Me the Breeze."

Well, now they call me the breeze, I keep blowin' down the road
They call me the breeze; I keep blowin' down the road
I ain't got me nobody, and I don't carry me no load...

By the end of the song, the whole main bar had moved to the banquet room…
Wooooooooohooooooooohoohooooooooooo… Mr. Breeze (big finish)!!!

They kept me on stage for the rest of the night and invited me back for the remaining two nights! When I got off the stage, Frank informed me, "Kid, you were heatsinking up there!"

I asked Dusty if they knew or could learn a few songs that Frank and I had been working on, especially "Revival" and "Southbound" by the Allman Brothers. It turned out that they knew both, and we were able to get Frank up there for a few songs the next two nights. The word got out to the surrounding area by the next night. Both nights were packed, mostly with bikers!

As it turned out, the bikers were in the area for some annual event that took place called "The Mother Lode Round-up." This was a series of events that took place throughout Calaveras County, Tuolumne County, and the surrounding area over the period between mid-April and mid-May. It consisted of rodeos, concerts, outdoor festivals, antique auto shows, and the famous "Frog Jump" in the nearby town of Angels Camp.

The frog jump is a commemorative event that honors author Mark Twain, who wrote *The Jumping Frog of Calaveras County* in a cabin that is a preserved landmark in nearby Tuttletown. It coincided with the annual biker group conventions held in the area, so they kind of merged. The bikers were able to partake in all the area festivities.

As we finished our last set Sunday night, Dusty mentioned that the guitarist was unable to continue with them after this show because he was going to be busy building his own home. This was not unusual as many in the area chose to build their homes due to lack of funds, but no lack of skill in the trades.

After the show, Frank and I were invited to the band's hotel room upstairs. As we entered, Dusty said, "There's our boys from Illinois!" with a big smile. She got up and grabbed me by the arm and said, "And this is our Mr. Mojo Risin', chonk-a-chew chon, chon." She laughed and sat me down next to her as she did her impression of my "Roadhouse Blues" improv. We were all sitting in a big circle on the floor drinking, laughing, and passing a few joints around. Then, out of nowhere, this big plate of cocaine gets passed and everybody's snorting a line and passing it on. I couldn't help thinking to myself, *I wish I had a syringe. What a waste!* I kept that sentiment to myself.

Then, the real shocker; Dusty pulled $400 out of her pocket and handed it to me. Surprised, I blurted out, "What's this for?"

She informed me, "The bar paid you. They wanted me to make sure you got it."

Wow! I was floored. Not only about getting paid for playing music, but with the integrity of these people. She could have kept the money for herself or split it with the band and I would have been none the wiser.

We continued to party until the crack of dawn when they informed us they had to leave. They lived in Mokelumne Hill about 40 miles away. So, they packed up their van and left, leaving the room to Frank and me. We were exhausted and we passed out in the two twin beds.

Within a few hours, we were both awakened out of a dead sleep by the phone ringing. I reluctantly got up and answered it. It was Dusty, "Hey, sorry to wake you up, but I gotta know. Do you and Frank want to join our band?"

I was in somewhat of a stupor, so I answered: "I don't know. Do I have to tell you now? We're sound asleep. Let me talk to Frank when we wake up."

When we awoke around noon or so, we weren't sure if we had dreamed the whole thing.

Frank and I accepted Dusty's offer and soon found ourselves driving to Moke Hill (as the locals call it) for our first rehearsals. Talk about a scenic drive. The route was sprinkled with an occasional bit of American history, too. There were the dilapidated ruins of a jailhouse from the 1800s near Angels Camp that incarcerated some pretty famous outlaws. Black Bart was one of the most famous in the area. Charles Earl Boles (his real name) was a stagecoach robber, famous for writing poetry and leaving it at some of his robbery sites. He was known as a gentleman and never fired a shot during his entire criminal career. When released from prison in the late 1800s, he disappeared.

We arrived at the quaint, historic town of Mokelumne Hill, once a Gold Rush mecca and boomtown, now a forgotten place, except for the tourists and bikers during special events throughout the year. Our first stop was the huge centerpiece of the town: the historic, antique, Hotel Leger (pronounced *Leeshea*). Dusty had arranged to meet us there.

The first two versions of the hotel burned down in massive fires that the town endured in the early and mid-1800s. Everything was original and authentic, built in 1875, including the floors, which creaked when you walked on them. The ornate trim and stained-glass pieces that hung behind the bar gave the place a mix of eclectic and Old West feel.

We sat at the bar and ordered a few beers from the attractive but slightly heavyset bartender Anita and waited for Dusty. When she arrived, she introduced us to her friend Anita. She invited Anita over after she got off work to "come and hang out with the band." Dusty took us on a tour of the place after Anita instructed her to warn us, "It's haunted, ya know."

The rooms were all filled with antiques from the 1800s. Everything from the bed frames to the desks, dressers, to pictures on the walls. The coolest room had a working roulette table from the era at the foot of the bed.

Dusty explained that they were the house band here and hosted an open mic on most Saturday nights. As we turned the corner to descend the staircase, I heard a young girl call my name. I stopped and turned around to see who it was. There was no one there. Frank asked what I was doing. "Nothing, just…never mind." Whoa!

Next, Dusty took us on a mini tour of the one-horse town, including an art gallery across the street owned by an artist and sculptor named Miles. The place was closed but what I saw through the window was the work of a skilled and talented artist.

Miles worked mostly with something called soapstone. He was fairly well-known throughout Northern California and did pretty well for himself. Dusty explained that he played sax, flute, harmonica, and percussion and he often sat in with the band when he was around.

She continued the tour, and we made our way over to a smaller saloon at the end of the block called "The Hole in the Wall." Hanging on the wall across from the bar were mostly forgotten, obsolete instruments that we had never seen before. Surprisingly, in the middle of the wall was a plaque with a gold record in it. It turned out that owner, Randy Sparks, was the founding member of a popular 1960s musical group, "The New Christy Minstrels." They had a few hit records, which oddly, I was familiar with. Randy had given up the whole music scene to settle down and live a simpler life.

From there, we went to Dusty's house. We unloaded our equipment and went into the living room, where the band's equipment was already set up. I noted pictures of rainbows everywhere throughout the place. When I asked about them, she said simply, "I've just always really liked rainbows." Okay.

The band would arrive shortly, so we just talked and got to know each other. I broke out my acoustic and showed her the song I'd just written on Venice Beach, "On the Coast." She loved it and recorded it on the reel-to-reel tape player that was also set up. She asked if she could write some words to it. Though I had written it as an instrumental, I figured, "What the hell; go ahead." This was all a new adventure, so I was open to trying new things. She put the headphones on, grabbed a pencil and paper, and immediately started nailing it.

Seagulls flying, ocean breeze a blowin',
You and I are so much more for knowing,
One another in this place and time,
Though the beauty all around us, can't compare to what's inside…

She almost wrote the whole thing right there and it fit the music perfectly. Then I handed Frank the acoustic and I broke out the Ibanez and we showed her some of the other stuff we had recently been working on like "Hotel

California." Her eyes lit up when Frank went into the intro, and she immediately jumped onto the mic.

On a dark desert highway, cool wind in my hair
Warm smell of colitas, rising up through the air
And up ahead in the distance, I saw a shimmering light
My head grew heavy, and my sight grew dim, I had to stop for the night
There she stood in the doorway, I heard the mission bell
And I was thinking to myself this could be heaven, or this could be hell
Then she lit up the candle, and she showed me the way
There were voices down the corridor, I thought I heard them say...
We harmonized...
Welcome to the hotel California
Such a lovely place, such a lovely face
Plenty of room at the hotel California,
Any time of year, you can find it here...

We wound up trading off verses on the lead vocal. The band started to show up and they went straight to their instruments, turned on their amps, and jumped in. There was "Catfish Bob" on bass, Joe Marino on drums, and Ron on keyboards. Dusty turned on the P.A., Frank and I cranked up the volume, and we went into a rough and rocky, albeit inspired, first take of the song. Then Dusty asked me to show them "On the Coast," and we worked on that. We discussed some good songs we could do that featured both male and female vocals. Two that I brought to the table were agreed upon immediately by the band, were Eric Clapton's "The Core" off the *Slowhand* album, and on the more obscure side, from my Matt's house days, Santana's "Love, Devotion and Surrender," off the equally obscure album *Welcome*. We were all getting into it and things were already taking shape. There was something magical about the experience and it felt as though we had stumbled into a fairytale of sorts.

Anita arrived with a brown paper bag in hand. When we finally took a break and Anita announced that the bag contained local, fresh-picked, psilocybin mushrooms. We all partook in the natural, mild hallucinogen.

Then, it was time to go back and work out the kinks in one of our biggest challenges—"Hotel California." I had a reasonable facsimile of the solo down but I had a hard time achieving Eagles guitarists Joe Walsh's and Don Felder's dynamic sound. It was going pretty well until the "shrooms" suddenly started kicking in. It became obvious when we noticed that we all had the same big, dopey grin on our faces. We started the song, and Dusty went to the mic...

On a dark desert highway, cool wind in my hair

Warm smell of colitas, rising up through the air
BWAHAHAHAHAHAHAHAHA!!
She started cracking up! "Okay, okay, let's try it again," and we'd start over.
On a dark desert highway, cool wind in my hair
Warm smell of colitas...BWAHAHAHAHAHAHAHAHA!! "What the hell is colitas anyway?"
...BWAHAHAHAHAHAHAHAHA!!

    Then, the entire band started cracking up. We all looked at each other and agreed to call it a day and hang it up. We put the guitars in their stands, turned the amps and PA off, and went outside.

    Upon stepping out the door, we were shocked to find that it was almost dark outside. We had completely lost track of time and found ourselves in the middle of a perfect, warm, Northern California night. The air was sweet-smelling, perfumed by one hundred different kinds of flowers in bloom—possibly one was colitas? There was a huge, yellow full moon that hung low in the sky and illuminated everything, like a giant lantern. We were drawn to it like moths to a flame. It shined off the rolling hilltops and painted the landscape with golden light as we all walked toward it. The stars were so close that you felt as though you could reach up and touch them. The velvet black sky created a contrasting background to anything the light touched. The dirt road we all walked on led west into the wilderness and the hills of "wine country," away from town and civilization. The scene was so surreal; I felt like I was in the shire described in Tolkien's *The Hobbit*. We came upon a huge, old tree.

    Being the lifelong, avid tree climber that I was, I proceeded to climb it. Everyone was looking up at me with big grins on their faces until their faces were too small for me to see. Higher and higher I went—so high that I started questioning if I should keep going. I did, and I made it almost to the top of the tree. I could see for miles of moonlit rolling hills, giant trees that were at least a century old, and we could hear an owl off in the distance.

    I sat there and soaked in the overwhelming sensory display of sights, sounds, and smells. Though I knew that the shrooms were enhancing my experience to some extent, I wonder if I even needed them at all. The beauty of the earth at that place, on that night, was intoxicating enough. It was an experience that I can't adequately describe with words. Everybody lay in the grass at the foot of the tree, silent, with me high above. We all just relished the sudden, full appreciation of the great gift of being alive on this awesome planet that we all had been blessed to be on. Truly blissful!

    On a sidenote, we would later learn that the "smell of colitas" was more in the house than outside ... It was marijuana they were referring to.

We all went back to Dusty's after our adventure in the wilderness. Frank and Anita started hitting it off. The other band members got ready to go to their respective nearby homes. Dusty offered Frank and I to spend the night rather than drive the 40 miles back to our apartment in Sonora. She also invited Anita to spend the night. Um, let's just say that first night, Frank and Anita didn't get much sleep, and neither did Dusty and me from listening to them. Dusty and I shared her pullout couch bed in the living room, and she hit on me.

She explained, "I know you probably like tall blondes, but I'm a tall blonde trapped in a short brunette's body."

I laughed but declined and told her about Laura and Jessica and at the time, I was still heartbroken and missing them. She understood. It turned out that she had a similar situation with her young son Dylan and his father. I asked if Dusty was her real name.

"No, it's Dorothy. Dusty is my stage name." We both fell asleep despite the "racket" coming from the other room.

Over the next week, we continued to rehearse and perfect our sound. One day, there was a knock at the door, and there he was, in all his glory—my cousin Ed! I introduced him as my cousin "who walked here from Chicago," so everyone was pretty amazed from the get-go. Ed had an extremely outgoing personality, and he immediately felt comfortable and inserted himself into any situation. He was quickly accepted by everyone. Ed enjoyed watching the band, particularly a little thing I came up with during the song "Hotel California."

Mirrors on the ceiling, the pink champagne on ice
And she said, we are all just prisoners here, of our own device
And in the master's chambers, they gather for their feast
They stab it with their steely knives, but they just can't kill the beast

… "Bump pa dump pum pum!"

On the record, there is a quick percussion riff here. I would jump on the conga that was almost always set up just to my right, and do the part, then jump quickly back onto my guitar. Ed was so tickled by me doing this, he would jump up out of his seat, pump his fist and yell, "Yeah, cuz!" every time I did it.

Ed got a job as a handyman and kitchen help at the Leger in exchange for room and board, so he hung out with us when he wasn't working. He wanted to be helpful and support the band, so he became our only real roadie.

Dusty felt we were ready to book some gigs. There were events coming up all over the area with the whole Mother Lode Roundup thing going on. The band needed a name, and it came to me almost immediately. "How about…Dusty Rhodes and the Rainbow Boogie Band?" I blurted out. Dusty had a big smile of approval on her face. Everybody gave the thumbs up and that was it. I realized later that it was inspired by Janis Joplin's bands "Big Brother and the Holding Company" and "Full Tilt Boogie" and incorporated Dusty's love of rainbows.

Our first gig was at the Leger, which was a good place for us to work out the kinks and develop material. Miles came back into town and joined us. He really added a lot to the sound, especially on songs like "The Core," with a great sax solo. To feature his flute, we learned "Can't You See" by Marshall Tucker Band, including a flute solo in "On the Coast." It fit and sounded great! The song "Never Knew How Much" was an obscure, newer Allman Brothers Ballad that had a sax solo in it. Miles was an all-around musician and would jump on the congas, shakers, sax, or flute—depending on whatever fit the song.

Soon, the band was playing out all the time. Most venues paid well because live music brought a big increase in business. Frank and I were making a living, however meager, playing music. We played outdoor fairs, and saloons in the surrounding towns of Modesto, Merced, San Andreas, and Stockton.

One day, Dusty came into rehearsal with an excited look on her face. She interrupted and announced: "I might have a really big gig for us. I'm waiting for a phone call to confirm." The gig was in the heart of wine country at the Sutter Creek Theater. The phone rang a short time later and when Dusty hung up, we had the gig! It would be the biggest audience we would ever play for. Little did I know what an understatement that would be.

We were part of a show that consisted of a handful of local artists, so we only had about 40 minutes. For us, that was only a handful of songs. Here was the set list we decided on:

The Core (Clapton)
Never Knew How Much (Allman Brothers)
Black Magic Woman (Santana)
On the Coast (Fiorito)
Hotel California (Eagles)
She's just gone (Fiorito—a song I wrote about my breakup with Carol)

On the day of the show, we arrived at the theater, and we went around back to load in. After setting up our equipment in a staging area backstage, we walked around to the front door to see what the place was like inside. It was like everything else in the area: quaint, vintage, and awesome!

As we walked down the center isle toward the stage, Frank, Ed, and I were struck by a huge banner that covered almost the entire width of the stage. It read "Live-KNGT Broadcast!"

Frank and I looked at each other, then we turned to Dusty, and I asked, "We're going to be on the radio!?"

Dusty had a big grin on her face. "Yep."

"Does everybody else know?"

"Yep."

"Why didn't you tell us?"

"I didn't want you guys to freak out."

"Well, that didn't work, 'cause I'm freaking out right now!" I exclaimed.

Frank and Ed laughed. Dusty assured me, "You'll be fine. Just do your thing, Chonker. Oh, and tonight we've got another gig across the street at Bellotti's restaurant in the saloon."

"Okay," I mumbled to myself, still in shock.

I walked backstage to start getting my equipment ready. I was nervous but also more excited. We were going to be on the radio!

The show went off without a hitch. In fact, a very cool thing happened during my song. "On the Coast." A white dove landed on Ron's keyboard and remained there for the rest of the set. It had escaped from the magician who did his act between sets. There was a photo taken that shows Ron playing and smiling from ear to ear, looking down at the bird. It was a good omen.

During "Hotel California," I did my little conga riff and Ed, who was sitting in the front row, leaped from his seat and did his thing. "Yeah, cuz!" A theater full of people and a live radio broadcast proved to be no deterrent to Ed's enthusiasm.

When the band wasn't playing in some of the bigger towns, we returned to a laidback, peaceful, picturesque rural landscape, filled with quirky, interesting, and eclectic people.

Two such people were Gus and Harlin. They were friends of Dusty's and lived on about 50 acres or so, about eight miles outside of town. "Gus and Harlin's farm," as it was known by all, wasn't really much of a farm, but they had what they needed to meet their needs. They were the first people I ever met that were almost fully self-sustaining and lived almost entirely off the land, the only exceptions being liquor and tobacco. They had a few cows and a few chickens and grew their own beans, sprouts, veggies, and weed.

They were two older men who lived a simple, organic life together. Were they gay? It never came up and it didn't seem to matter to anybody, including me. They were good people who enjoyed each other's company and the simple things in life. They were also on a tight budget and rolled their own smokes (and smoke), as did many people in the area. They would hitchhike or walk the eight miles into town once every few weeks for supplies.

Their home was one of the coolest things I've ever seen. It was very rustic and practical, adorned in antiques. But it was their living room that really blew Frank and I away. The walls were covered with antique farming relics, as well as authentic photos and paintings from the Old West and Gold Rush eras. The fireplace was handmade with rocks from the land and was lit and crackling due to a cold front that had suddenly moved in. The floor was made of huge pieces of slate that they laid themselves. But the real kicker was the back wall of the living room—twenty-five acres of pasture and rolling hills. There was no back wall. Just a segue into the beautiful Northern California landscape.

What enhanced the experience even more and etched it into my mind forever, was the brief but intense thunderstorm that hit while Harlin and I played chess. With the rainwater running off the roof, it looked like a pane of natural glass. It's the effect that they're going for when you see one of those big wall fountains in a high-end office building. This was the natural version.

We all spent the day in what felt like a time warp, enveloped in this simple, beautiful, surreal time and place that was Gus and Harlin's farm. It's funny how you can't really grasp the relevance of certain experiences in your life until much later. Gus and Harlin's farm became part of me, forever, as something inside of me yearned for simplicity, peace, and serenity. Maybe I should have gotten a clue that I had been looking for it in the wrong places, but of course, it didn't occur to me then.

Going back and forth between Sonora and Moke Hill became quite a pain in the ass, even though we were spending the night at Dusty's a lot. Frank and Anita became almost joined at the hip, so we decided to move to Moke Hill and found a cheap cabin for rent in the middle of nowhere. Frank, Anita, and I split the rent. It was on vast acreage owned by John Garamendi, a state senator who represented the area. It was an adventure just getting to and from the cabin.

Our driveway was a dirt road that was about two blocks long. Every morning, it would be blocked by 10 or 15 head of cattle. Frank would fly down this huge hill at them, threatening to hit them to move them out of the way. We laughed as they all panicked and scattered, mooing loudly in protest.

The feelings of missing Laura and Jess continued to grow despite the band's success, so I finally wrote her a letter, complete with pictures of the area, the band, and the cows. I wrote on the back to Jess: "These are Da Da's cows."

I would desperately check the post office daily for a letter. Every day the box was empty until, finally, one day, I opened it, and there was a letter! My heart pounded and I had a knot in my stomach as I opened it. Good news! She told me she felt the same way. She still loved and missed me, too, and so did Jessica. I was happy and relieved. I wrote often and Laura and Jessica's letters soon became the highlight of my life in Northern California.

Gathering storm clouds on the horizon

Ever since Frank and I escaped that wicked snowstorm in Nebraska, we had been on what I've described as a fairytale adventure and a natural high, well...mostly natural. It almost seemed too good to be true, and as the old saying goes, "All good things must come to an end." This was no exception.

The beginning of the end started when Dusty announced that she had to go back to the East Coast, where her family was from, to take care of some family issues. I don't recall the details but before she left, she said to me: "I know you're going to go back to Chicago eventually—aren't you?"

"Probably," I admitted.

"I've always wanted to go to Chicago. If I do, I'm going to look you up, Chonker."

"That would be okay," I assured her as we hugged, and just like that, she was gone.

After Dusty's departure, the band splintered off into other projects. Joe also played guitar and other instruments and had a side project called Deuce with his guitarist friend, Jack. They wanted me in the project, so to accommodate me, they started calling themselves "Deuce Plus One." They had some gigs booked but were nowhere near as busy as the band had been.

Bob and Ron started a new band, a little on the heavier and more commercial side, while Miles wound up moving his gallery to a more populated area and began putting more effort into his art and sculptures.

Soon, things started slowing down and boredom started setting in. For me, this was combined with being homesick and missing Laura and Jess more each day. Frank and I started spending our days at the Leger drinking gin and tonic, smoking pot, and hanging out at the pool. I think we bordered on alcoholism. We were both drinking like a couple of drunks, as was cousin Ed.

I recall one of Ed's drunken rants during this period, criticizing my uncle Lawrence (his father) for being an alcoholic, while ironically turning into one right before our very eyes.

Money started getting tight, too. Though I was still getting chiropractic adjustments, the workman's comp thing finally ran its course, and they stopped paying. We could drink for free when Anita was on duty but that ended when she got fired for doing exactly that. They were marking bottles, and she got busted out by the owner. Ed got fired for virtually the same thing, except he was stealing booze from the restaurant, not the saloon. Frank was still living off money his parents sent him, some of which was from the sale of the GTO. Anita and I wound up getting jobs. She worked at a mini-mart gas station a few miles out of town, and I got a part-time job as a groundskeeper for Garamendi's mother, who lived across the road from us. Once a week, I'd cut grass, trim hedges, pull weeds, and whatever else needed to be done.

The next step toward the end of our fairytale happened when Frank met a woman who knew a crooked dentist. She sold Dilaudid from one of the bigger towns in the area. Somehow, Frank found a connection for syringes too and soon he was "off to the races" again. He was just "chipping" at first. Chipping is defined as a period of less frequent, controlled drug use. Though I didn't partake in the Dilaudid or the needle at this point, I wasn't far behind. It was the first example of the fact that no matter how deep into rural country you go, there is always this "underground opiate society" that you'll eventually stumble upon if you're a "member." If you don't find it, it'll find you.

My unraveling began when I started spending the night at Joe and his wife Debbie's. While using their bathroom, out of habit, I looked in the medicine cabinet. There I found a full bottle of Tylenol #4 with codeine. I took a few and popped them before a gig. I remember starting to feel them as I took the stage, and I experienced that familiar warm surge of opiate-induced confidence. They seemed to enhance my comfort level on stage. I thought to myself; *Oh yeah, I remember this. I miss this.* Just like that, Pandora's Box flung open, and once again, I immediately became obsessed with using opiates.

Just like the Fanny May Mint Meltaway incident when I was a kid, I took two, then two more, then three, and so on, until the bottle only had about four or five pills left. And just like I had with the Mint Meltaways, I figured I might as well just take the bottle and maybe they wouldn't miss it. They didn't, that is, until Joe got a toothache.

"Hey babe, what happened to those painkillers we had? I thought they were in the medicine cabinet in the spare bathroom."

"They're not there? I may have thrown them out. I meant to, but I don't remember doing it," Debbie replied.

I was somewhat let off the hook by Debbie's poor memory, but there was that old knot in my gut again that hadn't been there for quite a while.

Then, "the straw that broke the camel's back" happened. I'm not going into details but let's just say that Frank and Anita participated in some criminal activity that I wasn't comfortable with. That made my decision much easier. It was, once again, time to "get the hell outta Dodge" and head home.

I called Laura and told her I was coming home. She said she couldn't wait to see me. She handed the phone to Jessica, who had turned three that July. She asked if I could bring some cows home when I came. I told her I would try but they were stubborn and didn't usually listen to me.

The next day, I got a one-way ticket for a Greyhound bus, said my goodbyes, and a few days later, got on a Greyhound headed for "sweet home Chicago." Frank and Anita got the hell outta Dodge too, and moved south to Santa Rosa, where Frank had some relatives.

It seems this was our version of the old Cinderella fairytale. Everything came together like magic for us, and we suddenly found ourselves at "the ball." Then, just as suddenly, the clock struck midnight, and we found ourselves turning back into pumpkins, mice, and peasants. Once again, we became two poor, lost, Midwestern drug addicts. Only difference? Frank had made up his mind never to meet face-to-face with Mike Lanfore, and stayed in Cali, while I went back home to continue my life with Laura and Jessica.

The second wall of the hurricane

Upon my return to Illinois, I remember the excitement of seeing Laura and Jess. We missed each other and were "in love" once again, that is, until the "honeymoon" wore off and it didn't take long for reality to set back in.

And so it was, with Laura and me, constantly breaking up and getting back together. In a way, it's what made our relationship work. It was a vicious circle we always found ourselves in. I didn't understand it at the time, but I think I do now. We had a true love/hate relationship, driven by our underlying low self-esteem. Deep down, we knew we weren't right for each other, but like all people who suffer from low self-esteem, we were afraid to let go. We were both victims of rejection. She would have thrown me overboard in a heartbeat if Russell had come back into her life, and I would have done the same if Carol reconsidered. I think we both felt trapped in the relationship. We had resentments that would flare up and we could be downright mean to each other.

Then there was Jessica, who made the situation even more complicated. I loved Jess. Laura and her family knew it, and admired that about me, though Laura didn't advertise her admiration, likely to prepare for the possibility that things wouldn't work out. Laura's mother, Rhoda, was the only one who let me know that she appreciated me. Once she told me, "I see the way you take care of Jessica, and I appreciate it, Steve."

It was one of the few things that made me feel good about myself back then. But she would also scold us on occasion: "You two need to quit monkeying around and get it together." Unfortunately, "getting it together" was a much taller order than anyone knew.

To make matters worse, a woman in the trailer next door to ours was a chronic pain patient who always had tons of prescription painkillers. This was my earliest recollection of Laura using opiate painkillers. "Getting it together" would have to wait. We both started buying pills from the woman, which for me would quickly lead back to doctor shopping, and pursuit of the ever-more elusive Tussionex.

We had burnt out all the pharmacies in the area, so I had to settle for Tusssionex's "second cousins": Hycodan and Hycomine. They both had Hydrocodone in them, but as Franko used to say, "Tussionex has a delicate blend of Hydrocodone and Phenyltoloxamine resin complexes," which gave it the extra kick that no other syrup had. This, of course, predictably led me back to eventually shooting heroin and cocaine again.

Paul, being on the Methadone maintenance program at Hines Veterans Hospital, was introduced to some interesting characters. One of these happened to be his counselor—John Lee. He was a black man whom I believe genuinely cared about my brother but was clueless about how to help him.

Another was Barry and his wife Nora who sold heroin and pills out of their mobile home. It became a convenient one-stop shop for all opiate needs. For coke, I went to Max's friend and partner in crime, Billy D, who continued to sell coke out of his father's house in the old neighborhood. The "eye" had passed and was about to give way to the second "wall of the hurricane."

I moved back into the mobile home with Laura, Jessica, Rhoda, and Leon, and worked a few odd jobs. Freddy bought a piece of land in the middle of the desert in New Mexico and moved there.

I had yet another feeble attempt to get a band together with neighborhood guitarist Dave Ackerman. The problem was, we were all too fucked up and chasing drugs around to be serious about music. I had officially turned back into a "garage band wannabe."

Unable to make any money playing music, I was forced to get a real job at a place called Rent-A-Color that rented TVs and VCRs. This was a fairly new concept at the time, but with the recent invention of VHS tape, it started to take off. Yes, it wasn't that long before this that you couldn't rent or own a movie. The only options—wait for it to be aired on TV or see it at the movie theater.

Bright and early, I'd start at the warehouse in Elk Grove, load up my company van with various-sized TVs and VCRs, and deliver and install them all over Hell.

And it felt like Hell, too, because all they had in the delivery vans was AM Radio. I would literally suffer through a myriad of pop bullshit such as "Who Can It Be Now" by Men at Work, and the particularly nauseating "Abracadabra" by Steve Miller Band. I'd endure these and many others just to hear the only four decent songs they played: "Waiting For A Girl Like You" by Foreigner, "Up Where We Belong" by Joe Cocker and Jennifer Warnes, "Rosanna" by Toto, and "Hard To Say I'm Sorry" by Chicago, which should have been mine and Laura's new theme song. By this time, I had turned moving out into an art form and could pack all my stuff within 20 minutes, including pictures off the walls...

Everybody needs a little time away, I heard her say, from each other.
Even lovers need a holiday, far away from each other.

Hold me now. It's hard for me to say I'm sorry. I just want you to stay.

After all that we've been through, I will make it up to you. I promise to. And after all that's been said and done, you're just the part of me I can't let go.

Another interesting part of the job was having to go into some really rough neighborhoods. I felt good about bringing a family living in the projects a new TV and VCR. They were appreciative, and their joy was something to behold when I got their unit up and running.

One day my brother heard an address that I had delivered to and got up off his chair and asked me to repeat it. After I gave him the address, his eyeballs about popped out of his head.

"That's Robert Taylor Homes, the projects. You delivered a brand-new TV and VCR into the Robert Taylor Homes!?"

"Yep, I've been there a few times. I rode the elevator up to the fourth floor with a bunch of black people, got off, and went to the apartment and installed their shit."

"Man, you're either fearless or crazy. You do know that ambulances won't even go there without a police escort? They must either think you're The Man or you're stark raving crazy!"

By then, my heroin and cocaine use had reemerged and started to escalate again. Surprisingly, cocaine gradually started to overtake heroin as my drug of choice. If I didn't have money for both, I would get coke and just get by on some cheap pills like Tylenol #4 to keep from getting dope sick.

My life had become a ritual of driving around doing installs, listening to bad AM radio, and shooting cocaine. I'd pull over and do a hit in the back of the van, wait for the rush to subside, then get back in the driver's seat and proceed to my next stop.

I would begin to experience delusions and paranoia, which led to me constantly looking in my rearview mirror and thinking that I was being followed by law enforcement. It's a wonder I never got into a serious crash with all the time I spent looking in the rearview mirror instead of at the road.

One day my brother Paul came to me with concern regarding my job at Rent-A-Color. He was concerned that while driving around all day with my van full of TVs and VCRs, something bad could happen while I was… say… in McDonald's eating lunch. He was afraid that I could… maybe…forget to lock my door, in which case, someone could… steal the van and the merchandise inside. I informed him, it could be much more lucrative, umm…I mean, costly to the company on some days, more than others. This was because on some days, I had more expensive items in my van than other days. He encouraged me to call him on the next day like that, and he would come… "help me out."

That day finally came. My first stop was a store on the South Side to set up a display. I had a shitload of large-screen TVs and VCRs and most of the merch was brand new in the box, which wasn't always the case.

I called my brother, and we put our plan into motion. I went to a local hardware store and made a duplicate key. I met Paul in the parking lot. When I came out of the store, my van had "mysteriously" vanished! I went back into the store, surprised and panicked. They called the police. I called my boss and explained what happened. After I had filed a police report, Paul came back in his car and picked me up. He was driven back to his car by one of his buddies. I believe we made a thousand dollars, and of course, the drugs began to flow.

This was one of several times I came close to overdosing. I wondered what he would have said to our family if I had ever OD'd and died. We never thought or talked about it because, of course, that only happened to other people and would never happen to us.

The Steve & Laura merry-go-round

As my drug use continued to progress, so did my character defects. One of these was jealousy. As I became more insecure, I became more jealous. This led to constant mistrust of Laura and regular spying. Spying in those days, mind you, was true espionage, not merely checking someone's phone. I used to literally sit in my car down the street from where Laura was, to see who came and went, and if she would leave with anyone. It wasn't like my suspicions were totally unfounded. Some of it was because I knew deep down inside that she had her eye out for something better. We both did, but because we were "looking for love in all the wrong places," "better" never materialized.

The breakup syndrome really started to escalate after Rhoda sold the mobile home and again rented a house right next door to a gas station on the corner of Green Street and York Road in Bensenville. Laura, Jess, and I lived upstairs, while Rhoda, Freddy, and Mark lived on the ground floor. Leon wisely moved out and moved in with his lifelong friend's family.

Laura and I got into a big fight that started with a series of arguments over the week. The walls and floors were thin, so her family heard the whole thing. It culminated in a big screaming match that resulted in Laura throwing a few items at me from across the room, including a big, heavy, novelty Zippo lighter of mine. I ducked, but it nailed me in the back. I picked it up and threw it back at her. It knocked something made of glass onto the floor and shattered it. This apparently is what triggered the ensuing attack.

Out of nowhere, her brothers burst in and came at me, yelling, "Keep your hands off my sister!" Although our fights had led to me being physically abusive at times, ironically, this wasn't one of them. I remember thinking, *Keep my hands off your sister? She just nailed me in the back with a giant lighter!*

Freddy attacked first. I just grabbed him by the shirt and used his momentum to throw him across the room, but as I did, I exposed my left side, which Mark, coming at me in a second wave, promptly nailed with a baseball bat. I went down with the wind completely knocked out of me. Now down and out, Freddy returned, and they both picked me up under each arm and threw me out and down the stairs just like in the old Western movies. As usual, I had everything, including pictures off the wall, in my car inside 20 minutes.

I moved back home with my parents and immediately adopted REO Speedwagon's hit, "Time for Me to Fly," as my and Laura's official breakup song. Every word personified our relationship, at least from my perspective.

You said, "We'd work it out"
You said that you had no doubt
That deep down, we were really in love
Oh, but I'm tired of holding on
To a feeling, I know is gone
I do believe that I've had enough

I've had enough of the falseness
Of a worn-out relation
Enough of the jealousy
And the intoleration

Oh, I make you laugh and you make me cry
I believe it's time for me to fly

Time for me to fly
Oh, I've got to set myself free
Time for me to fly
That's just how it's got to be
I know it hurts to say goodbye
But it's time for me to fly

It's time for me to fly...

    The song would snap me into reality and give me some inspiration to get me through the next few hours or so without her. But getting through the day without Laura also meant getting through the day without Jessica. Jess was going on four years old and would ask Laura, "Where's Da Da?"

    "He went back to California to see his cows," Laura would tell her.
    "Can we go to California with Da Da?"
    "Not right now, Jess; maybe soon."

    Honestly, I'm not sure what Laura told Jess. I would like to think that she wouldn't want to hurt our kid. The fact was, we were both hurting the little girl we loved, but we didn't know what to do, or how to stop, and it was about to get even worse.

    The year was coming to a close, and winter was upon us again. It was another bad one, too. One night, I was sitting at home, watching TV, when the phone rang. It was Laura. She announced, "I'm pregnant."

    "Do you know who the father is?" I jabbed back.
    "Who do you think?"

"I don't know, could be anyone."

"Real funny; it's yours, asshole."

"So, what do you want to do?"

Her response caught me off guard. "Well, since we're not together, I was thinking I would have an abortion."

"Well, If that's your choice, that's up to you."

"I think you should pay half for it."

"You know I don't believe in it, and I said I'd never contribute to one ever again. You can do what you want, but I'm not contributing to an abortion."

She angrily hung up on me, which by now, was standard operating procedure. She had the abortion, and the winter got a little colder.

Now, collecting unemployment (again), I began a pattern of letting my dealers hold my Ibanez and other musical and stereo equipment as collateral for heroin and cocaine credit. It seemed that at this point my sense of desperation when I ran out was increasing, likely due to the void Laura and Jess's absence created in my life.

Also increasing by then was my paranoid delusions and hallucinations from injecting cocaine. I would literally stand for hours, peeking out of the basement windows, seeing men hiding behind parked cars and dumpsters in the alley, hearing them whisper, and at times, even hearing their walkie-talkies. I would be waiting for them to kick in the door and arrest me.

My mother would often wake up in the middle of the night and in a sleepy, raspy, concerned whisper, she'd say, "Steven, are you still up?"

Trying to sound as normal as possible, I'd reply, "Yeah, Ma."

"You need to get to bed so you can look for a job."

"Okay, Ma, I will. I'm working on a drawing," I'd say, trying to pacify her that I was at least doing something semi-constructive.

But it wasn't me she was talking to. I was losing my humanity. I was like the monkey in one of those science experiments. "Let's see the effects of cocaine on the monkey's brain and how the monkey deteriorates and dies."

The drugs would finally wear off, and I'd be exhausted from standing for hours. The first rays of the sun would finally reveal the shapes I thought were people to be mounds of grass, tires, and various other inanimate objects. I was slipping deeper into drug-induced insanity.

Desperado, why don't you come to your senses?

On New Year's Eve, 1982, Laura and I were still broken up. It was probably the longest we had ever been apart since our relationship began; besides the time I spent in Northern California. My parents had gone out to a party at her brother Bill's, where they would be playing cards until the wee hours and likely spend the night. Earlier that month, my mother agreed to take out a loan for me from the life insurance policy she had (wisely) taken out on me. She likely figured she might need money to bury me, though I doubt she admitted that to herself. She and my father certainly couldn't afford it. The loan was to buy a car so I could look for a job. The check for $500 had come a few days earlier and sat on the kitchen table, waiting for me to find a car.

Enter my brother Paul, who stopped by to see what I had going on because he had apparently already blown his wad that day. We looked for some stashed money (slim chance), and during our search, we found a bottle of champagne in the closet, so we drank it. Now drunk, the alcohol buzz didn't satisfy, and instead, only lit the fuse for cocaine craving. Paul convinced me to cash the check and buy some quality coke that he had recently stumbled upon. The plan was to step all over it, sell it, double the money, and shoot some coke for free. It made perfect sense to my drunk ass, so we did it.

We got the coke and headed back to the house. We stopped and got the mix to cut it with and put some off to the side to shoot. We started to cut the rest and package it up into half and quarter grams. All was well until we were done packaging and started shooting the good stuff. Then, a funny thing happened…we ran out. Once again, I would have the lesson reinforced that I could not sell drugs because I was my own best customer. We started dipping into the stepped-on coke until it was gone, too. We were left wide-eyed, sweating, grinding our jaws, and wanting more. Paul left and said he would try to score some dope and come back. He never did. I sat there depressed and with strong cravings for more coke as midnight approached.

I celebrated the New Year, peeking out the windows at inanimate objects brought to life by cocaine. As my paranoia subsided, the craving for more coke got stronger. I was thinking about how I could get some money, when, out of the corner of my eye, I saw my replica 45-caliber pistol on my dresser. It was actually a lighter. I thought to myself, *it's got a strong enough resemblance to a real handgun.* In the dark, no one would be able to tell. I surmised, *I'll walk around and see if an easy opportunity presents itself.*

I figured a lot of drunks would be heading to their cars, leaving parties soon. I bundled up, stuck the gun (lighter) in my coat, and walked out the door to rob somebody. I walked west on Chestnut Avenue and saw a few people leaving house parties but no easy marks. I continued to Mannheim Road and crossed into the King's Plaza Hotel parking lot. It was not well-lit. Perfect. I circled around the parking lot a few times like a vulture circling its prey.

I turned my head and there she was. An older, heavy-set woman in a big fur coat. She was obviously drunk and was having difficulty navigating the snow and ice and finding her car. I observed her staggering around, digging in her purse for her keys. As she stumbled into striking distance, it was time to make my move. I gripped the gun-lighter tightly as I stood there…and stood there…and stood there… and stood there, frozen. It was as if my feet were frozen to the ground, which could have actually happened in that weather, had I stood there much longer. I couldn't move. I couldn't do it. No matter how desperate cocaine had made me, it wasn't enough to overcome the part of me that couldn't take advantage of an innocent person. I turned and walked the frigid half mile back to the house. She never even knew I was there.

I was getting hit straight in the face with a screaming winter wind that felt like it was trying to send me a strong message... *You can't go on like this.* A message that I apparently still wasn't ready to hear.

I can't remember exactly how it happened this time, but Laura and I got back together that month. I'm sure our addiction to each other had us Jonesin' pretty good by then, and we both caved. I moved back in, and Rhoda gave us her "get it together" lecture, and all was forgiven between Mark, Freddy, and me. I still didn't have a car, so I looked for a job in the area, which was surrounded by factories.

Unfortunately, there were no factory jobs, and the few that existed were being applied for by one hundred people, over half of whom were overqualified. Though Reagan was in the White House, the effects of the Jimmy Carter era were still being felt in the economy. Carter and I shared a love of peace and for The Allman Brothers Band, but that was about it. Nice guy—shitty President!

Desperate for income, with unemployment money about to expire, I wound up settling for a job in a fast-food restaurant right around the corner, making hot dogs, pizza puffs, and beef sandwiches. For the first time in my life, "Would you like fries with that?" became my oft-repeated mantra.

My brother Paul had remarried another Irish girl named Carie. She was a bartender at what used to be the Music Box Lounge, my dad's after-work hangout. They soon had a son, Vince, who was almost three years old by the time the "walls started closing in" on them. A phone call from Paul's lifelong friend Jim Black would be right on time and rescue them from the approaching "iceberg" that Paul's drug use was heading them for.

Jim had recently fled the endless party life with his wife Roberta and their kids. Previous summers had been a non-stop party. I believe the phrase "sex, drugs, and Rock & Roll" may have originated at Jim and Roberta's house. But, as with all parties, eventually, the party's over, and then it's time to clean up the mess. Jim and his family did just that. Jim offered Paul a job and a chance to clean up his life and get a new start in Southern California. This was one of the truths of my brother Paul's legacy. All who knew him would do anything for him.

In March of 1983, Paul took him up on his offer, and he and his little family moved to the L.A. suburb of Whittier. Paul, who had been driving "the big rigs" and worked construction, took a job at Jim's company, Safeguard, as a printer. They were a big company that printed checks. Not a bad gig and making pretty good money. He stopped shooting drugs and did a 21-day Methadone detox upon his arrival in California.

It was then that Laura dropped bomb number two on me. She was pregnant. Abortion wasn't even a remote possibility, so I was hit with a shot of reality. As Rhoda would say, it was time to "stop fooling around, pull up your bootstraps, and get it together." Again, that was much easier said than done, and I was struggling. I dialed the phone, seeking advice from my big brother.

In our conversation, Paul pointed out: "Every time you try to get your shit together, you keep running into those same old people, in those same old places, doing those same old things. You need to come out here, Steven. We're doing really good. We'll let you stay with us until you get on your feet. Then you can bring Laura and Jess out here."

It didn't take a whole lot more convincing. I was 23 years old, had another kid on the way, and it was time to get my shit together. Convincing Laura wasn't difficult either. She was ready for an adventure and was all for it. Rhoda wasn't thrilled but was supportive of anything that would help us get our heads out of our asses and be successful.

Second attempt at a geographical cure

In June of 1983, I embarked on my second attempt at getting it together in California. It had almost worked the first time—right? Maybe this time, in Southern California, things would be different.

Like any true dope fiend preparing to quit drugs, I went on a little "last hurrah" binge before I left for California. This included ripping off $250 from my childhood friend Ricky, whom I had convinced to go in with me on "a pound of some really good pot." In reality, I didn't have a dime. I used the money on an eight-ball of cocaine.

Then, at a party, I ripped off my friend Donnie for five or six quarter-bags of cocaine; by telling him I had a buyer, and I would be "right back" with the money. I went to Matt's house, about four blocks away. But I couldn't shoot coke there, so I went into the backyard and shot most of it behind his garage.

I was paranoid and sneaking around, hiding in the bushes when I heard voices. It sounded like Donnie and a few friends. They were looking for me. I watched from the bushes as they went to Diego's house and rang the doorbell. Diego came to the door, and I could hear him adamantly denying that I was there. He offered to let them come in and look if they wanted to. They declined but told him what I had done and encouraged him to call them if I showed up.

The next day, my spree continued, and I ripped off Barry and Nora for eight bags of heroin, again promising I had a buyer and would be "right back" with the money. I knew I'd never see them again. I had my Greyhound ticket in my pocket, and I'd be on a bus about 2,000 miles away in a few days.

I rationalized that what I did would force me to pursue my new life and never come back. Barry and a few associates would also be looking for me. In fact, I had to duck and dodge all that night because they were already looking for me. I shot most of it before stepping onto the bus. I did my last bag in the bathroom on the bus and still had a full day until I'd arrive in L.A. I had to kick a heroin habit on that Greyhound the rest of the way.

Upon my arrival in L.A., I was pretty dope sick. I remember getting off the bus and being reacquainted with all the pastel colors, stucco, palm trees, lizards, and exotic plants. Even though I wasn't feeling good, I remember thinking, w*ow, this is so cool. I'm going to live here,* and it took some of the edge off being sick. Southern California was such a stark contrast from the ranch-style houses and factories I grew up around in the suburbs of Chicago.

My nose started running, my eyes started watering, and I started getting chills. My hands had that powder-dry feeling that made it difficult to rub my fingers together. I was "turning back into a pumpkin." I don't mean to wear out the Cinderella metaphor, but at the time, it was my way to describe going into opiate withdrawal. It was a good metaphor for what it's like being an addict. Like in the story of Cinderella, the inanimate objects magically get brought to life by "magic dust" but when the clock strikes midnight, the magic wears off, and they return to their inanimate state. And so it was with drugs. When they wore off, I would again turn into a useless lump of flesh. Despite this, I felt inspired by my "totally awesome" (California speak) surroundings and was motivated to get through withdrawal and get on with my new life.

I had some time to kill, so I was walking away from the bus station to have a look around before I would catch another bus and then be picked up by Paul. I crossed the street, and in that instant, everything changed. Once again, I'm reminded of the film *The Wizard of Oz*. You know how the film goes from black and white to color when Dorothy lands in Oz? Well, it was like that, only the opposite. As soon as I crossed the street, my "film" went from color to black and white. Suddenly, I found myself in the land of dingy, litter-filled, peeling, sun-rotted paint, complete with winos, homeless, prostitutes, and hustlers. "We're not in Kansas anymore, Toto."

One of the hustlers spotted me instantly. He wore a bandana, had a goatee and an earring. With a thick Mexican accent, he asked if I needed anything. "I got that good boy and girl" (heroin and cocaine, if you recall), he said, sounding a bit like a used car salesman.

Funny how one addict can spot another from a mile away. The inspiration to stay clean was immediately out the window and replaced with that familiar overpowering craving that would shut down any part of my brain that would try to resist. I wound up in an abandoned building with him, and I did what I told myself would be the last bags of dope in my life.

Despite a bullseye on my forehead, a target on my back, and the sign on my chest that said, "Gringo idiot that's far from home and has no idea where he's at," somehow, I didn't get ripped off or worse. Do you believe in guardian angels? Mine definitely needed a crash helmet, even if she was a girl, Alice?

My brother picked me up at the bus stop in his new Camaro. It was a sharp-looking car. All cars looked good in California. They were easy to take care of and didn't rust or get beat by the weather like in Chicago and the Midwest. Paul looked good with his dark tan and cool, mirrored sunglasses. He was doing well, and it showed. "You sick?" Paul asked as I got in the car.

"A little. Nice car. I need smokes."

"We'll stop at the store around the corner," Paul said.

He then proceeded to give me the "lay of the land" about L.A. He explained that people were flakes and completely laidback and (with an annoyed tone) that good service was unheard of here. It was obvious that everyone who was at work didn't want to be there and couldn't wait to get off and go to the beach and "hang ten" or whatever it is they hang in Southern Cali.

Paul explained that getting people to do their job was like pulling teeth. "Really?" I laughed as we pulled in front of a convenience store.

I went in to get a pack of smokes and immediately experienced what Paul described. No one came out from the back room for almost 10 minutes.

Finally, some guy comes out and apologizes. "I didn't hear you," and sells me a pack of Newport. I got in the car, exclaiming, "What the fuck. I could've robbed the place blind!" Paul shot back, "See, what'd I tell you?"

We arrived at my new, temporary digs with Paul, Carie, and nephew Vince. I slept (though not very much for a few days) on their couch. I needed to be kept secret because, according to Paul, the property manager, Karen, was a "fucking bitch" and they would charge more rent for an extra person. Paul referred to her as the "Nazi property manager from Hell," always trying to bust tenants out who had people staying with them against the rules.

Paul and I both abandoned the needle and tapered our drug use back to our old standbys, marijuana and alcohol, which, combined with my excitement for a new life in a new and different place, helped me get through any lingering withdrawal symptoms. I was able to start sleeping a bit and started looking for a job when I wasn't being a built-in babysitter for Vince.

Paul helped me learn the bus routes and what areas had a lot of factory jobs. It only took a few days of riding the bus and filling out applications to find a warehouse job in Santa Fe Springs. I think the name of the city was Native American for "land of the stinky, yellow smog."

My eyes and nose would burn on the bus ride to and from work. I didn't care. The goal was to save money until I could bring Laura and Jess out there and get an apartment. I had come to L.A. to, once again, escape my addiction, and it was working. I stopped shooting dope and was saving money. After the morning clouds would burn off, the sunshine was bright every day in L.A. and so was my future.

As a result of hanging out at the pool, I befriended a young couple who lived across the way in the apartment complex. Maury and Jane were a typical young California couple with no kids. Maury was handsome with sandy brown hair, and Jane was a redhead with milky white skin (which burned frequently) and freckles. They were Buddhists and it was my first exposure to spiritual rituals that went beyond the "sit-stand-kneel" of the Catholic church. Jane tried to teach me how to chant (Nam-myoho-renge-kyo…) but I couldn't quiet my mind and sit still for more than 20 seconds, so we mostly just hung at the pool, drank beer, and smoked a lot of quality California bud.

I wanted to get Laura to L.A. before she had the baby, because if she had it in Chicago, it would be more difficult to make that transition with a newborn. Maury and Jane saw that I was getting impatient, so they invited me to live with them and offered to let Laura and Jess move in until we could get an apartment. They were good people who genuinely wanted to help us.

Laura and Jess finally arrived. It was a bit cramped, especially with a four-year-old running around. We stayed with them until we all got on Jane's last Buddhist nerve (Nam-myoho-renge-kyo, Nam-myoho-renge-kyo!), and just in time, we secured our first apartment in the complex adjacent to my brother's. The rent was four hundred and something a month, plus security deposit. It was a one-bedroom, and though the complex wasn't as big or nice as my brother's, like most apartment complexes in L.A., it had an outdoor pool.

Things were going pretty well, better than they had gone in a long time. We were paying our bills, keeping a roof over our heads, and food in the refrigerator. Laura got a doctor and kept all her prenatal appointments. Jess was already becoming quite a swimmer. I was going to work every day but, of course, we were cheating a little. Laura was still collecting public aid, and I may have collected a check or two from unemployment while I was working.

California was the land of plenty, not only for benefits but everything else too. On my way to the bus to work, I used to pass an apricot tree and put some fruit in a paper bag as part of my lunch.

My only problem in those days was at work. I worked at Bonanza Nut & Bolt. We shipped every size and type of nut and bolt you could imagine. Pulling, packaging, and shipping large amounts of huge nuts and bolts for a high-rise construction site was a bitch. Anyone who worked there for any length of time had back problems. That was some heavy shit that came in and out of that place. But the work wasn't my problem. My problem was being surrounded by California natives, that is, except for Ted.

Ted was originally from the Midwest, but you would never have known it unless he told you. He had lived in Cali for the past 13 years and completely "converted," including Hawaiian shirts and sandals. He sounded like a Cali native, too, frequently using words like "dude," "bitchin'," and "gnarly." Ted was the only friend I came away with from work. Despite his Californian disposition, we had that Midwestern bond. The rest of the guys all poked fun at me due to my Midwestern accent, which I was not aware I had. They called me "Chicaaago" and would say, "Hand me a baax, (box), will ya?" They made it sound as if I were from the Bronx, for Christ's sake.

Later, I came to understand that it was more than the accent. They hated and resented transplants that came from all over the country to "suck the golden nectar dry from the tree of California" and then flee when they got homesick, or after pillaging and plundering what they could. So, it wasn't just Mexicans who would use the system and resources, then go back to Mexico. In fact, most of the Mexicans who were there, had assimilated and were more respected, accepted, bona fide, and part of the California culture, than people like me were.

One of my co-workers that gave me the hardest time, was Blacky, a member of a small, insignificant biker club, the emblem of which he wore proudly on the back of his leather vest. He came complete with long blonde hair to the middle of his back, American flag bandana, heavy biker boots, and a chained wallet. He had the most seniority and was their best worker, so he could do no wrong.

One of the few good things about working there was the lunch truck ("roach coach"). But this was completely unlike the "roach coach" I had come to know in the Chicago area. The food was good, authentic Mexican and they cooked it right in front of you. I knew the difference, thanks to my high school friend Juan Garcia's mom. The real Mexican food she cooked for us was so much better than the Americanized Mexican food from fast food chains. No one was falling for the Taco Bell scam out there.

All it takes is a spark to start a fire

We started connecting with some of our neighbors: Laura, with a young single mom named Paige, whose two kids were slightly older than Jess, and me, with a fellow guitarist—Ken—who lived down the hall.

Ken had some amateur recording equipment set up in his bachelor pad and I would come home from work, grab my guitar, and head to Kenny's. We'd smoke a joint, have a few beers, and jam. We recorded a handful of cover songs, complete with cheesy drum-machine tracks.

Soon, I started buying my weed from a 17-year-old kid in the complex named Ricky. All was well in La La Land, until one Sunday when the kid happened to mention that his mother was on Tylenol #4 with codeine due to an ankle injury. It was like a switch got flipped in my brain. I remember that there was a short debate in my head, and part of my brain said, *do you really want to do this?* But that debate ended quickly, and the words flew impulsively out of my mouth without a second thought: "Can you get me a few? I'll buy them."

It was like a rerun of Northern California, only this time, I wasn't stealing them from a medicine cabinet. I convinced myself that I would just do a few on occasion and that would be it.

The next thing I knew, I'm popping a few pills here and there and then a few more. Then, out of the blue, my brain whispers the magic word that was buried in the recesses of my subconscious: *Tussionex.*

I thought to myself, *I wonder what the syrup scene is like here in Southern Cali.* And then: *With all the smog here, my bronchitis excuse is almost legit.* So that week, I looked in the phone book for a doctor in the area and I made an appointment for after work, telling Laura I had to work overtime.

Is there a doctor in the house?

The doctor finally came into the room. He'd been in practice for quite some time and looked to be in his 60s. My old routine (fake cough) kicked in and worked like a charm. When doc tried to write me a script for Robitussin, I informed him that it was ineffective and explained that only one syrup had ever really worked well for me—Tussionex. To my surprise, he'd never even heard of it and had to look it up in his PDR. He did so and wrote me a script for six ounces with a refill (Score!). He immediately became my new "primary care physician." It occurred to me then and there that California may just be "Virgin Tussionex Territory" because no one seemed to be hip to it. I had that "kid in a candy store" feeling come over me, but I knew I had to keep it cool. I loved our new life in Cali, and I didn't want to blow all the progress I'd made.

So, I embarked on a period of controlled abuse of Tussionex. At first, I would wait 30 days before going back to the doctor. I was trying really hard to avoid getting a habit, which I did for a while. But it was just too tempting to take advantage of the doctors and pharmacists of Southern California. I started losing control and doctor shopping. I quickly found a few more suckers. I would rotate doctors and pharmacies on a schedule. They were all clueless.

I started to get a habit again and felt sick when I'd run out. I'd usually have to wait at least a few days until I could crack another script, so I would be in withdrawal by that time.

I remember an incident that happened during one of these withdrawal periods. I was dope sick and left work early, around noon. At the bus stop, there was a young man who appeared to be physically, mentally, and developmentally disabled. I noticed that he had a prescription bag in his hand.

"Hey, got any good drugs in the bag?"

"Yep, I do," he said, not really understanding what I meant.

"What kind?"

He opened the bag and showed me several bottles of prescription meds. He explained to me what each was for to the best of his ability, which, as it turned out, wasn't great. The Haldol seemed to have the most potential as some kind of tranquilizer. I asked if I could have a few, and I'd give him a few bucks. He agreed. As I popped one in my mouth, his bus came, and I was left waiting for mine. Within a few minutes or so, I started feeling strange. I started having what I can only describe as intense muscle spasms, especially in my lower back. This led to my back being severely contorted (uncontrollably being bent backward), making it extremely difficult to walk. I knew I needed to get help, but I was in an industrial area surrounded by factories and office parks. As I walked down the sidewalk seeking help, I inadvertently got a harsh lesson on what it felt like to be physically disabled. This included a carload of teenagers that took the time to slow down and heckle me: "Hey retard, get the pole out of your ass. BWAHAHAHAHAHA!" as they sped off.

I was getting worse by the minute. Each step became a major endeavor, so I made a beeline for the next building I saw. Upon entering, I noticed several people standing in the reception area. They looked at me like I had the plague.

"Can I help you, sir?"

"Please call an ambulance."

"What seems to be the problem, sir?"

Not wanting to tell them the truth about the cause, I said: "I don't know. I can't straighten my back up!"

Judging by the way they were looking at me, I think they thought I was scamming them. "Well, we can't call you an ambulance but you're welcome to use the payphone and call one," pointing to two of them on the wall to my right.

"I don't have any change. Can I borrow a dime?"

A woman came out and handed me a dime. I could barely reach the slot or dial 911, but somehow, I managed to. Within minutes, the ambulance arrived and laid me on a gurney. I had to be honest about the cause of my condition, so I told them that I had accidentally taken a medication called Haldol, thinking it would "help my headache." They shot me up with a shitload of Benadryl and muscle relaxers, then transported me to the hospital.

I could feel my muscles starting to relax as I drifted off to sleep. When I came to, Laura and the doctor were standing over me. I asked the doctor out of curiosity why I had the reaction that I did. He explained that the medication is an antipsychotic that usually is best taken with another drug called Prolixin, which would have counteracted the side effects I experienced. Laura looked at me with a "That's what you get for being so stupid" look on her face. I took the rest of the day to recover fully.

Shortly after this incident, my problem of having gaps between prescriptions was solved as I stumbled upon the "magic Xerox machine" in the corner of one of the drugstores that filled my scripts. The copies it made were so good you couldn't tell that they were copies. I would make five or six copies of legitimate prescriptions and fill them at a variety of pharmacies in the area.

By this time, Paul had started some controlled indulging too. Even Franko came down from Santa Rosa to visit and took full advantage of the situation. In no time, we were all running around cracking Tussionex scripts throughout the area. My habit was up to three to four ounces a day at one point. As a result, I started pushing for eight ounces from my doctors. I could barely manage my escalating habit.

I always said that three guys from Chicago singlehandedly awakened the entire L.A. medical community to the abuse of Tussionex. They started getting hip to our game, and things started drying up a bit. Pharmacists would look at our scripts, and with a cold look on their faces, they'd say, "We don't have this in stock; try back in a few days," knowing we wouldn't.

Just when things were starting to look bleak, I met another guitarist named Allen in another building in our complex. It turned out that he had "chronic back issues" and had a doctor who prescribed him Dilaudid. Strangely, Allen's father had "chronic back issues" too and got these and other drugs from the same doctor, who, as it turned out, was crooked as the day was long. This guy made Dr. Kuch look almost legit. There were a ton of prescription narcotics flying off this guy's prescription pad. I asked if I could make an appointment with him, but Allen's dad wouldn't let anyone near his "golden goose."

Allen was a nice guy and the first addict I ever knew who was into the Bible. He and his daddy were from the South and still had their accents, albeit somewhat watered down from years in L.A. We both had a lot to lose from our drug use. Allen and his wife Lucy were separated because of it, and I could feel my new life beginning to hang in the balance and inching closer to the edge of a cliff.

Allen used to mope around, pining for her. "I miss my Lucy." "Lucy, Lucy, Lucy." He would talk about her endlessly. It got a bit pathetic. We were both getting sick and tired of the merry-go-round we were on and decided that "with Jesus's help," we were going to quit "cold turkey." Allen grew up in the Baptist church as part of his Southern roots. So, one day at his apartment, in desperation, Allen read a few passages from his Bible, and we kneeled on the floor with our heads bowed and our hands touching the book. We prayed to Jesus for the strength to stop using drugs. We proceeded to go through the next 48 hours sweating, in pain, and barely able to move, except to get to the toilet with dry heaves and diarrhea. For me, at the time, I found the comradery of going through withdrawal with a partner more helpful than Jesus. I had no particular spiritual beliefs at the time and Jesus was "just alright with me."

I went home to complete the withdrawal, and I remember being so sick that I couldn't move from the couch, even though I knew that a hot shower would afford some relief, however temporary. This was a cycle that I would find myself in again and again. I became a pro at detoxing myself, usually using a combination of Benzos and low-grade opiates.

My return to the needle and spoon occurred when Paul connected with a Mexican guy whom he met at work named Ray. We started going with him to cop dope in a seedy area of L.A. The dope we were getting was appropriately called "black tar" heroin. This was not powder but as the name suggests, it was a ball of gooey black tar. This stuff was so potent, we would literally nod out while cleaning the fit. You'd freeze in mid-nod right after shooting it. Your head would slowly sink into your chest and then toward the ground. Sometimes, the only thing that would snap you out of a nod from this stuff was falling off your chair or burning a hole in your pants with a cigarette. I can't tell you how many dope fiends I've seen come out of a nod, leaping off their chairs while flailing away at their smoldering pant legs.

We found ourselves on the merry-go-round once again with one exception—we refused to do coke. We felt as long as we didn't do cocaine, we could manage. At least our whole paycheck wouldn't be gone in a day.

Nevertheless, it still got me fired from my job at Bonanza. I started calling in sick or coming into work dope sick, and my performance suffered mightily. The job was already difficult and required physical strength and energy to work daily. Due to constantly being in and out of withdrawal, my strength and energy was dwindling.

S & L Quality Painting Services

My next gig came from answering an ad in the newspaper looking for a housepainter. I had done some house painting years earlier for a company called Campus Corps. They were known for hiring college students and young people and teaching them the business. It's where I met my friend Al, with whom I had the first Grateful Dead debacle.

I apparently interviewed well with the son (his name was also Al) of the father and son business—Griste Painting Services. I got the job.

His father was in his 60s and a housepainter all his life. He would tell house painting stories and make them sound like the coolest adventures ever—like how they would brush away the snow and paint exteriors throughout the cold Philadelphia winters. Nothing stopped them. He could mix paint and create any custom color a customer wanted. He and his son worked so fast that it was mind-blowing. I was a good painter, but I could never keep up with them. To watch them fly down the side of a house was mesmerizing. I learned a lot working with them, and it would come in handy.

My last day on the job was a good example of how impulsive I could be when I was dope sick. It was around noon, the sun was blazing, and I just couldn't make it another four hours. I couldn't stop my mind from imagining what it would be like to be free from the pain of being dope sick and working in the hot sun. I needed to find some dope and feel that relief. Like a zombie, I just walked up to the truck, and without a word, I left my brush, scraper, and putty knife—and walked away. This wasn't the first time I'd done this, but this time, I had a new baby on the way. I called Al's dad and had him mail me my last check. Just like that, I had my sixth stint back on unemployment.

Rhoda and brothers Freddy and Leon came out to stay with us to help out with the new baby coming. They got an apartment nearby. Leon and Freddy stayed for a while, but then Leon headed back to Chicago, while Fred headed back to his land in New Mexico. They drove out in a van that they bought. They wanted to sell it and fly back home. One day, near the end of my employment with Griste Painting, I remember thinking, *why am I doing this for someone else for $7 an hour when I could be doing it for myself?*

Laura was pissed that I quit my job, but I had been talking about starting my own house painting business, so we bought the van. Now, there was nothing stopping me. I came up with the company name: S & L (Steve & Laura) Quality Painting Services. I went to a local printer and had cards printed. Then, I went to a local home remodeling supply store and opened a business account.

The timing was perfect because I also had a helper who just sort of popped into our lives. A friend of Paul's had just come out from the old "hood" under similar circumstances as Paul and me. He was looking for a better life and trying to leave his addiction behind. Todd was a few years older than me and a few years younger than Paul. He wound up staying with Paul and Carie. He needed a job, and now, I needed help. With my last $80, I bought all the basic supplies and materials I needed to get started.

The next day, I drove around looking for houses that needed painting. The sun is brutal on houses in Southern California, so there were plenty. I had an idea about how to estimate and bid on jobs from observing Al's father, even though they did their best to hide what they were making. I started knocking on doors, writing up free estimates, for potential customers.

I'll never forget that first phone call and getting my first job. It was a widow who, at first, told me that due to recently losing her husband, she couldn't afford it. She knew the house needed it badly. I gave her a really good price, which included replacing her rusty, leaky gutters. She couldn't pass it up.

Getting my first job gave me that temporary surge of confidence, which would temporarily afford me some level of control over my use. Funny how that works. Experiencing a surge of natural pleasure would equate to temporary control over my drug use, but I could never sustain it.

The business started going pretty well. It could have been even better, but I didn't have enough help to handle multiple jobsites. I even enlisted the help of my young pot dealer, Ricky, on a few jobs.

We were all working on a job together, and I was standing on the top step of an eight-foot stepladder, when, out of nowhere, I lost my balance and found myself on the ground. Luckily, I wasn't injured, except for a few scrapes, but I didn't understand how I fell. I spent a lot of time on ladders and never lost my balance or fell. It bugged me all day. Later that day I found out why I fell when I got home and watched the news. They reported that a mild earthquake had hit the area at the exact time I fell off the ladder. I jumped up and told Laura, "That's why I fell!" It all made sense. I experienced my first earthquake!

One of our customer's dogs had a litter of purebred German Shepherd pups. Todd loved the breed, and once he showed interest, the guy didn't hesitate to offer him one of the remaining pups, complete with papers. The trouble was Todd had nowhere to bring the dog to, so the guy offered to keep him until Todd got settled and had his own place. Todd named him Brutus. He'd regularly visit the dog, take him for walks, and bring him over to our apartment.

Todd had done some roofing, so we were able to get a few roofing jobs, too. Talk about some hard work. If you've never humped shingles up a ladder and replaced a roof in the hot California sun, you haven't really worked!

One unseasonably hot day, we knocked off early. I came home and Laura was sitting at the kitchen table. Her eyes got really big, and she looked at me with an "oh shit" kind of look on her face. Just then, to my surprise, my brother came out of the bathroom. I looked at his face and saw it immediately. He was grinding his jaw back and forth and he looked "geeked."

"Okay, thanks for letting me use the john, Laura. I just stopped by to use the john. I really had to go. I'll talk to you later," he explained on his way out the door. I wanted to say something, but I couldn't. I just wasn't assertive enough to stand up for myself, especially when it came to my big brother.

I looked at Laura with anger on my face. "What the fuck are you letting him in here with that shit for?"

"I didn't know. He came to the door and asked me to use the bathroom. What was I supposed to say—no?"

"I don't want that shit in my house!" I yelled.

Apparently, Paul had met a coke dealer who lived in his complex. Louie was a nice guy, around my age, who worked a day job, but supplemented his income selling coke. Paul introduced me to him and soon, I started buying coke and snorting it with Laura. It was sort of becoming her drug of choice since PCP was scarce in the area. Amazingly, I was somehow able to maintain my recently acquired healthy fear of shooting it, at least for now.

"The best laid plans of mice and men"

Paul, on the other hand, found himself back on the full-tilt merry-go-round once again. It didn't take him long to crash and burn once cocaine was reintroduced into the picture. He started kiting checks from Carie's account, and then he put the final nail in the coffin by stealing and cashing some of the payroll checks that he printed at work.

For Paul, it was, once again, "time to get the hell outta Dodge!" I remember Paul being afraid that they would repossess their car because he hadn't made a payment on it in months. I have a vague memory of him catching a repo man in the act and threatening him with the infamous axe-hammer.

So, he (more or less) stole the car, and they drove back to Chicago. It was early November 1983 and my brother Paul, the person who invited me to come out and start a new life just months earlier, was leaving with his pregnant wife and son Vince. Just like that, they were gone. I'm sure Paul's lifelong friend, Jim Black, wanted to kill him. Burning bridges is "par for the course" for addicts. Jim and Paul never spoke to each other again, that I'm aware of. Paul left more disappointed people who cared about him in his wake. Todd moved in with us and slept on our couch.

About a week later, on November 9th, 1983, my second daughter was born. We appropriately named her Melissa after the Allman Brothers ballad. Technically, she isn't exactly named after the song, though, because we spelled it wrong on her birth certificate (all I had to do was look at the album cover...duh!). That's what smoking that good bud can do. So, legally, her name is Mellisa (Mel-Lisa). These days, it's kind of cool to find a new way to spell a common name, but in our case, it was just a mistake.

I made it to the delivery room, and I watched her being born. At one point, she shot out like a football, and the doctor almost "fumbled" and dropped her. No matter, she was beautiful and took after me. I saw her dark brown hair, long eyelashes, and brown eyes immediately. She was very alert too and looked me dead in the eyes as I held her in the delivery room. I always used to say that Melissa came out asking, "What's for dinner?" and "Can I borrow the car?"

Rhoda was rooting for us. She knew I loved Laura and the kids, and I would be a good husband and father if I could keep it together. She stayed until she thought Laura and I could handle things, then she headed back to Illinois. The support was gone, and we were on our own, 2,000 miles from home.

My drug use became a combination of Tussionex (though less available), Dilaudid, Percocet, and other painkillers from Allen and his father. Allen made an effort but soon relapsed, too. I was snorting cocaine and using my staples pot, and alcohol along with occasionally PCP (Laura finally found a connect) and "crank" (speed). In L.A., almost everyone did Crank.

Allen and I would go to his dad's house in Downey after his father would get his scripts filled, and cop pills. I soon learned that Dad had another little vice he engaged in, too—freebasing cocaine. I had never freebased before, so of course, I tried it. I remember it almost feeling like shooting it, but not quite. That's when I decided, *well, I'm already shooting Dilaudid, so I might as well shoot the coke instead of wasting it like this.*

It's amazing how thoughts like these would slip into my mind unchallenged, and soon, I'd be doing whatever my thoughts told me to do. So, my descent back into drug-induced insanity commenced. Cocaine had that unique characteristic of making you want to do more, and the more you did, the more you wanted. For me, the more I did, the more paranoid I became. And as it turned out, now I had some legitimate reasons to be paranoid.

Allen's father had learned that his MD connect was under investigation, which is how he discovered that his phone was tapped. I thought he was nuts at first, but once he pointed out a few strange things about the phone, it was apparent to me that there really was something unusual going on. Allen had a strict list of things he was not allowed to say over the phone when he called his dad. There were a lot of code words being used. For instance, the code word for Dilaudid pills was...hang on to your hat... "D's." I'm sure the feds were completely baffled by this.

"Balloons" for Jessica's birthday

One Sunday afternoon, I was getting something out of my van when I met a young Mexican guy named Jaime in the parking lot. I don't remember how we got on the subject, but it turned out he could get balloons of heroin right down the street. Using balloons to package heroin was very common, and still is, due to them protecting the dope with a watertight seal. I can't imagine how we got on the subject, though. How do you say to someone who's a total stranger, "Hey, can you get me some heroin?"

In short order, I was shooting heroin again and regularly. Things quickly got out of hand. Avoiding withdrawal soon became a full-time endeavor again, so I needed to slow down. I remember imposing one of my self-administered detoxes. Several days into it, I started to feel better, but still not great. Right on time too, because it was Jessica's fifth birthday, and we had promised to take her to Disneyland.

The morning of our adventure, as we were getting ready to go, I got hit with an untimely wave of sweats, chills, and low energy. I thought, *I gotta get something. I can't take my kid to Disneyland feeling like this.* So, I held up the trip and badgered Laura until she gave in and gave me some of the money, which was supposed to be for the outing, to get some dope. I went to Jaime's house and copped three balloons. I had to give him a line or two to snort. I shot the rest, and all was right with the world again.

We arrived at Disneyland somewhat later than we planned, but at least we made it. I took Jess on a ride called Magic Mountain, and upon disembarking—due to a combo of the dope, the food, and the ride—I promptly went to the bathroom and puked (or "hurled" if you prefer Cali speak). When I opened the bathroom door, still a little green around the gills, there was Jess with a big smile on her face. "C'mon, dad; let's go again!" I almost hurled right there at the thought of it.

"I think I should let Mom have a turn."

I was always walking the fine line between two completely different worlds of being a parent and being a junkie. It was quite a balancing act, but like a bad juggler, I was only able to keep the balls in the air for so long until they started hitting the floor.

The house of cards begins to collapse

My reunion with the needle, which led me back to shooting cocaine, made things start to unravel pretty quickly. I was copping coke from Louie in the complex where Paul and Carie once lived. I'd jump the six-foot-high wall that separated the complexes, then return to the safety of our bathroom.

Soon, I started noticing the same strange sounds and characteristics on our phone that I heard on Allen's dad's phone. We noticed it on Allen's phone too. This greatly increased my paranoia. Of course, Laura thought I was nuts, that is, until the feds indicted the good doctor and arrested Allen's dad. For my friend Allen, the clock struck time to "get the hell outta Dodge," and in the blink of an eye, he left town. Now, I was sure that they were watching me.

As my use and paranoia started spiraling out of control, I started to tear apart my "shooting gallery" (our bathroom) a little at a time. There was a piece of linoleum baseboard that had come away from the wall and I was sure there were microphones or cameras that were planted there. What started as a small piece of baseboard coming away from the wall became a huge hole in the wall, and most of the trim was removed. Things got so bad that when Laura knew I had copped coke, she would stop me from going in it until she and anyone who was there used it. This was because once I entered the bathroom, there was a good chance I wouldn't come out for hours. Laura was becoming more and more annoyed with me for tearing up the bathroom, but I would appease her by promising to remodel it, which, of course, never happened.

In a state of paranoid delusion, I would have my ear pressed against the door and could hear the detectives' voices on the other side of it.

"Ma'am, we're here for your boyfriend, not you. Just cooperate and tell us where he is, and we won't bother you or your kids." I waited for them to break down the door. In reality, there was no one there, let alone anyone saying anything of the sort.

What made matters worse was that around this time, Tony, the "Mafia wannabe" coke dealer, who was introduced to us by Jaime, started coming around. It was supposedly common knowledge, but never clear to me what, if any, mob connections he had.

Tony was an older, reasonably handsome but overweight Italian guy, who, of course, like most Italians, tried to play that "goombah" shit with me right away. It's a kind of presumption that "Hey, I'm Italian; you're Italian, so that makes us cool in our Italianess—right?" This is what Italian men do when they're either trying to express a feeling of comradery with another man or con him. In my circles, the latter was usually the case. I played along because the coke was good, and there were always a few freebies when Tony came over. This helped to distract me from the slightly creepy vibe that I got from him.

At that time, my main coke supplier was still Louie. I would call and arrange to meet him somewhere in the inner court of his complex. During these exchanges, we would sit and talk for a few minutes. Then, I'd make my buy and be on my way. In our talks, he would divulge a lot of personal information. This is how I knew that he wasn't a real drug dealer. He had no "dope dealer etiquette." You never disclose too much personal information to dope fiends.

In one conversation, he confided in me that he, too, couldn't stand the property manager, Karen, and avoided her like the plague. This was because his brother had been staying with him for a while, which she suspected, and she was always trying to catch him so she could charge him the extra rent. A seemingly harmless bit of information to the average person—right? But unfortunately for Louie, not to the diabolical, ever-scheming, desperate dope fiend mind. What happened because of that little "harmless" bit of information, only a select few people know about?

The elaborate schemes of a desperate dope fiend

After getting paid for a job we completed, Todd and I went on a coke binge that entire weekend. I don't remember where Laura was, but she had taken the kids and left to get some relief from the insanity that I'm sure constantly enveloped our apartment by then. We ran out of coke in the early hours of a Monday morning and sat at the kitchen table—sweaty, stinking, depressed, craving, and in the beginning of opiate withdrawal.

"How could we get more coke?" I thought out loud.

"We need to get some money," Todd replied.

"Yeah, but even if we did, Tony's not around and Louie's at work all day, and I don't want to take the chance of getting ripped off by some stranger."

"Think, Think!" I said, desperation breaking through in my voice.

Driven by strong cocaine cravings, we both sat there staring intently at the kitchen table; both of our dope fiend thinking caps were on tight and at their highest capacity.

Then, the light bulb went off over my head. "Maybe we don't need money."

"What do you mean?" Todd replied with a confused look on his face.

"Louie's at work all day—right?"

"Yeah."

"If we could get into his apartment, we could get at his stash. I'm sure he's got at least an ounce or two in there."

"How can we get into his apartment in broad daylight?" Todd asked dismissively.

"I don't know; let's think."

My mind went immediately to the obvious, and I pictured crawling in a window, but I quickly realized that wasn't likely. Even a pseudo-dealer like Louie wasn't stupid enough to leave his windows unlocked. Then, light bulb number two went off. I got a snapshot in my head of a scene from my days swimming at the pool when my brother lived there. It was fat-assed Karen walking down the sidewalk with her Cass Elliot-sized Mumu skirt and a giant ring of keys in her hand. My next thought was, *how do I get those keys?*

Then, it all rolled out before me, like a movie script in my mind. Todd smiled as if he could see the wheels turning in my head. "What are you thinking?"

"What if we got Karen, the property manager, to let us in?"

"How?" Todd asked, not as if he thought I had the answer, but just to encourage me and keep me thinking.

"I don't know."

I got out of my chair and started pacing back and forth. I remembered the seemingly meaningless information that Louie shared about purposely avoiding Karen so that he could avoid the conversation about the back due rent she felt he owed. Then, light bulb number three!

"I got it! What if I called her as Louie and told her my cousin was coming in from Chicago and asked her to let him in because I'm stuck at work all day?"

The wheels were cranking faster now! The strong desire for cocaine was searching every crevasse of my mind for every possibility. It reminds me of playing chess against the excellent players at Matt's house, scrutinizing and analyzing every possible move.

"I know he hasn't had enough contact with her for her to be that familiar with his voice."

Then I told Todd how and why Louie currently avoids her. It was perfect. Louie worked in a factory, so we even created some industrial background noises for effect, using a hammer and some metal objects. I looked in the phonebook, picked up the phone, and dialed the number. She answered, "Hello, (Can't recall the name) apartments. This is Karen. How can I help you?"

I went into acting mode and did my best Louie voice: "Hi, Karen. This is Louie in apartment 218."

"Hi, Louie. What can I do for you?"

"My cousin Steve is coming in from Chicago in the next hour or two, and I'm stuck at work today. I was wondering, when he arrives, if you could let him in."

"Sure, no problem."

Everything was going perfectly until she threw a curveball at me.

"Just one thing, though. I'll need to call you back at work, if you don't mind, just to verify it's you and everything. You understand."

I didn't flinch, stayed in character, and cracked a base hit into center field. "Oh, sure. I understand. Here's the number." Then, I rolled the dice, turned on the jets, and went for second base. I gave her the phone number to our apartment. Remember, this is 1984; there's no caller ID or easy way to verify a phone number for a business.

"Just ask for Louie Martinez in service," I instructed her.

"Okay, will do. Bye-bye" before hanging up.

Todd was listening on the extension in the bedroom. He burst into uncontrollable laughter, followed by a high-five. But our celebration was short-lived as we quickly got back into character to continue the ruse. As the phone started ringing, we made up a fictitious company name and did a quick, impromptu review of the script for part two.

Todd answered, "Timberland Manufacturing. Can I help you?" I grabbed the hammer and continued the rhythmic pounding on the metal piece, mimicking some type of industrial machinery.

"Can I speak to Louie Martinez in service?"

"Sure, let me transfer you." At the precise moment that Todd tapped the receiver, I stopped the pounding and picked up the bedroom extension. "Service. This is Mike. Can I help you?"

"Yes, can I speak to Louie Martinez?"

"One moment," I said, putting the phone down and taking a few steps away. "LOUIE!!" Then, running even further away from the phone in my Louie voice: "YEAH!"

"TELEPHONE!!" Four or five seconds later: "Hello, this is Louie."

"It's Karen. Okay then. Just have him come to the office when he gets here, and I'll let him in."

"Okay, thanks, Karen. I really appreciate it."

"No problem. Maybe you can give me a call later. We still need to talk about that other issue. Bye-bye." Click.

We both broke into giddy laughter and jumped around like little kids on the playground and high-fived again! We immediately got serious, remembering that we were only in the "top of the fifth" and there was still a lot of "ball to be played" for us to "win the game." I got back into character, and we started plotting the next few moves out loud.

"Okay, it's October, and I'm coming from Chicago on a Greyhound, so I should have a jacket on."

I threw dirty clothes into a suitcase and a duffle bag. I got dressed, grabbed my jacket out of the closet, and put it on, then my sunglasses. We just sat at the kitchen table and stared at the clock. We discussed all the details that we could think of. After about 25 minutes or so passed, it was time to go.

"Okay, here goes. Wish me luck."

I came in through the main entrance with my pleather jacket and sunglasses on, suitcase in hand, and duffle bag slung over my shoulder. I looked like I just got off a Greyhound. I stopped outside the door, took a deep breath, wiped away some of the sweat from my forehead, and walked into the rental office, where I was blasted by air-conditioning. Karen was at her desk; the giant key ring hung on a hook on the wall behind her.

"I'm here to see Karen," I said, pretending that I didn't know it was her. "Hi, you must be Steve, Louie's cousin."

"Yes, and you must be Karen. Nice to meet you." I reached out and shook her hand.

We traded a little more small talk, and then she committed another HUGE ERROR! "Well, I'll bet a nice hot shower would feel great about now. HERE'S THE KEY," she said (taking it off the giant ring). He's in 218. Follow the path out of the office to the left and it's the third set of stairs on your left, on the second floor. Bring the key right back after you let yourself in."

"Thanks, Karen. That shower sounds great about now."

As I walked toward Louie's apartment, my eyes got really big as I could hardly contain my excitement about the possibilities that now were laid into my hands. I couldn't believe I was pulling this off!

Then, I made a daring move and "went for third." As soon as I set foot inside Louie's door, it occurred to me that the hardware store was less than a block away. I dropped my bags, stepped outside, went to the end of the hall, descended the back stairs, and jumped the wall. As soon as I hit the ground, I flew full speed and made a beeline for the hardware store! Luckily, there was hardly anyone in there, and it only took about two minutes to make a duplicate key. I raced back as the alarm clock in my head was just going off, warning me that time was about to expire, and she would start wondering what was taking so long. I caught my breath and composed myself before entering the office and giving her the key back. I "stole third, sliding in, just under the tag!"

When I got back to the apartment, I tried my key to make sure it worked. It did. I then went to work and started my search for the cocaine. I methodically went from room to room, looking in every crack and crevasse that a bag of cocaine could possibly fit in. After searching all the other rooms, I stood in the only room left to search— Louie's bedroom. I fought off feelings of disappointment, reminding myself that the bedroom had more possibilities than the other rooms. I stood in the middle of his room, scanned and surveyed the entire room. I thought to myself, *where would I put it?*

I started with the closet and went through it with a fine-tooth comb. Then, under the bed, under the mattress, and every book. I looked behind pictures on the walls and on the sides of the mattress, box spring, and shelving unit headboard, looking for secret compartments he might have made. I even looked in the battery compartment of the alarm clock/radio on the shelf on the left side of the headboard. Nothing! Then, it dawned on me, and a feeling of dread and disappointment came over me. *He has it with him,* I thought. *That motherfucker keeps it in his damn car!* Then, I thought, *really? Would he be that stupid to carry around an ounce or more of coke in his car!?* I couldn't decide on that one, but I knew it wasn't there.

I gave up and was just about to go home to break the bad news to Todd, when something caught my eye. It was the box that his clock radio came in. It sat perched atop the headboard shelving unit. When I first came across it, I didn't give it a second thought because it was just too dumb that someone would keep cocaine in the box that their new clock radio just came out of. That's when it hit me like a ton of bricks—that clock radio wasn't new. It was dusty. It was at least several months old, if not more. I thought, *why would someone keep the box that their clock radio came in months ago on the shelf above their bed?*

I grabbed the box, sat on the bed, and opened it up. I slid out the two Styrofoam pieces that once held the clock radio in place. The back of one of those pieces had been hollowed out. In it, there was about a half ounce of coke staring me in the face! Columbo couldn't have done better detective work.

In the famous words of Chicago Cubs radio announcer Pat Hughes: "That ball's got a chance. It might be…it could be… it is… GONE!!" I felt like I just cracked a walk-off homer and won the game!

I made sure everything was like I found it, locked the door, and left. When I got back to the apartment, Todd met me at the door and anxiously asked, "What happened? Did you get in. Did you find anything?"

I tried to fake him out— "Nothing." But I couldn't contain my excitement and pulled the baggie of coke out of my crotch! "Except this!"

Again, we jumped around like kids on the playground, and Brutus took the opportunity to get his toy and bring it to us to play.

"Can you believe we pulled this off!?" Todd couldn't believe it.

Soon, Laura came home and learned what we had done. She couldn't believe it when I told her how we did it. Her response? "You better give me some of that before it's all gone," and "Don't go in the bathroom until I use it."

Todd and I proceeded to go on another cocaine binge for several days, tempered only by some heroin we copped from Jaime's guy. Those next few days, my paranoia went to a new level, and at night, I started running from hallucinations in the inner court of our complex.

I would hide from imaginary enemies in people's doorways and then end up knocking on their doors for help. Some of the neighbors started to really get annoyed with me, including Kenny. He no longer answered the door when I came over and purposely avoided me as much as possible. Things were unraveling quickly.

A few days into the binge, the doorbell rang. It was Tony. Laura welcomed him, and they sat at the kitchen table, snorting some coke that he had, while Todd and I continued to shoot the last of our spoils in the bathroom.

Todd left in search of some opiates to deal with the impending dope sick that we would inevitably experience when the cocaine wore off.

That's when Laura pulled me into the bedroom and said, "I have to ask you something."

"What?"

"Tony wants to know if he can take me to Vegas. He thinks I can win a lot of money with my luck with dice and cards."

So, we've finally arrived at that day in November of 1984 when I overdosed on cocaine…

Immediately upon looking into its eyes, I felt myself slipping away, and I could feel my heart beating irregularly. Then, it stopped beating. I felt the blood withdrawing from my brain and my limbs, and I began to lose consciousness. At that moment, I became overwhelmed with fear because I knew I was dying. It's hard to explain, but you just know. I knew I would not make it out of this. My eyes were locked with this being's eyes, and I couldn't look away. Seconds seemed like eternity as time seemed to stand still.

Was my time up? Was I about to share the same fate as Warren, Billy, and Leo? At the time, it certainly felt that way, but what happened next was nothing short of miraculous.

PART IV: HITTING BOTTOM - CONTINUED

Thirty-one seconds and beyond

As blackness closed in around me, and I felt the life force leaving my body, something strange happened. A bright yellow-white light came in through both picture windows in the living room and dining room. The light quickly spread to the entire apartment. It surrounded me, and as it did, my eyes were finally able to break the gaze of the man in black. I flopped out of the kitchen, and back toward the dining room. I stopped convulsing, felt my heart start to beat normally again, and I felt life returning to my entire body. I was able to rise off the floor to my knees. The ringing in my ears subsided, and my hearing was slowly restored. I heard what appeared to be crying in the distance that got louder and louder, sounding closer and closer. I realized that it was Jessica and Melissa standing behind me, crying at the top of their lungs. Apparently, they had witnessed the entire event, and it scared them.

Laura was now on her feet and was standing between the living room and the dining room with the same shocked look on her face. As the light slowly withdrew from the room, my faculties were restored.

I remember the first thing I did when I rose to my feet. I went to the spot where the man in black had been crouched between the stove and refrigerator and looked. He was gone, but I took note that the garbage can that was always there had been moved to the back of the room. I turned to Laura, and my first words were, "Did you see that guy?"

"What guy, Steve? There's no guy. You did too much coke and probably had a seizure."

I tended to my kids and assured them that everything was okay. They calmed down and stopped crying. I asked Laura, "Who moved the kitchen garbage?"

"I don't know. I didn't," she replied.

She turned and walked into the bedroom to pack and get ready for Vegas. She had already arranged for the neighbor, Paige, to watch the kids for a few days, and she got their things together. I sat in the dining room, still in a daze, trying to regain my composure and make sense of what just happened. I immediately started to second-guess myself and dismiss what occurred as just another delusional hallucination, but every time I did, I noted how different this felt. Most of my bad cocaine-induced hallucinations were at night, in the dark. This was in broad daylight, and I felt completely awake and conscious.

Laura and the kids emerged from the bedroom. "I'm going to take them over to Paige's. If Tony comes, let him know I'll be right back."

Tony returned with the eight ball that he promised, and they left for Vegas. Todd returned shortly after they left.

I told Todd about the seizure and the man in black. He laughed and said, "You're always seeing things that aren't there when you shoot coke."

I tried to explain the difference, but I couldn't. He pointed out, "Steve, if you were having a seizure, how would you know what was real and what wasn't?"

I couldn't explain that. I told him how strange the hit felt even before I injected it. His reply was a bit of a shock. "Sounds like a hot shot to me."

"What do you mean a hot shot?"

"A hot shot means old Tony may have been trying to take you out. Dealers do it to customers sometimes, for different reasons. They purposely spike the dope with some lethal shit. Seems like Tony wants your girl. Then again, it could've been that you just did too much coke and OD'd."

I didn't want to believe it, but I had to consider the possibility that Tony tried to kill me. A wave of the creeps came over me.

By early December 1984, the bottom dropped out pretty quickly. Laura didn't return when she was supposed to. Instead, she called to let me know that she was staying in Vegas a while longer. Todd and I went on another cocaine binge, and I continued to emotionally scar the neighbors. When we ran out of coke, we started kiting checks and buying stereo equipment and other items that we knew we could sell.

Ironically, I continued to cop coke from Louie. He confided in me, "I lost about a half ounce of coke, or someone ripped me off. I just don't know what happened."

"Wow. Really weird," I replied.

The next day, I used my key to get into his apartment and stole most of the Christmas presents out of his bedroom, including a diamond ring he bought for his girlfriend. I pawned the stuff as far away from Whittier as I could.

Laura came back briefly, but then quickly left again when she observed how in disarray everything was. We hadn't paid rent for several months and had just signed a new lease a few months earlier. She called, but I really don't remember much about the conversation except yelling at her, "Where's my kids?!" I felt hurt, and vulnerable, which almost always came out in the form of anger and rage. She told me that the kids were safe, but she had to get them away from me. I hung up on her and went to Paige's, but she said that Laura came and got them a few days ago, and she didn't know where they were (all a lie). She invited me to come in and see for myself. I declined, but as it turned out, if I had, they would have been there, hiding in the bedroom.

Todd and I scored more coke and went on another binge. I now had another dimension to add to my paranoia with the thought in the back of my mind that Tony wanted me dead and out of the way.

The first incident that included this new twist in my paranoid delusions happened about 2 a.m. I was running around the neighborhood, fleeing someone who was "trying to kill me." At one point, I went to a house where an older couple lived and woke them out of a sound sleep. I banged on the glass pane in their door so hard that I put my elbow through it and broke the glass. I saw the lights come on as they came to the door, and in panicked voices, they asked what was going on. I explained that someone was chasing me and to call the police. They actually opened their door and let me in. They were Christians, and their faith did not allow them to turn me away. I remember being impressed with this despite the state I was in. They comforted me and asked me who was trying to hurt me and why. I made up one of my instant lies. They had already called the police, and I heard the sirens as they got closer. I suddenly got up, made a beeline for the door, and took off, narrowly escaping arrest.

The following night, I decided to burglarize the drugstore on the corner. We were desperate for opiates to take the edge off all the coke we'd been doing. Todd wanted no part of it. "You go; I'll hold down the fort and wait here."

It was about 1 a.m. on a Monday. I staked out the place and the surrounding area to make sure that no one was around. I wondered if they had any alarm system, but even if they did, I knew where the syrups were and would be in and out quickly. I found a large rock and stood at the front door, debating whether to go through with it. Driven by the pharmaceutical treasures that awaited me inside, with a sudden burst of impulse, I hurled the boulder through the glass door. The alarm went off immediately and I wondered if it was connected to the police station. I wrestled with a piece of glass, which was stubborn and took too long to remove. The "alarm" in my head went off and I thought, *this is taking too long*. I decided to get out of there and monitor the place from afar to see if the cops showed up.

I waited in some bushes nearby. The coke was starting to wear off, leading to paranoid hallucinations as I waited. I noticed that as time went by, the alarm got weaker, until I could barely hear it. I waited in that bush for what seemed like forever. Nothing and no one came, except for an occasional passing car, so I deduced that there was probably no connection to the police station. It was time to make my move, but when the thought occurred to me that the police could be doing the same thing I was— staking the place out and waiting, it was over. I started hallucinating cops hiding in various locations, waiting to see if someone would enter the store. It was about 4 a.m. when the whole ordeal finally ended, and I went back to the apartment empty-handed.

The next day, the insanity continued. Todd would try to ease my mind and show me that there was no one under the bed, or in the closet, but the relief would only be temporary. Soon, even though it was broad daylight, the walls started closing in again. After shooting a hit, I knew someone was in my closet waiting to kill me. I slid the closet door open and jumped back. There, crouched in a dark corner of the closet, behind some clothes, I saw a man with a gun pointed at me. The bedroom window was open to air out the cigarette smoke, beer, and cocaine-induced body odor stench, which had accumulated in the apartment. There was only one escape—I leapt out the window to the ground two stories below. Luckily, I landed in the grass—well, mostly—except for my left heel. It unfortunately didn't make it to the grass and landed on the sidewalk.

I went down in a crumpled heap in the grass. When I went to stand up, my left leg buckled immediately, and in a wave of excruciating pain, I hit the sidewalk. I got up and began to hop on one leg, but I didn't get very far. I sat down on the grass, holding my foot and writhing in pain. Amazingly, all I could think about was the coke upstairs, so if I could just hop around the building to my front door, I could get to it.

Someone called out from a window, "Are you okay? do you want me to call an ambulance?" Within minutes I heard the siren, and a few of the neighbors were standing outside their apartments, whispering and staring at me. The ambulance arrived, and the paramedics put me on a gurney. Todd was watching from the bedroom window and yelled down to ask what hospital they were taking me to. "Whittier," I yelled back.

One paramedic asked me what happened, so I quickly made up a lie. "I bet my friend Todd that I could jump from two stories up without a scratch. Would've won the bet, too, but my left foot missed the grass."

They took me to Whittier hospital, where Melissa was born just over a year before. Upon arrival, it was apparent that I was in severe pain, so the nurse came in and administered a shot of Demerol.

After X-raying my foot, the doctor came in to talk to me. He asked what happened. I stuck to my story. He looked at me with a raised brow of concern. I don't think he believed me. He informed me that he would be back once he read the X-rays to see what was next. He turned to leave the room, but, at that moment, I saw an opportunity to address something that had been in the back of my mind and bothering me since it occurred; "Excuse me, doc."

"Yes?"

"I've got a question."

"Is it possible to have a seizure and totally lose control of your body, ya know, totally rolling and flopping around on the floor, but be completely aware of what's going on the whole time?"

"Yes," he replied. "There are certain types of seizures where this can happen. One type is a simple partial seizure. The person is completely conscious and aware but loses control of muscle and body movement. The motor and other symptoms can vary from one person to the next, but one can remain conscious and remember everything when it's over. Why do you ask?"

"It happened to a friend of mine not too long ago. He saw some strange things, and everyone told him that he probably dreamt or hallucinated them while he was unconscious and was having a seizure."

"Interesting...yes, well, it can happen. Relax now, and I'll come back once I've looked at your X-rays."

I felt vindicated. I knew I wasn't crazy, well, at least not about this. You could have a seizure like the one I had and remain completely conscious.

My mind refocused when I remembered that I still had almost a gram of coke stashed back at the apartment. It was starting to burn a hole in my brain.

The doctor returned with my X-rays in hand and showed me the pictures of my left heel.

"Your heel has split in two. You see this line right in the middle is the split. This is all supposed to be one piece. Then you can see from this other angle how uneven it is. This is the concern. We need to operate to fuse the two halves back together."

"Operate? When?"

"Now."

"Now?"

"Yes. The sooner, the better, before it heals and fuses back together by itself. If it heals that way, you walk with a limp the rest of your life."

I was feeling pretty good from the Demerol, and all I could think about was the coke stashed in the apartment.

"Can I come back later in the week to get it done?"

"Yes, but the sooner the better. The longer you wait, the more complicated the surgery will be. We will put a cast on it for now and get you crutches. Stay off it as much as possible. You will need some pain medication. When the shot wears off, you will be in pain if you put any weight on it."

"Okay, I promise I'll come back and get the surgery." Just then, the nurse came in and informed me that Todd was in the waiting room.

"We need to put a cast on and write a prescription for Mr. Fiorito."

As evening fell, Todd and I left to fill my prescription, then went back to the apartment. We shot the remaining coke, and I crutched around outside in my usual state of paranoia, hiding from my demons. Todd got so irritated with me, he left and went to a local bar to hang out and get a break from my lunacy.

Meanwhile, a neighbor called the police on me, and as they came up the stairs to knock on the apartment door, a small crowd had gathered outside at the foot of the stairs that led to the units on the second floor.

If you've ever seen the movie *Frankenstein*, you probably can recall the scene where the villagers have had enough of the doctor's evil experiments. They come to the castle with pitchforks, clubs, and torches to protest and lynch the mad scientist. Let's just say the only difference was the absence of pitchforks, clubs, and torches. They stood at the bottom of the stairs and started letting their displeasure with my presence be known.

I came to the door on crutches, in a cast, looking half dead. The officers informed me that several of them had called because of what they described as my "erratic behavior." The cops looked at me with pity in their eyes.

As they questioned me at my front door, the neighbors started getting louder and bolder. They started coming up the stairs, demanding my arrest, and that they wanted me removed from the complex. To my surprise, the cops turned on the angry mob, and one of them put his hands out and yelled, "Go home! We'll handle this! Mr. Fiorito pays rent here just like you, and he has rights!"

They grumbled under their breath as they broke it up and went back to their apartments.

"You look like you can use some rest. Why don't you just call it a night and stay in your apartment, Mr. Fiorito?" I promised I would, and they left.

With all the coke gone, and the Demerol worn off, the throbbing in my heel came on strong. I grabbed the bottle of 30 Percocet and dumped a handful out, stuck them in my mouth, and downed them with a beer. I lay on the floor with my foot elevated, drank beer, and watched TV until I fell asleep.

In the morning, Todd returned, and I told him about what happened with the cops and the neighbors. As we started talking about what we should do, what happened next would make our decision much easier.

Someone was at the door. Fearing it was the cops again; we decided not to answer it. We looked through a crack in the drapes and saw that it was Louie and another guy we had never seen before. After knocking several times, they finally gave up and left. Soon after, we made our decision. The visit from Louie was our cue that it was once again…you guessed it… "time to get the hell outta Dodge!" We grabbed some clothes, as well as anything that we felt was necessary or valuable enough to take with us, and we hit the road.

For the next few days, we lived out of the van and kited checks from my way-beyond-overdrawn and now-closed bank account. We mostly wrote checks for gas and food.

It was December 1984, and Christmas was just around the corner. "Merry Christmas?" I called and talked to Rhoda, and she told me that Laura and the kids were there. They had come back to Chicago for the holidays. How ironic that I was trapped in L.A.

Soon after, we were stopped by the cops for reasons that I don't recall. They searched us. They didn't find anything except the Percocet that I had a legal prescription for, but I would soon become aware of a California law that I had no idea existed. It turned out that in California, it was illegal to have track marks on your arms (or anywhere else for that matter). They noticed that I had long sleeves on. Only people with something to hide wore long sleeves in Southern Cali. They made me roll them up. My tracks were pretty terrible, especially on my left arm. They checked Todd, too, but his veins had all collapsed in the obvious places on his arms, and he had to find veins in unusual places. They let Todd go, but they arrested me and took me to L.A. County Jail.

There, they put me in the "bullpen." They didn't know what to do with me due to my cast and crutches. I shared the bullpen with several Latino gangbangers who were cool to me. My pain meds were starting to wear off, though, so I started squawking about that. The guards came and got me and put me in a holding cell.

Soon, the two cops who arrested me came in, sat down, and said the words that would stick in my head for the rest of my life: "We did a background check on you, and other than a few minor charges, you're clean as a whistle. What we've concluded, Mr. Fiorito, is, *you're a nice guy with a bad problem.* We're going to cut you loose on the condition that you get the hell out of L.A. and never come back. Deal?" I agreed.

So, from the L.A. County Jail, I called my ace in the hole— Albie. I told her that I was in trouble and needed to come home. She was obviously extremely disappointed, which should have made me feel bad, but it didn't. I was numb to those kinds of feelings. My only focus was on my needs and desires. I made up some bullshit that included being in a cast after "falling off a ladder." She explained that they didn't have the money. I suggested that she try to borrow it, and that Todd would pay her back as soon as we got back into town. She finally agreed to try and asked me to call back in a few hours.

They granted me an I-bond, so for the next few hours, Todd, the dog Brutus and me, killed time and drove around. We wrote the last of the rubber checks and took the last of the Percocet.

Later, I said a "foxhole prayer" and called Albie back. She came through. Back then, for two one-way tickets from L.A. to Chicago, I think it was around $400. The only problem was the flight she booked was leaving Los Angeles International Airport (LAX) in a few hours, so we had no time to spare.

Escape from L.A.

When we arrived and parked, it hit us: "What are we going to do with the dog?" We hated to leave him tied up somewhere, so Todd broke out his papers and started looking for someone to take him. He spotted a well-dressed guy with a silver Mercedes who was waiting at the terminal to pick someone up. Todd asked him if he wanted a purebred German Shepherd. The guy read the papers that Todd handed him and immediately said: "Sure, I'll take him." The man petted him, and Brutus wagged his tale. That was one lucky dog. He was liberated from a dope fiend, narrowly missed a trip to the animal shelter, and instead went home with a rich family—all in a matter of one minute.

But the cost of finding Brutus a home was being late and not being able to check our bags. So, we just left them and boarded the plane. There was nothing of any real value anyway. Mostly clothes, including my other boot, due to the cast on my left foot. But there was one thing that had a lot of sentimental value. My photo album. It had all my memories up to that point in my life in it. I had no choice; I had to leave it. When the plane took off, I felt a strange mix of regret and relief. As usual, the relief was short-lived; the regret was not.

We were held over in Denver due to the weather and were given cots to sleep on. Withdrawal started kicking in, so we became more uncomfortable and barely got a wink of sleep.

The next day, we arrived at O'Hare in Chicago. I got off the plane in a nasty maroon Dago-T, with one boot and on crutches. I think it was about 19 degrees outside, and there was about eight inches of snow on the ground. We were dope sick and freezing. Our jackets were left at LAX. My brother Paul was there, waiting to pick us up.

We let him know how sick we were and asked where we could get some dope. Then, we filled him in about the events that led to our departure.

It was a Sunday, so the only option was the V.A. to see if he could score some Methadone. We drove to Hines V.A. Hospital and Paul found a guy who sold us a 60-mg. bottle of Methadone, which we split three ways. Then, we drove Todd to his dad's house on the Northwest Side.

Paul confirmed that Laura was there and had the kids. He also informed me that my family decided that I should not stay with our parents and that I was not welcome there. I asked if I could stay with him and Carie for a few days until I could figure out what to do. "Absolutely not. Sorry, but Carie doesn't want you there at all."

For the first time in my life, I was not welcomed by anyone in my family. He asked: "Any friends that would let you stay on their couch?" "Maybe Diego," I replied.

So, he drove me to Diego's, which was now Diego and Holly's. They had gotten married and had a son and another one on the way.

More snow started coming down as we pulled into the driveway. Paul went in the trunk and got me a spare sweatshirt and stocking cap that he kept there for emergencies. I crutched up to the door and knocked on it. Diego answered the door. At that moment, Paul rolled down the window and yelled to me to call him tomorrow as he slowly rolled in reverse and made a smooth getaway out of the driveway.

Diego asked what happened to me. I told him I fell off a ladder in California while running my house painting business. "Bummer, man. Let me get a coat on, and let's go out in the garage and talk."

We went into his garage, he turned on a space heater, and we sat on a stack of drywall. He lit a joint, told me about the family he and Holly had started, and that he was in the process of turning the basement into a three-bedroom apartment. I told him I was happy for them, especially considering his illness. When I left for Cali, he was on dialysis, but he had since gotten a kidney transplant and was doing amazingly well, that is, except for one thing. I would soon find out what that thing was while telling him my California horror story.

I don't know what compelled me, and I don't remember exactly how much I disclosed, but I had so much built up inside me for so long it just kind of came out like puke. He was one of my best friends. If I couldn't talk to him, then who could I talk to? As some of the gory details started coming out of my mouth, I saw his eyes getting really wide. I also noticed that his face had gotten pale (more than usual). I stopped talking and was about to ask if he was okay, when he suddenly slid down the stack of drywall onto the floor and had a seizure! I remember getting behind him and holding his shoulders so that his head didn't hit the concrete floor. Apparently, the seizures were a side effect of some of the meds he was on to keep his body from rejecting the transplant.

When it was over, he snapped out of it as if nothing had happened. He then proceeded to say some of the most important words I've ever heard in my life. They went something like this…

"Steve, I'm sorry man, but you've got to leave. I can't have you in my life anymore. I've got a wife and kid and another one on the way. You had people here looking for you that threatened me. I just can't have that in my life. You have to go now. I hope you understand."

"No, I understand. I get it, man. I really do. Take care of yourself...and say hi to Holly for me."

And with that, I walked out the door and onto the street, stuffing the ache in my gut further down with every step. I had just been thrown out of one of my best friends' lives.

The snow started falling harder as I crutched my way up Roberta Avenue toward my sister Sue's house. I felt like George Bailey must have in the scene from the film *"It's a Wonderful Life"*, where he stumbles desperately through the snow, contemplating suicide. It was a big gamble, but it was my only chance. My big sister wouldn't turn me away if I showed up on crutches at her door—would she?

The sidewalk was buried under nine or so inches of snow, so I had to stay in the road, but it was still difficult crutching through the snow. Suddenly, a carload of teenagers who were joyriding and fishtailing on the snow-covered road passed by. They pointed and laughed at me as they passed. I noticed that one of them was my nephew, Gary. He looked at me dead in the face, so I'm pretty sure he knew it was me, but he was probably too ashamed of his uncle, the junkie, to make them stop and pick me up. I was once a mentor who got him into playing sports at an early age, but now, I'd become a source of shame.

I crutched the seven blocks to the house on Dickens Avenue where I had some of my best and worst times. As the house came into view, it brought a mixture of good and painful feelings. Feelings that were always just below the surface, waiting to erupt at any moment. Feelings that only occasionally surfaced as anger when I was provoked.

I stood at the door and rang the bell. Sue answered, and in her cold-shouldered voice, she asked, "What do you want?"

"Can I come in? It's kinda freezing out here."

Without saying a word, she turned her back and walked away, leaving the door open and implying without words, *yes, but it's not what I'd prefer.*

"I need someplace to stay."

"Well, you can't stay here."

"I don't have anywhere to go, Sue."

"Well, you should've thought about that when you were doing your thing out in California."

Word traveled fast through my family about mine and Paul's unraveling.

"What happened to your foot?"

"I fell off a ladder and shattered my heel"—now throbbing in the cold.

"You can spend the night and that's it. You've got to go tomorrow."

She gave me some bedding, and without saying another word, went to her bedroom and closed the door. I slept on the floor.

The next morning, as daylight slapped me back into consciousness of my miserable existence, I was awakened to my sister keeping her promise.

"Start figuring out where you're going."

So, I called Rhoda. Ever trying to keep Laura and me together, she informed me that Laura and the kids were at Linda's and that she would pick me up so I could see them. Rhoda was always there for me if I needed her.

By this time, withdrawal was "knocking at the door" as the Methadone started wearing off. I recalled that Paul once was on something called a "guest status" at a Methadone clinic. Clinics sometimes do this for people for various reasons if temporarily unable to get to their clinic.

The scam wheels started turning in my head, so I gave it a shot, and called H.I.P. House in Maywood. I disguised my voice and sounded as doctorly as I could. I said I was calling from a clinic I knew of in California. It worked. They went for it. I was placed on a seven-day guest status. 70 milligrams for a $5 fee per dose. I just needed to get to the clinic before they closed at 4 p.m.

Rhoda picked me up and drove me to Linda's in River Grove. I don't remember much, but I remember that I saw my kids, Linda and her kids, and Laura's brothers, Mark and Leon. Laura borrowed someone's car to drive me to the clinic in Maywood. By this time, I was getting dope sick. I can't imagine what Laura and I talked about after all that had happened, but I knew that she was my only hope of getting my sick off in that situation. Unfortunately, we caught one of the infamous area freight trains, and as a result, we didn't make it. The clinic was closed. Now what? I would have to come back in the morning.

We wound up at the Oak Park outdoor shopping mall, I think because of my past success "boosting" from stores and I was trying to get some money. Laura wanted to go home and didn't know what to do with me. She offered some PCP and a few Valiums from her purse to "take the edge off" of my withdrawals, until I could get medicated in the morning. Bad idea.

I popped the Valium and snorted the PCP. Unfortunately, the effect of this combination was to get me in touch with all those feelings that lay just below the surface and needed to come out. They did, and I started quickly spiraling into a state of despondency and depression. The fact that I'd made a mess of our lives, was magnified by the drugs. I remember crying. Then, I went into somewhat of a blackout and don't remember much else. Apparently, I had become suicidal and talked about killing myself. I felt like I was a big loser all my life, and it became abundantly clear to me that I would remain a loser until the day I died. I had lost everything that I cared about, so what was the point? Laura panicked, found a payphone, and called my brother Paul.

Paul arrived, and Laura handed me off like a bag of dirty laundry. Not knowing what to do, he drove me to the only place he could think of in the area.

Committed to?

I woke up the next morning and had no idea where I was or what time it was. I deduced that I was in the hospital when I noted my little gown and bracelet and saw the side table with wheels off to one side of the bed. On it were my cigarettes, but notably absent was my lighter. I got out of bed and grabbed a smoke out of the pack. I couldn't find my lighter anywhere, so I decided to venture outside my room in search of a light. It was dark and empty in the room outside the nurse's station. It looked odd, but I couldn't put my finger on why. Then I realized that it was encased in thick plexiglass.

"Hey, can I get a light?"

Over the P.A. speaker, I heard: "Sir, you're not allowed out of your room until 6 a.m. You have 15 minutes."

"What did you guys do with my lighter? If I had my lighter, I would've just smoked in the room, and I wouldn't have even come out here."

"You're not allowed to smoke in your room, Sir. Now, just go back to your room and when it's time, you can light your cigarette with the lighter that's on the wall."

I noted the lighter that she was referring to, so I walked up to it and lit my cigarette. "Yeah, fuck that," I said defiantly.

I took two drags off my smoke, and the next thing I knew, I've got two 400-pound gorillas on me, and my cig is being ripped from my mouth.

"Hey, what the fuck?!" I protested, as I was being escorted to a "rubber room." There, I was strapped down to a table and unable to move a muscle for the next four hours.

In case you hadn't guessed, Paul had me committed to the "looney bin"—one of the worst in the area—Madden Mental Health Center. They were able to contact HIP House and get my dose of Methadone, so at least I was medicated. Before they released me from my restraints, they made me promise that I would be a good boy, which I did, though I'm sure I had my fingers crossed behind my back.

I didn't realize it at the time, but I would find out later that afternoon that it was New Year's Eve. We were able to watch the ball drop on TV with *Dick Clark's New Year's Rockin' Eve* from Time Square. I remember sitting in the patient lounge next to a very chubby but attractive girl. How low can you go? Trying to pick up chicks in the looney bin! *One Flew Over the Cuckoo's Nest* was my favorite movie, and now, I was practically in it. Happy New Year from the looney bin! Thank God that 1984 was over.

After my 72-hour observation period was up, they were able to determine that I was no longer a danger to myself or to others. I'm not sure what magical criteria they used to make that determination. My parents showed up, and they released me to their care.

Once again, I became a grown man who lived with mommy and daddy at yet another apartment on York Road in Bensenville. I was relatively cool for a while, mostly due to limited resources and contacts. No one knew I was back in town, except Diego, and that was fine with me.

My father became my chauffeur. He retired and started collecting Social Security. He threw in the towel after making a last-ditch effort to pull things out financially and getting ripped off by his accountant "buddy," Harry Butcher, for seven grand. That was a lot of money for my father. Harry disappeared with my father's, and I'm sure, other people's money, never to be seen again. Had Paul or I ever caught up with him, he would have been found floating in a river. He was one of the few people in my life whom I felt justified taking out. Thank God I never got the chance.

The charade must end

My dad drove me to Maywood to get my Methadone for my week-long guest status. When that was exhausted, I started occasionally abusing pills and street Methadone again. In and out of withdrawal, I was getting "sick and tired of being sick and tired." My hands started to go up in at least a partial surrender.

I learned that Laura had taken my kids and returned to California with—to my surprise—Todd! Despite the feelings of hurt, anger, and betrayal I felt, for some reason, I wasn't as crushed by the Todd thing as I may have thought. Looking back, I think it's because I had slipped into survival mode. I actually felt sorry for them. As reality started getting clearer, I knew it wouldn't work, and what they were in for—more of the same. My head popped through the first layer of denial in January of 1985, and I realized that that's all any of us could ever look forward to—more of the same—insanity and chaos.

The hopeless, helpless feeling of being stuck with no way out led to my first honest cry for help, and as a result, I finally got honest with my parents. For the first time since being a kid, I viewed them as my allies instead of my enemies. That's how I had viewed them for most of my life—people from whom I had to hide everything and watch out for. People who would give me trouble and would get in my way. Suddenly, I saw them for who they really were—people who loved and cared about me, and who would do whatever they could to help me. This was a significant breakthrough.

I called them into the living room, and with my head down—eyes staring at the floor (I had a hard time with any eye contact back then under any circumstances), I said these important words: "I have a drug problem. I want to stop, but I don't know how."

My father just sighed and looked at me with helplessness in his eyes, not really knowing what to say. My mother recalled, "Your niece Deanna went through that program, and she's doing really well. What was the name? Gateway, I think. Why don't we look in the phone book?"

So, we did, and there it was, Gateway Foundation, with its symbolic circular maze logo jumping off the page. How appropriate. I surely was trapped in a maze that I couldn't seem to find my way out of. We called their intake number, but nobody answered. We were able to leave a message with the new technology that was sweeping the country—the answering machine.

I was in a state of complete defeat and humility. The question was, could I maintain it? I continued getting honest with my parents by explaining that I was getting sick, and as a way of detoxing myself, I needed to get some Tylenol #4 with Codeine. I told them where I could get some. I explained that I would let my mother hold them and dispense only three during the day, and two at night before bed, to take the edge off and make it possible to get some sleep.

It was impossible to sleep while withdrawing from Methadone. It was worse than any heroin withdrawal I'd ever experienced. They agreed to help me get and dispense the pills. My parents drove me and paid for them. Over the next several days, we followed the plan until the pills were gone. Now it was time to go the rest of the way "cold turkey."

The first night was the worst. I tossed and turned on the couch in hot and cold sweats until the sheet and blanket were soaked. Then, muscle spasms started kicking in, and my skin felt like it would crawl right off my body. My muscles ached, and my stomach started cramping. It was around 1 a.m., and I was smack-dab in the middle of Methadone withdrawal when what I consider to be my second spiritual experience in my life happened (though I didn't recognize either of the two as such, at the time). I reached over the back of the couch with my right arm and extended my hand in pain and desperation. Out of nowhere, I got this picture in my mind of Jesus standing there. I closed my eyes, reached out my hand to Him and I imagined His hand closing around mine.

The next thing I knew, I awoke suddenly to daylight streaming in the window above the sliding glass door and forcing my eyes to open. I was in the same exact position as when I fell asleep, with my arm over the back of the couch and my hand clenching the proverbial hand of Jesus.

Wait...what? Fell asleep? No way! I had been in that kind of withdrawal before and *there was no way you were going to sleep;* I thought to myself. I looked at the clock, and it was 6 a.m. Not only had I slept like a rock, but I had apparently slept for about five hours. *This was not possible,* I thought, and nothing short of miraculous.

I pulled myself up just in time to view the familiar sight and sound of my dad sitting at the kitchen table in his white undershirt, glasses on his nose, reading the paper, and tapping on his soft-boiled egg. The smell of my father (a mix of Old Spice aftershave, eggs, coffee, and cigarette smoke) filled my nostrils as I continued to ponder how I had fallen asleep. I felt so much better.

I poured a cup of coffee, bummed a Viceroy off my dad (yuk!), and when he was done reading the paper, I grabbed it and went to the horoscope, as I always did. This is what my horoscope in the *Chicago Sun-Times* said on that day, January 12, 1985...

The only way to cope with current emotional or domestic problems is to say that a time or cycle in your life is coming to a close. To do otherwise would be to continue a charade which every instinct is telling you must end.

Wow! Talk about being on the money. Astrologer Sydney Omar nailed it! I'm not sure if that was Sydney or God, but I knew it was speaking directly to me. I immediately cut it out with some scissors; then I was inspired to write this little limerick poem on a piece of thin cardboard...

Up until this cold wintery day,
You know that your life went astray,
This card serves to remind,
That the past that's behind,
Will help you to find a new way.

I combined the two back-to-back with clear box tape and turned it into a business-card-sized reminder that I carried in my wallet. That day, Gateway called us back, and I made an appointment at their outpatient office in the city. It was appropriately known as "The Maze," on Belmont Avenue and Broadway.

Stumbling blindly through The Maze

On Monday morning, my father drove me to my appointment, and as usual, words were scarce. The silence was filled up mostly with the drone of news radio in the background and only broken with an occasional commentary about whatever crap was being spewed across the airwaves.

The area was ultra-congested, and there was nowhere to park, so I was dropped off. I rang the bell, and a voice came over the intercom: "Yes, can I help you?" I told them who I was and that I had an appointment. I was buzzed in and filled out a bunch of forms until a fairly hot, older woman named Cindy came in and did my assessment. It was a no-brainer. They recommended inpatient treatment as soon as a bed became available. There was a waiting list (typical in the winter months), and it could be a month or two before that happened. In the meantime, they referred me to Central Intake on Lake Street and Ashland Avenue to finally surrender and get on the "odine" program.

"Odine" was a nickname that Lenny Rozak—one of Paul's runnin' partners and fellow Vietnam-era veteran—had given Methadone. I was also required to be on what was known as a "holding pattern." This consisted of weekly group and individual counseling at The Maze and daily phone contact on days when I wasn't there. Missing one session or phone contact meant losing your spot on the waiting list and going to the end of the list. My father finally found a parking space, came in, and it was all explained to him.

I wanted Cindy to be my counselor, but as fate would have it, my group counselor wound up being Stacey Balonick. Stacey was a no BS—tell it like it is—counselor. The lesson had officially begun—what I wanted wasn't necessarily what I needed. She and her sister Leslie were both recovering addicts and were pioneers in the early days of the field of addiction treatment in the Chicago area. Stacey and Leslie were both products of Gateway's residential treatment programs and now both worked for Gateway.

The field was still in its infancy and evolving in 1984. There weren't a whole lot of professional standards or regulations to speak of in the early days, and the addictions field consisted mainly of people in recovery.

A few days later, at my Central Intake appointment, I sat in the waiting room, sick as a dog. The "waiting room" was the right name for this place. You waited, and waited, and waited some more. There must have been what seemed like 100 dope fiends ahead of me. Finally, they called my name, and I was given a physical, I endured yet another assessment, and finally, I was given my first official, legit dose of Methadone. I was referred to a program called Interventions North Side that was near Diversey Avenue and Clark Street. This was convenient, with outpatient at Gateway being right around the corner.

I had to go to the clinic five days a week to get my dose (75 milligrams) and my two weekend pick-up bottles on Friday. I'd stand in line and show my clinic ID at the window, and the nurse would hand me my paper cup of the orange liquid. It was chalky, gritty, and had a bitter taste. Knowing that in about 25 minutes or so, I'd be going into a pretty good nod made the taste tolerable.

As the drug came on, any withdrawal symptoms would vanish. Then, I'd get that initial "kick in the chest" and shortness of breath, followed by what I can only describe as a familiar warm feeling of euphoric relief and well-being that would envelop my brain and body. My voice would get thick, low, and scratchy. Sure, I was high, but I was also stable, which meant I didn't have to go out and beg, borrow, and steal to get a fix.

My mother was so proud of me; she called my sister Mary Jo and announced, "He's starting to brush his teeth every day!" Mary Jo's response was less enthusiastic, "Ma, he's 25 years old; he's supposed to be brushing his teeth every day." The bar had obviously been lowered quite a bit by then.

I was trying to be good, but sitting around watching TV with my parents got a bit boring. My mother, I think sensing this, noticed in one of the local newspapers that auditions were being held for a local community theater group production. The play was a Neil Simon comedy-drama from 1970 called The Gingerbread Lady. They made it into a film in 1981 called *Only When I Laugh*. I was familiar with the film.

It's the story of Evy, who ruins her Broadway career and her life with alcohol, and winds up in rehab. Now, with her best years behind her, she comes home and tries to pick up the pieces and put her life back together. There are complications involving her teenage daughter and her socialite theater friends, one of whom is her best friend, Jimmy—a gay man who supplies most of the comic relief in the show. Things get further complicated when her good-for-nothing musician, ex-boyfriend Lou Tanner, comes crawling back after things didn't work out with the hot, young 18-year-old he left her for.

By the time I auditioned, Lou was the only role they hadn't filled, and the director felt I was perfect. I guess we could say I barely had to act at all. I could certainly relate to Lou's character apart from chasing the 18-year-old.

By then, I had traded my crutches for a cast shoe and then a regular shoe. But, as the doc in Cali warned, my heel didn't heal properly and was uneven. As he predicted, I walked with a limp. Luckily, that was easy to write into the show, which they did.

Another interesting thing about the play was that I tried to make amends with Diego by inviting him and Holly to opening night. I guess it was my way of showing him that I was trying to be somewhat normal and be the creative guy who he became friends with. I didn't know if they would come, but I got confirmation that they were there in a unique way. While on stage, delivering some of my lines, I heard a thud and a ruckus in the audience. For some reason, I knew it was Diego having a seizure. I remember thinking to myself, *oh good, Diego and Holly came.*

After the show, they told me how much they enjoyed it, and they confirmed that what I heard was, in fact, Diego having a seizure. I was glad they came. I took it as a gesture that they hadn't given up on me. However, what I did on closing night could have justified why they should have.

Somehow, I got left alone in the room with the box office receipts for that night, and not being able to withstand that kind of temptation, I took the money. In the investigation that ensued, I was never even a suspect, and it was decided that it was likely an audience member who somehow snuck into the room and grabbed the cash.

The good news was that despite the "slip," I was doing a bit better. I kept up with the obligations of the "holding pattern" at Gateway and was taking my Methadone daily.

Despite my improvements, one day after group, my counselor, Stacey, pulled me aside and informed me, "Uh, Steve, I want you to do a little more listening in group. You're talking too much and to be honest, your Methadone is doing the talking."

I didn't realize it, but Methadone made me chatty. This may seem insignificant, but it's not when you consider how shy I could be around people I didn't know. Though I didn't necessarily feel high, my personality was altered quite a bit by the drug. This is one of the issues with drugs that is typically misunderstood or overlooked by most people. Even when the user doesn't feel high, they are in a chemically induced, altered state.

On the other hand, there was some evidence of my being at least somewhat stabilized by Methadone. I bought a beater car from my old friend Brian. It looked like shit, but of course, it ran like a top. I met a girl named Ginny, and although she really wasn't my type, she had a hot little body, and we became "friends with benefits." I also finally got a job. I started working for an independent contractor who was a "jack of all trades" and did a little bit of everything related to home repair and remodeling.

I was doing so "well," I slowly drifted away from Gateway and fell to the end of the waiting list. A bed opened up for me, but I chickened out and didn't go. I told them I was going home to get my belongings and that I'd be back by 3 p.m., but I never showed up. My disconnection with Gateway was just fine with me because all I really needed was a job anyway—right? I was on a roll, and I felt, *I got this*, and I didn't need to go into treatment anymore.

My next cocky, impulsive move came in my next individual session with my Methadone counselor. Out of nowhere, I suddenly announced that I wanted to detox and get off Methadone. My counselor Jason, who was also a recovering heroin addict, was shocked by this announcement. After the initial shock wore off, he used a good analogy. His words would stick with me forever: "Steve, it's hard to contemplate hunger on a full stomach." He tried to convince me that it was too soon, and just because I had experienced some stability, it didn't mean I was ready to come off Methadone. But me, being the expert that I was (on everything), insisted, and so they started me on a 21-day detox.

As my dose got lower, I began to experience an addict's nightmare—discomfort. This, combined with money from my paychecks, quickly led to the me shooting heroin, and then cocaine again. It was amazing that no matter how well I was doing, it didn't take much to trigger me and quickly lead to a complete relapse. Things sank to a new low, fast. My fuck-buddy Ginny got a new job and needed a car, so I sold her mine. Nice—right? Yeah, except, then I promptly stole it back from her. Of course, I never saw her again. Rumor had it that her brother was looking for me and wanted to kill me. Get in line, buddy!

Then, there was our latest dope connection, Annie. She lived in the projects on Diversey Parkway and Clybourn Avenue. What is the lowest place you can imagine in the universe? If you answered "Hell," you'd be correct. This place was only one step above that.

Annie was the oldest dope fiend I'd ever met. In fact, she was probably the oldest dope fiend anyone ever met. Dope fiends usually didn't live that long, but the myth existed that heroin was a sort of preservative, and occasionally, you'd run into that ancient dope fiend who was older than dirt. They were like the undead, and short of driving a stake through their heart, nothing could kill them. Annie looked to be in her 80s but was really only in her 60s. She was overweight and literally looked like death warmed over. Her skin was pale white, her hair hadn't been washed in weeks, and she wore the same filthy house dress for days on end. After identifying you through the peephole, she would answer the door with syringes hanging out of her legs and a single drop of blood dripping down to her ankle. This was because most of her veins had collapsed, and it was very difficult for her to find one that she could shoot a hit into. She had pus-filled abscesses and sores on her arms and legs. A mix of body odor, urine, and God-knows-what stench constantly emanated from her. Her voice was raspy, demonic, and barely female.

The place smelled like pungent garbage and was a complete pigsty from top to bottom. It was littered with drug paraphernalia, and junkies were flopped out and nodding all over the place. Most were emaciated and looked like the undead. Female addicts would be turning tricks in one of the bedrooms. The term used for places like Annie's was a "shooting gallery."

AIDS, and the HIV virus that causes it, had been discovered not long before and had become front page news. At first, it was considered an illness that plagued only gay men. That changed, and by the mid-1980s, it had spread into the IV-drug-using community. There was still a lot of confusion and misinformation about how you could contract the virus and what the symptoms were. Many still believed that you could tell by looking at someone if they had it. Users were learning about the importance of not sharing needles, or if they did, cleaning them with bleach. It was one of the few things that smelled clean at Annie's. There was always bleach available. Good thing, too, because at that point, no one was disciplined enough not to share needles.

As things continued to unravel, so did any morals and values I still clung to. Don't ask why I didn't just stop the detox and admit that I couldn't handle it. The only words that come to mind are *pride* and *denial*.

My moral deterioration was well illustrated one day, while on Belmont and Broadway panhandling. After not doing too well, I got an idea to scam an old queer from the neighborhood whom I'd become familiar with. He would cruise up and down Broadway, trying to pick up male prostitutes and take them back to his house a few blocks away. I was familiar with him because he had propositioned me several times. My plan was to play along like I was going to let him have sex with me, until he handed me the money. Once in hand, I would get up and run out the door. Simple enough—right? Except for one thing: apparently, others had done the same thing to him, and he was ready.

So, when it was time to do the deed, I asked for the money. He resisted and tried to convince me to perform first. I finally wore him down and he handed me the money. I immediately got up and ran to the front door. The trouble was, it was locked, and you needed a key to unlock it. Same thing at the back door. I remember him standing up and watching me with an amused look on his face at my desperation, knowing there was no way out of his house without his assistance. I felt like I was in one of those teen horror films. Even the windows had bars across them that required a key to open, that is, except one. It was a small window that was on the back porch about a story and a half up from the ground. I opened it up, somehow managed to squeeze through, and jumped to the ground in his backyard. Luckily, this time, I was able to land on the grass, and not do any further damage to my heel, and I made my escape.

In yet another incident of my brazen insanity, I was arrested at the Oak Park Mall for trying to walk out of a store with a 24-inch TV in the box. Hey, I figured it worked with albums; why wouldn't it work with a huge TV? I went to court for retail theft and was put on one-year court supervision.

Around this time, I reconnected with Donnie and company. I gave Donnie some bullshit about why I never returned with his money that night, and all was forgiven. Of course, I had to pay him back. We were all hanging out with a traveling coke dealer who was staying at a local hotel on Mannheim

Road. These guys were nomads who would take up residence for some months in an area and then move on when they felt things were starting to get too hot.

One night, I ran out of money on a coke binge and did something I swore I'd never do. I hocked my beloved medallion that my parents made for me for $50 with Mr. coke Dealer. The guy suddenly disappeared along with my necklace, never to be seen again.

As my dose at the clinic went down to single digit milligrams, I became more uncomfortable and impulsive. Seemingly, out of nowhere, the idea popped into my head: *Call HIP House and get yourself on another guest status.* This time, I called it in from Northside Interventions instead of a California clinic—a bit riskier. The reason I gave was, I'd be in the area working construction and couldn't get to my clinic every day. They bought it. I called in a two-week guest status at 70 milligrams. I got my first dose the next day.

Sounds easy—right? But unless you've lived it, the life of a conman is full of stress and worry. Constantly looking over your shoulder, in fear of who would finally catch up with you, and not even being able to keep track of all your lies, or people you've burned and scammed. But for now, I got over again, and before I knew it, I was nodding and burning holes in my pantlegs, and all was right with the world once again. That is, until about my eighth day.

I showed up at the clinic with my five-dollar guest fee in hand. I stood in line, got up to the window, but something felt different. The nurse wasn't her usual friendly, jovial self. She told me to have a seat; the director needed to speak to me. I sat nervously in the waiting room. I thought about getting up and bolting, but I couldn't. I wanted that dope. I *needed* that dope! Soon, a tall black man emerged from the back offices. "Steven?"

"Yes?"

"Come on back here; let's talk."

I followed him to an office, and we sat directly across from each other. He stared intently at me with a sort of knowing smile on his face, as if waiting for me to speak.

I finally obliged him, as politely as possible; I asked, "Is there a problem?"

"You better believe there's a problem. You're in a lot of trouble."

"For what?"

"For what? How about committing fraud against the state of Illinois—that's what. I looked at your records and got suspicious, so I called Northside Clinic. They did not call you in on a guest status, and you're only on 7 milligrams, not 70."

I responded by pulling my five dollars out of my pocket as if I were flashing some big money in his face or something. "Do you think I could get one more dose?"

He chuckled. "Say what?! Can you get one more dose!? You should be asking, 'Am I going to jail?' not 'Can I get one more dose?' You've committed fraud, and I'm pretty sure it's a felony to be on more than one Methadone clinic at the same time. You're going to be banned from all Illinois programs until this gets resolved. You gonna be sick, my friend."

Though I was upset about not getting my dose, I remember thinking, *yeah, right. How are you going to ban me from all state programs?* But that's exactly what they did. I even went to a clinic in the far South Suburbs, and they knew who I was. I literally could not get on a Methadone program in the state of Illinois, and I'm sure there was a warrant issued for my arrest.

Within a day or two, I was starting to get sick, so in desperation, I bought some pills, which only bought me a little time. Not knowing what else to do, I called Gateway. They told me to come down to The Maze the next day, and they would see what they could do.

When I got there, they updated some paperwork on me. I weighed 118 pounds. I was hanging by a thread. I think they knew it, too. They probably sensed that it was now or never. I can't remember who, but one of the staff at The Maze sat me down and informed me...

"Steve, we have a bed available for you at our Kedzie facility."

"Okay, should I go home and get my stuff and come back tomorrow?"

"No, no! We feel you should go today, now. We'll call your dad, and he can bring your stuff later, and we'll get it over there for you. What do you say—you ready?"

"Okay. Can I just get some lunch from McDonald's? I haven't eaten all day."

"Sure. The driver has other stops before he can pick you up. Go ahead and get you some lunch but come right back."

He may not have realized it, but it was quite a gamble letting me walk out the door.

McDonald's was a few doors down, but before getting a quarter-pounder with cheese, I had a little stopover at the liquor store and picked up a pint of Peppermint Schnapps. In a futile attempt to take the edge off my dope sick, I sat in the alley behind The Maze, ate my cheeseburger and fries, and downed it with a pint of Schnapps.

That day, June 6, 1985, I was picked up at The Maze and driven to what was once a four-story apartment building on Chicago's West Side at 1706 N. Kedzie Avenue. Just like that, I was whisked away from the world that I grew up in and was familiar with. A world that I created of my own free will, which at first was fun and exciting, but within 12 short years, started crumbling and falling in on me. It wasn't a good world, but it was all I knew.

I didn't know it at the time, but upon entering the front door at 1706 N. Kedzie, I entered a completely new and different world. A sober world. A world in which I would often feel like "a naked baby, on a hill, in the rain"—a term that would accurately describe the fear, anxiety, and inadequacy I felt being clean and sober in those early days. I instinctively shut my brain off, knowing that if I thought too much, I'd talk myself out of it and run. When the vehicle came, I got in, and I officially became ... a "possibility."

PART V: HELP, A SHORT WORD BUT A LONG PROPOSITION

Kedzie House: Divine intervention

Upon entering the front door, the knot in my gut was somewhat eased when I noticed the warm, comfortable similarities to a home that I saw. However, I also noticed that there were some stark differences. On the left side of the room, there were a few offices. The only thing that disrupted the office feel of that side of the room was the upright piano against the wall.

I was directed to have a seat on a wooden chair, which was placed strangely in the corner, at the end of that hallway, between the living room and the dining room. It was appropriately called The Prospect Chair, because that's all you were at that point—a prospect, "a possibility", and a slim one at that—as I would come to learn. The Chair was a sacred symbol of Gateway's unique culture. It was used for people who were on their way in, and for some on their way out, while staff decided their fate.

I was told to remain in the chair until staff became available to process me in. I sat and watched as the kitchen workers came in and out while preparing dinner. People only glanced at me, but no one said a word to me. Someone walked past me, and I said hi. They said nothing back. I started feeling like I was in an episode of *The Twilight Zone*. Maybe I was dead or invisible? I was starting to feel that way more often. That's when someone came out of an office and informed me that I couldn't talk to anyone while on "the chair."

The alcohol I drank earlier that day, and the handful of pills I had taken the night before, were already wearing off, and I was feeling sick. My nose started running and my muscles began to ache. That's when I realized that I had been on that chair for quite a while. With a sigh of exhaustion, I leaned my head on the wall behind me. Almost immediately, someone with a clipboard in hand, who I assumed was a staff member, walked by and said to me, "We don't put our heads on the wall in Gateway, brother."

I quickly straightened my posture and took my head off the wall. After the tall black man rounded the corner and was out of sight, I remember thinking to myself: *Where am I, and what the hell did I get myself into?* What indeed.

The short answer is, I had gotten myself into a type of treatment setting, known as a "therapeutic community," or TC for short. For the next part of the story to be understood, the answer may require more explanation and a bit of history. So, here it is. I'll try to keep it as simple and coherent as possible.

The first TC for addiction was called Synanon and was started in 1958 in California. The model spread to other parts of the country throughout the 1960s, including a program called Day Top House in New York.

In 1968, Gateway Foundation was established in the Chicago area. These early TCs can best be described with two words—*experimental* and *extreme*. They were sometimes even referred to as a "cult commune." There is evidence that Synanon actually morphed into one and was the subject of several scandals in the 1970s, including the attempted murder of a journalist.

Early TCs seemed to have borrowed some structure and punishments from the military, while other aspects were loosely based on organized religion. There were strict rules and extreme consequences for violating them. It was typical in the early days of the TC to see residents with shaved heads, dressed in a diaper or a dress (if you were a male), or wearing a cardboard sign around their necks for days. You were only allowed to remove them to do chores, eat, and sleep. They were designed by your treatment peers and would reflect a variety of different issues and rule violations. Some were drawn by residents who had real artistic talent, and the signs were quite decent works of art.

Many of the methods used in the early days of Gateway's TC were jokingly known as "humiliation therapy." Though I'm sure there was some therapeutic value in these practices, some of them were discontinued as the TC evolved. Well, that's only partially true. They also decided to do away with some of the practices due to their not-for-profit status.

Gateway needed money, and as more potential donors to the program started getting tours, they would have to explain why most of the residents had no hair, and some were in diapers. Explain as they might, most potential donors didn't get it and were appalled. The likes of diapers and dresses were the first to go, followed by shaving heads or "haircuts," as they were called.

The terms *haircut* and *getting your head shaved* survived but became symbolic metaphors for getting confronted for inappropriate behavior. Signs were the last to go. It was said that one of my peers, Benny, received the last sign at Kedzie House before I entered treatment. Although some of the extreme practices were abandoned, the intense nature of TC treatment remained.

The simplest explanation for how a TC works can be found in the title, Therapeutic Community. The community—the rules, values, structure, and people in it—provided the therapy. When a TC is functioning properly, it provides an environment that is not only conducive to sobriety, but also supports and nurtures personal growth, and positive change. In other words, in the TC, it was time to grow the fuck up! One of the many TC concepts, "Grow or blow," represents the essence of what a TC is all about. Through intensive positive staff and peer pressure, you were going to do one or the other: conform to the values of the program and grow or leave. It was too uncomfortable to hang on to your old "dope fiend ways" in that environment.

One of the essential aspects of the program was the concept that we are our brother's—or sisters, as it were—keepers. Residents were encouraged to confront negative addict behaviors in each other but to use house tools and protocol to do it. Most of the treatment in a TC came from your peers, not the staff. The staff consisted mostly of former residents who had grown into peer leaders themselves and eventually became staff. Their role was primarily to oversee the appropriate functioning of the house and adherence to the schedule, as well as facilitate groups or other program activities.

At the core of the program are the values that are promoted in a TC. These values are rooted in the concept of "right living," which is the belief that there is a right and a wrong way to live life. Simply put, the wrong way was the way we were living, and the right way was the opposite. The belief is that addicts primarily have a life problem—a thinking, attitude, and behavior problem—which when addressed properly, would result in resolving the secondary problem, drug and alcohol abuse.

I remember, early in my treatment, getting into a lot of trouble for relatively small but constant rule violations. I confessed to my counselor, "I want to change. I guess I just don't know how, or what to do."

He replied, "Everything you were doing out there—do the opposite in here. If you were crying out there, stop crying. If you never cried, cry. If you couldn't be trusted, work on becoming trustworthy. If you were lazy, get to work."

I could certainly relate to most of those, especially being lazy. By the time I went into treatment, I had become one of the laziest people on the planet. I turned doing nothing while appearing to be busy into an art form at work. All the while, like a hawk, my eyes were zeroed in on that clock. No wonder time seemed to stand still whenever I was at work.

The TC approach also borrowed many of the principles from self-help programs such as Alcoholics Anonymous and Narcotics Anonymous. Participants took part in and were ultimately responsible for getting themselves well—thus the term "self-help." But this was best achieved with the help of the community and by rigorously following "right living" standards. This part of the concept is based on the principle that one alcoholic or addict can best understand and help another. The following are some of the TC concepts, house tools, and interventions that were used in our treatment at Kedzie House:

THE CONCEPTS
Act as if ....Change your behavior even if your thinking hasn't changed.
All feelings are valid........You can't control the way you feel, only how you respond.
Being up on your feelings..... Experiencing negative feelings.
Be careful what you ask for; you just might get it...You may not be ready for something you want.
Bust your image.............. Let go of masks we wore and images we projected (tough guy, etc.).
Care and Concern.............The spirit that should guide all confrontation of negativity.
Doing a bit..................... Doing time. Not invested in/sliding through treatment.
Drop your guilt .... Confessing verbally or in writing your rule violations/transgressions.
Fake it 'till you make it........ Change your behavior and your thinking will eventually change.

Flip the script .... Turning a confrontation around on the person bringing it.
Get on top of it .... Get it under control.
Grow or blow .... Mature or leave.
Growth before status .... Maturity before you get more trust, responsibility, and power.
Guilt will run you out the door... If you hang on to guilt/secrets, you'll eventually leave.
Horse concept .... If more than one person calls you a horse, it may be time to get a saddle.
If you're aware of it, take care of it... If you see something out of place, it's your responsibility.
Jacket (A) .... A reputation (usually negative).
Let it roll off your back .... Accepting something that you don't like/want to hear.
Re-round .... Come back to address something, usually at a better time.
Re-rounder .... A resident who's been in Gateway treatment before.
Role model-Pace setter .... A person who demonstrates the positive values of the program.
Seek and assume .... To confidently pursue a goal.
Stretching out .... Going above and beyond. Helping out/volunteering in a department that wasn't yours.
There's nothing constant but change ...... Learning to adapt to inevitable change is essential.
Think, think, think .... Think before you act and then think some more.
This is your house .... Promoting a stake in and ownership of our own treatment.
This isn't Burger King .... You can't have it your way in treatment.
To be aware is to be alive ...... Awareness of your surroundings and situations is essential.
Toughen up your baby gut ...... Take it like a man. Stop acting like a child. Cope with your feelings. Grow up!
We are a family .... The promoting of family values.
We are our brother's/sister's keeper... We have a responsibility to hold each other accountable.
What goes around, comes around ... What you put out there is coming back to you in some form. Karma.
When you come to the end of your rope, tie a knot and hang on... Hang in there when it's hard to.
When you think you're looking good, you're looking bad... Seeing through a "look-good artist."
You've got nothing coming ...... You have to start at the bottom. Nobody owes you anything.

You've got to give it away to keep it... You've got to help others as part of staying sober.

HOUSE TOOLS/STRUCTURE

Pull-up............... Making one aware of negative behavior and encouraging them to correct it.

Announcement....... A formal way of letting the entire family know something.

Need Slip .... A request to speak to staff about a need.

Drop a slip ....A written request to address someone in group who created feelings in you.

TPR (Booking, Write-up) .... A written accusation addressing a rule or value violation by you or a peer. If valid, it could result in a Therapeutic Peer Reprimand (TPR).

Morning meeting ...... Mostly a place to share good feelings and growth. A positive start to the day.

Department meeting... Weekly meeting addressing issues in the department you worked in.

Static group............Weekly meeting of the residents on the same caseload and their counselor.

Cluster group.........Otherwise known as "encounter group" to address/confront other residents.

Dropping guilt...... Admitting (usually in writing) all your rule violations/transgressions.

General meeting.... A special meeting with all staff and residents to address serious issues.

House closing...... The entire house is busted. No passes or privileges, G.I. (thorough cleaning), guilt-dropping sessions, etc.

RULE VIOLATIONS

Bad rapping.............Talking negatively about a person or the program behind their back.

Being encapsulated .... Being spacey and forgetful.

Coming off sick ...Lashing out. Abuse or critical comments, not out of care and concern.

Coming out the side of your neck.... Being sarcastic.

Carom shot.........Talking indirectly by saying things to another person that are really about you.

Confronting on the floor... Expressing negative feelings to someone about them outside of group.

Feedback and dialogue...... Responding inappropriately. Talking back.

Flagging............. Daydreaming and not being emotionally present in what you're doing now.

Having an attitude... Holding on to/displaying negative attitudes.

Having eyes...... Being attracted to someone. Flirting.

Hiding out .... Avoiding aspects of treatment that you're uncomfortable with.
Holding guilt .... Keeping secrets about yours or other's transgressions.
Kicking out .... A relaxed posture at inappropriate times.
Mugshot .... A mean or aggressive facial expression.
Negative contracts ... An informal or formal agreement to let someone slide/look the other way.
Profanity .... Usually only allowed in group or individual counseling sessions.
Punching holes .... Finding fault with the program.
Red Crossing .... Defending or rescuing someone being confronted about their attitude/behavior.
Rocks in your jaw ... Carrying an angry facial expression.
Selling a wolf ticket .... Provoking a physical fight.
Setting someone up to react ... Behaving in a way that you know will result in a negative response.
Shooting a curve .... Going around proper protocol.
Shooting dope on the family .... Shirking your responsibilities for others to take care of.
Shooting dry dope ...... Resorting to old/dope fiend behavior but not using drugs.
Spreading poison ...... Gossiping or spreading rumors.
Stuffing .... Avoiding work
Telling war stories ... Glorifying past drug use or related activities.

CONSEQUENCES

Assume the posture .... Confrontation stance: hands behind back, eye contact, legs slightly spread.
Bust .... Consequence that could include loss of privileges, status, etc. Usually two weeks.
Busted down .... Loss of status.
Busted to the Dishpan ... Learning experience, working in the kitchen all day. Doing a lot of dishes.
Busted to the Expeditors (spare parts) ... Whatever they wanted you to do with staff approval.
Busted to the Service Crew ... Back as a Service Crew member.
Confrontation .... Harsh critical feedback.
G.I. .... Military term for General Inspection. Extreme cleaning.
L.E. .... Learning Experience. All consequences were meant to be. Not punishment.
Loss of Pass .... Approval to go on a pass from the unit was revoked.
L.O.P. .... Loss of privileges including Pass, Phone, Visiting, and WAM, etc.

On Ban .... Off-limits. Having no contact with.
Prospect chair.......... Being made to sit in it meant you needed to reflect on why you're here.
Relating to the Scratch Sheet.... A record book that your TPRs were recorded in.
Smoking TPR .... Confrontation/TPR that included getting yelled at.
Talking to............... A verbal warning.
Talk contract.......... You had to be having a serious talk with other residents at certain times of day.
Therapeutic Peer Reprimand (TPR, sometimes nicknamed Medication) ... Negative behavior addressed by a panel of your peers, other residents, but could include staff at times.
7 to 7 work contract...... You worked (various duties) from 7 a.m. to 7 p.m., stopping only for meals.

I'm sure I left some out, but these are the ones that I remember.

I was finally taken off the chair by staff and taken upstairs, where I was given a delousing shower. At least the shower afforded me a little temporary relief from my increasing withdrawal symptoms.

Next, I was taken back downstairs and introduced to my "big brother," Scott Wolfe. All new residents were assigned a big brother or sister, depending on your gender (there were only two back then), whose responsibility was to hang with you, show you around, show you the ropes, and "pull you in" to how things worked. All that aside, their real responsibility was to keep you from leaving— "splitting," as it was called.

Scott was a strong, stocky, wide-faced, young white man in his twenties who was intense, loyal, driven, and seeking approval. Kind of a "ball-washer"—a nickname given to residents who constantly sucked up to staff. Scott reminded me of a friendly, energetic Pitbull. His tongue would even hang out of the side of his mouth on occasion when he was focused on something he was doing. That loyalty and intensity was just what I needed, because once Scott made up his mind about something, he was as tenacious as a Pitbull. I was his first little brother; therefore, I became his project. He was also very knowledgeable about how treatment worked, the house tools, and how to survive and thrive in the environment. Unfortunately for Scott, but fortunately for me, this was not his first rodeo. He had previously been in treatment in various Gateway programs both in the community, and the Cook County jail.

Gateway was one of the first treatment programs to bring treatment into the jails in Illinois. People who had been in Gateway's residential programs in the past were known as "Re-rounders." Re-rounders knew the staff and the ins and outs of the program. Scott liked to talk too, and he explained everything to me. We were on the same caseload, so he filled me in about our counselor, who I hadn't met yet. Scott warned: "Ron's a character. He can be a real hard ass sometimes…oh, sorry, I need to pull myself up…we're not allowed to swear, except in group. Anyway, Ron can be hard, but he can be your best friend if you're doing right. C'mon, I'm supposed to take you on a tour of the facility."

Just then, I noticed my father standing at the front desk with a green garbage bag and my guitar case at his feet.

"That's my dad. Do you mind if I go say goodbye to him?"

"Well, I'm not sure… ah, go ahead. I'll wait here. But just for a minute."

"Hey, Dad. Thanks for bringing my stuff."

"Oh, yeah." He looked away, trying to find something to say.

"They told me you can't have your guitar yet. They'll hang onto it for now. Do you have any money?" he asked.

"No."

"Here." He handed me some bills, which I quickly slipped into my pocket. It was $35, which I later found out I wasn't supposed to have. You had to earn the privilege of "Walking Around Money," or WAM as it was called, and the max you could carry was seven dollars.

"All right, I gotta go," he announced.

"I'll call Mom as soon as I can," I promised.

"Okay."

And with that, he turned and walked out the front door—no tears, no hugs, seemingly no emotions. But if you looked deep into his eyes, it was there. It was hard to tell with him. He never expressed how he felt, so you never knew. I'm sure he was glad I was there, but he likely didn't have a lot of hope that it would really change anything in the long run. Nothing had up to that point.

Scott and I continued the tour of the main floor. The kitchen was big and had professional restaurant equipment, including huge sinks (sometimes referred to as "the dishpan"), a sanitizer, huge refrigerators, freezers, and ovens. There was also an industrial-sized fan in the middle of the room.

Though the building was slightly rundown, the kitchen was spotless. Above the back door hung a lone sign that read, "Grow or Blow," an appropriate message for which I'd soon understand the reason.

Scott explained that this was his department, and he was a kitchen crew member; but he was "seeking and assuming Ramrod of the K-Crew." This meant that he let it be known to staff and residents that he wanted to be promoted to Ramrod of the Kitchen Crew.

Ramrod of a department was the direct supervisor of the crew in that department. Most departments also had a Department Head (or D-Head) and a Coordinator. These were known as "status" positions. They came with more privileges and "juice," or "informal authority" over peers (meaning, you didn't really have authority, when it came down to it) but also more responsibility.

The structure of the TC included a hierarchy that acknowledged personal growth by promoting people to more responsible positions. One of the TC concepts was "growth before status." There were ways to "campaign" or let it be known that you deserved and wanted status. One way was the "growth charts"—no, they didn't measure your height. They were drawn with chalk onto big chalkboards that were attached to the walls in the dining room. Each counselor's caseload would have their turn once per month to get up in front of "The Family" and present their growth. Part of the culture that Gateway promoted was that all staff and residents were members of a treatment family.

Residents would stand up by these charts and measure their personal growth by checking off their accomplishments on the hand-drawn graphs. I don't remember all the things listed on them, but some were privileges you had earned, like phoning, WAM, what your job in the house was. Also, if you were "seeking and assuming" anything like a promotion, transfer to another department, or some other form of accomplishment or growth, including how long you had been clean and sober.

Staff would get input from the house coordinators ultimately decided if you had enough personal growth to earn a status position. Occasionally, they would move someone into a status position who didn't necessarily deserve it, if they thought it would motivate that person to grow. At times, you could get moved into a position because of a "house need." In other words, if you were good at something, like laying floors, and some place in the house needed a new floor, you might find yourself moved to that department or promoted.

Scott deserved the promotion. He was one of the hardest workers in the kitchen, and the kitchen was notorious for being one of the hardest departments to work in. It was tedious, grueling work—and in the Chicago summer—it was also hot and humid. There was no air conditioning except for window units in the directors' and other select offices.

"So, the people I saw working in the kitchen when I was on the chair are residents?" I asked.

"Yep. You probably would have seen me, but I was busy working on dinner. We feed upward of 50 residents and ten staff three times a day. The whole place is run by the residents. This is our house. We do everything that needs to be done, including providing most of the treatment we get. Well, staff plays a big part in that, but most of our treatment comes from each other."

I just stared blankly and nodded my head. I had no idea what he meant.

"Don't worry; you'll see what I mean."

We came out of the kitchen and continued the tour of the ground floor. The dining room had eight-foot folding tables and chairs to seat 60 to 75 people. Another industrial-sized fan sat at the end of the room. Last was the laundry room. It had four laundromat-sized washers in front, and four dryers in back.

Opposite the dining room were three staff offices, a bathroom, and finally, at the end of the hall, the door that led to the backstairs. Only staff and residents with status could use them. Scott was neither of those, so he simply pointed it out, and we went back toward the doorway to the front stairs.

On our way there, we stopped at the piano, and he pointed out a wooden box that sat on top of it. It had a small padlock on it. He said he'd explain later.

The front stairs were directly across from the reception office, occupied by a male desk worker. Scott announced to him, "Relating up to take my little brother on a tour."

He introduced me to a guy, who was also a fellow resident. He explained that the office was known as the E.O., short for the Expeditor's Office. He further explained that the Expeditors were like the house police. Their job was to make constant runs through the house and make sure that everything in the house was in order. The status positions in their department consisted of the Shingle Expeditor, Chief Expeditor, and the highest level of status a resident could achieve in Gateway besides being staff, the "Big Kahuna" ... House Coordinator.

As we went through the doorway and headed up the stairs to the first floor, I noted a resident on the phone, sitting in a chair in an alcove to the right of the stairway. "I miss you too, baby. I got a pass coming in two weeks ..."

No matter how low you kept your voice, your words would echo through that hall. Scott whispered out of respect, "That's where you'll make calls from once you get your phone privileges."

"You mean I can't use the phone anytime I want to?"

"No, you have to earn privileges and request them after you complete certain goals."

"What kind of goals?" I inquired.

"First, you have to memorize The Gateway Philosophy and say it word for word in front of the family. It's in your packet. I'll help you get it done."

As we arrived at the door, he banged on it with his fist and loudly announced, "Brother on the floor!"

Scott explained that this was the "Sister's Floor," which was occupied by only female residents. It consisted of dorms and "The Sister's Lounge," furnished with a couch or two, comfy chairs, a coffee table, and end tables.

Down the hall, there were a few dorms and directly across the hall were the washrooms and showers, and a hallway that led outside to a balcony. At the end of the hallway there were several staff offices. On the left, just before the backstairs, was an office that housed the "Procurement Department."

Procurement's job was to solicit companies for donations. In other words, they were phone solicitors. Gateway relied on these types of donations for things they needed to operate. Because of their not-for-profit status, companies got tax write-offs for these donations. Scott explained that you had to have some good communication skills, and they didn't just put any dope fiend in Procurement. It was a small department and viewed as a kind of "cushy" office job. It was nicknamed "the penthouse".

Across the hall was the Business Office. We stepped in and Scott introduced me to two or three people who were working there, including the staff member who ran it, Alice.

Alice was an older, small, black woman. She could have used a booster chair in that big old desk she sat behind. She peered out at me over the glasses that barely clung to the end of her nose, and in a raspy yet squeaky voice, she asked, "How you doin' baby?"

"I'm okay. Thanks. It's my first day."

"You be all right. You pull him in right now, Scott."

"I will, Alice," he assured her, and we were on our way. Before we left, I noticed a huge sign on the wall that read, "There's nothing that can happen in this day that a drink or a drug won't make worse."

Interesting concept, I thought. I believed that alcohol and drugs made things better, but I was already starting to see things differently.

Next was the second floor. It was laid out exactly like the first floor, the differences being that all the rooms were dorms to accommodate the mostly male population, so there were no staff offices. Also, the balcony was set up with donated weights, so guys were out there lifting weights, or smoking cigs.

Last, but not least was the third floor, which Scott described as the aspiration of every resident in the program. It was known as "Second Phase." It was the re-entry part of the program.

You knew you had "arrived" if you made it to Second Phase. Residents worked, and some also went to school. You were there until you saved enough money to move out, or staff felt it was time for you to go. The Second Phase program had three or four staff, including a Program Director. The lounge area at the end of the hall had three payphones on the wall, a bench, and chairs. Adjacent was the Second Phase lounge. Second Phase residents had the option of eating on their own, or putting in a request to have a plate saved when they knew they would miss a meal due to work or job search.

Out of nowhere, a staff member poked his head out of an office and yelled down the hall, "Hey, Scott. His bags came. They're screened and ready. He's in 202 with the other new guy."

"Okay, I'll take him to his dorm! C'mon, I'll take you to your dorm and you can put your stuff away before dinner."

By this time, all the walking had not only started making my heel throb but sped up my withdrawal symptoms. I started to break into a cold sweat, and I looked a little green around the gills. I was getting sicker by the minute.

"Hey, you okay?" Scott asked, a look of concern on his face.

"I'm getting dope sick, well, more like Methadone sick."

"Oh, that stuff sucks. I'll let staff know. Maybe they'll let you see the nurse if she's still here."

Back on the second floor, we went into the dorm that I was assigned to—202. Sitting on the bottom bunk was a thin black guy who looked to be in his 30s. He looked up from his bag of belongings. "Hey, I'm Cleve."

Another young guy came out of the adjacent bathroom. He was an Irish, elf-looking kid, with what I'd describe as a light brown, "white-guy Afro."

"How's it goin'? I'm Brad."

We all introduced ourselves. Scott informed me that Brad was on Ron's caseload too. Brad pointed to the other bottom bunk and said, "That's yours,

Steve. I like the top bunk." They hadn't filled the fourth bed in the dorm yet, so it was just the three of us.

Cleve and I sat facing each other and rummaging through our stuff in our respective big green garbage bags. I noticed Cleve was sweating profusely and didn't look too good either. His skin was ashy and had a grey cast to it.

"You kickin' too?" I asked.

"Yep, about $350 a day heroin habit."

I could see that he, like me, had goosebumps all over his arms.

"I'm kicking 70 milligrams of Methadone."

"Well, neither of us is going to sleep too good for a while," Cleve lamented.

Brad and Scott started discussing which was worse, heroin or Methadone. Just then, someone poked their head in from another door, which came from the adjacent bathroom that 202 and dorm 201 shared, and put his two cents in. "The heroin will be worse in some ways, but the Methadone is worse in other ways. Neither one of you ma'fuckers is gonna sleep for a while. Hey, honey, I'm David. You're cute," he said, suddenly shifting into a gay voice while giving me the once-over."

Then he turned to Cleve, and in a sudden shift to Ebonics, straight from the hood, he said" "Wassup, my brother? You musta had some bank. $350 a day. Sheeet. You hada been slingin' (selling dope) —right?"

Within a five-minute period, David Grey transformed from a gay man to a black man, and then full-blown Latino! Oddly, the only voice that didn't come out of him was a skinny white guy, which is what he was. I would soon learn that these were not just voices, but distinct, separate personalities, all housed within his skinny ass. As it turned out, there was something even more interesting about David—he was a Re-rounder, and his first stint with Gateway was in the mid-1970s. He was a straight-up dope fiend back then, meaning, he was addicted to IV heroin and cocaine like me.

David would later explain that in those days, when you got to Second Phase, you earned what was called your "wings." This meant that you earned the right to drink alcohol "responsibly." David, who was now back in treatment, left drugs alone, but had now become what he termed "a soup-line, skid-row alcoholic." One of his main messages throughout his treatment was about the dangers of addicts who think they can drink.

"Hey, who do you think will be able to sleep first?" I heard Brad ask. They all debated the question while Scott showed me how to put my clothes away and fold them military style. I slipped the $35 my dad gave me into a rolled-up pair of socks in my drawer.

"Man, you can't sleep on that Methadone crap at all. I know people who were sick for over a month kicking it."

I thought about telling them the miraculous "falling asleep while holding Jesus' hand" story but didn't feel comfortable enough yet to share such an outrageous tale.

Then, the wagers began. "I got three bucks that says heroin man falls asleep before Methadone man." It was like the hardboiled-egg bet scene in the film *Cool Hand Luke*!

Sorry, guys. What's your names again?"

"I'm Cleve."

"I'm Steve."

"Okay, Cleve and Steve... just don't leave!" David said, as he and the others burst into laughter, and David made his way back to his dorm.

"Can you eat?" Scott asked.

"Yeah, I can always eat," I replied."

The way I ate, I should have weighed 300 pounds, but my metabolism was so high, I could never gain any weight. Cleve declined. His dope sickness was further along than mine.

"Try to get some rest, Cleve. C'mon, let's get ready for dinner, little brother," Scott announced.

Cleve curled up in the fetal position on the hard, military-style bunk, as if bracing for what was coming, as the rest of us headed out the door.

I ate my first dinner with my new "family". Introductions would continue, until I eventually met mostly everyone in the First Phase program.

The dining room was noisy and hot. People tried not to stare at me, and I tried not to stare at them, but I guess it's like the scene of an accident; it's hard not to look. After dinner, we were able to "kick out" (relax) in the living room; the TV was turned on and tuned to the 6 p.m. news. On our way there, Scott noticed my limp had gotten worse as the drugs continued to wear off.

"What's wrong with your leg?"

Immediately, the lie I had been telling started to come out of my mouth, but I realized that I didn't have to lie about it to Scott or anyone else in there.

"I shattered my heel when I jumped out of a two-story window in my apartment in California. I was shooting coke for a few days, and I was hallucinating. I hallucinated someone coming out of my closet with a gun in their hand. I would've been okay, but I missed the grass, and one foot landed on the sidewalk."

"Wow, yeah, I know about the paranoia and hallucinations. My thing was coke, too. I was big-time into it and was dealing ounces until I became my own best customer. Did you ever see the movie *Scarface* with Al Pacino? That was my hero. I wanted to be Tony Montana!" His eyes lit up as he spoke.

My eyes and nose were both becoming faucets as my withdrawal symptoms worsened.

"Man, you're in bad shape—aren't you? I'll introduce you to Ron. He should be on duty by now. I'll see if we can get you in to see Anita, the nurse."

Ron was the S.O.D. (staff on duty) that evening. Scott asked the desk worker to call Ron in the Director's Office, where the evening staff usually could be found during the summer. It was one of only a few offices that was air-conditioned. He explained that I was sick and needed to see the nurse.

"Have a seat. I'll call in there," the deskman responded.

We waited as I got sicker by the minute, and my foot continued throbbing from being on it too much.

While we waited, I asked about the wooden box with the small padlock on it that sat atop the piano. It was divided into two halves and two slots on the top. On one side were the letters "TPR," and on the other, the word "Slips." Next to it were blank slips of paper about 4 by 1.5 inches. Scott explained that these were some of the "house tools" and that residents were encouraged to hold themselves and each other accountable for old, negative, inappropriate behaviors as well as rule violations.

TPR stood for Therapeutic Peer Reprimand. They were referred to more commonly as "haircuts," "write-ups," or "bookings." He explained that they were usually investigated by an Expediter, and if found to be valid, the resident would later get confronted, usually by a panel of at least two or three peers, and a Coordinator. Your "peers" were residents who entered the program one month before, or one month after you. The evening was designated for these confrontations, and appropriately nicknamed "Medication Time."

The other tool: "Slips" were used to take someone to group who created feelings in you. In other words, if someone pissed you off, or hurt your feelings, you were not allowed to address them on the floor. Instead, you were encouraged to "drop a slip" on them and take them to Encounter Group or "Cluster Group," as it was called. These groups were on the schedule every Wednesday and Thursday.

Staff and coordinators would retrieve the slips from the box and decide who they wanted to put together in Cluster Group that week. They would decide which confrontations were more important or worthy than others. Slips that would get priority would, of course, be people who were identified as possibly coming to blows if they didn't address their issues.

Next, they would look at the issues that would produce the most growth for the individuals involved. The rest would likely be deemed to be issues that could wait or were just too petty. If they didn't deem your slip worthy enough, you likely wouldn't wind up in the same group with the person you dropped a slip on and would have to "sit on your feelings" for another week. The value of this would often be that you would learn patience and discipline, even if things were getting worse with that person. In some cases, the feelings would resolve on their own, either through talking it out with another peer or that person, or just letting it go because it was no big deal.

These blank pieces of paper also doubled as "Need Slips." If you needed something from staff that wasn't an emergency, you had to fill one out and turn it into the front desk or to a member of the Expediter team. You were not allowed to "drive up" on staff to ask for anything. You had to wait until they responded to your slip. One of the primary goals of treatment at Gateway was to transform people addicted to instant gratification into people who had patience and could delay gratification.

God sends the right man for the job

"Ron will see you guys now." We entered the director's office, and there he sat, the already-infamous Ron Orlando. Ron was a good-sized man with a light-brown, shoulder-length mullet with what looked to be blond streaks and a trim mustache. He wore a pastel, robin's-egg-blue linen blazer and pastel-colored T-shirt. His neck was adorned with several expensive-looking gold chains, and he had rings on the fingers of both hands. He had a dynamic and slightly intimidating presence. He looked up from his paperwork, stood up behind the desk and in a loud, gravelly, Chicago-Italian accent, belted out, "Hey, paisano! What, you don't feel good?"

"No, I'm getting sick."

"You're not gonna be a big baby—are you?"

"No, I've kicked habits before. I'll get through it," I replied, albeit slightly shocked by his question.

Treatment had obviously begun. Then, he suddenly softened. "Okay, Mr. Fiorito. Don't worry, we'll take care of you. You got a good big brother. Take him right up to see Anita. You don't have to tell the desk man to call up there. I'll call and tell her you're on the way."

He smiled and sang my name: "FI-O-RITO! What are you—Calabrese, Napolitano, or Sicilian?"

"Sicilian," I replied.

"Uh oh! Don't go tryin' to run shit around here."

"I won't," I said, smiling.

He came out from behind the desk, and I noticed his faded but expensive jeans and pointed-toe, snakeskin cowboy boots. I also noticed that his walk was sort of stiff.

"All right; go on."

As we left the office, I asked Scott, "What's wrong with Ron's leg?"

"It's fake."

"What?"

"He's got a fake leg. He lost it in a motorcycle accident."

"Holy shit!"

"Pull yourself up, brother."

"What?"

"Ahh, don't worry about it. Like I said, we're not allowed to swear except in group...I'll explain when we go through your orientation packet."

I just wanted to get off my foot and go lie down.

Pain and discomfort: The best medicine

Scott took me up to see the nurse, who doubled as the aerobics instructor. Anita was young, shapely, and so cute, even her short, boyish, haircut couldn't ruin it. How do you think she got guys down on the floor by 6:00 a.m. to do aerobics? She knew guys were probably more interested in looking at her ass than they were in aerobics, but she tolerated it to achieve the greater good of getting a bunch of dope fiends in shape.

After what was mostly a verbal interview and a slight physical, I walked out of there with a prescription for... multivitamins and aspirin. I could also have bed rest anytime I wanted until further notice. Cleve had been granted the same. I have to admit I was a little disappointed that I didn't come away with any good drugs, but in the back of my mind, I knew it was for the best and that it would have defeated the purpose of me being there.

For the next several days, Cleve and I spent a lot of time together, talking in the brother's lounge in the middle of the night. We bonded based on our common misery. We had a lot in common. We were both "a nice guy with a bad problem," as described by the LAPD. Although we had never shared this intimately with a person from another race before, the color of our skin was never an issue. Being two survivors of the "Titanic," known as addiction, became the only thing that was important. We couldn't afford the luxury of racism, which, you got the feeling, was true for most everyone at Kedzie House.

Whoever bet on Cleve being able to sleep first lost. Cleve didn't sleep for 11 days straight. I didn't sleep for nine, that is, if you don't count a little 15-minute cat nap here and there during the day. That was about all the sleep either of us got. It was mid-June, and it was already a hot summer. I remember intense lethargy and constant goosebumps throughout the day in a vicious cycle of hot and cold sweats. The industrial fan in the dining room didn't help much.

The department I was assigned to was The Service Crew. It was the department all new residents started out in. The Service Crew's function was basically to clean the house. No matter how spotless the house actually was—and it was—you cleaned it anyway. How many times could you sweep and mop a clean floor? It turned out the number was infinite. Dust was the equivalent of evil. If staff did a "house run" (an inspection) and found dust, anywhere, someone was in for it. We were being taught attention to detail and a sense of responsibility that was so extreme, we were told, "If you're walking down the hall and you see a matchstick on the floor, and you don't stop to pick it up, you're going to shoot dope again."

We were also taught the concept: "If you're aware of it, take care of it." And if you didn't, you were shirking your responsibility and leaving it for someone else to deal with. This was considered "old" or "dope fiend behavior," and we were said to be "shooting dope on the family." Developing a conscience and responding to it (instead of ignoring it like most of us usually did), was essential if we were going to have a shot at staying clean.

I guess I "shot a lot of dope on the family" that first week or so, due to being in withdrawal, and constantly going to lay down during the day.

There were three things that stood out about my early days in treatment: I was hallucinating from withdrawal and lack of sleep; my foot often throbbed from being on it too much; and I was having a hard time retaining information.

I remember starting to feel seriously concerned about the latter after attending treatment groups or one of the in-house 12-step meetings: Alcoholics Anonymous (AA), Narcotics Anonymous (NA), and Cocaine Anonymous (CA). During these and other groups early in my treatment, I would hear things that started to make sense to me, and that I knew were important, but five minutes after the meeting was over, I couldn't remember anything. I talked about this the first few times I ever spoke in a meeting. "I think drugs made me retarded," I proclaimed. Everyone in the meeting laughed, but I was dead serious. The first thing I was able to retain was a timely statement by the cute blonde, Debbie, who was the chairperson for the Sunday afternoon CA meeting. She always closed the meeting with the statement, "Bring the body and the mind will follow." Man, did I need to hear that! It was my first glimpse of hope that things would get better if I just kept showing up.

Unfortunately, the same couldn't be said for my foot. It was getting worse. One day, Anita looked at it and said, "We gotta send you to County"—the infamous Cook County Hospital. So, she made an appointment for me.

The night before my appointment was the first time I heard my name mentioned on "The Worksheet". The Worksheet was read every night before *"Clear the Floors,"* which is when most residents were required to clear the main floor with few exceptions. We were then required to get ready for bed until *"Lights Out.* The Worksheet consisted of the itinerary and house schedule for the next day and would include residents with appointments, departure and estimated return times—or instructions written to be given "call-back money." Remember, there were no cell phones. We had to find a payphone and to "call back when done" to be picked up by an approved house driver in one of the three house vehicles. Until you reached a certain status level, you were required to be accompanied by "strength," This was a peer who either had some status or who staff had some trust in. On occasion, the resident and their strength would relapse and split treatment together, but that was rare.

Every night, the entire Family would be called into the living room at around 9 p.m., and we would wait while the coordinators put the finishing touches on The Worksheet. Then, the staff on duty would review and approve it. Once approved, a copy would be put in the E.O. for the night monitors to copy onto the giant chalkboards that were on the walls.

The night monitors were two residents who stayed up all night, monitoring the facility with various duties, and then were allowed to sleep all day. All residents would have to pull night duty at some point. The pairings were dictated by staff, and they would pair people for a variety of therapeutic reasons, including learning how to communicate and bond with someone who you would otherwise never have spoken to in the real world.

While we waited for The Worksheet to be read, people would talk and joke around until someone got up and "gave it away." Giving it away was a term that was used when someone would share a song, a poem, or the like. This was also done in the morning at the beginning of Morning Meeting. I remember that we had a few decent singers and piano players who would get up and sing or play the piano in the living room and get us all going. We would start clapping or snapping our fingers, depending on the song. At the end, there was big applause from an entertainment-starved audience of addicts.

I was inspired by this, and I thought of my guitar sitting in the staff office, but I'd immediately get a knot in my gut and couldn't get up the nerve to play. Without drugs and alcohol in me, I was discovering that I had anxiety about performing in front of people. The "naked baby on a hill in the rain" syndrome (anxiety) was upon me. To make matters worse, I was also still going through withdrawal which magnified these feelings.

The COD (Coordinator on Duty) would emerge and ask for everyone's attention and then, read The Worksheet: "New brother Steve F. to go to Cook County Hospital—Scott W. as Strength. Take CTA there and call back $. Call back when done for P/U in the K-2."

The first time you heard your name mentioned in the worksheet, you felt like a celebrity or something. Well, more like you were alive and belonged there. I was officially part of this unlikely, 50-person family.

A new way to start the day—sober

The day would start with the night monitors doing wakeups at 6 a.m. The rule was "feet on the floor" by 6:15. You had 15 minutes to take care of your personal hygiene and make your bed military style. That meant no "snakes" (lines), corners creased and tucked. All beds had the same thin red bedspreads. Then, downstairs for breakfast by 6:30 a.m.

Once I started sleeping, I reverted to my old difficulty waking up. I would literally be half asleep making my bed at times; then I'd fumble and stumble my way downstairs for that coffee. Thank God we had real coffee. I'm not sure I would have made it through June without it. Breakfast ended at 7:15 a.m. and then, back upstairs to tighten up the dorms which would soon get a military-style inspection by the Expeditors. Remember, dust was the enemy! Then, back down to the dining room for Morning Meeting by 7:30 a.m.

As we all would start filing into the dining room, the energy in Morning Meeting would start out low-key most days. People would be talking in a low, almost whisper at first, as we waited for the Staff and the COD to emerge from the DO to formally start the meeting. The energy would build until someone would throw out the challenge: "Okay, who's gonna give it away this morning?" Then, the calls would start for specific people who usually sang material from specific artists. Motown was favored in those days. Some of the favorite songs of our black brothers and sisters were "My Girl," "Heard It Through the Grapevine," "Stop in the Name of Love," and "If You Don't Know Me by Now." They nicknamed these 60s and 70s standards "dusties."

"George, let's hear some Smokey!" referring to my peer George W., who almost always sang Smokey Robinson songs, albeit with shaky falsetto, and a bit "pitchy." He'd be trying to resist the family's urgings by putting a blocking hand up while shaking his head 'no.' It wouldn't take long, before he'd give in and "take the stage." Actually, there was no stage, just the hallway in front of the staff offices that ran the length of the dining room. Someone would yell from the back of the room: "What the family wants, the family gets!" George would start out by leading us in finger-snapping the tempo he needed.

People say I'm the life of the party 'cause I tell a joke or two,
Although I might be laughing, loud and hardy, deep inside, I'm blue,
So take a good look at my face,
You'll see my smile looks out of place,
If you look closer, it's easy to trace the tracks of my tears

  The lyrics of these songs began to come to life. As I thawed out emotionally, I started to feel the pain of missing Laura and my kids. Other feelings started to surface, too, including lust, which I started to feel for a few of my treatment "sisters." One of the first of these was Cynthia Brown.
  Cynthia had gotten into some trouble at Gateway's Lake Villa facility and was "rotated" to Kedzie House. I remember that she was busted when she arrived, and as part of her bust, they made her give one of the Kedzie House dogs a bath out on the deck. One of the more creative LEs (Learning Experiences) I've ever seen.
  What made my attraction to her particularly new and exciting was that she was black. I had never been attracted to a black woman before. Cynthia was of average height and weight, with curves in all the right places. She had beautiful full lips and a great smile. She had a sexy, raspy voice and dark, pretty eyes. Her personality had the diversity that I was starting to admire in a woman. She could be elegant, charming, witty, and funny, but she could also be hard, no BS, and that special brand of tough that most black women seem to possess. I officially had "eyes" for Cynthia, and though it was highly frowned upon by staff, it was a typical part of the drama in treatment. I let her know every chance I got too, and she'd often catch me staring at her in Morning Meeting.
  Some of my peers started to notice, and one of them pulled me over one day. "Boy, you better stop and pull yourself up. She's nothing but trouble."
  As it turned out, it would become nothing more than a harmless game of flirting throughout treatment. Cynthia and I would make jokes that referenced the Sydney Poitier film, *Guess Who's Coming to Dinner*, about how her mother would feel about having an Italian son-in-law, but that's about as far as it ever went. My "eyes" would eventually move on to more familiar territory with the arrival of a new prospect: a petite, cute blonde named Kathy.
  Eventually, during Morning Meeting, the SOD and COD would emerge. Staff would sit in the meeting doing paperwork, mostly keeping a low profile. They would let the a.m. COD run the meeting, including reading from the "Pull-up and Announcement Log." This log was a spiral notebook located in the EO. Residents could ask the desk worker to enter something in it for the next day's Morning Meeting. Pull-ups entered in the book were general issues

observed that the family needed to be aware of and take some kind of corrective action on. Announcements were typically personal things that you wanted to share, like sobriety anniversaries or other good news.

I put my first announcement in the book on my 10th day in treatment. The coordinator running the meeting would announce the author of the Pull-up or Announcement residents entered from the previous day…

"New brother Steve F. has an announcement."

I nervously got to my feet. "Good morning, Family."

"Good morning, Steve!" about forty-some residents replied in unison.

"I just want to say thanks for your patience and that two nights ago, I was able to sleep for the first time in nine days."

The family erupted in a wall of applause, woo-hoos, and whistles.

"Yay for that sleep!" someone yelled.

After my initial burst of confidence subsided, the "naked baby on a hill in the rain" quickly retreated to the safety of his seat.

Though I experienced withdrawal symptoms for over a month, after I started sleeping, my appetite returned with a vengeance. I will never forget the day early in treatment; I got my plate and sat down at the dining room table. My plate was so full of food, it was falling off the plate onto the table. I was shoveling huge mounds of food into my mouth and devouring it, as if I hadn't eaten in a week. I was so in the "food zone" that I had completely blocked out the other forty-some residents in the dining room. It was like I was in a food blackout. Then, it was as if I suddenly snapped out of it. I looked up and froze when I saw that almost the entire dining room was staring at me in silent amazement. I was so embarrassed. Another "naked baby on a hill in the rain" moment. I gained 23 pounds in just under one month.

My first shot of independence

The first sober event would be the 4th of July picnic. Families were encouraged to attend, so I invited my family. Somehow, one of them had gotten word that Laura and my kids were in town. Rhoda came through again and arranged for my family to pick them up and bring them to the picnic.

My memories are vague, but I do remember Jessica running to me when she saw me, yelling. "Daddy, Daddy, Daddy!" Jessica always had an unshakable sunny disposition that melted my heart as she put her arms around me. On the other hand, Melissa was more aloof and moodier. She was three years old and barely knew who I was. There was a definite need to develop a relationship with her. I remember feeling concerned about it. It would be a tall order in the situation that we now found ourselves in.

Speaking of not knowing who I was, another memorable moment that day was when my sister Mary Jo, who attended to show her support, looked me dead in the face and walked past me. I was shocked as she went by me. "Hey!"

She turned and did a double take. "Oh my God! Is that you, Steven?" With 23 pounds on me, and the color returned to my cheeks, she didn't recognize me.

The event was well organized and had activities planned for the kids and adults. I remember that we all had a good time, and the kids had fun too. It was cool to see everybody interacting with their kids and families. Albie seemed to be at peace knowing that "her baby" was safe and being "fixed."

But, just like that, it was over much too soon. The kids waved out the back window as they drove away. Once out of sight, the reality of how I failed my them settled over me, accompanied by a wave of sadness and emptiness.

As I continued to thaw out emotionally, my preoccupation with missing my kids and Laura grew, and at one point, started to interfere with treatment. Luckily, my counselor, Ron Orlando, was there with his highly sophisticated counseling skills to help. I like to refer to this technique as his "bitch-slap you back into reality" approach. He looked up from his paperwork at the end of our individual session, consisting of me whining for almost an hour, and said: "You need to pretend that you don't have kids right now. You didn't care if you spent their diaper money when you were out there using. Here's what you need to get through that *"capatosta,"* hard head of yours. Do what you gotta do for yourself, and the rest will fall into place."

He then advised me, "You need to focus on treatment and recovery right now, nothing else. If my mother got between me and my recovery, I'd cut her loose, and I love my mother dearly. Okay, time's up. See ya later."

I left his office thinking to myself, *wow, this guy is one cold-ass motherfucker.* But, as it turned out, he wasn't at all. He was 100 percent right.

Ex-drug users look to future

On Wednesday, July 24, 1985, Program Director Diane Schwartz called me and another resident into her office. Diane was an older woman with a big, ratted, 1960s, auburn hairdo. You could tell she was a wild one in her day. She and husband Chuck were now clean and sober and rode motorcycles. The treatment staff were role models for us and seemingly meaningless facts like that demonstrated that fun and adventure were still possible sober.

Both were some of the original pioneers of the TC in the Chicago area. That story could be an interesting book in and of itself. Apparently, one of the biggest heroin and cocaine busts of all time occurred earlier that day, and the *Chicago Sun-Times* covered it. As a side story, they decided to do an article on addiction treatment. I'm still not sure why I was chosen, other than they apparently wanted some racial balance, along with a newer, and an older resident who had been in treatment for different lengths of time.

John S. was an older black man who had an interesting feature that he would occasionally use as a reminder of his addicted past and what brought him to treatment. He had apparently got into a drug-related fight and had a bad scar on his nose where someone had tried to bite it off. We both signed some waivers even though they didn't use our last names. *Sun-Times* reporter Don Hayner entered the DO and sat down in a chair beside Diane's desk. The interview lasted about an hour. The article was titled "Ex-drug users look to future," and I believe it came out a few days later.

I was proud of being in the newspaper, but more importantly, after reading it, I had a sense that there was hope for me, even though I was still in pretty bad shape at that time.

No refuge, finally, from ourselves

As August approached, and the industrial fans continued to blow the sweltering heat around in the house, my treatment advanced, and I was finally able to come off orientation status. This advancement started with me standing in front of the family in Morning Meeting and reciting "The Gateway Philosophy" word for word. It was written in 1965 by Richard Beauvais, an early resident of one of the first TCs—Day Top House in New York. I stood up in the dining room in front of the family, and after being asked by a peer from their seat, "Why are we here?" I nervously recited the following…

"We are here because there is no refuge, finally, from ourselves. Until a person confronts himself in the eyes and hearts of others, he is running. Until he suffers them to share his secrets, he has no safety from them. Afraid to be known, he can know neither himself nor any other. He will be alone.

Where else but in our common ground can we find such a mirror? Here, at last, a person can appear clearly to himself, not as the giant of his dreams nor the dwarf of his fears, but as a man, part of a whole, with a share in its purpose.

In this ground, we can each take root and grow, not alone anymore as in death, but alive to ourselves and to others."

I know…it's a bit sexist. I'm not sure why Richard wrote it the way he did, but it did somewhat accurately reflect that most clients in treatment were (and still are) male. It has always been difficult to get women to seek treatment. The reasons for this could probably be the subject of yet another book. Funny thing is no one gave a shit about it back then. Female residents simply replaced the word "man" with "woman." Brilliant, huh!?

I'd like to tell you about the profound impact those words had on me, but if I did, I'd be lying. Though I was able to get some of it, back then, it was mostly just some nice words that I had to memorize to get off orientation and get more privileges and freedom. That freedom included phoning, visiting, and WAM privileges. My first 12-hour pass with "strength," was not far off.

One of my issues at this time was my inability to internalize much of the wisdom that was constantly being shared with me. Nothing sank in very far. I ran mostly on superficial, intellectual autopilot. This was probably for several reasons, not the least of which being lingering withdrawal symptoms. But the biggest reason was likely my stunted emotional growth, which had me emotionally at about 16 years old while chronologically being 25.

As I settled in and got more comfortable, I got back into some old behavior that had plagued me all my life. I had a hard time following the rules, and there were plenty of them. Some of the rules were a bit tight-assed in my book, and I obviously hadn't abandoned "my book" at this point. One rule I struggled with was that you couldn't touch the TV at all until you had a certain level of status. What if the volume was too low and I couldn't hear it!? Who was going to turn it up if there were no status peers around!? I was—that's who!

In most families, there's that sibling that you just don't get along with. In Gateway, this was a fellow resident who would be your arch-nemesis. Everybody had one…didn't they? This person would go out of their way to make sure you got every bit of treatment that you came for. Someone who had so much "care and concern" for you, that they would be hiding around every corner, waiting with pen and paper already in hand to "help" you.

Mine was Mark Narowicz. A big, greasy, creepy, pockmark-faced Polack, who always seemed to magically appear out of nowhere right at the precise moment I broke a rule. He'd have that crazy, crooked smile on his face that seemed to say, *I got you again*. He'd say something like, "Man, how many times does a brother have to tell you—you can't touch the TV?" Or, with that thick, ghetto Polish accent, "*Pool* yourself up."

As Scott eventually explained, "pull-ups" were yet another house tool. Any resident could issue a pull-up to any other resident. It was meant to make someone aware of their negative behavior and strongly encourage them to correct it. If someone started to lose it and started swearing, you might hear a fellow resident say, "You need to pull yourself up on that language, brother (or sister, as it were)." The proper response to a pull-up was "Thanks, I'll get on top of that" or just "Thank you." You'd be surprised, though, at the uncanny knack some residents had to make "Thank you" sound like "Fuck you."

John Clark was one of these. John was a Re-rounder who was an ace at camouflaging his rebellion and disdain for you or certain rules within the house tools. John became an important person in my treatment. More on John later.

I recall the "honeymoon" officially being over for me and hitting my first "brick wall" on one particularly hot and muggy day. They had worked us to death that day with a food order that came in. This was virtually a truckload of canned and boxed goods that would come in from time to time. We would form a human chain from the truck to the storage room and pass the boxes and gallon cans down the line. To attempt to make it fun, we would all yell out the food as we passed it to the next person; "corn giblets!"

Because of my history of laziness and the fact that my years of drug and alcohol use had seriously depleted me physically, low energy was yet another major barrier that I struggled with mightily in treatment.

I can't recall how, but a few days earlier I had gotten word that Laura and my kids had moved back to California to live with coke dealer Tony. I was devastated. I felt upset, hurt, and angry, and I wanted to give up on everything.

Then, like rubbing salt in the wound, later that evening, at the AA meeting, there was a lot of talk about God—a subject that, although I had cracked the door on, I still knew little about. I felt lost. People told me to "turn Laura over to God," but I had no relationship with God at that point, and didn't know how.

When the meeting ended, everyone headed outside to the deck or to the living room to chat and smoke. I just sat there alone, sinking deeper into a wave of depression, likely magnified by lingering withdrawal symptoms that would come and go. Luckily, one of the guys who came to the meeting from the outside came back into the dining room to get some coffee and noticed me sitting there. He came up to me and asked, "Everything okay?"

Depressed and filled with self-pity, and confusion, I answered, "Not really. I just don't know if this is for me. I don't think I can do this."

Looking back, I may have just been looking for an excuse to leave and go get high. I had always used drugs to cope with negative feelings.

He responded with words that were more intuitive than they were profound. He said, "I understand. Let me ask you something—was your life good when you were out there using?"

I didn't have to think about that for long. "No," I replied.

"So, what do you have to lose by trying this?"

"Nothing."

"I'll tell you what. I'll make a deal with you. You do everything these people tell you to do to the best of your ability for one year, and I'll meet you back here one year from now on August 17th, 1986, and if your life hasn't gotten better and you still want to go back out there and use, I'll go with you."

"Wow! You'd do that?"

"Yep, but you know what? I won't have to, because you won't want to. Give it a chance, brother." And with that, he walked away.

His words echoed in my mind— "Give it a chance." I had never given anything much of a chance to work in my life… that is…except drugs. I'd given them almost 12 years to work, and they didn't anymore. It made sense, even to an idiot like me, and I snapped back into reality. It's called Alcoholics Anonymous because everyone is anonymous. That guy saved my life, and I don't even remember his name. I wonder if he showed up on August 17th, 1986.

As time went by in treatment, all my issues started coming to the surface. I was lazy, dishonest, and immature. I also had low self-esteem, which I covered up with grandiosity and humor. As I later heard described in an A.A. meeting, I was "an egomaniac with an inferiority complex."

We are here because there is no refuge, finally, from ourselves. Until a person confronts himself in the eyes and hearts of others, he is running. Until he suffers them to share his secrets, he has no safety from them.

I was also in complete denial about most of it. I had a distorted perception of myself and the world…

Where else but in our common ground can we find such a mirror? Here at last, a person can appear clearly to himself, not as the giant of his dreams, nor the dwarf of his fears, but as a man, part of a whole, with a share in its purpose.

Though it was painful, I desperately needed that mirror.

I started to develop a "jacket"—a reputation. I was dubbed "The King of Rash" (short for rationalization), by my peers. A title that I'm sure was initiated by Mark Narowicz. In other words, I was constantly playing by my own rules. Upon noting this, my counselor, once again, was there to intervene with another simple yet profound observation that would stick in my mind like peanut butter sticks to the roof of one's mouth.

Ron observed, "Fiorito, you think you have all the answers; trouble is, they changed all the questions." I began to realize that I had the answers to the wrong questions.

He also developed a clinically therapeutic, individualized treatment plan to address these and other issues. He delivered it to me while passing through Morning Meeting one day as I was blah, blah, blahing to the family.

Ron announced, "Fiorito, your treatment plan is easy… NO and SHUT UP!!" The entire dining room erupted in laughter, including me. Getting fronted off by Ron always brought up mixed emotions for me—embarrassment, hurt, and humor—but most importantly—I felt he genuinely cared about me.

Now clean for almost three months, as the fog began to dissipate from my brain, realizations and self-awareness started to develop. Symbolically, two album titles from the days at Matt's house started popping into my mind on a regular basis: *Everything You Know is Wrong* and *We're All Bozos on this Bus*, both by the comedy group The Firesign Theater. They took on a whole new and more serious meaning. Hell, just about everything I knew *was* wrong—wasn't it? I started questioning myself for the first time in my life. The often-repeated treatment slogan "Your best thinking got you here," put it into more accurate terms. I started to realize, albeit on a somewhat superficial level, that as smart as I was, it never got me anywhere—an important early realization for me.

As far as being "Bozos" goes, we were all clowns of one sort or another. "Performing" and wearing "masks" to cover up our true feelings of inadequacy, fear, and sadness. Trying to fit in and please those around us while selfishly thinking only of ourselves and failing miserably at both. And now we were all on "this bus" together, trying to find our way to…I didn't know where…anywhere but where we came from. Again, Smokey Robinson depicted most of us in his hit song Tears of a Clown...

Now, if there's a smile upon my face,
It's only there tryin' to fool the public,
But when it comes down to foolin' you,
Now, honey, that's quite a different subject,

Don't let my glad expression,
Give you the wrong impression,
'Cause really I'm sad,
Oh, I'm sadder than sad
You're gone and I'm hurting so bad,
Like a clown, I pretend to be glad.

Now there's some sad things known to man,
But ain't too much sadder than the tears of a clown,
When there's no one around.

We were all covering up the fact that though we were smiling on the outside, we were all hurting on the inside. We were using drugs to cover up or change our feelings, run from life, cover up shame and pain, and avoid responsibility. We were master "avoiders."

Until a person confronts himself in the eyes and hearts of others, he is running. Until he suffers them to share his secrets, he has no safety from them.

I learned; that's what dope fiends do. But there was hope that by the grace of God, with the help of the staff, and each other, we could change.

In this ground, we can each take root and grow, not alone anymore as in death, but alive to ourselves and to others.

The push I needed out of my comfort zone

Weekends at Kedzie House were pretty laid back if you didn't have a pass. There were later wakeup and breakfast times, and no treatment groups. Most of us looked forward to seeing the people from the real world who would come in to chair the in-house meetings. NA was Fridays at 7 p.m., AA was Saturdays at 7 p.m., and CA was Sundays at 2:30 p.m. On Sunday mornings, you could sign up to go to the local Catholic Church for 9 a.m. Mass. Visiting, for those who had the privilege, was from 10 a.m. to 2 p.m.

On Saturdays, there was still a morning meeting. Everybody who had a pass had to "give it away" before they could leave. It was not optional. If you were one of those people with horrible stage fright who had avoided getting up in front of the family and giving it away, this was going to be your big debut. People would be up there sweating, stammering, and wringing their hands—trying to get through it. You just wanted to shoot 'em and put 'em out of their misery. We'd usually let them off the hook with an offkey version of "Take Me Out to the Ballgame," "Little Sally Saucer," or "The Itsy-Bitsy Spider."

Afterward, the TV came on, and people just hung out in the living room and watched it until lunch was made by a volunteer K-Crew. The real K-Crew usually had the weekends off.

This rare relaxation time happened only briefly during the week, for about an hour after dinner. Unfortunately, it was never long before an Expediter would interrupt any relaxation you were experiencing with these words: "Can I get a grateful brother to mop the dining room?"

Oh, how I dreaded those words every day after dinner. So much so, that I would sink low into the couch when I saw an Expediter come around.

Of course, this eventually backfired on me when they started taking notice. "Ah, brother Steve. You feelin' grateful today?"

"Yes, I am brother."

"Could you mop the dining room today?"

"I sure can, brother."

"THANK (fuck) you" (we all knew the code for *fuck you* was putting the extra emphasis on the word THANK).

"No, THANK (fuck) you, brother!" the Expediter replied.

Oh my God! You'd have thought that I just got asked to unload a semi-trailer by myself. I mean, the dining room (which included the kitchen and the hallway) was big, but it wasn't *that* big. It was indicative of how lazy I'd become. It was hard for me to do anything I didn't want to do.

So, after struggling through lingering withdrawal symptoms, laziness, lack of work ethic, and low energy all week, Saturdays were the closest thing to a shot of dope there was. To say I looked forward to Saturdays all week, would be an understatement. This is why what happened one particular Saturday morning turned out to be such a milestone in my early treatment.

I should begin by telling you how it all started. Due to my lack of ability to play my guitar early in treatment, my ego—the need for attention and approval from others—reverted to my old standby of drawing. I did a few drawings, and a few residents marveled at my "talent." Word got to the staff that I could draw, and that's what ultimately led to what occurred that day.

The SOD was Joe Michaels. He was a younger, good-looking, charismatic guy, who, looking back, had no training or counseling skills whatsoever. But then again, who did back then, especially at Gateway? He was a nice enough guy, wouldn't hesitate to bust your balls, and was sarcastic—which seemed to be a prerequisite to be a substance abuse counselor in those days. He saw one of my drawings, and it gave him an idea. He apparently called Director Diane Schwartz and got the idea approved before he approached me.

That Saturday morning, I had kicked back and got so comfy watching TV on one of the couches, I had almost melted into it and become part of it. Joe walked up and with a big grin on his face, said, "Hey buddy, how's it going?"

I looked up at him, almost startled due to my state of deep relaxation.

"Good," I said, without moving a muscle.

"One of the guys showed me one of the drawings you did. Pretty impressive."

"Thanks."

"Hey, c'mon. Let me show you something," and he headed toward the dining room.

"I talked to Diane about an idea and she liked it. C'mon, I'll show you."

I reluctantly unglued myself from the couch and followed him to what turned out to be the laundry room. When we arrived, he stood there staring at a blank wall above the dryers, his head nodding up and down in an affirmative motion with a huge smile on his face.

"See that wall?"

"Yeah." (We both now had huge smiles on our faces).

"What do you think about a big mural right there?"

"Yeah, that would be cool."

"It would—wouldn't it?"

"Yeah, I think it would," I agreed.

"Me too. I'll tell you what" as he pulled the giant staff key ring off his belt. "Here's the key to Operations. Why don't you go down there and see what you need and get started on it?"

I'm sure my smile had dropped off a bit here and was replaced by a look of shock.

Then, after resuming the big fake grin on my face, I nodded my head in agreement. "Okay, yep."

"Great! Go unlock OP and then bring me back the keys—okay?"

"Okay, yep."

So, I took the key ring from him and headed toward the boiler room, which is where the Operations Department was located. With that same fake-ass grin on my face, on my way past the living room, I glanced longingly at the couch, which still held my body's imprint where, just minutes earlier, I lay in a total state of cozy relaxation and condoned laziness. It was Saturday—dammit!

I re-composed myself and unlocked the door. I turned on the lights, and looked around at the workbench, shelves, and tools hanging on the wall.

"FUCK, FUCK FUCK!!!" I pulled myself up and walked back to give Joe the keys with my re-established fake grin. "Here ya go Joe."

"Thanks Steve. Check in and let me know how things are going once you're ready to start."

"Okay, Joe."

Operations was the department in charge of maintenance and repairs of the facility. Part of my advancement off orientation was that I had also received a job change to the OP crew. There were always people with backgrounds in the trades in treatment, keeping the house in a pretty good state of repair.

Now, here I was on my day off, having to do a project at the whim of some ex-dope-fiend staff member with visions of grandeur for, of all things, the laundry room! I was so pissed off, I honestly thought about leaving. It didn't take much back then. Don't forget, I was a guy who walked off jobs for no reason other than I didn't feel like being there. What made matters worse, I had no idea what to do for this mural. Now I knew why my brother Paul couldn't be an artist for a living. You just can't be forced to be creative. Or can you?

I sat there, mumbling obscenities under my breath. "If you want a mural there, why the fuck don't you do it!? What the fuck am I supposed to do?"

I was drawing a blank. As I paced back and forth, I noticed my reflection in the windowpane of the door. I had a Chicago Fest T-shirt on. It featured a not very detailed rendering of the Chicago skyline. The next thing I saw was a big roll of masking tape. Then, my eyes shifted to a shelf full of cans of spray paint. Then, it hit me! I would use the shirt as a model, and the masking tape and black spray paint to do an outline of the Chicago skyline! I saw a 1-by-2-foot piece of cardboard sitting on the bench and I thought, *I'll use that to make a stencil for the words Kedzie House, right in the middle of the skyline.*

I saw that one of the large rolls of masking tape was almost gone and I thought, *that's the perfect size for a moon in the sky.* But I would only do a half-moon with the outline of a face. I came flying out of OP like a man on a mission. I told Joe about my idea.

"Sounds cool: let's do it!" he encouraged.

I went back to get my supplies, which also included a metal yardstick for a straightedge. I grabbed a cup of coffee from the dining room that had been set out for the family, and next thing I knew, I was up on top of the dryers with my shirt off in the sweltering heat and humidity, using my shirt for a model. I was like a man possessed. I was into it! I had this surge of energy that I didn't know I had! It seemed to come out of nowhere.

Within minutes I was challenged by an Expediter doing a house run.

"Who cleared it for you to be in here doing that?"

"Joe Michaels."

"Did he clear you to have your shirt off and have coffee in here, too?"

"No, but I don't think he's going to care about that. Besides, it's like 100 degrees in here!"

I was right. He didn't care, and he gave the Expediters explicit instructions to "leave Fiorito the fuck alone" and that I could have as much coffee as I wanted.

I applied the masking tape until I had the skyline laid out. Once the outline was complete, I opened the window, put on my dust mask, and sprayed the black paint while using cardboard to protect the wall from overspray. I got the idea that instead of the bottom of the landscape being straight, I would make it look as though the whole city had been ripped out of the ground and was floating in the air. So, the bottom was jagged and got thicker in the middle and tapered toward the ends. An Expediter poked his head in. "Hey, it's lunchtime. Come on down and eat."

"Okay, in a minute."

"Looks good, man."

"Thanks. Wait 'til you see it when it's done!"

They had to practically pull me off those dryers to get me to stop and eat lunch, and then I was right back at it until dinner.

The mural was completed later that evening and turned out really well! I was proud of it, and I got a lot of compliments from staff and peers, but something much more valuable happened that day.

I learned that I could overcome and triumph over my negative feelings. I had never been able to do that before. I had been a puppet of my feelings for most of my life, up until that day. If I didn't feel like going to school or work, I didn't go. If I felt like running, I ran. If I felt like hitting you, I hit you. And if I felt like getting high…I got high. Sure, I had done things that I didn't want to do before, but always begrudgingly. I never completely overcame those kinds of feelings and transformed them into positive energy like I did in that situation, on that day. Even more important was the fact that I was acutely aware of what had happened and the significance of it. The realization made it an important learning experience and a building block of the foundation of a new identity that I somehow needed to forge of myself.

I talked about the experience, and my subsequent self-realization in meetings several times after that day. What I found was that talking about these realizations in meetings enhanced these breakthroughs even more. There's just some kind of magic in seeing other people's heads nodding as you're talking about things instead of just keeping them in your head. It's very affirming and validates their significance. I think talking about them in meetings helped to internalize these experiences and made them part of the new internal structure that I was slowly building.

The next day was Sunday, which was visiting day for residents who had earned the privilege and weren't on pass. There would be kids and family members running around the house until 2 or 3 p.m. If there were a lot of guests, it could get pretty chaotic.

All guests had to use a bathroom that was in the middle of the hall off the dining room. It was clearly marked: "Guest Bathroom." Because the strength in the house was thin due to people being on pass, residents would be asked to step up and perform some of the duties usually done by older residents. I was asked to do a house run.

A typical house run started at the front stairs, went through the upper floors, then down the backstairs to the back of the dining room, and through the remainder of the ground floor. As I made my way through the laundry room and dining room, I stopped to check on the guest bathroom, which was unoccupied. I flipped the light switch. I was somewhat shocked by what I saw.

It was trashed! The soap was out of the dish and in the sink, there was water all over the place, the floor was muddy, footprints were everywhere, pee was in the toilet and on the seat, and the garbage overflowed with paper towels onto the floor. One of the concepts we were taught in treatment was, "If you're aware of it, take care of it." This meant that it was now my responsibility to clean up this mess. So, I did, all the while thinking, *I'm going to put this in the Pull-up and Announcement Log and announce my good deed on Monday in front of the entire family.*

I felt at least I'd get a pat on the back from my peers and staff for cleaning it up, and come Monday morning, that's exactly what happened. The accolades that came from the family were personified in one of the shoutouts I received— "Showing growth, brother!" — and I was. Wasn't I? The true significance of this incident would come unexpectedly in the distant future.

Sober celebration delivers hope, not dope

It was the end of the summer of 1985. Not too long ago, I had stepped off a bus in LA and my world went from color to black and white. In some ways, it stayed that way right up until the day of the luau—a big Hawaiian-themed party at Kedzie House.

It was a beautiful summer day and there wasn't a cloud in the robin's-egg-blue sky. The entire house, including the deck and the backyard, was decorated. Most of the sisters and women staff wore flowers in their hair and some even had grass skirts on. Don't ask me where they got them because I have no idea. Everybody wore a variety of colored leis around their necks.

I remember stepping outside just in time for the Hawaiian music cassette to stop, and the surprise live entertainment to begin. Someone with a small electric piano started with the intro. Then, four black brothers, each with a different-colored lei around his neck, were all dressed in similar colorful shirts and black pants. Then, they started humming along with the piano. They snapped their fingers and moved in a choreographed rhythm to the music. In perfect four-part harmony, they quietly sang…

Oh how I wish that it would rain, woo oo oo oo,
Oh how I wish that it would rain, woo oo oo oo…

Then, their lead singer joined them and took center stage. He had on a white linen blazer, white pants, a colorful Hawaiian shirt, multicolored leis around his neck, and black Blues-Brothers-style sunglasses on. It was Ron Orlando! He confidently belted out:

Sunshine, blue skies, please go away,
My girl has found another, and gone away,
With her went my future; my life is filled with gloom,
So day after day, I stay locked up in my room,
I know to you, it might sound strange, but I wish it would rain.

And the boys answered back: *Oh, how I wish that it would rain, woo oo oo oo…*

The background vocals were perfect, as were the dance steps. They even had the hand gestures down. The Temptations and The Four Tops had nothing on these guys! I was inspired, and I wanted to be up there with them.

I'll never forget the sights, sounds, smells, and feelings of that day. A day the sun shone extra brightly, and the sky was bluer than I'd seen it in years. I'm sure I've fallen far short of describing the significance of that day. That's because it wasn't so much what was happening around me, as what was starting to happen inside me that made it special. I had been clean and sober for three months. I hadn't been clean and sober for three days since I turned 13.

Something came alive in me that day, as if my feelings broke through a barrier. I was starting to come back to life, and I was getting these spurts of natural pleasure on occasion. I was starting to recover. Now, it was time for my music to recover with me.

I finally started singing in Morning Meeting. I remember getting up in front of the family for the first time and with my eyes closed, singing "Statesboro Blues. It didn't win me a Grammy, but at least people knew I could sing. My song selection attracted the attention of the Staff on Duty—Jeff K., who was also a big Allman Brothers fan and a musician.

Jeff was a short, long-haired, bearded Jewish guy with a singing voice that made you think, *where the hell did that come from?* He was a drummer back in the day who still messed around and played on occasion but wasn't as serious as he once was. Jeff was known as the "Re-rounder counselor" because most of the Re-rounders who made it back to treatment after relapsing or re-offending (usually both) went to Jeff's caseload. This was likely because he was one of the few counselors who still consistently attended 12-step meetings. Most of the other staff relied solely on their treatment at Gateway to stay clean and sober. I should mention, this did not work out well for most of them.

He came out of the office after I finished; "Whoa! Fiorito can sing! Hey, I got one for you." He went into what turned out to be his old stand-by, "It's Not My Cross to Bear" by The Allman Brothers. One of my memorable moments in treatment was Jeff and I trading off verses on the song in Morning Meeting. I couldn't tell if the standing ovation we got was mostly due to the family sucking up to Jeff, or that we really sounded that good. Hey, a standing-o is a standing-o! I figured I'd take it any way I could get it.

I was starting to gain my musical confidence back, but I still had a long way to go. I remember the first few times playing my guitar and singing for the family. Out of nowhere, my leg would start shaking from nervousness. Talk about social anxiety. It became apparent that these were the kinds of feelings I used drugs over. I'm sure if I hadn't been in a drug-free, safe environment, I would have used. I just had to work through it. Eventually, I did, but initially, I could feel the uncomfortable self-consciousness trying to overtake me.

I did songs by my favorite artists like The Eagles, The Allman Brothers, John Lennon, and The Beatles, along with a few originals. Eventually, I developed a sense of confidence, and my leg stopped shaking when I played.

Growth comes from unexpected places

Though our scheduled gatherings were usually positive, one of the things everyone dreaded at Kedzie House was staff calling all the First Phase residents downstairs impromptu, into the living room or dining room. When that happened, it was usually serious. Once all residents were accounted for, staff would then order us to "assume the posture" (stand at attention with hands clasped behind our back). Each staff member would take turns expounding for 15 minutes or so, while we stood there sweating.

On one occasion, right after dinner, it happened. Staff started out with what I like to call the "This is your house" spiel. They pointed out how we needed to treat things with respect, and have gratitude for having the things we had, which were mostly the result of others' generous donations.

Then Rory Leonardi appeared from the dining room holding one of the Corelle dinnerware plates in his hand. Rory was my least favorite counselor in treatment. There was just something not right about him that I couldn't put my finger on. The word "snake" comes to mind. He didn't like me either, probably because I smelled how full of shit he was, and he sensed it.

He held the plate up high, so we could all see it and said, "Who could have done this!?" There was a huge wad of purple gum that had melted onto the bottom of the plate after going through the sanitizer. Everyone stood stoic, silent, and bewildered, well… everyone except me. I immediately recognized its majestic purple color, and realized it was mine. I remembered taking the giant wad of gum out of my mouth and sticking it to the underside rim of my plate. I intended to resume chewing it after dinner but forgot about it. Whoever was running dishes through the sanitizer didn't catch it, and this was the result. Apparently, my bad luck with big wads of purple gum didn't end in fifth grade.

When these types of confrontations happened, and they asked who was responsible, it was not a hypothetical question, nor one to be taken lightly. They wanted and expected the answer. If they didn't get it, no one was going anywhere until they did. I wanted to do the right thing for once in my life and I immediately felt this "tug of war" inside me. Before I could think of the potential consequences, I immediately shut my brain off, stepped forward, raised my hand in the air, and out of my mouth came, "I could have done that."

Somehow, I knew that if I thought about it too long, I would talk myself out of doing the right thing, so I stopped thinking and "impulsively" stepped forward and took responsibility.

Everyone was dismissed, and I was told to have a seat outside the DO until staff called me in. As everyone filed out of the room, I remember the smiles and looks of approval and respect I got from fellow residents.

This was the new culture that was beginning to have a positive effect on me. The new values of integrity and courage to step up and take your "medicine", were what was honored and respected in this place. These values started taking hold and replacing the "getting over" or "getting away with it" mentality I came in the door with. Don't get me wrong, those old ways were far from over, but at least they had some healthy competition.

I received my first bust to the dishpan, which I was sent to immediately. I washed and dried the remaining dishes from dinner, solo, which luckily, weren't many. After washing and drying the last dish, I announced to Ron that I was done. Apparently, he didn't feel that was adequate penance. He replied, "Hold on. I got something for you."

The next thing I knew, the entire family was coming into the kitchen, bringing stacks of clean dishes from the cabinets and setting them down for me to run through the sanitizer. All 45 First Phase residents crammed into the kitchen behind me per Ron's direction, followed by Ron with my guitar in his hands. Ron announced that they would serenade me as I worked. He played the opening chords and then the entire group sang "Louie Louie" to me as I did dishes. Even though I feared more consequences, I couldn't wipe the smile from my face due to the absurdity of what was happening!

> *A Louie, Louie, oh no, I said a we gotta go, yai yai yai yai*
> *I said a Louie Louie, oh, baby, I said a we gotta go....*

The song was brief because of course, no one knows most of the actual words to the song.

It wouldn't be long before I'd again need to rely on the same "positive impulsiveness" that I used in the gum incident, to save my treatment and quite possibly my life.

As I mentioned previously, Gateway's not-for-profit status required them to rely on donations, fundraising, and other ways to pay for the program. One of these was their annual raffle. They would sell raffle tickets practically year-round and then raffle off some nice prizes right before the holidays. All of Gateway's facilities would take part, and the residents of all three residential programs were pitted against each other in competition.

There was a big posterboard thermometer on the dining room wall that showed how much money Kedzie House had raised. It was updated weekly. High-selling clients would be rewarded with incentives like dinner and movie vouchers. They had us wearing Gateway vests, aprons, and hats, so the public didn't think it was a scam. It was a big deal. You didn't go out on raffle trips until they had some trust in you because they knew you were going to handle money. We were taught a little pitch, something like: "Would you like to help fight drug abuse today?" and sent out there to sell as many tickets as possible.

I couldn't wait to go out on my first trip, just to get out of the house, if nothing else. The day finally came, and I was told I was going out on the raffle trip and given my hat, apron, and a stack of tickets. I was excited!

There were two separate teams going out that day. One team was going downtown, and our team was going to the familiar Belmont and Broadway area. Gateway's outpatient program, The Maze, was just around the corner, on Clark and Diversey—my old Methadone clinic, *Interventions*. I realized we would be there around lunchtime. I started contemplating who would be hanging around the clinic or at the Golden Nugget restaurant across the street, selling their Methadone. Then, I remembered the $35 in my sock drawer.

Suddenly, that old switch got flipped in my brain. The wheels started turning and I couldn't stop. It was like trying to push back against a bulldozer.

As the two groups were preparing to leave, I made an excuse to the deskman to shoot upstairs to "get something I forgot." I grabbed the money, stuffed it into my pocket, and came back down. As everyone assembled in the living room, I was thinking about the high I'd soon experience due to my tolerance likely going down. I started divvying up the doses in my mind. I figured that I could get three or four doses out of 70 milligrams, keeping in mind that I didn't want to get so high that it would be noticeable.

The Strength for each team called out: "Let's get everybody into the vehicles and get rolling." So, that was it. I was going to get high. Everything I'd been through, and all the changes I'd made up to that point, would all go out the window. I remember thinking as I was headed toward the front door, *What's the point of being here if I'm just going to keep getting high? Wait...NO!*

I could feel the thought of that euphoric opiate high coming back. It had been kicking the door in and regained entry into my brain. As I got to the front door, I abruptly turned around. I again shut my brain off and stopped thinking, just like I had with the gum incident. Deep inside, I was aware of and feared my tendency to talk myself out of doing the right thing. It was always easy for me. Like a zombie, with my brain completely shut down, I made a beeline for the DO. I knew Ron was SOD that day.

My steps quickened as I knew I was running out of time. I practically crashed through the door as I burst into the office like someone looking for a toilet to puke in!

Ron looked up at me from his paperwork like I was crazy. "What's up?!" Still, in my Gateway T-shirt, apron, and hat, I ripped the money from my pocket and slammed it down on the desk. "Here, I was about to go get high."

Ron looked at me and smiled; "Okay, where'd you get the money?"

"My dad gave it to me when I first came in. I hid it in my sock drawer."

"Okay. Good man. You did the right thing. You know you're busted to the dishpan again, though—right?"

"Yeah, I figured."

"Very good, Steve, you showed a lot of growth. You got anything else in your dorm that I should know about?"

"No."

"Go take off your apron and hat and relate to the scratch sheet that you're busted to the dishpan per Ron Orlando. I'll put your money on the books for you."

One of the important lessons I learned in treatment was just because you did the right thing, it doesn't always mean there are no consequences. Just like in the real world, sometimes there's still a price to pay for being honest. The rewards would come later and be more meaningful. I had to believe that.

I'd like to attach some deep, philosophical meaning to why I did the right thing that day, but I really can't. In retrospect, the best I can surmise is that I just happened to be in the right place at the right time, and perhaps, somewhere inside me, I recognized that I could change if I just put in a little effort. Like my school report cards always said: "Steven could be a good student if he'd just apply himself". I just didn't want to do what I'd always done—blow it that early in the game.

After I got out of my bust, I started going out on raffle trips regularly. While out there selling tickets to strangers on the street, I made two important discoveries. First, I had the gift of gab and usually sold over 50 tickets every time I went out. There were people who would go out for six hours and sell 20 tickets, or less. Second, it was a great way to get girls' phone numbers. You'd be surprised at how many women were impressed that I was in treatment and willing to give me their phone number.

I met a little blonde cutie named Cheryl. We instantly hit it off and she gave me her number. I told her I had a weekend pass coming soon and we made plans to hook up. She was an acting major enrolled in college from a rural town in Iowa. She was pretty, happy, normal, sweet and unassuming. The fact that someone like her liked me was another early boost to my self-esteem. Cheryl was my first sober romantic relationship.

I felt that getting phone numbers was the true benefit of selling raffle tickets. I had no idea at the time how important my other discovery was. I was a natural salesman. I discovered I was good at reading people. This included how approachable they were and how to approach them. I also had a good sense of who wasn't approachable, and it kept me from wasting time on people who weren't interested. I would find people's "funny bone" and make them laugh, or at least smile, and quickly developed rapport with them. Once I did, I had them, and they would buy at least two or three tickets—they were $5 each. I didn't realize it then, but I was learning to use negative skills I'd acquired in my addiction in a positive way. Although there were other residents who were better than me, I just missed winning high seller for the week—twice.

Selling raffle tickets, as it turned out, was unexpectedly crucial in helping me develop self-confidence and rebuild my battered self-esteem. I can say that it turned out to be one of the most beneficial things I did in treatment.

When I first entered treatment, if someone would have laid out everything they did on a table and said, "You can pick only two. Which do you think will be most valuable to you?" I would have picked individual counseling and caseload group. Although I would have been somewhat right about caseload group, I would have been dead wrong about individual counseling. As it turned out, Ron was a terrible individual counselor. He mostly did paperwork during our individuals. He would pick up his head and look at me occasionally. "Uh huh. Uh huh." For one of my individuals, he took me to a carwash to get his Cadillac Gucci Seville washed.

I would have never guessed that selling raffle tickets and mopping the kitchen floor would have been the things that helped me the most in treatment, but in some ways, it was true. Selling raffle tickets, mopping, and other physical activities had huge hidden benefits to my low self-esteem and laziness, but the physical stress began to take its toll on my ailing foot.

I began to limp much more and found my foot throbbing so much that I had permission to get off it and elevate it in the evening. During my appointment at Cook County a few months back, they confirmed what I'd already been told in California. I needed surgery to rebreak the heel and realign the bone. They said whenever I was ready, they would do it. At the time, I felt I was too new in treatment and wanted to wait. Probably a rare, wise decision, but it was getting obvious that I couldn't put it off any longer.

Cook County Hospital: Where addicts go for gunshot wounds and more

As I sat on the examination table in my hospital gown, I remember thinking about drugs for the first time in months. After all, I was getting surgery, and surgery to an addict is a license to take narcotics. Talk about preoccupation—I probably should have been thinking about whether I'd walk with a limp the rest of my life, instead of what kind of drugs I'd be justified in taking. The exam room curtain swung open abruptly, snapping me out of my drug daydream. I looked up and saw several medical staff and a gurney. "You ready, Mr. Fiorito?"

"Ready."

Next thing I knew, I was being wheeled down the hall to the operating room while someone gave me the generic "what to expect" spiel. They parked me out in the hall and gave me a shot to relax me…Yeah, baby…was I ever relaxed… Demerol, I think. Possibly a vintage 1984. Mild, semi-fruity bouquet, with a moderate rush (kick in the chest), and medicinal aftertaste!

They wheeled me in, put the mask over my face, and it was done. The next time I opened my eyes, I had a newly constructed heel, and I was in a lot of pain, so I got a few more freebee shots of Demerol, compliments of the Illinois taxpayers.

The next day, I was picked up by some residents returning to the house from some appointments in the area. I was on crutches and in a cast shoe. I filled a prescription for Tylenol #4 with codeine, an antibiotic, and some kind of antibacterial foot soak at the hospital pharmacy. I also had instructions for taking care of my foot for the next three to four weeks.

Upon my return, I met with Anita, who confiscated everything and issued the orders that staff would need to follow. I was on light duty and could only engage in things that would not result in discomfort. If I experienced any, I had permission to stop whatever I was doing, go sit down, and elevate my foot. I also had to soak my foot daily for 30 minutes to prevent infection in my stitches and then replace the bandage. Though I would have preferred Demerol over Tylenol with codeine, it was all a lazy, dope fiend's dream come true.

Once I got off my crutches, I was put back on the Service Crew and couldn't do much for the first couple of days. I would go up to the second-floor brother's lounge and soak my foot for 30 minutes as instructed. Soon, 30 minutes became 40 minutes, then 45. It was so peaceful and quiet up there; it only made sense that I would take a little nappy. Sometimes, I would have trouble waking up and had to be woken up by an Expediter doing a house run.

"You cleared to be up here doing that?"

"Yep, per medical staff Anita."

"Okay," he reluctantly conceded with a raised eyebrow.

One evening, as dinner was being prepared, I was asked if I could help set up the dining room. I explained that I couldn't because my foot was bothering me. I then proceeded to head outside to the patio. After sitting on the deck for a while, I noticed the basketball on the ground and walked over and began to shoot baskets. Being the terrible shot that I was, I wound up chasing the ball around a lot. Little did I know, this scene did not go unnoticed by several of my peers.

Peeling a layer of the onion called denial

Another Wednesday brought about another group with Ron's caseload. As I hobbled toward the brother's lounge, I could see that our entire caseload (six or seven other guys) was already there and sitting in a typical loose circle. As I entered the room, everyone abruptly stopped talking as all eyes were upon me, and I started to get an uneasy feeling in my gut. I grabbed an open chair, and as soon as I sat down, everybody got up, bringing their chairs with them, and repositioned themselves directly across from me. The knot in my gut tightened. I felt like a guy who was about to face a firing squad. Then, Ron announced: "Benny's got an issue to bring up. Benny."

Benny L. was one of the most respected residents in the house. In fact, at one point, I called Benny my first Higher Power. After he told his life story to the family one afternoon (something we all had to do), my jaw was literally hanging on the floor in shock, followed by awe and inspiration. I remember thinking after his story, *if this guy can stay clean, I can.* I also thought it was a miracle that someone with his background could be happy and successful, which he appeared to be, at least as much as one could be in treatment.

Benny was once a high-ranking street gang leader for the Chicago-based Vice Lords. He did time in Pontiac penitentiary, where he was indicted and charged with 15 counts of murder for his role in the 1979 Pontiac prison riots. He was placed on death row at Statesville penitentiary. I don't recall all the details, but he was acquitted and given a chance to go to treatment. He took it. Now he sat across from me, looking ready to pounce.

"Steve Fiorito (he and I always addressed each other by our full names), we been watchin' you. Man, you're bogus. You playin' that foot, brother!"

"What?! I just had surgery!" I interrupted, almost jumping out of my chair.

Ron then interrupted me. "Just listen, Steve."

Benny continued, "I saw you tell the Ramrod of the Service Crew you couldn't set the table because of your foot. Then, twenty minutes later, you're out there shooting baskets!"

"Yeah, but..."

Benny interrupted, "I'm gonna turn it over to these guys, and they can tell you what they've seen."

I squirmed in my seat with discomfort, like a cornered badger.

Benny's little brother, James Minter, went first. James was a short, stocky, self-admitted "thug, hustler, gangster and a pickpocket" in the streets. However, in treatment he was what was known as a "therapeutic robot." James wanted to change so badly; he lived every moment in treatment by the book and followed the rules to the letter. He was surprisingly soft-spoken, speaking in mostly treatment lingo, and program slogans.

James would have handcuffed himself to Benny if they'd have let him. Benny was flattered and tolerant but slightly annoyed with his constant bragging and name dropping; "My big-brother Benny....". The general feeling was that when you saw James coming, you went the other way for fear that you'd be pulled up, or some other house tool would soon be used on you.

In his typical quiet, shaky voice: "Yeah, brother, I've seen you up here soaking your foot and sleeping, and..."

I again interrupted. "I have a doctor's order to be up here soaking my foot!"

"Yeah, but that doesn't give you the right to be sleeping—does it?"

"What else am I supposed to do!?"

Ron intervened again, a little louder: "Steve, just listen, man."

Next was James P., usually the comic relief of our caseload. He had a good-sized Afro and a sarcastic Richard Pryor-like sense of humor. He was truly a funny guy, and we had become friends, but just the same, he let me have it, as did my big brother Scott, and the rest of the guys.

"Doesn't your doctor's order say soak your foot for 30 minutes? Man, I've seen you up here for at least an hour a few times."

I became angry and defensive. The more defensive I became, the more confrontational they became. They were like sharks that smelled blood. They were circling, and I was bleeding bullshit badly. In a last-ditch effort to survive the "attack," I yelled, with arm outstretched and pointing at one peer's face: "Why the fuck should I listen to anything you say? You're an ASSHOLE!"

With that, Ron intervened one last time and yelled: "All right, that's it! Fiorito, sit on your hands, shut the fuck up, and listen!! You say one more word and I swear you won't go out on another pass until you're forty!"

This was apparently enough incentive to shut me up verbally, but in my mind, I continued cursing them out and listing all their defects. They went down the line until the last "bullet was fired." My denial, bound and blindfolded, was now slumped over, bleeding, and mortally wounded. The trouble is the symptoms of addiction are like cats—they have nine lives. Ron announced: "You're busted. I can't bust you to the dishpan with your foot, but we'll find something for you to do." I sat through the rest of caseload, pouting with my hands under my ass cheeks.

After the group ended, no one said a word to me as they went downstairs to get ready for lunch. It's like they sensed I needed to sit with my thoughts for a while to let it sink in.

I retreated to my dorm, which was steps away from the lounge. I sat on my bunk, replaying what happened in my head. I was huffing and puffing and running through the list of all the things I saw wrong with them in my mind, when suddenly, the first realization hit. I realized that I had not really listened to nor considered, one thing that was brought to me in that group. That was the story of my life. I hadn't ever *really* listened to anybody. I heard them, but never considered what people were saying to me. Whenever anyone would tell me anything, my pat response was always, "I know." In reality, I didn't know. It was important for me to start recognizing and admitting my character defects.

In that caseload group, I was too busy defending myself and focusing on "the messengers," not the message, and on the only defense I had—the doctor's order. Then, the second, and more important realization hit me. They were absolutely right. I *was* milking that doctor's order to avoid work and using it to get privileges that I really didn't have coming. Reality finally sunk in, and I admitted to myself that I was wrong. It was a rude awakening to think that I could have such a distorted perception of reality, and myself, but at the same time, it was a relief. Deep down, I think I knew it was the kind of awakening I came to treatment to have, and that, in fact, my life depended on it.

As it turned out, my bust was good for the house, too. I was relegated to the Operations Department, and I again put masking tape and spray paint to use. I made permanent Growth Charts for the dining room that no longer needed to be drawn by hand with chalk. I also made a bunch of new wooden plaques and signs for the walls throughout the house. They were mostly AA slogans like "Blind Faith," "First Things First," and the oft repeated "One Day at a Time." It's understandable when you consider how important it is for an addict to live life one day at a time. It was drummed into our heads over and over. One—Day—at — a —Time. Okay, I got it! It was a simple enough concept to understand—right? I would soon learn that though I understood it intellectually, I had no idea of its significance, or how to actually do it.

As fall snuck up on us, bringing temperatures in the 50s, I started to feel that old subtle excitement I used to experience as a kid. My love for the season seemed to run deeper than the obvious reasons of Halloween, the crisp air, and the turning leaves. Maybe it was that I was born in November. Fall was one of the things I missed the most when I was in Southern California. I realized that these feelings were magnified when I took my pain pills.

I started looking forward to medication time a bit too much. I felt myself slipping back into some opiate craving and it brought about yet another internal battle. I thought, *why did I come here?* It wasn't to keep using drugs. The day of truth arrived when I realized that my foot was no longer in that much pain. When medication was called that evening, I informed Ron (who happened to be on duty) that I no longer needed the pills, and that he should throw them out. I would just take a few aspirins instead. He looked a little shocked at first but smiled and said, "Okay, Steve. Good." Though it was only Tylenol with codeine, it was still a huge breakthrough for me. Had I really changed that much in less than five months? Only time would tell.

By this point in treatment, I had developed comfort and familiarity with most of my fellow residents. Of course, you gravitate to certain people that you feel are on your level, and relationships start to form. Being a white guy from the suburbs, I was most comfortable with people of my own ilk, and, of course, who had a sense of humor. That remained an important part of who I was, and in some ways, became even more important. It was difficult to get through a place like Gateway-Kedzie House without one.

I can't remember exactly when, but John Clark entered treatment sometime after me. John was overweight and had shoulder-length sandy-brown hair that helped hide the fact that his head was too big. He was older, in his late thirties I believe, and oddly, he had upper and lower dentures. I remember him sitting in the brother's lounge in his pajamas, wrapped in a blanket, no teeth, sweating his ass off, going through withdrawal when he first came in, just like Cleve and I had. John and David Grey became fast friends, which was typical for Re-rounders. They tended to gravitate towards each other due to having that common bond of previous experience that only Re-rounders had. Both had an edgy, irreverent sense of humor and became much of the comic relief for our peer group. I remember John leading games of "Porno-Hangman" on the chalkboard in the brother's lounge before lights-out. There would be words that only dope fiends would have in their vocabulary, like A_ SC_ SS.

"Ahhh…B?"

"Yep." A BSC_ SS.

"ABCESS!?"

"You got it, buddy! Tell him what he's won, Dave!"

"You've won a brand-spankin' new pair of plastic shower slippers, courtesy of Cook County Department of Corrections!" he said in his gay voice.

We'd be smoking cigarettes and telling an occasional forbidden "war story" and laughing our asses off! It was some of the first good belly laughs I remember having in treatment. We could laugh at how insane we were now that we were under this "umbrella" of safety.

John and David always walked a fine line between love and respect for the program, and irreverence and even disdain for it at times. This respect or disdain, as it were, was often directed at specific staff. For instance, Ron Orlando was one of those counselors you either loved or hated. His brash, outspoken "my way or the highway" style could easily be construed as arrogance and often was. John could take or leave Ron, but David hated him, that is, until something happened that would completely erase his hatred.

John was usually soft-spoken with a natural quiver in his voice, like he was always out of breath but then he'd surprise you with an infectious, deep, hardy laugh. He was an unlikely but natural leader who had a knack for pulling people together for whatever cause or purpose he might have.

He pulled some of the singers from the house together to form an acapella singing group. Now that we didn't have drugs, what else did we have? We were still above ground and had our sense of humor, music, and each other. We were forced to rely on our own natural devices to entertain ourselves.

John scouted out the guys who could really sing and I was one of them. He recruited George W. for his falsetto and Larry S. for his baritone. Frank W. was a straight-up thug and gangster on the streets. But in treatment, he was our brother, and the best damn singer in the house. When he sang "Up on the Roof" by The Drifters, you felt like you getting a professional performance. He'd get up in front of the family and start snapping his fingers. Everyone would join and start snapping theirs, bobbing their heads, and swaying in their chairs.

When this old world starts getting me down
And people are just too much for me to face
I climb way up to the top of the stairs
And all my cares just drift right into space

On the roof is peaceful as can be
And there, the world below can't bother me
Let me tell you now

When I come home feeling tired and beat
I go up where the air is fresh and sweet

From our chairs, the family would chime in the background vocals: *(Up on the roof)*

I get away from the hustling crowds
And all that rat race noise down in the street (Up on the roof)

On the roof's the only place I know
Where you just have to wish to make it so
Let's go, up on the roof (Up on the roof) ...

The song touched something inside all of us due to the program's demands for constant interaction with each other, exposure, intense scrutiny of our defects, and pressure to change. Each of us, in our own way, longed for that refuge that we could retreat to, even for just an hour or two. It was hard to find it at Kedzie House. Like I said before, even your private phone conversations echoed through the stairway for all to hear, no matter how softly you spoke.

It turned out that John knew every word of these old dusty doo-wop songs, by some of the late 1950s and early '60s artists and groups. The rest of us were familiar with a few but not all the songs, so John would direct us and show us our parts. John was the lead vocalist on most of the stuff but gave it up to Frank on a few, like "Up on the Roof." We would get together with staff's permission in an office, or the laundry room (when not in use) and worked on "Daddy's Home" by The Limelites, "Come and Go with Me" by The Del-Vikings, "Duke of Earl" by Gene Chandler, and others.

At times, we'd nail it, and we could feel what it was like standing on a street corner under the streetlight in the 1950s. After perfecting the harmonies and our sound (as perfect as it was going to get anyway), we needed a name, which I promptly came up with. George, Larry and Frank were black. John and I were white, so of course, the name of the group was…The Oreos.

John would get so nervous when we performed in front of an audience, the quiver in his voice would increase. Luckily, he would somehow stay in key, and it was mistaken for vibrato. We finally got our "big break" when another treatment program somewhere in the city was having a Halloween party and needed some entertainment. They heard about us and called the staff to ask if we could come and perform at their party. We, of course, accepted and were driven over by a house driver.

We laughed and joked all the way there that this wasn't exactly the limo ride we felt we deserved, but for now, it would do. It would be The Oreos' first and last outside gig.

The group was short-lived, but a great experience nonetheless and an early creative outlet. I really can't remember exactly why we stopped, except that we were dealt a big blow when Frank split treatment. The straight life just wasn't for him. It's a catch-22 though, because neither was the crooked life.

Cheryl went back to college in September. We wrote to each other regularly at first but then the relationship just faded and died a natural death.

Once again, I started going to my parents' and a few outside meetings on my passes. I was starting to get comfortable speaking in meetings and was learning all the "recovery lingo." I started coming to a lot of realizations about myself, my addiction, and my recovery, and I was learning to articulate them. I went to The Maze on Belmont and Broadway to a CA meeting on Tuesday's. But my favorite meeting was still the Friday night in-house NA meeting.

It was chaired (presided over) by Al R. Al was usually accompanied by his entourage of "NA elites"—people who had at least a few years clean. This included a guy we nicknamed "Orange Cary" due to his fake tan that had a slightly orange cast to it. He used what I believe was the first sunless tanning cream that came out, and it was bad.

Al was a throwback from the 1950s, complete with bouffant hairdo and leather jacket. He talked with a thick Chicago-Bridgeport neighborhood accent. Al missed his calling and should have been a stand-up comedian. He was seriously funny with a dry, sarcastic sense of humor, especially when it came to describing the trials and tribulations of addiction and recovery. He was one of the first people who made it okay to laugh at ourselves and the absurdities of an addict's lifestyle. He could also be very philosophical and insightful at times and would always close the meeting with some profound observation based on everyone's comments. He'd then end the meeting with the same one-liner every time: "And remember, dental work is part of recovery."

Though this was funny, it was also a harsh reality of early recovery for many. Our drug use and related lifestyles took a toll on our dental health. "Don't delay. Call a dentist today!" Al would say. He would have us all cracking up.

One observation that stood out to me went something like this...

"One of my big problems in early recovery was that all my memories were connected in some way to using drugs. If I thought about my past, I would automatically think about drugs. The cool thing about having five years clean is, I have a lot of good sober memories. Now, when I reminisce about good times, I can think about good times I've had clean and sober."

That was it! I had seen and heard enough. This guy had everything I wanted. One of the concepts expressed in the chapter "How It Works" in the NA text was...

If you want what we have to offer and are willing to make the effort to get it, then you are ready to take certain steps.

I looked up to Al, and I wanted what he had—his confidence that bordered on cockiness, his knowledge and wisdom, the respect he got from others, and his sharp sense of humor. As for the bouffant hairdo, that's where I drew the line—not my style.

After the meeting, though I was feeling intimidated and nervous, I approached him. "Hey Al, can I talk to You? I need a sponsor... and I was wondering if you could be my sponsor."

"Sure, we can give it a shot. Here's my number. Call me anytime."

He gave me his number and that was it; just like that, I had a sponsor, and a very cool one at that. I would also later, fortify my "sponsor arsenal" by acquiring a second sponsor at my CA meeting. I was officially "sponsored up" and loaded for bear!

Happier Halloween

Kedzie House was having yet another sober dance party, this time for Halloween. They had hosted several parties since I entered treatment and although I enjoyed them, I, of course, was much too cool to actually dance. I never did, didn't know how, and was intent on keeping it that way. The brothers in treatment were always trying to get me to dance. They grew up watching

Soul Train. I did not. An occasional glimpse of *American Bandstand* on my way out the door was as far as I made it into the dance scene.

This was a costume party, and we were all directed to dress up. That's right; it was mandatory. Part of treatment at Kedzie House was "busting your image" from the streets, and they did, every chance they got. A lot of us acted put out by the fact that we were being forced to dress up, but secretly, deep down, you could tell that people were really enjoying it.

One of my peers, Sue Ann, and I got to talking about what to do for our costumes, and we decided to be a pimp and a prostitute. This is when I learned a new term for prostitute— "ho" (street slang for *whore*). This probably wouldn't have gone over well with the staff since it was a little too "close to home" for some of the sisters. Many of them had prostituted themselves for drugs. So, we put the same twist on it that I had done when I worked at Bally. I was the ho, and Sue Ann was my pimp.

We had a gas putting our costumes together. The sisters all pitched in for mine, and dug deep (well, not really that deep) into their drawers to find the sluttiest stuff they had for me. This included a long brunette wig, black pantyhose, a sexy lingerie top, a leopard print purse, and nice-sized fake rack.

On the day of the party, the girls had a lot of fun doing my makeup. The finishing touch was the stiletto heels, but they also had to teach me how to walk in those things. When they were done, they walked me over to the full-length mirror in the hall, with shock in their eyes and mischief in their smiles. I was hot! Hell, I would have done me.

Sue Ann emerged from her dorm with her full-length fur coat, fedora hat with one feather, too much jewelry, and a thin penciled mustache. She saw me and fell over laughing. Downstairs, we continued to have fun with it.

Our first "victim" was James Minter. Sue Ann introduced me as Linda, a guest, who had come to the party. James smiled and introduced himself. The lust in his eyes was hard to hide. Sue Ann and I couldn't hold it in anymore and started cracking up. James recognized my laugh. His eyes got really big. "Oh my God! Oh my God! Is that you, Steve? Oh my God! You got me. Man, you really had me going." We even got a rare curse word out of him. "You asshole."

We continued to mess with people as guests started to arrive. Thank God for the people who would come to the house for meetings and events from the outside. They were out there in the real world, staying clean. They gave us hope that it could be done. One of them was "Pontiac Joe," a nickname given to him because of his many stints in the penitentiary in Pontiac, Illinois. Joe was a short, stocky, Italian, construction-worker type.

After he gave a lead and told his story at one of the meetings, we found out we had something in common. Or should I say, *someone* in common? Remember Annie, whose apartment was a shooting gallery where I used to cop dope? It turns out Annie was Joe's sister. I almost fainted when we figured it out. I couldn't believe that Joe could have a sister who was out there that bad, while Joe was in recovery for some years. He looked at the floor sadly and said, "I tried to help her numerous times, Steve. She just doesn't want it."

He described who she was when they were young and growing up together. It was hard for me to imagine, but she was a normal, healthy person at one time. I guess that was true for most of us. Very sad.

Our charade continued with another resident we fooled, Robert Randall. He was a big, slightly overweight black man, with a loud, rough voice, and an infectious, outgoing spirit.

One Saturday, I was doing a house run. As I walked past the entrance to the kitchen, my attention was grabbed by an animated figure in the dishpan, scrubbing the huge pots and pans used to cook for the residents of Kedzie House. I backtracked and watched in amazement as Robert vigorously scrubbed a pot that I could literally fit into. Suds were flying everywhere, and…he was singing! I stood there watching him for a while, mesmerized. I came up behind him and confessed, "Robert, I was standing there watching you, and I gotta say, you're the only person that could make washing some pots and pans look fun. I mean, I wanted to come in here and join you!"

He responded with some of the wisest words I would ever hear. He said, "Stevie, we, as dope fiends, are always trying to extract life out of life. Squeezin' it dry! What I've learned since being in recovery is, we gotta put life into our life. With the right energy and the right attitude, we can get enjoyment outta whatever we have to do in life!"

These are the kinds of philosophies that were imparted to me on a regular basis in treatment. I call it "junkie wisdom."

Robert had recently completed First Phase and had gotten offered a position as staff over the kitchen. He was a good chef, and food was his middle name. His response when he found out it was me inside that skirt was: "Can you cook? I'd marry Stevie if he could cook!" Luckily for both of us, I couldn't boil water back then.

Al showed up, his entourage in tow. They were all characters from the sitcom *Happy Days*. Al was, of course… "The Fonz." Not much of a costume when you consider that he dressed like Fonzie most of the time anyway. It was Friday, so as the clock neared 7:30 p.m., they announced that the meeting would be upstairs in the brothers' lounge. Al chaired the NA meeting as usual, but with a few twists. Instead of being surrounded by a bunch of dope fiends, he was surrounded by ghosts, goblins, a pimp, and a ho, as well as the most exotic characters possible by digging deep in one's drawers and closet.

Instead of ending the meeting with his usual public service announcement for dental work, he confessed, with what started as a serious tone, "Ya know, I've gotten a lot better in the five years I've been clean, but I know I'm still sick cause I'm sittin' here tryin' to look up Steve's skirt!"

The room erupted in laughter.

"Okay, let's end this thing and get back to the party," Al directed. We stood in a circle, held hands, and as we always did at the end of a meeting, recited the Lord's Prayer and the Serenity Prayer before descending the stairs to continue the music, dancing, eating and laughing. Albeit with some reluctance, we had all begun to accept our new way to party—clean and sober!

Birthday surprise

As another page turned on the calendar, I could see the little square on it that meant my birthday was in sight. I noted that it fell quite perfectly on a Saturday. I figured out that I would have a pass coming that weekend if I waited an extra week to request it. The stars were aligning, and everything was falling into place for a nice family party. This would not only mean seeing my family and an abundance of great food, but also a nice haul of gifts and some sorely needed cash on my books. I called my mom to let her know I'd be coming home that weekend and I'm sure I wasn't subtle in hinting at my expectations—homemade lasagna and banana cream pie!

To get a pass, you'd put in a request a week before. Staff would process the requests and either approve or deny them based on any number of things. So, in the weeks leading up to my request, I proceeded to "tiptoe" around. I believe the term we used was "walking on eggshells." I thought to myself, *I got this.* I would make sure they had absolutely no reason to deny my pass. I didn't so much as crack an eggshell in the weeks leading up to my pass request. As it turned out, my efforts did not go unnoticed.

Everyone who submitted requests lined up outside of the office their counselor occupied and entered one at a time to get the results of their request. My fellow "Orlando's Commandos" went in ahead of me for their results. I felt better about things after hearing "Approved" from Ron for each of them. He seemed to be in a good mood as he delivered each "verdict." As my turn came, I stepped into the office as Ron shuffled through the remaining requests. "Let's see, Fiorito...Oh, here it is." He looked up at me with a big smile, "No."

"Excuse me—what?" in shock, thinking I misunderstood.

"It was a no. You didn't get your pass."

I just stood there dumbfounded. "Okay."

I turned and walked out of the office, still in shock. The shock was replaced by anger. I'm sure my peers could see the smoke coming from my ears as I passed them. As I made my way down the hall, I got a few pats on the shoulder and words of encouragement; "You'll get it next time."

I sat on the couch in the living room and stared out the window, ("flagging"), thinking about leaving. Just as I was about to boil over and make a bad decision, several peers came to my rescue. James Minter, Scott, and Brad surrounded me. James brought the care and concern, Scott brought the strength and courage, and Brad brought the comic relief. "Between you and me, Ron can be a big dick!" Brad joked in a whisper.

I pointed out that I had done everything right for two weeks. I earned that pass. James responded with the painful truth, "Boy, you been walking around here on eggshells. You haven't dropped any slips or written any haircuts for weeks. Staff looks at that as avoiding treatment, knucklehead!"

He was right; I had emotionally disengaged from most of treatment because I didn't want to make any waves, and staff knew it. Fortunately, they talked me "off the ledge," and I was able to let it go and regain my composure.

In the weeks that followed my "birthday surprise," it started to become apparent that I wasn't the only one disengaging from treatment. There was an overall decline in slips being dropped and haircuts being written. This usually meant there was likely an increase in "negative contracts" in the house. A negative contract could be a spoken or unspoken agreement between peers, to look the other way when engaging in negativity. The house was getting "loose," but outside of a few occasional hints from staff, it was business as usual. Passes and privileges were still being submitted and approved.

One pass request that was approved was one of the coordinators—Ed Houlihan. Ed was a tall, soft-spoken, nice guy who was nearing the end of his treatment in First Phase. He was someone that, made you think, *is this guy in the right place?* He didn't present like a dope fiend in any way. I didn't get it. Why did he get his pass, and I didn't!? It reeked of favoritism, and I was jealous.

That weekend was like any other at Kedzie House. On Saturday morning, we all gathered in the dining room to send off the people with passes by forcing them to entertain us before they left. Ed couldn't sing a lick, so he did a sped-up, offkey version of "Take Me Out to the Ballgame," and he was out the door. The rest of the weekend was laidback and uneventful.

Monday morning rolled around, and as the first crack of sunlight streamed through the windows, it was back to the grind. The K-crew were the first ones to hit the floor and were in the kitchen preparing breakfast. The night monitors, fighting to stay awake, made the remaining family wakeups, and residents started to trickle downstairs, where we were hit by the usual Monday morning smell of coffee and breakfast sausage. After breakfast, we made our way back upstairs to tighten up our dorms. On my way upstairs, I noticed Director Diane Schwartz was heading into her office. She was never there that early on a Monday morning. Suddenly, the Expediters were up on the floors announcing, "Staff needs the whole family downstairs in the dining room immediately." I remember thinking, *Oh shit! What did some goof do now?*

The dining room was packed with residents, including Second Phasers, who were still in the house. We were all looking nervous and concerned, eyeing each other suspiciously and wondering who the culprit might be. We all knew that we were probably going to be told to "assume the posture" any minute, which meant we would be standing for the better part of an hour while staff lectured us. Sure enough, they emerged from the DO, Diane leading the way.

Oddly, we weren't told to stand for confrontation. Instead, with the three or four staff that were on duty standing behind her, Diane announced: "I called you all down here to deliver some bad news. Last night, Ed Houlihan was found dead. He died in a hotel room of an apparent overdose of heroin."

The silence that followed was deafening. Staff purposely didn't say another word for what seemed like a long time. They just scanned the room, looking into all of our faces. They wanted us to think about it, and let the words sink in. You could feel the shock that came over the entire room and could've heard a pin drop. I remember having a knot in my gut, accompanied by feelings of sadness and disbelief. *I just saw him standing right over there singing*, I thought. But the most predominant feeling was fear. We all lost friends and family to addiction when we were out there using, but this was different. We were clean and sober now, and this was a comrade in the fight we were in for our lives. Ed was the first person I knew who lost that fight. Months of battling and progress were over, just like that. In less than the time it took to sing "Take Me Out to the Ballgame," it was all over. It scared the shit out of me.

Staff took turns saying their piece and mostly reinforced the fact that one mistake could be our last, and that if we're not talking about our feelings, especially reservations about using, we could be next. Jealousy for not getting my pass was now replaced by gratitude and the feeling that it could have been me they were talking about that morning. I visualized Albie getting that phone call, and the knot in my gut tightened.

Then, "the hammer came down." This was TC slang for the house closing. They announced that the house was officially closed, starting immediately, and explained what it meant. In short, it meant that the whole house was busted. No passes, privileges, status, TV, etc. This included phone calls in or out, visiting, and turning in any WAM you had in your possession. The only exceptions were trips deemed absolutely necessary by staff, usually medical appointments, but they would now all require accompaniment by strength. We were virtually on lockdown. While the house was closed, we would GI the entire house from morning until night with breaks only for meals, in-house meetings, "guilt dropping," and group sessions. Dropping guilt was a form of confession by writing all our transgressions, big and small, on paper.

I don't remember much about the house closing, except that it was another event that kept me from setting foot outside the door for at least another three weeks. Christmas was coming, and we all wondered if the house would reopen in time for the holidays. I didn't have any major guilt or contracts, just small stuff like swearing, telling an occasional war story, and having "eyes" for Cynthia and Kathy. Everybody already figured that out anyway.

The house closing didn't last long, though it sent the message staff wanted to send" "Fully engage in treatment and hold each other accountable or there will be serious consequences."

By the time the house re-opened in mid-December, I was starting to get a bit stir-crazy. I went for almost two months without a pass. Word got around that there would be Christmas passes but that they would be given out sparingly to those who were "super-worthy." I figured, "Hey, what do I got to lose; all they can do is say no." They did, and I was stuck in the house again, which meant I would miss yet another Christmas with my family.

For some reason, this hit me especially hard, and it again drove home the realization of what a mess I had made of my life. I became somewhat depressed, but again, my peers came to the rescue. One of them said to me, "Steve, think of being in this place this Christmas, as an investment in your future Christmases. This year is a sacrifice so that you can be there for your family for every Christmas to come."

Once again, through the wisdom and words of others, I was restored to sanity, and I was able to accept it. Once I did, I was free from the sadness that kept me from experiencing the joy of the season. I was able to experience the Christmas spirit, albeit slightly diminished due to being in treatment.

Unfortunately, that spirit was suddenly interrupted one morning when I watched two men enter the facility who looked a lot like detectives, probably because they were. They stopped briefly at the front desk and showed the desk man their badges and some papers. Before he could call staff, they saw themselves into the dining room where they spotted David Grey. The room went silent upon the two entering.

"David Grey?"

David, caught off guard, looked up from his chair. "Yes."

"We have a warrant for your arrest."

They handed it to him and showed him their badges. They cuffed him and read him his Miranda rights as they led him through the dining room and out the front door.

Federal confidentiality laws enacted in the 1970s prohibited this from happening. So how did it happen? The desk man screwed up; that's how. He not only acknowledged David's presence in the program but told them precisely where he was. By the time staff came out to stonewall them with the federal confidentiality spiel, it was too late.

Afterward, Diane called the family into the dining room, and explained what happened, along with an explanation about the law, and how to keep it from happening again. The desk man acknowledging David's presence and his whereabouts in the facility was as good as an invitation to enter and arrest him.

Throughout her explanation, we couldn't help but notice the tall black man standing silently at her side. The man was a stranger to most of us, known only by a select few Re-rounders. Then, she dropped the bomb on us. She announced her departure from Kedzie House as our director, and that the day after Christmas would be her last day. In response to our sighs and long faces, she reminded us of the Gateway concept: "There's nothing constant but change." She explained that she needed a change. She had an opportunity at another Gateway program and decided to take it. Some of us couldn't help but think that Ed Houlihan's death was part of her decision. She then introduced the tall black man as her successor. His name was Arnold Muse.

Arnold was well-spoken, articulate, and though good-natured, was a bit of a perfectionist. He had worked in administrative positions at Gateway for some time, so he was no rookie at running things. He was a Harley-riding, cowboy boot-wearing, intelligent black man, who once did five years in prison for possession of two skinny joints in the early 1960s. In other words, he was sentenced harshly for being a black man. In retrospect, Arnold was an interesting man, but at the time, we thought he was slightly weird. He introduced himself and expressed his admiration for the job that Diane had done, and just like that, the Arnold Muse era at Kedzie House had begun.

Just as suddenly as he disappeared, David Grey reappeared several weeks later. He told the story of a new and unlikely hero of his—Ron Orlando. It turned out that Ron was the only person who came to visit him while he was incarcerated. Not only did Ron visit him, but he bought him cigarettes and put some money on the books for his commissary. And if that wasn't enough, Ron also pulled a few strings to help get David released. It turned out that many of Ron's family were in law enforcement. David was able to see the other side of the usually tough and cocky Ron. He got to see the big-hearted, compassionate, caring side, a side that we on his caseload already knew existed. He publicly thanked Ron in the form of an announcement in Morning Meeting.

When you come to the end of your rope, tie a knot and hang on

Staff took us Christmas shopping, and if we had no money, we had access to donations that the house was given. We had a really good time decorating the tree, singing, listening to Christmas music, eating, and opening presents. We bowed our heads as one of the sisters said a prayer of gratitude. First and foremost, we were grateful to be alive, and thanks to Ed Houlihan, we now had a deeper sense of appreciation for that simple gift. Then, the staff led us in a prayer for Ed and his family. The 12-step program concept "Some will die, so that others may live" now had a more personal meaning.

Good news! I finally got a pass approved for the weekend after Christmas. Not a moment too soon, either. If I had to spend another week in that place, I would have gone out of my mind.

I remember getting ready to go that Saturday, then heading to the dining room to "give it away" in Morning Meeting. On my way downstairs, who was walking toward me in the hall? None other than my archenemy, Mark Narowicz. He had recently been promoted to Expediter and was on duty doing a house run. We glared at each other as we passed and tried to be cordial.

Me: "Hey" (barely audible).

Him: "Hey" (even less audible).

It was the end of December, but while sitting in Morning Meeting, I swore I felt a mosquito buzzing around my ear. I turned to look, and it was a mosquito! A big Polish mosquito named Mark Narowicz. He leaned down, and in a creepy whisper, he said in my ear, "You need to re-round on your dorm. You got some dust on the dresser behind some of your pictures."

"God save us! Not the dreaded evil of the world—DUST?!" I jokingly responded. He remained stoic and never even came close to cracking a smile.

"Okay, I'll get it before I leave," I assured him.

After Morning Meeting, I went up to my dorm to get my things together and get ready to leave. I would need to get to the bus stop about two blocks away by about 9:40 a.m. I took a rag out of our closet and made a quick swipe behind my pictures on the dresser. I grabbed my coat and headed downstairs. I still had some time to kill, so I went into the dining room, grabbed a sweet roll leftover from breakfast, and sat at the dining room table, stuffing it into my face. I went into the living room, where someone had just turned on the TV. I killed another few minutes staring at whatever was on, with a few other residents. Suddenly, the big Polish mosquito returned and was buzzing in my ear once again. "You need to take care of your dorm before you leave brother."

"I already did."

"Well, I just re-rounded on it, and there's still DUST there."

"Well, I cleaned it," I insisted.

"No feedback and dialogue brother," he shot back.

"I'm not giving you feedback and dialogue; I'm explaining to you that I took care of the issue in the dorm."

"You need to *pool* yourself up."

"THANK you (Fuck you). I'll get on top of that!" I said, now getting aggravated.

With a frustrated look on his face that I'm sure would have resulted in my brutal murder had we been on the streets, he turned and walked away.

I sat for another few minutes watching TV and regaining my composure. I figured I'd better leave before I wind up belting this guy. I went to the EO, got my pass money, grabbed my bag, and left to catch the bus.

I felt instant relief as the cold wind hit my face while walking to the bus stop. As I got closer to North Avenue, I heard the Saturday morning traffic, already starting to build. I could also hear something else—a voice that sounded far off, and possibly in some type of distress. I felt like it was coming from behind me, so I stopped and turned around to see. There he was, once again—the big Polish mosquito, no coat on, waving his arms frantically over a block behind me, yelling: "Heeeeyy, Steeeeeve, come on baaaack!"

I couldn't believe my eyes. "Whaaat?" I yelled.

"Come on baaaack."

"I'm gonna miss my bus!"

"Ron wants to talk to you!"

"I'll talk to him when I get back."

"*Pool* yourself up brother. Staff needs to talk to you now!"

Begrudgingly, grumbling under my breath, I surrendered and started heading back. I assured myself that I would just get on a later bus. I walked in and related back in to the deskman. "Ron wants to see me?" He was SOD that day (imagine that). He called into the DO and instructed me to "Go on in."

I entered the office; my coat was still on and duffle bag in hand. As usual, he looked up from his mountain of paperwork, reached over, and picked up what was obviously a haircut. He then proceeded to read me the most trumped-up, inflammatory, exaggerated load of bullshit I had ever heard since entering treatment: "This is a TPR for Steve Fiorito for disrespecting a direction to re-round on his dorm, giving feedback and dialogue when this was pointed out, disrespecting a pull-up when asked again to re-round on the dorm, and…(just to put some icing on the cake)…being disrespectful in front of new residents." Nice touch to make me really look bad.

Ron looked up at me with a furrowed brow. "Any of this valid?"

"No, it's all BS Ron, I swear!"

Unconvinced, he snapped, "Okay," and called the front desk.

"Get Mark Narowicz in here."

Upon entering the office, Ron invited Mark to present his case. Mark gave a great performance, including closing arguments that rivaled the likes of *Perry Mason*. I laid out my defense, which included being framed by a guy who had it in for me ever since I walked in the door.

When the "gavel" came down, the verdict was announced: GUILTY AS CHARGED!

"Steve, there are four things on this haircut. Are you trying to tell me that you did not one of them!?"

"That's right; that's what I'm telling you. Not one thing on that haircut is true!"

The sentence was then handed down. "YOUR BUSTED TO THE DISHPAN."

Remember when I said, "If I had to spend another week in that place, I would go out of my mind"? Well, I was about to do just that. I immediately thought about the eight weeks I had spent in the house, followed by the thought of spending at least the next three weeks inside. The thought overwhelmed me, and I snapped. "Fuck that! I'm not doing it!"

"Go sit on the chair!" Ron commanded.

"You go sit on the fucking chair. I'm outta here!" I said, walking out and slamming the door as I left. As I made a beeline for the stairs, I barely noticed most of the family that wasn't on pass had gathered in the living room watching TV. They heard the whole thing.

I shot up the stairs and kicked open the door to my dorm like I was in some TV cop show. As I started to pull my stuff out of the drawers and put it onto my bunk, I inflamed and justified my anger by repeating over and over, "I've been stuck in this fucking place for two months and now it's gonna be another three weeks for some bogus bullshit? No fucking way!"

Meanwhile, Ron assembled a "posse" of residents to attempt to intervene on me. It was comprised of: John Clark, Tim Dacey, James P., and David Grey, people that Ron knew I was close to and were not on pass.

The "calvary" charged up the stairs once again to rescue me from myself. They entered the dorm as I was packing. Timmy started, "What do you think you're doin'?"

"I'm getting the fuck outta here; that's what I'm doin'."

John was next. "So, you're gonna just throw away everything you've worked for?"

I repeated my mantra about being stuck in the house all this time and now for some bullshit.

James replied, "C'mon Steve, you got to toughen up that baby gut. You're stronger than this."

From that point on, it seemed like everyone was just parroting treatment lingo and recovery slogans. "Take it one day at a time Steve." Blah blah blah.

It wasn't working. Their words bounced off me like bullets bounced off Superman. I tuned them out and kept packing. But there was one person who wasn't parroting clichés—David Grey. He knew a bit more about my situation after being in a group with me recently, where I talked about the damage I'd done to my family relationships. He decided to go another route, away from trying to be inspirational. Instead, he took the practical approach. He just kept repeating over and over, "Where you going Steve? Where you gonna go? You got no place to go Steve—remember?"

I got my remaining belongings into my "suitcase" (big green garbage bag) and got my guitar out of the closet and started heading out the door. David got in my face and just kept repeating his mantra.

Before I could even get to the stairs, the "nut finally cracked." David broke through the wall of denial and anger, and I pictured myself sitting on the corner of North and Kedzie avenues in the cold, waiting for a bus to.... where? I had nowhere to go. My family made it clear that I could never live with any of them again. They would have even more resolve once they learned that I split treatment against staff advice. It was like the scene in the film *An Officer and A Gentleman*. Richard Gere's famous line echoed in my head: "I GOT NOWHERE ELSE TO GO!"

Reality set in and I went to the prospect chair and sat down, just as I had almost seven months earlier—desperate and in withdrawal. I put my head in my hands, trying to get a grip on myself. Finally, I proverbially threw my hands up and I surrendered.

James and Timmy put their hands on my shoulders as they assured me, "You're doin' the right thing, brother. We'll take your stuff and put it in the EO." I nodded my head in agreement. I sat there staring at the floor, seeing some of the family out of the corner of my eye. I noted that look in their eyes that reflected, *You in some deep shit, brother.*

Then, a wave of humility came over me, helping me to regain perspective. Any place I had to go, people would be using drugs. I knew by the end of the evening I'd be using too. In the scheme of things, I wasn't going to die or fall apart from being busted to the dishpan and in the house for a few more weeks. I broke through and found myself in total acceptance of the situation. Again, this was new territory for me—working through, and overcoming my feelings, instead of sedating them with drugs.

A little while later, the deskman came out and said Ron wanted to talk to me. I got off the chair and went into the DO. Ron looked at me with a big grin on his face and extended his hand. Not to shake hands though. In his hand, he had a small bottle.

"Aspirin?" he offered.

"Sure. Why not?"

"One or two?" he asked.

"Just one."

"I figured you'd have a headache after seeing the way the veins on your forehead almost burst." We both laughed.

He pointed to a paper cup to get some water from the bathroom in the DO and we each swallowed an Aspirin tablet. I guess you could say that technically, I took drugs with my counselor that day.

He asked me what happened, referring to why I lost it the way I did. I reiterated my defense with more detail about how Narowicz fucked with me every chance he got.

"Well, you know I *have* to bust you—right? I mean, the whole family heard you."

"I know," I conceded.

"All you had to do was re-round with me, and we could have talked about it. If you ever need to yell at me like that, just let me know and we'll go for a ride in the Gucci and we'll yell our asses off at each other, but you can't do that in front of the Family. It's a bad message to send to them."

"I get it," I said solemnly.

"You're not leaving, right?"

"No, I'm not."

"All right, go on. I'll have a few of the guys help you bring your stuff back up to your dorm."

As I turned to walk out, he stopped me. "Steve," he pointed at his head. "Capatosta (Italian for hardhead), huh?"

Yes, even after seven months in treatment, my head was still hard.

Accepting the bust was huge for me. It showed that with a little help from my friends, I could overcome the self-defeating, impulsive behavior that had sabotaged me all my life. I was learning to cope with "life on life's terms" and accepting responsibility for my mistakes, but an even more important lesson was on the horizon.

Much more than a New Year's Eve dance

There were seven of us who were busted during the New Year's Eve party. This meant that we were going to be working our asses off, while everyone else partied. In the early afternoon, we were called into the kitchen by the new kitchen Staff—Robert Randall. He huddled us up and gave us one of his pep talks, as only Robert could. With that crazy, wild-eyed enthusiasm, he said, "All right, y'all busted—right?"

"Right," we all half-assed responded.

"Okay, so we should know by now that the best way to get through a bust is to have a good attitude—right!?"

"Right," with about the same level of enthusiasm.

"What?! I can't hear you!"

"RIGHT!" This time, with a lot more enthusiasm.

"So, we gon' have a really good attitude starting right now—right?!"

"RIGHT!"

"In fact, we gon' have the best damn attitude busted people ever had in the whole history of Kedzie House. RIGHT!?"

"RIGHT!!" Now we were pumped! Like some kind of spirit leaped into all of us.

"We gon' serve our brothers and sisters with a smile on our faces, a hop in our step, and joy in our hearts!" He was now preaching like a Baptist minister!

"THAT'S RIGHT!!" We now sounded like a football team in the huddle.

"All right, that's the spirit! I made a pot of coffee. Now get you some aprons on, and let's get to work!!"

"OKAY, let's do this!" we all fired back.

It felt like the same spirit came over all of us, as if we were on a mission to have a great time despite being busted. We laughed and joked as we sweated and toiled in the kitchen, preparing appetizers, dinner, drinks, and dessert for about 80 people. It was like we were in competition with each other to see who could have the best attitude. We busted out a great spread!

As guests started arriving, we went above and beyond what we were asked to do. We took guests' coats and hats and hung them up. We refilled everyone's drinks and brought them dessert. Everyone at that dance barely moved a muscle. We did everything for them, while simultaneously working behind the scenes cleaning, doing dishes, taking out garbage, and stocking whatever the party needed. We didn't miss a beat throughout the entire evening.

As I watched the revelers, I vicariously experienced their joy as if see through their eyes. The talk that Robert once had with me about "putting life into life" kept going through my mind. We had abandoned ourselves in the pure spirit of total service to others. With this came the unexpected gifts of peace and relief, due to being "free from the bondage of self," yet another often-repeated AA principle that now came to life for me. But the most important lesson was still yet to come.

As midnight approached, exhaustion set in. But we got a second wind when staff gave us permission to turn on the TV, so we could watch the ball drop in Times Square on *Dick Clark's New Year's Rockin' Eve* special.

It was about 11:45 p.m. when an Expediter announced: "Staff wants to see everyone who's busted in the DO now!" A sense of foreboding came over me, especially when I learned that the SOD was my least favorite—Rory. The Expediter's announcement had an ominous tone. We all gathered outside the door and knocked.

"C'mon in," Rory said from the other side.

We entered apprehensively and stood in a single-file row. Already assuming the posture for confrontation, we all put our hands behind our backs, out of habit. Sitting in Arnold's comfy chair and not behind the desk, Rory's beady eyes followed each of us in as we entered. With a look on his face that was stern but hard to read, he asked, "How'd it go tonight?" Afraid to commit to an answer that potentially would be wrong, we all mumbled things like "Okay, I guess" and "Pretty good."

"The reason I'm asking is because Arnold called and wanted to know. He wanted a full report. What do you think I told him?"

Again, some of us mumbled things like "I don't know," "It seemed to go pretty well," and "We had a problem with the sanitizer, but we figured…"

He interrupted, "Well…I told him you guys were awesome, and you busted this party out like you owned it! We had guests from the outside that went out of their way to tell me what a great job you guys were doing."

Smiles came across our faces as we all breathed a sigh of relief.

"You want to know what Arnold said?"

We listened attentively.

"He said to tell you that you're all out of your busts and you have your privileges back. Happy New Year! Now go enjoy the party. The rest of the family will pitch in to clean up. You guys are completely off the hook!"

We couldn't believe it. We looked at each other with a mixture of shock and joy on our faces. We all thanked him and yanked our aprons off as we left the DO.

We joined the family in the dining room, where most of their attention was on the wall-mounted 17-inch TV. We were met by several people passing out various noise makers. With the countdown to 1986 just minutes away, we explained to them what had just happened. They appeared just as shocked and happy as we were. All busted residents had never been taken out of their bust all at once like that. To the best of my knowledge, it was unprecedented.

The countdown began, and we all chimed in: "Ten, nine, eight …"

Suddenly, the memory of being locked in a mental institution the year before jumped into my mind. "…seven, six, five…"

Then, the memory of two years before that, when I almost committed armed robbery with a lighter.

A wave of gratitude came over me that I was at Kedzie House, celebrating with other addicts in recovery. I felt at home.

"Four, three, two, one…Happy New Year!"

1985 was officially over. A year that I will always refer to as one of the hardest, yet best years of my life. The year I at least started to pull my head out of my ass.

The noisemakers sounded, the confetti flew, and the hugs commenced! I, of course, tried to hug as many sisters as possible. Rory came out of the DO and wished everyone Happy New Year. The TV went off, the music came back on, and the dancing resumed.

Being the ace wallflower that I was, I immediately found a nice chair against the wall and did some quality observing from the sideline. As I sat there and thought, an important realization came to me. I realized that four days earlier, I had almost thrown my treatment and possibly my life out the window. It occurred to me that if I had done so, it would have been due to not living my life one day at a time. The crucial, bad decision I came close to making was based on focusing on the past and the future, and not being able to handle the moment I was in. A future, mind you, that did not happen at all the way I had envisioned it. I assumed that I would be busted for two weeks, then have to put in a request for my privileges before I'd be eligible to request a pass. As it turned out, I was busted for only about four days, and because I was given my privileges back, I'd be eligible for a pass that weekend, which I would finally take. I had the important realization that although I understood the concept of living one day at a time, I certainly wasn't doing it, and it almost cost me dearly.

Just then, my thoughts were interrupted by two tall black dudes who walked up and towered over me with serious looks on their faces. It was two of my fellow *Oreos*, George, and Larry.

"Yeah, ah, George and I were talking, and we decided it's time for you to dance, brother."

"What?"

"You heard him, Stevie," George chimed in.

"What do you mean?"

"Stand up. I want to show you something," Larry said, trying really hard to sound serious while fighting a smile that was just below the surface.

"You see that girl on the dance floor, dancing by herself?" he said, pointing at her.

"Yeah."

"You gonna dance with her."

"I can't dance."

"Yes, you can. We've seen you dance in your chair. Just do that standing up, and you'll be fine."

"I've never done it."

"Steve, are you lookin' at these people? Can't nobody dance up in here," George assured me.

"I can't."

"Don't make us do it, Steve. Go willingly, or we're going to *help* you."

"I really don't think it's a good idea."

"Okay, that's it."

And with that, they got on either side of me, picked me up off the floor by the elbows, and literally carried me out to the dining room turned dance floor, and placed me in front of the girl who was dancing by herself.

"Excuse me, miss, can Steve have this dance?" Larry asked.

"Sure," she said, grinning ear to ear.

We introduced ourselves when suddenly something from another planet started coming through the speakers. Next thing you know, I was… "just burnin, doin the Neutron Dance!" Oh my God! The tempo of this song by The Pointer Sisters gave you no choice but to dance. It grabbed you by the hips and started moving you around like a puppet! Of course, the comedian in me came out, making sure I protected my ego by not taking myself too seriously. My peers clapped, hooted, and encouraged me: "That's right, Stevie! You go!"

Suddenly, the mood shifted when The Commodores' *Brick House* played. Let's say things got a bit *funk-ay* at that time. The "funk" took me over as the beat was clapped by about 50 dope fiends. Then someone yelled, "Oh my God! What's he doin' now?! We gon' call that The Stevie Stick Dance!"

Thus, The Stevie Stick Dance was born. Actually, the "Stevie anything dance" was born. It was the first time I had ever danced besides dancing with Debbie Drexler at my fifth birthday party, and at my brother Paul's first wedding when I was ten. There were two things that I thought I'd never do because I thought people looked stupid doing them: dancing and bowling. Okay, well, at least I'd still never bowl—right?

Is God a Bears fan?

Once I got my pass, the pressure was released. Although, I admit, from that day forward, I never felt like I had my pass until I was on the bus and the wheels were rolling. Even then, I'd be looking around to make sure no one from the house was going to jump out from behind a seat and make me get off the bus. I apparently suffered from a form of PTSD ("Pass Taken by Slick Dope Fiend," or if you prefer, "Polack Terrorizes Steve's Day"). I'm sure these days I could get a legit script for Benzos for my "condition."

Upon returning from my pass, all was right with the world again, or at least, between my ears. How right with the world were things? The best year of my life to that point, 1985, was about to get a big exclamation point added to it. The Chicago Bears were going to the Super Bowl. That's how right! I had endured the worst decade and a half of football in Bears history, watching quarterback Bobby Douglas scramble for his life, then only to have hope dashed again and again by the likes of QBs Bob Avellini and Vince Evans. Now they were so cocky, they dared to release a video called The Super Bowl Shuffle.

We never missed a game that whole season at Kedzie House, and on January 26th, they went on to win Super Bowl XX, 46-10 against the New England Patriots! I even got to witness them lining up defensive lineman, William "The Refrigerator" Perry (The Fridge), as a running back and him scoring a touchdown! I took it all as a personal gift from God for being clean and sober. Speaking of God, I guess this is a good place to explain how an agnostic (and even, at times, an atheist) develops a relationship with God.

The closest I came to God as a child was sticking my head in church just far enough to grab a program so that I could fake my mother out, and she wouldn't know I went to Sun Drugs and bought candy with the offering money.

Since then, my spiritual experience was limited to foxhole prayers, Laura and I making our Confirmation so we could be married in the Catholic church (which never happened), christening my kids, and most notably, the "imaginary" holding of Jesus's hand while in severe withdrawal. Then there was the white-yellow light incident when I overdosed, but at that time, I dismissed that as a cocaine-induced hallucination. The farthest I'd ever gotten into spirituality could be best described as being hopeful at times that there was a God, and that Jesus was a nice concept but was… "just all right with me."

The piecing together of the God puzzle would be a long, slow process. I believe it ultimately takes a lifetime. For me, it started with three basic elements. Initially, people in treatment and 12-step meetings shared their experiences about their Higher Power. Then, there were the daily reflections being read at 12-step meetings from the book *Twenty-Four Hours a Day*. But ironically, it would be science that would initially crack the door of faith soon after entering treatment. This occurred after hearing a particular reading from the *Twenty-Four Hours a Day* book. The following meditation for the day cracked the door of faith, less than three weeks into my treatment…

Whenever we seek to worship God, we think of the great universe that God rules over, of creation, of mighty law and order throughout the universe. Then, we feel the awe that precedes worship. I, too, must feel awe, feel the desire to worship God in wondering amazement. My mind is in a box of space and time and it is so made that I cannot conceive of what is beyond space or time, the limitless, the eternal. But I know that there must be something beyond space and time, and that something must be the limitless and eternal power behind the universe. I also know that I can experience that power in my life. – June 25, Twenty-Four Hours a Day

What stood out and got me thinking, was the part about our minds being "in a box of space and time" and not being able to conceive of what is beyond it— "the limitless and eternal" —or infinity and "something beyond space and time." I started to contemplate the idea of infinity, which brought to my mind two simple questions: Where did the universe begin, and where does it end?

I immediately thought of the only answers that made sense to me. It didn't, and it doesn't! I started contemplating that the universe started from something, and whatever that something was, it too started from something, and so on, and so on, infinitely! This means the universe never started. Then, I started contemplating where it ends. As a visual aid to myself, I extended my arm as far as it could go and thought, *where my arm ends, something else begins.* I realized that the universe never ends!

The concept of a universe so vast that it had no beginning, and no end, boggled my mind. At that moment, I realized that there are things that are inconceivable to my finite mind. It was all I needed to ignite a small amount of faith. Then, I remembered God's proclamation from the Bible, in my brief occasional interactions in the church: "I am the Alpha and the Omega, the first and the last, the beginning and the end." The "puzzle pieces" fit perfectly.

The next phase in my spiritual development, started with another question: Could that have been God? This was due to the many stories I heard from fellow residents and people in meetings, describing what they believed to be divine intervention in their lives by their "Higher Power." They described incidents of survival and rescue which to them were inexplicable through conventional logic. I could certainly relate to many of them—driving on expressways and major roads, heavily sedated and nodding, while high on opiates, benzos, or other drugs, which often included weed and alcohol. Or being so paranoid while high on cocaine that I drove obsessed and fixated on my rearview mirror. This was the result of severe delusions and hallucinations that someone was breaking in from the trunk into the backseat to kill me.

I started realizing that these were just a handful of the many times that I should not have survived. I started to believe that something had protected, and even intervened on me, like there was a forcefield of sorts around me.

This realization was combined with a concept that I was introduced to by people in meetings. They said that we were "the chosen ones," meaning, we were actually selected by God to survive our addictions for some greater purpose. I didn't know if it was true, but it worked for me, and it was another piece of "the spiritual puzzle" that would eventually lead to a bigger picture.

Soon the God question became more present tense: "Could this be God?" Again, through other's accounts, I started to sense that God was working in and directing my life. From this, the daily (well, almost daily) practice of prayer and meditation (talking and listening to/ listening *for* God) began.

The talking part is easy for anyone to understand. I could be kneeling at the side of my bed in silent prayer or a nut wandering around mumbling to myself. At any given time, I could have been seen doing both. In either case, I can believe that I'm talking to God, but what about listening?

Very early in my spiritual development, I realized that there was no "bat phone" (a reference from the 1960s TV show *Batman*) to God. No one had ever received a call on the payphone from God that I knew of. I know I didn't. Rather, I began to recognize that God spoke through people, situations, events, and circumstances in our lives. I called this recognition of God's presence, "God glasses." The analogy I eventually came up with was, I had to borrow your "glasses" until a pair of my own was made.

I caught my first real glimpses of God through the eyes of my fellows. I got a piece here and there, from this person and that person, until I started to form a concept of a God of my understanding. It was perfect for me because the 12-step program encouraged this process instead of the "group think" of organized religion. I became a part-time "detective," if you will, on the case, searching for more evidence. I say part-time because at that time, I was too caught up in the struggle of learning how to live in the world sober to dedicate too much time to spiritual matters. This reading from the daily meditation *Twenty-Four Hours a Day* sums it up.

We know God by spiritual vision. We feel that He is beside us. We feel His presence. Contact with God is not made by the senses. Spirit-consciousness replaces sight. Since we cannot see God, we have to perceive Him by spiritual perception. God has to span the physical and the spiritual with the gift to us of spiritual vision. Many persons, though they cannot see God, have had a clear spiritual consciousness of Him. We are inside a box of space and time, but we know there must be something outside of that box, limitless space, eternity of time, and God. – April 27, Twenty-Four Hours a Day

Though I can't say I had "a clear spiritual consciousness" of God at that point, I had made a beginning and was on the path.

So then, the question is: Was the fix in? Did God ordain the Chicago Bears to win Super Bowl XX? I don't think so. God did his part through people, situations, events, and circumstances. It was ultimately the entire team making the right choices that God laid before them, that led them to victory. However, if you're from Chicago, "Da Coach," Mike Ditka, is considered the closest a mortal can come to being God Himself! Bearrrrzzzzzz!

Another name gets added to the guilt list

The natural high of the Bears' victory was short-lived when, on February 3rd, 1986, I was again summoned to the Directors Office. It reminded me of being sent to the principal's office and always resulted in me feeling, *What the hell did I do now?* On my way there, I had time to sort through my recent transgressions and try to figure out which one could have possibly warranted a trip to the DO. I came up empty, so the suspense was killing me. The deskman called me in, and I entered tentatively.

The first thing I saw was none other than Ron Orlando behind the desk, who just happened to be SOD that day. To his right sat my mother. I immediately realized that this was not going to be good.

"Have a seat, Steve." Ron directed in a quieter-than-usual voice.

"Your mother's here because she's got some bad news for you. Mrs. Fiorito?"

"Your friend Ricky died."

"What happened?" I said after allowing the words to sink in.

"He committed suicide. He shot himself," she said, beginning to weep. Shock and disbelief quickly turned into tears that filled my eyes. "Why?"

"We don't know for sure, but we think it was because of Phyllis's cancer. He just couldn't handle the thought of losing her."

Ricky's mother was diagnosed with late-stage cancer months earlier and was given only months to live. Months would, of course, turn into years, defying this prediction as it often does, but Ricky would never find that out.

Ricky had become a security guard in the footsteps of his father. He purchased a .44 Magnum handgun, also in the footsteps of his father, who was a Korean War veteran.

Don had firearms in his closet ever since I could remember. He would be in the living room cleaning them on occasion. Rick and I would sneak them out and look at them when no one was home. Luckily, we didn't become one of those tragedies that you hear about when kids find their parent's guns. To Don's credit, Ricky was taught how to handle a firearm and to "never point it at anyone." We were both always fascinated with guns. "Guns" was also our favorite thing to play as kids.

I found it ironic that now he was dead of a self-inflicted gunshot to the head. I just couldn't understand why he would do that.

My mother brought me some Kleenex, and I dried my tears and cleaned up my face.

"These things happen, Steve. I'm so sorry, man. You gonna be alright?" Ron asked.

"Yeah, I'll be alright. When are his services going to be?"

"They're on Wednesday."

Ron assured me that I could get a special pass to attend but I thought I should take a peer with me for support. I agreed.

My mother kissed me and said she'd see me at the services and left.

Still obviously upset, Ron approved some time off and let me go to my dorm but also encouraged me to seek support from my peers. I assured him I would.

I entered my dorm and sat on my bunk as memories started seeping through the wall of shock and flooding my mind. Everything from when we were kids to more recent events, like seeing Leon Russell and the Marshall Tucker Band. That was the last good time we had together. Inevitably, though, all the good times I initially recalled were swept away by waves of guilt that came crashing down upon me. The first and most obvious was ripping him off. Then, the fact that I procrastinated calling him to make amends. Now, I would never be able to. I guess the only consolation was hearing from someone that he knew I was in treatment and was getting help.

Another source of guilt, and in some ways, even more troubling, was the question: Had I been available to him, could I have stopped him from taking his life? A big part of me believed that I could have. He looked up to me and would turn to me for things that bothered him throughout our lives. Our entire relationship had always been conflicted and contradictory—an inconsistent mixture of protecting and helping him—then, at times, exploiting, hurting, and ultimately abandoning him. I was sometimes a good friend and a good influence on him, but other times, a bad friend and a bad influence. I remember getting some help and support for my feelings by talking about it in group.

At his wake, I walked in the door with a lot of unresolved guilt and remorse, just as I had at Warren's services. The difference was, I was clean and sober and had a clear head. This resulted in me feeling more "normal" and handling the situation better. At least I looked people in the eyes as I paid my respects to his family. This was new for me, as I hardly ever did while in my addiction. I was even able to get up the nerve to pull Phyllis over and have a little one-on-one talk with her.

I apologized for not being a better friend and not being there for him, and explained that I was in treatment, which she already knew. Then, in an attempt to get some answers from the person closest to him, I asked her "why?" She encouraged me to stay on the path I was on, and then sadly, she reminded me: "You know Ricky could never handle the world, Stevie."

This statement, along with Phyllis's facial expression, would linger and haunt me for some time to come. The longer it sat with me, the more I sensed some deep, underlying animosity and even jealousy. It was no secret that the woman who babysat me many summers didn't care for me once I got past the age of 12. It was as if her true feelings started leaking out and penetrating her cordial demeanor. *Why was my Ricky dead; shouldn't it be you?* And *why was my Ricky not able to handle the world and you were?* Whether I actually *could* handle it or not, remained to be seen. I was still only a "possibility."

Though I was able to get through the initial emotions from Ricky's suicide, I was in no way over it. Instead, I had to shelve it, get on with the business of treatment, and learning how to live drug-free. By this time, I and several of my peers had been promoted to Expediter. Soon, it would be our turn to run the show at Kedzie House.

Changes in values become changes in behavior

One Sunday evening, I was manning the front desk as people started coming back from their passes. I waited patiently to see my latest crush—Kathy Smith—walk through the door. Kathy was my usual type, a petite blonde with freckles, a nice body, and a pretty innocent face. She was the type that you would never suspect of being a dope fiend.

She arrived late and came in the door bundled in her coat, hat, and hood. Kathy knew I had a thing for her and would flirt back, as long as no one important was around to take note. As I signed her back in, I tried to flirt a bit and make some small talk about how her pass went. She gave me the bare minimum and appeared to be trying not to engage. That was the first sign that something wasn't quite right. After she got her coat and hat off, she scratched her nose. It was still winter, the air was dry, so no big deal—right? I waited to see if there would be a second scratch. There was.

The "orange-alert" warning light went off in my head. As she tried to disengage and walk away, I continued sucking her back in with small talk. I noticed the subtle difference in her voice too—just a hint of gravel. Then, I waited for it, and it finally happened—the third scratch! The "red alert" went off in my head, and I knew what only another heroin addict would know—she was high. Not super-high, but high enough for me to notice. She finally broke away and spoke briefly to a few other family members in the living room, before going up to her dorm.

I sat wondering what to do. Do I let her slide? Do I just talk to her and keep it between her and me (hold a "negative contract") or do I alert Staff? Letting her slide was eliminated almost immediately. Ed Houlihan's death cemented the belief that this would have been the equivalent of letting her kill herself. Talking to her one-on-one didn't seem to be a much better option.

What I had to do became clear …I had to bust her out. To do it, I had to leap that final hurdle over all the old values of being a "snitch" or a "trick." I picked up the phone, which now weighed 100 pounds, and reluctantly called into the D O to the SOD, which was … you guessed it…Ron Orlando.

"Hey Ron. I need to talk to you about something. Can I come in there?"

"Come on in," he growled through the phone.

Upon entering, I stumbled around a bit before coming out with it: "Kathy Smith just got back from pass, and I think she's high."

I told him the symptoms I observed.

"Okay, we'll get her down here and drop her. Good job, Steve."

Nervously, I said, "Can I just ask one favor? Can you not tell her that it was me?"

He looked at me and with that mischievous Ron smile, he replied, "No problem, I won't tell her."

"Thanks," I responded, relieved.

"Because you're gonna tell her" he announced.

"What?"

"You're gonna tell her Steve. But not now, in group. Now go to the piano and drop a slip on her. I'll take care of what's got to happen tonight."

"Okay," I mumbled reluctantly.

I went to the piano and picked up the pen, which now also weighed 100 pounds. I wrote the slip and held it with my fingertips as most of it dangled inside the locked box. I hesitated before finally releasing it into "the land of no return." There was no turning back now.

The next day in Morning Meeting, the COD called on people with pull-ups and announcements in the book. One of those was Kathy. She stood up, obviously embarrassed, and announced to the family that she had relapsed while on pass and asked that we "reach out" and help her get through it. The responses were positive and came in the form of supportive shoutouts from the family. I, on the other hand, slunk down a little lower in my chair.

That Thursday, as I walked toward the first-floor lounge where my assigned Cluster Group was, I remember thinking to myself, *maybe she's in another group* and *maybe there's more important slips that need to be dealt with. After all, she was busted and dealing with her relapse. What's the difference if she knows who fingered her or not?*

Who was I kidding? Did I really think that staff was going to overlook or trivialize this? As soon as I set foot in the lounge, my bubble was burst immediately. There she sat. She shot me a quick smile as I took a seat on the other side of the room. I had the usual knot in my gut that I had every Thursday during Cluster Group. You never knew who was going to "jump out of the bushes" with a surprise "attack" on you. I still had one shot though. Maybe they would run out of time.

No such luck. After only doing one other slip, the staff announced, "Steve Fiorito, you dropped a slip on Kathy Smith?"

"I did," I replied.

"Go ahead Steve," the staff directed.

"Kathy, I dropped a slip on you because…I wanted you to know… (I froze, realizing that I had never said anything like this my entire life) … I'm the one who told staff that I thought you were high when you came back from pass. It was hard for me to do, and I really struggled at first, but I've learned since coming here that if we really care about each other, we've got to hold each other accountable. I care about you Kathy, and I don't want you to keep using and die. I just wanted you to know that I did it out of care and concern."

The group's collective faces quickly went from shock to approval and respect.

"Is that it Steve?" staff asked.

"Yeah, that's it."

Her response went something like this…

"I just want to say thank you Steve. You saved my life. I had been using on every one of my passes and it was getting worse. I almost didn't come back Sunday. I was thinking of leaving treatment and giving up. If it wasn't for you busting me out, I probably would've left. Now I feel like I have a chance to start over in a way and get back on track. Thanks again."

A sense of relief came over me, and the tension in my neck and shoulders was immediately eased.

Staff then opened it up for comments from the group, most of which were supportive and encouraging. I got a few accolades, too. Although it was one of the hardest things I had ever done, I knew it was the right thing to do, and I felt good about it. By the end of that group, I felt respect from my peers and staff, but most importantly, I started respecting myself.

Once chased by police, becomes chief of police

Shortly thereafter, I was promoted to Shingle and then Chief Expediter. I had been in treatment for over nine months, and I was one step away from achieving the highest level of status there was, the level that my first idol in treatment, Benny L. had achieved—House Coordinator.

Staff brought the family into the dining room to announce job changes. As several of my peers were promoted to coordinator of various departments, I could feel it coming: the highest honor at Kedzie House! They called my name, and I stood up. Then, they announced my new position… "Medical Liaison?!" Huh? There must be some mistake! People clapped, and I said, "THANK you" (fuck you) as I sat back down. I looked over at James P., who was trying hard not to laugh. He knew what I was expecting and knew that staff had just purposely thrown me a big old curveball! Just like that, I had gone from the "Chief of Police" to the "Radar O'Reilly" of Kedzie House.

Although the Medical Liaison position came with coordinator status, it was the equivalent of being put out to pasture. You virtually hung out in the medical office, drinking coffee all day, doing whatever Anita needed done. Now, I had even more reason to set my sights on Second Phase. I was tired and had enough of the daily stress of "playing the treatment game." It was time for me to move up and get back into the real world.

Even more motivation to move on came when Second Phase resident Kevin was allowed to sit in one of the house groups. Kevin was a slightly older, good-looking, sharp-dressed, well-spoken black guy with high energy. He was a "role model pacesetter." We all looked up to him. He announced that he had found a job and just got hired that day. "Yay!!" We all erupted with applause! Then he told us who hired him. "McDonald's." And the group went silent.

It was hard to picture him in one of those funny little uniforms, flipping burgers. He looked at us with fire in his eyes. "I know what you're thinking, but I'm gonna be the best damn burger flipper there is, until I own that place."

"Right on, Kev, you go!" were the kind of comments heard; however, half-heartedly from the group in response. Nobody believed it, but we wanted to be supportive. We admired his level of humility, if nothing else.

In March of 1986, my "campaign" to be "rotated" (the term used back then) to Second Phase, started in earnest. Residents approached this in different ways. Some didn't need to do anything. Staff came and informed them that they were ready. Some were cool and dropped occasional, subtle hints, while others practically walked around the house with signs and banners that imparted messages like: *I've been in First Phase long enough and have experienced so much personal growth that If I grow one more inch, my proverbial head will be scraping the ceiling!* I, of course, was option number three.

Sylvester Williams, whose head literally almost did scrape the ceiling, was the Director of the Second Phase program. Syl (as most called him) was an extremely big and tall black man with an ominous look on his face. I had zero relationship with him because, quite frankly, he scared the shit out of me. His foot was as big as my entire torso.

Jeff K., on the other hand, was a newly promoted Second Phase counselor, with whom I did have a relationship. Our mutual love for the Allman Brothers Band was about to come in handy for me when he heard announced on a few local rock radio stations that Gregg Allman and his band were coming to Chicago and would be playing at the Cubby Bear Lounge on Addison and Clark streets. Jeff told me that he was going, and that tickets were on sale now in the standing-room-only venue. He suggested that I take my pass on that weekend and go. Ron would likely approve it, knowing Jeff would be there.

I got it approved, and I got my ticket. It was going to be my first time seeing live music in a club atmosphere, sober.

On the day of the show, I arrived early to ensure I'd get a good spot, close to the stage. The place started filling up as it came closer to showtime. There were folding chairs throughout the venue, but most people were content standing. I saw Jeff and a few of his friends who were further back and closer to the bar. Jeff acknowledged me with a big smile, and I could feel the excitement of seeing one of our musical heroes up close.

As I waited anxiously for the band to take the stage, my attention turned to a sharp-dressed woman who stood against the wall to my left. Our eyes locked as she smiled at me from across the room. Next thing I knew, she was standing next to me with two folding chairs in hand.

"Hi, you looked uncomfortable standing there all that time, so I brought you a chair. I'm Carolyn."

"I'm Steve," I said, helping her with the chairs.

Her feminine yet no BS bold approach made me smile. Carolyn was 100 percent woman, petite, fit, trim, and curvy in all the right places. She was beautiful and had a pretty face, an unbelievable smile, and big, curly, jet-black hair. She was funny, intelligent—and guess who one of her all-time favorite artists was? Gregg Allman! We compared our favorite songs, swapped trivia, and discussed the history of our beloved Gregg. I told her about "my friend" Jeff and I trading off vocals on "It's Not My Cross to Bear: but left out the details about where this took place, and who Jeff was. We also shared our thoughts about Gregg's tabloid marriage to Cher and subsequent divorce. Oh, did I mention Carolyn was black? I can't pretend that I didn't notice, but any barrier that it may have posed at one time no longer existed.

As Gregg and his band took the stage, Carolyn and I clapped and yelled with excitement. They opened with "Don't Want You No More" and just as on the Allman Brothers debut album, right into "It's Not My Cross to Bear." I shot Jeff a look from across the room and he returned it, both of us conveying obvious appreciation that he opened with the song that Jeff and I had once shared vocals on. He then shot a look at Carolyn and gave me the "pretending to be puzzled and concerned" look, while I'm sure, he was really thinking, *You lucky bastard."*

Between songs, I showed off my limited musical prowess by critiquing the guitar playing of "Dangerous Dan Toler." She was impressed when I explained how Gregg had stolen him from ABB guitarist Dickey Betts's solo project, *Great Southern*. As the first set ended, the best surprise yet …

"I'm going to the bar to get something to drink. Do you want anything?" I asked.

"Yeah, I'll have a 7-Up on the rocks with a twist of lime." I froze and looked at her, stunned.

"I don't drink," she explained.

"Either do I," I proclaimed for the first time in my life, without hesitation.

"Cool!" she smiled.

I made my way to the bar, looked up, and winked at God, mumbling, "Thank you" under my breath. I ordered two 7-Ups and had no desire whatsoever to drink alcohol. I held both glasses up for Jeff to see and mouthed, "7-Up." He nodded and smiled with approval. It was my first test, and I passed it, but I couldn't have foreseen the much bigger one that was coming just ahead.

During the band's second set, people pushed their way up to the front of the room. Our view became obstructed, so we stood on our chairs and regained a great view. We both got back into the music, when something caught my eye. The guy standing just to my right, who I was now looking down on from my chair, had something in his hand. As he opened it up, I could clearly see what looked to be about an eightball of cocaine. Then, with a straw, he took a big old snort from the pile. Carolyn saw it too and looked at me nervously. I just smiled, shrugged my shoulders, and looked back at the stage.

I checked in with myself, and other than the initial shock and fear which quickly dissipated, I was fine. I never looked at it again. I was too busy paying attention to one of my musical idols 15 or so feet in front of me, and a very pretty woman next to me.

At the end of the show, we waited in front of the stage for Gregg and the band to come out, as they were said to often do after shows in smaller venues. Danny Toler came out, but Gregg never showed. He had recently started making attempts to get clean and rumor had it he had been in and out of recovery. I guess this was one of his out periods.

As the room started clearing out, Carolyn and I decided it was time to go. We stood on the sidewalk on Addison Street and looked at each other with that "Okay, what now?" look on our faces. I clumsily blurted out, "Would you like to go out and do something sometime?"

"Sure, let me give you my number."

Knowing I was going to start cutting it close to my curfew, and that I had to get going to catch my bus, I also blurted out, "I gotta tell you something."

"What?" she smiled.

"I'm in treatment for addiction right now. I'm on a weekend pass. I've got ten months clean," I confessed.

"That's great! You should be really proud of yourself!"

"You're okay with it?"

"I'm okay; call me," she said as she walked away.

As I turned and started heading for the bus stop, she called to me, "Steven!" I turned around and saw that she was walking back toward me. When she got to me, she kissed me full on the lips. It was one hot kiss! "Call me—okay?" and she started walking away again.

"Okay, I will." I looked closely to make sure it was a real phone number before putting it into my pocket. In a state of natural high, I floated to the bus stop. Things were looking…up (pun intended)!

A buried memory surfaces

Several weeks later, my court date for retail theft had finally arrived. Had it really been over a year since I tried to walk out of a store with a brand-new TV?

I signed out and headed to my destination—the Cook County Maybrook Courthouse in Maywood. The last time I was in Maywood, I was being busted out of my Methadone scam. I was nervous because I never knew if a warrant had been issued for my arrest for the fraud I committed.

I got on the bus, and out of habit, I started to head to the back, but something stopped me. I spun into the first open seat in the front, right behind the driver. It was the first time I made a decision not to sit in the back of the bus. Just another sign of recovery. Everybody who has ridden the CTA on a regular basis knows what goes on in the back of the bus—drug and alcohol use.

I got off the bus and walked the block or so to the courthouse. I entered with the usual knot in my gut, and after checking in with the clerk, I slid into an open bench. A man came over to me and inquired, "Mr. Fiorito?" He introduced himself as my public defender and asked me how I was doing.

I told him that I was about to complete residential treatment, and I had been clean for almost a year. He smiled, congratulated me, and he stated that I had no arrests or pending charges. He said the judge would be pleased, my supervision would be over, and my case would likely be dismissed as of today. Just then, "All rise for honorable Judge McKinnley."

I sat there for what seemed like hours, waiting for my case to be called. I would sneak an occasional peek at the *Sun-Times* I had while being watchful for the bailiff, who would scold you if you were caught reading.

Just as my skinny ass started hurting from sitting on that hard bench, and I was beginning to wonder if I was in the right room, my case was called. "The court calls case number two one zero (blah blah blah), Steven Fiorito." I approached the bench from one side and my PD from the other side of the room. I stood at attention before the judge, knot in my stomach, and sweaty palms clasped behind my back as if standing for confrontation at Kedzie House. The judge read my records. Then, he smiled and looked up, peering at me over his glasses, and in a bold voice, he said: "Mr. Fiorito, I see that not only have you stayed out of trouble over the past year, but you've also taken the initiative to get help with your drug problem, at the Gateway facility. I want to commend you in front of this entire courtroom for having the courage to ask for help and taking the initiative to change. I wish you continued success. Your case is dismissed."

"Thank you, your honor." The PD smiled and nodded, eyeing the door as if to say, "You can go."

As I walked away, I could feel all the eyes in the courtroom upon me, but instead of it making me uncomfortable, I felt a new feeling—pride. I left the courtroom with my head high, my chest poked out, and with a sense of accomplishment instead of failure for once.

As I walked, admittedly a bit full of myself, down the sidewalk and toward the bus stop, my good feelings were suddenly interrupted when a big, tan beater Oldsmobile with a black vinyl roof pulled up alongside me. The passenger-side window came down, revealing a familiar face.

"Hey, Stevie! What's up, my man?" It was Lenny.

"What's up, Lenny?" I said as I leaned into the passenger window.

"I just got out of court."

"Me too," I replied.

"You need a ride? Get in."

Without even giving it a second thought, I got in the car.

"Where you headed?"

"Just up to North Avenue. I've got to catch a bus back into the city."

"I ran into your bro the other day at the VA picking up our "odine." I don't see him much these days. We both get take-homes, so we only have to show up twice a week."

"Yeah, I haven't talked to him in a while since I've been living in the city," I admitted.

"I've been getting some really good brown from the Ricans lately. If you got funds, we could cop some right now."

"No, I can't right now. I've been clean for 11 months and I gotta stay that way for a while."

"Court, huh? I get it. It's good to dry out every once in a while." We arrived at Harlem and North Avenues.

He pulled over. "Take my number. You need anything, give me a call."

I took the piece of paper and put it in my wallet. "Okay, good to see you, Lenny."

"I'll tell Pauly I saw you. You look good with some weight on you Stevie."

And with that, he drove away. I escaped unscathed and waited for the next eastbound North Avenue bus back to safety…and… wait … I can't remember getting on a bus…because I didn't….I wish what I said above is what happened …but it isn't. It's what should have happened, but it wasn't. I pushed down and blocked out of my mind for all these years what really happened that day. Until now.

As I sit here writing, what started out as a faded sketchy memory of what really happened that day, just kicked open the door of my subconscious mind, and through the haze of years, and drug-induced fog, the repressed truth surfaced. I wasn't sure at first, but then the memories came back strong and clear. The other story would have been so much easier to write, but I can't dismiss it as some false memory or something that happened at some other time.

What really happened that day was…I relapsed on heroin. One of the reasons I buried the truth was because I lied about it for years. I never told anyone. The other reason was, even as the vague memory started to surface, and I started questioning it, I dismissed it by recalling that I had no money for drugs and that Lenny certainly wasn't treating.

Then the key missing piece broke through. Before running into Lenny, I had gone downstairs to the clerk's office to get an unexpected reward that I had forgotten about—my $100 bail. Lenny's offer to go cop, combined with the surprise $100, caught me off guard, and was more than I could handle. Besides, *didn't I earn it and deserve a reward?* I thought at the time.

This is how addicts think, even after 11 months of intensive treatment. After not going to any meetings for two and a half weeks, the beam was broken, which I believe was the ultimate reason for my decision to use that day. The "strange mental blank spot" that's referred to in the AA Big Book, returned, and once again, I found I had no mental defense against the impulse to use, even after getting a huge pat on the back from that judge. Instead of going to my meetings, I had been going to Carolyn's every chance I got.

People often report a wide variety of reasons for their relapses. When it comes down to it, these "reasons" are for the most part, nothing more than excuses. The reasons are real, in that they may trigger the desire to use, but all can be overcome if the appropriate recovery tools or resources are administered. That day I found out, despite the progress I'd made, I still didn't have what it takes. Later, I would realize that this was a downside of the intensive, long-term treatment that I was engaged in. Because you're in a controlled environment or safe place daily, you can get a false sense of confidence about how easy it is to stay clean. It's much easier when you're around counselors, and people who are clean and sober, and talking about recovery 24/7. The trouble is, if you're in the real world on a regular basis, it's not that easy. This was the perfect storm that came together and became my recipe for relapse.

After we shot dope in his car on a side street, we went to Lenny's house for a while. The memories of what we talked about are vague, but he told me he had pick-up bottles of Methadone that were always for sale if I wanted any. He drove me all the way to North Avenue and Kedzie and dropped me off.

When I got back to the house, I felt so guilty, I'm surprised no one saw it on my face. I was still high but not to the point that I couldn't hide it. I was very conscious and careful not to scratch. I went to my dorm, and it was there that something clicked in my head. With my one-year anniversary just around the corner—this couldn't happen! So that was it. I decided at that moment *it never happened.* That's what I told myself as I shut the thick steel door in my mind tightly on it, locking away the truth.

Second Phase: Preparing to rejoin the real world

Myself and five of my peers—Sue Ann, Cynthia, Carl M., James P., and James Minter—finally completed First Phase. We were given our rotation ceremony—a rite of passage type celebration, acknowledging residents who had survived the rigors of the First Phase program and made it through.

The rotation ceremony was a roast of sorts, with hints of the popular *Dean Martin Celebrity Roasts* on TV at the time. Pete Piry, the Assistant Director of the Second Phase program, was the master of ceremonies. Pete, like Ron Orlando, was a character who took no prisoners, and like most of the staff, he had a chip on his shoulder, combined with a sarcastic, edgy sense of humor. As an added dimension to his character, he had only one usable arm. His right arm dangled uselessly from a birth defect. He would always tuck it into his front pants pocket. You got the feeling that Pete didn't really need the other arm and could whip your ass without it.

The rotation ceremonies gave staff a license to tee off and make sarcastic, humorous comments about us and our antics while in First Phase, in front of the entire family. In other words, it was just like any other day at Kedzie House. I don't remember everything he said when it was my turn to get up there, but I remember him saying, "Now that you're coming upstairs with us, until you find a job, you'll have plenty of time to wash the fuckin' Gucci!" referring to Ron's Gucci Seville, and poking fun of his caseload's willingness to please him by washing his car. Luckily, he always ended the humiliation with at least a few nice words of congratulations, acknowledging that you had survived the grueling rigors of First Phase.

After the festivities ended, I drove James P. and his two big green garbage bags home to Maywood. My parents bought me a car from their friends Maisie and Joe (the same people who lent her my airfare from Cali) in anticipation that I would get a job at GTE, where my sister was a supervisor and could pull some strings to get me an interview. The job was a paste-up artist, designing ads for the phone books. The plan was to pay them back once I got my Social Security Disability Insurance (SSDI) check of about $2,500 that had accumulated in an escrow account. In those days, addiction was viewed as a disability, and treatment was paid for by Social Security. Bad idea. Let's just say there were a lot of dope fiends relapsing with those SSDI escrow checks.

On the way to take James home, he looked at the AA guide for local meetings he could attend in the area. To our surprise there was an NA meeting going on that afternoon not far from his house at none other than Hines Veteran's Hospital. Who knew? All this time, a few buildings down from where junkies were selling their Methadone, in a room in a corner of one of the biggest, poorly run, inept excuses for a healthcare facility, recovery was actually taking place. It was a good-sized meeting, too.

We walked into the room like Richard Pryor and Gene Wilder in the movie, *Stir Crazy*. "That's right. We bad!" as all eyes were upon us. We emitted the vibe: *We Gateway graduates, motherfuckers. What you lookin' at!?* Both of us being well over our fear of speaking in a room full of strangers by this time, James and I both commented in the meeting. I don't remember my comment, but it was probably some bullshit trying to impress some girl. James's comment was based on some of the previous comments made, which I can't recall exactly, but I do recall the simple "junkie wisdom", word for word, that he ended his comment with. He said, "Why is it that we, as dope fiends, think we can do shit wrong, and have it come out right?" Mic drop!

Though the profound nature of the statement wasn't completely wasted on me, I didn't have a full grasp at the time of just how profound it really was. It was ironic that the guy who was mostly the comic relief in treatment, who always made me laugh, would leave me with such profound, simple wisdom. After the meeting, I dropped James and his big green garbage bags off at his mother's house. Sadly, I never saw him again.

We moved into our new dorms that Saturday, but our Second Phase adventure began in earnest when we started looking for a job. We all met upstairs in the Second Phase lounge on Sunday morning and had coffee as we waited for the vending machine on Kedzie Avenue to be stocked with the Sunday *Chicago Tribune*. Someone checked it earlier and they hadn't been there yet. Most of us usually read the *Sun-Times*, but everyone knew that if you were serious about looking for a job, there was nothing like the Sunday Trib.

I volunteered to see if the truck had come yet. Everybody wanted their own paper, so they all forked over their 50 cents. I walked about a half block down to the newspaper vending machines, and I could see through the window that they were there. I put my 50 cents in, opened the door, grabbed five papers, and slipped the money my peers had given me into my pocket. I thought to myself, *okay, I could use that $2.00.* Then my gut flipped, and a little guilt alarm went off in my head. I remember dismissing it by telling myself, *hey, the Tribune isn't gonna miss two bucks* and *my peers are getting what they paid for.* So, I thought, *No big deal—right?* What I would later refer to as "the progression of compromise" had begun.

Most of the time, I was able to keep the lid on my "heroin slip" with Lenny and keep it out of my mind. However, there were exceptions. One that stands out was when I received my one-year medallion at my home group, a CA meeting at The Maze. The husband and wife who chaired and co-chaired the meeting—Randy and Mary—ordered it for me, knowing my one-year anniversary was approaching on June 6th. When clean time anniversaries were acknowledged, Randy asked, as he did every Tuesday, "Is anyone celebrating an anniversary this week?" Several of us raised our hands and we all stated our names and how much time we were celebrating. He saved me for last, "Steve?"

"Hey, everybody. I'm Steve, and I'm an addict. Friday the 6^{th,} I celebrated one year clean and sober."

Loud applause and hoots erupted. I remember having to push down the guilt and the knot in my gut as I walked past people who clapped and cheered and I went up to get the symbolic pewter prize, that, in reality, I did not deserve. I was full of shit, and I felt it, but I couldn't bring myself to get honest about it. I had too much pride and ego in the way and too much freedom to lose.

Being in Second Phase brought about that freedom. Carolyn and I were starting to get hot and heavy now that I could see her almost anytime I wanted to. She would come by Kedzie House and visit. Everybody loved her, including my family. No one ever said anything to me about the color of her skin. My family was all very welcoming when we went to a family get-together at a German restaurant on Chicago's far northwest side.

Sex was good too, but with one slight hitch. Though she was very hip and progressive in her attitudes, Carolyn grew up in a strict religious household and was a good Christian. So, she was always conflicted and torn between following the dictates of her religious upbringing or giving in to her sexual desires and the chemistry we had.

I had my own issues related to sex. I was trying to forge a sober sexual identity that wasn't self-centered, but that also accepted and honored who I was sexually. I definitely wasn't ready for the Bible's recommendations. More to my understanding, I had read in the Big Book of AA about needing to stay away from extreme attitudes and finding some balance or middle ground when it came to sex. This rang true to me; however, sex was further complicated by the recent news that HIV/AIDS was no longer considered just a gay man's disease.

Research showed that IV drug users started testing positive for the virus at an alarming rate, as were their non-using heterosexual partners. I did share a few needles at the height of my use and had some unprotected sex here and there. Once I learned what the symptoms were, being prone to a bit of hypochondria, every ache, pain, and blemish that I experienced made me wonder if I had it. This worry would be exacerbated by more bad news that would soon come out about the virus—it could lie dormant for up to ten years. The HIV antibody test was fairly new, so I had no idea where to get tested at that time. Even if I had, I'm not sure I wanted to know my status at that point.

Cynthia, Sue Ann, and Carl got jobs within the first three weeks of entering Second Phase. James and I continued to pound the pavement and look in the paper. It was decided by staff that I couldn't have access to my car during the week until I found a job. I got a chance to use it when I drove Cynthia home to the far South Side.

She was hired by Gateway to work in the business office. Gateway had a strict policy that if you worked for them, you couldn't live there.

We had some fun with it on the way and joked that we would mess with her mother when we arrived and ask how she felt about having a white son-in-law. We would finally be able to have our *Guess Who's Coming to Dinner* moment. For what it's worth, her mother had no problem with me marrying her daughter.

One day, around July 1986, I went to my dorm after returning from my job search. A peer informed me that Pete wanted to see me. Of course, I started wondering what I did wrong. Typically, staff didn't want to see you unless you were in trouble. The door was open, so I walked in. "You wanted to see me, Pete?"

"Fiorito, you got mail," he said, handing it to me.

I immediately recognized the handwriting on one of the envelopes. It was confirmed when I saw the California return address. It was Laura. I went to my dorm and sat on my bunk with a knot in my gut. I looked up at God for a few seconds and then got the nerve to open it. I could tell there were pictures inside. I pulled them out and looked at them. I saw my girls getting older, and the pain in my heart, which had been dormant, came back with a full-force stab.

I don't remember exactly what the letter said, but the gist was they were coming home. Jess missed her dad, and Laura wanted me to be in my kids' lives. A tear rolled down my cheek as I went through the pictures. I practically memorized each one. Now, I had even more motivation to find a job.

James and I continued to pound the pavement daily, looking for work. For me, rescue came with a phone call from Mary Jo, who instructed me on who to call to set up an interview. I was to let them know that I was her brother. The strings had been pulled to get me an interview but, she warned, I still had to do well enough in the interview to get the job. I was fairly confident I wouldn't come off like a total moron, but my work history wasn't great, to say the least.

James would not be so lucky. With zero work history, but arguably a better work ethic than any of us, he continued his desperate daily search from the break of dawn until dinner time. I remember him coming back to the house Monday through Friday, just as dinner was being served, his tie loosened and shirt wet with sweat. We did all we could in group to encourage and support him, but I started to get concerned that he was getting close to an addict's dreaded two-word enemy— "Fuck it!"

Fortunately, soon after my interview, I was informed that I had the job. I was officially a paste-up artist—a type of work I had never done—and for the first time, it wasn't some form of manual labor. It was a new adventure. An adventure I would soon discover that I clearly wasn't ready for.

The first signs of trouble weren't obvious right away, but they slowly emerged. I was the only man in a department of approximately 12 women. There was one other man in the department, whose name was also Steve, but he worked second shift. He, too, was surrounded by all women. Most of them had been working together for years. So, not only was I the "new kid on the block," but I was also the "new only male kid on the block."

The large drafting tables accommodated two artists, so you were, in essence, assigned a partner. My partner was Bonnie—a hot, young blonde smartass, with a quick wit and sarcastic sense of humor. All the women were very good at their jobs. I, obviously, was not, and needed a lot of instruction and assistance. My supervisor, Dana, was hardly ever in the room, so most of my questions were directed at Bonnie and Pam, who sat directly in front of me. They were helpful at first, but after a while, I started to feel like I became an annoyance who interfered with their work. There was a quota of ads per day that needed to be met. A quota that I struggled to come near, let alone meet.

After a certain familiarity and comfort level was achieved, the sarcastic "inferior man jokes" commenced. My difficulties even extended to lunchtime. The entire department went out for lunch. I was not invited, so I would go to the cafeteria. There, I found myself sitting at a table alone with all the supervisors, sitting at another table in a corner of the mostly empty lunchroom. If I thought that dealing with the NA cliques was tough, they were a walk in the park compared to this. I felt self-conscious and trapped, so I started going out for lunch to the local McDonald's drive-through. This culminated in a daily work existence that can best be described as intimidating and stressful. My still fragile self-esteem was taking a daily beating, and this led to an almost constant state of anxiety. I was in the real world and out of my element—a fish out of water. In the "real world," I wasn't comfortable in my own skin.

I remember sitting in my car before work, with a knot in my gut, reading meditations for the day from both the *Twenty Four-Hour* and the *Day-by-Day* books, which I now kept under the seat. This was a commendable but inadequate attempt to alleviate my growing anxiety, and dread of walking into that place. I didn't realize it at the time, and I don't think the term was even used back then, but I had a bona fide albeit situational "anxiety disorder." In hindsight, I always felt I should have quit the job, but for some reason, I didn't. Later, I'd come to believe that reason was engineered by God Himself.

The day finally came that would offer the relief I sought, but at what price? It was Bonnie's 21st birthday. While she was in the washroom, Pam sent around a card for all of us to sign. As I handed it back to her, she asked, "Hey Steve, we're all going to (insert name of bar that is long gone and served lunch, here) for lunch for Bonnie's birthday. You want to join us?"

"Sure," I said, slightly shocked.

I can't remember the details, but I do remember that pitchers of beer were bought, 'Happy Birthday' was sung, and I drank. What choice did I have at that point? I was finally being let into the "secret club." Do you think I wanted to go back to being the "circus freak," odd man out by saying, "I'm sorry. Thanks, but I don't drink?" No way! Not to mention that having to lie about drinking a few beers was small potatoes compared to the huge secret of my previous relapse on heroin, already "locked away in the vault." This is a good example of the 12-step program slogan: "You're only as sick as your secrets." When you've got a big lie that you're holding onto, adding a smaller lie to "the pile" is easy to do. I also remember that the alcohol medicated my lingering social anxiety. All the justification I needed to drink was there.

The next day, I woke up on time, got ready, and went to work—all the while checking in with myself to make sure I was "okay." I remember thinking to myself, *Hmmm, no cravings to use heroin or cocaine or to go out and drink.* My conclusion? I was okay!

The following Friday, I was asked if I wanted to go to the same place for lunch. I agreed. Once again, I had a few beers. The next day was the same result, and again, I concluded, "I'm okay."

The third time, the circumstances were almost identical, with only two minor differences. I had four beers instead of two, and that particular Friday, I got paid. Was the outcome slightly different? No…it was extremely different! How different? After cashing my check, the next thing I know, I'm in Melrose Park, knockin' on Lenny's door. That's how different. I don't remember all the details, but I recall that I did some Methadone and shot some cocaine for the first time in well over one year.

It had been about 15 months since my world collapsed, and I asked for help and went into treatment. Now, in just a few short weeks, I found myself back on the merry-go-round that got me there.

Some of the newer staff were stuck working in the evening and ran groups for the Second Phasers that worked first shift. Pete usually left about 5:00-5:30 p.m. so I always made sure I didn't get back to the house until after that time. The last person you wanted to be around was Pete if you were dirty. Pete could smell someone who was using a mile away.

One day, I pulled up and "luckily" (now I understand that it wasn't luck at all) found a spot right in front of the house on Wabansia Avenue. I usually had to park at least a block or so from the house. To my surprise, Pete hadn't left yet and was backing down the driveway. I quickly ducked just as he got to the end of the driveway. I waited until enough time elapsed for him to make it out to the street and be on his way. My heart leaped into my throat when I heard his car stop and continue to idle at the end of the driveway. Now, almost sure he saw me, I thought fast and decided to play it off, acting like I was looking for something on the floor of my car. When I picked my head up above the dashboard, he was waiting to make eye contact. I smiled and waved. He nodded his head knowingly with that devilish grin on his face that said, *I got your ass.* He then proceeded to back onto the street and take off.

At that moment, I decided to come clean and confess. I knew Pete was on to me, and I couldn't carry the guilt anymore. I dropped it in group that night. My new counselor, Jackie Jackson (a recent Gateway graduate, of course), was running the group. She and the group commended me for being honest. After group was over, she called Pete, who instructed her to tell me that I could go to work the next day, but I was to come straight back to the house and meet with him. Staff would review my case and determine what came next.

The next day, I met with Pete and Jackie, and they informed me that I was on restricted movement until further notice. This meant that I could go to work and back, I could not be late, and that I was busted to First Phase on the weekends, including only attending the in-house meetings. I also had to have individual sessions with my new counselor, Jackie, at least twice per week.

Now that everything was out and being dealt with, soon, I was back on track in my recovery—right? WRONG! There was still one slight problem that I couldn't seem to solve… I still wanted to use. I couldn't shake the desire. I had opened Pandora's Box and couldn't get the lid back on and close it. This would be dealt with in my individual sessions—right? WRONG! You can only deal with what you're willing to talk about in treatment, and I wasn't willing to talk about it. I was too worried about getting off restrictions and felt that being honest about my continued desire to use would prolong them. So, I told Jackie what she wanted to hear and got off restriction in about a month.

During that time, Carolyn informed me that she had decided to move down South, which is where most of her family was. I was the only thing keeping her here, and the relapse, likely contributing to her decision. It was all for the best since Laura and Rhoda had recently moved back to the area with Jessica and Melissa after Laura finally crashed and burned in California.

I heard through the grapevine that she had temporarily lost custody of the kids after being busted with an ounce of cocaine. Luckily, Rhoda came to the rescue. She moved back to Cali to take custody of the kids. I remember feeling pissed off that no one even tried to contact me, though being in treatment probably wouldn't have helped my cause.

The details are a blur, but once off restriction, I started "chipping," a little heroin here and a little coke there. This, combined with Laura and the kids living in Elmhurst and my job being in Mount Prospect (the suburbs), were the catalysts that led to the decision that it was time to move out of Gateway.

Without warning, I left Kedzie House and moved back in with my parents, with the understanding that I would look for an apartment. I just received my Social Security escrow account check. Bad timing. It was around $2,500. I cashed it and immediately went out and bought a new acoustic guitar and case for about $500. I drove around with the remaining $2,000 in an envelope and my brand-new guitar in the trunk of my car. I was still chipping, and for the most part, maintaining, but my use was slowly increasing.

I remember thinking things like, *okay, you're in control. You don't have to use all the time. Stay in control, Steve!* I had to maintain, so I could reestablish myself with my kids. I was going to Laura's and hanging with them, occasionally taking the kids out. But what contributed to my demise was Laura's boyfriend Greg started selling coke, and I became a customer.

Soon, I started getting a heroin habit and would feel crappy, and my nose would run if I didn't have dope. As November approached, I told myself *"You have to stop."* The Gateway graduation was happening soon, and in my twisted mind, I still felt I deserved to walk across the stage and get that diploma. Somehow, I found the strength to put the brakes on and stop using.

Fake it till you (don't) make it

It was November 12, 1986, Gateway's annual graduation ceremony at what was then the Conrad Hilton Hotel on downtown Chicago's "Magnificent Mile"—Michigan Avenue. It was a huge, classy affair, complete with limos and tuxes. I remember crossing the stage, shaking CEO Michael Darcey's hand, and receiving my completion certificate. I felt like a thief as I escaped with "the goods" and walked back to the table I was seated at.

I continued celebrating with my fellow graduates. We laughed and reminisced about our adventures in treatment, and before the night was through, we all gathered for a Class of 1986 photo. We were all graduates of the college of "hard knocks." Ron Orlando used to say that diploma was worth more than any college degree. He was right.

It felt like my big mistakes were, once again, in the rearview mirror. I had to find a way to put them behind me and move on, but it was like the story that my sister Mary Jo used to read to me as a child—*The Tell-Tale Heart* by Edgar Allan Poe. Just when I thought the heart of my addiction was dead and gone, there it was again, beating ever louder and louder.

So, my attempt at cleaning up was short-lived. After graduation, the slow leak resumed and quickly escalated, until the dam burst. The roll of money in my trunk became like someone sitting in my back seat with a gun to my head. *Turn here, Steve. Now, get on the expressway. That's right; now drive. That's it; get off at Diversey."* Before I knew it, I was knocking on Annie's door again.

I continued to drive around "looking for an apartment," with most of my belongings from Gateway still in my backseat. My guitar remained in my trunk and was barely touched, let alone played. The white envelope that was not very well hidden in the hole of the spare tire, once filled with hundreds and fifties, began to shrink into a dwindling roll of twenty-dollar bills.

Whatever control I had was soon completely gone, and I found myself, again, fully in the grips of addiction. Guilt, shame, and remorse, for blowing over a year of treatment, were oddly absent. When you're in the throes of addiction, there is no time or room in your psyche to indulge in such emotions. You're too busy lying and manipulating to cover your tracks and getting that next fix. As soon as the poison was shot into my vein, any feelings still hanging around quickly vanished, and were replaced with the euphoria from the rush of cocaine, followed by the warm, false contentment of heroin. This is why I loved the "speedball." The mixture met all the needs of my addicted brain. No paranoia after the coke rush, and then into the warm cocoon of the opiate nod.

By then, I had reconnected with my brother Paul, who introduced me to his new connection on the West Side, Willie James. You usually went with whoever had the biggest bags, the best dope, and was the cheapest. At times, the only thing that mattered was who was the closest. It was mostly for this reason that I also reconnected with my Stone Park Hillbilly Mafia connection, Roy, who sold heroin and cocaine out of Lil' Abner's on Mannheim Road.

In November of 1986, I don't remember anything about my 27th birthday or the Thanksgiving holiday. I assume I spent them with my family. Still able to hide my use, no one knew I had relapsed at that point. Though the memories of those days were vague, I remember vividly what happened on Sunday, November 30th, at the end of that four-day weekend.

I bought 75 milligrams of Methadone from Lenny. I kept the bottle in my trunk and took an occasional gulp every now and then, between hits of coke that I was shooting in gas station bathrooms. I had still managed to hang on to my job at GTE, though my attendance had started to slip.

I had to work the next day, which was the reason I stayed close to home and decided to cop some dope from Roy at Lil' Abner's. I paged Roy from a payphone in front of the White Hen Pantry near my parent's building and waited. Seconds feel like hours when you're waiting to cop dope. No call. I paged him again. Again, the phone didn't ring, no matter how intently I stared at it. I remember getting ready to put my car in reverse and give up, thinking, *it's starting to get late. I should probably call it a night.* As I backed out of the space, the phone started to ring. I quickly pulled back in, jumped out, heart pounding, and answered it. It was Roy.

"This is Roy. Who's this?"

"It's Steve."

"Oh, hey Steve. Whadaya need?"

"I need three small pepperoni and two small sausage" (three $20 bags of coke and two $20 bags of heroin).

"I'm out of sausage 'til tomorrow."

"Okay, I'll just take the three pepperoni then."

I hung up the phone and jumped in my car. I pulled off Mannheim Road into the parking lot and looked for a good place to park. I knew when I came out, I was going to be shooting cocaine in the car, so I pulled in with my front bumper almost touching the building next door. The cars parked on either side would give me plenty of cover on three sides, with only my backside exposed.

As I walked in, Ray excused himself from the pool game he was in the middle of, and we walked to the bathroom. I forced some small talk with him, quickly handed him the money, and scored the three "snow seals" of coke. I opened one and the white powder sparkled teasingly at me. I put a small amount on my fingertip and tasted it. Numbing the tip of my tongue, it passed the test.

"I'm hearin' that people are likin' this stuff better than the last batch," he drawled.

"Okay, good. Thanks, Roy. See ya next time."

As I headed out the door, the knot in my stomach tightened. The butterflies in my stomach turned to gas, and I farted as I unlocked my trunk to retrieve my works, and a small plastic bottle filled with water from my secret stash compartment. As paranoia started kicking in, I surveyed the lay of the land, for one last check to make sure no one was observing me. I got in my front seat and checked my mirrors to make sure I had the "all clear" before preparing the hit in the spoon. Based on the taste I did, and the level of numbness my mouth experienced, I figured I needed to do a little over half a bag to get a good rush.

After drawing it through the cotton, I pushed the hit to the top of the syringe until the small drip appeared at the tip. I licked it off, adding to the numbness of my tongue. I checked my mirrors one more time before tying myself off. I penetrated my vein with a subtle "pop." The skin on my favorite injection site was getting scarred and covered with tracks once again. I pulled the plunger back and watched the blood cloud shoot into the syringe—I was in! I pushed the plunger slowly, being careful not to move one millimeter. Junkies know the slightest movement can mean the difference between getting a good hit and wasting it by going through the vein and into the muscle.

The ice crystal rush of cocaine flowing through the vein was the complete opposite of the warm rush of heroin, but they were somehow surprisingly similar when the drugs reached the brain. At the end of their respective journeys, both created intense euphoria.

As the hit coursed through my veins, the familiar smell of mint, pine and rubbing alcohol—mixed with blood and cells—filled my nose. The numb freeze that hit my mouth signaled the last stop before it would envelop my brain and body in intense euphoria. My jaw started moving from side to side and my teeth started to grind, and I became hyper-aware of holding on for dear life, as the "80-mph gust" of cocaine ripped away at me. I flung open my car door and leaped from the seat as my survival instincts instructed me, *Walk Steve. You've got to walk to make sure your heart keeps working.* It was a decent hit, and the drug was trying to pull me into a sea of death, as was typical with a good hit, but I resisted, and once confident that it did not have the teeth to take me, I was able to relax and enjoy the remaining 30 to 60 seconds of bliss I had left. I spent it pacing through the parking lot and in the alley behind Abner's until I felt it fading, and control of my breath, heartbeat, and consciousness returned.

I got back in my car, and as it all started to fade, it was replaced with intense craving to do another hit. My logical mind knew I couldn't. As I previously explained, if you don't wait until you completely come down from a hit, your next hit will be a dud and a waste. But out of nowhere, the part of my brain that was good at bullshitting me, jumped up to challenge logic. It said, *I think you may be able to do another hit sooner than usual. Don't forget, you have a good amount of Methadone in your system backing you up. And you have enough coke, so you may have to do a bigger hit, but you should feel it just fine.* It didn't take much bullshit to convince me to do something I wanted to do; so, it was settled—I'd do another hit in a minute or two.

I didn't go for long before getting the next hit ready. I dumped the remaining coke from the first bag, and the entire second bag, into the spoon. I hid the third bag in a secret compartment in my cigarette pack. I prepared the second hit and injected it. Everything that happened with the first hit happened with the second, only…TIMES FIVE!

I knew I was in trouble when my ears started ringing almost to the point of deafness. Then, the men started coming out of the shadows and this time I was able to make out what they were whispering, *"There he is. Let's get him!"* I knew I had to get out of there, so I exited the car, and walked toward Mannheim Road. I needed some alcohol as soon as possible, so I headed to the former discotheque, Stay Out All Night, which I still went to on occasion.

When I entered, I was blasted by the loud music and atmosphere. It was a Sunday, so the doorman didn't stop me to pay a cover charge, and I made a beeline for the bar. Carol was known to occasionally show up there, so I remember dreading running into her or any other normal person I knew, in the obvious state of panic and distress I was in. I shakily ordered my usual Southern Comfort on the rocks, pounded it down my throat, and ordered another. I was already starting to experience some relief—the booze did the trick.

As my hearing and vision started to return and I got my bearings straight, I started to scan the place, looking for familiar faces. I immediately recognized Debbie sitting directly across the bar. Debbie was a friend and neighbor of mine and Laura's when we lived in the Oasis Mobile Home Park.

She and her husband Al were around our age, and we became fast friends when Laura discovered a common love for snorting PCP. I obviously did not share this love but would do it on occasion when no other drugs were available.

Debbie was a bit of a dingbat, but she was also a vixen with a hot, sexy body. There was always a little underlying sexual chemistry and attraction that we were careful not to let Laura and Al see. She recognized me, saying, "Steve, oh my God!" and she flew off the barstool to come over and say hi. We chit-chatted about the usual stuff and quickly reported our relationship status. Apparently, like Laura and me, she and Al didn't make it and were divorced. I expressed my grief and disappointment, which of course, was complete bullshit. In the back of my mind, I was jumping for joy. It got even better when I asked who she was there with. She told me she'd come with a girlfriend who she thought had left without her, and asked if I could give her a ride home.

I became aware of the perfect scenario that was unfolding before me, a scenario that I used to always try to make happen when I used to frequent clubs and bars. Not only was it going to happen, but it was with someone with a great body, that I secretly always had the hots for. As 2 a.m. rolled around and the club was getting ready to close, I asked: "You ready to go?"

"I'm ready. You ready?" she replied with a lot of flirty innuendo.

"Yep."

We exited to the parking lot, and I looked for my car. Of course, it wasn't there. Then I recalled that I had parked at Abner's across the street. I explained to Debbie, and we ran across the street to the place I had parked. To my surprise and bewilderment, my car wasn't there either and there was another car parked in the spot. How could I have moved my car and forgotten where I put it? I was at a loss for an explanation. After checking the entire lot, Debbie started getting a look of concern on her face. I tried to play it off. "Hmmm, maybe I did move it to the Stay Out parking lot after all. I must be losing it," I chuckled. Reassured, Debbie chuckled too.

We bolted back across the street to the Stay Out lot that was now getting close to being emptied as people were leaving, making it much easier to see where my car was. After checking the entire lot and even an adjacent lot, it wasn't there. I apologized to Debbie and started thinking out loud, "It couldn't have been stolen. Who in their right mind would steal a 1980 Chevy Malibu?" It was one of the worst cars Chevy ever made. Then the only logical explanation hit me—it was towed! Someone may have observed me parking in Abner's lot but being at Stay Out. I knew where the tow lot was. It was next to my uncle's highway garage about a mile or so north on Mannheim Road. We walked there. It was our last hope.

When we got there, I climbed the eight-foot chain-link fence to the top to get a better view. It became apparent that it wasn't there. It was 3 a.m. Debbie had been a trooper through the whole ordeal. Then, a dude pulled up who recognized us from Stay Out and asked if we were okay. We told him what was happening, and he offered us a ride. It was time to admit defeat and let Debbie go. "You go ahead Deb. I gotta go back to Stone Park and keep looking."

"You gonna be okay?" she asked, concern in her voice.

"Yeah, I'll be all right. I gotta go to work tomorrow. I'll figure something out."

And that was it. I stood there staring and imagining what might have been as they sped off into the night. God played a cruel joke on me, and once again, drugs sabotaged me and interfered with me getting something I wanted.

When I got back to the area, I looked everywhere within a mile radius. Nothing. I thought about the wad of cash, a brand-new guitar, Methadone, and syringes were in the trunk as well as all my cassettes, photo albums, and other belongings in the back seat. It was about 4:30 a.m. and the only thing left to do was go to the Stone Park police station and report the car stolen.

I walked into a police station (voluntarily for once in my life) and completed the report. Just when I thought things couldn't get worse, they did.

"Mr. Fiorito, I'm sorry to inform you, but you have an outstanding warrant for your arrest, and we're going to have to take you into custody."

"What!? I came here to report my car stolen, and you're arresting me?"

"I'm sorry Mr. Fiorito. You have the right to remain silent. Anything you say…."

They patted me down and confiscated my belongings including my cigarettes, which contained a quarter gram of cocaine. I thought to myself, *well, as soon as they find that, I'm fucked!*

With my phone call, I of course called my mommy. It was about 5 a.m. when Albie came and bonded me out. As they returned my belongings, which included my cigarettes, I realized I caught a break. They didn't find the coke.

Albie looked tired and distraught as we got into her car. Paul and I had aged her beyond her years. She started questioning me and asked if I had started using drugs again. I of course, denied it and pointed out, "Hey, my car got stolen and I had an old warrant for my arrest!" It could happen to anybody, right? We methodically drove up and down every side street looking for the car until we ran out of time. We had to get me to work by 7 a.m.

If the next part of the story doesn't demonstrate the complete insanity that is drug addiction, then nothing will. On the ride to work, the quarter gram of cocaine in my cigarette pack started beckoning to me and I got hit with another wave of intense craving. I started plotting a way that I could shoot my last bag on the way to work. Impossible right? My mind, though tired from no sleep, drugs, alcohol, and all I had just been through, still found a way to grind out a plan. The sheer determination and ingenuity were incredible, even if it was for an unworthy cause. They say, "Where there's a will there's a way" especially when cocaine is involved. Then, it hit me! I remembered hiding a syringe in the bathroom at the small dive we used to hang out at on Grand Avenue—Carmie's. It was more or less on the way, so, I made up some bullshit reason to Albie why we had to stop there before I went to work.

On the way, I reminisced about more innocent times, when I was a kid, and the small building housed the penny candy store that my sister Sue sent us to on our candy runs. In a way, I had come full circle with my addiction—sugar to heroin and cocaine—an irony that was completely lost on me at the time.

Albie waited in the parking lot, while I went into the dark and dingy bar. I was immediately hit with the smell of the previous night's beer, cigarettes, sour mop, and just a slight hint of puke that hung heavy in the air. The smell of bleach mixed in there somewhere but barely put a dent in the barroom stench.

I went into the bathroom and felt above the paper towel dispenser, where a defect in the wood trim carved out the perfect hiding place for a syringe. It was still where I'd left it weeks earlier. It wasn't in great shape though, and I barely got the plunger to move in the barrel. Having no Vaseline, I had to improvise with the only emergency lube available—an old dope fiend standby—ear wax. I tested it and got the outfit as functional as possible. I found a bottle cap in the garbage and got some water from the sink. I went into one of the stalls and dumped the remaining bag into the bottle cap. I injected the mixture into my vein and waited for the familiar taste and smell. As it started coming on, it quickly dissipated.

The scenario that IV drug users dread became my reality, and put an exclamation point on the night, when I missed the vein with most of the hit. I immediately looked at the injection site for confirmation. There it was—a lump the size of a small golf ball. Having no time to dwell on my disappointment, I rolled down my sleeve, threw the outfit and other equipment into the garbage, and walked outside. I got into the car and conjured up some quick lie for Albie, and we continued to head to Mount Prospect to get me to work.

When I arrived, I had no way of knowing it would be my last day. You would have thought I'd have been fired by this point.

That day, I stole a bottle of prescription painkillers from a coworker's purse. I downed a handful of the pills with water. Since I was the only one who stayed back on break, they were bound to figure out that I stole the pills. I'm sure they had their suspicions about me. I had a knot in my gut for the remainder of my shift that she would discover them missing and make a big scene.

It would be the last time I would see their faces, particularly my supervisor Dana's face, except while watching the news months later. At that time, I would learn her fate. She would soon be shot to death in a mob-style hit, orchestrated by her husband. He would be charged and convicted. To be honest, I always thought Dana was a bitch, but never felt she deserved to die that way.

After I got home that day, I was still beating my head against the wall about what had happened to my car. I had a gut feeling that I was missing something. My obsession inspired the idea of calling Roy to ask him if he knew anything. I paged him, and he called back almost immediately. I told him the story of what happened. His response would confirm that there was a missing puzzle piece and a big one at that, which would solve the mystery.

"What kind of car was it?" he asked.

"A grey Chevy Malibu."

"Oh man! That was your car?"

"What do you mean?" I asked.

"One of the guys I was shooting pool with came in and said there's a car out there running with the keys in it and the driver's side door wide open right in the driveway with no driver in it! Like whoever was driving it, it was about to turn onto Mannheim. They went out and checked a few times. It was there for a long time, but when they checked on it around 3 a.m., it was gone."

Triggered by Roy's words, it all came back to me and hit me! I had suffered a cocaine-induced blackout. Remember when I wrote, "I knew I had to get out of there, so I parked, exited the car, and started heading for Mannheim Road"? That isn't exactly what happened.

Flashes of what really happened began penetrating my mind. I did head toward Mannheim Road but not on foot. Instead, I started the car and tried to drive out of there. As I reached the mouth of the driveway, the hit overpowered me. I knew I couldn't drive and was at risk of losing consciousness. That's when I threw it in park and exited the car, leaving it running with the keys in it. My initial thought was just to walk off the effects and then return to the car, but instead of the intensity dissipating, it increased, driving me to the need for alcohol as a quick comedown. By the time I made the beeline to the bar, I had blacked out and forgotten that I left my car running with the door wide open.

"Roy, I need my car to get to work. Please be honest with me. If you know who took it, please help me get it back," I said, desperation in my voice.

"Steve, I swear—none of the guys in that bar took it. They were just amazed every time they looked out there and saw it was still there and running. I would get it back for ya if someone I knew took it, but they didn't."

"Okay, Roy. Thanks. Let me know if you hear anything."

I was still in shock from the memory of what really happened. I didn't know how much cash was in the car because I wasn't keeping track. All my possessions and a brand-new guitar and case were gone just like that.

As I further descended into insanity, I could no longer function normally. Now, without a car, I just stopped showing up at work. Dwelling on my misfortune was only interrupted by the thought of needing a car. There was only one person to call in my world—Brian Kasman.

Brian once again came through with a cheap, beater Chevelle. The body looked like shit, but everything worked, and the engine ran like a top. Unfortunately, the car did nothing but give me the means to drive myself deeper into the abyss of addiction.

My next plateau would be a new low, even by my fellow addicted brother Paul's standards.

Right before Christmas—I stole my parents' microwave oven and TV. My parents were on a fixed income, and for all intents and purposes, they were poor. I brought the items to my latest connection who Paul had hooked me up with on the West Side—Willie James.

Paul worked with Willie, but he sold dope from his house on the side. We would go there on Friday's and Paul would sometimes blow his entire paycheck on dope. Paul was livid when he found out what I did. My parents figured it was either me or my brother who took their stuff. Paul of course knew he didn't, so that left only me. Apparently, my sister Sue's most recent husband Dave was with him when they got the call from Albie.

"That little son of a bitch!" Sue exclaimed. Paul and my brother-in-law Dave set out to find me. They knew right where to look too, and they staked out Willie James' house. Sure enough, they saw me walk out the front door and head to my car. I got in it and drove away, and a brief car chase ensued until they got me to pull over. I remember feeling embarrassed and thought to myself, *what the fuck is Dave doing here?*

After pulling over, I tried to run, but they cornered me, grabbed me by the shirt, and pushed me up against the wall of someone's garage. They threatened to beat the shit out of me if I didn't get the microwave and TV back.

"Where are they?" Paul yelled.

"I traded them to Willie James for some dope."

"Get in the car. Let's go!"

They escorted me into Dave's car, and we drove back to Willie's. Once there, Paul went in, and Dave and I waited in the car.

"What the hell's wrong with you Steven? Your parents are old, and they don't have anything. How could you do something like that?"

My response was robotic and one of many auto-responses I used to have cued up, but ironically, it was also true. "I don't know," I said in a sincerely bewildered tone. Why did I do anything? The million-dollar question.

In a few minutes, Paul came out with the microwave, and Willie James followed close behind with the TV. They put the appliances in the trunk as Willie shot me a look that reflected pity. I overheard Paul promise to pay $50 on payday, which is what the dope I got was worth. Paul thanked him profusely, and Willie assured him that everything was cool, and he went back in the house. As they drove me back to my car, Paul talked to me like I was a retarded child.

"You can't do that shit Steven. Mom and Dad are old. What are they going to do without a TV? They can't go out; they don't have shit. Don't ever do anything like that again."

"I won't," I promised, and I meant it, but by now, I knew I couldn't keep promises, whether I meant it or not.

They dropped me off by my car and drove away. I felt the few seconds of guilt that I was capable of, and then my mind went back to what was important—how I'd get my next shot of dope.

After getting some money, I found my way back to Willie James' house a day or two later. As my addiction continued to spiral out of control, I became obsessed and using became my only priority. If stealing my parents' microwave and TV wasn't proof enough, what I was about to pull next left no doubt.

By then, I had stopped going to work and wound up staying at Willie James' for several days on a cocaine binge. I used just enough opiates to keep me from going into withdrawal. Willie was a nice enough guy, but he was a dope fiend and so was his girl. They had a toddler son who walked around with poop in his diaper constantly. They rented a house off Chicago and Lockwood Avenues, in the heart of "the hood" on the West Side. Paul and I were often the only white people in the entire area. I remember walking to the store on Chicago Avenue to get cigarettes and being vaguely aware of being the only white person in the hood. Meanwhile, they were robbing and shooting each other daily. I get the feeling that my brother was right about why I was never bothered. They either thought I was completely crazy, or I was "The Man."

When I ran out of money and shot my last bag, I started to experience a deeper than usual desperation. Because of the TV and microwave debacle, I had no credit, and I knew it. I had no hustle that would fly in an all-black neighborhood, and no resources, except one—my car.

I thought, *hey, I can get another beater*. So that was it. I traded my car for about $150 worth of mostly cocaine. I agreed to bring him the car title the next time I came over, as I once did with my little sex-buddy Ginny.

As night fell, and I shot the last of the cocaine, I slipped into my typical hallucinations and paranoid delusions. Willie, his girl, and a few of their friends were in the bedroom upstairs doing their drugs while I was down the hall in the bathroom doing mine. The delusions came in the form of hearing their words, slipping through from under the door: "I'm sick of that white boy. He makes me nervous and ruins my high when he does too much coke. He's probably out of dope by now and is gonna start begging. I say we should get rid of him."

Of course, they probably never said any of that, but I never knew for sure. In any case, once I thought they were going to kill me, things quickly got pretty insane. I was going to slip down the stairs and then out the door, until it occurred to me that I had no car. No matter. I had to get out of there, even if it meant walking through the entire West Side at night, in the cold with no coat. I got about halfway down the stairs, but because it had gotten dark, I began to hallucinate people at the bottom of the stairs. I was trapped on the stairs. I crouched down so I would be a smaller target and turned toward the bottom of the stairs. That's when I saw my only chance to escape—the stairway window. I wouldn't have time to unlock it, open it, and crawl out. I'd have to leap and crash through the glass like in the movies. I remember thinking I'd be cut up and hurt when I hit the ground about 15 feet below, but it was my only chance of surviving the situation I was in. I crept down a few more stairs to get into position. I put my hands over my head and positioned my arms over my face to take most of the impact. I felt the sweat dripping from my forehead and could smell my strong, chemically induced body odor.

"Ready, set…JUMP!" I closed my eyes, but nothing happened. I tried again, but again, I didn't move. I knew I didn't want to do it, but the longer I sat there, the louder the voices got. I knew I had to make my move, but when I tried to straighten my legs and leap, I couldn't. It was as if someone had me by the ankles and wouldn't let me do it. I sat in that position for about an hour. Then, the bedroom door opened, and Willie came toward me. Before I could think anything, he was upon me. He passed me on his way downstairs. "Hey, we were wondering where you were. How you doin'? You okay?"

"Yeah, just a little paranoid" I replied as I snapped back into reality.

"You doin' too much of that coke without a break. Go on and git you some of that Jack Daniels upstairs. That'll mellow you out."

And just like that, I snapped out of it. Good thing too. When I think back on what would have happened if I had gone through that window, I get a knot in my gut. I know I would have died. If the glass and the fall didn't kill me, Willie James and his friends would have had to. There was too much dope in that place for them to have the cops and an ambulance come. Talk about the stairway to Heaven; that would have been mine. Or maybe, more like the stairway to Hell.

I took his advice and went into the bedroom and poured some whiskey into one of the plastic cups. Willie's girl and a few other people tried to be pleasant but were probably leery and annoyed with me. I know I would have been. As usual, I was able to clear the room by my presence and cocaine use. You'd have to be crazy to want to be around me when I was in that state.

I found myself sitting there alone, downing Jack Daniels out of a plastic cup. As I scanned the room, looking for dope that someone may have left, my eyes zeroed in on something that jumped out at me—my keys. Memories of what I did to Ginny flashed into my mind. Could I really do it again? Getting caught could result in my murder, or at least a good ass-whoopin' and getting thrown out in the cold on the West Side of Chicago at night.

I went down the stairs to see where everyone was and if I had a clear path to the door. Everyone was in the kitchen, which was in the back of the house, and the path was clear. I crept back upstairs and reluctantly picked up the keys. I walked quietly down the stairs, keeping a sharp ear out for anyone coming. I was even able to grab my coat from the bedroom. The coast was clear, and I picked up my pace to the front door. The door was a challenge with several locks and two chains. The second chain was my last hurdle. I pulled on the door and the cold December air hit me as it opened. I did it! I was out.

Luckily, my car was where I remembered parking it days earlier. Now the question was after sitting outside in the cold for days, would it start? The temperature had dropped quite a bit since I parked it. I put the key in the ignition and turned it. It didn't start. I panicked and wondered if I could get back into the house and put the keys back without being noticed. I pumped the gas a few times and said a quick prayer, which included my buddy, Brian. "C'mon, fucking Brian. You're a great mechanic—right?!" And I turned the key again. It started! Brian Kasman came through again in ways he'd never know.

I pulled away, drove past Willie James' house, and looked to make sure no one was coming out the door. No one did, but I was looking in my rearview mirror at least until I was out of the hood and hit the affluent suburb of Oak Park. I not only had burned a bridge for myself, but also for my brother, who never went to Willie James' house again.

Ain't but one way out

Once I was able to take my mind off my getaway, it occurred to me that I had nowhere to get away to. I was no longer welcome at my parents' after stealing from them. I wound up in the parking lot of my parent's apartment on Armitage and Mannheim roads. I was almost out of gas when I arrived. I reached into my right-front pants pocket and pulled out a one-dollar bill. I had to decide if I should put it in my gas tank to keep the heat going a little longer or get something to eat at the 7-Eleven up the street.

A wave of exhaustion came over me and I cranked the heater, locked the doors, and crawled into the back seat. I covered myself with some old clothes and newspapers I had on the floor and decided I would just crash out until the gas ran out and the cold woke me up.

Within minutes, out of nowhere, I started to sweat profusely. The cocaine I had been shooting had finally worn off, and as it did, I started to feel the opiate withdrawal it had been masking. Cocaine had also masked the fact that I was starving, which I was now painfully aware of. I started getting hot and cold sweats and bad chills. I was shaking uncontrollably. The sleepy feeling that I had experienced minutes earlier evaporated and was replaced by the restlessness of insomnia. I was miserable. I thought about my parents and even though it was 2 a.m., I felt compelled to ask if I could just come in out of the cold until morning. I had nothing to lose. Once they saw how sick I was, and knew my situation, they would cave in as usual, and let me in, right?

In the film, *The Basketball Diaries* with Leonardo DiCaprio, there is a scene where the main character Jim is dope sick and tries to get his mother to let him in and give him some money. She has the door cracked with the chain on. She refuses to give in, and she calls the police on him.

I was about to experience a variation of that scene. The only differences were that I wasn't asking for money, she didn't call the police on me, and instead of intimidating her with anger, I tried to get her to feel sorry for me and make her feel guilty. "Ma, please, I'm sick. Just let me stay until morning."

"I can't," she replied, her voice cracking in agony.

"Please, Ma. I'm freezing. I'm really sick. Look, I'm sweating in the middle of winter."

"I can't. Go get help Steven."

"Get help? Okay, I will, but I can't right now. Are you going to let me freeze Ma?"

"Hold on," she said, now starting to cry.

She walked away and while she was gone, I tried to get the chain off, but it was on correctly and I couldn't. She returned and pushed a blanket through the space.

"Go get help, Steven," she said, now sobbing as she closed and bolted the door.

For the first time in my life, it didn't work. They didn't cave. My father never even spoke to me or came to the door. I turned around with the blanket in hand and returned to my car.

As I sat there, wrapped in a blanket, staring at the gas gauge that was on E, the realization of what a complete failure I was, once again, set in and took hold of me. I was a failure as a son, as a father, as a brother, as an uncle, and just at life in general. And now, even after being given a second chance, I was a failure at recovery. Throughout my entire using history, I could say I never had a problem with depression, until that night.

A deep depression that I never felt before enveloped me. For the first time in my life, I felt like giving up, and I became suicidal. I thought it was the only way this nightmare that my life had become was ever going to end.

At that moment, if I'd had a gun, I'm sure I'd have used it on myself. Luckily, I didn't, but I did have a syringe.

At some point in a junkie's travels, they will eventually hear the urban myth that you can kill yourself by injecting a syringe full of air into your vein. The air bubble will travel to the brain, and boom, you'll fall over dead. I got the syringe out of the glove compartment, and stared at it, thinking about the peace that I thought would follow after it was over. Being the selfish addict that I was, the thought of how it would affect others I cared about never entered my mind.

I pulled the plunger all the way back so that the entire barrel filled with air. I reminded myself again that I just wanted this all to be over, but as I moved the needle toward my vein, Franko's words from a conversation we once had, jumped into my head...

"Kid, you know you can die by shooting too much air into your veins. But you couldn't do it with these little diabetic syringes that we use."
"Why not?" I inquired.
"They don't hold enough air to kill you. They would just probably cripple you and make you a vegetable for the rest of your life."

Those words probably saved my life that night and were the only reason I didn't try to kill myself. I certainly didn't want to be a vegetable and be in that state for years. So, I pushed the plunger back into place, put the cap on, and returned it to the glove box. I drove to 7-Eleven, gas needle on E, and spent my last dollar on some Hostess Cupcakes to stuff in my face.

Soon, daylight crept over the horizon. Later that day, I was notified (can't remember how or by whom) that there would be a family meeting that night to discuss my situation. Out of options, I agreed to attend. My family would meet at my parents' apartment, and we would eat dinner, and then have the meeting. I was never one to turn down a free meal, so I agreed to attend.

Johnny the drapery man puts his foot down

I was nervous and though my family tried to make small talk, the mood was tense during dinner. My sister Susan, in typical form, gave me the cold shoulder and didn't say a word to me. After dinner, we all went to the living room where my fate would be decided by them. I can't remember how the conversation went, except that my sisters were adamant that I could not stay with my parents. Susan was the most vocal about this, probably due to finally coming out of some of her own denial and divorcing Gerhardt. She was also the behind-the-scenes matriarch of the family and started to throw her weight around a bit. It could be said that she started bullying the discussion. My father, of course, sat quietly and listened as everyone else monopolized the conversation. He tried to introduce a plan for me to stay, but Susan insisted that I had to go, and it didn't matter where. That's when my father stood up and I witnessed one of the four times he ever showed anger in my life. At that moment, my father's proverbial foot came down hard on top of Susan's... "This is my fucking house, and I'm his father, and I say he's staying here!"

Everybody turned white with shock, and the room became silent. Then he turned to me and continued: "You can stay here, but the only thing you're allowed to do is get on that phone every day until you get back into treatment—nothing else! No social life, nothing! Eat, sleep, and work on getting back into treatment; that's all. Got it!"

"Yes," I answered, almost in a whisper.

Susan and Mary Jo left without saying much. They obviously weren't happy, but respected his decision, or at least the fact that he had made one.

I pulled Paul off to the side and explained what happened with Willie James. He told me he planned to stop going there anyway and warned me not to go back. He said he'd tell him that I left the state if he talked to him. Then he gave me some final words of encouragement before he left: "Don't blow it."

My mother brought me a pillow and blanket, and my parents went to bed. I lay there watching the TV I had just stolen and returned. I was 27 years old and once again found myself living on my parents' couch.

The next day I got on the phone as promised and called Gateway. Winter was not a good time to get a bed in inpatient treatment. They had no beds and there was a waiting list, but because I was a graduate, I was at least on a "short list." They recommended that I call some of my peers and get some support and encouragement from them. It took a lot for me to swallow my pride, but I finally did. I can't remember exactly who I talked to, but they encouraged me to get back to meetings, come to Kedzie House, and hang out. I hung up the phone after getting a glimmer of hope. However, it was short-lived, and things quickly started moving in the wrong direction.

My father had put his foot down but unfortunately, wasn't very good at keeping it down. He wasn't around during the day and was hanging on to his business by a thread. The move from his long-time location at Belmont and Narragansett Avenues, combined with his age, and the absence of any help from me or my brother, started to take its toll and signaled the beginning of the end of North Oak Drapery Service. He was already collecting Social Security, so retirement was just around the corner.

Though I was careful not to attract too much attention, by staying close to home, I slipped back into almost daily use. Things progressed and came to a head in early January when Paul and I went out to "get cigarettes" while at a family gathering. We went all the way into the city to Annie's, and copped dope. All I remember is that it was arctic, as in frigid cold, and my car had been leaking oil (as most of my cars did). The engine was loud and obviously struggling in the frigid temperatures. It seized and locked up. We wound up catching the last bus to the end of the line and we had to call someone to come and pick us up and drive us home.

Now that I had no car, my options became limited. I remember shooting cocaine in the bathroom with the shower running, pretending to take a shower. My mother would knock on the door, and ask, "Did you fall in?"

I was once again dependent on borrowing her car, which she was pretty stingy with. I would engage in some small-time hustles on foot throughout the day for money. This would all lead to a situation that would become yet another source of lingering shame and guilt.

I had been out hustling all day and had scored a pretty good amount of coke. I even got money to rent a room at the Carriage House—a seedy hotel across the street on Mannheim Road that was frequented by prostitutes and dope dealers. It was a little after midnight and I was out of coke. I left the room and walked home. On my way, I was hit with an intense state of craving. Out of money, and without a car, the wheels started turning in my coke-fiending mind and scheming how I could get more coke.

My father was away on one of his now more frequent fishing trips. This meant I'd be able to con Albie more easily. I came up with my story: I'd tell her that I needed to pay some people I owed money, or they were going to kill me. She couldn't refuse that one. When she went to the bathroom, I saw my opportunity. I pretended to be on the phone and the actor took "center stage," making it sound as serious as a heart-attack.

"Okay, okay. I'll find a way to get you the money!" I said in ear shot of Albie as she came out of the bathroom.

She looked at me with concern: "What's going on Steven?"

"I didn't want to tell you, but if I don't get these people their money tonight, they say they're coming here and they're going to kill me."

"They know where we live?" she asked.

"Yes."

"How much do you owe them?"

"Two hundred dollars, but he says he wants at least half tonight. Can I borrow your car? I've got to find a way to get some money."

"It's after midnight, Steven. Where are you going to get money?"

"I don't know, Ma, but I gotta try!"

She looked at me with worry on her face and said the words I wanted to hear: "I'll pay them. Where do we have to go?"

"The city—Diversey and Clybourn."

"Let's go!" her worry now turning to anger.

She put her coat on and her scarf over her head and grabbed her purse. We got in her car and drove to the projects.

When we arrived, I had her park in a secluded row in the parking lot of the adjacent Diversey River Bowling Alley and told her to wait. She handed me the money out of her purse. I told her I'd be right back. As I exited the car, I could see the fear and worry in her eyes. She asked, "How long will this take?"

"I should only be a few minutes or so," I said, shaking off the effects of seeing that look on my mother's face. I returned to "zombie mode" and the mission at hand—get the dope!

I walked across the Diversey Parkway bridge to Annie's, leaving my 68-year-old mother alone in a dark corner of a parking lot, in the projects at 1:00 a.m. I was oblivious to this and had only one thing on my mind—drugs!

When I arrived at Annie's, I couldn't restrain myself and shot several speedballs. By the time I returned to the car, it was 2 a.m.

Albie exclaimed, "What took so long?"

"The guy wasn't there, so I had to wait for him." The lie rolled off my tongue without a thought.

She lectured me about the money they didn't have and that I needed to get back into treatment before my father put me out on the street. I played her my "I know" tape from my "dope fiend library" of generic responses, pacifying her while I thought about the remaining speedball I had in my pocket. I had a tough decision to make: Should I do it when we get back or wait until morning.

This incident would signal the beginning of the end. The bottom was about to drop out and total loss of control was about to take over. For me, total loss of control meant I would not be able to hide my using from anybody, and I would start stealing anything that wasn't nailed down.

It reminds me of the old black and white werewolf films. After the man realized what was happening to him during the full moon, he warned the woman he loved, "Please go. I don't know what I'll do. I might even…hurt you."

Now I had become like the man in that old film. I couldn't control what I'd do. I couldn't guarantee that I wouldn't hurt people I cared about. Even my own mother.

It was the dead of winter, and there were still no beds available at Gateway. In desperation, I called Westlake Hospital in Melrose Park. They had a 28-day inpatient program there and they had a bed available. There was a problem though—if you didn't have insurance, you would be billed thousands of dollars for it. I had an insurance card in my wallet but figured it was no good since I left my job. I was wrong. As it turned out, my insurance was still valid because technically, I was never fired. I had always questioned why I didn't quit that job at GTE. Was this the reason that I held onto that miserable job? I remember thinking, *could this have been God?*

My father bought me a pack of smokes and drove me to Westlake. He stayed until they processed me in. I'm sure he left feeling relieved that I was finally in a safe place getting some help. His relief would be short-lived.

As a result of my intake assessment, the MD ordered me to be medicated with Methadone, and because of the cocaine withdrawal, Valium. Big mistake! Valium made me as snaky as hell. I became bold and slippery on the drug. It also made me horny.

After they fed me, I proceeded to my first activity on the co-ed unit. I joined my fellow patients in the community room for group. There, I saw a little hottie sitting across from me. We exchanged smiles, followed by a round of the flirting game, "Caught You Looking at Me." We continued to flirt throughout group until "the entertainment" portion of the evening began. As it turned out, a few times a week, a psychiatrist who was affiliated with the hospital, Monte Meldman, would sing and perform on keyboard for the patients. This would require quite a bit of audience participation. His belief was that this was very therapeutic for the patients, and I'm sure it was, provided you weren't high as a kite on Methadone and Valium.

When group was over, I finally got a chance to talk to the object of my affection. We both knew that we had little time or opportunity to get to know each other, so we dispensed with the formalities. In fact, we dispensed with everything that wasn't absolutely necessary. There would be no time for normal courtship rituals, so cutting to the chase seemed almost appropriate. Before clearing out of the dayroom, she slipped me a note with her room number, inviting me to her bed after lights out. She said that after a certain time, there would only be one nurse at the nurse's station to get past.

At the suggested time, I tip-toed to a good vantage point of the nurse's station. Just like her note said, there was only one nurse on duty. My chance finally came as she got up and attended to one of her duties, which required her to turn her back. I shot silently past the station to the hall where the female rooms were located. I found the room number and opened the door. The light from the hall showed four beds. She sprung up in her bed with a smile on her face and raised the covers showing her scantily clad body, inviting me to join her. I did, making sure the door made no noise as it closed behind me. I was also able to make out the beds that were occupied by her roommates.

As we started to fool around, I quietly asked about them. She assured me that they were sleeping and even if they weren't, they were cool. I don't remember if we used a condom, but we took care of business, after which I slipped out the door, making my way back to the room that I shared with a few roommates. I crept to the end of the hallway and again waited for a chance to get past the nurse's station. As I watched the nurse, I saw her go into her purse for something and then put it back under the counter near where she was sitting. Then she got up and went into a backroom. I saw my chance to get past her, but then I got an idea. I would reach over the counter and see if I could grab some money out of her purse. I would pretend I didn't feel well if she came out of the back before I had a chance to make the grab.

I went up to the counter where her purse was on the other side and listened for signs that she was coming. The sounds I heard confirmed that she was nowhere near coming back, so I reached over the counter and grabbed her wallet. I opened it and saw a modest stack of bills, which I grabbed and slipped into my pocket. I closed the purse and slipped back to my room. In the bathroom, I counted the cash, which totaled $80. The wheels started turning in my head. *How can I get some dope in here?* I couldn't do anything at that time, so I would have to sleep on it and find a way tomorrow.

The next day, as I was in the dining room eating breakfast, I looked for my new friend but didn't see her. As I finished breakfast, one of the staff asked me to come with them, saying that another staff member wanted to talk to me. As we walked toward one of the offices, I saw my friend through the glass, sitting in another room with her coat on, talking to two staff members. She was crying. It dawned on me that we were busted. Someone ratted us out.

When I entered the room, the director and two security guards waited for me. They informed me that I was being discharged. Several fellow patients had identified me as the person who snuck into the girl's room, and they strongly suspected that I had taken money out of the night nurse's purse. They asked if I would mind if they searched my belongings and my person. I declined (the money was in my pocket). They asked if I wanted to call anyone for a ride since the snow drifts were four feet high, and it was pretty cold outside. I called the only person left who would even talk to me—my father. I, of course, made it sound like I was an innocent victim of mistaken identity. He agreed to come and get me. Security escorted me to the lobby with my big green garbage bag of stuff that they had so kindly packed up for me, and I waited. It started snowing as I saw his car pull up to the entrance of the hospital.

What a huge disappointment I must have been to him, though he never said a word to that effect. I opened the back door and threw my Hefty bag in the back seat, then got in the front passenger side.

"Where are we going? You know your mother won't let you come back by us," he informed me.

That was a good question, and to be perfectly honest, I didn't have the answer. I know where I wound up but have no idea why I was there, or how I got there. It's completely blacked out of my memory.

I wound up alone at a White Hen Pantry on York Road in Elmhurst Illinois. One possibility is that I went to Laura's, who lived in Elmhurst at the time. She either wouldn't let me in or threw me out in the cold at some point. In any case, I remember having my bag of belongings with me and being at a payphone outside the store, calling people to see if I could get someone to pick me up and help me. I got nothing and no one. I was freezing. I looked down and noticed a patch of ice next to me on the sidewalk, and it gave me an idea—I would fake a serious injury and get a free ride to a hospital. That would at least get me out of the cold for a while. I made sure no one was looking and lay down on the sidewalk. I waited for someone to pull up or come out of the store, whichever came first. Someone pulled up, and I began my performance. I moaned until a man who looked to be in his late 30s came over. His girlfriend then got out of the car, and they both asked me what happened. I told them that

I've fallen down, and I can't get up. Okay, I didn't say it like that, but that was the gist. They said they would alert the store clerk to call an ambulance.

When the ambulance arrived, I faked a back injury, pretending that I couldn't move. So, they loaded me onto the gurney, strapped me in, and put me in the ambulance. I told them that I'd slipped on the ice and fell. They transported me to Elmhurst Hospital.

I occupied one of the emergency room beds and I was interviewed by hospital staff. One of the nurses took my vitals and she noticed the track marks on my arms. She alerted the attending physician. He asked me about the marks. I saw an opportunity to get a free dose of Methadone with my stay, so I got honest about my addiction. I told him that I was starting to go into withdrawal, which was at least partially true, as I soon would be. He assured me that they would help me and informed me of the 28-day program there. He said they would keep me for observation overnight but asked if I wouldn't mind meeting with one of the treatment staff for an evaluation in the morning. I agreed.

After being dosed with Methadone, I slipped into the safe, comfortable, familiar cloud that I loved more than life itself and drifted off to sleep.

Groundhog Day (same shit, different day)

The following morning, I was interviewed by the drug treatment staff. I was obviously qualified and admitted to the treatment unit. Once there, I was medicated with another dose of Methadone, and once again, someone made the fatal mistake of giving me Valium. I can only speculate that they were concerned about potential cocaine withdrawal. Or, I may have complained that the dose of Methadone was too low, so they gave me the Valium to shut me up. In any case, it was like the movie *Groundhog Day*.

That night, after lights out, I did almost the same thing I did at Westlake. Though I didn't have sex with a fellow patient this time, in many ways, the things I did were bolder and much worse.

As the lone nurse sat at the nurses' station doing paperwork, I crawled silently the length of the counter past her and slipped into the back room, where the staff kept their belongings. Her coat and scarf were hung up on a coat rack, and next to it on the floor was her purse. I carefully opened it and pulled out the wallet. Again, I grabbed a modest stack of bills and put them into my pocket and slipped back into my room, which had two beds but was only occupied by me. Oddly, the amount was the same—$80. Was it a thing with nurses that they carried around $80 in their purse?

What I did next went far beyond what I did the first time. I thought, *how could I get some dope*. I wondered if Roy would deliver since he was only about 10 minutes away. I got change for the payphone and managed to sneak off the unit. I called from the lobby. To my surprise, Roy answered and agreed to deliver the drugs outside the entrance but refused to come into the hospital.

I sat in the lobby in my hospital-issue pajamas, trying to keep a low profile. Within 15 minutes, I saw the familiar headlights of Roy's classic '64 Impala pull into the driveway. I met him outside, and we did the exchange, which was mostly cocaine but enough heroin to bring me down. It also included a brand-new syringe. I needed to get back on the unit undetected, and I'd be home-free. Somehow, I slipped back onto the unit and into my room.

I had the whole room to myself as I proceeded to fix and shoot my first hit of cocaine. You'd think that at some point in all this, it would have occurred to me that I was wasting my last chance at life. Unfortunately, that thought never occurred to me. It was my second treatment program in three days, and I was shooting cocaine in my room!

By my third hit, the delusions and paranoia started setting in. It was official—I was completely insane. I heard detectives outside the door talking to the hospital staff about me and waited for them to come through the door. They never did. Out of cocaine, I tried to find my way back to reality, so I cooked up the bag of heroin and shot it into my vein. It took the edge off but didn't completely neutralize the major flood of coke coursing through my veins.

By the time I finally fell asleep, it was 5 a.m. I crashed hard from the drugs wearing off, combined with pure exhaustion.

Just one hour later, at 6 a.m., I heard an angel calling my name, "Steven, Steven…Steven."

As I slowly awakened, I realized it wasn't an angel, it was a nurse. "Steven, you have to get up."

As I opened my eyes, I saw that my bed was surrounded by staff, which included two or three security guards. It was like that scene in *The Wizard of Oz*, where Dorothy's coming to after her ordeal. Maybe like in the film, they would inform me that it had all been a bad dream.

"What…what's going on?" I asked.

"You need to get up, Steven. We know what you did last night."

"What do you mean? What did I do?"

"You went off the unit and out of the hospital. We saw you on the security cameras. A nurse had money taken from her purse, and we saw you on camera coming out of the staff area last night."

"We have to discharge you, Mr. Fiorito," one of the program staff interjected.

"Let's go, Mr. Fiorito. We'll help you get your things packed up," a security guard chimed in.

Because I had nowhere to go, and the snow drifts were now six feet high, they helped me to make some calls to other programs. From the list of referrals I was given, only one had a bed available—Grant Hospital on Lincoln Avenue in Chicago. The hospital social worker got on the phone and expressed my severe need for treatment. They agreed to hold the bed until I arrived. The staff allowed me to call my father, and I don't remember how I explained the situation to him, but nonetheless, he came and got me.

I again found myself in the hospital lobby, waiting until I spotted those other familiar headlights pull up to the entrance. As I trudged through the snow to the car, Hefty bag in tow, all I could think of was the small amount of cocaine I still had left and when I would come down enough to be able to feel it. I was oblivious to how perilous and hopeless my situation had actually become.

Third time's a charm

Upon arrival at Grant hospital, I used the bathroom that was near the elevators. There, I saw a good spot to stash my remaining coke, spoon, and syringe. I hid them in a window well that was about seven feet or so off the ground. We rode the elevator up to 5-East, the drug treatment unit. Once there, my father said goodbye as if he were dropping me off at a job interview and disappeared behind the elevator doors. Again, I was in the hands of strangers, who I'm sure my father hoped could help me, but by now, he had to be having serious doubts that anyone could.

I was once again interviewed, and the typical assessment questions were asked. The intake staff introduced me to Mark, a male nurse to whom I was assigned, and I was told that I would meet my counselor, Bill, in the morning. Mark was a skinny guy who struck me as being gay, but not overtly. He was mostly bald, with a Fidel Castro-like beard, and a turtleneck sweater. You got the feeling that he was an anti-establishment, anti-capitalist, anti-gender, anti-whatever throwback from the Beat Poet era.

The next day, it didn't take long to realize that this program was different than the previous two. Though they medicated me with Methadone, they wouldn't give me so much as an aspirin, no matter how much I whined and complained. They also followed me everywhere I went.

I remember them grilling me, "Where are you going now, Steve?"

"Um, to the bathroom, if that's okay."

"Sure, go ahead," a smiling Mark would say. When I came out, there he was, sitting there waiting for me.

As the cocaine left my system over the next few days, I started experiencing paranoia. I was sure Mark hated me and was out to get me. The fact was, they were on to me. They had likely gotten the scoop from Elmhurst staff and my father about what happened at the previous two programs, and they were doing everything in their power not to let it happen again.

Eileen

From the first time I laid eyes on Eileen, I fell head over heels in lust with her. She was a freckled, curvy, smart, sexy nurse whose curly black hair was a bit on the wild side. She dressed in the same style of "hippie-gypsy" that I was, or at least thought I was. She was irreverent, had an edgy sense of humor, and exuded genuineness and confidence in everything she did. She pulled no punches and didn't tip-toe around anything. If you asked her a question, you'd better be ready for the answer, even if it hurt your feelings, but she wasn't mean-spirited. She had a genuine desire to help addicts. My attraction to her would be a good thing, as it wasn't just based on her physical attractiveness but also on the fact that she was in recovery from alcoholism for ten-plus years. I would gravitate to her as much for the valuable raw truths she would deliver to me, as I would her great knockers, shapely figure, and pretty face.

My counselor Bill was a kind of a stuffed shirt, and nurse Mark was—well, Mark. Eileen became my confidant and go-to person whenever possible. We connected right away, and she infiltrated my defenses and got me talking about myself. I think she, like many I'd met in these places, saw potential in me that I didn't see in myself, and I certainly hadn't realized at the time.

As I began to settle in, it became apparent that most of the patients on the unit were rookies and were clueless about treatment and recovery. I saw my chance to feel like "a big fish in a small pond" and expound on my advanced knowledge of both. You couldn't go through a program like Gateway and not come away with a deeper understanding and insight into addiction and recovery than most people had. However, I still had no idea how detrimental my ego was to my chances at actual recovery. This did not go unnoticed, and I was soon dubbed "The Patient Therapist" by the staff.

I became very helpful to my peers, spouting insightful advice and feedback, in and outside of group. Soon, my ego would inflate even more. I became a treatment "folk hero" by talking a peer out of leaving treatment who had his bags packed and was at the elevators. I got a few big pats on the back from staff and peers alike. Even Eileen was impressed, though careful not to pat me on the back too hard.

On Wednesday and Friday evenings, staff on duty would take us to the NA meetings on the ground floor. The Wednesday meeting was small and held in one of the smaller rooms. The Friday meeting was held in a huge conference room and was usually packed. It would start with a short lead (testimonial from a guest speaker) on Step One of the program, and then the meeting would take a break for people to socialize or get coffee and refreshments. Upon returning, everybody would break up into smaller circles in the room. At times, there would be eight or ten groups, with up to ten people in each group. It was challenging but also interesting to hear people talking in the group behind you while listening to someone in your group.

It was called Friday Night Alive, an appropriate name due to the social nature of the meeting. There was always a lot of pretty women, so I liked the meeting right away. Unfortunately for me, there was a huge distraction that needed to be dealt with. While attending my first meeting, I remembered the cocaine and works I'd hidden in the bathroom. By my second meeting, I had scoped out a way to slip away without being noticed by the staff, who would sometimes wander off while we were at the meeting. Without giving it a second thought, I reached up and felt the spot where I'd left the contraband. Everything was still there. I put the drugs and works in my sock and headed back to the meeting. When I got back to my room, I stashed the stuff in a drawer.

I went on autopilot and started going through the motions in treatment with only one thing gnawing at me from the back of my mind—how I could shoot that stinking cocaine. It didn't take long to realize there was only one place that you had privacy for long enough to do it—in the shower. Fortunately, I was only five or six days into my treatment when I did it. I think in the back of my mind I needed to just get it over with so I could get on with treatment.

Thank God it turned out to be a terrible experience in every way. First, I once again, partially missed my vein with the hit, so the rush was minimal and brief. Secondly, the feelings of depression and guilt that followed were magnified by the cocaine. I decided almost immediately that these were two feelings I never wanted to feel again. I broke the needle off the syringe and threw it and the related paraphernalia in the garbage.

With this incident behind me, I was ready to get on with my treatment and recovery. Not so fast! Unfortunately, I was still nowhere near out of the woods. I was in strong denial—out of touch with the reality and the dire nature of my situation. I was cocky, argumentative, defensive, and even belligerent at times. I failed to complete assignments or even come out of my room. Part of this was due to experiencing insomnia as they tapered my dose of Methadone, which, in my estimation, was already too low. I frequently complained but to no avail. The medical director, Dr. Michael Baldinger, was unsympathetic to my complaints. Apparently, he had experienced drug-seeking behavior in patients before (gee, ya think?) and was unmoved by mine.

In retrospect, the medication issue was secondary. The real barrier that kept my recovery as a vague and somewhat out-of-reach concept, was my distorted view and addictive thinking. I just couldn't get my bearings straight, and I was all over the place. I still couldn't differentiate what was important for my recovery from what was unimportant or what was real from what was fantasy. This wouldn't have been so bad, but what was worse was, I felt that I was okay and on track. That's the problem with denial—you don't know you're in it. So what if I shot a little cocaine a few days ago while showering in the treatment center—doesn't everybody? Like I've always said, does a crazy person know they're crazy? Usually not.

Staff and my peers started catching on and confronting me. Even the "rookies" figured out that although I knew a lot about addiction and recovery, I was applying almost none of it. It's kind of like a guy who reads a diagram on riding a bicycle but has never gotten on one and started peddling. Intellectually, they know how to ride a bike, but do they really? No. That was me at that time.

So, my counselor Bill sat me down and in his infinite wisdom (or maybe he just lucked out), gave me the perfect assignment—24-hour silence. I also had to journal my feelings through the whole thing. I was given a small cardboard sign to pin to my shirt that said, "My assignment is to be 'brain-dead for 24 hours. So, I'm not ignoring you. I'm just doing my assignment."

Unfortunately, I only lasted for about three hours. I asked someone to "pass the salt" at dinner. When they informed me that I had to start the assignment over, I became defensive and belligerent and refused.

In the "Big Book" of AA, the chapter on "How it Works" says:

"We stood at the turning point. We asked His protection and care with complete abandon."

I've always said that the only disagreement I have with this statement is that it should be plural, as in *turning point(s)*. I believe that there are usually several key events or milestones on one's recovery path that are crucial. My failure in treatment up to that point would bring me face to face with one of those turning points the very next day.

Open Report

On January 29th, 1987, an event would occur that would have a lasting impact and would change me in a profound way. I know the date because for some reason that I'm still not sure of, I possess a copy of my entire treatment file from my stay at Grant Hospital. It may have been standard practice in those days to give the patient a copy of their entire record upon discharge.

Open Report was a therapeutic, clinical exercise that consisted of a review of each patient's progress (or lack thereof) by the entire staff. It was usually done every week. Doesn't sound like anything special—right? But here was the kicker: the staff sat in a circle with the patients in rows behind them. As they reviewed each case, the patients were not allowed to speak at all. In other words, it had the feeling that they were talking about you as if you weren't in the room. The staff did a great job of not looking at or acknowledging the patients the entire time. They would pass the patient's chart around, and upon receiving it, each staff member would make comments about their experience with that patient and their view of their progress. The comments were generally positive, encouraging—and sometimes—even entertaining. It usually took at least five minutes or more for someone's chart to make it around the room.

My first experience was unremarkable. I hadn't been there long enough for the staff to get to know me. The second time around, it was an entirely different experience. In under two minutes, my chart made it around the entire room. Some staff just shrugged their shoulders, said nothing, and passed my chart to the next person. The comments that were made, were very brief and went something like this...

"He won't listen."
"He's not engaged."
"I don't know what to do with him."
"He's still in the grips of his addiction."

"I don't know what to say."
"He's treatment-wise, but that's about it."
And the one that had the deepest impact...
"I don't know if we can help him."

Here is what the actual case note said that was written in my chart that day:

"1/29/87   3:30 PM
#2 & 3 Open Report: Not engaged in tx. Will not listen to feedback. Talks a good talk, Tx. wise. Still into blaming the world for his drug problem. Until he opens up, he has no chance for long-term recovery."

I'd like to give the author credit, but I couldn't make out the signature on the note.

After the meeting, we were able to go to our rooms for an hour of rest and relaxation. As the meeting disbanded, we were allowed to briefly ask questions and share our feelings with staff about their comments. I remember reaching for my old standby defense mechanism of humor. The "class-clown" jumped in to save my ego and hide my feelings, and I made jokes about their comments, minimizing and dismissing them.

I turned and headed for my room. Upon entering, the voices of people in the hall became muffled, their words indistinguishable, and as the door closed behind me, I was met with a sudden, eerie silence. I was completely alone. My roommate had just moved out, so I had the room to myself. Suddenly, as if a dam burst, the staff's words exploded into my mind, especially...

"I don't know if we can help him."

"I DON'T KNOW IF WE CAN HELP HIM!"

At that moment, a monumental realization broke through. I was the sickest patient on that unit, and up until that moment, I didn't know it! If my treatment had ended that day and I had left, I would not have stayed clean, and I would have died. Then and there, my wall of denial crumbled, and the truth came crashing in on me! Overwhelmed by the pain and fear of my realization, I fell to my knees and started to cry.

Then, I said the first sincere prayer I had ever said in my life. It went something like this: *God, if you're up there, you've got to help me because I'm going to fuck this up. I can't do this on my own, so if you're there, please show me the way.*

It was the sincerest cry for help I had ever uttered. At that moment, my "hands" proverbially went up, and a sense of complete surrender came over me, including total acceptance on a deeper level, that I couldn't use drugs ever again. The line from "How it Works" in the AA Big Book and meditation from the *Twenty-Four Hours a Day* book sums up what happened to me that day…

"We stood at the turning point. We asked His protection and care with complete abandon."

You must admit your helplessness before your prayer for help will be heard by God. Your own need must be recognized before you can ask God for strength to meet that need. But once that need is recognized your prayer is heard above all the music of heaven. It is not theological arguments that solve the problems of the questioning soul, but the sincere cry of that soul for strength and the certainty of that soul that the cry will be heard and answered – Twenty-Four Hours a Day, November 12

It's hard to explain, but it's like stepping into another dimension, a new reality, and a new state of being. I felt this huge weight come off my shoulders; the burden of obsession with drugs was finally being removed—by God—not by me. Suddenly, I became acutely aware of the stark difference between wanting it and becoming it!

I knew I could never achieve this on my own. I tried so many times. It was as if a switch flipped inside me, and I found myself no longer in the problem, but suddenly propelled into the solution, and I was acutely aware of it. Don't get me wrong, the solution would be fraught with problems of its own (I call those "good problems"), but I was committed in every fiber of my being to staying in the solution, no matter what it would bring.

This is the "spiritual awakening" that Step 12 in the AA program talks about, and I had heard about in *so* many meetings. I understood it intellectually, but now it was actually happening to me. A sense of relief and peace came over me that the world could neither give nor take away. I always describe that moment in the following way: "The walls literally could have come down around me and I wouldn't have budged from that spot I was kneeling in. I felt completely protected and safe."

I now knew what it was like to be Samson when he trusted God as he pushed the pillars from their foundation and collapsed the Philistine's temple of Dagon. He had absolutely no fear of his own physical destruction because he was assured that his soul was safe in the hands of God.

After being stuck in a cloud of lies and distortions for the first nine days of treatment, I was suddenly enveloped in the truth, and like they say, "The truth will set you free."

That night, at about 1 a.m., I came out of my room after having my usual bout with insomnia. Eileen was on duty. My spiritual awakening put me on an introspective quest to better understand why I relapsed. God provided me Eileen, who was the perfect person to have that discussion with.

"I know I had my faults, but I was in treatment on my own. I wanted to stay clean, and I liked going to meetings. I had good counselors and good people all around me. What went wrong?"

She intuitively knew the answer and reached for the book—*Alcoholics Anonymous*—which lay on the table next to us. She held it up with the cover facing me and said: "You weren't working the program. You may have been working some Steve Fiorito version of it, but you weren't working THIS program!" she said, holding the book up with that clever, wise, Eileen smirk on her face. It could have been a commercial to market A.A.

I realized that I did pick and choose what parts of the program I was comfortable working, while the rest, I dismissed and ignored. She also pointed out that I had extremely low self-esteem and tried to cover it up, rather than face it and work on it. She bluntly proclaimed, "Deep inside, you think you're a piece of shit—don't you?" This was something I couldn't see and wasn't ready to come to grips with at the time.

"I don't think it's that. I like myself enough. I just wasn't doing the right things."

She agreed, but again, reiterated her statement. This observation would linger in the back of my mind and haunt me from time to time, well into the future. I didn't really feel that badly about myself—did I?

Silence is golden

The next day, I let it be known that I was ready to do my 24-hour silence assignment. Below are some of the highlights from my feelings journal while doing that assignment:

I'm very hurt by my evaluation. I'm said to be "in the grips." I would say that's very true considering I am still using one of the worst chemicals you can use every day. It's very hard and confusing taking Methadone every day and trying to recover. Maybe some people don't understand that here, but I think at least 1 person I found does. My nurse Mark. I think I have to get closer to Mark.

I don't like not being able to talk to everybody. Especially now when I'm feeling so down. I would really like to talk to Greg or Cisco or Terry about the way I'm feeling. Sometimes I feel like I'm not going to make it, then I feel I know I can do it, because I want to. I don't want to use anymore, and I feel like I'm going to be ok. And what's really scary is, I know this is it. I feel if I don't make it this time I will die. Something else that bothers me is no one seems to care. Counselors walk by as I'm writing here in the library. They all seem to know I'm having a hard time but none seem to show any concern. I don't know, maybe I'm paranoid.

Well to sum it up I'm starting to feel like there's hope for me again. I feel like the hyperactive Steve starting to calm down. Starting to think that I can start to concentrate on why I'm here more other than just to detox.

I was thinking about cocaine today for the first time in a good sense in a while. I actually not only didn't feel any craving for it today, but I started feeling the fear of ever using it again setting in.

I've decided that I think I know what I have to concentrate on while I'm here – Me – why I relapsed, and how I'm going to keep it from happening again.

I relapsed pretty simply because I wasn't working a program of recovery. The program I was working was my own design.

There will be no more Steve the counselor. I'm going to start to be honest about myself and my shit and let all of you counsel me.

Reading these thoughts brings up mixed feelings for me now. I'm a little embarrassed by my immaturity, obvious self-pity, and attention seeking, not to mention my poor writing skills. But I'm also sympathetic, understanding, and tolerant of what that young man was going through. It was confusing to take Methadone—a drug I abused regularly in my addiction—while trying to forge a sober identity and recover. At the time, I didn't realize how important it was to have a different relationship with myself and see myself differently. Despite this, somewhere in my ramblings (some of which I did not include here) peeking through, were the beginnings of a solid foundation in recovery.

I no longer wanted to use drugs, including Methadone. I was truly "sick and tired of being sick and tired." I also recognized the need to abandon my initial plan to just "detox" in that program. I needed to focus on myself and stop inflating my ego by coming off as an expert and counseling my fellow patients.

The silence assignment was almost as groundbreaking as Open Report was. I could hear myself think and feel my feelings for the first time in a long time. I saw clearly how my constant chatter was a distraction that kept me out of touch with my feelings, and how the "class clown" helped me avoid the unpleasant aspects of my reality. The value of listening, not only to others, but to myself, became clear. Listening and understanding started having more value than talking and being understood, especially in that early stage of recovery.

In the days that followed, a clear message emerged from statements I made that were documented in several group notes. *I'm not going to let anyone bring my program down,"* and *"I'm serious about wanting to recover."*

This was the beginning of an important fundamental belief that I was constructing, which would become the foundation of my recovery…

I COULD RECOVER no matter what others thought of me, or how wrong I was, AS LONG AS I DIDN'T PICK UP A DRINK OR A DRUG!

I had always heard that the first step is the only one we must work perfectly. I finally internalized this essential principle of the first step—don't use, no matter what! I clung to this new understanding like a drowning man would cling to a life preserver. It was the only thing I knew for sure back then.

On January 31, 1987, my parents came for a family session. They announced their new tough love stance, which meant, I could never live with them again. They were supportive of my plans to return to Gateway or The Men's Residence—a halfway house in Rogers Park, on the North Side.

So far, my attempts to get back into Gateway weren't having much luck. Their beds were filled. After initially talking to Syl about returning to Second Phase, I wasn't hearing back from him.

My dose of Methadone was reduced to 3 milligrams and on February 2, 1987, I would be given my last dose of Methadone. I believe it was a placebo and likely had no Methadone in it, as was typically done in those days.

The next day, I would finally hear back from Syl, who informed me that there were no beds available in the Second Phase program; however, one was about to open up in First Phase soon, but I needed to come in for an interview. He also let me know that I might have to spend "a month or two in First Phase" before returning to Second Phase. I remember feeling disappointed. I really didn't want to deal with TC house tools and drama, but at that point, I figured "beggars can't be choosers." I could suck it up for a month or two. I made an appointment for that Friday.

On Friday, February 6, I walked to the bus stop to go to my appointment at Gateway. I immediately got my first test. Only one other person sat on the bench waiting for the Clark Street bus. A freaky looking young white guy, who after making some small talk, proceeded to light up a joint and pass it to me. I immediately knew what to say: "No thanks. I don't smoke."

Looking back, this was an important response not only for obvious reasons, but it also showed that I didn't give a shit about what he thought. I felt no pressure to make up some excuse about why I wasn't smoking. In the past I would have, because I wouldn't have wanted him to think I was a pussy or a square. My head was in the right place for the first time in a long time. Within ten minutes, his role in my life would be over. My only priority was to stay clean, no matter what. I was getting stronger in my resolve day by day.

Another good thing about my response was that it's what I needed to learn how to say if I was going to stay clean and sober. Despite experiencing mild withdrawal symptoms, which would unfortunately be with me for quite some time to come, albeit on and off, I was able to fend off the offer to get high.

For some reason I have no recollection of my interview at Gateway. I know I was accepted back into the program upon my discharge from Grant Hospital after 21 days of treatment.

On Sunday, February 8th, my family came to visit me for the first time and brought my kids. Jessica was eight and Melissa was five. I was nervous, especially about seeing Jess because she was old enough to understand some things, so I decided to tell her the truth about why I was in the hospital.

My mom cut my hair in my room, and while she was cleaning up and Melissa was occupied with some objects on my dresser, I saw my opportunity to sit down with Jess. I started with a simple question.

"Do you know why daddy is in the hospital?"

With a mischievous grin on her face, and much to my surprise, she shook her head yes.

"Why?" I asked.

"Because you take too many drugs."

She obviously understood the gist of the situation and that should have been good enough, but as is typical of me, I tend to overexplain things. She quickly lost interest and moved on to the really important business at hand: "When are you going to be able to take us to the park?"

"Soon," I assured her and her sister, who suddenly became interested.

When the visit was over, I walked my parents and my kids to the elevator. As I made my way back to my room, I felt a glint of hope as I realized that I had family who still cared about me including two daughters who loved and needed me. And because my emotional "thawing out" had begun, I could actually feel some gratitude for those things.

The next day I went to my last group session and expressed my concern that my daughters were being raised by drug abusers. I received feedback and well wishes from the staff and my peers.

The following morning, on February 10th, I was discharged from Grant Hospital and walked to the bus stop, green garbage bag in tow. On that morning, I read what would become one of my favorite meditations in the *Twenty-Four Hours a Day* book…

Like a tree, I must be pruned of a lot of dead branches before I will be ready to bear good fruit. Think of changed people as trees which have been stripped of their old branches, pruned, cut and bare. But, through the dark, seemingly dead branches, flows silently, secretly, the new sap, until with the sun of spring, flows new life. There are new leaves, buds, blossoms, and fruit, many times better because of the pruning. I am in the hands of a Master Gardener who makes no mistakes in His pruning – Twenty-Four Hours a Day, February 10

As I rode the buses to Kedzie House, I sensed that spring was just around the corner. I also sensed, albeit ever so slightly, the new leaves, buds, blossoms, and fruit that lie just below the surface inside me. I had hope. The Grant Hospital program had done its job and put me back on the path of recovery. Once again, I became "a possibility."

Return to Kedzie House

Sitting on the prospect chair was a humbling experience no matter what the circumstances, but my experience was doubly humbling. As I sat in the hard wooden chair for the third time in my life, watching members of my new treatment family walk past, I realized that many of them had entered treatment just as I had completed it. They looked up to me as a "role-model pacesetter." Now they were running the house and would soon be giving me directions and ordering me around. I felt ashamed and embarrassed. I had a knot in my gut that only a proper dose of humility could ease.

I was taken off the chair and put back into my old dorm 202 and placed back on Ron Orlando's caseload. There was no big lecture from Ron. He welcomed me and said he was glad I made it back. There are many who never do. He simply said, "Let's get it right this time." Indeed. But getting it "right" would be difficult. The treatment slogan "When you think you're looking good, you're looking bad" comes to mind. If that's the case, wouldn't the opposite be true too? The answer is just ahead.

The first thing I did was make a simple announcement that I put in the Pull-up and Announcement Log for the next day's morning meeting. When they called on me in that meeting, I stood up and said, "Good morning family."

"Good morning, Steve," 40 or 50 residents replied.

"I'm grateful to be back, and I thank the staff for letting me come back. My announcement is…DON'T DO IT IN FRONT OF ME! I will hold you accountable. I'm not going to hold anybody's guilt, so if you're going to break the rules, don't do it in front of me. Thank you."

"Thanks, Steve," they all replied.

As I sat back in my chair, I noted the puzzled look on some of their faces. This was the advantage of being a Re-rounder—you knew how the TC game went and could foresee some of the typical traps and pitfalls. As it turned out, this particular group would be quite a bit more scandalous than my first family. That simple announcement would save me from a lot of grief and unnecessary bullshit, because for the most part, they would heed my warning and didn't do their dirt in front of me.

However, I noticed one guy that didn't look puzzled at all. Instead, my announcement brought a big grin to his face. As the meeting broke up, we made a beeline for each other. His name was Mark Storch, a big strapping redhead, of German descent. Being a fellow Re-rounder, he totally got it.

Mark was in treatment fighting a case that could result in him doing some time in prison, so his motives for treatment weren't exactly pure. I think the idea of recovery grew on him as we went through treatment. Our connection was immediate and based upon not only our shared edgy sense of humor, but also our love/hate relationship with Gateway and the TC. We both had unique insight into the absurdity of some of the things that went on in the TC culture.

Mark and I became fast friends and would have much of the same dynamics in our relationship that John Clark and David Grey had from my first Gateway family. As Re-rounders, we had a keen sense of who's who, who's about what, and well-developed "bullshit meters." We would frequently look across the room at each other, rolling our eyes and trying not to laugh at the same things—mostly look-good artists, trying to brownnose the staff and gain brownie points. As Re-rounders, we both were coming to realize that these "points" were worthless and would not lead to recovery. We shared a common but mostly unspoken wisdom, that the house tools and other TC stuff would get "the plane off the ground" but wouldn't "keep it in the air." We started to look to each other for sanctuary. Our friendship would become like an island surrounded by a sea of therapeutic robots, try-hards (Franko would be happy that I used one of his terms), and wannabes.

One of these therapeutic robots in whom I took a special interest, was Willie Ripple (yes, that's really his name). Willie was a short, stocky, penitentiary-built guy with glasses, of Italian descent. He, like David Grey, grew up in a predominantly black neighborhood and could be talking to you in the King's English one minute, then flip a switch and be talking black street jive/Ebonics the next. He was funny and fun, with the same irreverent sense of humor as Mark and me. But after his last bit in the penitentiary, he was dead serious about wanting to change his life and recover. The trouble was, as I would soon find out, he was going about it completely wrong. He was beyond a therapeutic robot. Willie was what we called a "therapeutic warrior"—using house tools to do battle with everyone and everything around him, believing that this would keep him clean. In a rare case of genuine wisdom on my part, I knew that it wouldn't. That approach could work for some, but it wouldn't work for Willie. The TC is not a one-size-fits all situation. Some benefited by immersing themselves in the TC and house tools because of their background and issues. But Willie had different issues and needs—and he got lost in the TC stuff. So, I did my therapeutic duty, as it were, dropped a few slips on him, and brought him to group. One of those confrontations went something like this...

"Steve, you dropped a slip on Willie," the staff running cluster group announced.

"Yeah. Willie, I've been watching you around this house and I'm concerned that you're missing the money. You run around here holding everyone accountable but yourself. You're not here to save everyone else. You're here for you, and to figure out what's wrong with Willie. That therapeutic warrior shit isn't gonna keep you clean out there. Believe me, I know. You'd better start paying more attention to Willie and less to everyone else, or you're heading for a relapse. That's all I got."

"Do you want to respond, Willie?" the staff asked.

Willie responded in a typical and predictable way, and though I don't recall his words, I do remember that he was defensive, justified his behavior, and even tried to turn it around on me a bit. Typical therapeutic warrior tactics. He received mixed feedback from other peers and staff. I remember thinking to myself, *hey, no skin off my nose if you don't get it. I did my part.*

I believe I took him to group one more time and that was it. I pulled the plug. I had learned by then not to keep trying to force a square peg into a round hole, so I moved on.

Several weeks later, Willie got his first 12-hour pass. His ETA was 9:00 p.m. I remember looking at the clock and seeing that it was 9:10 p.m. No

Willie. By 9:30 p.m., still no Willie. By the time we had to clear the floors, there was still no Willie. He never came back from pass.

A.A. stands for attitude adjustment

As I readjusted to the rigors of the TC, the foundation that began January 29th in Grant Hospital remained intact. I found myself going back to it again and again. It was my "ace in the hole." No matter what I did or didn't do in a day, if I didn't pick up a drink or a drug, that day was a success. From that basic premise, the next level of my development would evolve—losing my fear of treatment consequences. I realized that they couldn't hurt and could only help me. I knew that the real consequences were awaiting me outside the doors of 1706 N. Kedzie, and if I didn't get this right, they would soon be upon me again, and I wouldn't likely survive another relapse. I came so close to death during my relapse, it was only by the grace of God that I made it back. The removal of this fear helped me to be more of my real self, in treatment. I was no longer trying to hide parts of myself to impress staff or avoid consequences. I was free to be the selfish, cocky, fearful, egomaniac with an inferiority complex that I really was. Hey, in some circles, those traits describe genius!

Remember the question I posed earlier about that treatment slogan? The opposite would be "When you think you're looking bad, you're looking good." Was it true? For me, I think it was. The more honest I was, the more myself I was, the more flack (treatment) I got from staff and peers.

Mark Storch really became important at this point, and I think I was for him too. We kept each other sane through the contrived drama of the treatment game. We continued to find humor in the absurdity of it. Storch and I were irreverent and even somewhat rebellious at times, especially me, as it became obvious that I was going to remain in First Phase beyond the one or two months I was initially told. Still, I left the decision entirely to staff to tell me when they felt I was ready. I never petitioned to go to Second Phase like I had the first time I was in treatment. But it wasn't easy once I came to the realization that it would ultimately not be the answer for me and wouldn't keep me clean.

Besides Storch, another way I started coping with the situation was: once I started getting passes, I took the North Avenue bus to Wells Street and hit an AA meeting at The Mustard Seed every chance I got. I didn't know it at the time, but "The Seed" was a world-famous Alano club.

Alano clubs were places that rented space and had meetings throughout the day and evening, seven days a week. It became a haven for me, and it became apparent that AA and NA meetings were the thing that was going to keep me clean, not house tools. I not only had a place to dump all my trials and tribulations of being back in Gateway and other typical early recovery issues, but I was listening and learning how others were staying sober on the outside. Don't get me wrong, I was grateful and had a lot of respect for what Gateway did, but dare I say, I was starting to outgrow it. As a result of my growth, my patience would start to be tested by staff and peers alike.

This was especially true for a counselor named John Servitch —yet another recent graduate hired fresh out of treatment. John was new to Kedzie House. He was a tall, good-looking guy with a chip on his shoulder. Every morning, he would come in and I'd pass him in the hall, say "good morning," and he would ignore me. After seeing him in action around the house, it became apparent that he was a big jagoff. I never said good morning to him again, and instead, would say *fuck you* in my head when I'd pass him in the hall.

Now ordinarily, this is not what emotional growth would look like, but, in my case, it was. In my first attempt at recovery, I always either looked up to people and put them on a pedestal or looked down at them and felt they were beneath me (as if that were possible). This was especially true for how I viewed the Gateway staff. It was almost a form of hero worship. This is typical, especially for people new to treatment and recovery. Then, because they were mere mortals, they would invariably let me down, and I'd be disillusioned. Now, I saw them as equals, people with good qualities and bad.

When reflecting on this realization, I used to say, "At that point in treatment, the staff could have all gone home and taken a nap. I didn't rely on them for my recovery or my well-being anymore." This was growth for a person who not long ago in Grant Hospital, craved attention and approval from staff.

My fate was dependent on two things only: God and myself. For the first time in my life, I started taking responsibility for my own success or failure. I started looking people straight in the eyes. My newfound sense of self was challenged more often as my fellow residents started dropping slips and taking me to Cluster Group. Several of these stand out as significant to my development.

The first was when a new resident dropped a slip on me and took me to group for disrespecting his pull-up. Hardly a reason to drop a slip on someone. He was obviously trying out his newly acquired house tools. John Servitch was the staff presiding over the group. After the guy brought the confrontation, my response pressed "Jagoff" John's buttons. So, he cut me off, stood up, pointed at me, and angrily yelled across the room, "Fiorito, you're gonna shoot dope again, the minute you leave this place!"

I thought to myself; *What a terrible thing to say to a resident in treatment. Who the fuck does this guy think he is?* I laid it all on the line and took a stand for myself...I shouted back? "Why John? Because I disrespected a pull-up!? You walk around here every day with an attitude and a chip on your shoulder, but that's okay!? If I'm going to shoot dope again for disrespecting a pull-up, you're definitely going to shoot dope again!"

The group braced themselves, sensing that the "hammer" was about to come down on me. To everyone's surprise he responded, "Ya know, I could put on my staff hat and bust you down, but I'm not going to do that. I don't want people to think I can't take criticism. I'll give you enough rope to hang yourself with Steve. Group's dismissed." I walked away to get ready for lunch unscathed, having just dodged a bullet—albeit a "rubber treatment bullet."

In another incident, someone dropped a slip on me, and his confrontation went something like this, "Yeah, Steve. I've been watching you around this house, and man, you're a liar!"

He then proceeded to give me several examples that he observed of my lying. I don't think he, staff, nor anyone else was prepared for my response. The first time I was in Gateway, I would have gotten defensive, gone into therapeutic warrior mode, and tried to undermine his credibility. That's how you played the treatment game. But since I was no longer playing the game, my response was brutally honest: "I know I'm a liar. It's one of the reasons I'm here. Most times, I don't even realize I'm doing it. It just kind of comes out like puke. I know I need help with this. Anybody got any suggestions?"

The group sat stunned in silence for a few seconds. Then somebody raised their hand, and the staff called on them.

"So, you say you don't realize you're lying when it happens. What about afterwards? Do you know you lied after you do it?"

"Yeah," I replied.

"Okay, then I have a suggestion for you—go back and clean it up. Once you realize that you lied to someone, go back and tell them so, and tell them the truth. I'll bet after you do that a few times, you'll think twice before lying."

The staff and peers agreed that it was a good suggestion, and so did I, and I assured him that I would try it.

My first opportunity to try that suggestion presented itself within a day or two with the surprise appearance of my "little brother," Sherman. He was the last of several little brothers I was assigned to in First Phase in my previous treatment. Sherman was a tall, light-skinned brother, who was somewhat unusual in that he was well-spoken. His drug of choice was ironically, "Sherm Stick," which was basically a cigarette dipped in liquid PCP. Sherman was one of those smart, funny, mixed-race guys, who didn't fit in anywhere. I knew that he too had relapsed after leaving treatment, so it was good to see him outside by the basketball net, talking to an Expediter who was doing a house run. He apparently wanted to talk to staff about getting back into treatment. Who was SOD? None other than Ron Orlando.

At the time, we were "functioning" in our jobs around the house. No one was allowed outside during job functions unless their job called for it, and they still had to relate to the deskman to leave. Without giving it a second thought, I told the deskman that I was "relating out to talk to my little brother" and that Ron cleared it. The desk man bought it without question.

I walked outside and gave Sherman a hug. He was shocked to see me, and we both acknowledged our relapses. I told him Ron was on duty (Sherman's counselor too) and that he should talk to him about coming back. I ended our visit abruptly when I realized I had to get back to my job or I'd be pressing my luck. "All right, I'll talk to you soon little bro'," I assured him.

As I related back into the deskman, my conscience hit out of nowhere: *That's what they were talking about in that group. You just did it, Steve. Okay, now go back and clean it up like old boy suggested.* At first, I thought, *really?*

You're not really going to do that—are you? Then, my newly acquired fearlessness kicked in and I thought, *"Why not? What have you got to lose?"*

Fear of treatment consequences removed, I went back to the window, shut my brain off, like I did when I copped to the gum incident in my first treatment, and said to the deskman: "Brother, I just told you I had permission from Ron to go outside and talk to Sherman. That was a lie, I didn't. I'm sorry."

He looked at me in a mild state of shock and paused, not knowing what to say. He finally uttered; "Thanks Steve, I appreciate your honesty brother."

I walked away feeling good about myself. Of course, the deskman still wrote me up.

I must say, I was a bit surprised when the Expediter on duty that evening investigated it: "Ahh, Steve, at 2:20 p.m., *could you have* lied to the front deskman about having permission from staff to go outside?"

"Yes, I *could have* done that," I replied.

The "could have" thing was TC lingo. They knew that dope fiends often had a hard time admitting stuff outright, so the term "could have" made admitting wrongs a bit easier. When "medication" time rolled around, I was summoned to one of the small offices to take my "medicine" for the infraction.

The three-person panel consisted of two Coordinators which usually meant it was going to be serious. Sure enough, they "smoked" me. Smoker TPR's were very dramatic and made a deep impact, that is, if at least one of the people doing the smoking was any good. I came to realize that though difficult to take, they were an effective therapeutic tool because hard-core addicts don't hear with their ears; they hear with their guts. Words were only useful if they were able to penetrate beyond the ears. If you could penetrate the gut, you had a chance of making a profound impact that might stick.

A typical smoker would go something like this: "Assume the posture brother."

"The posture," if you recall, was standing up straight, legs slightly spread, and hands behind your back. You must look straight into the eyes of the person talking. If your eyes strayed, they'd call you on it— "What are you looking at? I'm over here brother." Then they'd begin; "Yeah, Steve. This is a TPR for lying to the deskman AND CONTINUING TO PRACTICE YOUR SLICK AND DEVIOUS DOPE FIEND WAYS!" at the top of their lungs.

Then back to a calm demeanor. "I don't know what it's going to take after all this treatment. Maybe you'll have to be ONE OF THOSE THAT DIES OUT THERE STEVE! MAYBE YOU'LL NEVER GET IT STEVE!!"

It was pretty intense. Then, they'd pass the TPR slip to the next person on the panel and he or she would say/shout their piece.

Afterwards, the lead Coordinator said, "Relate to the scratch sheet that you were given a smoking TPR by me and…" (whoever the other two were).

As I started to walk out of the room he added: "But we appreciate your honesty brother. You're showing some growth."

I remember walking to the EO feeling good about myself. I had two or three more incidents where I had to clean up a lie I told, and that was it. It worked just like dude had predicted. I started becoming aware of lies before they rolled off my tongue. I'm not saying I never lied again, I was just less impulsive about it. I had developed an awareness of what I was about to say that I never had before. This was another small but important step in my growth.

Fear begins to take its toll

As my self-confidence and self-assurance continued to grow, unfortunately, so did my fear—a fear that started back in my first stint in Gateway—the fear of HIV/AIDS. The news made it clear that IV drug users were now neck and neck with gay men for contracting the virus. This appeared to be supported by the number of people in treatment with me who had it. There were several peers who did not try to hide the fact that they were HIV positive.

I remember a Latino guy who started chairing the NA meeting on Fridays who was HIV-positive. He used to start every meeting with, "Hello, my name is Efrain and I'm grateful for HIV." He would explain that if it weren't for HIV, he wouldn't have gotten clean and sober. His story was remarkable because he was sick with symptoms of full-blown AIDS, but his symptoms all but vanished after he got clean and started taking care of himself. I can't recall if he was on AZT—one of the first experimental drugs that was supposed to at least slow down the HIV virus's progression into AIDS—but he was healthy.

I started to experience weight loss, blemish breakouts—mostly on my face and chest—headaches, fatigue, and various other mild symptoms. I was sure I had the virus, especially when I would constantly check the glands in my neck in the mirror and they appeared swollen at times.

There was a new test for antibodies to the virus and I wanted to get tested, but fear of being positive created mixed feelings, and part of me didn't want to know. The stress and fear started to grow, and this combined with continued mild withdrawal symptoms (these lingering symptoms would later be given a name and referred to as Post-Acute Withdrawal Syndrome or PAWS for short), resulted in mood-swings, impulsive behavior, and lashing out.

The staff and fellow resident's response to this was more intense treatment—the "heat" was turned up a few degrees. I became more defensive and combative. At that time in my treatment, I stayed in a perpetual state of being busted to the dishpan and then to spare parts. I was also "smoked" a lot.

One particular TPR that stands out from that time and had a profound impact on me, was when a peer yelled— "HOW MANY MORE NIGHTS WILL YOUR MOTHER CRY HERSELF TO SLEEP!?"

This triggered flashbacks to the time I had left my mother alone in a car in the middle of the night at Annie's, while I selfishly shot cocaine at her apartment. I was consumed with guilt and would get a knot in my gut every time I thought about it.

Eileen's words started to echo in my head: *You think you're a piece of shit—don't you?* Was she right? Maybe I did, and what's even worse, maybe I was. In any case, her words finally sunk in, and I realized that I had extremely low self-esteem that I had covered up most of my life.

Timely visit from an old friend

As the stress became overwhelming, my treatment continued to spiral out of control. I was again busted to spare parts, meaning the Expediters could get you to do whatever they wanted to during the hours of 7 a.m. to 7 p.m. As I was mopping the front stairs, I heard an old familiar voice at the front desk. It was "Mr. Therapeutic Robot" himself—James Minter. He worked a strict program on the outside, visiting the house regularly to speak to new residents, he spoke at in-house NA or AA meetings, or whatever he needed to do.

While I was putting the mop and bucket away, I saw him walking toward me with that "therapeutic robot" look on his face.

"We need to talk, brother," in a tone that was more serious than usual.

He went to the EO window and related to the deskman, "Me and my peer Mr. Fiorito are relating down to the boiler room. It's cleared from staff on duty. C'mon man. Let's go down here," as he motioned to the boiler room door.

We both found a chair and sat directly across from each other. James looked me dead in the eyes and asked, "What's going on with you, brother?"

"What do you mean? Nothing," I replied.

"That's not what I'm hearing. I'm hearing you all over the place, being disrespectful and can't accept a pull-up."

Then he cracked the façade and broke through. James was a firm believer in the treatment concept, that if you were acting out, it was because there were feelings you weren't talking about.

"Man, something you ain't talkin' about, and you better get to talkin' about it right now before you get your ass thrown outta treatment."

I realized he was right, and I knew what it was. I looked up from the floor and looked him in the eyes. "You're right, James." I hesitated, trying to find the words. James waited patiently.

That's one thing James was—patient, as evidenced by his perseverance in his never-ending job search. On the brink of giving up, he landed a job at Brach's Candy Company, making $11 an hour—better money than any of us. He endured all that frustration and disappointment, and God rewarded him.

"Go 'head, man. What is it?" he asked.

"I think I've got the thing," I confessed.

"What are you talking about? What thing?"

"Ya know, the thing—HIV. The AIDS thing."

What happened next almost knocked me off my chair. He never hesitated or even blinked.

"So?"

"What do you mean so? I said I think I got HIV."

Unfazed, he repeated, "So?"

"What do you mean so? If I got it, I'm gonna die."

Again, without blinking: "So?"

"So? I said I'm going to die. I'm not even thirty."

Again, without hesitation, he said, "We're all gonna die, Steve. No one gets to choose when or how they die. What makes you think you're any different? You think that gives you the right to go around acting like an asshole? Sorry, I'll pull myself up (because he swore). If you're gonna die, you're gonna die clean and sober, and doin' the right thing."

Boom! He was right. His words cut through my denial like a knife and snapped me back into reality. I realized that no matter what, I still had a responsibility to my kids, my family, my peers, myself and to God to do the right thing. We talked for a little while more and then we gave each other a hug.

"Thanks James, I needed to hear that."

Once again, I had been restored to sanity by one of my peers, and once again, I worked Step Three and turned my will and my life (and my fate) over to the care of God.

This was a crucial turning point in my second treatment, and my attitude did a 180. I was busted to the Expediters and many of them would "come off sick" on you and give you the most horrendous job they could think of. If you didn't have the right attitude, it could easily run you out the door.

At 6 a.m. the next morning, a newly promoted Expediter named Darren woke me out of a sound sleep. "Hey man, c'mon, get up. I got a job for you."

Darren was an 18-year-old black kid. He had obviously gotten the blessing to fuck with me from his supervisor Bruce, who was the Chief Expediter at the time. Bruce and Darren were likely holding some negative contracts with each other.

I sprung out of bed with a smile on my face, much to Darren's surprise. "What do you need me to do, brother?" I asked, with a positive attitude, that this youngster couldn't understand.

"I need you to come on downstairs and clean this dumpster."

There were two jobs that were considered the worst jobs you could be asked to do at Kedzie House: cleaning the grease traps in the kitchen, and the absolute worst— cleaning the dumpsters.

Darren handed me my supplies, which consisted of a bucket, some cleaning products, rubber gloves, and a toothbrush. The toothbrush was old-school, hardcore Gateway and hadn't been done to anyone for quite a while.

As we came onto the main floor, I noticed a familiar form sitting on the prospect chair with his face to the wall. It was Willie. Staff came and took him off the prospect chair and I noticed his face was sporting two black eyes. I tried to make eye contact, but he made a distinct effort not to look at me. He finally gave in, and I smiled and gave him the thumbs-up as I headed out to my duty.

It was a warm, sunny morning. I used a step ladder to climb into the dumpster. I started singing as I scrubbed the inside of it inch by inch with that toothbrush. I was glad that Willie came back, which lifted my spirits even more, and I thought, *there's no way in the world this young punk is going to break my spirit*. I had a great time cleaning the dumpster that day. It was almost a spiritual experience. I felt that nothing earthly could hold me down. I had officially risen above one of the worst, most absurd, demeaning TC consequences in Gateway.

Deja vu

My continued emotional growth was further confirmed when, on a Sunday, during family visiting, I was asked to do a house run. I came down the backstairs, and after checking the laundry room, the next stop was the guest bathroom. I flipped the light switch on and immediately had a Deja vu. The soap out of the dish and in the sink; there was water all over the place, the floor was muddy, footprints were everywhere, pee was in the toilet and on the seat, and the garbage overflowed with paper towels onto the floor. It was an exact replica of what the guest bathroom looked like in my previous treatment when I did a Sunday house run. I did the same thing and cleaned the entire mess up, but this time, though I thought about putting the announcement in the Pull-up and Announcement Log like I'd done the first time, I decided not to.

Although it was the same exact situation and even looked the same, there was a significant difference—my motives. I was no longer interested in getting a pat on the back from anybody but myself. My first time in treatment, I did a lot of right things, but unfortunately, often for the wrong reasons. This time, I did it because it was the right thing to do, and I wanted to change. I didn't need validation from others. I finished by wiping the pee off the toilet seat, throwing the toilet paper in the toilet, and flushing it. I turned out the light and walked away and never told one soul that I did it…until now.

Taking a stand for who I was becoming

As I continued my growth and the development of parts of myself that had been stunted by addiction, I started to believe that with the help of God, I was not only on the right track, but that it was the *only* track there was for me. If I wanted to live and have a quality life, I had to continue to do the right things to the best of my ability, while having faith that God would continue to show me the way. Easy to say it and believe it, but my conviction to my new way of life would soon be put to the test, when one of my roommates would challenge just how sincere my changes really were.

Curtis was a short, stocky, black man, recently released from the penitentiary and given an option for treatment in exchange for early release. It was obvious that he, like many others, was just doing a bit in exchange for less prison time and had no real interest in recovery or change. Usually, I just avoided these types, as I'm sure they avoided me. Unfortunately, because we lived in the same dorm, it was impossible to avoid Curtis. Also, as he got more comfortable with me, he started showing his true colors more and more. Remember my announcement, "Don't do it in front of me?" Well, he started doing exactly that, so as promised, I started holding him accountable. He figured out that I was the one writing most of the haircuts, and it was particularly obvious when it came to infractions he committed in the dorm.

One day, after one such write-up, he confronted me while we were alone in the dorm. I reminded him that if he didn't want to be held accountable, he should pull his weight in the dorm, and not do his other dirt in front of me. Curtis had a crazy smile that made it hard to tell if he was really smiling or just showing his teeth like a rabid dog. With that crazy smile on his face, his response went something like this: "You know what? I really don't mind going back to the penitentiary. Penitentiary is like a second home to me. I can do a two-year bit standing on my head. So, you better back off."

"You threatening me?" I asked.

"I'm just telling you like it is. You take it whatever way you want," he responded as he walked away.

I'd be lying if I said I wasn't intimidated. I mean, the guy slept in the bunk beneath mine. Then, an old treatment slogan jumped into my head: "If you don't stand for something, you'll fall for anything."

I thought about what James said to me in the boiler room a few weeks back. If I'm going to die, it's going to be doing the right thing. Curtis' response made me angry. I decided that I wasn't going to take his shit, and I needed to take a stand for my recovery. I went to the piano and dropped a slip on him.

I sat in the Cluster group and looked around the room at the faces. It was always interesting to try to guess who dropped a slip on whom before group started. I noticed Curtis was there. They did a few slips, and upon concluding the last issue, staff read the next slip. "Steve, you dropped a slip on Curtis"?

"Yes, I did."

Curtis looked surprised.

"Go ahead, Steve," the staff instructed.

"Yeah, Curtis. I dropped a slip on you for that bullshit you tried to pull on me the other day in the dorm. I admit, at first, I was intimidated by your threats, but the more I thought about it, the more I knew I had to drop this slip on you. I relapsed and almost died out there. I'm here to save my life, and I'm not gonna let you or anyone else stand in my way. You said the penitentiary is like a second home to you, and you could do two or three years standing on your head. First, it's a shame that you're that comfortable with prison. You should work on being comfortable with the outside and with recovery. Either way, I wanted to tell you—do whatever you gotta do, and I'm gonna do what I gotta do. If you violate the rules, I'm gonna hold your ass accountable. If you're gonna kill me or whatever, then so be it. At least I'm going out trying to do the right thing for once in my life. That's all I got for you."

Curtis's response likely surprised the entire group. He confessed that he was struggling with a penitentiary mentality, and he didn't know how to change. He got great feedback from peers in that group who reached out and gave him good suggestions. The best feedback came from a peer who was a fellow ex-con. He made a huge impact on Curtis that day when he pointed out:

"Curtis. I heard you said you could do a two-year bit standing on your head. I understand man, but did it ever occur to you that one day, that cell door might close and never open back up? I know we never think about that—do we? What would that be like, to never be able to see your wife and kids again except through glass or an occasional visit? You need to think about that, brother."

Curtis's eyes got really big. You could almost see the light go off over his head. "You know, I never thought about that," he admitted.

After group, Curtis pulled me off to the side. "I want to apologize to you," he said in a low voice. "I thought you were just a therapeutic robot who was trying to impress staff, but now I see you're serious about change, and I respect that. I'll do better at taking care of my stuff in the dorm."

"Thanks Curtis. I appreciate that."

Curtis did kind of a 180 after that group. It had a profound impact on him. I felt good that I had the courage to drop that slip on him, and it had an unexpected positive outcome.

I've always referred to the people I was in treatment within 1987 as "my second family." As it turned out, the announcement I made in morning meeting upon my return— "Don't do it in front of me" —paid off at key points in my treatment. As I said before, they were pretty scandalous. By the time the house closed, the guilt and negative contracts were so thick you could cut them with a knife. When the hammer came down, and the house finally closed, the guilt-dropping sessions revealed some pretty juicy stuff. The results were pretty serious, too, and several peers were given the boot and shown the door.

Storch and I rolled our eyes and cracked jokes through the whole ordeal. We only had some minor stuff, mostly related to smoking cigarettes, me playing my guitar on the backstairs at unauthorized times (great natural reverb) and bad-rapping staff and peers.

Another result that I must admit at the time brought a smile to my face (and Storch's) was that Darren and Bruce split treatment together. To put a little icing on the cake, they stole petty cash from the EO on their way out. But the "cherry on top" came sometime later with the arrival of the morning paper.

It turned out they were both involved in an armed robbery and wound up shooting each other. They survived but were likely looking at some serious prison time. After reading the article in the paper, I remember the old TC slogan popping into my head: "If it doesn't come out in the wash, it will come out in the rinse." I guess it was time for the rinse for those two.

After reading the article, I couldn't help but think Darren might have been wishing he was in a nice hot dumpster with a toothbrush. It was just one of many examples that culminated in my belief that you never really get away with anything. Karma's a bitch and she'll have her day eventually. Part of my growth was eventually outgrowing my pettiness and feeling sorry for people like Bruce and Darren. But I admit, at the time, I wasn't there yet.

Early gifts from God

My continued emotional and spiritual growth, though not free from occasional setbacks, was also validated by events that occurred. One event that reinforced my feeling that I was doing the right things most times happened when my father asked if I could take a trip with him up north to Herbster and Eagle River, Wisconsin. He was going to drop off my niece Amy and nephew Jamie so they could spend most of the summer with their grandmother Elma and husband John. Then, he would stop in Eagle River on his way back to check on "Uncle Paul," who was now in his 90's and was starting to fade.

Uncle Paul wasn't anyone's uncle except Florence, my father's first wife who passed away. His driving skills had declined significantly, and the powers-that-be were getting ready to pull his driving privileges. He would have no way to get to town and get supplies and would need to rely on others. This was going to be extremely difficult for a man who never relied on anyone for anything most of his life. My parents had requested that I be allowed to go because it would likely be the last time I would get to see Uncle Paul. Also, there was a lot of driving that my father, who was 75 at the time, would need help with. The trip would require me to be excused from treatment for about five or six days, which, to my knowledge, was unprecedented for a resident while in First Phase, especially with the house being closed.

Surprisingly, they approved the trip. I took it as a compliment and a reward for the progress I had been making. Most of my early rewards were simple pleasures in the emotional and spiritual realm. When they would happen, I felt God was whispering to my soul.

After dropping my niece and nephew off, and visiting for a few days in Herbster, it was time to make our way to Eagle River. My father and I found ourselves alone in a car for the first time since I'd gotten clean. I'd like to tell you that the awkward, long silences were behind us, but that wasn't the case. Though I had improved, my father was still not much of a communicator. There was plenty to talk about related to the landscape and the changes he'd witnessed over the years of driving through the state of Wisconsin. We also talked about his history with Uncle Paul, and his current situation.

I couldn't help but ask about the chipmunk story, a bit of folklore I had heard throughout my childhood and how Uncle Paul had befriended the animals. The story was, they would go into his pockets to get peanuts and eat them on his lap. My father confirmed the story but said that he didn't live in that house anymore, and he had no idea if he was still "friends" with the local chipmunks. I resigned myself to never being able to confirm the story or see it for myself. I remained skeptical and felt it was at best, an exaggerated tall tale.

As we pulled into the driveway, it was obvious that it was not the same house on the sprawling wooded acres I remember going to as a kid. We let ourselves in through the unlocked (typical of small towns in Wisconsin) front door. Uncle Paul got up to greet us. He had obviously aged, was not as tall and was much thinner than I remembered him. We exchanged greetings, then he and my dad sat at the kitchen table as I went to the car to bring in our bags.

After bringing in the bags and locking the car (like a good city slicker) I couldn't help but peek into the backyard. There, I saw an old wooden chair that faced a tree with a magazine rack next to it. *Was it true?* I thought to myself. I grabbed my cheap camera out of the car and stuck it in my front shirt pocket.

My dad and uncle Paul were still at the kitchen table, deep in conversation. One line is the only recollection I have of his words. "Dey come in de evenink," he said with a thick Polish accent. He was referring to fishermen who would stop in to check on him to see if he needed anything, after a long day of fishing on the lake.

I went to the counter, where I saw a basket of fruit and grabbed an apple. As I did, I noticed another basket filled with peanuts in the shell. I grabbed a handful and headed to the backyard. It was a beautiful sunny day with birds chirping everywhere. I sat in the chair with the peanuts in my left pants pocket, grabbed a *Great Outdoors* magazine, and started reading. Nothing happened. Minutes went by. Still nothing. I was about to give up when I thought I'd give one more thing a try. I grabbed a peanut from out of my pocket, put it on my thigh, and resumed reading.

Suddenly, my attention was drawn away from the article I was reading to a rustling sound coming from above in the tree. Then, the unmistakable sound of tiny claws scurrying across the bark. I looked up and saw a childhood fairytale becoming a reality! Here comes the chipmunk in short bursts down the tree, stopping abruptly from time to time to sniff for danger on its way to the ground. My new friend continued toward me hesitantly, still uncertain if I was safe. It retreated to the safety of the tree trunk several times before finally throwing caution to the wind. It really wanted that nut! The next thing you know, it climbs up my leg, opens the nut, and begins eating it right there on my leg! I was so excited that I almost forgot about the camera. *Could I do it?* I thought. It was worth a shot. I slowly reached for the camera in my shirt pocket, pulled it out, and took the shot. I captured it perfectly!

The trip, the event, and the photographic proof were, to me, all gifts from God. Rewards for being clean and sober. The message from God became clear: "I will now let you experience the things that have real value in your life that you would never have experienced the way you were living." The photo of that chipmunk eating that nut on my leg was more valuable and meaningful than a photo of any celebrity would have been.

After returning from my trip, the house re-opened, and I was able to start having a little fun. Several of my peers were fellow musicians, including Conrad Perez, who played piano and sang. He was a younger guy, so he was into the "New Wave" music scene, which at that time included artists such as Talking Heads, Billy Joel, Foreigner, and Blondie—to name a few.

The music these artists made had some of the elements of the classic rock I'd grown up listening to and playing but was quite different in some ways. Most of the songs were very polished and overproduced, and none relied on long, self-indulgent guitar solos. If there were solos at all, they were brief and very structured. In fact, the guitar was being rapidly replaced by keyboards and synthesizers.

Conrad pulled us together to form a little Kedzie House band and asked me to play the only string instrument—bass guitar. I told him that I'd never played bass before and didn't have one. He told me to relax; I'd be fine, and he did. So, I had my first experience playing bass. I also sang some of the material.

The band consisted of a piano, synthesizer, sax, a few female background singers, and me on bass. We alternated lead vocals on different songs. We had a lot of fun rehearsing, and our biggest gig was playing at one of the Gateway graduate's weddings.

After the house reopened, I resumed going on meeting passes frequently. I went to the Mustard Seed every chance I got. There, I heard a recurrent theme, "I don't want to go back out there and die of this disease."

Though I certainly related to this being likely if I relapsed again, I started to realize that I could not rely on the fear of dying to keep me clean and sober. Though I had that fear, it would not be enough. I found an even better motivator that was growing inside me—I wanted to live! Not just exist or survive—cockroaches can do that—but really live. In other words, I wanted to see if I could create a sober life worth living. The challenge genuinely started to intrigue me. I felt that with God's help, there were no limits to what I could achieve. A hunger for a better life started to awaken and grow in me.

Progress not perfection

Just when it looked like I was on my way to sainthood, something—well, actually, someone—came along to bring me right back down to earth and remind me that I was still an imperfect sinner, with a list of flaws and character defects that weren't going anywhere any time soon. The one that was my Achilles heel—women—became abundantly clear to me.

I believe Penny was the first intern ever at Gateway. I guess you could say this was one of the early signs that Gateway was evolving and becoming less radical. Penny was studying to be an addictions counselor at Harold Washington College. She was a light-skinned, intelligent, well-spoken, pretty, young black girl with a body like a Playboy centerfold. That is not an exaggeration! When she was introduced to the family, I looked over at Storch, who, as usual, was reading my mind and was already staring at me with a sarcastic grin on his face from ear to ear. Both of our eyes got wide with a look on our faces like *I'll race ya to the dessert table!* Luckily for me, as it turned out, she preferred thin Italian guys over big, brawny Germans.

I think I sealed the deal when she stopped by at the end of her shift to watch the band rehearse. It became obvious that her intense stares were not just coincidental glances. The message in those stares was total lust, and I countered with some lustful stares of my own. Of course, it was strictly prohibited for an intern to have any type of relationship with a resident outside the program. Yeah, and that rule was going to stop her and I from hooking up about as much as one of those three-foot toddler gates was going to stop a freight train.

It started out with some innocent excuse to hook up outside the facility. I think she wanted to check out a meeting, so I took her to an open AA meeting. Next thing you know, we're at her apartment on the North Side, ripping our clothes off. After that, we started hooking up on my passes.

One of our rendezvous was a day at the beach. She picked me up at our usual spot and we headed to North Avenue beach. She packed some snacks and drinks for us. On the way there, she was drinking what appeared to be fruit punch out of some container that had a built-in straw. I didn't think anything of it, until I started smelling the distinct odor of alcohol. It was confirmed when I kissed her. Apparently, the container was filled with a homemade wine cooler. It didn't faze me, and I had no problem with her drinking alcohol. She knew I didn't drink and never offered it. Our discrete relationship continued.

What was supposed to be "a month or two" in First Phase had now become five months. I had made up my mind that I would do no petitioning and would leave the decision completely up to staff as to when they felt I was ready to go back to Second Phase. That day finally arrived when Jeff K. tapped me on the shoulder and asked, "You feel like you're ready to go back upstairs?"

"What do you think? I decided to leave it up to you guys to tell me."

"We think you're ready. Do you?"

"Yeah, I think I've gotten all I'm going to get out of pull-ups and Cluster Groups," I replied sarcastically.

Jeff smiled. "Okay, then I want you to set up your interview with (the Assistant Director) Laura."

Moving forward with flaws in tow

Later that night while doing a house run, I was passing the pay phone in the Second Phase hallway. I looked around and realized there was no one on the floor. I decided to sneak a quick call and share the news with Penny. Luckily, the phone was only feet from the house-run sign-off clipboard, so if anyone came, I would have a reason to be in the vicinity. I made the call, and I let Penny know the good news. Just then, I heard someone with keys coming down the other hall from the backstairs. I abruptly hung up the phone, quickly moved to the clipboard on the wall, and pretended to write on the log just as staff Sheila Jackson rounded the corner. Sheila was a street-tough, street-smart, black woman with an edgy sense of humor. She was not to be messed with. She turned the corner and made a beeline for me with an intense look on her face.

"Were you on that phone?" she asked accusingly.

"No!" I lied through my teeth.

"Yes, you were. You were on that phone."

"No, I wasn't. I swear." I was now laughing and trying to play it off and make it a joke.

She wasn't budging. "You were on that phone. I can tell by the look on your face."

"Sheila, I swear I wasn't on the phone," I said, still laughing.

After a few more exchanges, she finally relented and started walking away and I continued with my house run. I heard her faint voice echo as she went down the stairs, "I know you were on that phone."

I felt bad for lying, but there was no way I was going to spend my last few weeks in First Phase busted. The next two weeks, every time I ran into her, she'd look me in the eye and say: "You were on that phone; I know you were." I, of course, continued to deny it. I knew I wasn't going to shoot dope over it.

My interview for Second Phase was done by Laura Reed, and, of all people, my least favorite counselor, Rory. He wound up asking me a tough question that completely caught me off guard. I guess that's why he was there.

"What would you do if you relapsed again, Steve?"

It was just *so* out of the question; I couldn't even entertain the thought for one second. I gave the only answer that my mind would allow. "I'm not going to."

"But what if you did?" Rory pressed.

"I'm not going to," I repeated.

We had several more of those exchanges before I finally relented and allowed myself to consider the possibility. "I guess I'd come back here."

They both almost leaped out of their chairs and simultaneously shrieked, "Noooooooooooooooooo!"

Then Rory continued, "Steve, there's really nothing more that treatment can do for you. If you have a slip, you can call your sponsor. You don't have to stay out there and keep using."

I guess I understood their point, which was, if I used again, it wouldn't require five months of treatment. They, like me, recognized that I'd outgrown the TC stuff and gotten as much as I could get. Nonetheless, I think they failed to consider that the level of loss of control I typically experienced would require nothing less than total confinement, and that was if I were able to make it back at all. It was likely that I wouldn't require five months of treatment because I would require a morgue instead. It was a moot point as I still felt deep down that relapse was not an option.

Pete Piry hosted my second rotation ceremony to Second Phase. As he ended his roast of me, in a style that could best be described as a cross between Don Rickles and Richard Pryor. He pulled a gift from his pocket. Then, with a shift to his more serious, somber tone, he gave me some words of wisdom, as only Pete could. "Steve, I brought you a gift from Acapulco."

It was a coin. With sincerity and earnestness in his voice, he said, "I want you to keep this coin in your pocket at all times, and if you ever find yourself needing to get the last word, I want you to reach into your pocket, pull it out, and let it remind you to…SHUT THE FUCK UP!"

This was followed by his typical outburst of maniacal laughter! The house fell out laughing, me included. He had us going for a minute there. Just when we thought he was going to say something heartfelt and sentimental, he'd pull the rug out from under us. There was nothing like some good old TC treatment humor to help you forget that the odds of staying clean were stacked against you. Unfortunately, in those days, only about ten percent of IV drug users were successful and stayed clean.

As I moved to my new two-man dorm on the third floor, I was excited to meet my new roommate Greg. He was a short, stocky black guy who seemed to be doing well. He was working and had a good head on his shoulders, so we hit it off right away. However, a damper was put onto my mood of celebration when Storch returned from court later that day.

As he walked toward Willie and me in the dining room eating dinner, his long face had bad news written all over it.

"I gotta do two years, guys. I gotta turn myself in Monday to begin my sentence," he reported.

He couldn't beat the case he'd been fighting throughout our time together, and now it was time to "pay the piper."

Although I had a knot in my gut, I didn't show it and tried to be strong and positive for my friend. Willie jumped in to rescue my loss for words: "You can do that standing on your head. You'll only do a year with good time, and they'll probably give you some credit for being in here."

"Yeah, it could've been worse. I was looking at six years," Storch added, trying to find something positive to focus on. Storchy grabbed the plate they put up for him and we had what looked to be our last meal together.

Second attempt at employment clean and sober

After responding to a want-ad in the *Chicago Tribune*, I landed my first job in the suburb of Bensenville. The job was with a small picture framing company that framed and prepared the type of commercial artwork you see in large office buildings. Unfortunately, I had no transportation. My dad, who was now retired, came to the rescue, and let me use his car while I saved for one.

On my way to work, I drove through the town of Des Plaines passing the historic, second ever McDonald's. I also passed the slightly less famous Des Plaines Alano Club. I had heard of it around "the rooms" but had never been there. I'd pass by in the early morning before it opened and in the evening on my way home. It wasn't likely I'd be checking it out though, as it was all I could do to make it back to Kedzie House, eat dinner, and get to group on time.

The job entailed multiple duties, from cutting glass, frames, and vacuum-mounting posters and prints, to packaging orders and shipping them. When you were working on an order, you'd move from station to station until the order was complete. It was a fast-paced work environment and was about to get even faster after the owners landed two big commercial accounts, one being Merrell Chase Art Galleries in downtown Chicago.

Soon after starting work there, I noticed that there were no chairs in the place. The members of our small crew would literally have to find a box to sit on to eat lunch, which was the bare minimum required by the Department of Labor. The floor was concrete, so you needed some comfortable shoes because you were on your feet almost the entire time you were there.

As Merrell Chase and other new orders started pouring in, the overtime hours started to increase, as did the need for speed. The job was exhausting, and my feet would be sore by the end of the day.

The owners, Rich and Joan, were a married couple who were around all day, so you got the feeling you were always being watched. Rich was a good guy, but Joan was a bit of a bitch. Whenever co-workers and I got a chance to talk without one of them being in earshot (which was rare) we started to grumble about the excessive workload and wondered when they would hire a few new people to accommodate their expanding business. It never happened. At least, not while I was there, which, as it turned out, wasn't very long.

As I came to the end of my probationary period, on a Friday, I was called into Rich's office.

"Steve, I'm sorry, we're going to have to let you go." Followed by the usual vague bullshit: "Joan and I just don't feel it's a good fit."

I was caught off guard. I made some mistakes, but nothing major. I was still learning the multifaceted position and was getting good at most of the tasks.

"Okay," I said, at a loss for words.

"Here's your check for the previous two weeks. You'll have to pick up your last check for this week next Friday or I can mail it to you," as he handed me my check.

I agreed to pick it up. I grabbed my coffee cup from the sink area and walked out the door. As I made my way to my car, a voice spoke to me in my head. It said, *"You're a loser, Steve. You can't even keep a job clean and sober."* An interesting side note: the voice wasn't mine.

I felt the knot tighten in my gut, as the pain of failure kicked me in the pit of my stomach. As I drove out of the parking lot, the voice whispered, *C'mon Steve. You know your dad was right. You haven't got the stomach for work. You know there's only one way to get rid of this kind of pain—get you some dope!"*

Next, I felt a strong case of the "fuck-its" coming on, and my paycheck started burning a hole in my pocket. Then, out of nowhere, a snapshot of the Des Plaines Alano Club popped into my head and another voice said to me, *"Go there, now!"* So, I shut my brain off (as I had learned to do in treatment) and made a beeline for the place.

When I got there, I turned my brain back on and all the second thoughts hit, such as: *I've never been here"* and *"I don't know anybody.* I ignored them and walked through the door. To my surprise, the place was empty, except for one person—the custodian in charge of cleaning, making the coffee, and performing other duties that kept the place going.

"What time is the next meeting?" I inquired.

"About a half an hour," he said, looking up from wiping off the tables.

"You mind if I just hang out and wait?"

"No, go ahead. Make yourself comfortable."

So, I sat in an area that was set up like someone's living room in an overstuffed lounge chair, grabbed a magazine, and pretended to read it. I looked up and noticed all the program slogans: the 12 Steps and 12 Traditions, and the preamble to the AA Big Book "How It Works" on the walls. Their words delivered a measure of relief and comfort, but I was not out of the woods.

Soon, people started to trickle in and set up chairs for the meeting. I introduced myself and exchanged pleasantries with a few people and the meeting of about 15 or so people was called to order. They opened with the chairperson introducing himself and the meeting, the reading of the Preamble and the AA Promises by various members, followed by the chairperson's questions: "Is this anyone's first meeting of Alcoholics Anonymous?" No takers. "Is this anyone's first time at this meeting?" I raised my hand.

"Can you introduce yourself"?

"I'm Steve. I'm an addict and an alcoholic".

"Welcome Steve," the room all chimed back in unison.

As the meeting unfolded and several comments were made, I realized that though I felt safe and at home, I wasn't really feeling a whole lot better about my situation, so I decided to speak up. This would prove to be one of the biggest decisions of my life.

I told them the whole story. When I was through, the support started pouring in. Some of the things I heard in response were: "You need to give yourself a lot of credit; you came here and didn't go use," and "It took a lot of courage to come to a strange place and share what you shared with a bunch of strangers. I don't think I could've done it if I were in your shoes."

Then, probably the most helpful comment of all: "Don't worry about it, Steve. We all got fired from our first job sober. You'll get another job. You did the right thing!" Most of them laughed and brought a smile to my face.

After the meeting, the help and support continued when I also expressed concern to a few members who stuck around to talk. I told them that I really didn't know why they fired me. I thought I was doing okay, which probably bothered me more than anything. I was given a suggestion by one of the guys who heard me say I needed to return for my last paycheck.

"Ask him to tell you the truth about why they fired you, and tell him why you need to know," he advised.

He suggested that I tell Rich the truth about being in early recovery and that it was important that I know the real reasons I was fired, to avoid taking my mistakes into my next job. I thanked him and agreed that I would do it, though I really didn't have any intention to.

I left the meeting with a new perspective and felt completely different about things than when I walked into the place. My hope for the future was mostly restored, and I had stronger confidence in my ability to stay sober after experiencing failure. What at first felt like total failure was put in its proper perspective with the help of the people in that meeting who pointed out that it was nothing more than a temporary setback.

When I went to get my check the following Friday, I surprised myself by following the suggestion I was given. I told Rich the truth about myself and that knowing the real reason I was fired would be a great help to me. As soon as Rich heard my story, he almost tripped over himself apologizing, as if I was an orphan toddler and he had thrown me out in the street in the middle of winter.

"God, if we had only known your situation. Let me talk to Joan. I'm sure she'll be willing to give you another chance."

"No, no, no—that's okay! I don't want the job back; I just wanted to know what I did wrong," I said, stopping him as he turned to go find Joan.

"Well, if I'm being honest, you were too slow. With the increase in orders, we needed someone who could move a bit faster."

"Okay, thanks. I appreciate your being honest with me."

He handed me my check and that was it. I got in my car and reviewed his feedback in my mind. I concluded that his expectations were somewhat unrealistic, especially for $6.75 an hour, and that a more realistic solution would have been to hire more workers. I felt the only way I could have done the job any faster was to run from station to station. I concluded that I wasn't the right person for that job and accepted the outcome as a blessing in disguise.

Doc—The right thing for the right reasons

As my freedom increased, I continued to see Penny on the sly, but I also expanded my horizons in my recovery too. I started going to different meetings besides the Mustard Seed and Grant Hospital. One meeting was at a new place called The Serenity Club. It was an old warehouse that was rented out by an older AA guy named Doc. He, his wife, and a few others, remodeled and transformed the place into a combination of a sober dance club, Alano club, food stand, and halfway house. When a dance wasn't going on, the dance floor doubled as a huge meeting space.

Doc happened to be the lead speaker at one of the first meetings I attended there. He told his story, which I found amazing and inspirational, especially how he came to Chicago from New York City. He and his wife found themselves stuck in New York for years. They hated it. After they both got sober in AA, Doc woke up one morning and made up his mind that they were getting the hell out of "God-forsaken New York!" Where to? Chicago. They had visited once or twice and fell in love with the city. Doc said that the only plan he had was to trust God and the AA program, so he "turned it over to God," bought a one-way bus ticket, put some toiletries and one change of clothes in a small bag, and put their last $50 in his pocket. He kissed his wife goodbye and told her he'd send for her when he got settled.

He arrived at Union Station and walked the eight blocks to the club that he'd heard so much about—the infamous Mustard Seed. He sat in meetings, drank free coffee, and told his story. The outpouring of support he received was phenomenal. The people at the Seed took care of his every need. They fed him, clothed him, got him a job, and someone put him up on their couch until he could get his own place. He was soon able to bring his wife out from New York!

After she arrived, he stumbled across the opportunity to rent the old warehouse (cheap) from the owner who was in the program, and The Serenity Club was born. This story, combined with hearing much wisdom about the 12 Steps in a few previous meetings, confirmed that this was the guy I wanted to be my sponsor. Doc was an old alcoholic, and I was a young heroin and cocaine addict, but it didn't matter. By then, I was doing most of the right things and for the right reasons. As my priorities got clearer, I realized it was what he had to offer my recovery that was important, not his clever wit, or drug of choice.

At our first serious meeting, I told him my story over some food in a booth at the club. I confessed all. As a result, we identified how my "way with words" had gotten me into trouble in my past attempt at recovery. I asked him if I should stop talking in meetings for a while and just listen, totally willing to do whatever it took. His response was the type of wisdom only found in someone truly in recovery. He furrowed his brow at my suggestion and looked up, pausing for a moment to think. Then he said, "No, I don't think you need to do that. You have a lot of good things to say, Steve. But here's what I want you to do: After you comment in a meeting, ask yourself three questions. What did I just say? Why did I say it? And am I doing any of it? That's the one restriction I'll give you—you're not allowed to talk about anything you're not doing." He dubbed this technique a "spot-check inventory."

I agreed. It was not only a way to check in with myself about my motives, but also a way to discipline myself into talking only about things I was doing, not abstract recovery concepts, which I was good at, but ultimately did me no good. This was part of how I faked myself out last time. It was like the 24-hour silence assignment in Grant Hospital as a way of focusing on my true thoughts, feelings, and motives. I believe this is the goal of today's "mindfulness," though I'm sure someone will "rebrand" it and call it something different by the time this is read.

I finally had a real sponsor who met with me on a regular basis, taught me how to work the steps, and apply the program in my daily life.

A call from Oprah

I was unemployed and had my face in the paper daily in the Second Phase lounge while drinking my morning coffee. My daily ritual was interrupted by an Expediter who came to inform me that Arnold Muse wanted to see me in his office. As usual, I had that old feeling I had as a kid about to get his ass paddled. I thought about Penny and started getting nervous. When I got to his office, it turned out to be something completely unexpected. Arnold informed me that *The Oprah Winfrey Show* was going to be calling and talking to residents in preparation for an upcoming show they were doing called "When Social Drinking Goes Too Far." They were looking for people to be on the panel who would answer the questions Oprah, and the audience would ask. I was one of the residents selected by Arnold to be interviewed by phone.

When my turn came to be interviewed, the producer asked me a bunch of questions. I think they just wanted to make sure that I could express myself in a reasonably intelligent manner, and that I wasn't a moron.

A few days later, the residents who had been interviewed were called into the dining room. Several of us were chosen for the panel that would be on the stage. I wasn't one of them, probably because my drug of choice wasn't alcohol. I was, however, chosen to ask a question from my seat in the audience.

In those days, Oprah's show wasn't as spontaneous as it may have appeared to viewers. Those who were approved ahead of time to ask a question of the panel had tape on the side of our seats so Oprah could identify us.

The day of the show came, and we were driven to Harpo Studios. We were directed to our seats on stage and in the audience. Tape was applied to the side of the seats of those designated to ask questions, and one of the producers gave us a general overview of how things were going to happen.

Soon, Miss Winfrey came out and gave us all the "Oprah pep talk." She asked if there were any questions and that was it. The show started and went until the commercial break. Upon returning to live TV, she came alongside my seat, as my hand was raised, and she called on me. I stood up and as the camera zoomed in on my face, I introduced myself to Oprah as if I were in an AA meeting: "Hi, I'm Steve and I'm an addict," something that no one else did.

Realizing this, made me suddenly freeze and go blank for a second until I somehow stumbled over the words and spit my question out. Here I was, a guy who sang and played guitar in front of tons of people, getting nervous about asking a question that was preplanned in front of a camera. To this day, I have no explanation, and no recollection of the question I asked.

After the show, on our way back to Kedzie House, we all laughed and joked about the show, including me doing an imitation of myself stammering over my question. It was pretty funny. In reviewing the show, overall, I thought it was pretty lackluster and unremarkable. Oprah's show was usually interesting and entertaining, but this episode was pretty forgettable. It would, however, yield an interesting surprise for me later that day.

A blast from the past

As I walked to the Second Phase lounge with some clothes I was about to iron, I heard one of the payphones at the end of the hall ringing. Out of the corner of my eye I saw one of my peers answer it and paid no further attention, knowing it had nothing to do with me. No one in my life had ever contacted me on those phones and didn't even have the numbers. To my surprise, the person who answered the phone put it down and walked toward me.

"Steve Fiorito."

"Yeah," I responded.

"It's for you."

"It's for me!? Who is it?"

"She says her name's Mary DeWitt."

My jaw about hit the floor. I took the phone.

"Mary?"

The voice on the other end was unmistakable.

"Hey mister. How's it going?"

My heart pounded nostalgically upon hearing that voice.

"Good! Wow! How did you know I was here?"

She proceeded to tell me that she was changing her child's diaper with her back to the TV, when suddenly, she "heard that unmistakable voice" (I apparently have one too). She continued, "I thought, I know that voice. I turned around and sure enough, there you were, on Oprah!"

She said that during the show, Gateway was identified as being involved and that it was mentioned that some of the panel members were in treatment at the Kedzie facility. She got the number from directory assistance and called. Her call was answered by the First Phase desk man, and she asked for me. Luckily, he was willing to violate my confidentiality and informed her that I could be reached on the payphones upstairs and gave her one of the numbers. This time, the desk man's violation of confidentiality was a good thing and didn't lead to anyone's arrest.

We spent the rest of the time catching up. She was married and had two or three kids. I confessed to being in treatment for the second time. Then, she gave me the scoop on Cal, which was not good. He was still using, which was one of the reasons they split up. I could feel the deep sadness in her voice when she spoke about him, and when we remembered losing our beloved Warren to addiction nine years earlier.

I guess you could say it was one of my early realizations that our addictions deeply affected many around us in ways that we never considered. Most addicts are oblivious to this. I don't remember everything we talked about, but I do remember the best thing about our conversation. She told me she was proud of me, which made me feel good because I knew she meant it.

Drapery Cleaning Service

I went back to my daily ritual of drinking my morning coffee with my nose in the want-ads. One ad jumped off the page at me for a drapery installer for a company called Drapery Cleaning Service. I leapt to my feet and went to the phone. I called and one of the owners answered. I gave him a brief synopsis of my experience. He informed me that the position was still open and scheduled me for an interview. I finished my coffee and prayed, pleading with God that I needed a job, which I'm sure He already knew.

On the day of my interview, I arrived, résumé in hand, and introduced myself to Gene and Jerry, the two owners who also happened to be brothers. Both looked to be in their 50s or 60s. They recognized my name and knew of my father's drapery business, which I think scored a few points with them. Unfortunately, my application did not. It was a load of made-up crap that included working on a fictitious aunt's farm in Wisconsin, a fictitious factory that went out of business, and of course, working extensively for my father as a drapery installer, which was quite exaggerated. My real work history sucked, and for the most part, couldn't be used. The truth was, I'd been unable to work for the better part of the last two years due to being in and out of treatment.

I had a lot of trouble filling out the application because I had to make things up as I went along and plug in dates that needed to be accounted for. By the time I was done, my brain hurt. I gave the application to the girl at the counter and waited until Jerry stuck his head out of his office and called me in.

Upon entering, I sat facing his desk. He had my application and resume in hand and read some of the history aloud to me. He then looked over the top of his glasses and imparted these words of wisdom that I will never forget.

"Well Steve, this résumé is a bunch of bullshit, and quite frankly, I wouldn't be able to tell if you were an axe murderer or not from this. I will say: I *do* get the feeling that you know how to install drapes and blinds though."

I was stunned and caught off guard by his frankness. He continued, "A year on your aunt's farm, a company that's out of business."

I had no choice but to double down. "Well, I know it doesn't look very good, but it's all true."

"Okay," Jerry said, shaking his head yes, while squinting at me with a furrowed brow, trying to read me.

There was a long pause. "All right, we have one or two more people to interview and then we'll decide. We'll call you and let you know. Thanks for coming in." He stood up and reached across the desk to shake my hand.

"Thanks, Jerry; I'll look forward to hearing from you." With that, I turned and headed out of his office and out the front door. On my way out, I ran into his brother Gene and told him it was nice meeting him.

"Give your dad our regards Steve."

"I will; thanks again."

As I got in my car and started driving back to the house, I realized that there was no way I was getting that job…unless…there was one chance.

What if I called him and told him the truth? I thought. It didn't take me long to realize I had nothing to lose, so I looked for a payphone, and pulled over on Cicero Avenue at the first one I spotted. I picked up the phone, dug a quarter out of my pocket, but I almost chickened out until I reminded myself that I had nothing to lose. I dialed the phone and Jerry answered, "Drapery Cleaning Service. This is Jerry. Can I help you?"

"Jerry? This is Steve Fiorito."

"Yes, Steve, what can I do for you"?

"I was thinking about what you said about my résumé being bullshit."

"Yes?" he said inquisitively.

"Well, you were right; it is. The truth is, I'm a recovering alcoholic and I've been in treatment and in a halfway house for the past year and a half. I figured I'd call and tell you the truth since I knew there was no way you were going to give me the job if I didn't. I just need a chance."

"Okay, good for you. I appreciate you being honest and you're right; there was no way I was hiring you the way you left it." Then, after a bit of a pause, he said, "If you want the job, show up Monday morning at 7 a.m. It's yours." ... It took a few seconds for it to sink in.

"Okay, I'll be there. Thanks Jerry!"

Okay, maybe I wasn't completely honest with him, but I figured heroin and cocaine addict might be too much honesty and have defeated the purpose.

I see this as an early example of my decision-making getting better, not just because of the new values being instilled in me, but also the fog clearing up in my brain. Not only did my instincts kick in and guide me to the right thing to do, but I was also able to push myself beyond my comfort zone and do it.

Mission accomplished. I got the job! It would be important to my recovery and my development in *so* many ways. It was yet another example that the longer I stayed clean and did the right things, the more doors would open for me. Most importantly, I started viewing these events in a spiritual way. It reinforced in me the sense that God was guiding me and taking care of me.

My supervisor wound up being Gene, not Jerry. As it turned out, Jerry was more the accountant and handled the business end of things, while Gene was the overseer of daily operations.

The installer that was leaving trained me for two weeks. John was interesting. He was going back to school full-time. He had me do all the driving while he read and did homework in the passenger seat.

One of the benefits of the job was getting to take the van home nightly, including weekends. At the time, I still used my father's car to get to work during the week, but I had no vehicle on the weekends. The job and the vehicle became the lifeline for me being able to continue to build a relationship with my kids and stay in their lives. I now officially became "Weekend Dad."

Regardless of the challenges before me, my faith and the distinct sense of being led by God continued to grow. Although I still relied on other's interpretations, I was in the process of developing a relationship with a God of my own understanding. I started to embrace more and more the concept that as long as I stayed clean and did *most* of the right things (yes, I didn't always do the right thing), the way would open for me.

As I continued attending meetings and growing along spiritual lines, I was outgrowing treatment. I knew I was ready for the real world with my ace in the hole in my back pocket, which was: "Don't pick up the first drink or drug, no matter what, even if your ass falls off!" I once heard that in a meeting.

Unfortunately, what wasn't growing fast enough was my savings account. I was saving as much as I could but was still short of what I needed to move out. God was about to help me solve that problem in short order.

PART VI, MIRACLES HAPPEN

Recognizing the signs from God

I walked down the hall toward my dorm and heard what was by now, the familiar sound of one of the payphones ringing. Once again, out of the corner of my eye, I saw one of my peers answer it and paid no further attention, again, knowing it was not likely for me. Outside of Mary, no one ever contacted me on those phones. But once again, to my surprise, the person who answered the phone put it down and walked toward me.

"Steve Fiorito."

"Yeah," again I responded.

"It's for you."

I started having a déjà vu... "It's for me!? Who is it?"

"It's your mother."

My first thought was, *who died?* I slowly made my way to the phone and picked it up.

"Hey Ma. What's going on?"

"They found your car."

"What!?"

"The police found your car. They found it parked on a side street on the West Side of Chicago."

"Oh my God! You're kidding! Where is it?"

"It's impounded in a police lot on the West Side. Here's the address and the phone number...."

I grabbed a pen and paper and wrote it down. "Does it run? Is my guitar, my tapes and my stuff still in it?"

"I don't know but they did say that there was a fire in the interior. I don't know how bad."

"Okay Ma. Thanks. I'll call and go over there. I can't believe it!"

Albie, being a devout Christian, gave all the credit to whom it belonged. "That's God Steven. Anything is possible with God."

I agreed, hung up the phone, and went to my dorm to get some change to make the call. On the way, an overwhelming feeling of gratitude came over me. I don't know if it was a voice in my head or just a feeling, but somehow, the words that were conveyed to me by the voice said, *Okay Steven, I feel you're ready to get back some of what you lost now.*

I fell to my knees and tears welled up in my eyes as I thanked God for making His message clear to me. I thought about my picture albums, my guitar, and the money in my trunk. I wondered if they were still there, but I didn't really care about the material things. The sign from God was all I cared about, and it was enough for me.

I told staff and called to make the arrangements to check it out. The police told me that the keys were not found in it, and if I had a spare set, I should bring them along with the title. I didn't have any keys, but I did have the title. They also told me that the car wasn't drivable and that the interior fire appeared to be deliberately set and was pretty bad. All I wanted to do was open that trunk!

I jumped in my van and took a hammer and the biggest screwdriver I had out of my toolbox. Then, I remembered what else was in that trunk—a bottle of Methadone, syringes, and other drug paraphernalia—hidden in a secret taillight compartment. I got a knot in my stomach.

Upon my arrival, I presented the proper identification and the title. I was given a document that included the spot it was located in. My heart started racing when I spotted the familiar shitty grey box—the 1984 Chevy Malibu.

I stopped and got out with the hammer and screwdriver in hand. The first thing I did was open the driver-side door, and as I did, flashbacks hit me of that night when a shot of cocaine overwhelmed me and led to the car's fate. I remembered the feelings of hopelessness, being out of control, and drowning in cocaine-induced insanity, that had pushed my life to the brink of death. I snapped back into reality and continued with the task at hand.

The interior was badly burned. Next, I opened the rear driver-side door and looked on the floor, where most of my belongings had been. There was nothing but more charred interior. Then, the last chance for recovering something of value rested with whatever the trunk held. I thought about the bottle of Methadone and what I was going to do with it.

I centered the screwdriver on the trunk lock and struck it hard with the hammer. It pushed in slightly. I hit it again even harder. It pushed in further. The third time was the charm and sent the lock disappearing into the darkness of the trunk. I lifted the lid and immediately saw that the guitar was gone. I thought to myself, *shit, they went into the trunk*.

The next thing I thought about was the white envelope I had my cash in. It was in the same spot where it had been that day, in the center of the spare tire, facing up with the end of the envelope torn open. It appeared undisturbed. It hadn't budged throughout my relapse except to peel off twenty-dollar bills for drug purchases. I slowly leaned the two feet over the trunk, until I could see down into the envelope. I remember saying to myself, *did they see it? Did they see it? Did they see the money?* ... No, they didn't!

A wad of rolled up cash was staring up at me. They missed it! Thank God for my messy trunk! Once they found the guitar, everything else just looked like worthless trunk crap—a spare tire, jumper cables, maps, oil cans and the like. I grabbed the envelope and pulled out the wad of cash. There was $600 in twenties just sitting there all that time. I realized that the money would be a nice chunk of what I needed to move out of Gateway and into my own apartment, and I again thanked God.

Finally, it was time to face the Methadone and the syringes, which symbolized the demons that had almost ended my life. I opened the compartment and there it all was, just as I had left it. I pulled out the small plastic bottle of orange liquid that likely still contained about 40 milligrams of Methadone. I unscrewed the cap, looked up at God, and thanked Him for giving me the strength to do what I was about to do. Then, I proceeded to slowly pour the contents of the bottle out. I watched it hit the ground and splatter before disappearing into the dusty dirt. Then, I took out the three syringes and broke the needles off, one by one. Franko and I had done this before but somehow, I knew that this was different. There was a power greater than myself at work and I could feel it. Dumping 40 milligrams of Methadone on the ground was something I could never have done without the strength of my Higher Power.

I closed the trunk as well as I could, got into my van, and drove away, symbolically catching one last glimpse of the last remaining relic from my addicted past in the rear-view mirror. It was a fitting end to that part of my life.

The feelings of gratitude and pride I experienced could have been expected, but there was another unexpected feeling that I also experienced that day—revenge! I actually felt a sense of revenge against addiction, like: "Fuck you addiction! I'm not falling for your bullshit anymore!"

Drugs had lost their appeal and no longer had power over me! It felt great! I shared the whole experience with my sponsor and in meetings. The 12-step program had become a place where I started realizing that what I used to view as coincidence or luck was actually God's divine intervention.

Moving on with an attitude of gratitude

Once John left Drapery Cleaning Service, I was on my own. The job got more difficult not only physically, but also mentally, as I had to solve problems on my own without the benefit of John's experience. I called Gene a lot in those early days at work, and though he seemed slightly annoyed at times, I sensed he was glad that I cared enough about not making mistakes to call him. I also had to find my way around the city and suburbs using a paper map. There were no commercial GPS systems in 1987. As I adjusted to the rigors of going to work every day, and working hard, good sleep became essential. I would go to bed early, sleep like a rock, and get up early to get to Belmont and Cicero avenues, get my stops for the day, map out my routes and load up my van. I usually needed gas and would fill up at a station across the street from the shop.

I started to develop familiarity with the people who worked there, including a young attendant around my age. We would shoot the shit as I stood in line to pay for my gas and get my receipt from him. Receipts were important for me to get reimbursed for gas. The guy always seemed like he was trying to impress me. One day, before I was about to take off and get on my route, he came up to the van with something in his hand. I rolled down the window and he handed me a stack of blank receipts.

"Hey, I just wanted to give you these. I remember you telling me that you get reimbursed for gas. I figure, you're a cool guy, so this will give you some extra money in your pocket."

"Okay, thanks. I appreciate it!" I said, playing along.

I thought to myself, *no way. Gene catches me doing something like this, and I can kiss this job goodbye.* I shoved the receipts under the clutter on the "desk in my office" (the engine cover in the van) and drove away, never giving them a second thought.

About three weeks later, while I was loading up, Gene called me into his office. "What are these?" he said accusingly, holding up the blank receipts.

I got an instant knot in my gut. "The guy at the gas station gave them to me. I forgot all about them."

"You never turned one in?" he asked, his eyes staring into mine.

"No Gene. I just didn't know what to do when he handed them to me, so I just shoved them under some paperwork and forgot all about them."

"Okay, because you know that if I can't trust you, we have nothing."

"I know. I would never do that to you."

"Okay. You got a lot of stops today. You'd better get going."

"Okay."

He tore the receipts in half, tossed them in the wastebasket, smiled, and shook my hand. I could tell he believed me.

I started learning the value of being trustworthy in treatment, but this incident really brought that value home. This man actually trusted me with his business... me!

Surprisingly, a lot of what I learned in treatment started coming into play in my daily life. I admit that I never thought any of it had anything to do with the real world, and it doesn't, that is, unless you stay clean long enough.

The emotional skills I was developing got another early test when I had a particularly cranky old woman customer. She was my last stop, and I was trying to get home at a decent time, but it wasn't going well that day. I installed her draperies, and as was customary with certain fabrics, I had some wrinkles to steam out. Once she realized this, she started standing over me and critiquing my work. "What about this one?" she crowed, pointing to a small but stubborn wrinkle with her shriveled, arthritic finger.

This went on and on for the better part of an hour and I was losing patience. I explained to her that the drapes had to hang for a while before all the wrinkles would come out, and that I had steamed them as best as I could for now. She continued to complain and berate me. I was just about to go off on her when the image of Pete Piry handing me that coin from Acapulco popped into my head and him saying: "Fiorito, when you think you have to have the last word, reach in your pocket and pull out this coin and let it remind you to... SHUT THE FUCK UP!"

I reached into my pocket. The coin was there. I pulled it out, squeezed it tightly, and I didn't say another word. I kept steaming the drapes until she finally relented. I outlasted her. She got tired of standing and I let her win. Or at least I let her think she won. In reality, I won—another battle over myself.

Working hard while still going through Post-Acute Withdrawal Syndrome, led to the need for a minimum of eight hours of sound sleep, which suddenly started being regularly interrupted by my roommate Greg. He started coming into the room at around 2 a.m. to get things out of his drawers. At times, he'd be digging in the bottom of the drawer and would even turn the light on, like he was looking for something. Or he'd prop the door open so he could use the light from the hallway. After this started happening more frequently, I started throwing some hints by acting concerned.

"Everything okay?" His answers were short, and he seemed annoyed with me for asking. I remember thinking, *this guy's shooting dope*. After this happened several more times, I decided that I needed to have a talk with him before I went to staff. I got my chance that Saturday morning when I walked into the Second Phase lounge. He was just finishing up some breakfast and got up to turn off the TV. We were the only ones in the lounge and seemed to be the only ones awake on the floor.

I approached him. "Brother, we need to talk."

"About what?" he snapped back.

"About you waking me up in the middle of the night. I've got to get up early and go to work and I have a hard enough time doing that as it is."

"That's not my problem. I live there too."

"What do you need from your drawers at two in the morning anyway?"

"None of your damn business," he barked as he got up from his chair.

"Well, to be honest, I think you're using brother," I said, as I got up from mine.

"Mind your own fucking business." He now moved toward me and got up in my face. I got right back in his. "You are my fucking business, when you start affecting my sleep."

Out of nowhere, he took a swing at me, but I pulled my face back and he only caught a small piece of it. I countered with a hard right to his face, after which it was full-blown on! We were both landing blows about each other's face and head and started to wrestle for position. It was loud enough to wake two of our peers out of a dead sleep. They came into the room in their underwear and pulled us apart.

Staff was called and came upstairs. They put us in separate empty offices, and Pete was informed. As it turned out, he was in his office down the hall, but apparently didn't hear the altercation.

We were called in one at a time and interviewed by Pete and his new staff member, Jennifer. I told them what happened and that I suspected that Greg had relapsed. I was told to go back to the office and wait. After about fifteen minutes, I was escorted back to Pete's office. On my way there, I noticed Greg had been accompanied to our dorm by two Expediters and staff Jennifer. He was packing. I remember thinking, *well, that was the right call. He swung at me first. I only swung back in self-defense.* But there were no witnesses.

Upon entering his office, Pete asked me to have a seat. With a look of concern and sadness, he said, "I'm sorry, I gotta terminate you, Steve."

Initially, I was shocked and in disbelief. "Why? I hit him in self-defense. What was I supposed to do? The guy's waking me up in the middle of the night relapsing, and I'm going to work every day trying to do the right things. All I did was try to talk to him about it and he became hostile."

Pete interrupted, "Steve, Steve, Steve. I know. I believe you man. We were getting ready to drop (urine test) him. We suspected he was using. We know you're doing good, but unfortunately, I gotta terminate you anyway." He leaned closer to me and almost in a whisper, he said, "How would it look if the white staff (his new counselor Jennifer was white) terminated the black guy and not you?"

My reaction was even more proof I was growing and changing. The old Steve would have been pissed about that reasoning and would have argued vehemently, but I was very much in a "humility zone" based on recent events, including my car being recovered. The realization came over me that it was time for me to go, and that Gateway had taken me as far as they could. I'm sure I surprised Pete with my response: "I understand. I'm grateful to Gateway for letting me come back and get my life together. Thanks for all your help."

I feel the need to mention that once again, my "white privilege card" was nowhere to be found.

With that, I got up, went to the dorm, and packed my belongings. Greg had already been escorted downstairs. As I was packing, I thought about where I was going. I assumed I would need to call my parents and tell them what happened. They knew I was doing well, but I'm not sure if they would have been too thrilled about me coming to live with them, no matter how temporary it may have been. Then it dawned on me: *I'll call Penny and see if I could stay with her while I save the rest of the money for my own place. That way, I could stay in the city, continue making my meetings, and get to work much easier.*

I called her and told her what happened. She agreed and we arranged for her to pick me up at our usual rendezvous spot. Again, I walked out of a treatment program with my big green garbage bags in tow, but this time, it felt different. It felt like it was the right thing—it was time to move on.

Progress: A small bed to an even smaller couch

Living with Penny in a studio apartment and sharing her full-sized bed was a bit tight. I wasn't there most of the time due to work and seeing my kids, and neither was she, due to work, school, and her internship at Gateway. We were like two ships passing in the night…and having sex when we *did* see each other. It was great, that is, until I started noticing something—she always smelled like alcohol. In fact, I started noticing that she was often drunk. This was a huge turn-off, as it always had been for me and although it wasn't as if she was using my drugs of choice, it probably wasn't a good idea being around someone who was abusing alcohol almost daily. After just over a month, I couldn't take it anymore. I didn't know what to do, so I called someone I trusted—my "brother from another mother"—James Minter, whose wisdom had always pulled me through.

Just as I suspected, he gave it to me in the raw, without holding back. "Boy, you must be crazy. You need to get out of there ASAP!"

I knew that I called the right person when he offered to let me move in with him and sleep on his couch. He urged me to "Get out now brother, before the sex makes you change your mind."

He was right. I couldn't look her in the face. I just wasn't at that growth level yet when it came to that stuff. So, I packed up my things and wrote her a note that was brief and to the point. "*I'm sorry. I can't do this anymore. Hope there's no hard feelings. Thanks for everything - Steve.*"

I hightailed it over to James's apartment on Grandville and Winthrop avenues. Not the best neighborhood, but beggars can't be choosers—right?

I wound up living with James over the winter. Nothing remarkable happened during this period except that parking was a bitch, especially with a van. I'd wound up having to park five or six blocks from the apartment at times in the snow and frigid temperatures.

James and I both worked, so we didn't see a lot of each other. But when we did, we always had good conversations at his kitchen table about whatever was going on in our lives.

As I learned to consistently show up for work, I also learned how to work hard every day. My training at Gateway helped but couldn't totally prepare me for the busy seasons at Drapery Cleaning Service. November 1st through the first of the year was the worst. Everybody wanted their drapes cleaned for the holidays. As a way of coping, I invented a little game I would later refer to as "The Work Game," a kind of work-related version of the AA slogan "One Day at a Time." This is how I played it: I would show up for work and tell myself, *Today, I'm going to put 110 percent into this job, but tomorrow, I'm going to screw off and take it easy.*

The next day would come, and I'd repeat the same mantra, like people do in AA when they put off taking that drink for just one more day. I would do this daily until I'd find myself getting through the entire week without taking it easy or screwing off.

The fact that I was finally living my life *one day at a time* was really driven home when I went to work one Monday morning. I had a lot of stops that would take me from the North Shore to the Far South Suburbs. I was taking the bagged draperies off the rack, and loading them into my van, when, I had a realization that stopped me dead in my tracks—I was singing! That may not sound very significant, but it was very significant for me. I was hit full force with the sudden realization of the stark contrast between who I used to be, compared to who I was becoming. I realized that I had never felt good or sang on a Monday morning at 7 a.m. at any job in my life. My Monday mornings had always been spent in a hangover-like haze from the weekend, out of dope, and out of money, with the shittiest attitude possible, thinking to myself, *Shit, I gotta do this all week again and it's only 7:12 a.m. on Monday? Fuck!*

I didn't think like that anymore, so I didn't feel that way. I only had to do this for today, actually, only for right now. There was no "all week" anymore. I can't say I had all the energy I needed though, and I still relied heavily on my "medication"—coffee.

As I mentioned earlier, I didn't know it at the time, but I was experiencing something that would later be identified as Post-Acute Withdrawal Syndrome, or PAWS for short. PAWS was a set of physical and psychological symptoms that anyone with a severe enough addiction problem would likely have to deal with, after any severe withdrawal had ceased.

The duration, intensity, and type of symptoms one would experience, would depend mainly on how severe their addiction was, and what drugs were used. I had my share of typical symptoms but the worst of these was low energy. I would run out of energy quickly and be "running on fumes" for a good part of the day. I would become extremely lethargic and tired. Constant yawning and eyes watering became the norm for me.

Luckily, there was coffee, which, looking back, was a gift from God. I used it medicinally in my early recovery. If it weren't for those little dark roasted beans, I don't know if I would have made it through that time. I guess we could say by using a mild stimulant, I was engaged in another early version of MAT (Medication Assisted Treatment) though not an opioid replacement.

There but for the grace of God go I

On February 2nd, 1988, I finally hit that milestone—I'd been clean and sober for one year! My "home group" was Tuesday NA in the basement of Lakeview Lutheran Church on Addison and Broadway. I was looking forward to getting my one-year medallion that night, and this time, I really deserved it.

At about 1 p.m., I made one of the stops on my route in a nice area of the Chicago suburb of Oak Park. I rang the bell several times, but no one answered. Gene had a strict protocol that included going to a payphone and trying to call the customer. If they didn't answer, I was to try to contact Gene and get the okay to go to my next stop. It was a big job, so I didn't want to have to come back to the area once I moved on. I remember driving to a main street looking for a payphone and coming across a bar, which I knew would have one. Back in the day, not every business had a payphone and there wasn't one on every corner. You kind of knew which businesses would likely have one, and bars were one of them. I walked in and tried to call the customer. No one picked up the phone. As it rang, I turned and started scanning the bar, mostly to see if there were any poor slobs drinking at 1 p.m. There was only one. He turned on his barstool and I got a good look at his face. I recognized him instantly and my heart sank. It was Rick—a guy I was in Grant Hospital with.

I flashed back to the group where he told his story, and he broke down crying. You could feel his desperation as he described how he and two lifelong buddies owned a successful bar, and how they used it to hang out, get away from their wives, and escape life. They would buy each other, and customers rounds. They were "the big men on campus," that is, until the story took an ominous turn, and cocaine entered the picture. Before he knew it, he had drained his kid's college fund, was in hock up to his ears, had been neglecting his family, and his wife was ready to leave him. When he finished and it came time to give him feedback, I gave it to him in the raw. "I hate to tell you, Rick, but you gotta get out of that situation, sell your part of that bar, and cut your buddies loose (who were still using) if you really want to stay clean and sober."

His response was riddled with excuses, denial, and was disappointing. He made a valiant effort to backtrack and admit I was right, but it reeked of insincerity. I remembered walking away after the group ended, thinking; *No way, that guy's not going to be able to let go of that bar and make those kinds of sacrifices.* As it turned out, I was right.

One year later, he sat in a bar, drinking, and bleary-eyed at 1 p.m. on the day that I was going to get my one-year medallion. I walked up to him.

"Hey Rick, is that you?"

"Stevo!! Wow! How you doin'?"

"I'm good. Working as a drapery installer. I had to use the payphone to call a customer."

"Well, you don't have to ask how I'm doing—right? I fell off a few months after leaving treatment. My wife and kids left after that. You were right. I should've gotten out of it. We still have the bar, but it's not doing very well."

"I'm going to get my one-year medallion tonight at my home group. Can you believe it? I'm one year clean today, Rick."

"Good for you. Congratulations! You look good. You put some weight on…You look good."

"Why don't you come to my meeting Rick? If not tonight, next week? Here's the address…I gotta go. Come to a meeting Rick." I slipped him the napkin I'd written the address on.

"You're right. I should. I'm gonna try to make it next week."

"Okay, you promise?"

"I promise," he said, his speech slightly slurred but still convincingly.

"Okay, I gotta go to work. I'll see you next week—right?"

"You got it. I'll see you next week."

Literally, and metaphorically, I walked out of the darkness of the bar into the light of day. As the cold, crisp air hit me, so did the sadness of knowing I'd never see him again. I reminded myself what the program had taught me— *There but for the grace of God go I*—and it helped to ease the sadness.

Real recovery: The gift that keeps on giving

That winter, sleeping on James's couch, I saved the rest of the money I needed for my own place, including money for a TV, stereo, and other amenities, including a new Washburn acoustic guitar.

As the snow melted with the coming of spring, it was time to search for my own place. I started looking in the paper, and making appointments to see apartments, but my lack of experience and still deficient self-esteem kicked in. I remember thinking: *Who's going to rent an apartment to you—the sick dope fiend with bad credit and no work history to speak of?"* Like I said, beggars can't be choosers and at the time, in many ways, I still felt like a beggar.

I remember seeing apartments with the paint peeling, cracked walls, or worse, and thinking, *No big deal. I used to be a house painter. I can paint it.* In one place the kitchen sink was so unlevel that I actually tilted my head and torso to the left as I walked up to it. I told the landlord, "No big deal, I'll still be able to wash dishes—right?" He shook his head in agreement with a big grin on his face and said something in Greek to himself. Probably, something like, "What a chump. He's actually okay with that lopsided sink?"

I was obviously desperate, but something stopped me from jumping at the first few offers I got. Good (God?) thing, too, because I saw an ad for a one-bedroom apartment in Portage Park, a much nicer area off of Irving Park Road and Milwaukee and Cicero Avenues. It was a nice neighborhood with a big Sears department store on the northeast corner, plenty of other shopping and restaurants, and even a game room less than half a block away. Most of the buildings were vintage Chicago with renovated nice apartments in them.

I immediately felt I was out of my league upon arrival at 3939 North Lamon Avenue. The apartment was on the second floor of the two-story, four-unit building. As I climbed the stairs, the smell of new carpeting mixed with home-cooking filled the air. The owners were a husband and wife in their fifties. The door was open, and the wife greeted me, "You must be Steve."

"That's me," I replied smiling, attempting to cover up my nervousness.

She introduced herself and explained that her husband was showing the apartment to another prospective tenant and that they should be done shortly. She informed me that I was the last person they'd be showing it to. We stood in the living room and after I completed the application (complete with fake landlord references), she asked some standard questions. The place became even more attractive when she told me about the monthly rent. It was reasonable and really made me glad I didn't take any of the initial offers I had gotten. Not only were some of those places dumps, but they were also overpriced.

As we made small talk, I simultaneously scanned the place. It was beautiful. All the wood in the place, from the hardwood floors to the crown molding that bordered the entire ceiling in every room, had been recently refinished. The living room and dining room were bright and sunny with the new blinds open on the refurbished windows. I couldn't help but comment on how beautiful all the wood was. She explained that she and her husband did all of it. It was by far the nicest place I had seen. The more beautiful I realized it was, the more my hopes sank, until finally, they were all but dashed when her husband entered from the kitchen, wrapping up his tour with a young woman.

She was well-put-together and well-spoken, smacking of that new term, "Yuppie" (Young Urban Professional). Some of the comments he made to her made me feel like she had it in the bag. We all exchanged introductions. Her name was Jennifer and as she headed out the door, he told her that I was the last person they were showing it to; they'd be deciding by the end of the week and would call her.

Then, he took me on a tour of the apartment, pointed out the unit directly across the hall, and explained that a young woman about my age lived there. As the tour ended, he gave me the same spiel he had just given Jennifer. We shook hands, and I left thinking; *No way am I getting that apartment; they're gonna give it to Miss Yuppie.* I put it out of my mind, but I liked the area and thought about concentrating my future search there.

By Friday, I had forgotten all about the apartment and had appointments set up to view some places the next day. Sunday was now my day to pick up my kids, so that was out for apartment hunting. Laura and the kids had moved into the kitchenettes on Wolf Road and Lake Street in Northlake with Laura's boyfriend Garner. The same apartments that I visited frequently as a kid when Sue and Gary rented their first apartment there. The place had gotten badly run down and had become "The Barrio." I have nothing against any race or ethnicity, never have, so I'll let you draw your own conclusions.

When I came home, James gave me a message he had received. It was from the owner of the apartment on Lamon. I thought about not calling him back because I knew he was just calling as a courtesy to let me know that they gave the apartment to someone else. I guess I was curious to see if I was right about them giving it to Miss Yuppie, so I called. The landlord answered.

"Hi, it's Steve Fiorito returning your call."

"Oh, hi Steve. Steve, my wife and I talked it over and we decided to rent the apartment to you, so if you still want it, it's yours."

I was in shock and almost fainted! "Really? I thought for sure you'd give it to Jennifer, especially after you told me that there was another young woman who lived right across the hall."

"Actually Steve, that's one of the reasons we chose you. We didn't like the idea of two young women living alone across the hall from each other in that building. We felt we wanted a man there, just in case. We also felt you were a nice guy, and we liked you." I was a nice guy! Even LAPD thought so!

After hashing out the security deposit, and move in date, I hung up the phone. I was still in shock and couldn't believe what had just happened. I turned to James and told him. We hugged, and both acknowledged the many miracles we had both experienced since getting clean. His almost $12-an-hour job with no work history, my job, and now this, were no longer simply luck. We now recognized them as the miracles they were—blessings from God that rewarded our efforts to change our lives. The "Red Sea" was being parted for both of us.

Having my own place not only made me feel like I was on the right track with my recovery, but it meant I had somewhere to bring my kids to spend the weekends. It would be a good thing for them to have a place to escape, since it became apparent that Laura was still using drugs, and as it turned out, her new boyfriend Garner had a serious alcohol problem.

He would come out and talk to me when I'd pick up or drop off the kids. He was older than me, so he'd try to come off like a big brother. I think he meant well, but it irritated me when he would occasionally slur his words, while being condescending, and borderline scolding me for occasionally being late picking up or dropping off the kids. When he found out I had just moved into my apartment, he went out of his way to give me some things I needed.

Once I got set up with my new stuff, combined with whatever hand-me-downs I could get from my family, I still had a lot of holes to fill furniture-wise. So, I went to a second-hand store and got some cheap crap to fill in the gaps. I figured they were just temporary, and I'd replace them a little at a time with each paycheck. So much for that plan—it never happened. When I woke up one morning and realized it, I took all the stuff down to the dumpster and threw it all out. I knew that the emptiness in my apartment would motivate me to fill it and stop procrastinating, and I finally did.

It was very symbolic of what needs to happen in early recovery—letting go of a lot of old useless stuff, experiencing the emptiness of the void it creates, and filling that void with the real quality things that life had to offer.

I loved my apartment and would come home and *attempt* to cook. After dinner, if I didn't go to one of my meetings, I'd pick up my guitar and work on a song I was writing, play a record or cassette tape on my new stereo, or watch TV if there was anything good on. Unfortunately, as with all love affairs, the honeymoon would soon end, and so it was with my love affair with my apartment and the things inside of it.

I'll never forget the first time it happened. I came home and, after dinner, sat on the couch. I stared at my guitar, but I didn't feel like playing. Next, I looked at the stereo, but I didn't feel like listening to music. So, I turned on the TV, and flipped through the channels, but there was nothing that interested me, so I shut it off. I just sat there staring at the blank TV screen as darkness began to fall. The silence in my apartment became deafening. It was official—for the first time in my new life, I was bored—a scary feeling in early recovery, a feeling that typically led me to drug-seeking in the past.

I became so uncomfortable; it was almost like a panic attack. I hadn't been bored in quite a long time, so it caught me off guard. I was immediately able to identify boredom's connection to relapse. I could sense that thoughts about using were "just around the corner." Luckily, there was something else literally just around the corner on Irving Park Road—a game room! I got up, reached into my pocket, and pulled out a twenty-dollar bill. I bolted out the door to the game room. Twenty bucks got you a lot of pinball and Galaga (arcade games) in those days. I came home about 11 p.m. and went to bed.

Mission accomplished, but at a price. I couldn't stop and buy lunch for the rest of the week, so I had to get by on peanut butter and jelly sandwiches with some fruit on the side. I figured it was a small price to pay to avoid a possible craving to use. Two weeks later, it happened again and once again, I flew out the door and spent my last twenty bucks on games. Then, a few weeks later, it happened yet again. I sprang to my feet, pulled a twenty out of my pocket, and headed for the door, but this time, I stopped dead in my tracks and thought to myself, *I can't keep running to the game room and blowing twenty bucks every time I feel bored*, followed by, *I like my quarter pounder with cheese and fries, and I don't like having to eat peanut butter and jelly for lunch.*

I had also started picking up my kids on the weekends, and due to my financial limitations and not having many options, I started taking them to, of all places, the Town and Country Bowling Alley. I used to make fun of bowlers when I went there to shoot pool or buy dope. I found myself doing just one more thing I thought I'd never do—bowling.

I became more aware of God's sense of humor, when I struggled to keep the ball from the gutter as it rumbled down the lane. I was officially a "square"! Well, at least in some ways. In those days, bowling was relatively cheap, and it was all I could afford. Then, I'd give my daughters quarters, and they would try to grab a toy or stuffed animal with the crane claw game. They got pretty good at it. They had a lot of practice due to one of the machines also being at the local, infamous truck stop, *Steak & Egger* on Mannheim Road. There was nowhere better to get a good breakfast, cheap. The owner used to give them both a handful of quarters to play the games in the place. Nice guy.

I started paying Laura twenty-five dollars a week for child support. It's the best I could do at the time. Money was so tight; my budget couldn't accommodate blowing twenty bucks in a game room on a Wednesday night.

Lacking experience managing money, I'd often put off paying some of my bills to have money in my pocket for my kids. It wasn't long before I started getting "red notices" in the mail, threatening to shut off my phone or electricity. Commonwealth Edison was especially shrewd about wanting their money and eventually sent me a surprise in the mail—they required a $100 deposit to keep the juice flowing to my little "bachelor pad." The nerve!

I figured out pretty quickly that occasional boredom in early recovery was probably normal. And whether it was or not, I was going to have to deal with it. It was just a feeling, and I didn't spend almost two years in treatment to let my feelings run me around like that. So, I sat my ass on the couch, turned the TV on, and stared at whatever was on until I got tired and went to bed.

The next day, getting ready for work, I noticed the feeling was gone. I learned a valuable lesson: I didn't always have to respond to and do something about the way I was feeling. I could just accept occasional negative feelings and ride them out. Tomorrow was a new day, and I could start over.

After building what was now a bona fide, however fledgling, and imperfect program of recovery on the foundation of just not picking up a drink or a drug *(even if yer ass falls off)*, I found myself still dealing with occasional triggers to use. They were pretty manageable though and were more like little "yip-yip" dogs occasionally nipping at my heels. I would describe them more as *thoughts* about using than *cravings* to use. I discovered that along with my occasional bout with boredom, something else that I couldn't have foreseen started to send me down a path that I didn't want to go down—gas station bathrooms. Due to what I did for a living, I found myself in them much more than the average person would. I'd have to stop on my route occasionally while on the road. They were quick and easy, in and out, then back on the road.

In my addiction, they were perfect to shoot dope in. They were everywhere, they were private and rarely would you get disturbed by anyone. I'd lock the door and set up my dope, works, spoon, and equipment on the flush box. Then I'd get a hit ready, get water from the sink, sit on the closed toilet seat, tie myself off, and shoot my dope.

It's amazing that you don't hear more stories of dead junkies being found in gas station bathrooms. I could see the headlines: *Family Vacation Ruined when Father and Son Find Dead Junkie in Gas Station Bathroom.*

While taking a leak, I'd find myself passing the time scanning the flush box. I'd see if there were any soot marks from the bottoms of burnt spoons, any crumbs or drips of dope that had dried, or even any spilled powder. It was fun in a sick sort of way at first, that is, until I saw my first rocks of coke that someone left. Then, one day, I saw an outfit in the garbage and a dope tinfoil wrapper on the floor. I knew I needed to start doing something different.

On that day, I decided that I would no longer use gas station bathrooms when I was on the road. Instead, I started going into restaurant bathrooms, where I saw no signs of drug use ever again. Another potentially big problem, solved with a simple adjustment.

Post-Acute Withdrawal Syndrome also continued to pose a threat to my recovery. The greatest example occurred soon after I moved into my apartment. I remember coming home late with not a lot of time to get to my Tuesday NA meeting. I was exhausted and thought about not going. I remember being in my bedroom and looking longingly at my bed; *Boy that looks good. Just to be under those covers all comfy and warm right now*. Then, just messing around, I did a belly flop into my bed. The next thing I knew, I was waking up in the same position I'd landed in—fully clothed. I had no idea what time it was. I sprang to my feet and noticed it was still dark. I wondered if I was late for the meeting. When I looked at the clock, it dawned on me that it was 5 a.m. I had been laying in that position without moving a muscle for ten hours.

The following week, it happened again—I was too exhausted to go to my meeting. Again, I looked at the bed and thought about how good it would feel to be in it, but this time, something totally different happened—a warning "alarm" went off in my head. I reminded myself; *this is exactly how it happens. This is what they're talking about (people who relapse). Get your ass in that kitchen, heat up some water, jump in the shower, and make some instant coffee. You're going to your fucking meeting Steve!"* So, that's what I did.

I remember the meeting being especially good that night, with the lead speaker and comments being more profound than usual. They all seemed to be speaking directly to me, and the things I was dealing with at the time. I made a comment that I had heard many variations of on many occasions in meetings: "I almost didn't come to this meeting tonight, but I'm really glad I did."

I proceeded to share the story of why I wasn't there the previous week and how when it almost happened again, I kicked myself in the ass and found a simple solution to overcome a potential threat to my recovery. Again, I thanked God for the little dark roasted bean.

I had gotten through a handful of minor threats to my recovery without using, but one of the biggest threats was just ahead and would ambush me at a moment of weakness when I least expected it.

My second big test

The term "Thank God it's Friday" was magnified as I came to the end of a very hard work week. It was one of those weeks where if it *could* go wrong, it *did* go wrong. Routes were filled with construction delays, customers were fussy, hardware was missing to reinstall jobs—well—you get the picture.

So, I was relieved to get to my last stop and finally put an end to the week. I was looking forward to my Friday night meeting at Grant Hospital. I arrived at about 5 p.m. and found the woman, who looked to be in her fifties, oddly, still in her bathrobe and house slippers, with what looked to be a turban wrapped around her head. The job was an easy install, and I knocked it out in no time. I had to pee, so before I cleaned up and collected the check, I asked to use the bathroom. The woman directed me to it. I went in, lifted the seat, and started peeing. Just when I thought nothing else could go wrong, I found no need to scan this flush box for remnants of drugs because staring up at me were two huge plastic bottles. I read the bottle on the left first.

PRELUDIN
75-Milligrams
500 Tablets

Then the bottle on the right…

PERCODAN
Oxycodone Hydrochloride/Aspirin
500 Tablets

I couldn't believe what I was seeing—almost the pharmaceutical equivalent of my drugs of choice! Most people know that Percodan is an opiate painkiller, but many may not be familiar with Preludin (Phenmetrazine). It was soon to be all but discontinued due to its history of abuse potential and addiction. It was known on the streets as the "Cadillac of speed." Though similar, it was not an amphetamine and didn't have some of the less desirable effects of increased heart rate and jitteriness. It had an intense euphoric effect like cocaine and was often referred to as "a pharmaceutical, pill form of cocaine." It dissolved easily in water and could be injected intravenously.

I looked up, still peeing, and whispered to God, "You've got to be kidding. This is a joke—right?" Followed by: "Why you doing this to me?" I think it was the sheer number of pills that made the wheels start turning in my head. I'd only seen that many pills on a pharmacy shelf to fill a bogus prescription. It occurred to me the reason for the woman's appearance this late in the afternoon and the turban—she had cancer, likely late stage. Then, the unthinkable happened. I was triggered, and the old "tapes" started playing in my head. I couldn't stop them!

I started thinking about how I could get those pills out of there without her knowing. *My socks,* I thought. It would be awkward, but it could be done. Then, I tried to justify it by lying to myself: *I'll just sell them. Those Preludins go for twenty bucks a pill on the street and the Percodan five bucks each!* Then, sane, recovering Steve finally jumped up and employed the technique that I'd been taught for just this kind of occasion. It was called "Playing the tape all the way through." I thought, *"Sell em? Ha! Right! You could never sell drugs Steve. You were always your best customer—remember?"*

As the tape played, it became a movie in my mind, and I saw clearly the events that would likely occur if I walked out with those pills. The first thing is, when she noticed her pills were gone, she'd immediately call Gene.

You're losing your job and your vehicle, which means you're losing the ability to see your kids, I thought. Then, I got the image in my head of shooting up the last pill, followed by swallowing the last handful of Percodan. I pictured myself in my apartment for days with 15 or so unanswered messages flashing nonstop on my answering machine, mostly from my kids and Laura. In my mind, I saw the image of myself—pale, gaunt, sweating profusely, in intense opiate and speed withdrawal, and scheming how I was going to get more drugs.

I snapped back to reality and said to myself out loud, just above a whisper: "No thanks! I've come too far to throw it all away." And with that, I zipped up, flushed the toilet, picked up my mess in the living room, got the check, and "got the hell outta Dodge!"

When I got to the van, I sat there stunned for a minute and thought about what had just happened. That's when I realized I had just experienced a miracle. I'm not just calling it that; it truly was. You might think, *"What's so miraculous about walking away and not stealing someone's pills?* For a normal person, nothing—and believe me—that thought did cross my mind. But then I realized, *I ain't Joe Normal."* I'm an addict, and I was never able to use my own power to walk away from that level of temptation—quality drugs, within arm's reach—when in my addiction. I had no more power to do what I did than a magnet had to coming within a few inches of steel without sticking to it—a metaphor that I used to tell the story in meetings for the next few weeks. I was convinced that only "a power greater than myself" could do that. My message in those meetings was, "God's power is real!" Just like it says in Step Two of the program: a power greater than myself had restored me to sanity!

After sharing the story in meetings, a few people corrected me. Preludin was actually going for about $35 a pill on the street! The drug was written about in the book by Kim Wozencraft and was made into the film *Rush*, that I mentioned earlier, featuring Jason Patrick and Jennifer Jason-Leigh.

A curse is lifted as creative energy is restored

A guy who regularly attended my Tuesday home group was stuck in a 1960s-time warp. He would dress in tie-dyed shirts, bellbottoms, sandals and some colorful headbands. He was a little weird, so he didn't connect well and was kind of a loner. One day in the middle of the meeting, he announced, "I got two tickets to see the Grateful Dead tonight at Poplar Creek, but I have no way to get there. Anyone with a car who's interested, let me know."

It was a no-brainer— "I'm interested," I said without batting an eyelash!

"I'll give you money for gas," he offered.

"No need. I have gas," I assured him, and we jumped in the van and headed to the show, which was about 45 minutes away. On the way there, I told him the story of all my past failed attempts to see The Dead. I heard God's voice whisper; *Here's another gift I feel you're ready for now Steven."*

When we got there, we caught a few minutes of a Deadhead NA meeting attended by many sober Deadheads. We sat back on the lawn on a beautiful summer night and saw the show. And just like that, the "curse of the Grateful Dead" was lifted. I was *grateful* that I finally got to see them before I was *dead*, and as it turned out, before they were *dead*. Puns intended.

I started volunteering to sit at the desk on Saturday mornings at the Mustard Seed. This was an ideal setting to expand the creativity that had been sabotaged by my drug use. It started to simmer and bubble to the surface. I invested in some spiral notebooks, and I started writing lyrics, poems, and songs again.

I knew that what I had experienced in Gateway was special, and even back then, I felt compelled to tell the story. I had a sense, or should I say a premonition, that the subject of recovery from addiction would soon become a hot topic. A movie needed to be made. Why not mine? So, I started writing a screenplay after buying and reading a book on the subject. I outlined the story of a guy— loosely based on me, and his partner in crime—loosely based on Franko, and how they hit bottom after robbing a dope house. The main character then goes into treatment in a TC and turns his life around. I sat at that desk every Saturday morning and wrote an outline, scenes, and dialogue.

As the addict recovered, so did the artist. I began to realize that I had been in my own way all along, due to my addiction. Now, the sky was the limit! My aspirations started coming into focus and becoming more clearly defined, along with specific parts of my identity—who I really was. I was an artist, dammit! My appetite returned to put a band together.

Unfortunately (or fortunately, depending on how you look at it), my parade was rained on, and my desire to join a band and play in clubs was bitch-slapped into reality by other musicians in the program. The first thing they asked when I sought advice about playing in bars and clubs was, "How long have you been clean?" At the time, I had around a year and a half. "You should wait until you have two years or so. There's plenty of people in the program to jam with in the meantime." was their consensus. So, that's what I did.

One of my first jamming partners in the program was a guy named Nick, who was also an aspiring singer/songwriter who played mostly acoustic guitar. We shared stuff we were working on and wrote a song or two together. As a result, I stumbled upon my ability to arrange music by piecing his songs together, writing bridges, and filling in missing pieces of his songs, both musically and lyrically. We went on the "program tour," playing a few covers and a few of our originals at program-sponsored events.

As my creativity blossomed, others around me did as well. Another guy I met in meetings had always aspired to be a recording engineer and have his own recording studio. Now that he wasn't spending his money on drugs, he started buying recording equipment. Kenny had no idea what he was doing, but he started experimenting and figuring it out, and I was ideal as his first "guinea pig." Many of us were just groping around in the dark, trying to find our creative way, as it were. It was a perfect fit.

You've got to give it away to keep it

By this time, I started checking out different meetings. One that interested me that I had heard about from friends at the Mustard Seed, was called *The Pacific Group*. It was held at the Pacific Garden Mission in downtown Chicago on Thursday nights. Unbeknownst to me at that time, I would get so much more from attending that meeting.

One Thursday, after the meeting, while standing outside smoking a cigarette, a person I had seen in other meetings struck up a conversation. "Hey, I've heard you speak at meetings. You're a good speaker. You know there's a detox unit in the YMCA across the street? They're always looking for speakers to share with the people in detox. You should go check it out."

Step 12 says *Having had a spiritual awakening as a result of these steps, we tried to carry this message to addicts and to practice these principles in all our affairs.*

An important part of what keeps us clean and sober is helping other addicts. We were told we needed to "give it away to keep it." So, I called the place.

The person I talked to on the phone confirmed what my fellow AA said, "Yes, we're always looking for people to volunteer and speak to the patients. It's hard to find people willing to do it."

He asked how long I'd been clean. I told him 16 months.

"Great! Can you come Wednesday at seven? It's for an hour. Speak, then open it up for questions and comments the last 15 minutes."

On my way to my first meeting, I was thinking about and planning what I was going to say. All the important things I had been through and learned about addiction and recovery started racing through my mind.

Upon my arrival at the unit, I signed in and filled out some paperwork. The staff on duty took me on a quick tour, then, pointed to a door and said, "They're in there waiting for you. Good luck."

I walked into what was a dingy day room with no windows, and fans blowing hot, stuffy air around, reminiscent of Kedzie House. I immediately remembered what it was like to be in treatment. I looked around the room at the faces of about 20 or so people, mostly men with a smattering of women. Some were sweating and fanning themselves, while others had sweatshirts on and likely had the chills. A few looked like they would keel over at any moment.

I wish I could tell you what I said, but I can't remember. I do remember that I poured my heart out to those people and gave them my best effort.

On the ride home, I could almost feel their pain, and I remembered what it was like to be in their shoes, followed by a sense of gratitude that I no longer was, along with renewed determination never to be again. Without that kind of contact, it's easy to forget what it was like to be in that situation.

A few days later, I got a phone call from the director, who thanked me for coming. He said that the patients got a lot out of my talk and were buzzing about it the next day. He said this was the first time he had ever seen that response from the patients. He asked if I wouldn't mind coming back next Wednesday. I told him that I really enjoyed it and I'd be happy to come back.

It was the third time in as many weeks that someone told me that they got a lot out of what I said. Earlier in the week, I had gone to a meeting at the long-since-gone Martha Washington Hospital. Someone came up to me after the meeting and told me he got a lot out of my comments. He said it was exactly what he needed to hear, and it really helped him.

These incidents were not only a boost to my self-esteem, but also served as guideposts to let me know that I was still on the right track. Of course, there was a tad of ego and pride mixed in too, but at that stage of recovery, it's to be expected. The downside of this feedback was getting a big head and losing your humility. Luckily, I still had plenty about living sober that kept me humble.

At my next visit to the detox, I was shocked when I saw 20 new faces in the chairs. Then it occurred to me—it was a five-day detox, which meant every week there was going to be a new group of patients. When the director offered to make the volunteer position mine for as long as I wanted it, I accepted. It became what I did on Wednesday nights and an important part of my recovery.

Because I had a different audience every week, I began to develop and get down a well-honed spiel. Every week I crafted and revised my message until it was almost perfect. One aspect that I found a way to address was, no matter how eloquent or powerful my talk was, I would start to lose them after about

30 minutes. I remembered how difficult it was to be in withdrawal and retain information, no matter how good the information was. It's nearly impossible. So, I addressed that issue by starting my talk with this little speech...

"Hi, my name's Steve, and I'm an addict. I've got some good news and some bad news. The good news is, I've got about 45 minutes to tell you some things that might save your life. In that time, I'm going to tell you everything I know and give you a lot of good information. The bad news? Unfortunately, you won't remember most of what I say. So, if I only had 30 seconds to tell you what I thought would help you, here's what I'd say: Don't pick up the first drink or drug even if your ass falls off, go to meetings, and get and work with a sponsor. Thanks for listening."

And with that, I would get up from my chair and leave the room. The patients would be dumbfounded. Just when they'd start grumbling things like ""Is that it?" and "Did he really just leave?" I'd re-enter the room announcing: "Just kidding. I have more." I'd get at least a chuckle out of most of them every time, which would engage them for the remainder of my talk. Then I'd continue with, "That's really how *simple* recovery can be. But it's not *easy*." I'd explain the difference between *simple* and *easy* and get on with the rest of my talk.

I didn't realize it at the time, but my volunteering at that detox would be the foundation for profound changes in my life that would soon come to pass.

Sticking my toe in the relationship pool

At this point in my recovery, my love life was superficial, and pretty lame. In other words, it was perfect for me. It was about all I could handle. My first "love" interest was a casual thing limited to Friday night dates. I would pick Linda up at her parents' due to her recent divorce from her husband. I'd drive her to her meeting at the Independence Park Fieldhouse, then drive up Irving Park Road to Lincoln Avenue to get to the Grant Hospital meeting. Afterward, I'd pick her up and we'd go for dinner at The Harris on Irving Park Road with others in recovery who would come from several meetings in the area. Then, if she felt up to it, we'd go back to my apartment for some "heavy petting" (she wasn't ready for intercourse, and I was used to having "blue balls" by now anyway) after which I'd drive her home.

After a relatively short stint, she ended the relationship abruptly when I picked her up after her meeting. I responded by pointing out that I felt she still loved her ex-husband, which she adamantly denied. I pressed her several times to admit it, but she wouldn't. In the middle of my "interrogation," I had an important realization. I realized that it didn't matter what the reason was. All that mattered was that she didn't want to see me anymore. I stopped myself, apologized to her, and shared my realization. I drove her home and that was it.

I talked about it in meetings for about a minute, and I was over it. Like I said, perfect—nothing too serious. I started learning in meetings that God didn't give me anything I couldn't handle. I had already passed much bigger tests.

On a side note, I ran into her mother in the grocery store some months later and asked about Linda. Her mother informed me that she had re-married her ex-husband. Intuition on target!

Being a normal male of the human species, albeit a recovering one, the never-ending quest for female companionship was still always somewhere in my mind. I walked that fine line, as did many in recovery, of learning how to be alone, versus fear of being lonely. I started going to AA dances that were held regularly on Saturday nights at St. Gregory's Church on Ashland Avenue. It was awkward sitting alone, so I'd walk around a lot, scoping out if there was anyone I could ask to dance. Dancing was still a challenge, but I knew it was one of the few ways available for me to meet someone.

I started seeing Eileen at the Grant Hospital meetings, and St. Greg's dances. She seemed surprised to see me (likely shocked that I was still clean) though she would try not to show it. I finally got the nerve to share a cassette of the song I wrote about her and started recording with Kenny.

She of course was very cool about her response, saying that she was impressed and flattered without ever really addressing the obvious crush that I had on her. She'd always ask, "How long have you been clean now Steve?" followed by, "You're doing great; keep it going." It felt more like a gentle reminder that I needed to stay focused on my recovery and not her.

I continued to feel Eileen was "out of my league," but just the fact that I was attracted to a woman like her, made her an important part of my development. She was sexy, pretty, unique, spiritual, intelligent, with a sharp wit and a biting sense of humor—the kind of woman who would have intimidated me (and two-thirds of the male population) in the past. It was testimony to my increasing self-esteem and self-image. I started to see myself as worthy, and capable of handling a relationship with someone like her.

I'd like to tell you that I then embarked on only mature, intimate pursuits, with only the finest female specimens on the planet, but I'd be lying. I just wasn't there yet. Being the work in progress that I was, I often found myself chasing skirts around the program trying to get laid. For me, the term Sex, drugs and Rock & Roll" morphed into "Sex and Rock & Roll." Good thing the program asks only for *progress, not perfection.*

One of these pursuits led me to a newcomer who started coming to my Tuesday home group. The chemistry was apparent from day one when we immediately began playing "the eye contact game." You remember, the one where you look at someone until they feel you staring at them, and they look at you? Then you look away. Then it's their turn to stare at you and you try to catch them. I made sure to make some witty comments, to demonstrate my recovery prowess. When I finally introduced myself, she was impressed, especially since she was going on only two months clean. We hit it off right away and instead of going out with the group after the meeting, I invited her to a private "recovery lesson" over coffee. She was so intrigued by the lesson, she decided to "stay after class" for more "recovery wisdom" back at my apartment.

In the program, the name for what I was doing is "thirteenth stepping"—using one's recovery to get into someone's pants. I justified having sex with her because I was also really trying to help her stay clean. Unfortunately, the problem is that newcomers tend to have low self-esteem and having sex with them contributes to and exacerbates this. Also, they are emotionally fragile and become attached quickly. If it's not reciprocated, they get hurt—badly.

Though I'm sure people at the meeting suspected, no one said anything to me directly. I did get a few eyebrows raised when I declined going out for coffee a third straight time.

By the fourth week, she had failed to show up at the meeting, and she didn't return my calls. She was gone, "back out there" relapsing, a reliable source reported. I felt terrible and embarrassed.

After the meeting, I went home and thought about having to face people in my home group and it made me feel very uncomfortable. I thought about what other meeting I could find on Tuesdays. *Wait! What are you thinking!? That's your home group!* I reminded myself. It was an important part of my recovery. It was *my* meeting, and as I heard someone say in a meeting: "I earned this seat, and I'm not going to let anything, or anybody, run me out the door."

To complicate matters further, I'd recently been elected GSR (Group Service Representative). This meant I now had the responsibility of attending the monthly area meetings at Martha Washington Hospital and bringing back fliers of upcoming events from that meeting, for my group. It also consisted of me putting in, and picking up, the group's N.A. literature orders every month.

I wasn't going anywhere, so I decided to face my feelings and whatever "music" I might encounter from fellow NA members at the meeting. I confided in a few members I was close to the mistake I made. They understood. The "music" was mostly in my head, so there was no significant harm done to my relationships with people at the meeting.

I didn't want to be in that situation or feel those feelings ever again, so I had a talk with myself and made a pact that I would never date anyone in the program again. Yeah—right! I quickly realized that although quite admirable, this was a lofty goal that was probably unrealistic. So, I modified it to only dating women with one year or more of clean time. Again, the "bullshitting myself meter" in my head went off, so I finally settled on nine months.

That was it. It felt more realistic, and if someone had nine months clean, they were no longer considered a "newcomer," and could be responsible for the decisions they made regarding their recovery.

My pact would be tested in a few weeks, when another cutie showed up at the meeting. At the break, she made a beeline for me and struck up a conversation that started with "I really got a lot out of what you said."

My response: "Thanks. So, how long have you been clean?"

"I'm going on three months," she replied.

"Good for you. Keep coming back because like they say, it gets greater later. Hey, I really need to talk to a few people, so I'll talk to you soon."

And with that, I got the hell out of there, grabbed one of my buddies at the meeting, and struck up a conversation.

Although I didn't get laid, I walked away with something much more valuable. I felt like a grown-up. I began to develop something that had always been missing from my life—self-control. I was finally able to live up to the commitments and agreements I made with myself. This ability would prove to be extremely important in the not-too-distant future.

Katherine

My "trolling" the St. Greg dances finally paid off in July of 1988 when I met Katherine. We danced all night together and she gave me her number before we parted ways. She was petite, pretty, and somewhat exotic, with an athletic but curvy build and curly hair to the middle of her back. She was an interesting young woman who was in recovery from an eating disorder (bulimia) not substance abuse. She had gone through the groundbreaking inpatient eating disorder program at Parkside Hospital.

It was becoming nationally known for its pioneering work with people with eating disorders. The program would soon become even more famous when it would admit the likes of Elton John and other celebrities. I knew little about the illness, but I knew that people with eating disorders usually attended OA (Overeaters Anonymous) support groups, which used the same 12-step model as AA, NA and CA. As a result of our relationship, I would learn about food plans, portioning, weighing foods, and eating sugar or white flour being the equivalent of me relapsing on heroin. I quickly learned that people with eating disorders, use food like alcoholics and addicts use alcohol and drugs.

Several other things that made Kathy interesting were that she was a Recreation Therapist on an adolescent psychiatric unit at a local mental health center. She lived in an apartment in the Lincoln Park area, and drove this huge, classic 1970 Olds 98 convertible. She almost needed a booster seat to drive it but drove it like an Indy-500 racecar driver. She used to love to play "the traffic game" as she called it, weaving in and out of traffic, jockeying for position. She was always looking for the "hole-shot" in the adjacent lane to blow around whomever was in her way, which was usually everybody. It was kind of fun to be in the car with her when she drove, watching her jam on the gas pedal with her tiptoes, and if it weren't so damn scary, I might have even enjoyed it.

Our relationship quickly went to the next level when sex started, which was almost immediately. I found myself spending a lot of time at her apartment. She even had a nice Yamaha nylon six-string guitar that I would play when I was there. We would watch PBS together, while snacking on fruits and vegetables, though I noted that her snack was a lot of fruit that took up the better part of a good-sized serving bowl. Something just didn't seem right about the amount of fruit in that bowl, but I didn't know enough about the disorder to question it. I discovered her favorite show was the classic *Doctor Who*, which had a cult following similar to *Star Trek*. I never became a big fan, but after a while, the surreal time-traveler grew on me, and so did Kathy.

A new path leads to new opportunities

I will be renewed. I will be remade. In this, I need God's help. His spirit shall flow through me, and in flowing through me, it shall sweep away all the bitter past. I will take heart. The way will open for me. Each day will unfold something good, as long as I am trying to live the way I believe God wants me to live. – Twenty-Four Hours a Day, January 3

Recovery is like a thousand-piece puzzle. It's easy to get frustrated in the beginning when nothing fits together, and no picture is coming into view. But, if we're patient, vigilant, and stay with it long enough, the pieces start fitting and a picture finally begins to emerge. As the picture became clearer to me, so did my ability to articulate it to others in my comments and conversations in and around the program. This did not go unnoticed by my fellows in the program, and I was soon being asked by some of the chairpersons at meetings to be the lead-speaker, or "give a lead" as we would refer to it.

"Leads" followed the initial formalities in a meeting. This included some readings from the program text that outlined the who, what, and whys of the program. The chairperson would then give a brief introduction about the speaker, who would then give a 15 to 30-minute talk, usually followed by a five to ten-minute break. The basic format was: What it was like (your addiction). What happened (what brought you to the program)? And what it's like now (what has your recovery been like?)." After a break, the meeting would be open for comments. The chairperson would close the meeting by asking everyone to join him or her in the serenity prayer and the Lord's prayer, or in NA, the less-spiritual "Just for Today" (more of a statement than a prayer), as the program sought to distance itself from being perceived as religious. All would stand holding hands or arms around each other's shoulders, until the final chant of "Keep coming back. It works if you work it!" was proclaimed in unison.

After giving a lead at one meeting, I saw an old familiar face approaching me—It was Menzo McCray. Menzo was a peer of Benny L.'s, and although he was in the peer group ahead of mine, our treatment at Gateway overlapped enough for us to form a relationship. We had a special bond due to me following in his path throughout my entire treatment. From the dorms we were assigned, to the departments we worked in, including neither of us making House Coordinator after being Chief Expediter. Menzo also got thrown out of Kedzie house for fighting just like I did, along with my buddy Timmy Dacey, who threatened to throw Menzo out a window during a Second Phase group they were in together. We used to joke about it when we'd run into each other. I'd say to him, "They got me on the Menzo McCray plan!" and we'd both laugh.

After the meeting, he said to me: "That was a great talk, Stevie. You've become a really good speaker. Listen, I got a line on a potential job, and I think you'd be good at it."

"What job?" I asked.

"Doing what I do at Weiss Hospital. I work for a company called Lifeline. It's a 21-day inpatient program. I'm the Milieu Therapist on the unit."

"What's that?" I asked.

"It's basically a three to eleven shift so the counselors can go home. I run some light evening programming and take the patients down to the AA and NA meetings two nights a week. I make house runs through the unit to make sure they ain't burnin' the place down. I'm really just a paid babysitter and my job is mostly just to hang out with the patients, play board games and cards, share my recovery, and encourage them. They have a big contract with Amtrak and just got a new contract with the Ford Motor Company, so they're getting ready to open a second unit in Hyde Park at Chicago Osteopathic Hospital."

"Do you need a degree in counseling or anything?"

"Nope. Just a high school diploma and two years clean. It's pretty good pay too, due to it being second shift. You interested?"

"Yes, I am. I passed the GED, but I don't have my certificate because I never took the Constitution test, and I only have 18 months clean."

"The GED should be fine. Just tell them you have two years. You were clean for almost a year the first time—right?"

"Yeah, eleven months."

"Okay, well, that'll work. Here's the number."

He scribbled it onto a scrap of paper he had in his pocket.

"The person you need to talk to is the director, Nancy Peterson. Oh, and drop my name, they like me."

"Okay. Thanks Menzo!"

"Good luck Stevie."

"Hey Menzo…by the way, what's a milieu?"

"It's French for patient environment or some shit."

"Okay, whatever!" We both laughed and walked away.

Would I continue on "the Menzo McCray Plan" and follow in his footsteps even after treatment?

I thought; *Would a regular guy like me really be able to walk away from forklifts, factories, and tools and be able to get paid for sharing my recovery and helping addicts*? It still seemed a bit absurd, but part of me started to believe it was possible. After all, wasn't that what I was? A "possibility?"

If I said I was excited, it would fall short of capturing what I felt. I was scared, but in a good way. Were there things that were possible for me that I never thought were possible? I sensed that I was standing on the edge of a cliff of sorts and was about to jump into the realm of the unknown. That day, I felt myself reaching beyond just being a possibility. I was going to go for it!

The next day, I did as Menzo suggested and called Lifeline at Weiss Hospital. When I spoke to Nancy Peterson, I dropped Menzo's name, and he was right; she loved Menzo and raved about him. She directed me to the newly hired director of the new program, Blythe Smith, and gave me the number.

I contacted Blythe and told her that Nancy referred me. We talked on the phone and set up an interview at Weiss Hospital. The new unit was almost ready to accept patients. Nancy and the medical director, Dr. Greenberg, wanted to be in the interview since Blythe was also a fairly new hire.

When I arrived for my interview, I was a little intimidated, but not so much by the interview itself, but by the women doing the interviewing. Each in their own way, Blythe and Nancy were knockouts! They could have both been supermodels. They looked to be in their thirties and were well put together. Nancy was a tall brunette and was more outspoken, take-charge, and no holds barred. The kind of person who might speak recklessly at times. She tried to hide her pretty face with some black-rimmed nerdy glasses.

Blythe was more of a classic Irish beauty with long wavy strawberry blonde hair and freckles. She was as dynamic as Nancy but in a more subtle, and less intimidating way. Like Eileen, these women were new territory for me. I was slightly intimidated, but I was intrigued and impressed with them.

Dr. Greenberg looked to be approaching middle age. He was a handsome man with a year-round tan. I had already heard about him in my travels. He had a reputation for being "heavy-handed" with the prescription pad, meaning, he was quick to write narcotic scripts for patients. Information like that traveled around the rooms of NA, AA, and treatment pretty quickly.

They asked me about my addiction and recovery, how long I'd been clean, and some general questions about the 12-step program. They gave me a few hypothetical situations I might run into with patients. I don't remember the exact questions they asked or the situations they presented, but they must have liked my answers. The next day I got the call from Blythe—I got the job!

When Blythe called me, it would be the beginning of a succession of many firsts for me. She said, "We were very impressed with your knowledge of addiction and recovery and felt like the patients and the staff will benefit from it. You'll be a great asset to our team. We'd like to offer you the job as the milieu therapist at the Chicago Osteopathic Unit."

After two years of intensive treatment, it was only fitting that I should have some insight into those subjects, but still, I had never heard anything like that in my entire life from a new employer. She told me that the unit would open next week and asked when I could start. That's when another first would happen in my life. "I'll have to give my current employer at least two weeks' notice." It would be the first time in my life I'd work somewhere for one year or more, and the first time I'd give an employer any notice that I was leaving.

I called Kathy, then Albie, and shared the news. Albie was bursting with pride that her son was going to be a "milieu therapist," or a therapist of any sort, for that matter. I'm sure she would have settled for me doing just about anything for a living, as long as I wasn't poisoning myself with drugs anymore.

I took the next step in my development. I plugged my proverbial nose and jumped into the deep end of the pool of the unknown. Sensing God's guidance and power through it all, helped to alleviate any fears I may have had.

"We hate to see you go."

The next day at work after loading my van, I told Gene I needed to speak to him. We went into his office, and I gave him the news. I told him that it was a great opportunity, and I had to take it. His response was very supportive. "Of course you have to take it. I wish you all the success in the world in the next chapter of your life. The work you'll be doing is *so* important."

"Thanks Gene. I'm giving you three weeks' notice. I wish I could give you more time, but the unit will be up and running by next week and they'll need me to train at Weiss Hospital for a week or so before I start."

He then delivered the last in a series of firsts, and probably the best one of all… He said, "We hate to see you go Steve. We appreciated all your hard work and your integrity."

Wow! I couldn't believe my ears. I almost wanted to say; "You talkin' to me?" I had never heard anything like that said to me by an employer. They usually said things like: "Don't let the door hit you in the ass on the way out" or "No, we don't owe you any money. You owe us money!"

It was a happy ending to the chapter in my life titled "Menial Labor." I guess another first was that I'd be making a living with my mind instead of my hands and my back. What an honor and a privilege. What a gift from God.

There's nothing constant but change

While training at Weiss Hospital with Menzo, he immediately passed some words of wisdom on to me that came in the form of a warning: "Being in this field isn't a replacement for working a program of recovery."

Apparently, this was a common "rookie" mistake that led a great many recovering counselors to relapse. From that moment on, I became acutely aware of this pitfall and made every effort to avoid it. This would be more challenging due to the change in my hours, which brought about some unavoidable changes in my life, and in my program—some good; some, not so good.

One good change was that while at one of the monthly area meetings at Martha Washington, they held elections, and I was elected North City-Area literature chairperson. My duties included getting literature and other NA-related materials ordered from the GSRs of the meetings in the Chicago area known as North City. I would purchase those items from the NA Central Office in the suburb of Oak Park and fill the orders at the monthly area meetings.

Luckily, I had been saving my money (something Albie preached my entire adult life) to buy a car and insurance once I left Drapery Cleaning

Service. My new position had my trunk full of NA literature, cassette tapes, books, information pamphlets, key tags, and various other NA doodads.

Some of the not so good changes were, I had to stop attending several meetings that had been the cornerstone of my recovery, including my Tuesday home group and Friday at Grant Hospital—at least until I could establish some days off. I was forced to find daytime meetings, so I started attending meetings at The Mustard Seed, and a place called the Lincoln Park Alano Club (LPAC).

My new schedule also required me to give up my volunteer position at the Lawson YMCA detox. Before I did, one good thing that happened was I got my first sponsee—a young black guy named Tony. He pulled me over after my last talk at Lawson and asked me to be his sponsor. I immediately recognized the important signs that he was serious about recovery and his hunger for a better life. I had that same hunger, and I think it's what attracted him to me. I told him to call me every day, and if he didn't reach me, to leave a message.

This was the first of only a few "rules" I established for my sponsees—they had to call me every day, no matter what was going on in their lives. The key to utilizing a sponsor was getting used to picking up the phone and calling, whether you needed to or not. I knew it would only be a matter of time until they needed to. The desire to use would come, and they would pick up the phone, or give in to it and pick up a drink or a drug— "call or fall" if you will.

Tony was a good first sponsee and followed my suggestions to the letter. We'd meet for coffee or dinner, talk about our history and our addiction, and how to work the program. I had him read the chapter on Step One and gave him the first assignment I'd ever given, to write a one-page essay on what the step meant to him and how to work it. I learned the hard way about the difference between working it and merely understanding and talking about it.

I recognized how sponsoring him was helping me as much as it was him. I also recognized the need to make sure my ego was not overblown. I knew that if I were going to stay clean while helping other addicts, I would always have to watch for the potential for overblown ego, grandiosity, and "holier than thou" attitudes. I, of course, suffered from all three, but was able to keep them in check enough to stay clean. It made it easier to stay humble seeing newcomers "crawling" through the doors at meetings. They were constant reminders of where I came from and could easily return to if I got cocky.

One day while watching TV, I saw a trailer for a new movie that was coming out. This confirmed my intuition was on target once again about the hot topic that treatment and recovery were about to become. On August 10, 1988, the film *Clean and Sober* starring Michael Keaton was released. I went to see the film with a group of recovering friends, and we loved it. It nailed most of the important themes about addiction and recovery. Of course, being real addicts in recovery, we were quick to point out and be overly critical of the few subtle inaccuracies, mostly due to trying to cram too much into a two-hour film. But for the most part, they did an admirable job. Morgan Freeman was perfect as the typical treatment counselor—a delicate blend of tough love and no bullshit mixed with nurturing and caring.

I remember having a knot in my gut during key scenes, especially when Keaton's character, Darryl, calls his mother, and tries to manipulate her into giving him his inheritance money. His desperation came through as he tries to convince his mother that it would be better before she and his father die, so that he could "put it to use now." As her heart breaks at the realization that her son cares more about the money than he does her feelings, he gets angry at her and demands she "stop crying." How dare she cry and make him feel guilty! It was an accurate depiction of how extremely selfish and insensitive to other's feelings, addicts can be while in the grip of addiction. I couldn't help but be reminded of leaving Albie in a car at 2 a.m. in the projects, and a wave of unresolved guilt poured over me. Just because we're recovering and doing well, doesn't mean we've made peace with all our past demons yet.

The film brought up mixed feelings. Though I loved and enjoyed it, I felt jealous and discouraged that my instincts were right about the subject of addiction and recovery for a film being a good idea. But I was too late and was beaten out by someone else. I realized that I felt this way about my music too.

It was a pattern I'd experienced all my life—the "Beautiful Loser." I was always "a day late, and a dollar short." I felt that if I hadn't gone down the path I did, I could have filled the niche of the Midwestern acoustic-rock artist that was filled by the likes of singer-songwriter, John Cougar Mellencamp. I coined a phrase to describe the "boats" I felt I missed because of my addiction: "The John Cougar Syndrome." I felt I was a better songwriter.

The release of *Clean and Sober*, combined with changes to my schedule, took the wind out of my sails a bit, and I never finished the screenplay. However, I would move on to other creative endeavors.

With my recovery came a glimmer of hope that I was still young and there may still be room for one more artist from the Midwest. I pursued my new career while I continued to play, write songs, record, and daydream about putting a band together that played mostly my original music.

Becoming a member of SA

As if this time in my life wasn't challenging enough, another change that hit was Doc sold the Serenity Club and moved out of the city. Though we tried to make it work, it was just too difficult to connect as my life continued to evolve and get busier. I started looking for a new sponsor and found one at an NA meeting I started to attend.

Mark had a clear strong message and held nothing back. He was a dynamic speaker with a very convincing delivery that made you buy into recovery without reservation. I was impressed by him and asked him to be my new sponsor after I heard him give a second lead. He agreed.

Over the next three weeks, we spoke on the phone and I gave him the "made for TV" version of my story. He invited me over to his apartment later that week to sit down and go over the 12-steps, the text, and the NA program.

When I arrived, Mark greeted me and introduced me to his wife and kids. I believe he had three small children at the time. His wife Lori took my coat and made some small talk before hanging it in the closet. She was petite and had a pretty face. Oddly, there was some kind of immediate "vibe" I felt that made me a little uncomfortable. It wasn't a bad vibe. It was a sexual chemistry vibe. Luckily, it was interrupted by his kids loud obnoxious introduction, as one of them crashed a toy airplane into my thigh. I quickly did everything I could to disconnect from the strange energy and followed Mark into the family room, where we got down to business.

Mark went to another room to get the NA text when Lori poked her head in and asked if I wanted something to drink. I told her I'd take a can of Coke, and as she left to get it, I felt the energy switch back on. I quickly grabbed the energy, punched it in the face, kicked it in the nuts, and buried it in the ground—hopefully, never to bother me again. Just in the nick of time too, as Mark came back with the book, and Lori with a can of Coke. She smiled warmly as she handed it to me and then left the room.

We went through the steps, and I shared my interpretation of each one and how they worked for me. Mark did the same. I told him about me volunteering on Saturdays on the desk at the Mustard Seed. His facial expression changed to a look of concern: "Isn't that an AA club?" he asked.

"Yep, I go to both. Sometimes I'll hit a CA meeting too, but there just aren't that many."

"Oh," he said, sounding disappointed.

"Why? Is there a problem?"

"Well, kind of."

"What is it?" I asked, somewhat baffled.

"Well, it's just that I work an NA program. It's all I really know about. I don't know anything about AA's program or the literature, so I can't really help you with any of that. Let me think about it and I'll get back to you."

When we were through, I started to leave, and Lori was there with my coat. As she handed it to me, she again gave me that just a little too warm smile, and again I felt the vibe.

Wow, that was weird, I thought, as I got into my car.

Several days later, Mark called and informed me that he couldn't sponsor me if I continued to volunteer at the Seed and attend AA meetings. I liked Mark. The talks we had about recovery were good and I felt they were helpful, but I felt the same about the other fellowships and my volunteering on the desk at The Seed. I told him I'd have to think about it and get back to him.

I had heard about it, but this was the first time I'd come face to face with the leftover resentment of NA members for the way addicts were treated in the early days, before Narcotics Anonymous was formed.

In the 1950s, addicts had no choice but to attend AA meetings and were treated like second-class citizens. They had to sit in the back of the room and listen but were not allowed to comment.

Mark was what was known as an "NA purest." It went beyond just not being familiar with AA and their literature. Mark and others like him, had a kind of disdain for AA and anything related to it. I think they felt it was some kind of show of loyalty to the NA program to shun anything AA–related. They didn't realize that what they were doing by carrying this "torch" was keeping a 35-year-old resentment alive. Many of these people also became known by another nickname, "The NA Police." Some would even go so far as to interrupt someone in a meeting who was quoting the AA Big Book. They'd say things like, "I'm sorry but that's not NA-approved literature."

I remember thinking; *You've got to be kidding! Remember when you didn't know your ass from a hole in the ground a few years ago? Now you're going to tell people what they can and can't say?!*

I asked several people about what they thought of the Mark situation and got mixed feedback, but the majority did not agree with his suggestion. The feedback that stands out most was… "Does it help you in your recovery to volunteer on the desk and go to some AA meetings?"

I didn't have to think too long for that answer: "Yes."

"Then, if he's your sponsor, shouldn't he be encouraging you to do things that help you in your recovery?"

That was it, I made my decision. "Mark… (to be said like Donald Trump), you're fired!" I called and told him my decision and repeated the feedback I received almost verbatim. He said he understood, and that was the end of Mark being my sponsor, but not the end of his story as it related to me.

This issue was kind of the "straw that broke the camel's back" and it became a catalyst for me. I was on a mission from that day on, to stand up for mine—and all recovering people's—right to say and do whatever they felt necessary to stay clean and sober. I felt that no one should be trying to "police" or censor that. The old, rebellious defiant Steve, came back into my life once again, however repurposed in a positive way. I even incorporated this statement into the beginning of all my talks when asked to speak at meetings, which started happening more frequently: "Before I start, I just want to say that I've been seeing some controversy in these rooms lately that has me concerned. I just need everyone to know right now: I'm not in NA, I'm not in AA, and I'm not in CA. I'm in SA…SAVE STEVE'S ASS ANONYMOUS! And I'm going to say whatever I need to say in order to save Steve's ass and recover. If someone doesn't like it, they can KISS STEVE'S ASS, and they should work Step One! Remember—you're powerless over what comes out of my mouth!"

This would usually get big laughs, and sometimes, applause. I could tell that most of the people in meetings were in total agreement with me, and they were glad that someone had the balls to finally speak up. I was developing this fearlessness to say what was on my mind, and although it was still a double-edged sword at times, it felt really good!

It was official—my reputation in meetings for being a no BS, tell it like it is, rebel pot-stirrer was cemented. Again, my experience in Gateway deserves the credit for developing this part of my personality. I had always withdrawn from and avoided conflict and controversy, but I no longer feared it and instead viewed it as a necessary challenge. One that I was now up to and ready for.

Lifeline

I thought I hated Chicago, but in reality, I knew little to nothing about it. It was only fitting that my discovery of "the real Chicago" should include the great Hyde Park on the South Side. I now worked in the heart of Hyde Park at Chicago Osteopathic Hospital at 52nd and Ellis. The area had a style all its own, and was a unique mix of hip, classy, funky, old-world, and black and white people. It was quite the melting pot and known for being a mecca of sorts for interracial relationships. It wasn't unusual to see interracial couples walking down the street holding hands. At the time, it would have been a bit unusual in most other areas. The neighborhood also boasted the likes of the University of Chicago, the Museum of Science and Industry, and some funky little clubs, restaurants, and diners. I got the feeling, walking down the street, that this was what Martin Luther King Jr. had envisioned for race relations, and I felt part of something unique and special every time I was there.

Soon after starting work, I discovered a famous neighborhood cafeteria-style diner to eat dinner at—called Valois. It had been around forever and was within walking distance. More importantly though, it was also within my budget and the food was good.

Back on the unit, I couldn't have asked for a better team of people to work with in my first position in the addictions counseling field. The staff consisted of six counselors, an intake coordinator, two family therapists, a psychiatrist, a recreation therapist, an administrative assistant, and a nursing team. The public relations consultant, Earl Cannamore, was known as "Brother Earl" and gained notoriety for his *Street-Smart* series of films on addiction and recovery-related topics. We were a microcosm of the community—a racially balanced group, that had a nice mix of professionalism and (thank God) humor.

I had to wear a shirt and tie, which helped me look and feel professional. I was more than willing to wear the tie, and it would be a while yet, before I'd discover how much I really hated them.

We had a nice balance of recovering and non-recovering staff. The head nurse, Jim, was in recovery after losing his nursing license for diverting and abusing prescription opiates. He earned his license back and was one of the leaders on the unit. We had a lot in common. We were both "relapsers" who made it back and had a lot of firsthand knowledge and wisdom about addiction and recovery. We both attended regular meetings and worked the program.

Then, there was our program director, Blythe, who always showed all of us plenty of respect. She was nurturing but was also a leader who wasn't afraid to roll up her sleeves and get done whatever needed getting done.

And one final sign from God that I was in the right place—there was a ping-pong table in the patient's dayroom. That's right. Part of the job that I was getting paid for was playing ping-pong with the patients. It wasn't long until I got my form back from the hours spent playing in Jim and Jeff's basement, and I established myself as the "ping-pong king" of the unit, that is, until Jim came in the dayroom one day while I was on duty and picked up a paddle. It was close, but he beat me. We had some exciting games, and the patients would enjoy watching some of the intense matches between us.

Once the patients started pouring in, the team quickly started operating like a well-oiled machine. I can recall being in those early staff meetings, reviewing cases and being able to contribute. My perspective from being a recovering addict and having all the lessons of my relapse close at hand.

I could sense the respect from my colleagues and my self-esteem climbed another crucial step. I remember thinking, *Maybe I could become a counselor.* Blythe took note too and soon let me know that she had the utmost trust in my clinical understanding and judgement, albeit still developing.

The wheels started turning early in my career, and I started seeing ways that I could do more than just babysit patients. I began to see holes in the program and ways to plug those holes and improve it, practically and clinically.

One of my early suggestions that was adopted at both units was being able to document in the patient's records. The milieu therapist wasn't allowed to write in the patient's chart. Only medical or clinical staff could. In staff meetings, I would report significant interactions that I had with clients the previous evening. The trouble was, I usually didn't start my shift until 3 p.m.

Blythe quickly realized that the valuable information I had should be accessible to the primary counselor when they came in to start their shift, not just nursing notes, which were usually things like: *Patient reports trouble sleeping due to headache"* and such. It was my idea to have medical or clinical staff sign behind anything I wrote and use the opportunity to teach us clinical language. Blythe got it approved by Nancy Peterson, and they started letting us chart in the patient record. Now, counselors could come in and read about significant interactions I had with their patients. Much better than hearing it at the end of their shift when I came in and they were getting ready to leave.

I also observed that patients had too much downtime, watching too much TV on the nights they didn't attend the 12-step meetings. I got permission from Blythe to run what I named "The Hazelden Pamphlet Study Group."

Hazelden was a famous treatment center in Minnesota that was (and I believe still is) also the largest publisher and distributor of addiction and recovery-related materials in the country. Their pamphlets were typically 12 to 30 pages, focused on various addiction and recovery related subjects. They were written by people in recovery as well as medical, substance abuse, and other mental health professionals.

Our counselors would give their patients specific pamphlets to read and write essays on as part of their treatment plan. I picked four or five of the subjects that seemed most important to me and started formulating ways to present them. The ones I remember were, "King Baby," "Barriers Against Recovery," "Letting Go of the Need to Control," and "The Dry Drunk

Syndrome." I read them thoroughly, underlining the highlights that I thought were most important to discuss with the patients. This would usually only be about five or six points the pamphlet made. I only had an hour, so I learned to manage the time efficiently. The groups would always go overtime, and the discussions were lively, with no one looking at the clock. This told me that what I was doing was effective and was engaging clients in treatment.

I even started utilizing the new-fangled dry-erase board on the wall behind me, to illustrate or emphasize points I was making. They were starting to replace most of the old chalkboards, that were still refusing to become obsolete. The groups were a hit with the patients. Feedback from the staff was often things like, "My guy Ralph P. really got a lot from your group last night."

As my confidence grew, I even started bringing a little TC to the program when I came up with the "King Baby of the Week" award. Somewhere, I had acquired a black and white button with the black outline of a pacifier on it that I used to pin to my shirt. Counselors would joke with their caseload, "If you don't stop whining, I'm going to make you wear Steve's King Baby pacifier button." When the staff started actually doing it, the patients mostly took it in stride and were good sports about it.

One of my early challenges came when one of the more beloved counselors left and was replaced by a new counselor who, let's just say, lacked experience. His newly inherited caseload figured this out pretty quickly and became like sharks who smelled blood and began "circling." As I walked through the unit, one of his clients cornered me in the hallway.

"I asked my new counselor if he thought I should have only one sponsor or more than one. He said I should get as many sponsors as I can. What do you think of that Steve?"

My personal feeling was that I totally disagreed and thought that it was bad advice, but I recognized that there was something bigger at stake than my opinion about sponsorship. I chose my words carefully when I responded: "Well, let's see. Some people think you should have multiple sponsors, and some think you should have only one. When you have more than one, some people say you'll go to the one who will give you the answer that you want to hear rather than what you need to hear. You have to decide what sounds like it would work best. I suggest that you ask people in the meetings and get a variety of opinions, then decide. Remember, you can change your mind if something you're doing doesn't seem to be working for you and try something else."

"Thanks Steve; that helped."

I felt like I did the right thing, and that the priority was not undermining a member of my team and the therapeutic relationship he was trying to establish. The patient would find his way one way or another about sponsorship.

Could I really become a counselor? I think I was becoming one, whether I liked it or not. I had the feeling of my path being directed by God.

Freddy

Being new to the field of addiction treatment, I would need to work through personal bias and feelings while maintaining a professional approach. This would prove to be challenging at times. You couldn't deny or change your personal feelings about patients or even co-workers; you were going to have them. Particularly with patients, you were going to like some, and dislike others. Obviously, it was not going to be therapeutic to let on that you didn't like certain patients, or treat them unfairly, or differently, because of your personal feelings. My Gateway treatment experience helped with managing personal feelings about someone in an appropriate way. We had to manage our feelings, or we wouldn't survive in that environment.

However, it was a little trickier with patients you liked. The lines were a little more blurred. Were you just being helpful, or spending too much time and attention on someone simply because you liked them?

This was the case with Fred M.—a patient who entered Lifeline and with whom I had a lot in common and likely over-identified with. He was an IV heroin addict, a guitarist, and from my neighborhood in Franklin Park. He was a few years younger than me but knew a lot of the same people I knew, or at least their younger siblings. He also knew of my family and that my uncle was the highway commissioner of Leyden Township. We bonded right away, and I remember feeling that I really wanted him to succeed. That's why I was very disappointed when he relapsed after completing 21 days of treatment.

The good news was, he made it back and did a second stint at Lifeline. In that treatment episode, Fred disclosed he had a secret that he didn't deal with the first time in treatment. He had an eating disorder. He compulsively overate.

Toward the end of his second treatment, his counselor decided to bring his family in for a session. Fred and I had bonded, and he requested that I be part of that session. His counselor asked me, and I agreed.

In the session I met his parents, younger brother, and his sister. His parents expressed their thanks to me and confided that Fred looked up to me and that I had helped him a lot. I felt honored. I had gotten thanks from patients before, but this was the first time someone's parents ever thanked me.

Fred only had about a week left in treatment, so his parents were given permission to bring him his guitar and a little Pignose amplifier. He showed me some original riffs and songs he'd been working on, and I showed him some of my stuff in his room while visiting with his family. His musical tastes were a bit heavier, but we had some artists for which we shared mutual adoration.

After his family left, Fred asked me to be his sponsor. I agreed but only after he completed treatment.

Once Fred completed the program, he moved out of his parent's house in Franklin Park and rented an apartment in the city. Kathy suggested that I tell him about a combo OA/AA meeting that she sometimes attended at LPAC on Saturday mornings. I had resumed volunteering at the Mustard Seed on Saturday's once my days off were established, so I had to find someone to cover for me so that I could accompany him to the LPAC meeting the first few times. The plan was to eventually return to the Mustard Seed for my meetings after I felt Fred was comfortable going on his own.

Little Miss Muffet

The meeting at LPAC was packed, and for good reason, it was a surprisingly good meeting. Listening to the comments gave me a new respect for people who recovered from eating disorders. They couldn't just completely walk away from food (their "drug") like I could with drugs and alcohol. They had to change their relationship with food into a more normal, healthy one. I realized that you had to be working a really good program to do that.

Once I started attending, I got an unexpected surprise when I saw David Hoffman in the meeting. He, like Fred, was an IV heroin addict who also had an eating disorder. I introduced Fred to David and both of them to Kathy. I think it was Fred who would later refer to Kathy as "Little Miss Muffet" or "Muffet" for short. It was fitting if you know the old nursery rhyme...

> *Little Miss Muffet,*
> *Sat on a tuffet,*
> *Eating her curds and whey,*
> *Until along came a spider,*
> *Who sat down beside her,*
> *And frightened Miss Muffet away.*

In this case, it should have read, *Bingeing on her curds and whey... until she purged and vomited in the toilet.* Soon, "Muffet" would become a generic reference used by the three of us to refer to any petite cutie in recovery from an eating disorder.

On the weekdays, it became harder and harder to get up from the comfort of Kathy's cozy Lincoln Park apartment and go home to my empty cold apartment, miles away. It was also very convenient to hop on Lake Shore Drive from her place and zip straight to work. I started having more clothes in her closet than in mine. I was practically living there, and my beautiful apartment started growing dust and cobwebs.

Then, out of nowhere, things started changing in our relationship. I couldn't put my finger on it, but she became distant, and I started feeling this disconnect that I couldn't explain. Being the communicator that I was becoming, I tried talking to her about it and asked what was wrong. She blamed her eating disorder and said she was struggling with her food plan. I accepted her explanation and backed off, but over the next week or so, I didn't see any improvement. So, I had another talk with her. Her response was the same. The situation seemed to be getting worse, and my intuition was on high alert. I felt the pain of a possible breakup may be on the horizon, and I remember thinking to myself that it would be much less painful if I ended it with her, rather than her breaking up with me. However, I felt this would be cowardly and a cop-out, and I cared about her enough to give it a chance and see it through.

But what if I did and it didn't work out? That's when I had a heart-to-heart talk with myself. I asked myself, *if this doesn't work out, are you going to be able to handle it?* I realized that my answer needed to be *rigorously honest*, and that this was no time to bullshit myself. I also understood that by handling it, I meant, *are you going to stay clean and sober, no matter what happens?* I knew I was still very vulnerable emotionally, but I was also committed to staying clean and sober "even if my ass falls off." Since this fell far short of my ass falling off, my answer to myself was a resounding— *Yes!* I was starting to trust myself and my decision-making, despite my occasional impulsiveness. So, that was it; the decision was made. I would stay in the relationship and see it through to whatever end may be in store.

Within days, Kathy shared some good news with me. Her mother had made a down payment on a house for her on the far Northwest Side. She was going to be a homeowner! As a result of this, her demeanor improved and so did our relationship, for a little while. But as with all "honeymoons," this one soon ended, and her demeanor went back to being depressed and distant.

Kathy had a moving date set up for Saturday, October 15[th,] which was a week away. I asked my sponsee Tony to help, and he agreed. Unfortunately, by this time, I had decided that I had enough of the way things were going and had another serious talk with her. I realized that what was going on with her felt a lot like what had happened with Linda; so, whatever was wrong really didn't matter anymore. It just wasn't right. I expressed my frustration with the mystery about what was wrong, simply stating to her, "But something is."

She seemed concerned that I was going to duck out on helping her move after already renting a truck, and a deadline set to be out of her apartment. I assured her that Tony and I would still help her move. We discussed options for the relationship and decided that once she moved into the house, we would take a break, give it some space, and see where we stood in a few weeks.

Not so Sweetest Day

Sweetest Day is a made up "holiday" that was started by a bunch of candy companies in Cleveland in the 1920s. They were obviously trying to sell more of their product. It rightfully all but disappeared but made a resurgence in the Midwest in the 1980s.

That Saturday was not only moving day. It was also Sweetest Day. The irony of this would soon become clear. So, Kathy and I played along and got each other a card and some small token of our affection. I'm sure I didn't get a girl with an eating disorder a box of chocolates—sorry candy companies. One of my gifts was a song I wrote for her. I somehow wound up with her Yamaha acoustic guitar at my apartment and wrote the song on it. It was one of the better songs I'd written at the time and was appropriately called "Katherine."

Luckily, Kathy didn't have a ton of stuff. The hardest thing to move was going to be her king-sized waterbed. What a pain in the ass! We got the truck and humped her stuff in three trips. On one of the trips, when we pulled up to her new house (about a three mile straight shot west on Irving Park Road from my apartment), there was a little gift bag on the front steps. She scooped it up and brought it into the house. When I asked about it, she said it was "nothing", just a little house-warming gift from her mother. Aww…how sweet.

We finished as dusk peered over the horizon, and the crisp autumn air started getting chilly. Tony waited outside as I put some finishing touches on the move and got ready to say our goodbyes, hoping they were only temporary. I came across some Taco Bell fast-food shopping bags in a corner. I pulled them out and asked about them. She was obviously embarrassed and told me they were old and from when she was in her full-blown eating disorder. She said she used them as a reminder of how bad things had gotten.

We couldn't get the bed frame put together, but she started filling the mattress with a garden hose anyway. I looked around at the stack of boxes and realized she likely wouldn't get the bed put together by herself and would have to sleep on the couch in the living room. I thought it might be a little spooky being in a big new house alone, so I offered to stay and at least put the bed together and get it set up in the bedroom. She declined my offer, insisting that I had done enough, and she reminded me that I had to drive Tony home. I realized she was right, so we said our goodbyes, and I gave her a kiss with the plan being to call me in a few days once she got settled.

Tony and I got in my car and drove away. On the ride to Tony's, we talked about the situation with Kathy and me and how I applied the program to it. I told him about the conversation I had with myself and how I made my decision to see the relationship through.

I thanked him and gave him the money that Kathy had given me to pay him for his help. I dropped him off and told him to call me tomorrow as usual, then headed back to my apartment.

Upon arriving, I climbed the stairs and started to process the day in my mind. As I unlocked my door and stepped in, my thoughts narrowed to the last hour or two. I got as far as taking one arm out of my jacket when I suddenly froze dead in my tracks in my living room. With my other arm still in the jacket it hit me: *Man, that was odd that she turned down my offer to put her bed together. I had an electric screw gun; she only had screw drivers.* Then, the next thought was *She almost seemed in a hurry to have me leave.* That thought was followed by pondering the little gift bag on the front steps and her strange behavior when she picked it up and brought it into the house. The "dots" started to connect. Two plus two, plus two, was starting to equal six!

Then, I remembered her talking on occasion about a co-worker, Jack, who she often worked closely with at the hospital. Her occasional references to him were reminiscent of Linda talking about her ex-husband. An old familiar knot formed in my gut, followed by a wave of jealousy—something I thought

I was over and didn't feel anymore. The wheels started to turn in my head, and I slid my free arm back into my jacket.

I contemplated getting back into my car and driving over there, but a debate ensued in my mind. I didn't want to be *that* person anymore. I started to feel like who I used to be when I was with Laura—a person so insecure that I believed I had to lie, cheat, and spy on someone to maintain a relationship. I took my jacket off and was about to throw it on the couch when, despite my attempt at restoring myself to sanity, the knot in my stomach tightened. I made the decision. I had to know. I grabbed my jacket, put it back on, and went to my car. I drove down Irving Park Road like a man on a mission.

When I arrived, I pulled in about a half block away from the house. I got out of my car, and the first thing I noticed was a car in the driveway. My heart started pounding, and the knot in my stomach began to make me short of breath. I walked up the driveway, then up the steps to the front door. It was open, so I let myself in, and I could hear them talking in the bedroom. I made a beeline for the bedroom door. When I opened it, what I saw was Kathy and Jack sitting cross-legged on an area rug on the floor, finishing up some Chinese carryout they had eaten. Behind them—the put-together and freshly made waterbed. Twenty more minutes, and I'm sure I would have walked in on them doing more than eating Chinese. I stood and stared at her as anger boiled up into my eyes. I did what I came to do—know the truth—and now I knew it. The knowledge brought no relief. I turned around and walked out of the house with the knot in my stomach, now much worse, and headed back to my car.

Kathy followed me, crying and apologizing, saying over and over, she didn't mean to hurt me. I responded, but due to being in an anger blackout, I can't remember what I said. I was so full of hurt and anger that everything from that point was a blur.

I drove to Irving Park Road and started heading east back to my apartment, almost three miles away. The feelings of hurt and anger surged and intensified when I realized that I also felt used. *Why didn't you get him to move you!?* I remember thinking. I stopped at a red light and turned my head to the right and saw a bar's beckoning neon sign above the door and in the window. Then, out of nowhere, I heard the voice of a person I thought didn't exist anymore: *You won't be able to get rid of this pain. There's only one way to get relief from it. Go on, park your car, and head into that bar. Have a few drinks. You'll feel so much better. You don't have to do any heroin or cocaine.*

The light changed to green, and I jammed on the gas pedal like I was fleeing and eluding the cops, but I couldn't shake the thought. Luckily, I didn't have to stop again because miraculously, every light turned green the rest of the way back to my apartment! God? Looking back, I'm convinced it was. The perfectly timed green lights had never happened before or since.

When I got back to my apartment, I frantically paced back and forth. The hurt and anger were still overwhelming and the voice in my head continued to try to convince me that some alcohol would be okay.

I realized that it was time to ask for help, so I pulled the little black book out of my wallet and started looking for phone numbers. I started with my recently "fired" sponsor, Mark, but there was no answer. Then, I must have called six or seven other people. No one answered though I may have gotten one or two answering machines. Remember, it's 1988. There were no cell phones and not everyone had an answering machine, so the phone just rang and rang until someone either picked it up, or you hung up. I came up empty. It was, after all, Saturday night, and Sweetest Day. I stopped picking up the phone and tried to calm myself, and talk myself down, but it just didn't work. I was still overwhelmed by my feelings and still in danger.

It was getting late, and by then, calling people meant I might be waking them up. I gave it one last try and dug deep into my phone book. Finally, someone picked up the phone. Who? None other than my brother from another mother, my oldest confidant since I had first gotten clean, my peer, my own personal "therapeutic robot," my conscience—James Minter.

"Boy, it sounds like you done got yourself in deep this time brother. First Penny; now this. God's tryin' to tell you somethin'. Maybe you better slow down chasing these skirts around for a while."

It was so good to hear his "by the book," cliché, program-slogan ass. His blend of simple wisdom and common sense was exactly what I needed to hear. It grounded me by getting my priorities straight and giving me the hope that I needed. *"This too shall pass"* and *"Everything happens for a reason."* He also humbled me with questions like: "God's got a plan for your life. Do you trust God's plan, or do you think you got a better one?" Only program people had this kind of grounding wisdom.

We talked on the phone until almost 2 a.m. When we hung up, I immediately noticed that the pain and anger wasn't gone, but it had dissipated enough to be tolerable. I was able to call it a night and go to sleep. James would sometimes describe himself as an ex-pickpocket, a thief, and a dope fiend. But that's not who he really was. He really was an unlikely angel, sent into my life by God.

I woke up the next morning and made myself some coffee. As I drank my first cup, I engaged in my typical morning ritual of reading the *Day by Day* and the *Twenty-Four Hours a Day* books, desperate to read something that would take me out of my pain. I was startled out of my quiet, meditative silence by the phone ringing. I picked it up and there was an odd silence on the other end. Then she started to speak. Her quiet, apologetic voice cut me like a knife. I immediately hung up the phone hard, as if to slap her in the face. It felt good. It felt even better when the phone immediately rang again, and I knew it was her. I had played this game with the best—Laura—and I sensed that she was desperate to explain herself, so it gave me great pleasure to slam the phone down on the receiver again after she got only two or three words out. Immediately, the phone rang yet again. I picked it up and listened this time and heard her say: "I'm so sorry I hurt you. I didn't know what to do. I didn't mean for it to happen; it just did. I…" SLAM went the phone down again, and again!

The next time she called back, I picked it up and while pacing back and forth in my living room, I finally responded, yelling, "How could you do this to me?!" SLAM! I hung up on her again. The phone immediately started to ring again. I picked it up, and as my pacing quickened, I yelled, "HOW COULD YOU DO THIS TO ME?!" SLAM went the phone.

But this time the loud crash of the phone seemed to jar something in my brain, and from it sprang a realization of the absurdity of my statement. So, as if to demonstrate just how absurd and childish I was being, I purposely continued my temper tantrum rant aloud to myself… "YES, HOW COULD YOU DO THIS TO ME? ME…STEVE…GOD'S GIFT TO ALL WOMEN!!"

Suddenly, it was like I was outside of my body, looking at and listening to myself. I started laughing at how absurd that sounded. My façade began to crack, and the truth started to reveal itself. It was my ego that was hurt more than my heart. I realized that I had never caught a girl cheating on me in my life, and even though I knew Laura did, I never caught her. I realized that my false pride was what really hurt.

I picked up the phone, which by now had stopped ringing (she apparently had finally given up) and called her. I was still hurt and angry, but I was able to have a civil conversation with her and hear her out. She confessed that her food was more than just a bit off, and she had actually been in a full-blown relapse for months. She also confessed that the Taco Bell bags I found were recent and a part of that relapse.

As far as the cheating goes, it was one of those things that just happens. They worked together, wrestling crazy adolescents to the ground and restraining them until security could put restraints on them and take them away. Apparently, this created some kind of deep bonding experience for them, and they fell for each other. So, she didn't maliciously do anything *to me*. Once I took myself out of "the center of the universe," I realized that I was just collateral damage of something that happened to all concerned.

Now we had to figure out what we were going to do about the Saturday meeting. I had to keep attending with Fred, at least for a while longer. She agreed to find another Saturday meeting for a while.

As the dust settled, I realized that humping her shit across town was still a sore spot for me. I asked why she didn't get him to move her. I don't recall her explanation, but I remember it didn't make me feel any better about it. Before we ended the conversation, she reminded me that I still had her guitar and asked me to bring it to LPAC next Saturday and leave it with Vince, the custodian. I agreed, and we hung up; however, after thinking about it, I thought of a way to reconcile my feelings of being used. I called her back and informed her that I was keeping the guitar as payment for moving her. She was not too happy about this, but was reluctant to argue about it, at least at that time.

When Freddy and I showed up at the Saturday meeting, she was there. She pulled me off to the side and asked for her guitar. I reached into my old Steve bag, which was still readily available when needed, and dug my heels in.

"I'll give you your guitar back when you give me $75 for moving you," I offered. She agreed. I never saw the money, so I wound up keeping the guitar.

I purged the pain of the incident by talking about it in meetings until I'm guessing, people were probably sick of hearing it. I didn't care. I was learning what it meant when they said the oft-repeated slogan, *"This is a selfish program."* I was going to say what I needed to say and take care of myself regardless of what people thought.

Navigating the ups and downs of early recovery

That fall I started to bond and hang with a group of fellow NA members. A few were musicians, and one was my friend Gwen's boyfriend, Steve Goodman. Steve was related to the "King of Swing" bandleader of the 1930s and '40s, Benny Goodman. The heavy metal singer-songwriter and guitarist's music was quite different from his famous relatives. Gwen's brother, Guy, played drums, so again, I was asked to play bass, but this time, I was writing original basslines, albeit with some direction from Steve.

I also started developing a strong friendship with fellow Ron Orlando caseload-peer, Bob R. He had a daughter around Jessica's age, and we got together a few times with our kids while in our roles as weekend dads.

After one meeting that Bob and I regularly attended, we'd all head to a small restaurant on Clark Street just across the street from where the infamous Saint Valentine's Day Massacre occurred. They made the best banana-strawberry shakes. When I couldn't find parking on the street, there was a Walgreens parking lot behind the restaurant that I would park in.

About 9 p.m. when we finished our usual ritual of dinner, dessert, laughing, and "shootin' the shit." Afterward, we all went to get in our cars.

I got in mine, started it up, and put it in reverse to back out of the space I was in. Nothing. I stepped on the gas a little harder, but the car wouldn't budge. I tried putting it in drive with the same result. "Fuck!" I yelled, punching the steering wheel and thinking *the transmission went out!* I knew this meant I'd need to get a car because there was no way it would be worth replacing a transmission in a beater car. My focus became about how I was getting home. Realizing that Walgreens had a payphone right outside the entrance, I exited the car and made my way toward the phone. On my way there, I came across an older, tall, thin black guy, sitting on the curb smoking a cigarette. He noticed I was having trouble and asked, "Car trouble?"

"Yeah, I'm going to have to get it towed."

"Won't stay runnin'?"

"No, it runs; it just won't go into gear."

"Sounds like the tranny."

"Yep," I agreed.

"If you want, I can take a look. I used to work on cars for a living. Sometimes, with older cars, it's the linkage and isn't that difficult to fix."

"Okay," I said, thinking, *It's worth a shot.*

We headed over to the car, and he crawled underneath it.

"You got a hammer or a tire iron?"

"Yeah, in the trunk," I said, now hoping that it wasn't serious.

I handed him my lug wrench out of the trunk while he remained under the car. He brought the wrench under the car and began banging something with it. At that moment, I realized something didn't feel right. I was certainly no Brian Kasman, but I knew that no one had ever fixed a transmission problem with a tire iron. It suddenly dawned on me that I was being scammed!

He placed the tire iron next to his right leg as he lay there with his legs spread apart. I thought about kicking him in the balls so hard, he'd be gasping for air until midnight, then grabbing the tire iron and using it on him if I had to. Then, a funny thing happened—the ex-dope fiend in me identified with him, and I felt a strange admiration for him. I thought, *"What a great scam. Why didn't I think of that?"* He slid out from under the car and announced, "Yep, that's all it was. I fixed it. So, you think that's worth a few bucks? Whatever you can spare is cool. I wouldn't even ask, but I'm not working right now."

"Sure. Mind if I get in and try it first, though?" I replied.

"Not at all. Go ahead."

I started it up and put it in reverse. I felt a sense of relief as I backed out of the space. Then I put it in drive and drove to the end of the lot. I turned around and drove back toward him, as he stood and watched proudly, with a look of accomplishment on his face. I thought about flooring it, driving past him, and flipping him the bird as I sped by him, but something stopped me. I pulled up alongside him, rolled the window down, reached into my pocket, and peeled a twenty off the wad of bills that was there (it was Friday, and I just got paid), and as I handed it to him, I said, "Thanks, brother."

"You're welcome, brother. Glad I could help," he replied.

As I drove away, what just happened started sinking in. The admiration and amazement with the scam wore off, and I felt a little sick to my stomach. I was embarrassed and ashamed. I felt like a fool. *How could I have let my guard down like that?* I thought. I should have "smelled" that guy from a mile away. I hadn't felt this kind of feeling since the time I got conned out of my entire income tax check at a carnival when I was 19.

Then, the voice I now identified as God, spoke to me in the back of my mind, *"That's how it feels, Steven. That's what it feels like to be a victim of the kind of things you used to do to people. You never thought about how it affected them; now you know."* I knew that was the purpose of what just occurred, and I felt okay about it, except one thing that still bothered me: How did he do it!?

The next day I called my brother Paul. He was familiar with the scam. Apparently, he pulled the cotter pin out of my transmission linkage with a pair of pliers. He then leaves both under the car and positions himself between the "Vic's" car and the nearest payphone. He offers to help. The tire iron is for effect, and to have a weapon in case things go sideways. While under the car, he puts the cotter pin back in, and *voila*, your major tranny problem is solved! Only a complete jagoff wouldn't feel obligated to give him a double saw.

The winter of 1988 was pretty unremarkable other than trying to navigate being a weekend dad and developing my skills as much as was possible in my role on the unit. I continued to sponsor Tony, Fred, and two or three others who would fall off and relapse. I'd never hear from them again. Storchy and I started writing to each other and I allowed him to call me collect from the joint. This contributed to my feeling more like a grown-up, but the icing on the cake came when I got home from work and checked my mailbox.

When I saw an envelope from Com Ed in the stack of mail, my heart sank. I thought, *What now?* I tore it open knowing that it wasn't my monthly bill. I read the letter as I walked to my apartment. *Dear Com Ed Customer. Due to your payments being on time for the past 12 months, we are reimbursing the deposit you submitted. Thanks for being a good customer.*

Sure enough, there was a check for one hundred dollars attached. I of course needed the money, but more importantly, it was more reinforcement that I was becoming a responsible adult, and my self-esteem jumped another notch.

Unfortunately, while most things were improving, I was still dealing with being lonely after Kathy and I parted ways. I did manage a few unmemorable one-night stands, well, except for one. It happened when I went to an NA convention being held in the city.

While there, I ran into my ex-sponsor's wife Lori. When I asked about Mark, the news was not good. They were in the middle of a nasty divorce, and she was trying to block his rights to see his kids. She accused Mark of molesting his children. According to Lori, he had also relapsed and was out there shooting dope again. I expressed my shock and sadness to hear this.

Though I was genuinely saddened by the news about Mark, I admit that I couldn't pass up what seemed like a rare opportunity to get her number. The vibe was still there, and I likely wouldn't get another chance. It was obviously there for her too, as she offered me her number without me asking for it. I called her the next day, and we planned to get together the following Friday night.

When Friday came, we went to an Italian restaurant, then back to my place for a little "dessert." We wound up on the floor in my living room making out, until I suggested we go into the bedroom. She agreed but had one little request before we did…she suggested we both… "brush our teeth."

"Okay?" Good thing, she brought her own toothbrush to the event because I only had my kids' and mine in a cup on the sink. I reluctantly followed her into my bathroom, and we loaded up our brushes with paste, stood in front of the mirror side by side, and brushed our filthy little teeth. As it turned out, the sex was just as anal. No, not anal as in *anal*, but anal as in OCD! I saw this as a necessary learning experience. I learned that sometimes "dead rats" come in pretty packages! That was our first and last date.

I imagine that this is one of those things that women ponder when they're out with their friends: "He said he'd call me, but he never did. Jerk!"

Did you tell them how you made us brush before sex—and that sex sucked!? No, not sucked as in *sucked*, but sucked as in bad!

On a side note: I was able to verify that Mark relapsed but not the other accusations. I would come to realize that women often lie about their kid's fathers to get custody or wield power in a divorce. I'm not saying this was the case, but it was certainly possible. Mark did not strike me as a child molester.

Christmas Fiorito style returns

Once upon a time, in a treatment center far far away, someone said to me that I should think of being in treatment on Christmas as an investment in Christmases yet to come. It, like many predictions and "promises" that were made in my early recovery, came true.

My addiction had pulled me away from what was always an especially warm and wonderful time in my family. Christmas was always filled with joy, music, great food, friends and family. There was also a bit of "low budget" seasonal magic that my siblings always tried to provide for me when I was a kid. Whether it was taking me to see Santa or creating hoof prints in the snow that went clear across our garage roof (Yes, they actually did that!) they always found a way to make Christmas a little more special.

I, like most kids in that era, waited with great excitement as the season approached, for holiday movies, specials, and shows like *A Charlie Brown Christmas* and *The Grinch Who Stole Christmas*. Woven into the season and my psyche was a Christmas soundtrack—music by classic artists such as Johnny Mathis, Burl Ives, Andy Williams, Bing Crosby, and Perry Como that enhanced the joy of the season. Sadly, my addiction had reduced my interest in the holidays to little more than a way to score money for drugs.

Although the days of the huge Fiorito Christmas parties with extended family and friends had passed, we were able to recapture a good measure of what was likely gone forever. There were still enough of us and enough kids to give Christmas that old-time feel. At least it felt that way to me, likely due to the emotional thawing that continued over the almost two years that had passed.

Being clean and sober left me little choice but to reinvest emotionally in the season that had always brought me so much joy as a child. I had a deeper appreciation for my family and the history and traditions we carried through the years. I'm sure that me being clean and sober also had a calming effect and was a relief to my family, freeing them up to have more joy as well. As I recall, even Paul was in one of his periods of stability and seemed to be doing okay.

So that year, we did the things that made Christmas a warm, special time. We had a grab bag (that I could afford to participate in), the Christmas music played, everybody talked over each other like an Italian family should, and the kids ran around laughing and screaming in seasonal excitement, combined with too much sugar. Best of all, Albie cooked her ass off.

Mary Jo and I got a laugh from everyone when we reminisced about switching Frank Zappa and The Mothers album, *We're Only in It for the Money* into *The Andy Williams Christmas Album* jacket, (same record label so they looked identical). We will never forget the look on Albie's face when the psychedelic sound effects started coming out of the speakers instead of Christmas music. Her response was classic and cracked us all up: "I think there's something wrong with my record!" she said with shock on her face.

We had all the traditional seafood that I grew up watching my father and older brothers prepare including clams, periwinkle snails (or the Sicilian name that we used, *babbaluci*), the traditional antipasto tray, spaghetti with meatballs and sausage, and calamari. These were delicacies to me, though I would later learn that most of them were chosen because it's what they could afford. My parents didn't have money and always did the best they could around the holidays, which looking back, was pretty darn good. However, it fell short of my standards. I rarely got that big expensive gift that I asked Santa for. I was finally able to appreciate what we had and see "the cup" as "half-full," instead of focusing on what we didn't have and seeing it as "half empty."

Now, as my dad reached just beyond his mid-seventies, it was up to Paul and me to open the clams. Some of us ate them raw but plenty were for baking for the lightweights who like to cover up the taste of fish with breadcrumbs and Italian seasonings.

There were two rites of passage in my family, and oddly, both happened at the Fiorito Christmas party. The first was you had to try a raw clam. This went for women as well as men. You weren't truly a member of our family until you slurped one of those slippery little devils off the half shell. I'd suggest a few drops of Tabasco and lemon before they'd endeavor. The family was lenient, and you were allowed to spit it into the garbage if you were a wimp and absolutely had to. At least you gave it your best shot!

The second rite of passage for the young men was shucking (opening) clams. No easy task. As my nieces got older, it was fun to pull their boyfriends off the couch with the inviting words, "Hey! Capatosta! Put this apron on, grab a sharp knife, and get your ass in here!" You were considered a boy and not a man until you shucked your first clam. Again, tolerance was abundant for novices who would inevitably slice their finger open, or some other appendage. Of course, you were then banished from the sink area and told to have a seat with the womenfolk, who were preparing the breadcrumbs for the baked clams and the calamari, like the little pansy-ass that you were! Besides, we didn't want you bleeding all over the clams.

I had just turned 29 years old, and I was finally becoming a man. Hey, better late than never!

Amelia

Lit a cigarette, watched the smoke float through the room.
It drifted off and led me to your face.

I can't say that I remember what I did to usher in the New Year in 1989, but I can tell you what I didn't do—use alcohol or drugs. I'm also pretty sure of what I did on New Year's Day—I went to a meeting at the Mustard Seed. I remember it was cold outside because everyone had tons of winter garb on. Some Chicago winters saw Jack Frost not simply "nipping at your nose" but ripping your entire face off!

I remember the meeting was standing room only. The chairs along the back wall were filled, which was rare. I must have got there early because I had a seat in one of the main sections by the chairperson's desk, facing the back wall. After the lead speaker and the break, the meeting opened for comments, which I'm sure consisted mostly of people talking about not drinking the night before, with a few relapse stories of some that did, sprinkled in.

As the meeting went on, the Seed filled with smoke. This was back in the day when you could light up anywhere you wanted. I lit a cigarette and watched the smoke float through the room. It drifted off and led me to a woman's face who was sitting along the back wall. She was attractive, with brown hair and faded freckles, just as any trace of summer had by then. She raised her hand and was called on to comment.

She said she was in Chicago from Los Angeles to be with her mother, who lived here alone. I remember thinking, *why would anyone want to come to Chicago from LA at this time of year?* The sad answer was revealed in her comment. She began to cry as she talked about recently losing her brother to a rare illness. He was only in his mid-thirties as I recall. I could feel her pain and my heart went out to her.

When the meeting ended, I stood in line (of mostly guys) to give her my condolences. She mentioned to me that she grew up on the North Shore but hadn't lived here for years, and that the city had changed so much, she didn't know where anything was. I saw my chance and I took it...

"If you'd like, I'll take you on a tour, show you around, and reacquaint you with the Windy City."

"I'd like that," she said, smiling, despite her puffy eyes from crying.

"Let me give you my number. I'm staying with my mother at the Belle Shore Apartments on Bryn Mawr Avenue."

She then proceeded to hunt for pen and paper and jotted her info down.

"What are you doing Friday?" I asked.

"What did you have in mind?" she replied.

"Maybe we could get some dinner and find something to do."

"Okay, I think I'm free. Call me."

I did, and we made a date for Friday night.

On Friday I picked her up at the historic Belle Shore Apartments. It was a Chicago landmark, recently converted to condominiums. It was once a hotel with quite a rich history, which of course I knew nothing about. When I went into the lobby, I was greeted by a doorman to whom I gave the apartment number and my name. I stood there as he rang upstairs.

"Miss Hamilton, there's a Mr. Fiorito to see you…..I'll send him up."

He directed me to the elevator and the floor the apartment was on. The lobby was ornate and fancy. The smell was sweet and heavy, mixed with old antique wood and faint expensive perfume. A knot of intimidation started forming the minute I walked in and continued to grow into nervousness in the pit of my stomach. Luckily, the intrigue overrode the nerves, and I rode the elevator to the appropriate floor. I knocked on the door and waited nervously.

"Who is it?" I recognized her voice. Amelia had a unique voice that could be described as a child's voice but mixed with overtones of something very sexy. Kind of a cross between Shirley Temple and Marilyn Monroe.

"It's Steve." The door opened and there she stood, in some kind of casual yet classy, unique hippie garb, that looked great on her, but at the same time made you wonder; *Who is this woman?* I, on the other hand, was dressed in classic midwestern, Franklin Park grease-monkey attire: jeans and my pleather bombardier jacket. The same jacket I wore shooting heroin and cocaine. In fact, if you put your nose in either armpit, you could still get a very faint scent of the paranoid cocaine-induced body odor, that once permeated it.

She took me by the hand and brought me through the hall of the elegant, classy, but cozy apartment, decorated with antiques, family heirlooms, and pictures. We went into the living room to meet her mother, where I suddenly became *Steven*. Albie would have been pleased.

"Mother, this is Steven. Steven, this is my mother—Arlene Hamilton."

"Nice to meet you, Steven," she said as a formality but with what felt like a hint of sincerity. She grilled me a bit, under the guise of being casually curious, which I was no stranger to, but always unnerved me, nonetheless.

Arlene Hamilton was five foot and a few inches mix of classy, yet down-to-earth woman. She was feisty and assertive, but not in a mean way, with utter confidence in the words she spoke. Back then, she was just another mother who intimidated me, made me uneasy, and probably didn't like me.

Amelia, sensing I was uneasy, rescued me: "We have a reservation, Mother. We don't want to be late." Then she pulled me by the hand into her bedroom to finish getting ready. I got my first dose of criticism since leaving treatment, albeit more subtle than I was used to: "Is that jacket real leather?"

"No" I said, realizing it for the first time. She came up to me and felt it and made a frowny face. "We need to take you thrift store shopping my boy."

"My boy" was an appropriate term, as I would discover that Amelia was 11 years older than me. I would be 30 that November and she would be 41 in April. Up close, I could see the chinks in the armor of her youth— crow's feet and lines on her face, but to me, this made her more interesting and sexier. Her more rugged, slightly weathered beauty would begin to grow on me and further reinforce my discovery that tight-skinned, young girls—or "Barbie dolls" as I would later refer to them—weren't my thing. I had officially outgrown my attraction to young, tan, California blondes.

She continued brushing her hair in the mirror, which was not cooperating, likely due to the static electricity in the dry frigid Chicago air. Giving up, she ran into the adjacent bathroom, apparently to douse it with "product." Then, she hurried out, grabbing my hand once again.

"C'mon. We'll take the back elevator; it'll be quicker."

We raced through to the back door, shooting past her mother, who barely had time to say anything as we raced by. "Don't be too late Amelia!"

We went out the back door to what used to be the small, gated service elevator back when the building was a hotel. We said goodnight to the doorman and made our way to whatever vehicle I was sporting in those days. Amelia made a sarcastic comment about my car, to which I replied, "Maybe I can find a better car at the thrift store when we go." I made her laugh for the first time.

On the way to the restaurant, we talked mostly about me. I told her that I was coming up on two years clean and sober, what I did for a living, and about my kids. She seemed genuinely impressed and confided that she had only been sober for several months. This would violate the agreement I had made with myself, but somehow, I felt she was different.

She gave a brief overview of her drug history, which seemed typical and even somewhat tame for the times she began using in—the 1960s and '70s. She said she had only gone off the deep end recently when her brother Charles died after open heart surgery in June of 1988. She started doing Quaaludes and drinking a lot to kill the pain. She realized she needed to stop, so she turned to AA because she knew others who stopped drinking through the program.

Whether or not she was an addict or alcoholic was questionable. The AA program only requires a "desire to stop drinking" to qualify. She may have just been using the program as a form of support to deal with the loss of her brother. That was for her to figure out. She and Charles were close, and though he was younger, somewhat of a hero to her. At dinner, I would find out why.

Her brother, Charles James Hamilton, was a talented artist. He was an actor, a musician, and a songwriter. His credits included being in the original cast of several groundbreaking plays on Broadway. He had various other stage, TV, and musical credits, including appearances on several popular 1970s TV series. Amelia cried as she described who Charles was. I'd soon observe that she would cry every time she spoke about him.

As we finished dinner, I explained that I was a musician and a songwriter and had done some theater in the past. I threw out the miniscule two feathers in my musical cap, one being my adventures with the band in Northern California and the second being my current recording of original music. She seemed intrigued. "I'd love to hear some of your stuff."

"If you'd like, we can go back to my apartment, and I can play you some stuff that I'm working on."

The light went from yellow to green, "I think I'd like that," she smiled.

We drove the short distance to my apartment. Once there, we went upstairs, and I played her several songs including the recently completed "Katherine," and other tracks I had done in the studio with Kenny.

I put my guitar back on its stand and sat on the opposite end of the couch facing her.

"I love your stuff. You've got a great voice. You need to get out there."

I was encouraged because I sensed her comments were sincere and she wasn't just blowing smoke up my ass. As I learned more about her, those comments would become even more meaningful.

"What about you? You haven't told me anything about yourself. What do you do?" I asked.

"I'm an actor," she replied with a matter-of-fact tone.

I remember thinking to myself; *How cute. She's probably done some local theater, a few commercials or something.*
"Okay, but I meant…ya know…what do you do for a living?"

"I'm an actor," she repeated.

She went on to list some of the things she had done which, like her brother, included several Broadway plays. She also did some TV, including made for TV movies, several of which received much critical acclaim.

I remember thinking to myself; *Okay, she really is an actor.* Though I was impressed, I wasn't totally "star struck" because I wasn't that familiar with most of the things she'd done, that is until she uttered these words… "I was nominated for an Academy Award for Best Supporting Actress."

This definitely got my attention. "Really?! For what film?" Her answer put me in a state of shock! When she told me the name of the film, I about fell out of my chair! *Who is this woman?* Indeed!

The second shock wave hit when she told me the character she played. My mind immediately flashed back to one of my favorite scenes, where the absence of a bra showed a well-defined outline of some very shapely tits, and I realized it was her! Amelia Hamilton! Older, slightly weathered, and a bit more meat on her bones, but it was her!

"Oh my God! I had such a crush on your character!"

"Really!? What did you like about her?" she said, now smiling, knowing that her character had such an impact on me.

"I loved the free spirit that she was and, well… she…I mean you…were… sexy as hell! She… I mean, you… really turned me on."

She knew she had me now, so she played me like a fiddle. "What did you find sexy about her…I mean… me?" she laughed playfully.

"Well, that scene where you wore that T-shirt and no bra."

"Yes, and…?" she continued toying with me.

"Well, to be honest, you had some really nice tits," I confessed.

She smiled with a sexy gleam in her eye and delivered a line that I'll never forget: "And now those tits are sitting across from you on your couch."

"Yes, they are" I said, trying to normalize the conversation as much as possible before completely losing it.

With that, we both started laughing. She was genuinely amused by the whole exchange. My laugh, on the other hand, was more nervous and sought to break the blinding sexual tension that was building.

I instinctively slid across the couch to make my move and looked for any sign of recoil from my advances. There were none. We kissed passionately and I took her into my arms. We took a breath, and she commented: "That was nice. You know I'm not the character you had a crush on—right? I'm Amelia."

"Yes, I know," I assured her, and our relationship took off like a rocket. These words I'd later write captured the essence of the moment…

On our very first night
Held you in my arms so tight, but still, I couldn't find the words to say
Thought I stole your heart, hope it's not just another part, you were acting out, in a scene, from some romantic play

The plot thickens

As I continued to find myself at the Belle Shore Apartments more and more, and our affection for each other grew, Amelia shared more of herself and her life. As it turned out, her wounds were not just about the death of her brother and hero Charles. There were other painful wounds and scars that afflicted and damaged her. Unfortunately, her story was just as sad and tragic as it was unique, charmed, and triumphant. After her initial success, her life became a series of rejections by an ex-husband, ex-lovers, and Hollywood.

I learned that she'd been married and divorced in her 20s from a man in the music industry. He had a list of credits and eventually went on to produce several famous artists. It was the old story of just being too young to be married.

Then there was her long and sometimes difficult relationship with her boyfriend and fellow actor, who would eventually become quite successful. According to Amelia, she helped him make the connections that contributed to his success. She watched his career take off while hers sputtered.

Her Oscar nomination was followed by a series of bad choices, bad scripts, and bad bounces that didn't go her way. Other TV projects were critically acclaimed, but none of her roles in those productions was "juicy" enough to really get her over the hump and make her a household name.

In the strange land of Hollywood, they talk about getting your "big break" as if it's all you need to do. What they don't tell you is how to sustain yourself in that world and how it's what you do *after* your "big break" that is of the utmost importance.

Amelia was a free spirit and did things her own way. This might be a good thing if you live in a hippie commune, but in Hollywood, it can be deadly. Her recklessness, combined with a bit of bad luck, resulted in her going from being a rising star who was the talk of the town, to becoming "Amelia who?"

The comedy that made her cry

In the early 1980s, Amelia got the chance to audition for a film that did pretty well at the box office and was also loved by critics. It would have likely breathed life into her career and got her back on track. The film was a dark comedy starring some big names. The directors were torn between Amelia and another actress for the role. After numerous call-backs, she came very close, but ultimately, the other actress got the part. Amelia said she was devastated and exhausted by the whole ordeal. This, combined with problems in her relationship with her actor boyfriend, led to not only increased substance use but also to the two biggest career blunders she would make. To escape the negative feelings that these circumstances created, she and a female friend took an impromptu extended hiatus to Italy.

Upon her return to LA, she made things worse by agreeing to open and operate the West Coast branch of her youngest brother Dan's art gallery in California. Dan was an artist who turned into a successful gallery owner in New York. When the California gallery failed, and she was ready to get back to her career, she learned, as many others had, how short Hollywood's memory is.

There were, however, at least a few recent bright spots. Before coming to Chicago, she had a supporting role in a film that starred some up-and-coming young actors and was soon to be released. She had also auditioned for a role that she thought looked pretty promising. I remember seeing the script lying around my apartment, which, by this time, may as well have been hers. She spent the night often and would return to her mother's only on occasion. She even started using my phone number as a contact number, not only because she was there so much but also because I had an answering machine, and I don't believe her mother did at that time. The words finally just came out of my mouth, "Why don't you just move in?" So, she did. I even let her record the outgoing message on the machine so her voice would be on it.

I remember shortly after Amelia moved in, coming home to the first message I received. I played it and was surprised and slightly awed. It was film critic Gene Siskel, who was at the height of his popularity with the movie review show *At the Movies,* that he did weekly with his partner and fellow critic Roger Ebert. Siskel said that he heard that she was in town and to give him a call, and he left his number. I went from a feeling of awe to a little twinge of jealousy. It was a sign of things to come. When I asked Amelia about him, I tried to keep my feelings under wraps, but it leaked out a bit. Instead of reassuring me, she laughed and said in a matter-of-fact way: "He's just a friend dear." She exited the room, leaving me to grapple with my insecurity. She knew I was the only one who could overcome it.

A few days later, we returned with the spoils of a long day of thrift store shopping. She was completely redesigning my wardrobe. Kind of an early rendition of Bravo TV's *Queer Eye for the Straight Guy,* only without the "queer" aspect. I went from "Franklin Park tough guy" attire (rock shirts and cowboy boots) to multicolored sweaters, jeans, and penny loafers.

We barely noticed the machine beckoning from the living room end table with its blinking red light. When we played the message from a woman who was one of the casting director's assistants, informing Amelia that she got the part! We hugged and kissed and decided to make reservations for that evening at one of the finer dining establishments on the North Side to celebrate.

Upon our return that evening, another message was waiting. This time the news not only wasn't good, it was devastating. It turned out, the woman had made a terrible mistake, which she explained in the message. It wasn't Amelia who got the part. She apologized profusely. I don't remember the details of how the mistake happened, but what a colossal blunder. The woman obviously felt terrible, but it didn't help the huge letdown and disappointment that we both experienced. Getting this role could have also led to more work in the sequel that wound up being made. Just another day in Hollyweird huh?

Despite these disappointments, the good news was we were in love. This would present many significant challenges, especially for me. It was a state of being that I had not experienced since I was 17 years old. The only women whom I had ever felt this strongly about were Mary and Carol. I don't count Laura because although I loved her, we were more addicted to each other than in love. Now, those feelings were for a worldly, vivacious, flirtatious, sexy older woman, who was trying desperately to get her once-promising acting career back on track. It was intimidating and it scared the shit out of me. My relationship with Amelia brought to the surface my remaining insecurities, lack of confidence, self-doubt, and low self-esteem. In many ways it was like being back in treatment at Gateway.

Though I had gotten through the initial tests, it was time, once again, to face the "second wave" of fears and barriers that this relationship presented. A quote from one of her letters sums it up...

I love the way you don't run away from me as some kind of "other" person, but you love me as somehow a part of yourself that you want to know and own more and more.

My relationship with Amelia was a constant challenge to become more and better than I ever was, and not only in the "recovery world," but in the real world. Was I up for that challenge just two years into my recovery? The challenge wasn't just our relationship, but everything associated with it. As challenging as my relationship with Amelia was, it was also exciting!

Meet the Hamiltons

My first encounter with Amelia's family came when we were invited to her mother's for dinner. Her immediate family consisted of her mother Arlene, older sister Judith, brother-in-law Bob, nephews Andy, and Conner (Brett), and younger brother Dan. Judith was the typical social worker type, ironically, with a pretty substantial alcohol issue. Come to think of it, I guess it's really not that ironic and unfortunately it is more common than people think. Her husband seemed mostly irritated with her, like they had always had an argument in the car on the way to wherever they were going. Her nephews were both good kids. The younger of the two, Conner, decided he wanted to be called Brett out of the blue (he just thought it was a cool name) so we obliged him. I guess you could say he was a pioneer and ahead of his time, in that although he was born Conner, he "identified as Brett."

Dan was an intelligent, low-key, quietly creative guy who had a good head on his shoulders that included good business sense. He was laidback and unassuming. All went to the best schools and had thoroughbred type values, manners, and etiquette. They were upper class, but were they snobs? Anyone who met the previous description was a snob to me when I was younger, but I started to realize that it was my own low self-esteem that put people into those categories. I admit I felt pressure to be charming, witty, and intelligent when I was around them. I'm sure those qualities were somewhere in me, and I did my best to bring them out, but mostly I felt like a guy who was "tripping" as gracefully as he could over himself. I always felt that "first day on the job" nervousness in the pit of my stomach around them.

We arrived early and Amelia's mother was entertaining some women friends in the dining room. After introductions, Amelia went to do something, so I sat in the living room and observed them unnoticed. I reached into the inside pocket of my new thrift store-purchased tweed sports jacket and pulled out a small notebook and pen. I started to carry these with me most of the time, as song lyrics, poems, and other creative ideas started coming to me, seemingly out of nowhere. My observations inspired me to write the following poem...

Snobs

Stuffy old women in careful conversation,
Careful not to cross the boundaries of words
that had taken years of constipated living to erect,
Stuffy, wrinkled, well-pressed, old women,
Painted thick with makeup and too much lipstick,
Doused with pungent, sweet perfume,
Articulate in their wheezing,
Polite in their dying.

At dinner, the main course was leg of lamb with mint jelly in a small dessert dish. I had never seen nor had any idea what to do with the emerald-green blob before me. Nor did I know what to do with the array of small and large forks and spoons on either side of my plate. Luckily, I didn't spread the green blob on my bread. I kept a cool exterior to cover up my ultra-nervousness inside. As Arlene led us in saying grace, I wisely decided to wait until I saw what others did before doing anything. I was somewhat taken aback when I saw someone apply the jelly to their meat, of all things.

To make matters worse, an image of me ravenously shoveling food into my piehole in treatment at Gateway popped up uninvited into my mind. I thought to myself; *Too bad you people missed that. Then you'd know who I really am!* My mind always had a way of torturing me in this manner. Kind of my own private "theatre of the absurd" in my head.

Judith interrupted the "play." "So, Steven, you have two daughters?"

"Yes, I do. Jessica is nine and Melissa is six."

"What beautiful names."

"Thanks. They're both named after songs by my favorite band—The Allman Brothers."

"Oh," she replied, obviously not terribly familiar with their music.

Dan, being close to my age, was, and jumped in to rescue me. "Two great songs!"

I was also relieved to witness Amelia throw all proper etiquette out the window as she reached across the table and grabbed a hunk of food. Her mother promptly scolded her, and I was able to catch my first glimpse of the lifelong power struggle that was their relationship. This was displayed by Amelia's constant rebellion against Arlene's control and correction, which always tried to push Amelia to be her best. What a disappointment I must have been in comparison to her accomplished actor boyfriend. I'm sure the current success of his film career rubbed salt in the wound.

They continued the dinner table small talk, which included how their family had always been musical and used to do family sing-alongs around the piano just like in old movies. They discussed how Charles had been the one to continue to pursue music in a serious way.

Then the subject abruptly changed; it seemed to steer away from the subject of Charles. This is when I learned that the entire family were followers of a sect of Christianity known as Christian Science.

Christian Science was developed in 19th-century New England by Mary Baker Eddy, who in 1875 wrote the book, *Science and Health*. The book proclaimed that sickness is an illusion that can be corrected by prayer alone. They viewed disease as a mental error rather than physical disorder, and that ill health requires correction of the beliefs responsible for the illusion. The "science" was the practical application of Christian beliefs to life and health. It seemed extreme at the time, but as a person who was on a spiritual journey, and an ongoing quest for spiritual growth, I was open-minded about it. Something that I had to consider was they were all healthy as horses and had received minimal if any medical treatment their entire lives, of course, except for Charles. Christian Science intrigued me but also challenged the realist in me.

I had experienced both: mystical divine intervention and practical, earthly help; though at the time, I don't think I realized it. Both heavenly and earthly angels had rescued me.

Something else that really helped with my bouts of spiritual confusion was this meditation from the *Twenty-Four Hours a Day* book…

Fret not your mind with puzzles that you cannot solve. The solutions may never be shown to you until you have left this life. The loss of dear ones, the inequality of life, the deformed and the maimed, and many other puzzling things may not be known to you until you reach the life beyond. "I have yet many things to say unto you but ye cannot bear them now". Only step by step, stage by stage, can you proceed in your journey into greater knowledge and understanding – Twenty-Four Hours a Day, December 3

It remains one of my favorites in the book, giving me permission to admit and accept my human limitations.

Exploring the Chicago entertainment landscape

When the weekend rolled around, the weeks that I had the kids, we started taking them on whatever adventure we could afford. This included swimming at Amelia's mother's, thrift store shopping, out to breakfast, or staying in and making meals ourselves.

On the weekends that I didn't have the kids, we'd look in the local newspapers to find something to do on Friday or Saturday nights. This would usually vary between films, local theater, and occasionally live music. The Chicago theater scene was exploding. Not only with the more mainstream Second City, Steppenwolf, and Royal George theaters, but there were also a thousand small theater companies popping up doing original productions.

A few that stand out in those early days of discovery of the Chicago scene, were The Annoyance Theater's *Co-Ed Prison Sluts,* and Torso Theatre's *Cannibal Cheerleaders on Crack.* These plays were R-rated, irreverent, over-the-top farces, that were not only very funny, but also had strong social, and political messages that were foreboding about the inevitable doom of humanity.

The Neo-Futurists' *Too Much Light Makes the Baby Go Blind* was a little lighter fare that improvised 30 plays in 60 minutes. The show can best be described as organized chaos. A timer is set for 60 minutes and 8.5-by-11 sheets of paper, numbered one through thirty, hung on a clothesline above the thrust-style stage area, positioned in the middle of the audience. The audience would yell out numbers and the actors would jump to reach the chosen number off the line, pull it down, and read the title of the play written on the back. It was similar to the more-modern TV show: *Whose line is in anyway?* which was likely based on TMLMTBGB (as it was sometimes referred to). After reading the card, the cast scrambled to arrange the set and props and get the right personnel on stage to perform the short, improvised play. The closer your seat to the performance space, the more likely you were to be dragged onstage and used by the cast.

The Neo-Futurists rented space above a funeral home. They took no reservations and usually started at 10 p.m. Lines would form around the corner, trying to get in to see the show. It was not uncommon to have a handful of people who already had a bit too much to drink. This would add to the rowdy, unconventional atmosphere of the show. It was quite a unique experience.

In April of 1989, Amelia scanned the show section and there it was, jumping out at her from the pages of the *Chicago Sun-Times.* It was the last film she made. The film had recently been released and was playing at most major theaters in the city and suburbs. We made a date out of it to see the film at a theater downtown, then go to dinner. It turned out, she didn't want to pay to see a movie that she was in, which she didn't tell me until we were in line.

She asked to speak to the manager. Though I got her point, I could feel the embarrassment welling up inside me as we waited to speak to the manager.

I tried to talk her out of it, insisting that I'd pay, but she would not be dissuaded. The manager came out from the back. "Yes, how can I help you folks?"

"Hi, I'm Amelia Hamilton, and this is my friend Steve. I'm in the film (which shall remain nameless) and I feel funny about having to pay to see a film that I'm in. Could you comp us and let us see the film for free?"

My heart sank into my stomach and the knot in my gut tightened in anticipation of the debate that was about to ensue—Amelia's logic versus the rest of the world's. To my surprise, the manager recognized her from the film and replied: "Sure Ms. Hamilton, I understand. Consider yourself and Steve our guests." With that, he escorted us past the barrier into the theater. What a relief.

Amelia had never seen the film, so we were both seeing it for the first time. It was a groundbreaker for its time—a dark comedy that mercilessly attacked and poked fun of subjects that were usually treated seriously.

I liked the film and found it to be edgy and different. Amelia didn't love it, and I felt one of her reasons was a bit petty and self-righteous. She said they used a slightly "fish-eyed" lens to shoot the adults in the film to purposely make them look like foolish, incompetent caricatures. I would never have noticed it if she hadn't told me. I pointed out and reminded her that her character and the other adults in the film *were* "foolish, incompetent caricatures," so why wouldn't they do whatever they could to enhance that point?

As we exited the theater with the throngs of movie-goers and continued to critique the film, Amelia collided with a man who almost spilled his soda all over her. It was someone I knew— Johnny Mars.

Mars was a local disc jockey on the radio station WXRT-FM.

"Hey Steve! How's it going? Did you guys see (untitled film)?"

"Yeah, what'd you think?" I asked.

"I loved it," he proclaimed.

"Me too!" I replied.

We all proceeded to critique the film, Amelia being the biggest critic. Mars tried to convince her that the film was great, and Amelia expressed her displeasure about the fish-eyed lens used. Mars disagreed that the lens was used, when out of nowhere as if he was suddenly hit over the head with a frying pan, he said: "Wait. Was that you in the film?"

"Yes," Amelia replied.

Mars exclaimed to me: "I thought, 'this woman looks like the (her role) in the movie!' And it's you! Wow!"

Even though Johnny was a local celebrity, you could tell he was still a little shocked and awed as we said our goodbyes and we headed off to dinner in beautiful downtown Chicago.

Later that summer she would finally land a role in a film that was being shot in Chicago. The movie featured a Rock & Roll legend who happened to also be on tour at the time with his band.

After we went out for breakfast with the kids one Sunday, Amelia had to go to an actor's warehouse on the North Side to pick her wardrobe for the film. My daughter Melissa was in her "kitty phase" at the time and often spoke of wanting to be a "kitty deliverer" when she grew up. Amelia tried to correct her. "You mean you want to be a veterinarian." We cracked up after Amelia was immediately and sternly corrected by Melissa, "No, a kitty deliverer!"

So, Melissa spotted a sweatshirt with a kitty on it and picked it out for Amelia. Amelia promised to wear it in the film as a tribute of sorts to Melissa.

Unfortunately, as it turned out, the film was terrible. They contemplated not releasing it at all, but it finally got released in the UK, where they predicted it would do better than in the US. Maybe they thought Brits would find a terribly written script with an American theme more interesting than Americans would. I'm not sure if they were right, but they finally released it in the US, where it officially flopped. I never saw it, so I had no idea whether she kept her promise to Melissa and wore the kitty sweatshirt or not. The film was so bad, it only made it as far as VHS, and never even made it to DVD.

UPDATE: I bought the VHS for $5 (plus free shipping) on eBay. Boy, did it suck! She wore the kitty sweatshirt that Melissa picked out for one scene.

I think, looking at the evidence thus far, you can assume that my ego was as big as a house due to my live-in girlfriend being an Academy Award-nominated actress. I'd be lying if I said this fact meant nothing to me. Exactly what it meant would become much clearer soon, but at that time, I could have cared less about that aspect of her. I was head over heels in love with her. In fact, her acting career would soon become more of a thorn in my side and a threat to our love than anything.

Pressing onward while others around me fell

With just over two years clean and sober, my life was becoming full and exciting, and on top of that, I got my energy back to live it. All PAWS symptoms, especially lethargy, were completely gone. The oft-repeated program slogan "It gets greater later" was becoming my reality. I realized that as long as I stayed clean, kept God in my life, continued attending meetings, and worked the program, there was no limit to what I could accomplish.

Unfortunately, the blessings I was experiencing were not being shared by many of the peers I was in treatment with. Besides Storch being locked up, the bad news started trickling in. Several more peers were in the penitentiary, including Willie, Brad L., and my big brother in treatment—Scott Wolfe.

Scott would be my first big lesson (besides myself) that someone could have good insight, give guidance, and be helpful to others, but not be able to apply their wisdom to themselves. Several others had relapsed too, including the talented Conrad Perez and another piano player—the first person who ever spoke to me at Kedzie House, with the famous words, "We don't put our heads on the wall in Gateway brother"—Clarence Lumpkin. He relapsed and died in a car crash. They said he was being chased by police when the crash occurred.

But the worst news of all was David Grey. The person responsible for stopping me from making a huge mistake by leaving treatment, thereby probably saving my life, was found in a hotel room dead of an overdose.

Although David and I hadn't spoken for a while, we had that forever bond, and I carried the sadness with me for weeks. It's difficult to describe what it's like to feel profound sadness and immense gratitude simultaneously, but it's what I felt. I knew that only a few bad decisions and wrong moves and I could have wound up in any of their shoes.

Closer to home, in my world, was my brother Paul. I got the scoop on him from his wife Carie, or my sister Sue, who was close to Carie. She would pass the news on to me. Paul was at the end of one of his stable cycles and was starting to slip. He still had one foot in "normal" before going off the deep end.

It wasn't long ago that it was hard to stay away from my brother; now, it was hard to be around him. Though he never tried to get me to use with him, I knew I had to keep my distance and was only around him in the presence of other family members. Even though I felt strong in my recovery, based on our history, he still had the most power to get me to say, "fuck it," and suck me back into that lifestyle.

By no means were things perfect in my world. I was still on the planet. I had changed, but the world hadn't. In September of 1989, we got the bad news we all figured would come at some point—my father was diagnosed with lung cancer. He'd been smoking since age 13. He did finally quit smoking. It was the first time I'd ever seen him without a cigarette in his hand since I was born. He was 77 years old and given the option of surgery to remove one-third of one of his lungs. They said it would give him about two more years and that he was too weak for chemo or radiation. My sister Mary Jo didn't think it was a good idea and advised him to skip the surgery and go fishing. He opted to get the surgery. As the situation unfolded, Mary Jo wound up being right.

Lifeline to recovery or bedsheet to addiction?

At work, I was getting a staff perspective of what I had seen as a client in residential treatment. It was a natural cycle of a program going from what we referred to as "top-heavy" to "bottom-heavy." A top-heavy program meant most of the patient population had been there for the better part of their stay and had made some significant progress in their treatment and recovery. The new patients coming in would benefit from this for obvious reasons. Unfortunately, as those patients completed the program, new patients would come in to take their beds, and the program would eventually become bottom-heavy. When this occurred, all it took was one negative, clever, outspoken addict, to be a "ringleader," to turn the unit from a place of treatment and recovery to an almost prison-like environment. The negativity would then spread quickly because the patients who were otherwise neutral would get enveloped and sucked into negativity, due to having few skills to resist.

In Gateway, the program had some built-in mechanisms to deal with this phenomenon, such as house-closing, GI, cancellation of passes and privileges, guilt-dropping sessions, etc. Unfortunately, in a 28-day hospital program, these things were almost impossible to implement due to the brief length of stay. Also, the patients at Lifeline were paying for treatment with insurance from their decent paying jobs. They weren't desperate, broke, homeless, or avoiding incarceration like most of the Gateway population was.

In September of 1989, the perfect storm of negativity came together, complete with a loudmouthed female ringleader, and for the first time, we had a pretty negative group of patients. Some of their antics included staying up after lights-out; cross-talking and other disruptive behaviors in groups; falling asleep in, or missing groups, falling asleep after dinner; being difficult when being woken up to attend in-house 12-step meetings; faking illness to drug seek; or to get out of anything they didn't want to do—and so on.

As far as I was concerned, it was on. With my background, I was not about to back down from a bunch of dope fiends practicing their addiction in treatment. Soon, Blythe and the rest of the staff were "in it to win it" too, and we all rolled up our sleeves and commenced to do battle.

We were determined to take our unit back from a handful of negative patients who didn't want to change. Even the nursing team was onboard, scrutinizing every reported ache and pain, dispensing not so much as an aspirin or bedrest without the utmost scrutiny. The patients would have to be half-dead to get either. I started confronting patients in their dorms who tried to duck out of meetings, saying, "I don't feel good."

"That's okay; don't feel good downstairs in the meeting. Let's go!" For the more full-of-shit patients, I became their addiction's worst nightmare.

They knew we were onto them. It was all coming to a head, and just when it seemed we were starting to get the upper hand, they fought harder and showed they weren't going to give in that easily.

In our next staff meeting, we brainstormed what our next moves should be. "Steve, what do you think?" Blythe asked, hoping I would come through with the insight they needed. At the risk of sounding conceited, at Lifeline, I was like the brokerage firm E.F. Hutton in the TV commercials. "When E.F.

Hutton talks, people listen." It wasn't that I was so great, as it was having experience in treatment and recovery that non-recovering staff didn't have.

My input was based on my TC experience: "You have to identify the ringleader and maybe one or two of the more negative patients and show them the door. It's the old 'kill the head of the snake' thing. Then, you start working with patients who are positive about how to set boundaries, confront negativity, and encourage their peers who are on the fence. That'll straighten the rest of the unit out pretty quickly. I think we all know who the ringleader is (don't recall her name), and I have a list of the key players if you want to hear it."

Blythe and the rest of the staff agreed, but Blythe expressed concern that she'd have to run the decision by the regional director, Nancy Peterson, before she could terminate anyone and that she'd get back to us.

Unfortunately, before we could execute our plan, "Ms. ringleader," possibly sensing that the hammer was about to come down, pulled out all the stops, and pulled an unexpected, desperate dope fiend move. She convinced all the patients on the unit to stage a sit-in and hunger strike in the dayroom. That Saturday, when I went to get the patients for lunch, they refused. Blythe had to be called in on her day off to intervene.

When she arrived, they presented her with a list of their demands in writing. I'm pretty sure handcuffing and muzzling me was on it. Blythe tried to talk some sense into them. She explained the concept of "no pain, no gain," and that treatment is not always comfortable, but to no avail. They dug their heels in even deeper and demanded to speak to Nancy Peterson. Then, they proceeded to lock themselves in the dayroom and refused to open the door until Ms. Peterson was on site and ready to hear their complaints.

Later that day, Nancy Peterson arrived and went in to intervene on her own, leaving Blythe and the staff out of the negotiations. After more than two hours, she emerged from the dayroom and announced she would review their complaints and make some decisions by Monday. In the meantime, she got the patients to resume a somewhat normal schedule.

On Monday morning, Nancy came onto the unit and began executing the very plan we had discussed in our staff meeting—killing the head of the snake. The only problem was…it was the wrong snake!

That morning, Nancy Peterson earned her reputation as a shrewd bitch, and shook up our program to its core, by firing Program Director Blythe Smith and two other counselors who she identified as being "too hard on the patients."

It was my turn next, and she called me into what was Blythe's office.

"Have a seat, Steve. I need to let you know that we've decided to make some big changes to the program here. Blythe Smith and (two other counselors whose names escape me) will no longer be here. We feel we need to create a new culture here and that the previous one was too hard on the patients. Your name has come up as one of the people who is part of that culture. I know you mean well Steve, and being a person in recovery from addiction, I know you want that for all the patients, but not all of them want recovery. It's their money Steve. If they want to waste it, that's up to them. So, what I'm saying is, if they don't want to go to the meeting, they don't have to. Do not force them."

Then, the words that will stick in my head until the day I die: "In fact, if they want to hang out the windows from their bedsheets and smoke crack, you let them—got it? Are you going to be able to do that Steve? Because if you can't, this isn't the right place for you to work. So, what do you say?"

There were only three words that came into my mind. They hung there, in big, bold letters, sort of like the Hollywood sign. And they took up all the space in my mind—FUCK YOU BITCH! But, to my surprise, as I opened my mouth to say them, this is what came out instead: "Sure, I can do it. If that's how you want things—no problem."

She replied, "Okay, good. Then you still have a job. That'll be all then. You can continue whatever you were doing."

I walked out the door and down the hall in a slight state of shock and disbelief, not only about all the changes that occurred in the blink of an eye, but also my response. I was angry, especially about Blythe being fired. She was an awesome person and a great leader who had the entire staff's loyalty and respect. She really cared about the patients, and she was being punished for it.

However, I realized that in that office I had immediately gone into survival mode, and I actually felt pretty good about how I handled it. The old me would have said those other words, and I'd have been out of a job. I had an apartment, bills to pay, child support (through a verbal agreement with Laura at that point), and a starving-artist Academy Award-nominee to support.

The injustice of life had again reared its ugly head, and I realized that it was still one of the hardest things to deal with in life. That day, the patients won, and the staff lost that battle—right? Wrong! Addiction won. The patients lost. We can only speculate about what happened to that group of people. Maybe some were as blessed as I was and got a second chance. But for some, it may have been their one and only chance. And they blew it and wound up being another grim statistic, at least in part, due to being in a bad peer group.

I immediately felt a wave of gratitude as the faces of Benny L., James Minter, Scott Wolfe, David Grey, and John Clark flashed across my mind. I was in treatment, at least for my first stint, with a strong peer group who helped save my life. They weren't perfect, but they respected the program and engaged in treatment as was required, most of the time. I immediately started looking in the newspaper for another job.

Northwest Youth Outreach

I was quickly rewarded for my decision not to compromise my values. My search for a new job led me almost immediately to an ad in the paper for several positions available, including "entry-level counselors." I was familiar with the agency because it was the same agency that had once reached out for me when I was in high school; Northwest Youth Outreach (NYO), which they would soon change to Youth Outreach Services (YOS).

I was excited about the possibility of working with teens. I must have been out of my mind! After all, it's where it all started going downhill for me. I figured if I could rescue even one kid and their family from going through the hell of addiction, it would be worth it.

I arrived and was surprised to find myself in a group interview with eight or nine others looking to fill several available positions. The interviewers consisted of Executive Director Gene Renaldi and Director Rick Velasquez, whom I recognized immediately as the outreach worker who roamed the halls of West Leyden when I was in high school. Also in attendance were several program managers from different offices located throughout the city.

At that time, NYO was the biggest provider of services for adolescents and their families in Chicago and the suburbs. Their services ranged from community outreach to regular and intensive outpatient (OP or IOP) substance abuse treatment services. They also offered psychiatric and psychological services with an emphasis on family therapy. One primary philosophy of the agency was to effectively treat adolescents; you must treat the entire family.

The outreach department was a unique feature of the agency. Those workers were the lowest paid but went into the trenches daily where kids hung out, including schools, parks, fast-food joints, and anywhere else you'd find teens. They did their best to get them off the streets and invited them to several drop-in-centers in the neighborhoods that NYO operated in.

I was one of several people hired that day as an entry-level treatment counselor to...um... develop their new IOP program at their Kedzie Street office. No experience? No problem! This would be a sign of things to come as I would soon discover that "baptism by fire" was part of the culture at NYO.

I think one reason I got hired was telling the story about how Director Rick Velasquez reached out for me back in the day when he was an outreach worker. They got a kick out of the fact that I was once a client, albeit briefly. Addictions management professionals love to hire people whose success they feel they had a hand in. In my case, they absolutely didn't.

In October of 1989, I resigned from my position as milieu therapist, after giving two weeks notice for only the second time in my life. I had mixed feelings about leaving Lifeline. It was my first job in the addiction treatment field, and I had grown close to and bonded with several of the staff. However, I'd be lying if I said that I didn't take a great deal of pleasure in turning in my letter of resignation. I kept it professional, but I did take one subtle parting shot at Nancy Peterson in the middle of the letter: *I am grateful for the experience I have had working for Lifeline, and at least in part, regret having to leave.*

My resignation was a strong enough message that I was NOT okay with letting patients "hang out the windows from their bedsheets and smoke crack."

Baptism by fire

I was no longer a milieu tech and was officially a substance-abuse counselor. I was welcomed to the field unceremoniously with a good swift kick in the nuts! To give you a good idea, let me start by saying that up until I started, NYO had no IOP program. They had outreach, education, and regular outpatient. I was the pioneer selected to develop and run their new, more intensive level of care. Why did they need it? Because they discovered that they had some really sick dysfunctional kids, who came from dysfunctional families—and that regular outpatient wasn't enough to effectively treat them.

Luckily, I had a great team of people to work with, starting with my IOP partner, Jackie. Jackie came from another unique program of NYO's, a foreign exchange program that swapped counselors from other countries with American counselors, for stints in various countries abroad. Jackie was a young, short, stocky blonde from Scotland, with a tough no BS exterior, but a complete softy on the inside that often showed, despite her efforts to hide it. With her Scottish accent, she'd say to me, "Would it be advisable to go out back and *puff Billy* now, Mr. Fiorito?" Interpretation: Is it time for a smoke break?

Then there was Terry—a young, fair-skinned, plain-looking natural beauty. The survivor of a horrendous past that quietly struggled with depression but used her dry, sarcastic sense of humor to cover it. Terry's jokes were so dry, you really had to pay attention, or she'd slip one past you. You'd be walking down the hall later and the joke would hit you, and you'd start laughing, thinking, *Oh, that's what she meant!* Her desk was next to mine, and we shared a file drawer. In it, we created what we called the "Major Dweeb File Folder."

This came about from NYO's phone-screening system. Whenever we took a call from a distraught parent or a kid who was court-mandated to our services, we had to complete a phone screening form. Our job was to get parents to schedule assessments and get them into whatever level of care we recommended for them. As you can imagine, getting some of these people to keep an appointment was like getting a Beatles reunion to happen. They'd often cancel or no-show. With persistence (and sometimes threats) we'd get some of them in, but some of them gave us a major runaround. Terry and I deemed these as "Major Dweebs." Dweeb was a popular term in those days, so we decided to make it an acronym for *deliberately* and *willingly exhibiting evasive behavior*. I can't remember the exact criteria, but once we deemed you a Major Dweeb, your prescreening got put in the folder and we stopped wasting our time on you.

Next was Michael—a seasoned counselor several years older than any of us, who had a low-key demeanor, combined with a sharp sense of humor. Michael imparted much wisdom and experience to the rest of us. One unique skill that he taught us was how to interpret family drawings that we would have the clients draw. He was a master at this and used it with all his clients. From these bad, often stick-figure drawings, he could tell you who was who, and what was going on in that family. It was amazing. He would point out things such as where each family member was positioned in relation to each other, who had hands or feet and who didn't, who had eyes open or closed, or even who had no eyes. He'd also note the size of each character, and what activity or event they were engaged in. Michael was our team's unofficial leader.

Unfortunately, the official leader was hardly a leader at all. In fact, it didn't even feel like she was part of our team. Mary was a flake, who was constantly out running personal errands under the guise of going to "important program manager meetings" and such. Mary wasn't a bad or a mean person (thank God, because that would have made working with her unbearable); she was simply "missing in action." Being sarcastic, clever, irreverent people, a lot of our inside jokes were about Mary. We were all secretly glad she was out of our way and off our backs. Mary was a minor inconvenience, but soon, events led to our dislike of her becoming more intense and more justified.

Jackie and I brainstormed a six-week curriculum for our IOP groups. We had a variety of topics and formats with a few holes to fill here and there, which we decided to wing it and improvise. Of course, those turned out to be some of our best groups and we would soon learn that adolescents respond better to spontaneity than to structure.

I remember spontaneously doing a talk on communication styles that I dubbed "The Anger Mask." It included an overview of passive, aggressive, passive-aggressive, and assertive communication characteristics. I was whipping this whole diagram up on the dry erase board and I just got in "the zone" with it. The zone was a place of deep understanding and insight that I didn't realize I had, until I'd find myself in it. By the end of my presentation, I had a well-put- together diagram of what I was talking about.

Afterward, it was time to break and "puff Billy". The kids left the room, and I followed but noticed that the intern, Chris, had stayed behind, and was writing something at the table in the back. When I asked what he was doing, he said: "I'm copying that. That was really good. Have you done that before?"

"No, that was the first time," I replied. I decided to join him, announcing, "I'm going to copy it too; that's a keeper." We both spent most of our break copying it off the board. As I did, I thought: *Where the hell did that come from?* It was like this divine wisdom had possessed me and was working through me. This would be the first of many of those times. It would become the first of many handouts and worksheets I would create as a counselor.

Despite developing insightful materials, I would soon discover the challenges of working with adolescents and their families. Besides the typical difficulties, like having to call DCFS to come and intervene with a kid who disclosed sexual abuse at home, or convincing a runaway to return home, there were also more unique situations each of us would find ourselves in. For instance, the Middle Eastern family on my caseload that had me negotiating and navigating the relationship between the hardcore Muslim parents and their Americanized teenaged daughter.

Luckily, as bad as NYO was about "throwing you into the middle of the pool to either sink or swim," they were equally as good at providing constant training and education to their staff. I got such a great education at that place on everything from advanced pharmacology to family therapy.

But no amount of training could prepare you for the unique situations you would occasionally find yourself in with this population. I remember talking to the group about different healthy ways to expand consciousness without using drugs and giving examples such as reading, music, film, and other forms of healthy adventure, when one of the client's hands shot up. I called on him, "Yes David." His question? "But without taking acid, how else could you see your friend's head melt?"

This immediately earned the giggles of his fellow group members. I froze like a deer in the headlights for a second, caught off guard, and momentarily stumped by the question. I looked over at Jackie, whose eyes had opened as wide as saucers. Her face seemed to say, *I hope you're not looking at me for an answer to that one; it's all yours.* Lucky for me, I had actually seen my friend's head melt while on acid on more than one occasion. Picturing this in my mind finally led me to the obvious answer: "Well David, the real question is: why do you need to see your friend's head melt?"

Now, he was stumped. Jackie breathed a sigh of relief as she watched me becoming an adolescent substance abuse counselor right before her eyes.

Another challenging situation I found myself in was when one of my clients, Chris, started chronically relapsing after he had been doing well for some time. At the time, he had a lot to lose, including possibly looking at some substantial time being locked up in juvenile detention. In a one-on-one session, I challenged him to dig deep and try to be as honest as he could about why he was continuing to use, despite the consequences he faced. He put his head down and thought for a few moments. He then gave me a brutally honest answer: "I just don't care. I know I should care, but I just don't," he confessed.

Again, I was speechless, and I thought: *What can I say about that? What do you say to someone who tells you they don't care about what happens to them?* My brain searched desperately for an answer until, out of nowhere, the answer came like a lightning bolt. I realized that the "I don't care attitude" was an acquired adolescent defense mechanism, which led me to the obvious answer again in the form of a question. "When did you stop caring Chris?"

He looked up at me, perplexed. "What do you mean?"

"I mean, when did you stop caring? You didn't come into the world not caring. No one does. You cared Chris. You cared about being fed; you cared if your diaper got changed; you cared about your mom and everything else Chris. When did you stop?"

He looked back down at the floor for a while until he mumbled toward it. "When my parents got divorced."

Immediately, I came back with, "What Chris? I didn't hear you."

"When my parents got divorced!" he yelled as he looked up at me, tears rolling down his face.

"Right. I understand," I empathized. Then I leaped to my feet, again as if possessed by some unknown entity and grabbed a marker. I wrote the word CARE on the board. I spontaneously saw the acronym in my mind and wrote: *Can, Acquire, Respect, and Enthusiasm*. I explained to him that the same way he practiced not caring, he could practice caring and again acquire the ability to care. We discussed some things he would need to practice to achieve this.

I remember feeling relieved and that I had done my job—I had given hope to a teen who presented a seemingly hopeless situation.

I'd soon get another sign that I was becoming a counselor at the NYO Christmas party. I got a huge stroke from Executive Director Gene Rinaldi in his "Christmas state of the agency address" to the entire staff. In it, he mentioned standouts or "stars" of the agency and detailed what they did to deserve his attention; the last one on his list, to my surprise, was me.

But the homage he paid me was somewhat different than any of the other accolades he doled out that evening, "And then there's Fiorito, who deals with the most difficult of our clients in the IOP program. We just send the kids to Steve and don't ask any questions," he said looking away and closing his eyes. The entire staff erupted in laughter, and I felt my ego inflating a bit. However, I would soon learn that just like anywhere in life, especially in the field of counseling, what is inflated by pride can be easily deflated.

Adolescents were one of the most difficult populations to work with, and one of my biggest challenges in working with them was yet to come. It would decide whether I really belonged in the counseling field or not.

At times, clients had little or no family involvement and were unable to attend groups due to scheduling conflicts. Such was the case with Kim, a 17-year-old "drop-off"—a kid whose parents would come in for the initial assessment, but then, for any number of reasons, you'd rarely, if ever, get them in the door again. The term "drop-off" implied that they dropped their son or daughter off on our doorstep, said, "Here, fix my kid," and drove away, like we were a Chinese laundry service.

My initial meetings with Kim alleviated some concern about this, when it became apparent that she was brighter, more capable, and more mature than most seventeen-year-olds. She was articulate beyond her years and could hold an intelligent conversation. She caught on quickly and understood the detriments of her substance abuse that I was imparting to her, especially to her future, which looked bright. She was like a sponge, and she seemed to hang on my every word. I thought, *When the student is ready, the teacher shall appear.* I was impressed that she had stopped drinking and using immediately. She appeared to be ready to fend off any peer pressure and to change her life. Apparently, this was not the only thing she was ready for.

The first change I noticed was in her words. She seemed to be sending hints and flirting with me at times. She would make statements like, "If I want someone as together and good-looking as you in my life, I've got to be together first." I could dismiss these comments as her looking up to me as a role model, that is, until the clothes she wore to sessions started changing significantly from sweatshirts, jeans and tennis shoes to skimpy tops, short skirts and heels. Her change in dress revealed that she was mature beyond her years in more ways than just emotionally. She was built like a twenty-five-year-old with curves in all the right places. She was also pretty and blonde.

"Well, she was just seventeen, you know what I mean."

The first line of the famous Beatles composition started popping into my head, and I started to feel like I was getting drawn toward the edge of a cliff, and about to go over. It all culminated at the end of one individual session. I can't remember her exact words, but I remember they were nothing short of an invitation. I played it off and tried to make a joke as she walked away.

My toes were now dangling over the edge, with little chunks of cliff starting to break off and fall. I got a sense of what it was like for Wiley Coyote as he realized the Road Runner had tricked him again. That's when I sat down at my desk and did something that had become an important tool in my recovery and had gotten me through other significant challenges I had faced. I had a heart-to-heart talk with myself. It went something like this…

Me: "Do you want to be in this field?"

Me-2: "Yes, I have a meaningful career for the first time in my life that I'm proud of, and I think I'm actually good at it."

Me: "Okay, then that means you absolutely cannot fuck clients! It's non-negotiable; it's off limits. Do you understand and accept this!?"

I thought hard and even saw pictures in my mind of driving a forklift and installing drapes and blinds. In this case, I also should have pictured the inside of a jail cell, but for some reason that didn't occur to me.

Me-2: "YES, I ACCEPT THIS!" I proclaimed to myself.

Me: "Then you know what you have to do—right?"

Me-2: "Yes, I do."

Kim came to her next session dressed even hotter than the week before. At the end of the session, as she got up to leave, I called her back into the office. I said, "Kim, when you come to session from now on, I want you to go back to wearing jeans and tennis shoes. No more short skirts and heels—okay?" She looked a little shocked. "Okay."

She turned and walked out of the office and that was it. I breathed a sigh of relief. I was officially a counselor.

Return to The Big Apple

At home, Amelia was getting restless with the Chicago film scene. She informed me that she was going out to LA to look for work and get some of her belongings out of storage. She was also going to get her 1963 Chevy and drive it back here. She felt if she had a car, it might help her find work. Fearing I would lose her to Hollywood, my insecurity started to return, and we started fighting a lot. She responded by putting my concerns into their proper place and proceeded to dump them back into my lap: "Your problem honey; figure it out."

Upon her return, she found that the car didn't help much, and this led to a big decision—she decided to move back to New York, which meant after all that, she had to sell "the death trap!" This was my nickname for a car that I felt had no business being on the road. Having a car in Manhattan was the equivalent of having to take care of a new puppy and your elderly grandma, while working two jobs, and going to college. There was virtually nowhere to park on the street. The street-sweeping laws were ridiculous and required you to move your car every other day, or face tickets or towing. As a result of her announcement, we got into a huge fight, and she wound up moving back home with her mother.

On the upside of this turn of events, it helped me write the third verse and finish the song I was writing for her. Since getting clean and sober, I found my songs would almost always write themselves right up to the third verse, and then, I'd usually struggle. This song was no exception but upon its completion I'd eventually record my second complete song.

My relationship with Amelia gave me the sense that I might be a "diamond in the rough." However, at that time, I felt more "rough" than I did "a diamond". The creativity, pent up by years of addiction, continued to swell and find its way out. One part of the song asks...

> *Was it all just another show?*
> *Another script you were reading from, just to get you through.*

It certainly felt like it. But as it turned out, it was not the end. We were in love, and although we no longer lived together, we made up, and our relationship continued. She moved back to New York in April, and I was officially in my first long-distance relationship. How could I handle that? The same way I handled everything in those days—one day at a time.

Chief Seattle's Reply

The year 1990 would prove to be important. It was full of changes, adventures, highs and lows. With a foundation of three years in recovery under my belt, I was about to experience important emotional and spiritual growth, along with an expanding awareness of the world around me, which until I got clean, I never paid much attention to or noticed. The caring that I had referred to with my adolescent client Chris, was happening to me.

Like it says in the AA Promises: *We will lose interest in selfish things and gain interest in our fellows. Self-seeking will slip away. Our whole attitude and outlook upon life will change.*

Caring became an unexpectantly interesting phenomenon, and a process that continued to expand the longer I remained in recovery. I started caring about my kids, then the staff and my peers in treatment, then myself, followed by my family. Then it started to expand, and I started caring about my community, the city of Chicago, then the country, until finally, I started to care about the world and the planet. With this ever expanding "giving a shit," came an unexpected emotional price, especially when I became acutely aware of how in trouble the planet really was—it made me sad and angry.

My newfound love for the planet came to a head at the place that Freddy and I often went to drink coffee, hang out, and talk recovery—Café Voltaire on North Clark Street. I remember going there alone on a Sunday in April and grabbing something to read while I ate my eggs espresso. This, along with going to the laundromat and washing clothes, became enjoyable rituals for me.

At times, I enjoyed the peace and solitude of being alone and I no longer felt lonely. The gentle whirring of the dryers, the warmth, the smells, and occasional people-watching while reading the newspaper, became a meditative relaxing experience for me.

The reading material I grabbed that day was a special publication celebrating what I believe was the first global Earth Day ever. A few pages in, was an article called "Chief Seattle's Reply." It was supposedly the chief of the Puget Sound Indians reply to then President Franklin Pierce's offer to buy the tribe's land and set them on a reservation. I later learned that it was likely embellished and only loosely based on anything the great chief said.

I always had a soft spot for the plight of Native Americans. It started with a very poignant commercial from the early 1970s. It depicted scenes of pollution, culminating with people in a car throwing litter out the window at the feet of an American Indian, adorned in full Indian dress from before the turn of the century. He turns and faces the camera to reveal a single tear rolling down his cheek. Heart-wrenching.

Then there was the 1971 film *Billy Jack*, which was one of my favorite movies at the time. The underlying theme is the half-breed, ex-Green Beret, Kung Fu Master hero, who stands up for and protects the mistreated peacenik college students in a southwestern town. He does this mostly by kicking the asses of the white racist rednecks, who harassed and intimidated them.

Being a Chicago Bears fan and one myself, I always identified with and rooted for the underdog. I also developed a hatred for littering that is still a pet peeve of mine. These things planted the seeds of empathy for Native Americans that came to some sort of fruition that day.

Here is just a piece of that article that I read as I ate my eggs…

"How can you buy or sell the sky, the warmth of the land? The idea is strange to us. If we do not own the freshness of the air, and the sparkle of the water, how can you buy them?

Every part of the earth is sacred to my people. Every shining pine needle, every sandy shore, every mist in the dark woods, every clearing, and humming insect is holy in the memory and experience of my people. The sap which courses through the trees carries the memories of the red man.

The white man's dead forgot the country of their birth when they go to walk among the stars. Our dead never forget the beautiful earth, for it is the mother of the red man. We are part of the earth, and it is part of us. The perfumed flowers are our sisters, the deer, the horse, the great eagle, these are our brothers. The rocky crests, the juice in the meadows, the body heat of the pony, and man all belong to the same family.

So, when the great Chief in Washington sends word that he wishes to buy our land, he asks much of us. The great Chief sends word he will reserve us a place so that we can live comfortably to ourselves. He will be our Father, and we will be his children. So, we will consider your offer to buy our land. But it will not be easy, for this land is sacred to us.

This shining water that moves in the streams and rivers is not just water, but the blood of our ancestors. If we sell you land, you must remember that it is sacred, and you must teach your children that it is sacred and that each ghostly reflection in the clear water of the lakes tells of events and memories in the life of my people. The water's murmur is the voice of my Father's Father."

As I continued reading, out of nowhere, as with the Indian in that commercial, a tear began rolling down my face. At that moment, I experienced an awakening of how much I loved and appreciated the beautiful planet we lived on. Simultaneously, I was experiencing the pain and sadness of the realization of how we were taking it for granted and trashing it.

The incident at Voltaire inspired a creative burst and I went home and wrote most of this song. Of course, I mean all but the third verse, which I likely struggled to write for the next month or two.

Chief Seattle's Reply

There once was a man who knew the truth,
Brother to the eagle, he was one with the earth,
And the white man forgot from where he came,
Bought the land and his soul which were one and the same

The water, the blood of earth and of man,
The perfume of flowers, the trees, and the sand,
So you think you can buy these with a wave of your hand?

So you dug and you sawed for what you thought was your need,
Shunning natural laws that you still do not heed,
And you'll reap what you sew 'cause you've planted the seed,
Of selfishness, hatred, power, and greed

And you said to the Chief, "Let us show you the way,"
But you needed to listen, not teach on that day,
The earth is the mother of mountain and man,
You've all but destroyed with a wave of your hand

The sight of your cities pains the red man's eyes,
You've turned into haze; what were once the blue skies,
The clatter and noise, insults the ears,

Of the great Chief, I know, from beyond, he still hears,
And the rains from the heavens are really his tears

They say that the meek shall inherit the earth,
But I think it's the Red Man because from their birth,
No one's surpassed their love for the land,
That you've all but destroyed with a wave of your hand

And you said to the Chief, "Let us show you the way,"
But you needed to listen, not teach on that day,
The earth is the mother of mountain and man,
You've all but destroyed with a wave of your hand

In the beginning of this book, I told you how the beauty of the planet and beautiful weather had slipped into the background, and I barely noticed them. All at once, my awareness and appreciation came back, full force. I wasn't alone in experiencing this awakening either. In 12-step meetings in the spring of each year, I'd hear what I'd later refer to as "the weather comment." Inevitably, on a beautiful spring day, someone would comment about the weather as if it were the first time they'd ever noticed it. It would usually go something like this: "I was walking down the street today, and the birds were chirping, and the flowers were blooming, and the sun was shining, and I thought to myself: 'Wow! What a beautiful day! I'm glad I'm alive!'"

As the emotional thaw of recovery continued, my spiritual connection to the planet and the universe did too. Those of us who didn't use it as a flimsy excuse to get high, developed a deep appreciation for the simple beauty of nature and pleasures of just being alive.

Hello, old friend

After the Saturday morning meeting at LPAC, I decided to head over to the Mustard Seed to catch another meeting and see who was there to hang out with. About two-thirds of the way there, I looked at my watch and realized that they were probably between meetings, but I decided to stop by, just to see who might still be hanging around. This was something I did on occasion, since my social life revolved around the people who frequented a handful of local Alano clubs and meetings. I was disappointed when I saw only one solitary figure emptying the ashtrays from the previous meeting.

As I watched him from behind, his short stocky build and walk seemed familiar to me. He bent down to empty several ashtrays into the larger can, so I saw his profile from across the room. I called out, "Willie?!" He turned immediately and answered, "Yeah?!" as if startled out of a daydream.

"Oh my God—it's you! I thought it looked like you, but I couldn't see your face. What are you doing here?"

"I just got out of the joint."

We walked to each other and gave each other a hug. I called out his self-proclaimed nickname: "Big Daddy Woo Woo!"

"I heard you had some time to do."

"Yeah, I caught one of my cases on that pass I went on that I almost didn't come back from. You know your counselor, Ron Orlando, busted me down and took my pass. I felt the punishment didn't fit the crime, so I appealed the bust to Arnold. He gave me my pass back. I almost died on that pass!"

"Wow! I don't think I knew that story until now. Ron was a ball-buster, but he was usually on the money. I remember the day you made it back though. Sitting on the prospect chair with two black eyes!"

I laughed. Willie didn't. I continued, "I'm in contact with Storchy. He writes and calls me collect sometimes. He told me you guys had been writing."

"Yeah, Mark told me that you guys were keeping in touch. He should be getting out soon," Willie replied.

"Yep. Next month, I think."

"I heard you're a counselor."

"Yeah, I'm working with adolescents at Northwest Youth Outreach. I'm studying for my certificate in alcohol and drug counseling. Storch told me in his last letter that he has two of the books I need to study to take the test. I've been meaning to call his mom to arrange to go over there and pick them up."

"I've got a degree in counseling. I just finished it in the joint. I really need a job. Are they hiring over by you?"

"They're always hiring. That place is like a counselor puppy mill. They're huge. They have like five or six locations. Here's the address and phone number." I wrote on a piece of paper that I had in my pocket. "Talk to Mary Morgan and I'll put in a word for you."

Within a week Willie was hired and assigned to the now growing IOP program at the East Office with me.

Soon after Willie was hired, tensions started to build as our "fearless leader," Mary, was missing in action more and more. Luckily, our actual leader, Mike, stepped up even more and made decisions when we were unsure about how to handle situations that would arise, and with the adolescent population, plenty did. When Mary was there, we started overhearing heated discussions between her and Mike, seeping from under her office door. Jackie's eyes would get like saucers, and Terri would just give me the subtle raise of her eyebrows. Mike would emerge and give us the "I'll tell you all about it, after she leaves" look, which we all knew she would, and usually sooner than later.

Then one day, he emerged from one of those meetings with a different look on his face. He was huffing and puffing and obviously distraught. One of us immediately asked, "What happened?"

Mike's response? "She fired me."

"She what!?" Jackie exclaimed, her eyes now popping out of her head.

"She fired me," he repeated.

We all jumped up from our desks in a state of shock and encircled him as Mike began to clear out his desk.

"Why?!" Jackie exclaimed.

"Too many philosophical differences," Mike replied, combined with the old standby when there's no legitimate reason— "It's just not a good fit."

In reality, Mike was calling her on her bullshit and was likely to start going over her head and blowing the whistle on her. She likely viewed him as a serious threat to her position.

The anger boiled over in all of us. You could feel that it was about to explode, when Jackie proclaimed with her fiery Scottish temper, "We'll strike! We'll all march over to the main office straight away and let them know that we refuse to work with that bitch anymore, and Michael needs to be reinstated!"

Everyone agreed, the torches were lit, and pitchforks were grabbed! Mike expressed his appreciation for our support, but being the level-headed professional that he was, tried to dissuade us from doing it.

After he got his stuff, we said our goodbyes and hugged and that was it. After Mike left, the talk of going to the main office to protest the decision was rekindled and quickly reached a boiling point again. Jackie, Terri, and the intern Chris had gone as far as putting their jackets on and were ready to walk just over a mile on Irving Park Road to the main office, until I stopped them.

This is what I said to them; "Listen, I'm just as upset as you are about this, but I can't walk out of here and take that kind of chance. I have an apartment, bills, and two daughters. I can't afford to lose this job. What we need to do is outlast her. I'm making it a goal to still be here after she's long gone."

It worked. Everyone started to calm down, get their heads on straight, and get back to work, albeit begrudgingly.

As Jackie and I started to prepare for that evening's IOP group, Mary called me into her office. She announced that she was leaving for the day (what a surprise!) and noting that Willie hadn't come in yet, she informed me that she did not want the kids to know that Mike was fired and instructed me to inform Jackie and Willie of this directive. Mike had a good relationship with our kids and would always talk to them when they came to group, so there was a good chance they'd ask about him. I assured her I would, and she left. I passed the directive on to Jackie right away, then Willie upon his arrival.

Later that evening, in an NA meeting, I talked about the incident and noted that I had been "the voice of reason" that day. Imagine that. Me, the voice of reason. Miracles really do happen.

The following Monday morning, I walked into the building, and as I headed down the hall to my office, I noticed Mary's door was open, and Wille was standing across from Mary, who was seated at her desk. She called to me as I passed. I turned around and stuck my head in.

"Can you come in here once you get situated?"

"Sure, let me go drop off my stuff, and I'll be right in."

Upon entering her office, I looked at Willie's face and saw fear.

"What happened here on Friday?" she asked.

"I'm not sure what you mean."

"When I came in today, one of your kids was here for a family session and asked me why I fired Mike. He said Willie told them. I asked you to tell everyone not to tell any of the kids that Mike was fired."

"And I did," I replied, looking over at Willie.

"No, you didn't Steve," he proclaimed.

I had to gather my wits due to being caught off guard and in a temporary state of shock by his blatant lie.

"Yes, I did Willie, and you know I did."

"No, you didn't Steve," he doubled down.

I couldn't believe what I was hearing. I helped this guy get a job and now he was throwing me under the bus to cover his mistake. After a few more rounds of "Yes I did; no, you didn't," Mary had heard enough and sent Willie out of the room. She asked me again, and I explained that I *did* tell Willie and even repeated what Mary had told us to say if anyone asked, that Mike "was no longer at NYO and had moved on." I added that Willie was lying, and that he was likely afraid of getting fired, since he was still in a probationary period. I further stated that had I forgotten to tell him, I'd have had no problem admitting that. That seemed to make sense to her, and that was the end of it.

Willie and I were friends and were now hanging in the same circles and going to meetings with the same people. Realizing that Willie was afraid to lose the job he desperately needed, led to a kneejerk lie, and helped me to forgive him and let it go. It was put even further in the rearview mirror, when our mutual friend, my confidant and main man throughout treatment, Mark Storch, was released from prison. It felt like we were "getting the band back together." The only thing that lingered and bothered me was that Willie never admitted it, even outside of work. He never apologized, that I recall.

Love letters from New York

I received my first letter from Amelia early in May 1990. We talked on the phone after she left, but neither of us had a ton of money for that, so writing letters seemed a better option. Besides, she was from that era where people actually wrote letters to each other...

Hi Baby,
I've got a great view from my kitchen window down to the street. There's the NYC Skate Shop (headquarters for skateboarders - I get a free show @ 5 PM every day) and I can see a store called "The Smoke Pit" (?) From what I can see it's a kinky leather scene store. I'll have to check that out. From my front (living room) I can see trees from Thompkins Sq. Park across the street.

She went on to tell me that she bought a fiddle and bow from a thrift store on payments and that she owed $80 on it. *Barely scraping by and she buys a fiddle! That's my girl,* I thought.

When you come you must bring your guitar and we'll play in the park. And we'll take the Staten Island Ferry (just 5 cents) to see the Statue of Liberty.

It's one of the things I loved about her—she was this educated, worldly actress, while at the core, there was this vagabond gypsy, just like me. I'd kiddingly refer to her as "my bag-lady girlfriend" as she also had a propensity for garbage picking (mostly furniture) and restoring things. She asked me to send her a tape of music I was working on. Little did she know, I was laying down the rough tracks to her song "Amelia" and hoped to surprise her with it.

Please come to me in my dreams. You can if you try. I'll be looking for you my darling man. Kiss me,
(your) Amelia

I started planning my first trip to the Big Apple for June, but as my father got sicker, some in my family started questioning whether going to New York for nine days was a good idea. I made my decision after stopping by my parent's apartment to install a handrail so that my dad could go up the six or eight steps to the front door and sit outside.

The handrail was very significant and symbolic to me. My mother told me later how much my dad appreciated and used it. To me, it represented the turning of the tide and me finally doing something important for the man who was there for me all my life. My dad—Johnny the drapery man—did everything from picking me up from the police station at all hours of the night, to giving me his last five dollars. I had finally become a man, and for once, I was the one with the tape measure and the screw gun in my hand. The handrail was perfect, strong and sturdy. It contributed to the quality of what little life he had left.

I talked to him about where I was going in New York to visit Amelia, and I asked about where he spent his first eight years of life. It was near Amelia's neighborhood. His eyes lit up when I said that I wanted to see where he lived as part of my trip. He gave me his address which I can't recall. I remember the intersection of 103rd and Broadway near the East Harlem area.

He reminisced and shared some of his childhood memories as only my dad could. I could almost feel what it was like to be living in that time. Now, I was even more intrigued and excited to go, and after our conversation, though he never said it, I got the distinct feeling that he wanted me to go.

My mom and sister Sue expressed concern that he might pass away while I was gone. I explained that it would be okay if that happened, because I felt it was more important to both of us that I not only went to New York to see where he lived, but that I was finally living the life I was capable of, and he was proud of that. It would be a kind of full circle for him. As his life was coming to an end, he would revisit, through my eyes, where it began 78 years ago.

Culture Shock!

I decided to take the train to New York. Metra was fairly inexpensive back then, and I figured I could see the sights, since I had never been east of Indiana before. I'd have almost 20 hours to kill from Union Station to Penn Station, so I brought my Walkman and assorted cassette tapes with me. I guess I was just trying to keep my mind off the butterflies in my stomach that had formed when I realized I was really going to New York to see Amelia. I hadn't seen her in over a month. It was all new territory for me.

As I made my way through Pennsylvania, I was struck by the beauty of the state. The landscape of lush green rolling hills was peppered with old-world church steeples, ornate buildings from the turn of the century, and some even earlier. It looked sort of like I imagined it after the American Revolution.

Upon arrival at Penn Station, everything changed after I set foot out the doors and onto the street. The quietude of the train, and hypnotic rhythm of the train going over the tracks, was replaced by the urban noise pollution of horns honking, people yelling, and every other type of noise you can imagine.

I remember thinking, *Welcome to The Big Apple,* when out of nowhere, two cabs drove from opposite directions straight at me, almost colliding head-on in an attempt to get my fare. They got out of their cabs and started arguing violently and threatening each other. I stood there, bags (a real suitcase, no more big green garbage bags) and guitar case in hand, with my mouth hanging open. I decided to go with the slightly less violent Middle Eastern guy.

"Ver you goink?"

I told him the address.

"Oh, you goink to de East Village. Are you ardist or acdor?"

"I'm a musician."

"Same difference," he quipped back.

The small talk suddenly ceased when I noticed that my little friend was doing about 100 mph and making some lane changes that would have rivaled the best of the Indy 500! I had forgotten all about my desire to see Amelia as I realized I would never see her again, because…I was gonna die! I closed my eyes and awaited the inevitable crash and explosion.

The next time I opened them, I was expecting to be in heaven (wishful thinking?), however, what I saw couldn't in a million years be mistaken for heaven. I felt like I was in a deranged demented circus—a "freakshow" of sorts. The sidewalks were packed with every kind of person from every corner of the world you could think of.

When I got out of the cab, the beautiful bouquet of spring was interrupted, and my nostrils were immediately assaulted with the unmistakable smell of garbage. There were businessmen in suits with briefcases in hand, stepping over homeless people sleeping on the sidewalk, passing people with green mohawks, the leather clad, to the scantily clad, and about every 60 feet, someone sitting on a stoop, in a garbage-picked chair, or just on the sidewalk, shaking change in their cup and begging: "Spare a quarter"? I immediately bought a T-Shirt that I saw being sold, that read, *No I Don't Have a Quarter!*

I was able to see firsthand what the song "The City," by Fleetwood Mac guitarist-singer-songwriter Bob Welch, was talking about…

Well, there's something wrong with New York, it's a prison without walls,
I won't set foot there, I just don't like that place at all,
Now, you might call it sophistication, but I say time is running out."

"Two dolla' and fifty cent please."

I paid him, and the cabbie from Hell sped off to terrorize his next victim.

The street was packed on both sides with small shops that mostly alternated between basement to street level. Typically, the three floors above were dwellings like Amelia's. Each shop was a unique, creative brainchild of the owner and specialized in something very specific. I remember a button shop that sold only buttons. Every shape, and color of button that was ever made in the universe was in that store. My curiosity got to me so, yes, I did go in.

As I came up to Amelia's building, my mouth was hanging wide open, but as the initial shock wore off, I was able to feel the creative energy, excitement, and pulsating overflow of humanity that Greenwich Village was known for. It had become famous for being a Mecca of new progressive ideas, whether political, artistic, or cultural—such as gay rights and racial equality. It became the center of the "Bohemian" movement (socially unconventional artsy types). A kind of East Coast version of what San Francisco was in the 1960s, it was famous for its alternative culture including The Beat poets of the 1950s (Beatniks) and the experimental Living Theater and Theater of the Absurd.

It was in essence a creative smorgasbord of all the arts and played host to a plethora of famous actors, writers, artists, and musicians—since before the turn of the 20th century. Amelia fit right in.

I rang her bell and as she buzzed me in, the butterflies in my stomach reached their peak. She opened the door and gave me that smirky smile that she sometimes used to try to control her feelings for me, but her eyes could never lie, and they would sparkle with passion.

"Good. You brought your guitar!"

"Of course I did. I never leave home without it."

After we both unleashed that repressed passion onto each other for forty seconds or so, I told her about my cab experience. I went to the window that overlooked the street and expressed the feelings that the city brought up in me, good and bad.

"Wow! People just step over the 'bumskis' sleeping on the sidewalk?" I said, narrating it as it happened on the street below.

She smiled ear to ear and seemed to delight in sharing things that were now old to her, but new to me. At times, she lived vicariously through my excitement and I'm sure it brought her back to a time when it was all new and exciting. I believe it's one of the reasons she was attracted to me. Lately, it all seemed so laborious, frustrating, and disappointing for her.

"Listen to what I learned on the fiddle."

She broke it out and played some simple tune for me.

"Very nice! Listen to my new song, 'Chief Seattle's Reply'!" I told her the story of the inspiration as I took my guitar out. Then I played it for her.

"That's a great song. You need to record that!"

Her apartment was decorated in "struggling artist Bohemia"—a mixture of antiques, modern art, and practical what-nots. This included a chair that she garbage picked and refinished. Then, I looked up and noticed her Oscar nomination plaque hanging on the wall. It was the first time I had ever seen it.

It was a nice-looking plaque that didn't quite represent her mixed feelings about it. It represented accomplishment and failure, all at the same time.

"Your plaque looks nice there."

Then, right as the idea popped into my head, I blurted out; "If I were you, I'd put it to use and start teaching acting."

This would be the first of many times I would suggest to her that she give up chasing around a career in films and teach instead. Unfortunately, she wasn't quite ready to let go of the dream.

My first trip to New York was filled with new adventures like taking the Staten Island Ferry, and seeing the Statue of Liberty, but just walking around the Village was enough of an adventure.

This included dinner in Soho, and shopping and lunch at the shops on St. Marks Place. I bought a cool Doors T-shirt there, but the real bargains were the black markets on the sidewalks on Broadway or Canal Street. Amelia tried to discourage me from buying a nice travel bag because the locals all knew that a lot of the suitcases, bags, and clothing items were once people's luggage. In other words, they were stolen.

Later, we visited her brother Dan at his gallery and went to dinner with him and long-time partner Sharon, at their apartment Bleecker Street. Amelia also surprised me with comps that she received from the Steppenwolf Theater Company to take me to my first Broadway Play. The production of the classic book *The Grapes of Wrath* starred Gary Sinise (Forrest Gump's friend) and Lois Smith (too many to list). What a great first Broadway show! They had the coolest special effect I've ever seen in a play—a thunderstorm, using real water raining down onto the stage. The technical director and the cast created a great optical illusion of being caught in the downpour. The rain fell only into a trough downstage that couldn't be seen by the audience. It created an effective illusion that the entire stage was getting rained on. It was impressive.

Afterwards, we went backstage and met the cast, though I met Sinise only briefly as he fled his dressing room and the theater. I spent most of the time with Lois Smith, a great American actress with a huge resume of films, television and theatre. Also backstage after the show was Constance Shulman, who was very recognizable at the time for a series of commercials she did as "Patti Mayonnaise" for the food giant Kraft. I said, the only thing I could think of at the time, "You're very funny in those commercials." She thanked me.

My first major exposure to celebrities was topped off by having lunch with several theatre and film people including Rae Dawn Chong, best known by most people as the mixed-race daughter of Tommy Chong of Cheech and Chong, the famed drug culture comedy duo. By this time, she had made a name for herself for television, film, and theatre roles. I was a bit starstruck not only by her radiant beauty, which was even more vibrant in person than it was on the screen, but also by the fact that I had just seen her in a film called *Tales from the Darkside*. She was beautiful in that film and had some very hot love scenes. She was a sweet girl, with a warm infectious smile.

The next day was a perfect opportunity to see the place where my father spent the first years of his life. I took the bus and got off at that corner of Broadway at 108th Street. The area seemed very Latino and a bit dicey, but I didn't mind. I guess that's the upside of being an ex-junkie—you can feel comfortable in the worst neighborhoods.

I got off the bus and walked the block or so, to the address my father gave me. As I got close, I started to see a row of the original five-story buildings that I knew were there when my father played on this street. You could tell, not only by how rundown they were, but also by the style of architecture and the detailed ornate trim. For a moment, I felt what it was like to be back there right before the Roaring Twenties kicked in.

As I came to the end of that row of buildings, there was just one more building—a big modern building at the end of the block on the corner. It was then that I became saddened by the realization that my father's building was gone. It had been torn down to make way for this building. I believe it was a nursing home if I recall. Though I was disappointed that his building was gone, I took solace in the fact that parts of the block were still intact as they were when he was there, and that I was able to get a sense of what it was like in that neighborhood when it was inhabited by mostly Italian immigrants.

The only blemish on the trip came a few days before I was to take the train home. It happened at a dinner party Amelia hosted at her apartment. In attendance there were ten or so local actors, artists, directors, and other film and theater industry people. At first, I sailed through, playing a few songs on my guitar accompanied by Amelia. She harmonized background vocals on one or two that we had learned when we lived together. I think they genuinely appreciated my songwriting abilities. I also think they were impressed that I was a counselor that worked with teens. However, soon after dinner, I seemed to hit a wall and I "turned back into a pumpkin."

As people gathered in different rooms of the small apartment, the conversations became very worldly, philosophical, historical and even political. These were subjects that I had no experience, or interest in at that time. I was out of my league, and I started to withdraw. My only escape was to the two rooms that remained, which soon became nowhere to run to, when they too became occupied by Amelia's friends. To make matters worse, Amelia not only didn't protect me in these situations, but would even throw me under the bus and kind of pile on, by putting me on the spot, or laughing at a misstatement I'd make. I felt embarrassed and out of place, but I found a way to keep my low self-esteem and insecurities at bay, and get through the evening by relying on simple, yet powerful wisdom and truths I had acquired through my recovery.

Unfortunately, with my ego still being somewhat fragile, it resulted in anger, fighting, and bickering after everyone left. Most of the anger was about her "hanging me out to dry" and how unimportant I became when it came to the pursuit of her acting career. I felt betrayed. I believe we didn't speak for a day or two before I went home. Soon after my arrival home, I received a letter. An excerpt from it is below…

Today I was thinking a lot about myself and my personality and wondering why you love me when I seem so obnoxious to myself. Don't get me wrong. I love how I am when I'm alone, but then, thinking about how I act around other people just makes me cringe. I'm really tortured. I think I need to go to charm school. Why do I need to impress total strangers, people I don't care anything about?

Why indeed Ms. Amelia? I guess "tortured" was an appropriate word. She was torn between a dream that almost came true, and still could, and the true love of a man who was only a "possibility". I didn't even qualify for a credit card at the time, and possibly, never would. A dream that would have appeased her mother's expectations and possibly mended the hole in her soul left by Charles's death. She again faced becoming the forgotten "Amelia who?" Ironically, it was around this time that another actress's star was on the rise. She had a striking resemblance to Amelia when she was young. Was this another sign from God that it was time for her to stop chasing the dream? Honestly, I felt it was. I could hear the Hollywood elite in my mind: *Who needs a 42-year-old Amelia Hamilton when we've got a 26-year-old lookalike?*

As the summer temperatures increased, and the clothes on women decreased, I would find being in a long-distance relationship more challenging. I was a young man, newly sober, horny, and had never been in this situation before. Sounds like excuses—doesn't it? Maybe, but it was my reality at the time. I started to wonder if our love could survive the challenges we faced.

Go and tell your father about Me

After arriving home, I was driving through the old hood on my way to the expressway when, out of nowhere, the voice of God said to me, "Go and tell your father about Me." I say it was the voice of God because it's the only explanation that makes any sense. It certainly wasn't me telling me to go tell my father about me. That wouldn't make sense because my father already knew about me. I had just passed my parent's apartment on Mannheim Road, so I pulled into a parking lot, turned around, and headed back to their apartment.

When I arrived, my mother was in the kitchen cooking and my father was in the living room watching TV. I gave my mother a kiss and stole a taste of whatever she was cooking. I explained that I was passing through and thought I'd stop by to see how they were doing. I told her about my trip, and she likely responded with some "Albieisms," which I'm sure included "Shave that shit off your face" and "I hope you're saving your money."

I went into the living room, where my dad was watching TV in his pajamas and robe. This was completely out of character for him as it was late afternoon and went against his daily ritual of shaving, dressing, two soft-boiled eggs, and reading the paper for an hour. Of course, the morning cigarette had been eliminated soon after his cancer diagnosis. He looked gaunt and pale and had lost more weight from the last time I saw him.

I told him about my trip to New York and broke the bad news about his building being gone, but that some of the adjacent buildings were still there. Then I said the most important thing I had ever said to my father: "Ya know, it occurred to me that I never heard you say anything about God my entire life. I don't even know if you believe in God or not."

I was relieved by his response, "I believe in God."

"Do you ever talk to God or ask for His help?" I asked.

"I've always had my own private relationship with God," he responded.

"Good! I'm glad to hear that. Because, you know that God is the reason that I'm sitting here right now, clean and sober and talking to you—don't you? It was God's power, not mine, that finally allowed me to stop using drugs. I just wanted you to know that."

Surprisingly, he responded, "I know."

"Okay, well, that's all I wanted to say. I gotta get going. I'll talk to you soon."

"Okay, see you later," he said.

It was the last time I would ever see him, and the last words we would ever speak to each other. Within days, he became bedridden. I heard that the last words he said were to my mother… "You're beautiful."

On July 17, 1990, he passed away in the ambulance that my mother called when he started severely laboring while trying to breathe. I believe they call it "the death rattle." My whole life, Johnny the Drapery Man hardly said two words to me, but somehow, that wasn't so important to me anymore. Any wound that was once there seemed to have disappeared. More importantly, our last words were so meaningful that they seemed to make up for years of bad communication. For that, I have always been grateful. This was the song I wrote soon after his death as a tribute to my father…

Silent Man

The silent man gets the call at 2:00 a.m.
Awakened from a dream, of how his life once had been,
And the cop on the line says "Come and get your son,
He's in trouble once again, and we caught him on the run," caught him on the run

So half asleep, he shuffles out the door,
Going through the motions, you can tell he's done this before,
And the steam from his breath fogs up the dashboard light,
But he braves the bitter cold, Chicago winter's night, cold Chicago night

My old man arrives like I knew he would,
Not a word to say to me, he knew it wouldn't do any good,
'Cause I could never seem to make his trips worthwhile,
'Cause the trouble just got worse, as the years went slowly by, all those years went by

Silent man,
You never had much to say but now I understand,
Silent man
Now I realize, you said more with your eyes, than any words can

Then one day my troubles they did pass,
I think he knew it all along, he knew it just couldn't last,
And I'm thankful that he finally got to see,
Before he drew his last breath, a change come over me, all the change in me.

Silent man,
You never had much to say but now I understand,
Silent man
Now I realize, you said more with your eyes...than any words can, Silent man

  The song wasn't quite finished, so I wasn't able to play it at his services. Throughout the ordeal, my brother Paul was a basket case. He was totally distraught and spent most of the services hiding out in the kitchen of the funeral home or elsewhere, chain-smoking cigarettes, and yelling at the kids. I could see that he was absolutely in a perpetual state of discomfort. I guess I can attribute some of his behavior to having a longer and in some ways, a more meaningful relationship with our father, but most of it I attribute to Paul being in active addiction at the time of my father's death.

Meanwhile, I was greeting people at the entranceway, telling stories about my father, remembering the good times, comforting my mother, and intermittently visiting the casket and shedding tears. In other words, I was grieving like a normal person. It was a stark contrast how my brother and I handled our father's death. I felt our roles starting to reverse. I felt like I was his big brother, and to be honest, it felt awkward and uncomfortable.

A few weeks after his services, I stopped by for a dual purpose: to see how my mom was doing and to ask for my father's mandolin. Being the only serious musician in our family, I figured it was only right that I should have it. Besides, I was thinking of using it in the studio on the song "Amelia," which I was getting ready to start recording with Kenny. I never played mandolin other than plucking around with my dad's here and there, but I'd figure something out. When I told her that I had come to get the mandolin, she informed me that it was already spoken for, and she'd given it to my sister Mary Jo.

"What?!" I exclaimed.

"Well, she'll keep it safe so it can be kept in the family."

"But I'm the only musician in this family, and you gave my father's mandolin to Mary Jo, who's never picked up a musical instrument her entire life!?"

"I'm sorry, but we felt it was best."

"You did!? Well, I think it's best if I leave!" And with that, I stormed out the door, cursing under my breath.

I got in my car, incensed as I drove away. This was the last straw. My discontentment with my family had been building for some time. It started with my sister Sue calling me at work and stating what amounted to: "This is what we decided we're doing with daddy's services, and this is how much you owe." No one asked for my opinion or input, and some of the expenses I felt were uncalled for. This is how it had been all my life, and in the past, it was justified for obvious reasons, but now, I was a responsible adult, and I wanted to be treated like one and have some input in these matters.

Then there was the time that I tried to borrow someone's car to see my kids because my car needed repairs. No one would do it. After three years of being clean and sober, they still didn't trust me. Time to think and talking about it in meetings helped me realize why I was so upset. Not only was I insulted, but my family often unknowingly made me feel like the person I used to be and worked *so* hard not to be anymore. My family could still make me feel like a lying, thieving, junkie who couldn't be trusted. Everyone else in my life made me feel respected and trusted. Some people even started to look up to me. It was starting to bring me down, and the mandolin was the last straw.

Ron Orlando's statement, "If my mother got between me and my recovery, I'd cut her loose," started to make a whole lot more sense. People in meetings helped me see it but also reminded me that I had spent many years as that other person and had only been this person for just over three years. They also reminded me that my relapse had really shook my family's trust in me. With all these things considered, I still made the decision at that time that it was in my best interest to distance myself from my family. I don't think I put it in exactly those terms then, but I was in the process of building strong self-esteem for the first time in my life and it just wasn't good for me to be around them.

Within a month or so, they started noticing that I wasn't showing up for birthday parties, so my mother called me. Luckily, I was able to explain my feelings without losing my temper. She got it. She said she would talk to Mary Jo. Three days later, she called and informed me that my sister agreed with me and wanted me to have my father's mandolin. We patched things up, and to the best of my knowledge, no one in my family ever made me feel like a junkie again. Of course, Albie continued to treat me like her "baby," but I accepted that this would always be true, no matter how long I stayed clean, or how old I was. To this day, I have not pawned the mandolin and still have it.

Visit from a *Ghost* brings about a spiritual epiphany

At work, it was time for the annual summer "NYO Funfair." I was selected to represent the east office, which included attending weekly brainstorming meetings at the main office. It was there that I met Angela. She was a young exotic woman of Greek descent, in her early 20s, with beautiful dark brown hair to the middle of her back and big brown eyes to match. She wore a lot of hippie jewelry and was especially fond of wearing many bracelets. She was very shapely, but preferred jeans and cowboy boots over dresses and heels. She was a sexy, gypsy tomboy, who loved to laugh and actually made me laugh. She caught my eye, and we hit it off immediately. I was attracted to her physically but still in love with a woman that lived in New York City. This, being uncharted territory for me, put me in a state of emotional confusion unlike any I'd ever experienced. I was lonely and bored, so I figured what's the harm in having a buddy to hang out with. I asked her out and she accepted.

On our first date, we went to see the newly released film, *Ghost*. Some called it a "chick flick" but as an artist, I began to outgrow those "rules," and the limitations they imposed. Art was either good or bad, it was entertaining, or it wasn't. The film had gotten good reviews, so I felt it was a good date flick.

As it turned out, it was a good film that I enjoyed, at least in part because it revisited a familiar theme that, for some reason, appealed to me as a child. One of my favorite movies as a kid, oddly enough, was the musical *Carousel*, starring Gordon MacRae and Shirley Jones. I liked the musical score well enough, though I would come to dislike musicals as a teen, as I began to find it ridiculous that characters suddenly burst into song in the middle of a conversation. What did appeal to me was the idea of a person coming back from the dead as a ghost and interacting with their loved ones, and others in the story. *Ghost* had this theme, albeit with a few different twists.

Near the end of the film, the "bad guy" gets what's coming to him for the treachery he's been involved in against those in his life. He gets killed in a fateful accident while running from the ghost of the man he murdered. After he dies, he leaves his body, then, turning to see it lying there, lifeless and bleeding, he realizes what has happened. Then, some spooky sounds begin getting louder and louder. From below him, a group of ghostly black figures surround him, grabbing him, and dragging him away, presumably to Hell.

At that moment, it was like getting hit in the head with a baseball bat! The scene triggered a memory that came flooding back into my mind. My heart began pounding and I could feel my hands getting sweaty. For the first time, I realized, without any doubt, that what I had experienced in California was not a cocaine-induced hallucination—it had really happened to me!

I was shocked to discover a figure sitting crouched between the stove and refrigerator where Laura and I always kept our garbage can. I noticed that this person (or whatever it was) was dressed in black from head to toe. I saw that it had three very distinct parts to its dress—a shroud, a hood, and a veil— that covered its entire face.

"That almost happened to me," I mumbled to myself almost involuntarily.

"What?" Angela asked.

"Nothing. I'll tell you after the movie," I whispered.

We watched the sad but beautiful ending of the film, although I had difficulty focusing as flashbacks came into my mind in clear focus about what took place that day in 1984. We left the theater with tears running down Angela's face. She got some tissue for her face and as she composed herself, asked, "What did you mean when you said, that almost happened to you?"

I told her the story of my overdose in California, and about the strange hooded being dressed all in black who seemed to have the power to make my heart stop. I told her about the light that came through both picture windows that brought me back from the edge of death. I explained how I had dismissed it as a cocaine-induced hallucination, even though I knew it felt different than any other cocaine hallucination or delusion that I had ever experienced. I explained that I had put it out of my mind until now. That scene in the movie brought it all back, and for whatever reason, it finally became clear to me, and I finally accepted the truth that it had really happened.

Angela sat listening with her mouth hanging open and her eyes getting wider and wider. Growing up in a very religious family (in all that jewelry, the cross could always be found somewhere), she reassured me and said, she completely believed that it happened to me.

After our date, I drove Angela home and went back to my apartment. Once inside, I fell on my knees, my eyes filled with tears, and my heart filled with gratitude to God as I acknowledged all the rewards I had received in my recovery. I thanked Him for intervening and saving me that day.

In the days that followed, I talked about the realization of my spiritual experience with friends and in meetings to mostly supportive but some mixed reviews. The biggest skeptic, of course, being the "anti-Christ" himself—Mark Storch. Mark was slightly atheist but mostly agnostic like I had been. He rolled his eyes and said, smiling, "Sounds like ya had some pretty good coke there." Most supportive was Amelia, who, being a Christian Scientist, absolutely believed it happened and treated it as a normal everyday occurrence, like getting a visit from a relative. It cemented my faith in God and challenged my long-held belief that the only Hell was here on earth. I realized that there very well could be a terrible place that bad people's souls went after they died.

Also, people's comments in meetings about recovering people somehow being "the chosen ones" was reinforced. Apparently, God put a little extra effort into choosing me. I couldn't decide if that was a good thing or a bad thing. At times, I still felt that I was a disappointment to Him.

Music takes center stage

My relationship with Fred continued but had morphed into a friendship. I suggested that he get another sponsor and that his eating disorder made it important to find someone who was also dealing with both food and drug addiction. He followed my suggestion, so I was officially no longer his sponsor.

We both continued to attend meetings at LPAC. This led to the discovery that the custodian, Vince, was a pretty good guitarist. Based on this common interest, Fred and Vince started hanging out and jamming between meetings. Then Vince started inviting Fred over to the apartment he shared with his girlfriend Dee, and they would jam there. These jam sessions soon turned into songwriting sessions. I happened to be passing through LPAC for one of these sessions, and they called me into the back of the club.

"We've been putting some music together. Come on back here and listen to this and tell me what you think," Fred asked. I agreed.

Vince and I were already acquainted through my attending meetings and recently doing an LPAC-sponsored talent show called "The Java Jive" hosted by The Old Town School of Folk Music—a very nice little venue a few blocks from the club.

Vince knew I could play, but we were in different worlds musically. Vince was very punk and new wave influenced by bands like Siouxsie and the Banshees, The Clash, Elvis Castello, and the Pixies. Fred's influences were heavier, as in Motorhead, ACDC, and other artists on the heavier side. Though their musical tastes were quite different from mine, they apparently had enough respect for my abilities to ask my opinion.

I grabbed a chair and listened attentively. What I heard were fragments of songs they had written that were pretty good but went nowhere in terms of song structure. I, of course, didn't say that, and instead said, "Sounds really good!" I remember adding in my mind: *Not my kind of stuff but not bad.*

"Fred tells me you played some bass."

"Yep. For a few bands."

"These songs need some basslines. You want to play some bass for us? I have a little rehearsal space above my apartment, well, actually, it's an attic that we're turning into a rehearsal space."

"Sure, I would if I had a bass. Get me a bass, and I'll come and play."

"Okay, deal!" Vince proclaimed.

"Okay, we'll see what we can do," Fred added as he glared at me. Fred still had a low tolerance for anything that didn't go exactly his way.

I remember walking away thinking, *Yeah, right. You're never going to get me a bass,* and I put it out of my mind.

Surprisingly, I'd come to LPAC, and after meetings, they'd be back there jamming away. Every time they saw me, they'd ask, "When are you gonna play some bass with us?"

I'd answer with my pat response. "When you get me a bass."

It was like a little game we'd play with each other for a few months until one day, the game ended. I walked into LPAC, and Fred and Vince announced: "We got you a bass!"

"Okay, when's the next rehearsal?"

"Six o'clock tomorrow at my place. We'll order a pizza. Here's the address," Vince said as he grabbed pen and paper.

"You got an amp, too—right?" I inquired.

That's when I got my first dose of Vince's sarcastic sense of humor.

"No, we're going to put a very large megaphone in front of your guitar. Yes, we have an amp for you."

The following evening, I arrived and broke my "no coffee after 6 p.m." rule when Vince showed off his and Dee's new espresso coffee machine. Vince was the first person I'd ever known with his own espresso machine, and being the coffee lovers we all were, we indulged in a few café lattes before ordering pizza. We plugged our guitars in, and a creative explosion occurred! It was like a dam had burst. All that pent-up creative energy flooded Vince's living room.

The music could best be described as "Blondie and the Pretenders meet Judas Priest and Black Sabbath on steroids while shooting a speedball!" The music would later be referred to by some of our musical peers as "Classic, power pop, punk, metal." It was a far cry from the classic rock songwriter I was becoming, but I realized that this was something that made it fun for me. I could throw caution to the wind. I had nothing to lose. If I couldn't cut it, it would be no big deal. My true musical identity would remain intact. So, I went for it, no holds barred, and it was a blast! I also brought something important to the table where Fred and Vince's songwriting abilities fell short—musical arrangement. They had a bunch of pieces of songs. I often became the arranger who weaved those pieces into coherent songs with a beginning, middle, and end. I would also write just enough to connect some of those pieces.

When we finished working on the material, Vince asked, "You in?"

"Yeah, I'm in," I replied. It was still Rock & Roll, and it was fun!

Then we went out the back door and up the back stairs, and Vince and Fred took me on a tour of the attic.

"Fred and I are working on soundproofing this," and he showed me what they had completed. "You wanna come over Saturday? We got a bunch of old carpet remnants and more foam rubber we found in the alley. We're going to finish soundproofing it so we can start rehearsing up here."

"Okay."

The space was adequate but a bit tight. Then we walked into a dark storage area lit only by the fading daylight streaming through a single window at the front of the house. It was unusable due to having no flooring to speak of.

"Too bad we can't use this," I said.

"Yeah, it's actually bigger, but it would be too much work to make it doable. And anyway, it's haunted," Vince added nonchalantly.

"Haunted?" I said in knee-jerk disbelief.

"Kid, it really is," Fred chimed in.

They proceeded to tell me stories of hearing footsteps and other sounds and seeing shadows coming from the area constantly.

"We've named the ghost Iz," Vince confessed. I remember thinking, *Cool name for a band.*

Once we got it soundproofed, we appropriately named the space "Big Stinky." Let's just say some of the materials we found in the alley to use for soundproofing should have probably stayed in the alley.

Next, we needed a singer. Once I got the feel for the dark, spastic, manic, in-your-face nature of the music, the lightbulb went off over my head, and one person immediately came to mind—David Hoffman. I remembered the dark, intellectual, philosophical poetry he shared with me. It fit perfectly.

I brought the idea to Vince and Fred, who were leery. "Can he sing?" Fred inquired.

"I don't know, but if he can, his lyrics are perfect for this stuff. We won't know unless we audition him." They both agreed.

"I'll talk to him and see if he's interested."

When I talked to David about singing in a Rock & Roll band, his response was immediately, "Fuck yeah. I'll do it!"

But beneath that front layer of excitement and exuberance were already hints of insecurity, doubt, and debilitating fear. I'd later learn that this was the bond that Fred and David shared that the rest of us couldn't understand. It was, at times, referred to by them as "fat boy syndrome." Both had struggled with their weight and compulsive overeating for a good part of their lives. It deeply damaged their self-esteem, especially David. His fears and insecurity would become palpable and difficult to hide at times. Fred also had been bald on top by age 20. Fred's insecurity would show itself as anger, and there were times when his temper would be difficult to control. Though he was still chunky, Fred had slimmed down, but David remained somewhat obese and was somewhere in the vicinity of 250 to 300 pounds. He had successfully kicked over 100 milligrams of Methadone "cold turkey," and now it was time to go for the gusto. He agreed to come to "Big Stinky" and audition.

It was a Sunday afternoon late in August. Big Stinky was particularly hot and stinky, so we had the fans on high. We set up a mic and stand, plugged it into the PA, and awaited David's arrival. He showed up and we engaged in some small talk, then pointed out the mic in the middle of the room and told him that it was there just in case he was inspired to try some stuff, but there was no pressure on him to sing. He encouraged us to play, and he would just observe for now. He proceeded to sit in the lotus position, cross-legged on the floor as if he were about to meditate with the Maharishi Yogi. He pulled out a steno pad and a pencil, placing them on the floor in front of him. We played one of the shorter pieces we had been working on—not so much as a stir from David.

"What do you think?" Fred asked with a slight "tone" that really meant, "What? Are you just gonna sit on your fat ass like a fucking lump?"

"I like it. Sounds great. Got any more?"

"Sure do," Fred assured him. "Let's do that new one we've been working on."

I started it with a repeating, rolling bassline. Then, Fred jumps in with some screaming two-string bends, then Vince joins me until the change that would accommodate the verses. Then, the second change that leads to a crescendo and back to the opening line and repeat. Again, David barely moved a muscle. Then, finally, a stir. "Could you play that again?"

"Sure," Fred said in his best appeasing voice, typically used to cover up his impatience. We played it again. This time David grabbed the pad and pencil and began feverishly scribbling into it as we played. When we finished playing, he was still writing, until he looked up briefly and ordered, "Play it again." Fred, Vince, and I looked at each other with bewilderment on our faces. "Okay," Fred said, and I started the intro. Fred jumped in, then Vince, then, right at the change, we were shocked as David suddenly lunged at the mic from his position on the floor, like a rattlesnake striking its prey, and belted out the words to what would become the song; "Twisted Little Lilies," our little ditty about anorexia and bulimia...

The nearest little Jilly, she is such a twisted filly
Thinking of being fat, running like a maniac

Twisted little lilies in her garden
Deadly body sculpture plan

A lunatic in tragic flight she rides her bike all day and night
Skin atrophied and tight, seems such a haunting fright

Twisted little lilies in her garden
Necromantic body alchemy...

Fred and I looked up from our instruments and turned our heads to look at each other simultaneously. Our mouths were hanging open and our eyes were as wide as saucers. Then, almost as if it was choreographed, we both smiled from ear to ear and simultaneously nodded our heads "yes" in approval. Vince got it and was also smiling.

Then, to the second change that builds to a crescendo, David sang...

Always running here and there and never getting anywhere
Will she ever get it clear that she will always hear
Those sounds frightening clear ringing in between her ears
Of those little flowers that have gone their way before her?
Twisted little lilies in her garden! ... David belted out at the crescendo!

From there, Fred erupted into a guitar solo that was on fire, subconsciously in celebration of finding our singer! It fit perfectly. The experiment was an unlikely success.

David's lyrics were dark, raw, intelligent, and interesting with just the right amount of mystery, as in; "What the fuck is he talking about!?" But that was the cool thing; he was always talking about some reality of human existence, inspired by his study of Eastern philosophy while doing a stint in the penitentiary. It was never just putting together lines of clever mumbo-jumbo.

David wrote the rest of the lyrics to "Twisted Little Lilies" at home...

Haunting the strangest leer when looking in the bathroom mirror
Will she ever get it clear that she's skeletoid and queer?

Twisted little lilies in her garden
Deadly body sculpture plan

A little birds blink to eat finds her standing near the sink
Sticking fingers in her throat playing such a sickening note

Twisted little lilies in her garden
Necromantic body alchemy

Always running here and there and never getting anywhere
Will she ever get it clear that she will always hear
Those sounds frightening clear ringing in between her ears
Of those little flowers that have gone their way before her?

Twisted little lilies Auschwitz volunteer
Twisted little lilies skeletoid necessity
Twisted little lilies Auschwitz volunteer
Twisted little lilies skeletoid necessity

We had found our singer, that I would later describe as our "screaming poet." Now, if we were serious, and we were, we needed a drummer.

Creative explosion at Big Stinky

Finding a drummer would prove to be more of a challenge than we'd imagined. The problem was, we didn't really know where to look. I think we put an ad in the *Chicago Reader*, a weekly publication that covered the arts scene in the area. Though it had a classified section that included bands seeking musicians, it wasn't the best place to advertise for serious musicians. A better place would have been the monthly *Illinois Entertainer* magazine, but I don't think we knew that then. Luckily, we all hung out in the Wicker Park and Lakeview areas, both Meccas for artists and musicians. Wicker Park was the closest thing Chicago had to New York's Greenwich Village. There were posters plastered all over everything for bands shows at local venues in the area.

At the corner of Belmont Avenue and Clark Street, was the second home to Chicago musicians—Guitar Center. We plastered the place with fliers.

It finally paid off when we got a good handful of inquiries, and we started setting up auditions at Big Stinky. Unfortunately, most were disappointing, and either just didn't have the skill level needed or were heavy metal-oriented and too heavy-handed. We needed a drummer who could keep up with the manic music we were creating that darted abruptly from metal to punk, to pop, and beyond.

Frustration started setting in as the last audition for the evening arrived. Doug was a skinny guy, but all muscles without an ounce of fat anywhere on his body. We found out that there was a good reason for this; he was a bicycle messenger who sped around the streets of downtown Chicago daily. I swear I never felt Doug's ass, but I saw him in his little bike-messenger speedos, and believe me, it's no exaggeration when I say his ass was as hard as a rock! He was of Irish descent and had a ruddy, pasty white complexion, which was further accentuated by his jet-black hair that looked so good, it almost looked fake. It was the healthiest looking thing on him besides his glutes.

He had an impressive résumé, including being classically and jazz-trained and having been offered the chance to step in for the band, Cheap Trick, while they were on tour when their drummer became ill. He declined the offer. He also declined to go on tour with Kool and the Gang. None of it meant a thing to us, we just wanted to know if he was right for us, and so far, no one was.

Our hopes sunk slightly lower after he set up his drum kit, which could best be described as "circa 1965, Ringo Starr." It was so basic; I think we all felt: *There's no way this guy can be that good. He just doesn't have enough drums and cymbals.* Compared to the other drummers who auditioned, Doug's kit looked as anemic as his pasty complexion did.

If the saying "Looks can be deceiving" hadn't been invented yet, it would have been invented that day. I can't remember what songs we did or in what order, but it became obvious that not only did Doug get it, but he brought something extra to the music, like tasty well-placed high-hat strikes in unusual places. There were quick tight snare rolls in places where other drummers had just thumped and plodded through. Because of his jazz background, he was able to pick up on the subtleties in the music and enhance them. I liken what Doug brought to the music to what John Densmore did for The Doors music—he added another dimension to it and made it more interesting than it was.

It went great! We had a gas hearing some of the material as a more finished product. However, it appeared we had a new and unexpected problem: Was Doug too good for us? Maybe, but he put our minds at ease when he confessed that he was bored with typical predictable rock music. He found our music unique and intriguing, so it met that criterion perfectly. We had found our drummer! There was just one tiny thing I almost forgot to mention…Doug was a raging, practicing alcoholic, complete with blackouts and regular hangovers. Hey, nobody's perfect right?!

Through early fall we continued to work on the material. As we did, excitement about the band started to swell and we even had a little audience, mostly comprised of friends of the group who started cramming into Big Stinky to watch us rehearse. This included Mary, a female friend of Dee's who had a penchant for photography. She took pictures of us rehearsing and started developing promo material for the band, but we needed a name.

We all had ideas for the band's name. I had two possibilities in mind; Iz, after the ghost that haunted Big Stinky, or Humans, which I felt was the only thing we all had in common. Fred hated the name because there was a popular new wave band at that time called The Human League, and he felt it sounded too much like them. I argued that it didn't and everyone else agreed. Doug's choice was Alloy, which represented our blend of different musical styles being a strength of the band. Not bad. Fred had two names that he was torn between. His first choice was Flaming Purple Dildos, and his second was Firetruck. My response to "Dildos" was "no way" but it kind of grew on me. David's was Switchblade Caress, and Vince's was Barking Sidewalk. How do you spell PRETENTIOUS? I thought I was going to puke! Because of this dilemma, we decided to write them on slips of paper and draw one out of a hat. Mary Captured the drawing on film. Drumroll please… FIRETRUCK it was!

I was relieved and admitted that I would have refused to be in a band named Switchblade Caress or Barking Sidewalk. In retrospect, I think we may have missed an opportunity by not calling ourselves Flaming Purple Dildos. It was ballsy and catchy, but also risky.

Ultimately, I think Firetruck was the right name for the band. Our music was like we were racing to put out a fire of sorts. If we meant it in terms of a child's toy (how I always viewed it) that worked even better for me. The band was our desperately needed toy that helped four of us sustain our recovery, and for one to possibly start his. The band was an essential creative outlet. We were unlikely playmates, from different musical "playgrounds": Freddy, the heavy metal lead guitarist; Vince, the punk-rock rhythm guitarist; me the classic rock bassist, Doug; the jazz drummer, and David; the "screaming poet" with no musical background to speak of. We all desperately needed to make it work…

So, we did!

Before we knew it, we had seven songs and were ready to record a demo that we could shop around to venues. The most interesting of these was inspired by the powers of the world going to war over oil. It was appropriately called "Driven (by oil)." It was arguably our best song. Vince wrote most of the music for the verses. However, when it came to the chorus, he kept the same tempo as the verses. I didn't like it and felt it needed more than just a chord change, so I played with it at the break.

"Try it like this," I suggested and sped it up, playing it with more of a "surfing music" feel. We all liked it, and the term "Nuclear Surfing Music" was born...I think? Well, at least I think we coined that phrase. David actually started interjecting the words, "Let's go surfing now; everybody's learnin' how," into the live version before Vince's solo. Here are David's haunting apocalyptic, and now somewhat prophetic lyrics...

Driven (by oil)

Scorpion's tail, very queer
Reaches out from a chariot of fear
Breast plates gleaming, copter blades screaming
Suddenly, a new orange star appears

Driving tanks, the sands of time
Insecticide soldiers spray new crime
Armored locusts torch this land
Prophecies reach up through the sand

Driven, driven, driven, driven, by oil

Eschatological age is near
In Bagdad he could appear
Beginnings in the halls of fear
Masters of the maggot's line

Meeting with the worms of crime
Speaking in blistering rhymes
Oil and gunpowder ritual lines
Awakening him from another time

Driven, driven, driven, driven, by fear!

That was as far as we had gotten on the song. So, on the last line, Fred announced, "Smoke break!" and he and Vince set their guitars in the stands with the last chord still ringing through their amps. David plopped into the only comfy chair in Big Stinky.

We knew the song needed a bridge. I hadn't taken my bass off, and for whatever reason, Doug decided to keep lightly riding a cymbal, possibly inspired by Fred's ringing but slowly fading chord. The combination of these two elements made it hit me out of nowhere, and I started playing this bassline.

Doug and David looked up at me and started grinning from ear to ear. They heard it too. Out of nowhere, I found myself writing the bridge we were looking for. I called Fred and Vince back in from the backstairs from their smoke break.

"I think I found our bridge. Let's take it from the second verse into the chorus right before the break."

We did. "Now just let that last chord ring, and Doug, keep riding the cymbal like you were." He did, and I went into the bassline I'd written. Fred and Vince then joined in, Vince with some haunting stuff, and Fred with a helicopter-like scratching sound on his strings. It was perfect! We let it build until I suggested we take it back into the chorus.

Here are the rest of the words after the bridge and Vince's solo:

On the cosmic ocean lies
Lord and master of flies
Dreaming in his foulest breath
Nightmare landscapes of death

Steaming hills of burning flesh
Dante's hole, nothing less
Melting concrete twisted pyres
Amidst the rise of new hellfire

Driven, driven, driven, driven, by fear!

The song brought out some of our most creative moments, but it also brought out our tendency to argue. I was starting to realize and accept that arguing is an inevitable and necessary part of the creative process, especially in a band with five distinctly different personalities.

The first big argument we had was between Doug and me, over when to come out of the bridge and back into the chorus. This would be the first clear example of a trait of Doug's that at times would get on all our nerves—he was a know-it-all, especially when it came to music.

Being the only one of us who had any formal musical training to speak of, Doug would often don his "musical expert" beanie when we disagreed about anything musical. Usually, we would capitulate, but this time I knew I was right. In short, he felt like his drumroll back into the chorus needed to wait until after an even sixteenth measure of the bridge. That didn't feel right, and I felt the roll needed to start earlier.

He proclaimed, "We can't do that."

"What!? What do you mean we can't do that? We just did it!" I yelled. "It's a rule in music. You have to wrap up on an even number before you change."

"Who told you that!?"

"I told you—it's a rule in music."

"There are no rules in music, and if there are, they're meant to be broken. Just ask The Beatles!"

Being the Beatles fan that Doug was, that pretty much shut him up, but we decided to put it to a vote, which is what we did when we couldn't agree. We wound up doing it my way.

Unfortunately, this would be a sign of things to come, and as the "honeymoon" started to wear off, more arguing ensued. A likely contributing factor was the five of us being cooped up in Big Stinky all winter, working on and writing new material.

Once, Fred was so pissed off at me, he stabbed a piece of Styrofoam soundproofing on the wall repeatedly with his guitar. David threatened to pound Vince's face in. Doug would complain, "Are you going to play or just tune?"

I saw a sign in a store that said, "Steve's Rules: Rule #1: Steve is always Right. Rule #2: If Steve is wrong, see Rule # 1.". I bought it and hung it above my amp.

Speaking of The Beatles, we were slowly becoming them. Not musically of course, but relationally. As I had come to learn, out of most negatives in life, comes something positive, and the band's growing discourse was no exception. Something very positive and lasting would eventually grow out of it as the band's "pot" continued to percolate!

The Fort

The day I was promoted to treatment coordinator at NYO was a great day…well, kind of. The pay raise and acknowledgement of my developing leadership skills were nice, and it would look good on a résumé. It was another testimony to how far I had come. However, the downside was that it was not at my beloved Kedzie office. I was transferred to the Proviso office located on First Avenue and the Eisenhower Expressway in a big office building near the border of Oak Park and Maywood. This was the office that Angela worked out of, so that would make our relationship more accessible and convenient.

I was always honest with her about Amelia. She was "okay" with it: however, I was beginning to learn that when women say they're "okay" with something, it really means, "I'll tolerate this bullshit for a little while, but then it had better change, or I'll kill you."

My disenchantment with NYO as an agency had officially begun. As I said, I started to see that they really were a "counselor puppy mill"—churning out counselors, while encouraging them to move on to other agencies. It seemed cheap labor was the goal. The only exceptions were the executive staff and a handful of managers that were referred to as "sacred cows." Everyone else was expendable "counselor currency," to be spent and abruptly thrown here and there to different offices, at their whim. Ultimately counselors would benefit from this practice by toughening up their skin, and learning to adapt to change, but those who did not benefit, and in fact suffered as a result, were the clients.

Imagine working hard over several months to bond with an adolescent and their family, only to be abruptly yanked out of their lives and replaced by someone fresh out of college, who may be of a different gender. The gender of the counselor could be extremely important in some cases. I'll let you figure that out on your own. I understand that at times this couldn't be helped, but that was not the case most of the time at NYO.

Luckily, my office change would coincide with an offer to share the rent three ways on a house-for-rent in Oak Park by an AA friend—Bob H.

Bob was someone who I started to develop a strong friendship with. He was a guitarist and singer, though a bit folksier and more bluesy than me. He was also an actor and a writer. He had a dry, witty, slightly dark sense of humor, with just the right amount of silly mixed in. We hit it off immediately. He had approximately the same amount of sobriety too. His drug of choice was alcohol, and ironically, he worked for a top-notch downtown restaurant as a bartender. He made good money and, due to his seniority, could set his own schedule. All of this, combined with no longer being in the throes of alcoholism, made conditions right for him to follow his dream of becoming a filmmaker. So, he enrolled in Columbia College, known for its excellent filmmaking program.

Due to my ever-expanding life that was mostly happening outside of it, my apartment was again growing cobwebs. Between the band, going to meetings, going out with friends, working with sponsees, dating (kind of), and spending time with my kids, I was once again hardly ever there. I think my rent had also gone up to $550 a month by this time and the rent at the house was just $500 split three ways. I just couldn't afford to throw that kind of money away on something I no longer needed. This made the decision a no-brainer—it was time to let go of my beautiful sanctuary.

My apartment was an important symbol of my early progress in recovery, but now it had become a burden that kept my life from moving forward. My growth had allowed me to see and accept this and let go. The Gateway concept "There's nothing constant but change" was once again in play, but now I was much less fearful and moved forward into the unknown more confidently. I knew as long as I kept not picking up that first drink or drug (even if my ass fell off) as my ace in the hole, things would work out.

The move to Oak Park went smoothly with the help of Storchy, other friends, and a few sponsees. The huge drafty old house was somewhat in disrepair and needed both an interior and exterior paint job. The three bedrooms upstairs were decent and where Bob, me, and our third roommate Toby spent most of our time when we were home.

Toby was also in recovery and was a long-haired hippie, save the whales, hug a tree—type guy. He mostly kept to himself, although he had his girl (fellow tree hugger) over often. They were a little odd but harmless. They seemed to get under Bob's skin and irritate him for some reason.

Bob and I nicknamed our new home "The Fort", due to it reminding us of a childhood fort you would make in an abandoned house that you may have stumbled upon. The basement had a natural reverb and was ideal for writing a few new songs. My songwriting was getting better, judging not only by my own standards, but by the response I got from others whose opinions I trusted.

Just when I started getting somewhat comfortable in my new role and living arrangements, I got thrown another curveball. I was transferred to the main office as a treatment counselor. This was a slight demotion and took my high-flying ego down a few notches—probably a good thing. I felt it was, at least in part, the result of an incident that had occurred just before the transfer.

A group of treatment clients were supposed to get parental permission slips signed to go on a field trip to the Cook County Jail in Maybrook. Some clients got it done, but others didn't. When the day came to go, I would have had to go through a lot of changes to get what we needed to pull it off; so instead, I decided to cancel the trip. To my surprise, I caught flack for this.

The "powers that be" felt I should have made more effort to obtain the missing permission docs, and I should have run the decision by my supervisor Lauren, who in typical NYO fashion, was usually nowhere to be found on Fridays, and this was no exception. I could have paged her, but I felt comfortable with the decision. They never said it, but I believe it's why I was transferred. Also, my salary was probably getting in that "We don't want to pay anyone this kind of money" range.

This meant that I would now be under the supervision of one of the biggest "sacred cow" managers in the agency—Leo Thomas. For my entire albeit brief career, my instincts as a counselor had been trusted and respected... until now. I was about to have the first controlling micromanaging supervisor of my young career. As bad a manager as Mary Morgan was, she mostly stayed out of our way. This would not be the case with Lee.

It started with him insisting that the clients address me as "Mr. Fiorito." Though this was an agency-wide policy, it was loosely enforced at most offices, and personal preference was allowed. I felt it was too formal, like wearing a suit and tie. Both made me less accessible and more of an authority figure to adolescent clients. I presented this argument, but I would soon learn that there was no argument that could stand up to "Leo logic." It was his way or the highway. He even went as far as to tell me where to sit and what to say (word for word) in family sessions I had scheduled with some of my clients.

Then there was the skit we wrote for the Christmas party. I'm sure I didn't earn any points with him when I portrayed him in the spoof play that we wrote and performed at the party. It was co-written by me and three other staff members from the main office. We cast 12 staff from four different offices in roles. The name of the play was "A Family Systems Christmas," spoofing the popular TV show *The Simpsons'* special called, *Christmas with the Simpsons*.

Leo was bald on top and had thick black rim glasses, so I bought one of those bald-on-top wigs and the thick black rim fake frames. My parody of him took sarcastic swipes at all his idiosyncrasies, which of course, included his need to be in control. The play got big laughs all the way through, especially my portrayal of Lee. I thought Gene was going to fall out of his chair, but when I looked out into the audience, I noticed that everyone was laughing except Lee. The best he could do was muster a forced smile, behind which were the subtle signs of, "We'll see who has the last laugh."

Ultimately, because of the move to the main office, I lost my seniority and consequently my ability to take my vacation through the Christmas holiday when I planned to spend it in New York with Amelia. Fortunately, having to postpone my trip until after the holidays would be a blessing in disguise and would lead to one of the coolest experiences of my early recovery.

Sober in the recording studio

Firetruck had eight or nine original tunes, and we were ready to record a demo. Dave found some guys, who like many, had made use of the vacant space for rent in the city. The recording studio was down the street from The Golden Apple restaurant, where we often ate breakfast. Perfect! Except for one thing—we could only get the studio starting on Thursday January 3rd.

That morning, we set up our equipment in the studio, then met for breakfast at The Apple. Breakfast was like being in high school again. We were on a great adventure, and we all sensed it. The excitement was palpable and magnified by the fact that we all probably drank too much coffee. We were so loud and obnoxious. At times we'd get stares and raised eyebrows from the patrons at the tables that surrounded us. The only problem was, I had planned my second trip to New York leaving from Union Station on January 6^{th,} which meant I had three days to get my basslines down before I left.

I didn't know it at the time, but on January 3rd, 1991, our first day of recording, Doug, somewhat reluctantly, would join our sober adventure. I would later learn that it was his first day of sobriety. Fred had "twelve-stepped" him the night before. This was the practice of helping another addict or alcoholic to get sober. Fred brought him over to his apartment to spend the night and "dry out." He also poured the booze that Doug had stashed down the drain. Doug would later attribute one of his motivations for getting sober to the band, proclaiming, "You guys inspired me. You were having such a good time without using drugs or alcohol, I felt like it was time to get with the program."

Getting sober is one thing; staying sober is quite another. Doug had some previous attempts at staying sober and going to AA, so he was not exactly a rookie. We all kept our fingers crossed that this time he would stick with it.

The high energy carried over from breakfast into the studio, and we laid most of the music down in one take in a live-studio format, meaning: with all of us in the same room, like a live show, but minus David's vocal. He watched from a vocal booth, as we laid down the bulk of the music for seven songs. We left two out that we felt were still in need of polishing and development. We opened with what would remain the first track on the demo, "Asphalt Playground," David's little tribute to young gangbangers and incest? Here are some of David's lyrics about the dark reality of the streets…

Standing on the corner, lookin' like no fool, signifying clean, on the drama team
Other bangers pass, makin' him out an ass, needs to save his face, can't live in disgrace

Won't let him snooze, go gunnin' for his crew, screaming at the moon, they'll pay until June
Lucky little fool, thinks he'll never lose, splitting from his turf, stupid little jerk

Bastard little children of the night,
Walk toward heaven with hope, outta sight,
Cadillac dreams clean and mean,
Hot dry snots inner city streets,

Hair full and mean, leather jackets scream,
Livin' dyin' dreams, dirty fuckin' jeans,
Flames ringing clear in any fat cat's ear,
Makin' faggot friends and it's only from fear

The highlight of that first day in the studio was "Twisted Little Lilies." The song had an abrupt, "stop-on-a-dime" ending, that we always had to do over to nail it. Someone would always fuck up and bleed over. In the studio, it would mean we'd have to do the whole song over, which would become a challenge, particularly for me, with that continuous rolling baseline. We nailed it on the first take! This did not go unnoticed by us as we all froze like statues and smiled from ear to ear. Doug immediately laughed, which got picked up by one of his drum mics. We decided to leave it in the final mix as part of the song.

The next day, David laid down all the vocal tracks. The only song we had any background vocal on was a song called "Why Say No," our tribute to the never-ending quest to get laid. All of us piled into the vocal booth to add a shout of the words "Oh, yeah!" Also, David's main squeeze at the time, Linda, entered the booth with David to add a track of a conversation with her rejecting David as he attempted to convince her to fuck him.

Day three was adding guitar solos, and what-not. We had been given access to a sound-effects library, which thank God, we used wisely and didn't go overboard with. We added an air raid siren to the intro of "Driven," and a nuclear bomb blast at the very end. On "Twisted Little Lilies" we went with an odd combo to accompany my opening bassline—a fussy baby starting to cry, combined with sparse hands clapping. The combination made it sound like the baby was getting slapped. It fit perfectly with the demented nature of the song.

The only other notable thing about the day was that as Fred neared the end of the grueling overdub session, he sort-of "ran out of gas," creatively speaking. Try as he might, he could not find the groove in the solo for the song "Tears in the Rain." This was David's little testimony to being outmaneuvered and outclassed by a woman in a Corvette, while he chased her on his Harley in a rainstorm on "The Magnificent Mile," Lake Shore Drive. After six or seven tries, he called me over: "Stevie, you want to give this solo a shot? I'm toast right now." I took the guitar, with Fred's strap still on, slung it over my head, and put the headphones on. They rolled the tape, and I nailed it on the first take.

The only other thing worth mentioning involved Fred's friend Bob Becker, who was the leader of a band called Faith Dealers. The band was already out there playing the Chicago club scene. He was with us that second day, and not only provided encouragement and guidance to us but lent us some of his musical talents. He played the second solo on David's song about the spiritual battle between good and evil, "Zoroaster's Dead Angels." Then, of all things, piano, on our obscure little tune about being an IV heroin addict called "Frosted Breath." It was one of my personal favorites probably because Vince and I were the primary writers. David's lyrics were haunting and provocative...

Dreams away, flags unfurl, never weep, in these streets
Frosted breath, pane of glass, this needle speaks, of relief

I will always speak to you of graves and decay,
Lies and dismay
I will make you speak of me like a lover and a friend,
One whose always been

It will show me nighttime fears in the middle of the day,
Wild winter's day
And this little space I know it's floating to my head,
Paisley pinks and red

Colors in, shades of gray, lasting springs, of decay
Plastic mimes, float in tune, softly cry, of this ruin

I don't know but if I could I'd find myself someday,
Along this way
I don't know but if I could I'd find a better way,
A way today
I don't know but if I could, I'd go back in time,
Split from my crime
I don't know but if I could, I'd find a friend today,
Ask them the way

All tracks were completed by Saturday, and I would have to leave the final mix to the rest of the band while I was in New York. They were able to put a quick mix on cassette for me so I could have something to listen to on the train, and to show Amelia when I arrived. I also had another cassette for her, a belated Christmas gift of her song, "Amelia," which was as done as the makeshift Kenny studio with the bad drum machine would allow. The contrast between the two tapes was huge, and I wondered what Amelia's reaction would be to the departure from my typical classic rock style.

A different kind of men in blue

My second train ride to New York would treat me to a different visual feast. The rolling hills and church steeples of Pennsylvania were now snow-covered. Every mile was like a Christmas card and gave me a subtle, underlying sense of joy, something I experienced a lot in those days. These were simple times, full of simple pleasures, that I began to appreciate more and more, especially with the fear of life all but removed. Between the stress, problems, and the "grey days" of nothing special, were these times with no yearning and no hunger—mostly just a sense of contentment and peace. Was this the natural high I'd heard about in meetings? It most definitely was one of them. It may not have been like shooting a speedball, but it was almost constant now, not elusive and fleeting like shooting dope. Little did I know, the natural high experience was about to be taken to a whole new level.

My arrival at Amelia's apartment started in a familiar way—mad passionate sex, followed by the usual bickering and arguing. I gave her my belated Christmas gift on cassette tape. Her eyes welled up with tears. She loved it. Who wouldn't love a song that was written and recorded about themselves—and a pretty good one at that?

"You're a good songwriter Steven. You need to do something with it," she encouraged.

Then she heard Firetruck's stuff, and she was wowed. She totally got it, which surprised me, but shouldn't have. Her brother Charles's stuff was pretty dark too.

"Sounds like stuff that would go over well at CBGB's. You should bring them a tape."

CBGB's was a local venue that was the home of the American Punk/New Wave music scene. I was only vaguely familiar at the time. It launched the careers of acts such as The Ramones, Blondie, Patti Smith, and Talking Heads—to name a few of the more well-known artists.

I didn't bring them a tape. Why not? Because I was still green and clueless about the music industry, and I was "born yesterday" (in some ways, literally). Should I have brought them a tape? Absolutely. Chalk it up as the first in a series of bad management decisions for Firetruck.

Beyond that, there was nothing remarkable about my second trip to Manhattan until two days before my departure. It was Friday, so Amelia told me to look in the local paper to see if any shows playing in The Village interested me. I picked up the paper and spotted a show called "Tubes." I can't remember why, but I just had a feeling based on the name and the brief description that it would not be your ordinary play. Also, because it was still in previews, it would be cheap. When a show was in previews, they asked only for a donation to be determined by the patron. I remember thinking that the price was certainly right, and the theater was right down the street from Amelia's apartment.

When we arrived at the funky, somewhat small and cramped La MaMa Theatre, they sat us near the stage at one of the 30 or so small two-person high-top tables that filled the place to the back of the theater. Against the back wall was standing room only or barstools if available. People often grabbed the barstools and brought them up to the tables, cramming three or four people at a table that only fit two comfortably. The place was dark, dingy, and reeked of old booze and cigarettes; so, it was more like a bar than a theater.

Hanging from the ceiling, there were multicolored plastic tubes, about three inches in diameter. Some of them dangled low enough for the audience to reach. People started noticing that if they listened to the tubes, they could hear strange music and talking, or someone on the other end would strike up a conversation if they spoke into some of them, thus the name of the show—Tubes. By showtime, the place was packed.

The lights went down revealing three musicians decorated in blacklight paint in a cage above the stage. They immediately started playing their instrumental soundtrack for the show, which was a cool mix of futuristic space-rock and jazz fusion. The excitement started to churn in my stomach immediately. Then, multicolored stage lights came up and backlighting revealing the shadows of three bald men from the waste up, each playing his own drum and taking turns joining in with the music. The other musicians stopped playing, and the three took over trading off individual drum solos. Just when you started thinking "these guys are serious musicians" and you were at a futuristic music concert, the first hints of comedy came through when one of the men's shadows shows him eating a banana, then smoking a cigarette with one hand, while continuing to drum with his other. The laughter commenced.

The screens lift from the stage to reveal that the three bald men are all blue. All are wearing protective welding face shields, which they promptly lower, to protect their faces from a stream of tri-colored blacklight water, that suddenly starts emitting from small holes in their chest plates onto their drums. It splashes all over and one of the men grabs a blank canvas and hangs it up, so that all three can splatter it, adding their color from their "drumming paint brush." It's passed back and forth until covered sufficiently by all three artists, which is when they end the piece, with the three of them simultaneously pounding the last heavy beats in unison on their drums, followed by abrupt silence. They raise their arms above their heads, drum mallets in hand, in victory! As the audience erupts in applause, one of them slaps a price tag of $25,000 on their painting, which took all of two minutes of drumming to create. The enthusiastic applause mixed with laughter is interrupted as the band in the cage above starts their next tune, moving the show to its next scene.

Amelia and I looked at each other, our faces reflecting the same shocked, excited amazement, at what we had just seen. At that moment, I think we both knew we were seeing something very special.

We got the distinct feeling that our bald blue friends were from outer space and were discovering and revealing to us the absurd nature of the society we live in. This was particularly true of their swipe at "fine art." Whether it was paintings made haphazardly by spitting onto a spinning canvas, or sculptures made of a marshmallow-like substance regurgitated from one of their mouths, the price tags slapped on these "masterpieces" were outrageous.

In yet another skit, they discover some old carpet bags containing wigs with curlers in them, bathrobes, and old lady house slippers. As they put the robes and wigs on and try to figure out what to do with the slippers, an intricate set of multicolored fluorescent PVC tubes slowly emerges from a hidden place on the stage. The three men look at it curiously, then to the audience, which gives them no answers but plenty of low, steady laughter.

Suddenly, the one with the slippers in his hand gives the open end of one of the tubes a whack. It emits a vibe-like sound. Excited by the discovery, one of the others takes off his slippers and strikes another one of the tubes, which echoes out a different note. They soon find that the two notes sound good and complement each other, until finally, all three men are playing the strange tubular instrument as the musicians above them join in for accompaniment. As their experiment continues, they stumble across such classics as, "Crazy Train" by Ozzy Osborne and "Like a Virgin" by Madonna. Again, the audience response was a mixture of awe at their musical talent, the uniqueness of their instruments, and laughter at their sarcastic wit.

Then came the audience participation parts of the show, which I would venture to say were the most unique ever seen at that time.

By the end of the show, I sensed the audience experienced a mixture of exhilaration and emotional and mental exhaustion, but you're not quite done with this rollercoaster ride. Instead, you're about to experience an ending that the term "grand finale" was made for, and you were certainly not ready for.

From the stage, the three men walked across the high-top tables (sometimes barely able to fit their feet between the drinks, ashtrays, and empty glasses), stepping over patrons as they made their way to the back of the theater. When they got there, they stood on a half-wall at the very back of the room as three giant roles of bright white paper descended from the ceiling. The men then proceeded to unroll the paper as strobe lights began flashing and house-music starts playing. The bright-white paper intensifies the effects of the strobes, and you can barely stand to keep your eyes open during this intense visual assault. The paper soon becomes a mountain that covers the audience and must literally be pushed forward, to avoid drowning in the sea of paper that is building. This was not tissue paper in these early shows, so you literally had to use some arm strength to push it forward to the table in front of you. It could be described as really scary if it weren't so much fun!

As the audience wrestled to push the mountain of paper toward the stage, the three made their way back to the stage and slipped back into the abyss of space and time from whence they came. The house lights came up, a recorded soundtrack started playing, and it was over.

Of course, most of you know, if you haven't been living under a rock these past 35-some-odd years, that I'm talking about *Blue Man Group*. Amelia and I saw the original show with the creators and original Blue Men: Matt Goldman, Phil Stanton, and Chris Wink—while it was still in previews. I paid eight dollars to see that awesome show, which was all I had in my pocket. I must admit that I felt a bit guilty about it, like I had just stolen something. We both knew when we left the theater that we just experienced something rare and unique as we recapped some of our favorite moments of the show.

This was confirmed a year later, when I sat down to watch *The Tonight Show* with Jay Leno, and there they were. I jumped up and yelled to Bob, "Hey, there's those blue guys Amelia and I saw when I was in New York!"

I was amazed when I saw the show in Chicago years later and realized that aside from a few minor changes, the show was almost identical to the original show I saw at the La MaMa. One difference was the bit with the wigs, robes, and slippers, which was short lived. No one I know besides Amelia has ever seen it. I believe they decided they didn't need the premise of house slippers to explain the paddles they used to play their tubular instruments. The paddles were simply part of their discovery when they first discovered the instrument. They also eventually stopped doing the paper at the end of the show, which was replaced by gigantic beach balls that fall from the ceiling for the audience to bounce around the theater. I guess they wanted to be more environmentally friendly. I'm glad I was able to experience that original intense, environmentally unfriendly, politically incorrect ending. It was significantly more intense than anything they do currently.

The show wound up being a fresh, unique, "multi-sensory extravaganza" that featured an incredible mix of great percussion, original music, art, satire, comedy, sarcasm, visuals, and film—all laced with just the right amount of political and social commentary about the absurdity of the human race. It was an awesome experience on many levels. The most important one to me was an intense natural high from the show. So much so, that I commented to Amelia on the way home: "Wow! If anyone doubts that there is such a thing as a natural high without drugs, they need to come and see this show. I think anyone in recovery would benefit from seeing it." I didn't realize at the time how prophetic and foreshadowing that idea would be.

Wicker Park's groundbreaking Indie Rock scene

Upon my return from New York, I got to hear the final mix of the seven-song demo. I and the rest of the band gave it mixed reviews. There were definite problems with the recording quality. The thing that irritated me most, was the mix of "Frosted Breath." Becker's piano was pulled so far back in the mix, you could barely hear it. Fred's scratching on his strings overpowered the subtleties of the song. I wanted to scratch his eyes out when I heard it. Despite these issues, the energy of the band and the songs came through loud and clear.

Our explosion of pent-up creative energy stood out even more against the backdrop of the popular music of the times. Bands like Depeche Mode, Culture Club, The Human League, and Flock of Seagulls dominated the airwaves at that time. I started referring to it as "British Fag Rock.". If British Fag Rock was Christ, then Firetruck was certainly the anti-Christ.

We weren't the only ones, who were sick of being lulled to sleep by this "barely able to call it Rock & Roll" muzak. We didn't realize it at the time, but we were part of the rebellion against music that contained lazy Caribbean sounds behind new-age synthesizers with drippy lyrics, like; *Do you really want to touch me; do you really want to make me cry?*

Firetruck was at the beginning of a growing underground movement, which was in complete defiance of the new wave movement of the 1980s. To understand its origins, you must understand what was happening in the mid-1980s in Chicago's Wicker Park and the surrounding areas.

First, there was a surplus of cheap warehouse-like space, resulting from a huge decline in U.S. manufacturing. Then, there was this non-profit organization called The Near Northwest Arts Council (NNWAC). This non-profit was dedicated to assisting struggling artists in an area that used to be inhabited by thugs, pimps, prostitutes, the homeless, and junkies. It suddenly started getting infiltrated by actors, theater companies, artists, filmmakers, musicians, and independent recording studios and labels.

In Wicker Park and surrounding communities, bands like Urge Overkill, Smashing Pumpkins, Jesus Lizard, Liz Phair, Naked Raygun (to whom we were often compared) and Firetruck, laid the groundwork for the post-punk, *indie,* and *alternative rock scene* to come.

Bands got tired of waiting around for their "big break"—a major label record deal—and decided to make their own breaks. The DIY (do it yourself) music rebellion was underway in Chicago. We were unwitting pioneers amid a musical revolution that would lead to the birth of such genres as alternative and grunge rock. Indie labels and studios started popping up all over the area.

Unfortunately, we experienced some of the downside of the booming "Wicker Park scene.". Everybody and their brother became a sound engineer, a director, or a producer. There were many wannabes mixed in with those who were truly developing creative geniuses. For us, it was hard to tell the difference. The good news was that what our recording lacked in engineering and sound quality, for the most part, made up for with raw creative energy.

Vince, studying to be a commercial artist at the time, designed the cassette cover and our unofficial manager Mary put together a promo package and we got it out to local clubs. We landed our first gig at a favorite Chicago nightspot called the Avalon Nightclub, albeit on a Tuesday night and not on the mainstage. Lucky for us, the place was pretty packed from front to back every night. The monthly NYO newsletter for February even promoted the band...

Steve's back from New York and playing his first public gig with the new band in town "Firetruck." Ask him to explain the name and what exactly is a screaming poet.

We were officially part of the Wicker Park club scene. Dropping off promo packets at clubs and venues, slapping up posters on light poles that were crowded with a million other band's posters, and anywhere else they would fit. I was the poster designer, and I started spending a lot of time at the now-defunct Kinko's. Soon, we were booked into several local clubs over the next six weeks.

One show that stands out from those days was at a club called Czar Bar on St. Patrick's Day. There was nothing we did musically that stood out, but rather it was related to my personal life at the time.

By then, I had given myself permission to be a single guy, and date anything that moved. I even started sleeping with the new receptionist at work while still seeing Angela, who worked at the Proviso office. Meanwhile, I met the older sister of my Big Brother from Gateway, Scott, and started sleeping with her. To complicate matters further, I was still in love with a woman who lived in New York. I felt like a tightrope walker in the "circus of confusion."

All three Chicago women knew about the Czar Bar show and decided to come. The women didn't know each other and would be scattered throughout the good-sized St. Paddy's crowd, so no worries—right? Except I didn't count on one thing—David being in one of his mischievous prankster moods. Being my closest confidant at the time, David knew about my antics and had met all of them. So, he reserved a table near the stage where he proceeded to seat all three women as they arrived. Then, after executing his diabolical little plot, to rub salt in the wound, he pulled me off the stage as I was doing a last-minute equipment check and brought me to their table.

"Hey, Stevie. I thought your friends would have a nice view of the stage from here," he said with a crooked, mischievous grin on his face. I smiled to cover up the fact that I was panicking and squirming inside. "Good thinking. Thanks David," I replied while giving him the death stare through my smile.

To make matters worse, we started to notice a pattern with Doug of being late to gigs, which brought about the inside joke that the band should change its name to "Where's Doug?" Apparently, being sober for two months does not make a lot of old alcoholic behavior just magically disappear.

I continued to play off the double knot in my gut as nonchalantly as I could, while introducing everyone.

"Well, enjoy the show ladies," I said, as I slunk away. Backstage, I was able to share my feelings: "You fucking asshole!" David just laughed as we took the stage.

Once I set foot on stage and strapped my bass on, all knots and cares immediately vanished, and it was all about the music. From what I remember, we had a great show. The only casualty of David's little prank was Scott's sister, who figured things out and consequently told me to piss off at the break. Ironically, Angela and Karla, who worked for NYO at different offices, remained unaware that I was seeing both of them. Well, it was probably time to "thin the herd" anyway. Sorry, couldn't resist that one.

Sex

This seems to be the right place to address this subject. I started wondering about the reasons for the apparent absence of it in my story. Luckily, it's not that my sex life has ever been boring. Quite the opposite. Okay, well, there were some moderate droughts, mostly at the height of my addiction.

The first reason for the absence of details is…it's none of your fucking (pun intended) business! It's known as "intimacy" for a reason. It's something that's between you and the other person, or other people, as it were. In other words, I don't "kiss and tell." People did not share their bodies with me, thinking that someday, our experiences would be plastered all over the pages of a book. Also, this book is obviously not about sex; it's about recovery from addiction. The old adage "sex sells" comes to mind, but to me, that's a "tabloid-ish" copout. I'm hoping "recovery sells" too. But, make no mistake, for most of us, recovering from addiction and recovering sexually go hand in hand.

As the AA 12 & 12 book says in reference to sex; *Some of us needed an overhauling there.* I will admit that, at least in part, I replaced drug addiction with sex. There was a period in those early days that I "chased a lot of skirts," though I'll stop short of labeling myself a sex addict. I like to think of it as a "sexual awakening" of sorts after I stopped using drugs. A closer description might be a "womanizer," but that term irritates me if I'm being honest. When two consenting adults have sexual relations, why is the man accused of using the woman? Why is the woman never accused of using a man for sex? Why doesn't the term "manizer" exist? The biggest solution in dealing with a "womanizer" is a mature woman with good boundaries who doesn't engage sexually with someone before really getting to know them.

It reminds me of the old toilet seat issue. Why is it that I'm responsible for putting the toilet seat down when it's your ass that's going to get wet if you sit on the toilet without making sure the seat's down? Not to mention, I need the seat up. I actually had that argument with Amelia once.

It takes two to tango, and I feel that men, at times, are viewed as somehow responsible for women's sexual conduct. People understand this concept when we try to shift blame onto a rape victim because of the way they dressed or behaved and that it somehow invited and condoned criminal behavior from another person. If all parties involved are adults and are consenting, they all need to take responsibility for their own sexual conduct.

To complicate matters further, there was the ever-present fear of HIV/AIDS. Sex became this tightrope walk between being an uninhibited free-spirit and making every effort not to contract the virus. Any kind of sexual encounter that involved multiple partners (there were a few in those days) was followed by months of paranoia and volleys of testing at the health department. Looking back on it, it was quite stressful and could have made someone with less coping and stress management skills vulnerable to relapse.

I was still in the middle of an ongoing learning experience when it came to sex and still prone to a lot of impulsive, old behavior. This was never more evident than when David and I were driving through Wicker Park late at night after band rehearsal. We were flagged down by a street prostitute as we drove by. This was pretty common at that time of night on that strip of North Avenue. David suggested that we turn around and pick her up and see if she'd do us both at the same time. Against my better judgement, I agreed. We both started laughing like little school kids on the playground who were about to steal someone's lunch money. The girl agreed and we went through with it.

Afterward, a typical men's locker room mentality prevailed as we critiqued our experience. However, after I dropped David off at home, and I was left with my thoughts, I started to feel guilty. It occurred to me that I had likely just contributed dope money to what was probably a fellow addict in the throes of her addiction. This did not sit well with me, not only as a recovering addict, but also as a new substance abuse counselor. I never did it again.

This was just one incident in what would be an ongoing struggle—how to enjoy sex without feeling guilty. It was a difficult road to navigate at times, but it helped to have developed some basic rules that I was somehow able to stick to: No sex with minors, no sex with newcomers in recovery, and no sex with clients in treatment (or their mothers). With these rules as guiding principles, if there was an attraction and we were mutually consenting adults, sex was on the table as an option.

I admit that because of being a young horny guy, it started to interfere with my long-distance relationship with Amelia. I loved her, but it became difficult to remain true to her. I started to consider ending the relationship.

Several months later, to try to get my mind off of Amelia, Storchy suggested going to see a movie. We went to see the newly released *Dances with Wolves*, a film that would become one of my all-time favorites. When "Stands with Fist," played by Mary McDonnell, makes her appearance in the film, her resemblance to Amelia gave me a knot in my gut. This did not get by Storchy, and he glanced over at me out of the corner of his eye to see my reaction. He smiled and chuckled as if to say, *Ain't this a bitch? We come to see a movie to get his mind off her, and there's some chick in the film that looks just like her.*

After the film, on the ride to get some food, I confided in him that Amelia was the best sex I'd ever had, along with the fear that I would never have anything as good ever again. He looked at me and imparted these words of wisdom: "I understand your fear Steve, but the next person's not going to be better or worse; they're going to be different."

It was the beginning of an important understanding about good sex—that one needed to be able to adjust one's "sex-pectations" of others in relationships. It was the wisest thing Storchy ever said to me, followed by one of the funniest. As we looked for somewhere to eat, he demanded: "Don't take me anywhere to get a lettuce sandwich. I need real food!" This referred to healthier changes I started making to my diet, mostly from being with Amelia but also from hanging around with people with eating disorders.

Unfortunately, it would be one of the last good conversations Mark and I would have. Our relationship was about to take an abrupt and steep nosedive.

Northwest Youth "Over-reach"

While the band was being promoted at work, I was not. My conflicts with my supervisor Lee, continued to grow (post-Christmas party) and finally came to a head in a way that shook the very foundation of the "new me." In March of 1991, I was fired from NYO by Leo Thomas. The reason? The same bullshit they told Michael: "It's not working out" and "It's just not a good fit." I was furious. Those are reasons you fire someone who's on probationary status, not someone who's worked there for almost two years and been promoted twice. I knew we didn't like each other, but would he really fire me for that? Maybe, but I didn't think so. Maybe they found out that I was sleeping with the receptionist Karla and Angela at the Proviso office, and they didn't want the potential drama. Or, as I said before, maybe they felt my salary was getting a little too high. In any case, it was the second time I'd been fired since getting clean and sober, and it hurt my pride, my ego, and my self-esteem. It brought me down quickly and hard. It didn't make me want to go out and shoot heroin to cover the pain, but going from the "golden boy" who "we just send the kids to Steve and don't ask any questions" to being fired, had me confused.

Suddenly, I found myself immersed in a deep pool of self-doubt. For the first time since entering the counseling field, I started seriously contemplating whether I wanted to be in it or not. After being approved for unemployment benefits, I decided to take a break from the field and give myself time to think.

Luckily, our landlord approached me and offered me a nice cash side job painting the exterior of "The Fort." The house was huge and old, it had wooden siding, and it was in bad shape. The prep work alone was a massive undertaking for one guy, but I had all summer to do it.

Soon after, to rub salt in the wound, I remember getting a call from my brother Paul, who saw my setback as an opportunity to "talk some sense into me." His goal was to "help me" see the light, become a truck driver like he was and make better money than I ever had in my life. To do this, he presented the case that my life really hadn't changed or improved very much from when I was using drugs. He pointed out that I was collecting unemployment, not making good money even when I was employed, didn't have my own place, and still wasn't married. I felt insulted and defensive because I knew deep down, he was wrong, but I just couldn't seem to find the words to explain why. I hung up the phone and experienced another wave of self-doubt.

On the surface of things, this time in my life did resemble my standard operating procedure when I was using, as he mentioned. Then it hit me, and I realized what the significant differences were. I picked up the phone, called him back, and set him straight...

"Hey, it's me. After I hung up with you, I realized that what you said bothered me. Then I realized why. I know on the surface, things may look like they did when I was using, but there's a few big differences. I used to be in those situations in the past because I had no choice. Today, I'm clean and sober, and because of that, I have choices that I didn't used to have. I'm choosing to be unemployed and collect benefits for now. I'm choosing to live with roommates, people I chose, because I want to save money and realized I didn't need all that apartment. And I'm doing a job I'm good at and that I feel good about. I don't want to drive a truck, even if I would make better money."

There really wasn't much he could say after that. When the call ended, I felt good that I was able to find the words to explain the differences between who I was today and who I used to be, even though they looked similar on the surface at that time.

There would soon be another situation that would require me to take a stand for myself and set some necessary boundaries that involved my best treatment buddy, Mark Storch. As the novelty of him being out of prison wore off and our lives started going in different directions, we started to grow farther apart. Me being in a band and him attending meetings less often, contributed to the situation. Also, as my faith in God increased, his atheism became more and more annoying to me, as I'm sure my faith did for him.

Tension started to mount between us and culminated in a phone call that I got from him late that spring. Surprisingly, I am unable to remember what it was about, but we got into a heated argument that escalated and led to him screaming at me in a manner that could best be described as violent and threatening. An alarm went off in the back of my mind, alerting me that he had crossed a serious line with me. My response?...

"Who the fuck do you think you're talking to? No one talks to me like that! We're not in seventh grade on the playground! I don't need to have anyone in my life that talks to me like that!" And with that, I slammed the phone down and hung up.

That would be the last real conversation I would have with him with the exception of a chance encounter we had while walking from LPAC to the 7-Eleven store to get cigarettes later that summer. At that time, my suspicions were confirmed that the tension between us wasn't just from growing apart. Mark had relapsed, big time. He had lost a ton of weight and looked terrible. He tried to play it off as intentional weight loss, but a dope fiend can't fool another dope fiend. Our encounter was cordial but brief. I know he must have been ashamed. I walked away once again, with that dual feeling of sadness mixed with gratitude that it wasn't me.

"A three-hour tour, a three-hour tour"

Amelia's struggles in The Big Apple continued, so she settled for a theatre production being done at a good-sized theater in Ohio. It was a classic American play. Amelia was one of the female main characters, whose counterpart was none other than Tina Louise, famous for her role as Ginger Grant in the 1960s' TV sitcom, *Gilligan's Island*. However, in a phone conversation with Amelia, I learned that Ms. Louise viewed her "fame" from the show as more of a terrible curse than anything. Though the show only ran for three seasons from 1964 to 1967, the reruns continued to play all over the world. Because she was still viewed by everyone and their brother as her role of the movie star castaway, she was absolutely typecast.

Amelia invited me to the play, and due to Chicago not being more than a long drive to the city the play was in, I was able to arrange the trip.

The drive was another peaceful, meditative experience, beautifully lined with fall colors. Upon my arrival, Amelia and I engaged in our typical hot, passionate sex, followed by petty bickering and arguing. The play opened the next day, and she informed me that Tina had invited us to dinner that evening. I responded, "Cool," and proceeded to sing the Gilligan's Island theme song: *A three-hour tour, a three-hour tour....*

Amelia looked at me like she wanted to kill me. "Okay, let's talk."

"What?"

"When we go to dinner, whatever you do, do not bring up *Gilligan's Island*. It's a very sore subject for her."

"No problem. I was always more of a Mary Ann guy myself anyway."

"You promise?"

"I promise."

I had no problem not bringing up the show. My biggest fear was accidentally calling her Ginger. She had always been Ginger to me.

When we arrived at the restaurant, Tina was already there and had gotten a table, which we were shown to by the hostess. There she sat, Ginger…I mean…Tina! See what I mean!? She stood up to greet us as we approached.

Surprisingly, she was as tall as she looked on TV. She was still very sexy with a few more lines on her face. That only made her sexier to me. Amelia introduced me, and I immediately dove into some small talk and asked about the play in a deliberate attempt to steer away from bringing up *the professor and Mary Ann, here on Gilligan's Isle.*

I don't remember how it happened, but some part of the conversation led Tina to tell us about a recent trip she'd made to Japan. She described a slew of difficulties she experienced on her trip…

"I finally got to my hotel room in the middle of the night. I was exhausted but needed to unwind a bit before trying to sleep, so I got in bed, grabbed the remote, and turned the TV on. What do you think was on the TV? *Gilligan's Island* with subtitles! There I was, on the TV, twenty-five years younger, blathering away in Japanese! I immediately changed the channel and thought, *I can't escape that show no matter where I go!* I mean, I'm thousands of miles away in Japan—right? And there's that stupid show!"

I turned and looked at Amelia as if to say; *It wasn't me,* and to get some kind of permission to respond. I got no such permission and instead got a shocked, blank stare from Amelia that was impossible to read.

Tina then went into a rant about how the show ruined her career, and she had nothing to show for it. She said the pay sucked, and they got no royalties, which I believe was being litigated in the courts at the time. Then, to add insult to injury, the reruns of the show haunted her everywhere she went.

My response was sympathetic and supportive, and I remember coming away from that dinner feeling sad for her. The 57-year-old actress was well past her prime and was obviously tortured and being eaten alive by resentment. Too bad that she wasn't an alcoholic or an addict. She could have used the program.

Urbus Orbis

Back in Chicago, at least several times a week, the words "Urbus Orbis" would be on my mind and in my eyes. The words were made up and, as I would later learn, were code for "Got any weed?" Was I being tempted to smoke some weed on a weekly basis? No. In fact, the term probably hadn't been used to ask that question since the 1970s.

As Wicker Park and the surrounding neighborhoods became our artistic stomping grounds, we began to carve out "our places" mostly to eat. Recovery involves a lot of eating, and as bachelors, a lot of eating out. I call this aspect of my recovery "food adventures." These adventures were made possible by the diversity of the City of Chicago's eclectic melting pot of cuisines. We would roam the city after meetings, and randomly wander into Thai, Indian, German, Tapas, Italian, Greek, Turkish, and other ethnic eateries.

I don't recommend those in early recovery partake in the Turkish espresso. After just one, our hair stood up on end, we were talking a mile a minute, and we all broke out in a bead of sweat on our foreheads. I swear, we needed to hit a meeting after we got out of there! "I think we just relapsed," we joked as we left the place.

We would go into places that served foreign cuisine and ask the wait staff, "So, what's good?" Then, we'd blindly follow their recommendations. We were on a great adventure, so why not food, too?

When we weren't exploring the food terrain–or at Guitar Center, The Alley, or Café Voltaire in the Lakeview area–we could be found inhabiting the bohemian, artsy Greenwich Village-like area in the center of Wicker Park. It was becoming filled with art galleries, studios, small no-name theaters, clubs, bars, and eateries. The gentrification of the area had begun. The cooler the neighborhood got, the higher the rents and mortgages went. Before gentrification got a stranglehold, some of my favorite eateries were Sophie's Busy Bee (great, cheap, real Polish food), Earwax Café (eggs espresso, organic veggie breakfasts, and caffe lattes, served by pretty girls with hairy legs and armpits, wearing combat boots) and the Hollywood Grill (dine with junkies, pimps, prostitutes and artists, in this neighborhood melting pot), to name a few.

But the hub, at the center of it, the heart and soul of Wicker Park, was Urbus Orbis, the coolest, funkiest coffee shop in the land. We got to know the owner/operator, Tom, from frequenting the place. It only took about a year for me to finally ask the question, "Hey, Tom, what does Urbus Orbis mean?" I wasn't at all surprised by the answer. Tom was an urban, intellectual stoner, hippie-type throwback from the Beatnik era. He was the "Sam Malone" of Wicker Park's version of *Cheers*. As such, he presided over a cast of characters who could only be described as eclectic and unlikely to be in the same room together outside of this "commune."

The place was huge, with a U-shaped bar, tables, couches, comfy second-hand chairs, and a backroom that was sometimes used as a performance space. It was just the right amount of messy and unkept, with newspapers and magazines strewn about the place, art for sale covering the walls and the aroma of strong coffee and cigarettes with an occasional hint of weed.

Tom, like Sam Malone (and many bartenders) was a community healer/caretaker/therapist of sorts and fulfilled different needs for different patrons. Once he got to know our small entourage, he took an interest upon learning that we were all sober ex-junkies and ex-alkies. He zeroed in on me when he found out I was not only an ex-heroin addict but also a counselor.

He pulled me into his office and confided in me that he had a friend, a local artist, struggling with heroin addiction and needed my help. I don't recall if I gave him my number or not, but my first meeting with Adam was in person. Tom introduced us and we sat at the corner of the bar and had a long talk.

Adam chain-smoked, and pounded cups of coffee, which likely contributed to his already sweaty shaking hands due to heroin withdrawal. I remember being concerned about his health as he appeared skinny, gaunt, and pale. HIV/AIDS was always a looming possibility for all IV drug users. I gave him my standard heroin-withdrawal pep talk, the same one given to me once upon a time: "Don't be a fucking baby. Buck up and get through it!" I agreed to be his sponsor. We planned to meet at an NA meeting the next day. The band became his sponsor as we all took Adam under our proverbial wings.

It was the Serenity Prayer

As the band got more gigs and started developing a small following, albeit still mostly program people and friends, we started developing a show. This included opening with a poet named Mikey who we met in A.A. meetings. Mikey was a slightly autistic, idiot savant type straight out of some dark underground comic book. He had thick coke-bottle black-rimmed glasses, wore a stocking cap and combat boots no matter the weather, and lived in the projects where I used to cop dope from Annie. If we thought David's lyrics were dark, we hadn't heard anything like Mikey's stuff. The best way to describe Mikey's poetry was demented and psychotic. You felt like you were getting a peek into the mind of a serial killer. In reality, Mike was sober and harmless...I think. He'd read one of his poems and segue us into a sick, demented, but somewhat structured noise explosion that we used as an intro to our opening song at gigs.

We decided it was time to go for the gusto, and we sent a promo package to one of the biggest local venues in Chicago—Cabaret Metro. Metro was one of the "brass rings" for local bands. Many spent years rehearsing and refining their music and never set foot on the Metro stage.

Seven months after putting the band together, Firetruck was booked at Metro for a July 17, 1991, show. Okay, it was a Wednesday, but it was still a huge feather in our cap.

On the day of the biggest gig of our lives, we all dealt with our nerves the best we could. Fred went through his typical pre-show ritual of masturbating (privately, not in the presence of the band) and drinking a cup of warm milk.

When we arrived backstage, we were greeted by the sound crew, who did a sound check with us. They asked if we wanted a DAT (Digital Audio Tape) made of our show, which of course we did. During our soundcheck, they gave us some semi-bad news—my bass couldn't go through the mixing board due to my amplifier being a vintage Custom (complete with gold Lamé upholstery) with tubes instead of transistors. This meant that the audience and the band would hear my bass fine in the room and on stage through the monitors, but they would have to pick it up from the room mics and couldn't be recorded through the sound board. We still wanted the tape.

Mary put together fliers with photos and the lyrics to most of our songs. She distributed them and prepared her camera as we finished our soundcheck.

When we got to the dressing room, we got a shock when the first thing we saw was a large ice bucket full of a variety of beers! Upon closer inspection, our shock quickly turned into relief when we noticed that the beer was all non-alcoholic, mixed with sodas and bottled water. Apparently, they knew we were all sober. *Very cool*, we all thought.

Time dragged and nerves set in (cold, sweaty palms were the worst for me) as we waited and heard people start to file into the club. Right before we went on, we all stood in the middle of the room, arms around our shoulders just like we were in a meeting, and we said The Serenity Prayer. Then, one of the crew came back and asked, "You guys ready?" We were as ready as we were going to be. We grabbed our axes and headed for the stage.

The MC went to the mic and announced, "We've got some great bands for you tonight, starting with a band making their debut on the Metro stage. Please help me welcome…FIRETRUCK!"

Their breasts and sheets and penises and vaginas and balls and blankets will be bathed in the red from my eye curtain incarnate. And their stomachs will redeem my yellow eye curtain with bile as their expectorations of liquid soft will transform to solid hard. And from inebriation to torture, from climax to death, the exact reversal of my spiritual transformation. Now, to that future then, when small will be small enough to be large. I must conserve hand energy though, to be able to grasp the cup and its dregs for my final escape and the mocking nausea, because when I do my damage one fine night, I will not be convicted by a jury of dogs!

B I G   N O I S E (which simultaneously released a lot of that nervous energy)!!!

The song we opened with was a newer one called "El Loco," a little ditty about a Latino convicted murderer, gangbanger, and "warrior priest," serving time in the Chino prison in California. The song was driving and intense. Apparently, so much so, that Vince immediately broke a string.

After the song ended, Vince scrambled to change the string as David improvised, bantering with the audience to buy us some time. It seemed like an eternity for Vince to change that string, so Fred saved the day by handing off his "AK-47, Frankenstein-monster assault guitar" (that he made out of spare parts) to Vince. Fred then grabbed his vintage Gibson Explorer (which I nicknamed "the coffee table guitar") and plugged it in. Not a moment too soon either, because David ran out of things to say and in desperation ended his blathering with, "Hey girls show us your tits! C'mon, show us your tits!" Once Vince was ready to go, he introduced the next song, and we moved on.

As it turned out, that was the only hiccup, and the rest of the show went smoothly. When we got off stage, we were as giddy as school kids. We had pulled it off! Mikey pointed out to us; "It was The Serenity Prayer" as an explanation for why things went so well. We all agreed.

Another big show we did around that time, was a benefit to "save" a college radio station, WHPK, out of the University of Chicago in Hyde Park. The station played an eclectic mix of music and was completely run by the students. The entire weekend event was broadcast on the station. We shared the bill with some big local names including Smashing Pumpkins.

It seemed we were always right on the proverbial heels of the Pumpkins, playing in places where they played the night before or after. This is as close as we would get to the soon-to-be national act. I remember seeing their stepped-on, beer-stained setlists when setting up equipment for a show.

No one knew who was going to "make it" and who wasn't in those days. We all hated Liz Phair's music, but she wound up being one of the success stories from those days. In any case, the benefit must have been successful. The station still exists at the time of this writing.

This show was important for a number of reasons. For me, it made clear who our audience was—college students. But because of David being almost forty, I thought, *how are we going to sell ourselves to college students?* That's when it hit me—*Uncle David!* I thought. You know, that weird mysterious hipster uncle some people have, with the cool adventures and stories from their younger days. David was by far the most interesting person in the band and the ingredients were there to build an intriguing mystique around him. I could envision the kids sitting around, getting stoned and trying to decipher what the hell Uncle David was talking about, as they were unraveling the complex, deep philosophical meaning of lyrics the likes of "Zoroaster's Dead Angels" ...

Mandalas secret pleasure lay
In Kundalini's spiral ray,
Driving up evolutions play

Soon tune will reveal
New levels to feel
Sex appeal, drug meal

Purity's boring rhymes
Old virginal crimes
Sex appeal, drug meal

Twisting children's play

Call sacred signs
Profanity's eye rays
Fades innocence away ...

While solving the mysteries and puzzles, they would also be getting a history or Eastern Philosophy lesson on any number of intellectual subjects. Firetruck's music was tight, youthful, hard, and driving. But the real appeal, that made us stand out from the rest, was "Uncle David" Hoffman's lyrics!

These shows emboldened David to attempt to pull some strings with a celebrity who he had crossed paths earlier that year—Sir Elton John.

Elton had started his recovery from addiction and an eating disorder at the world-renowned Parkside Hospital. He started going to some of the meetings that David went to, including the Saturday morning OA/AA at LPAC. He decided to write to his "buddy" Elton. Here is some of that letter:

Mr. Elton John, I hope. Sir.
Find enclosed one demo tape. We're called Fire Truck ..." He goes on to whine about the lack of quality production and ends with— *"We think we have raw talent. We need production, backing, and money."*

Well, at least he didn't pull any punches or dance around the issue: How about writing us a big fat check Elton!?

So, I had this epiphany. The appeal of Firetruck became completely clear as to the direction we should go and what we should be promoting. The band had a manager in a practical sense, but no one to direct the band's path. I started emerging as that person. Unfortunately, when I brought up my vision to the rest of the band, it mostly fell on deaf ears, the deafest being Fred's.

Fred had issues, one of which was related to his ego (imagine that—an addict with ego problems). He wrote a lot of the music so that was his focus. He really didn't get the "Uncle David" thing and took himself and the band too seriously, musically speaking. He didn't see that we were basically like The Doors, in that, without Jim Morrison, we were just another Rock & Roll band. His response was one of those crooked Freddy smiles accompanied by the Freddy death stare. The message: *Cool, Steve but shut up and play bass. You're drinking too much coffee.* I couldn't believe they didn't get it, and I experienced my first wave of disillusionment with the band. Tensions continued to grow.

Café Bustelo

As I previously indicated, Fred wasn't the only "egomaniac with an inferiority complex" in the band. As my issues with the band's lack of direction started to grow, ironically while experiencing success, egos started to flare up, and tension started to build. It's an old story that you've seen on those *Behind the Music* shows. The Beatles were probably the most well-known from my era. The big red flag was when Fred and Vince got into a fistfight before a show.

To avoid the fate of the Fab Four, the band sought out a location where we could meet regularly to air our differences and facilitate some "group therapy" for the band. It was open to any of our friends who wanted to join us.

Doug and our mutual AA friend Tom M. attended the small Wicker Park Lutheran church on the corner of Hoyne Avenue and Lemoyne Street. The pastor agreed to let us use the basement for our meeting. We checked it out and noted that it had a kitchen, a few coffee pots and accessories. It also had a few bricks of the Puerto Rican espresso coffee—Café Bustelo, that we decided it would be okay to break open. We set up an eight-foot folding table and seven or eight chairs around it in the middle of the room, and we were all set.

Souped-up on strong coffee, we set out to "get our minds right," iron out our differences, and maybe even resolve a childhood trauma or two if we were lucky. We started meeting on Fridays at 7 p.m. The first meetings were mostly bitch sessions for the band, but we quickly realized that others in attendance really didn't benefit from that, so we grasped for some type of structure that would accommodate everyone. The format that we were all familiar with was Twelve-step meetings! So, it morphed into some semblance of a bastardized AA meeting. We rotated chairing it, but it really ran itself.

What emerged, besides our band and relationship difficulties being aired, was a kind of irreverent challenging and questioning of some of the principles and dictates of the 12-step program. In other meetings we attended, we found ourselves sitting there and biting our tongues while philosophies from God to cliché program concepts, got shoved down our throats. By this time, we were all feeling pretty rebellious about some of the more generic aspects of the program. The banter was pretty irreverent, and the loose informal format of the meeting made it easy to do. Not to mention being infused with a pretty good dose of caffeine from drinking too much Puerto Rican espresso.

We would read a daily devotion from the *Twenty-Four Hours a Day* book in the beginning of the meeting and David would jump out of his seat and yell things like "Bullshit!" Then, go on to state his case and share his experience with whatever concept he was challenging. We would laugh, crosstalk across the table, and argue about some of the principles of the AA program and of life in general. This would have been fine except for one thing; my sponsee Adam attended the weekly meeting with me. During one meeting, Adam finally chimed in and ridiculed an important aspect of the program, which I can't recall. That's when it occurred to me that our irreverent and unconventional approach may be hurting him. After all, he was in a very early stage of recovery and didn't have the experience the rest of us had. After the meeting, I pulled him off to the side and had a "sponsorly" chat with him…

"I heard what you said in the meeting tonight and it concerned me. It made me realize something that I think I should set you straight on. We've all gone through the program and worked the steps. You haven't. Because of that, we have sort of earned the right to challenge and make fun of certain aspects of the program. Deep down we know the program saved our lives. In other words, we've gone through the program, not around it. You haven't worked it enough, and I don't want you to think that you can avoid some of the work that the program suggests. Maybe this isn't a good meeting for you right now, and you should consider finding another one on Friday nights. It's not a real meeting."

He got it and agreed. Although he enjoyed our irreverence and edgy humor, he admitted that it probably wasn't what he needed to hear at this stage of his recovery.

The incident made us realize that we needed a more traditional format for the meeting. This was further affirmed when local artists and musicians started to show up after hearing about the meeting through the grapevine.

One man in particular stands out. Local artist Dave S. made his first meeting and told his story of typical alcoholic drinking and his desperation to stop. He had been struggling to stay sober, so he finally decided to give AA a chance. He planned his first meeting after calling the Chicago AA office. When he showed up, no one was there. Apparently, the meeting didn't exist anymore, and no further information was available.

The next week he called and got information about another local meeting. This time, there was a sign on the door that said the meeting had moved and changed to a different day.

His third attempt was slightly more successful, but when he arrived, he noticed that he was the only man at the meeting. It was a women's group. They were nice enough to let him stay, but he admitted that it was a bit uncomfortable, and likely for them as well. He was about to give up when he heard about us through a friend of a friend.

He expressed relief after arriving and seeing us all sitting around the table. After sitting down and listening to us, he realized that we were sober musicians and artists. Dave knew he was "home," and he became a regular member of our group. Fellow artist Adam hit it off with Dave right away. They wound up renting a loft on Milwaukee Avenue and turned it into a studio where they would both churn out works of art, clean and sober.

Even though it wasn't our intention, we had started an AA meeting. God has a way of inserting His will, despite our intentions. After a handful of local addicts and alkies started showing up, we put it to a vote and wound up putting it in the Chicago AA Meeting Directory.

What started as a private "therapy group" to air Firetruck's grievances, had officially become an AA meeting. We needed a name for the directory listing. That was a no-brainer...and "Café Bustelo Group" was born.

Interventions

At the end of August of 1991, I was engaging in my usual Sunday morning ritual at Earwax Café. This was usually eating my eggs espresso, drinking coffee, smoking cigs, and peeking over my newspaper to get a glimpse of the waitresses while trying to block out the view of their hairy armpits.

Unemployment benefits were going to end soon, and it was time to find a job. I perused the wanted section, and one job listing jumped off the page at me. I recognized the agency as being the same one whose Methadone clinic I attended before I went into treatment. Interventions was looking for a counselor for their inpatient treatment program in Lincoln Park, the heart of Chicago's North Side. At this point, I still wasn't sure if I wanted to continue in the addictions field, so I said a prayer and turned it over to God.

After attending a meeting at LPAC, I was surprised to learn that the program was in one of the three-flat residential buildings less than a block away. I decided to check it out and walked to the Sheffield Avenue address.

I was greeted by a resident working at the front desk. He called back to the staff on duty, who came out and greeted me. I explained that I saw the ad in the paper and inquired about the position. He informed me that the position was still available and instructed me to complete the application which he would forward to the director, Colleen Nitka.

We had a brief conversation about the program and the population being young men ages 17 to 25. It was a TC model similar to Gateway. My ears perked up and I remember thinking that the position would be right up my alley. I mentioned that I never knew the program was there, even though I attended meetings right down the street. He laughed and said: "That's good news. We try to keep a low profile around here. We got 'grandfathered' into this neighborhood before it was zoned as residential, and some of our neighbors aren't thrilled that we're here. I'll pass your application on to Colleen."

The next day, I got a call from her and set up an interview. The interview was a breeze as I learned that the regional director Leslie was not only a Gateway graduate herself, but her sister Stacey was my very first counselor at The Maze on Belmont and Broadway. I told her the story of Stacey pulling me over and telling me to talk less and listen more, because my "Methadone was doing the talking." Leslie was obviously tickled that I was one of her sister's success stories. I also learned that two of my Gateway mentors worked there: Benny L. and Howard P.

Gateway's programs had churned out many second-generation pioneers in the addictions field, like Leslie and Stacey and a lot of good clinicians too. I have never knocked formal education, but TC people just understood the dynamics of addiction, treatment, and recovery on a deeper level than any school could teach. Colleen and some of the other non-recovering staff would, however, create a much-needed balance to contrast and complement all who were products of the Therapeutic Community.

After my interview, I think it was obvious to them that not only was this modality of treatment my forte, but as a 31-year-old man in recovery, I would also be a good role-model for their population. I was hired immediately.

Because of the way the job sort of fell into my lap and it being walking distance from LPAC, I remember thinking; *Okay God, I got the message.*

Step 11 of the 12-step program says: *We sought through prayer and meditation to improve our conscious contact with God as we understood Him, praying only for knowledge of His will for us and the power to carry that out.*

Was doing this work God's will for me? Maybe. I wasn't totally convinced back then. All I knew was I still wanted to be a recording artist! I resumed my career as a substance abuse counselor on September 16, 1991.

I was soon able to take the certification test I'd been studying for, to become a certified addictions counselor. The problem was, the test I studied for was considered obsolete and was replaced with a new, more up to date test. I quickly recognized that the questions were not what I had studied. Luckily, I had enough clinical insight and understanding to wing it and pass the test. But there was one more catch—I technically was not a high school graduate. This would have interfered with my ability to be hired, until I explained to Colleen that I had passed the GED exam but needed to take the US Constitution test to receive my diploma. I had never gotten around to it.

After conferring with Leslie, they devised a way around this. The program had a tutor that came weekly to help some of the guys achieve their GED. I got a study guide from her, she was able to administer the test, and luckily, I passed it and finally earned my GED.

I'll never forget getting my GED diploma in the mail. It caught me off guard and I began to cry as I released forever the pain from one of my biggest past failures—high school. As the tears ran down my cheeks, I flashed back to a collage of memories, like; running from security through the halls, staggering from the nurse's office under the influence of drugs to escape Dean Paske, pulling an ounce of marijuana out of my pocket in his office, the police leading me out of the school in handcuffs, and a few other unsavory memories. I was 31 years old when I got my high school diploma. To some, the piece of paper in my hand may not have meant much; to me it represented redemption.

One of my biggest regrets had always been my high school years. If I could have, I would have approached them completely differently. Instead of running around the halls in a daze, and escaping every chance I got, I would have been on the chess team, a thespian, and an art major. I would have laughed at peer pressure to do wrong and brushed it off my shoulder like it was a flea. I would have had no problem standing up for myself and showing whomever I needed to "the hand," like I finally did when I made my announcement to my second family in Gateway: "If you're about bullshit, stay the fuck away from me!" I couldn't go back and redo high school, but this was the next best thing.

The new job couldn't have been timed any better, as it coincided with a move back to the city. Bob and I had both had it with Toby, who became increasingly more irritating. Bob approached me about looking for an apartment on the North Side. I was all in due to the new job and it wasn't long before he found a reasonably priced, spacious two-bedroom at 4208 North Lincoln Avenue. Bob continued film school and bartending at the restaurant. Both were downtown, so the move made sense for him too.

Upon starting my new position at Lincoln Park Interventions, I felt like a fish placed back into water. My comfort and familiarity with the TC environment kicked in immediately. They paired me with an experienced counselor, Carl Scroggins, who also ran the family education program. He quickly recognized my knowledge and understanding of TC dynamics, so following him around and observing didn't last long. I came in one morning, and he informed me, "You're running group today," throwing me right into the middle of "the pond." I think he knew I could "swim" and I did not disappoint.

My days of being mentored ended abruptly and they assigned the next four clients who entered treatment to my caseload. The "caseload from Hell," as I would lovingly refer to them, came into being. Caseloads were typically four to six clients and allowed us to give a lot of attention to each individual.

Once again, I was "baptized by fire" with my first client, who was a twenty-year-old, gay black prostitute heroin addict named Anthony. His mother was also a heroin addict and a prostitute. Anthony started using heroin at the tender age of nine! He never met his father. He came in, looking like he had just crawled out from under a rock. He had extremely long fingernails and his out-of-control afro made famous fight promoter, Don King, look well-groomed. Piece-a-cake! No problema! My response was to look for the magic wand up my ass, but I quickly discovered that I didn't have one.

Next was Max. Also in his early twenties, Max was a South Side, Irish alcoholic who identified himself as a racist, white supremacist that hung with, and aspired to being a "skinhead"! I remember thinking, *"Gee, this will make for an interesting dynamic in caseload group."* Max's parents were interesting too. They were divorced and his father was likely an alcoholic but stopped drinking on his own without treatment or AA. His mother never drank except for holidays. So, was she a normal person? It appeared so, until Max told me the details of his mother's holiday drinking. He reported that when she did drink, she drank all the men in the family (all heavy drinkers) under the table and usually blacked out. It occurred to me that his mother was likely alcoholic too. She was just an alcoholic who didn't drink most of the year. Not typical but totally feasible. Her story cemented my developing understanding of the wide variety of patterns addicted people have. Simply put, not all addicts and alcoholics use or drink every day. I didn't. I couldn't afford to.

Then came Mike, whose drug of choice was anything that got him high. He was a product of the foster care system after he was removed from his home due to sexually inappropriate conduct with his younger siblings. Mike was "damaged goods" and was hurt and angry at the world, and justifiably so. Mike never had a father in his life and was rejected by the one person who was never supposed to reject him—his mother.

Last, but not least, was Lamonte. Lamonte was a quiet unassuming young black man who was completely a product of his environment. He grew up on the West Side in one of the roughest neighborhoods in Chicago. Outwardly he had a gentle disposition, but it was mostly a facade. In reality, he had a fortress of thick walls around him, behind which was a ton of trauma, hurt, and anger. Lamonte was never going to let you know how he really felt inside. Sharing your true feelings where he came from, could get you killed. My colleagues agreed that I had my work cut out for me.

Once again, I would build a reputation for being fearless, with the kind of intuitive clinical insight needed to "work well with difficult clients."

I think some of the things that made me a good counselor for the hard cores was, not only having been one myself, but also, realizing that these rough parts of their exterior were symptoms of their addiction—defense mechanisms that helped them survive in the streets. My job was to get them to recognize this, abandon these "masks," defenses, and survival skills—and replace them with recovery and life skills. I nicknamed this process "Finding the chewy marshmallow center within." I came to understand that the "real person" was in there somewhere, and I would find that person through being fearless in showing my genuine love, care and concern for them, while balancing it with my no-bullshit, "tell it like it is" style. It was pretty effective in that setting.

I learned that there was always something to love about every client. I found that when you don't honestly love and care about your clients, they sense it, see you as a phony who can't help them, and tune you out. We would say it jokingly, but I felt that I was "on a mission from God."

I soon discovered that one of the key advantages of working with clients on a daily, instead of a weekly basis, was being able to build on successes and sustain progress, despite occasional setbacks. I developed the ability (likely from my own treatment experience) to start over with clients every day, meaning; however confrontational I'd gotten with a client today, I was able to come in the next day, holding no grudges whatsoever. This had an important effect on clients by demonstrating that there was a way back from mistakes and that resolution and reconciliation was possible. These are paths to healing that addicted people are typically incapable of while in active addiction.

I began to recognize that resolving conflict in a healthy way was an important life skill for these young men to acquire. This seemed to be a good indicator of their growth, and ultimately, their ability to remain clean and sober. Conflict resolution was important in a more practical and immediate sense too. It was essential in getting a bunch of young, addicted men through treatment, without beating each other's ass and getting kicked out of the program.

Conflict resolution became a special interest and a forte of mine. Using mostly my instincts and experience from my treatment, I developed an experimental group technique.

I would have the group members in a circle and put the two that had the conflict directly across from each other inside the circle, spread far apart, with me seated in the middle between them. I would allow them to air their grievance with each other across the room with no limits on what they said, but they had to stay in their chairs and look each other in the eyes when speaking. They were not allowed to say anything without making eye contact. It's hard to be a jagoff tough guy when you're looking into someone's eyes. The conversation would initially be aggressive and peppered with profanity.

After each volley, they would each move their chair two feet closer. They would eventually find themselves facing each other, with only me between them. I would not block their path to each other but would be strategically positioned in case I needed to get between them. On the last volley, they would literally be so close, their knees were almost touching. At that time, I'd require them to extend one arm and put one hand on the other's shoulder.

As you might imagine, by this time, the conversation became much more civil, and even empathetic toward each other. By the end, there would usually be no sign of conflict remaining. I'd encourage them to shake hands, and give each other a hug. They were commended for their efforts and the other group members would applaud, then give comments and supportive feedback.

I recognized the significant therapeutic value this had, not only for the clients with the conflict, but for the rest of the group. We all witnessed two guys who were ready to fight—that started out yelling, insulting and cursing each other out—become civil and end up hugging and shaking hands. You would literally feel the conflict and angry feelings evaporate from the room.

I continued developing my clinical insight and intuition. I understood clients' pain and defenses on a deeper level, and I became emotionally fearless and able to "get in the ring" with the most negative, destructive emotions clients had and help them work through them. I would roll up my sleeves, going toe-to-toe with their addiction and insanity. Many clients were the product of parents who abandoned them or made them feel unloved and unwanted. My approach promoted healing through "Tough love". I loved them "unconditionally" (Never been a big fan of that term). Well, almost unconditionally. There are always conditions with love, (i.e., if you light me on fire, I probably won't love you anymore). This was combined with drill sergeant-like discipline. It was a powerful combination. For some, I became the father they never had.

I became an emotional "exorcist" of sorts, willing to do battle with client's demons. They knew I understood them, and I wasn't afraid—a very important quality to have if you want to be an effective addictions counselor. If substance-abusing clients sense the least bit of fear, they will run roughshod over you. It's built in to their manipulative nature.

As I became more comfortable, I became more creative and took more healthy risks. I developed intense controversial groups such as all-night candlelight marathons, where clients' defenses would be worn down by sleep deprivation, and they would self-disclose their worst secrets.

Another was a candlelight visualization group that I called "My Life in Five Years if I Stay Sober." Clients were asked to visualize and describe in detail what they wanted their lives to be like in the future, and what they wanted to get out of recovery. Some clients were so detailed in their visions that they could tell you the color of the lettering on the side of their truck while visualizing owning their own company.

Another group I was particularly good at, having had some acting experience, was a "psychodrama" group, where I would roleplay their drug of choice and try to talk them into using. I would select clients who I felt were getting cocky and felt they were "relapse-proof."

Sitting directly across from them in the middle of the circle, I'd start out with meek and non-threatening questions. Then, I'd tell them how much I missed them and ask if they missed me. When they'd try to deny that they did, I'd turn up the heat and remind them of why they "loved" me so much. I was especially good at playing heroin or cocaine for obvious reasons. I would eventually wear down their defenses and they would cave in and admit being triggered to use. Another advantage of being in a residential setting was being able to work with anyone who was triggered by these roleplays and help them work through any cravings to use. This had the added benefit of showing them that they could survive craving without using.

There were other roleplaying sessions such as "The Mcbistro Death Group." The group was named after the first client we performed it on whose nickname, "Mcbistro," was given to him by his counselor. The group was a mock funeral for clients who were struggling mightily in a last-ditch effort to save them from unsuccessful discharge. The client laid across several chairs with their eyes closed as staff and clients came to pay their respects at the "coffin," one at a time, softly speaking about their feelings and regrets for the "deceased." It was very powerful. The group usually had quite an impact and helped them recognize the seriousness of their situation.

Director Colleen got her knickers in a twist when she heard about the controversial group, until she saw the results. Several clients who experienced it made a complete turnaround and successfully completed treatment.

These treatment approaches were intense, but also very effective. Though they often opened client's emotional wounds, they also facilitated healing of those wounds and promoted lasting recovery. It was one of the advantages of the safe environment that a long-term residential setting provided. Many of these approaches would not work in an outpatient setting and could even be dangerous.

Luckily, I was flanked by a staff team that, despite our different personalities, backgrounds, and styles, possessed similar qualities and abilities.

The groups I developed were only a few of many examples of the creative approaches the staff team brought to the program, enhancing client treatment experiences and making the program something special. Each of us brought something different and important to the table.

Lincoln Park Interventions also had additional programming that Gateway didn't have, such as family education, vocational programming, and its "specialty focus groups": sexual abuse survivors, adult children of alcoholics or addicts who grew up with addicted parents, and feelings group, which focused on developing coping skills. Like at NYO, there were also constant training opportunities for the staff, both in-house and off-site; these helped us develop the skills to address these complex and difficult issues.

We were a special, unique and dynamic treatment team. Lincoln Park Interventions gained a reputation throughout the addictions field in Illinois at that time as the gold standard for addiction treatment.

To see some of these young men turn their lives around and become productive members of the community was what made doing this work so rewarding. Much more valuable than any paycheck I ever got was the fact that I had found a worthwhile purpose for my life.

"No matter how far down the scale we have gone, we will see how our experience can benefit others. – The AA Promises

Although I was still in pursuit of my aspirations of being a recording artist, I was blessed to be in a profession that I felt was making a difference in the lives of addicted people. Despite my resistance, a growing sense started to emerge that quite possibly being a counselor was my true calling.

A poinsettia at Christmas time

In December of 1991, the first signs of "trouble in paradise" began to emerge. Although I had earned the respect of Colleen and the rest of the staff for my leadership, insight, and creative approaches with difficult clients, ironically, I was simultaneously starting to draw Colleen's scrutiny. Colleen was a young program director, and though she had a lot of respect for the TC model, she wanted to move away from "old-school treatment" and toward some of the new approaches that were evolving at the time. Approaches like motivational interviewing and others identified and emphasized client strengths (strength-based) instead of identifying, attacking, and eliminating weaknesses.

An incident that highlighted this clash of "old school verses new school" happened as the Christmas season approached. The house was decorated in lights and holiday whatnot. Potted poinsettias must have been on sale because there were a lot of them all over the facility. Most of them were healthy and were two to three feet tall.

One day, shortly after I arrived at work, it was brought to my attention that one of my new clients, Marshall, was constantly getting written up by his peers for leaving his belongings lying around and forgetting them. This included treatment-related homework and other important items. After speaking with him several times about his chronic forgetfulness, I decided to give him an LE (learning experience). For the next two days, he would carry one of the potted plants around with him everywhere he went.

It was surreal and somewhat comical to watch him walking down the hall or entering the dining room with the large plant in his hands and then having to explain to his peers why he had to have it with him everywhere he went. Colleen came in the next day and called me into her office. The conversation went something like this…

"Steve, why is Marshall walking around with a poinsettia?"

"It's his LE. He has to carry it with him wherever he goes for two days."

"Steve, this isn't Gateway."

"I know that."

"Okay, if you can explain the therapeutic value of your client carrying a poinsettia around, I'll let it stand."

My mind immediately recalled Ron and my entire treatment family cramming into the kitchen singing "Louie Louie" to me. I explained that having unique, memorable treatment experiences has a significant, valuable, and lasting impact on clients. I also pointed out that taking a humorous approach was non-threatening to a client's fragile self-esteem, and due to the nature of the issue of forgetfulness, the intervention made perfect sense. I asked her: "Do you think that Marshall will ever forget the time he had to carry a poinsettia around for two days?"

She let the LE stand, but the changes in the field of addiction treatment were right around the corner and barreling straight at us.

I was a product of the Gateway "tough love" counseling style, and as such, often approached my work with clients in this manner; however, I started realizing, even this early in my career, that to survive in this field, I would need to incorporate a variety of skills and approaches into my counseling repertoire. Try as I might, nothing was going to stand in the way of "progress."

Despite being at odds with Colleen at times, I was promoted to senior counselor. Soon after, I embarked on the biggest challenge of my career to that point, when I took over the family education program. I remember revising the program and placing the emphasis on the family's constant struggles related to "support versus enabling." My program made clear the difference between the two, and helped client's parents and families learn how to start supporting recovery and stop enabling their loved one's addiction.

The highlight of my efforts was when a client, who had a chronic history of treatment failures and relapses, celebrated two years clean. He came back to Lincoln Park to visit on occasion, and I asked him to be a guest speaker for my family program. During his talk, he explained how his parents attending my program made the difference that led to his current success in recovery. They had finally stopped enabling him and informed him that they would no longer bail him out of jail or any other trouble he found himself in related to his drug use. He knew they were serious, and he explained that this took away the "ace in the hole" he always had in the back of his mind—that his parents would come to the rescue if he needed them. Once that "safety net" was gone, he took the program and his recovery seriously, resulting in his two years of sobriety.

The program was a success. I had reached another career milestone.

1991 – A Christmas story

In 1991, I had special plans for Christmas, one of only a few that I didn't spend with my family. That year I spent Christmas with Amelia and her family in Washington DC. No, I wasn't quite ready to run for office, but it was another sign that the self-conscious, unworldly, Franklin Park regular guy, who Amelia had to teach how to dress, was finally being accepted by her family.

The first big sign happened months earlier when Amelia suggested that I call her mother to see if she wanted to go to see a movie or grab a bite to eat. So, I called Arlene and "asked her out." She accepted and chose to go see the movie *Frankie and Johnny* with Al Pacino and Michelle Pfieffer.

The "date" was going swimmingly well, until the hot sex scene in the film. I admit, I became a bit uncomfortable when Michelle throws Al against the wall and starts grinding him from behind before their highly erotic sex scene explodes on the screen. I dared not take my eyes from the screen to check on the state of Arlene's face, but I did catch a glimpse from the corner of my eye. She was smiling, though somewhat reservedly. I had to remind myself that Arlene was a class act, but she was no prude. She had seen her daughter almost completely naked sitting on her co-star grinding away in one of her early film roles. Amelia was not shy about disrobing in front of the camera.

So, getting invited to their special Christmas holiday plan was further proof that I was in. I had also ended all my little flings by this point. Despite my confusion and struggles to be faithful, I did love Amelia. They rented a house that accommodated the entire family plus yours truly.

I remember the family going out Christmas shopping while Dan and I stayed back playing Scrabble. Whatever advantage Dan may have had in terms of vocabulary, I matched it with my ability to play the board for the most possible points per turn. He beat me by only two points, 304 to 302—a moral victory for sure. Amelia was genuinely impressed that I had given Dan a run for his money. "He beats everybody, and you almost got him!"

I was becoming a more intelligent person, and I was unapologetic about it. I discovered that I valued a good vocabulary, mastery of the English language, and words. For me, this was another sign of my growth. In my addiction, I was immersed in a culture that did not value conventional intelligence, and for years, I denied this part of myself. Fortunately, I had a solid foundation due to having quality teachers who found ways to help me learn despite my rebellion and troublemaking antics. Later, I would find out that those teachers did so much more for me than I ever knew.

The highlight of the trip was attending the famous Washington National Cathedral to see their world-famous production of *Handel's Messiah*. What an awesome production it was, both musically and visually, in this huge, beautiful, world-famous cathedral. Who could have ever guessed that I, a regular guy, former junkie, from blue-collar Franklin Park, would be having all these awesome experiences this early in my recovery?

I was finally becoming comfortable in my own skin, no matter who I happened to be around, and without drugs. I became acutely aware that I was more capable than I thought, and that I was a person on equal ground with all other human beings—no better—no worse. The importance of Amelia's celebrity status (albeit diminished by this time) made me realize that for most of my life, I either looked up to people as better than me or looked down on them as not as good as me. My brushes with celebrity and interactions with Amelia and her family, combined with my growing faith in God, helped me to get a more realistic view of myself.

Here at last, a person can appear clearly to himself, not as the giant of his dreams, nor the dwarf of his fears, but as a man, part of a whole, with a share in its purpose.

In my addiction, I often looked down at the floor and barely made eye contact. Now, I looked at people's faces and into their eyes when I talked to them. I had officially become a child of God. I always was, but now I knew it.

No longer ruled by fear

At the very beginning of this book, I quote a Pink Floyd song from one of my favorite albums, *The Dark Side of the Moon*: *Breathe, breathe in the air; don't be afraid to care.* Somehow, without realizing it, I had become "afraid to care." This was a major catalyst that led to my pursuit of being "comfortably numb," yet another Pink Floyd song title.

For the first 25 years of my life, I found myself driven by fear, including the fear of rejection, change, and the unknown—to name a few—but mostly fear of failure and its flip side, fear of success. The risks associated with caring scared the hell out of me. The underlying feelings of: *"What if you reject me?"* and *"What if I fail?"* permeated my entire being and often immobilized me from taking the action needed to make my life worth living. I found that drugs eased these fears and made the consequences I received for not caring more tolerable. Ironically though, through my years of chasing the comfort that drugs provided, I made an important discovery—it stopped working, the scales tipped, and it became more painful not to care than it did to care.

Although caring had its share of pain, it also had some great rewards that I had missed out on. In my recovery, I reinvested in caring. I found the rewards far outweighed the occasional pain, consequences, and setbacks. I would finally learn and accept as truth, and internalize, a famous quote: *Happiness is not the absence of pain.*

I wrote the following poem. It sums up the changes I had experienced from who I once was, to who I had become, and was still becoming.

Fear

The chalkboard, wooden desk smell scared me,
Though I told myself a lie about it at the time and pretended it didn't.
"Clean your Room! Grab a broom!" Zoom, zoom, zoom,
And I watched you all moving so fast, talkin' about the past,
About the loves that didn't last,
And I was afraid, but I still couldn't tell you.
You see, I just wanted to run, play in the warm bright sun,
Feel the wind blow through my hair,
Ride my bike without a care,

And your big world it scared me so,
But still, I couldn't tell you though.
Then the day came I could run no more, from the big world that you put me in,
So, I took some stuff, then I took some more, which enabled me to run again,
And from that day on, I ran so fast,
I couldn't see what I was running past,
Because I was blind, in all my strife,
I was running away from my own life,
Until I ran smack into a mirror,
Which helped me see myself much clearer,
So, I stopped, and I looked you in the eyes,
And finally, the words I uttered,
Which stuck in my throat like rocks, but soon they flowed like melted butter.
"I'm afraid," I said.
I'm afraid of your big world with its "Clean your Room! Grab a broom!"
Zoom, zoom, zoom, "I'm afraid."
And the words hung there in the air,
Dangling in front of my face like scary little monsters,
Dancing and laughing wildly, drunk with insanity.
Then, suddenly, a huge hand descended from the heavens,
A great, warm, and powerful hand,
And it cupped the mad, tiny, monsters in it,
And kept them in for just a minute,
Then, opened up and to my surprise, released a thousand butterflies,
And then a voice came from the sky, so I thought at first, then I realized,
It was speaking through your lips and eyes.
And the voice said.... "I have intervened for you many times in the past, though you did not recognize me due to your blindness. Now that you see more clearly, I have revealed a part of myself to you so that you might replace your fear with faith. For faith is the key to your human condition. You cannot escape the chalkboard, wooden desk smell. Your whole life on earth is but a classroom. A school for you to learn to overcome selfishness, greed, hatred, fear, and ultimately, your humanness. Even through the chaos and turmoil of life, you must learn to stand in faith and not run, in fear. Go now in faith for ye shall not see me nor hear from me again in this manner until the end."
And the hand ascended back into the heavens.
Now sometimes I'm still, and sometimes I run,
I work, and I play in the warm bright sun,
And the wind still blows through what's left of my hair,
And I drive in my car without a care,
And I'm not afraid anymore.

I would no longer run away or hide out from life in a quest to avoid pain, but rather, I'd roll up my sleeves, face whatever life brought my way, and turn the results over to God.

"Until a person confronts himself in the eyes and hearts of others, he is running."

I can't say that I became completely fearless but fear no longer had the power to immobilize me and sabotage me the way that it had all my life.

When I was in treatment, one of my peers, Mike G., used to say: "I care but I don't—know what I mean?" This bit of junkie wisdom, passed on to me by a fellow dope fiend in treatment, finally clicked when I realized it meant that I could be passionate about all that I endeavored in life while letting go of and turning the outcomes over to God. Yes Mike, now I know what you mean!

God has never given me more than I could handle. In January 1987, in a treatment center, I fell to my knees and said the first real prayer of my life. Though my previous treatment wasn't a total waste and laid a foundation, my recovery really began in earnest on that day in Grant Hospital.

My faith has not been perfect. I would continue to struggle at times with over self-reliance and intellectual pride. Ultimately though, I learned that my faith and trust in God was the only thing I had to turn to and rely on.

Another important aspect of overcoming my fear of life was the support system I developed. God always put the right people in my life at the right times. No matter what mistakes I made or what I attempted to accomplish, the people in the program always had my back. I never felt alone anymore. The "naked baby on a hill in the rain" had all but vanished from my life.

Promises kept

In just five years, the universe unfolded a wave of cosmic messages and surprises. They were hidden until I started trusting God and stayed clean and sober long enough to receive them. I found myself embarking on one adventure after another. My life started feeling like I was on a roller coaster, but in a good way. I knew I'd be okay, as long as I didn't pick up a drink or a drug. I had a sober support network comprised of ex-counselors, sponsors, recovering friends, and family, who could help me get through anything that life could throw at me. I'll give myself some of the credit for putting in the time and effort to develop that support system. It doesn't happen by osmosis.

My spiritual development allowed me to *wear the world as a loose garment,* as is says in the *Twenty-Four Hours* book, and I began to experience an underlying inner peace that *the world could neither give nor take away.*

I still experienced the emotional ups and downs of any human being on the planet, but I was never stuck for long. I was able to work through negative situations and feelings quickly and continued to move forward. I began to trust God more as months turned into years, and I began to recognize His purpose in ALL events that occurred, whether they were "good" or "bad." If I needed evidence of this, I needed look no further than my own life and recovery.

The A.A. Promises proclaim…

If we are painstaking about this phase of our development, we will be amazed before we are half way through. We are going to know a new freedom and a new happiness. We will not regret the past nor wish to shut the door on it. We will comprehend the word serenity and we will know peace. No matter how far down the scale we have gone, we will see how our experience can benefit others. That feeling of uselessness and self-pity will disappear. We will lose interest in selfish things and gain interest in our fellows. Self-seeking will slip away. Our whole attitude and outlook upon life will change. Fear of people and of economic insecurity will leave us. We will intuitively know how to handle situations which used to baffle us. We will suddenly realize that God is doing for us what we could not do for ourselves.

Are these extravagant promises? We think not. They are being fulfilled among us—sometimes quickly, sometimes slowly. They will always materialize if we work for them.

I've seen people in recovery who, like me, have experienced most or all of them, and I've seen others, who are experiencing few if any of them. You get out what you put in. I endured and got through a lot of pain in my early recovery, both physically and emotionally. Before I completed the fourth and fifth step with my sponsor, my life had already changed in miraculous ways.

By the end of 1991, with God's help, I had experienced not only most of the AA Promises, but also "the miracle" I'd heard about on occasion in the program of Narcotics Anonymous. It says: *Don't quit until the miracle happens.*

The miracle they're referring to is when some of us wake up one day and realize we are no longer plagued and tormented by any desire to use drugs. It's truly miraculous when you consider that at one time, my whole life revolved around getting high.

My addiction and recovery "in a nutshell"

Earlier in this book, I asked an important question:
"Was it exhilarating enough? No, unfortunately, it wasn't. Why not!? Why the hell not!? WHAT THE HELL WAS WRONG WITH ME!?"

Why weren't the things that brought me the most pleasure and excitement as a teenager, enough to stop me from falling into the pit of addiction? I have the answer, but before I share it, let me break down some of the related issues.

When people talk about the factors that cause addiction, things like genetics are often emphasized, and in many cases, rightfully so. But what about "early onset"—starting too early? This factor doesn't get near the attention it deserves. I believed that I was genetically predisposed to addiction by my grandfather. As it turns out, I couldn't have been more wrong. The main cause of my addiction was *early onset*. My brain and personality weren't fully formed yet. I had no way of coping with The Traumatic Trifecta that I experienced, so I turned to the only thing I knew—drugs, and they worked…for a while.

My drug use interfered with developing the things that would make success and happiness possible. The typical adolescent brain has no way of foreseeing or caring about those things. Adolescents' brains aren't developed enough, and they don't have enough wisdom or experience. Try as they might, parents are limited in what they can do. So don't waste your time doing things that are ineffective. Instead, seek professional help early and stay with it as long as possible. Don't expect quick fixes or miracles.

Also, take a lesson from Carol Decino or Mary DeWitt's mother, and remove them as far away from the problem environment(s) as you can. This, in combination with counseling, has the best chance of being effective.

I find it ironic that although the first three or four years of my drug use were the most innocent, fun, and seemingly harmless, in some ways, they were the most destructive. Those early years laid the foundation for what would be a crippling life-long illness and set me up to eventually have to battle for my life, a battle that I would no doubt have lost, had it not been for the Grace of God and the divine intervention I received.

Of course, there are other contributing factors, some of which are unique to each individual. I had the proverbial "addictive personality" that people often refer to. When something felt good to me, I wanted more and had difficulty stopping whatever it was.

There were several other key vulnerabilities too. At the risk of blaming, growing up with parents like Albie and John, who lacked effective disciplinary interventions, contributed to my inability to develop enough sorely needed self-control. Yelling and lecturing were ineffective. I got good at tuning everybody out. As another line in the Pink Floyd song "Comfortably Numb" says, *"You are only coming through in waves. Your lips move, but I can't hear what you say."* I heard words, but was unable to consider what people were saying to me.

I also became an ace at blaming, justifying, and rationalizing my behavior. These "skills" contributed to stunting emotional growth and maturity.

The NA basic text says: *We did many people great harm but most of all we harmed ourselves. Through our inability to accept personal responsibilities we were actually creating our own problems. We seemed to be incapable of facing life on its own terms.*

While in treatment, I realized that I *did* create most of my own problems, either through my actions or my inaction, but in my immature, drug-induced, distorted mind, I was sure it was all your fault.

So now I think I should answer that important question about why the natural pleasures and good things in my life weren't enough and weren't able to save me... *"WHAT THE HELL WAS WRONG WITH ME!?"*

What was wrong with me was...I was simply too far gone. Scientifically speaking, my brain chemistry had already changed in profound and significant ways. By age 17, my addiction was already a "runaway train."

Sue and Gerhardt's intervention helped, but it was "too little, too late." It wasn't enough. In fact, the mixed messages of Gerhardt's substance abuse, combined with his traumatic exit from my life, ultimately became more of a contributing factor to my addiction than a solution.

So, now that I've taken you on this long and complex journey, there needs to be some "punchline," a great "secret to success in recovery" —right? Well, I've got some good news and some bad news. Most people like to hear the bad news first, so here goes: Everyone's path and addiction is different; therefore, the secrets to their path for success in recovery will be different. No one can predict what will happen while on that path, so although the science is important, recovery is as much an art as it is a science. I liken it to modern dance—some choreographed steps mixed with a lot of improvisation. For example, it's unlikely that someone will be pulled off a comfy couch on a Saturday morning and made to create a mural on a laundry room wall, but there will likely be other events that will have a significant impact in their recovery.

Quality treatment will always result in having a significant impact on clients. An analogy is getting the "lightbulb to go on" over one's head. But I've found that this won't be sufficient. The real "trick" to recovery, if you will, is KEEPING IT ON! Another good metaphor that illustrates the typical barriers would be to look at recovery as an airplane flight. Getting the plane off the ground is very important, but then, one must keep it in the air and stay on course. The hard part for most addicted people isn't GETTING clean; it's STAYING clean. The "destination" is a significantly better, drug free life.

With that said, I guess the good news is there are some typical ingredients I can identify that appear to be essential to recovery. I will attempt to summarize the key ingredients in my "recipe" for recovery…

Hitting bottom

Pain has always been, and still is, the greatest motivator for change. Unfortunately, people who suffer from addiction must be in enough pain and discomfort before taking the kind of action necessary to recover. As the NA basic text says, we must be *sick and tired of being sick and tired.* What brings this about can vary greatly.

Another consideration is the number and types of *enablers* one has. These can also vary and range from loved ones to the criminal justice system or just the amount of money one has access to. As the AA book *Twelve Steps and Twelve Traditions* states: *In time, all his protectors either flee or die, and he is once more alone and afraid.*

It seems the best these enablers can do is postpone pain. The longer an addict avoids and postpones the pain of addiction, the more severe that pain is when it hits. All those involved with addicted people should do all they can to allow addicts to experience the consequences of their choices and lifestyle.

I was also able to sense some of what the program refers to as "yets" (likely future consequences) that were just around the corner if I didn't stop using—the biggest of these being prison. It wasn't until I lost everything and everyone and had nowhere to go that I finally sought the help I needed.

Seeking professional help

First and foremost, I admitted the need for and sought professional help. DO NOT—I repeat—DO NOT try to recover on your own. My history of trying to stop or control my use on my own was all the evidence I needed that this would never work. I realized a long time ago that without the help I received, I would not be here today. Luckily, we had a family member, who had gotten that same kind of help I needed. All we had was a phonebook back then. Calling and asking for help was the first step in me actually getting help. I almost didn't get help due to my initial inability to follow through.

Being placed in the right level of care for my severity of substance abuse

Thank God for the treatment staff who recognized that I needed long-term residential care but also utilized the services that were available until a bed in a residential setting became available. When I finally made it into inpatient treatment, I was afforded the time I needed to get my head out of my ass. I had to be removed from easy access to alcohol and drugs and put into a safe environment *long enough* to promote healing of my mind, body, and spirit.

The brain chemistry problems—and subsequent thinking, attitude, and behaviors associated with addiction—must have *time to heal* and reverse as much as possible. This can take months or even years, depending on the severity of one's addiction. The brain can't heal if you continue to re-injure and damage it. If you take a cast off a broken leg too soon, it won't be healed.

Ironically, this "safe" nurturing environment was complemented by a heavy dose of intense confrontation. Confrontation, when balanced with the spirit of "care and concern," can be very beneficial. Through these confrontations, I was able to break through several layers of denial (lies I told myself and I believed), which always had me going in circles and kept me stuck.

Here at last, a person can appear clearly to himself, not as the giant of his dreams, nor the dwarf of his fears..."

This was not just in Gateway. I can't emphasize enough the importance of experiencing "Open Report" at Grant Hospital. To all the "strength-based" proponents out there who don't believe in confrontation because it might "shame" the client, imagine the outcome if that day in open report, the staff would have all passed my chart around and talked about what a great guy I was. I have no doubt I'd be dead and not be writing this.

The concept is known as "tough love." It's old, but far from obsolete. It was first introduced in a 1982 book by the same name, written by Pauline Neff. I, and many others, believe tough love is still the best approach for the treatment of substance abuse disorders. The "tough" is necessary to combat the symptoms of addiction. Without it, an addict's symptoms of addiction will flourish, run roughshod over everyone, and they will not get better. The "love" is for the real person who is in there somewhere, held captive by their addiction. Both (in the right amounts and at the right times) are essential.

The NA basic text says: *We believe the sooner we face our problems within our society, in everyday living, just that must faster do we become acceptable, responsible, and productive members of that society.*

This simply means we can't live our lives under the safe "umbrella" of treatment and must eventually reintegrate back into society. I believe the reentry model used at Gateway was important in achieving this. The treatment community learned years ago that releasing someone from a highly structured environment, back into an environment with no structure is a recipe for disaster.

<u>*I engaged in treatment and worked on myself*</u>

I didn't just take up space and occupy a bed in treatment. I bought into and participated in the program. Unfortunately, this had some unforeseen negative as well as positive effects. I got caught up in playing "the treatment game" and lost sight of the ultimate goal—recovery from addiction.

Fortunately, by my second round of treatment, I stopped avoiding my character defects and started taking responsibility for and working on them. I became more aware of my true feelings and motives and gave myself much needed permission to be brutally honest with myself and with others when necessary. The treatment culture valued having "thick skin" and being able to handle criticism and confrontation, as well as the harsh "curveballs" that life can sometimes throw at us. They forced us to "toughen up our baby guts." This contributed greatly to my ability to live "life on life's terms" today.

Developed/practiced work ethic

God put me in the right place by directing me to Gateway, Kedzie House. Looking back, it was like a general store of everything I needed, not the least of which was physical labor on an almost daily basis. By the time I had to handle employment situations in the real world, though I still had a way to go, I had already made significant strides in being able to not only handle working hard but also excel and become more promotable.

I was eventually able to heal an old "wound" inadvertently made by my father when he proclaimed: *You'll never be able to get up and go to work every day! You haven't got the stomach for it!* My life today is a daily testimony that says, "You were wrong! I do have the stomach for it!"

Today, that guy with the sudden burst of energy, who was up on the dryers in the laundry room at Kedzie House, is no longer a rare anomaly but a daily occurrence. My conscience no longer allowed me to be at work without putting 100 percent into whatever I was doing.

Experienced emotional growth/maturity

I'm reminded of the name of an NA meeting on the North Side called *Show Up to Grow Up*. I knew from the moment I read it in the Chicago meeting directory that it summed up what had happened to me. I always knew how to "act like" an adult, but I eventually developed the ability to actually be one. This included being able to handle my responsibilities, being more trustworthy, and coping with occasional setbacks.

An important element of my growth was developing healthy self-esteem. By developing my self-confidence, I became "self-actualized," which for me, meant I developed a deep fundamental belief that I could influence my own destiny. I no longer saw myself as a helpless victim of circumstances beyond my control, being buffeted about by life.

Another essential part of my growth, was the ability to challenge my own thinking. I lost the fear of calling myself on my own bullshit. This was demonstrated in several crucial "heart to heart" talks I had with myself, which led to some good decisions that allowed my recovery to continue and progress.

I also came to the important realization: An addict's life gets better before they do. We may get a good job, an apartment, reestablish family or intimate relationships, etc., but the brain has not caught up yet and has not healed sufficiently. In early recovery, we may not feel sick, but even though we may be feeling better, we're still not well.

A good example is when I got my first apartment. I could have easily been misled by the vast improvements in my life and mistaken them for me being ready for more than I could handle. My "addict brain" started telling me all the cool things I could do now that I had my own place. Luckily, "Recovering Steve" jumped in to slow me down and have one of those crucial "heart to heart" talks with myself. I reminded myself to keep my life simple and manageable; *Man, you better slow down. All you're gonna do is go to work, go to meetings, pick up your kids on the weekends, and that's it for a while!*

Another important result of my growth was abandoning the "blame game." I realized that others were not responsible for my problems, my happiness, and the outcomes in my life.

I never forgave Albie and John for "what they did to me and didn't do for me" because…I no longer had to. Instead, I emotionally and spiritually outgrew any "injury" that I thought was there. This meditation says it best, though most may have to read it slowly and several times for it to make sense…

"I must overcome myself before I can truly forgive other people for injuries done to me. The self in me cannot forgive injuries. The very thought of wrongs means that myself is in the foreground. Since the self cannot forgive, I must overcome my selfishness. I must cease trying to forgive those who fretted and wronged me. It is a mistake for me to even think about these injuries. I must aim at overcoming myself in my daily life and then I will find there is nothing in me that remembers injury, because the only thing injured, my selfishness, is gone." – Twenty-Four Hours a Day, May 3

In essence, it means grow emotionally, stop blaming, let go of your unrealistic expectations of others, and take personal responsibility for your life; and just like that, most "wounds" inflicted by others disappear. I started seeing my parents as ordinary people with flaws and problems, not just as my parents.

<u>Developed sober relationships and a recovery support system</u>

Initially, my mother and my daughters Jessica and Melissa were important catalysts for me to get help. But despite how much I loved my mother and my kids, I would not be here today if it weren't for the relationships I developed, both in and out of treatment, especially with other recovering people. We had a special bond. We were survivors of a Titanic-like disaster and had made it into the "lifeboats." I remember hearing in the program that *Some must die so that others may live* and that we were *the chosen ones*. I didn't know if that was true or not, but I can tell you that it helped to believe it. It made me feel special and grateful when I realized that I survived something that has taken so many off the planet. I'd eventually come to believe that I was "chosen" for a purpose, which was slowly being revealed to me the longer I stayed clean.

No one can sustain the level of motivation needed for long-term recovery on their own. We face too many overwhelming barriers, obstacles, and unknowns. Those who believe they can do it on their own are fooling themselves. Although I didn't approach my relationship with a sponsor "by the book," I utilized sponsorship in important ways at crucial times in my recovery.

<u>Learning important lessons from mine and others' relapses</u>
Unfortunately, relapse is a common, defining feature of addiction disorders. However, I think it's important to say that relapse is not necessary and not recommended as a way to enhance recovery, internalize important concepts, or take recovery more seriously. Too many never make it back. I almost didn't. But if I'm being honest, if one does make it back, it can be the catalyst that propels a person into more committed and solid recovery. It certainly had that effect on me. I sometimes wonder if I could have acquired the necessary level of vigilance and commitment to recovery without relapsing the way I did. I guess I'll never know the answer to that.

The people who do make it back to meetings to talk about it (like me) are very important. Those of us who relapse are often in meetings searching and discovering for others, the secrets of the program, albeit the hard way. First and foremost, we'd hear, "I stopped going to meetings." But there are also any number of more subtle factors discovered and shared.

Upon my return to sanity (by the grace of God), I realized that I suffered from a hidden reservation that ultimately led to my undoing. I thought that I would somehow be able to stop using if I needed to, due to the time I'd spent clean and in recovery, that somehow, I'd be able to draw upon this and use it to stop if and when I needed to. This miscalculation almost cost me my life.

Distorted perceptions like overblown ego, combined with hidden reservations (secret desires) about using, are a deadly combination. This is why "rigorous honesty" is so important.

After my relapse, I was able to clearly see the level of vigilance needed to keep my recovery on track. We must "surrender" daily, which simply means that every day when our feet hit the floor, we must remember that *we have a disease* (or condition, if you prefer) *for which there is no known cure. It can however be arrested at some point and recovery is then possible.* We must never forget the wisdom shared with us in the AA text: addiction is *cunning, baffling, and powerful. Without help it is too much for us.*

The most important result of my relapse was accepting the need for total abstinence from all major mood-altering substances. Why? The answer can be complex and could (will) be the subject of another book, but the simple answer is the inevitable loss of control and the resulting unmanageability I'd eventually experience. I had to accept that without total abstinence, I had no chance of success. There was no "safe drug" or "safe way" for me to use.

That sign I once saw in the business office on my first day of treatment: *There's nothing that can happen in this day that a drink or a drug won't make worse,* became mine. I owned it, and I carried it with me everywhere I went, just like I do with my wallet or my car keys. Once I fully accepted that I could not pick up that first drink or drug and was able to re-commit to it daily, my recovery and my new life evolved from that basic foundation.

We'd do well to try to avoid or reduce the triggers that lead to drug cravings, but this is not always possible. All externals are an excuse for relapse. No matter what happens on the outside, the real battle is internal—thoughts and feelings. It's not the events in life that lead to relapse as much as the permission we give ourselves to seek relief by drinking or using drugs, to numb the feelings created by those events. The bottom line…*Don't pick up the first drink or drug, no matter what, even if your ass falls off!*

<u>Re-socialization</u>

The ability to socialize with others sober that started in treatment, continued and went to the next level in the 12-step programs. The more I showed up at meetings, the more the social aspects of the program evolved for me. It started off just showing up and speaking up in meetings, which quickly led to going out for coffee or dinner afterward. There were always special events like dances, conventions, and retreats, etc. I attended my share including the first ever CA (Cocaine Anonymous) convention in Chicago in 1985.

After the Grant Hospital meeting on Fridays, a bunch of us would go out to Giordano's across the street, push three or four tables together, and order pizza. We would tell war stories and laugh our asses off. When you stop using drugs, you begin to realize that all you have left to entertain yourself are your natural abilities. So, our tongues got quicker, and our wits got sharper. Afterward, a smaller group of us would walk a few blocks to the Three Penny or the infamous Biograph Theater to see a movie.

We rediscovered Chicago in all its glory; its history and beauty that once eluded us, now seemed to be coming alive to us. This included the restaurants, the landmarks, the architecture, the Water Tower, and the beautiful skyline. Lake Shore Drive, Michigan Avenue (The Magnificent Mile) and

Marshall Fields. Then there were the neighborhoods (ethnic melting pots) with their diverse ethnic histories, each with its own unique feel and culture.

But it wasn't Chicago that was coming alive. We were. I was able to see and feel it all and I started falling in love with the city that I once thought I hated and couldn't wait to get away from. I found it ironic that I now felt disdain for LA, the "utopia" I had once escaped to. My "geographical cures" never worked because wherever I went, I brought the problem with me—me!

I began to make important connections with people in the program. Some were merely acquaintances based strictly on program-related stuff like; mutual admiration of our recovery progress and were limited to in and around the meetings we attended. Others were based on common interests such as music, art, theater, acting, and other creative endeavors. I slowly regained the ability to connect with people, and I was developing friendships based on the right things: common interests, shared values, and our common quest for recovery.

The boredom that was once a major threat to my recovery became a distant memory that I can hardly recall. It was replaced by always having something to do and someone to do it with.

Weekly recovery-oriented structure/routine

I once heard in a meeting a great example of the power of addiction. A man stated, "I got a disease that's trying to kill me any way it can. Addiction is so powerful; ten minutes after we're dead, it'll still be standing over us, seeing if it can't get one more lick in." I think this aptly illustrates the level of vigilance that's required to stay clean and sober, at least for the first few years or so.

Addiction is a full-time problem. When recovery is approached like a part-time job, it just doesn't cut it. To be vigilant means to be on guard and regularly invest and engage in the solution. The AA Big Book clearly states, "Half measures availed us nothing." The fact that I remained clean and sober shows that I must have been doing over half of what was suggested for me to do. The following describes the things that my early recovery consisted of...

Every week, I attended my Tuesday home group at Lakeview Lutheran Church, the Friday Night Alive at Grant Hospital meeting, and the Mustard Seed, mostly on Saturdays. Meetings were seven days a week, so I could pop into any meeting any day of the week and often did. I continued to meet with and work with my sponsor. The slogans "First things first" and "This too shall pass" were probably the most important for me. I had always struggled with keeping my priorities straight until I started incorporating "First things first" into my life. When hard times hit and things didn't go my way, "This too shall pass" reminded me that however bad things seemed at any given moment, as long as I didn't use, I'd get through it and things would get better.

One of the most important aspects of my recovery was, I showed up, meaning I showed up at the right places consistently, and I stopped showing up at the wrong places. I had a choice, and I chose to show up at the places that made and strengthened those connections, enhanced my recovery, and my life. I believe in the old saying: *Eighty percent of life is showing up; the other twenty percent is what you do after you get there.*

And just what did I do after I got there? The answer to that question will reveal one of the most important tools of recovery anyone has—their mouth! My ability to express myself well was one of the most important things I did in my recovery. This took time, practice, and the ability to face and overcome "social anxiety" (caring too much about what others think of us). We don't have to be scholars or intellectuals to do this, just be willing to be honest and "tell it like it is." If someone is sitting in meetings like a bump on a log, "just listening", my advice is start sharing before it's too late.

Finally, I read the *Day by Day* and *Twenty-Four Hours a Day* meditation books religiously every morning and sometimes throughout the day. Addicts are usually not known for being well-read. The good news is that the reading we must do as part of a program of recovery isn't too extensive and can be kept very simple. Taking a few minutes each day to read a daily meditation book, or a paragraph in the text, doesn't require a lot of effort or time. Those words ground and focus on what's important—our recovery—no matter what's going on in the world around us. This also addresses two important characteristics of addiction that must be addressed: preoccupation and obsession with using. We must retrain our brains. I cannot overemphasize the importance of a daily reflection book, not only in my recovery but in my personal as well as spiritual development. These readings, along with daily prayer and meditation, were, and still are, instrumental in my development and helped me make the important transition from being agnostic, and as I said earlier, at times even atheist, to becoming the spiritual person I became.

<u>Service work and working with others</u>

I continued volunteering at the front desk at the Mustard Seed on Saturday mornings. I answered the phone, which typically consisted of giving meeting schedules and times, or someone who needed a ride to a meeting. Occasionally, someone would call to ask for help with an alcohol problem. When that happened (and it did), I was trained to interrupt the meeting and see if I could get someone to volunteer to go to them and intervene (12th Step them) in whatever way they could.

My next service position was being elected treasurer (still hard to believe) of my Tuesday home group. That's right, I collected and held the seventh tradition money *(Every N.A. group ought to be fully self-supporting, declining outside contributions)* for the meeting. I was elected as the literature chairperson for the North City area of Chicago. I supplied literature for all meetings in that area.

My service positions made me feel useful and an important part of what happened in the program. My service position at Lawson YMCA, along with sponsoring people in recovery, opened the door to me becoming an addictions counselor. I'm extremely fortunate to have the privilege of making a living helping others achieve recovery.

<u>Time</u>

This is probably the most misunderstood, underestimated, and overlooked, element of recovery from addiction. A few important analogies I use are *Recovery is a marathon, not a sprint,* and *Recovery is a twelve-round fight, not a three-round fight.* There is no instant gratification in recovery from addiction. Most of the important rewards don't happen right away. This is why so many don't make it very far. The program slogan, *"It gets greater later,"* is something that newcomers need to hear often and take to heart.

For me, enough time being sober led to three very important things. First, I overcame one of the biggest enemies of my recovery and, I might add, an enemy that I knew nothing about until well after defeating it. At around 18 months, Post Acute Withdrawal Syndrome (PAWS) was all but gone, especially the lethargy I had experienced throughout my entire early recovery. Suddenly, I experienced a surge of energy that I not only needed to live day-to-day life, but it far exceeded that level.

The second thing— "the miracle" happened. As I've previously mentioned, I had completely lost any desire to use drugs.

Finally, the third important thing that happened which I may not even have realized if it wasn't for a rare question from one of my clients. He asked: "When did you start enjoying your life sober? When were you really happy?"

I thought it was an excellent question, and I had to think about it for a minute. I explained that there were really two answers. One answer was that in some ways, as soon as I was over acute withdrawal, I started to experience happiness albeit in spurts. I explained that I had a lot of fun and good times even while in treatment, but I knew that wasn't really what he was asking. He was asking for more ongoing, steady happiness, that wasn't so intermittent. "Three years," I answered. I explained that's when I had gotten the basics of daily life down, and God started opening the doors to more opportunities, adventures, fun, and enjoyment. Thank God I stuck around long enough for those important things to happen to me.

<u>Developed a relationship with God</u>

Finally, if I had one big "secret of my success" to share, it would obviously be my relationship with God. I realized years ago that I have too much evidence of His power manifested in my life to chalk it up to coincidence. When I started to sincerely ask God for help, I started getting the help I needed, and in ways that I never did before.

I don't wear it on my sleeve, I don't proclaim it to everyone I meet, and I certainly don't stand on the street corner and shout it into a bullhorn. Those things are for someone else. My assignment from God is to help addicts recover from addiction. I'm the guide on the first leg of their journey. I just lead them out of the wilderness. After that, I turn them over to God. As I said, I believe this is my true purpose and the reason I was saved in 1984.

Talking and listening to God throughout the day, otherwise known as *prayer and meditation,* became a habit similar to brushing my teeth. He would communicate His will for me through other people, circumstances, and experiences I was having in my life. Once I was "tuned in to that station," the messages became clearer and frequent enough to alleviate my fears of life and facilitate change. On a regular basis, I prayed for God's will to be done and accepted whatever the outcome was, as best for me, and all concerned.

"We stood at the turning point. We asked His protection and care with complete abandon."

He sent His *protection and care,* but God didn't send me a lightning bolt or a puff of smoke. He sent me the right people! There are several crucial "turning points" in my story, where people "talked me off the ledge," inspired me, motivated me, and, in essence, "restored me to sanity" when I could not have done so myself.

There are also those events throughout my story that can't be explained with conventional logic and can only be explained by divine intervention from something greater than me. A few examples of this were being able to sleep while in the middle of Methadone withdrawal, the golden light entering our apartment and restoring me from certain death by the hooded being in black, and finally, walking away without taking those pills from a cancer patient.

As I said early on, "The God puzzle" is a life-long endeavor. So, I just keep following where my faith leads me, trusting that when the time is right, *more will be revealed.*

So, I guess we can say that "in a nutshell," I suffered from physical, emotional, and spiritual bankruptcy and stunted emotional growth and immaturity. It led me down a path of constantly seeking comfort, relief, and escape from unpleasant feelings, most of which, I was creating. My pursuit of pleasure and comfort ultimately led to even more pain and discomfort. I was finally able to see and admit this and get help, which pulled me off that "hamster wheel" and put me on a new and better path.

My subsequent recovery was simply that I finally grew up and accepted the responsibility of staying clean. I learned to live life on life's terms as a necessary part of success and happiness. My efforts helped me change my self-image, develop self-esteem, and, most importantly, ultimately replace the pleasure I once got from drugs and alcohol with natural pleasures through self-improvement, pursuing higher education, a more meaningful career, and bringing old hobbies and interests back into my life. I even took some healthy risks and expanded into some new territory—writing!

One of my old high school friends recently made a list on social media of people we went to school with that had unlikely outcomes in their lives. I was on that list. He wrote, "Steve Fiorito—A writer!? This is a guy who couldn't write and turn in a paper if his life depended on it when we were in school!"

As miraculous as that may be, I think it's important to mention that my recovery has been far from perfect. As stated in AA's "How it Works": *"No one among us has been able to maintain anything like perfect adherence to these principles. We are not saints."* I've made mistakes throughout my recovery, but I made enough good decisions, when it counted, to keep my recovery on track.

Though most of my progress was initially confined to the treatment and recovery world, I was able to transfer that progress into my endeavors in the "real world" and move my life forward. I believe this is where a lot of people's recovery gets stuck, bogs down, and stalls. Too many are content "resting on their laurels" and stagnate in "the rooms" (meetings). In my opinion, this is one of several major causes of relapse for recovering people with multiple years clean and sober. Moving one's life forward could mean any number of things, ranging from going back to school to becoming more involved in church, etc., depending on the individual. I am grateful for the power to live life and all the great gifts and opportunities that God has given to me.

Sometimes, I can feel Albie and Johnny the drapery man, looking down on me smiling, and in my mind, I can hear them say the words they were never able to say to me in this life…*We're so proud of you.*

LA 1984 revisited

I've seen the needle and the damage done. A little part of it in everyone.
But every junkie's like a setting sun.   – Neil Young

I can still vividly recall that warm, sunny California day in 1984, with the Santa Anna winds swirling through the inner court of our apartment complex. When I think of how close I came to never experiencing the awesome adventure my life became, I feel a deep sense of gratitude. If I had died that day, I would have been just another dead junkie who never amounted to much, another California "setting sun" that set much too early—yet another grim statistic who never reached my potential or even knew what I was capable of. The "beautiful loser" who left his kids and his family behind to bear the grief, the suffering, and the lifelong scars.

During my second treatment at Gateway, my counselor Ron Orlando said something very controversial to me—okay, well, even more controversial than most of the other things he said to me. He said: "If you go back out there and start using again, just get a gun and blow your brains out. Get it over with so your family can bury you and get on with their lives."

I know this sounds harsh and even inappropriate for a counselor to say to his client, but when put in the proper context of the times, the TC culture, and where I was at on my journey, it was on the money and exactly what I needed to hear at that time.

The only thing worse than dying that day in 1984 would have been to continue in that slow, cowardly suicide (every addict knows what I'm talking about), dragging my family and kids along for the long and painful ride. As it turned out, I was capable of so much more than I ever could have imagined. Thank God I was given another option—*Recovery*—and I chose it.

Although some days are easier than others, there isn't a day that goes by that I'm not completely aware of the fate I avoided, the blessings I've received, and that I don't experience a deep sense of gratitude even amid the pain and chaos of life.

"There should be joy in living the spiritual life. A faith without joy is not entirely genuine. If you are not happier as a result of your faith, there is probably something wrong with it. Faith in God should bring you a deep feeling of happiness and security, no matter what happens on the surface of your life. Each new day is another opportunity to serve God and improve your relationships with other people. This should bring joy. Life should be abundant and outreaching. It should be glowing and outgoing, in ever widening circles.
– Twenty-Four Hours a Day, Sept. 22

My life has certainly yielded all those things. I feel that God has got me and is ultimately in control, which brings me back to the spiritual question: Does God control outcomes? Though I gave a partial answer to this when I talked about my beliefs regarding the Chicago Bears winning Super Bowl XX, to expand a bit…yes…sometimes. He did in 1984 in California. I believe in divine intervention, but I don't claim to understand God's motives—when and why He does, and especially, when and why He doesn't. Maybe it's the prayers of others that we never even knew were prayed that influences His decision.

I recently reconnected with a schoolmate, David Pikel, and his mother Esther. I went to school with David since kindergarten. Esther was the grade school assistant librarian I wrote about early in this book who intervened on my friend Mark and me in the library. At an event I recently attended with them, Esther shared with me that several of my grade-school teachers drove to my childhood home and prayed for me as they sat in their car in front of my house. Hearing this brought tears to my eyes, and I became overwhelmed with gratitude, knowing that these people, to whom I gave so much grief, were asking God to intervene on me. Then there was Albie's, and many others' prayers that were apparently answered. This is what I meant when I said that my teachers did more for me than just give me a good education.

My feeble attempt at reaching out for the hand of Jesus while going through withdrawal on my parent's couch was my first real attempt to connect with a power greater than myself.

Looking back, I believe that God intervened on me that day in 1984 because he had a purpose for my life—to help save other souls from addiction. So, no matter how great of a songwriter I became, I was not meant to do it for a living. Instead, I was called to do something for a living that's more valuable to God. Every year on November 11, I am reminded of this.

As you look back over your life, it is not too difficult to believe that what you went through was for a purpose, to prepare you for some valuable work in life. Everything in your life may well have been planned by God to make you of some use in the world. Each person's life is like the pattern of a mosaic. Each thing that happened to you is like one tiny stone in the mosaic, and each tiny stone fits into the perfected pattern of the mosaic of your life, which has been designed by God. – Twenty-Four Hours a Day, November 11

By writing this book, I have shared with you God's masterpiece, a work in progress that I still am. So, until God's final stroke is made…

I will try to help others. I will try not to let a day pass without reaching out an arm of love to someone. Each day I will try to do something to lift another human being out of the sea of discouragements into which he or she has fallen. My helping hand is needed to raise the helpless to courage, to strength, to faith, to health. In my own gratitude, I will turn and help other alcoholics with the burden that is pressing too heavily upon them.

Prayer for the Day

I pray that I may be used by God to lighten many burdens. I pray that many souls may be helped through my efforts.—Twenty-Four Hours a Day, May 29

Most of the time, God gently guides us to what is needed to keep us on the right path and have a successful life. It could be a few spoken or written words here, a road sign there, or an event that seems coincidental or inexplicable. Unfortunately, other times may require a catastrophe or two to get our attention. But unless we see things through spiritually trained eyes, we will miss God's messages and guidance, or as we used to say in Gateway, we'll "miss the money." It's up to us to read the road signs in our lives, make decisions, and act accordingly. God is "Da Coach" with the supreme game plan. We are "the players" and must execute it.

My journey has led to an important realization: God wants us to be happy, joyous, and free. He doesn't just want us to trudge through life, bearing our burdens and doing our duty. When I've executed his plan for my life to the best of my ability is when I've been the happiest.

This leads me to one of the main points of this book, which requires that I make one major correction—the title of this book is wrong…

We are here because there is no refuge, finally, from ourselves.

Although I completely appreciate Richard Beauvais's point and his attempt to get addicts to face their inner demons, live *life on life's terms,* and to stop using drugs and alcohol to run away from responsibility (and ironically, possibility and opportunity), as it turns out, there is one refuge, finally, from ourselves…

…that one is God. May you find Him now.

The eternal God is your refuge. He is a sanctuary, a refuge from the cares of life. You can get away from the misunderstanding of others by retiring into your own place of meditation. But from yourself, from your own sense of failure, your weakness, your shortcomings, whither can you flee? Only to the eternal God, your refuge, until the immensity of His spirit envelopes your spirit and it loses its smallness and weakness and comes into harmony again with His.
– Twenty-Four Hours a Day, November 30

EPILOGUE

The adventure continued as 1992 would prove the Gateway slogan "There's nothing constant but change" to be one of the absolute truths in life. The changes started with me breaking up with Amelia over the phone. I loved her, but I could no longer handle being in a relationship with someone who, for the most part, wasn't physically present in my life. However, this would not be quite the end for us, and there would be one more chapter that I'll get to shortly.

In February, I met an awesome woman named Beth, and we embarked on a relationship that would also last four years. Beth was a tall, sexy redhead. She was a welcome "breath of fresh air" in my life and a much-needed change from the constant arguing and bickering that my relationship with Amelia had become. Beth wasn't in the program. She drank socially and even smoked a little weed on occasion, but by then, it didn't bother me in the least and created no temptation. We had a lot in common, particularly music. Beth was a good singer and sang background on several of my songs in the studio.

Another big musical change came when I was introduced to Dave Schreier. Like Kenny, Dave had a home studio, but Dave's equipment was up-to-date and superior, and he knew how to use it. We recorded my original material and the demo for the unplugged band that Beth and I put together with mutual friend Stacey Earley. I named the band Elsie's Porch, in honor of my days hanging out at Matt's house playing music with Diego and company. We featured my originals and a few cover tunes. We played mostly small venues, with a few big gigs here and there. One of the memorable gigs was an annual Chicago event called Around the Coyote, which showcased the work of Chicago painters, sculptors, and other artists. Elsie's Porch and other future musical endeavors became possible only after my departure from Firetruck.

For that, I blame lack of direction and poor management for the band going nowhere and the ultimate failure of capturing, packaging, and marketing the "lightning in a bottle" creative explosion that we were. You can drag your thirty-something-year-old friends around to gigs for just so long until things fizzle out. Vince was the first to leave and started his own three-piece band called Hip Deep Trilogy. I would lovingly refer to them as "Sheep Dip Trilogy," which, of course, irritated Vince. Doug's wife, Jodi, on keyboard, replaced Vince. As irritating as Vince was at times, his guitar and writing ability were essential to Firetruck's music. The band also replaced me and carried on for a little while but eventually splintered off into various other projects.

We all remained friends and continued to see each other at meetings, particularly, Café Bustelo Group on Friday's. We did a few reunion shows in the years that followed, but the coolest thing related to Firetruck happened some years later when we all met at Bustelo to celebrate Doug's 10-year-sober anniversary. Most of us had not been to the meeting in years for one reason or another. I was shocked when I walked into what started out as a bitch-session/group therapy for the band and saw 70 or 80 people that now packed the church basement. The only one not in attendance was David Hoffman.

David had struggled to stay clean and continued to chronically relapse for years. He later admitted to shooting heroin at times while a member of Firetruck, including in the bathroom, at our first gig at Avalon Nightclub. Opening night jitters became severe anxiety for him, while for me, they had become a sense of excitement and adventure. This is symbolic of the stark difference between being in recovery and being stuck in addiction.

David moved back to the St. Louis area and though we stayed in touch via email for some time, he stopped responding to my messages. I've never confirmed it, but I have a feeling that David is no longer with us. His story still makes me sad. He was such a unique, awesome person, who thought so little of himself. He never completely made peace with the "fat boy" he once was.

Another big change happened when the "progress" in the addictions counseling field I spoke of earlier reared its ugly head. In the Spring of 1992, the entire staff was called into the dining room at Lincoln Park. The "managed care" era was officially upon us. What it meant was; insurance companies now called the shots when it came to length of stay in treatment. Someone sitting behind a desk who never even met the client could now override a trained professional's clinical recommendation. The days of keeping people in treatment for as long as they needed to be, were over. The term "managed care" was a thin veil for the reality; "It's all about the money, and we don't really care if you recover or not." They, of course, put a positive spin on the changes.

Interventions President and CEO Peter Bokos, came to break the news to us. He shed tears as he informed us that our six-month or more program had officially been slashed to 90 days starting immediately. Hell, most clients didn't even get their heads out of their ass for 60 days. My "caseload from Hell" were all in treatment for eight months or more before they were ready to leave.

The type of treatment that saved my life was quickly becoming a "dinosaur," as they say. Don't get me wrong, the changes weren't all bad, but the limitations on length of stay would ultimately determine whether some would recover or continue on the merry-go-round of addiction. As I mentioned, time is an extremely important element in healing the addicted brain, and now, addicts in treatment would have considerably less of it.

While me and some of my peers, like Benny and Willie, joined the fight against it, many others succumbed to it.

Mark Storch died of "health complications related to his addiction" sometime after my last encounter with him. He and Willie remained in touch until the end, and I recently learned that Willie was with him at his deathbed when he passed away. Tears filled my eyes when Willie reported reciting *The*

Sinner's' Prayer with him. The staunch atheist accepted Jesus Christ as his Lord and Savior before taking his last breath. I played two songs at his services.

Willie and I continued our friendship. Despite an occasional falling out, the bond of brotherhood we shared was stronger than any worldly disagreement we may have had. Willie passed away in 2021, but I didn't hear about his passing for months. I don't have any other details.

Still, others tried to be helpers but ultimately couldn't keep their own recovery on track. David Grey worked for the court-affiliated agency TASC that once saved Benny's life but ultimately lost his battle when they found him in a hotel room, dead of an overdose.

John Clark helped many by taking over his father's halfway houses—Bill's Family—after his father passed away in 1993. John formed Jack Clark's Family with his sister Denise and her husband Larry. They expanded to multiple locations. Much to their credit, they did so in neighborhoods that most Chicagoans wouldn't set foot in. Unfortunately, John's chronic relapsing finally took its toll, and he died in 2010.

These brothers' roles in my life were brief but profound. David Grey kept me from leaving treatment. Mark and John's sense of humor kept me sane enough to get through treatment before I was "restored to sanity" (as much as is possible for someone with my past) and let me know that music, laughter, and fun, was still possible after we get sober.

There were, of course, other success stories besides Benny, Willie, and myself. The "burger flipper" Kevin, whom we all snickered at when he announced getting hired by McDonald's, went on to become regional manager of the entire Skokie area. He wasn't kidding when he said, "I'm gonna be the best damn burger flipper there is, until I own that place." He came pretty close.

Another success story is my Gateway roommate Curtis A. He surprised everyone by staying clean and opening several barbershops on the West Side of Chicago. Last I heard, he was still doing well.

Then, there was my first client at Interventions, Anthony W. He stayed clean and was hired and promoted to regional manager of a national grocery chain. He was transferred to NYC, where he continues to thrive, and from what I've heard, has a wife and kids. After hearing of several cases like his over the years, I'm waiting for someone to write the book *I Was Gay Until I Wasn't Anymore*. I'll buy that book the minute it comes out!

As the years went by, other casualties of addiction (whether directly or indirectly) began to mount. In 1996, the list would include my brother Paul, who technically also died of "health complications related to his addiction." But I feel the primary cause was his failure to stop using drugs. I believe he could have recaptured much of his health if he could have gotten clean and learned to take care of himself. Willie and I facilitated a family intervention on him, followed by one led by my Gateway counselor, Ron Orlando about a year later. It resulted in him entering treatment at Gateway's Lake Villa facility. Unfortunately, he only lasted four days and returned home which wife Carie allowed, despite my advice not to until he completed treatment. My family and I cut them off for the next two years. He eventually lost control during that time, which led to Carie filing for divorce. He went downhill quickly after that.

I remember feeling a glimmer of hope when he agreed to attend an NA meeting with me. Unfortunately, any hope I had evaporated when I noticed him squirming in his chair and watching the clock. He couldn't wait to get out of there. I'll never totally understand why. He had no life and nothing to lose at that point. I remember the hopeless feeling of powerlessness that came over me—realizing at that moment that he was beyond help.

Before he died, I visited him in the hospital for the last time. I looked into his eyes and saw overwhelming fear. It was as if he finally realized he was dying and that he wasn't going to be able to bounce back like he always had. I tried to reassure him: "It's okay man. Just let go. God forgives you. I know he does because I forgive you, and if I can forgive you, I know God does."

Those would be the last words I would say to him. I wrote a poem that was printed and became his Mass card at his memorial service. Within months, an old picture of his daughter Carly sticking a flower in his face inspired the opening line to the song I'd write and record about him...

Coffee Can Drummer

Faded memory, of your face I see, in a picture that I found from days gone by,
Makes me sad to see, all the casualties,
Of an era, where we tried to fly too high,

I can still recall, how we'd risk it all, to chase a feeling always out of reach,
What did you let go? Guess you'll never know,
Were the things you wanted so far out of reach?

All you wanted,
All you needed, was in front of your eyes,
All you wanted,
All you needed; how could you be so blind?

What was once a game for you somehow changed, and became most important in your life,
Twenty years went by, as you lived your lie,

Tryin' to keep a good home and a wife

Whatever happened to the coffee can drummer?
House of the Rising Sun strummer?
How could you leave it all behind?

And we felt so small, as we watched you fall, cause all of us just stood by helplessly,
And your mother cried, on the night you died,
As she prayed beside your body, on her knees

All you wanted,
All you needed, was in front of your eyes,
All you wanted,
All you needed; how could you be so blind?
Brother, how could you be so blind?
Faded memory, of your face I see, in a picture that I found from days gone by

Next was Franko. His mother called me one day in a panic, not knowing what to do as Frank finally hit bottom in California. I suggested getting him home, and I'd help him get into treatment. She followed my advice, and I was able to pull some strings and expedite a bed in an inpatient program.

Meanwhile, his brother Max was getting married soon, and a bachelor party was being thrown at one of our old haunts, the Grand Bowl in Franklin Park. Frank had just gotten out of treatment, so he asked if I would go with him for support. I agreed.

At first, being in the old hood and seeing some old faces was nostalgic, but the nostalgia quickly wore off, and it became apparent why my presence was necessary. Excessive drinking and drug use soon surrounded us. I started feeling like I was in an episode of *The Twilight Zone* and stuck in a time warp. It occurred to me that everyone was talking about the same things they were talking about in high school. I was waiting for the blacklight posters to fluoresce, and I thought I might have an acid flashback at any moment when the song "Karn Evil 9" came through the speakers. The lyrics, *"Welcome back my friends to the show that never ends"* reflected how I felt. At the risk of sounding "holier than thou," I realized that I had outgrown all of this. I wanted to get the hell out of there, and I felt relieved when we finally did.

Frank's parents had followed my advice to the letter with one exception, as in Paul's case, I told them: "DO NOT let him live with you. Make him go to a halfway house when he gets out of treatment." They, like Carie, didn't follow that advice and they let him move in. On July 27th, 1998, they returned home to find Franko dead from a heroin overdose. We all did our best, but it was too little, too late.

Cal was next, when, in 2003, he was found frozen to death, homeless, and sleeping under a bridge in Michigan. His death was likely the result of an overdose. Brian thought the police in the area had something to do with it and may have beaten him and left him to die. This story was never confirmed.

Cal would leave me with one last memory of better days when we all got together in 1999 at a reunion for Brian's surprise 40th birthday bash at the VFW hall in Northlake. We all posed for a picture that included Cal, Brian, Danny Diaz, me, Mary, Pam, and a few others. We had not all been in the same room together for years. Missing was Juan, who we never located after Warren's death, and of course, Warren.

Brian had married my cousin Dee, and she pulled off this monster surprise party. He was so surprised; his face turned beat red when he entered, and I thought he was going to keel over from a heart attack. Luckily, he didn't that night, but sadly, in 2012, he would.

Brian died much too early at the age of 53 of a "heart attack," but I believe the real cause was years of alcohol and drug abuse. Brian confided in me not long before he died that he needed to drink 10 beers just to fall asleep. I encouraged him to stop drinking and get help. I said I'd help him any way I could, but I never heard another word from him about it.

He is sorely missed by all. I've never seen so many people who came to say goodbye at his services. The stories heard were all similar and almost always included what Brian did for others. He would go out of his way not only for family and friends, but total strangers. He would literally give the shirt off his back if you asked for it. Dee moved out of state after Brian's death. I continue to miss them at family events to this day.

Later that year, Diego would lose his long fight with kidney failure. But his story is much more of a success than a failure. He miraculously survived a long stint on dialysis and two kidney transplants. No one thought he would survive for as long as he did—but with the love of his family, strong faith in God, and sheer will to live—he lived for 36 years from when his ordeal began at that summer party. He and Holly managed to raise three awesome sons. One of my biggest regrets was that I never reconnected and played music with one of my musical soulmates after I got clean.

Finally, the last of my old "gang" was Danny Diaz, who died in 2018, just after turning 60—a feat only accomplished by Danny, myself, and Juan Garcia from that group of male friends. Again, whatever the official cause of death was, didn't matter. Alcohol killed Danny, plain and simple. You just can't drink from age 13, the way Danny, Brian, and Cal did, without devastating consequences eventually catching up with you.

These untimely deaths remind me that although recovery mainly emphasizes emotional and spiritual health, the importance of physical health should never be taken for granted.

After moving the Interventions program from Lincoln Park to the suburb of Woodridge, I took on the role of a sort of pseudo-rec-therapist for the young men I worked with. Interventions had lost a court battle with the lawyer who lived next door. Just like that, Lincoln Park Interventions was no more and became Woodridge Interventions.

I had no problem joining in when I took them for rec time, that is, until the guys tried to get me on the basketball court. I thought I was going to die! I joked that the only way I'd play basketball with them again, is if they had an ambulance on standby.

This was a result of my cigarette habit. I started getting headaches and feeling generally crappy from smoking. I remember thinking to myself, *I didn't get clean to feel crappy.* I decided then and there—I had to stop. But how? I had been a smoker since the age of 13. I had always thought of myself as a smoker but that had to change. I refer to this process as "reinventing ourselves." I find it to be essential not only to recover from addiction, but for life in general. At different stages, for various reasons, we will no longer be able to hang onto the idea of who we thought we were and used to be.

I was reminded that although I was an artist and a musician, I was also an athlete. I was once again able to forge a new self-image, combining the nonconformist, irreverent artist-musician with the healthy, nonsmoking, non-drinking/non-drugging athlete. This, combined with my growing interest in natural wholistic alternative therapies, led me to a naturopathic doctor named Sue Mardoian. She gave me a $60 acupuncture treatment, putting a needle in each wrist for 20 minutes. I have not smoked a cigarette since.

So, now I think I should wrap up the part of my story that involves Amelia. I said there would be one more chapter, and here it is. Just as the "honeymoon" was over, and the magic faded for Beth and me, out of the blue, Amelia called me. What she said to me during that call was everything I had wanted to hear from her when we were trying to keep our relationship alive.

She said she missed me, she loved me, and I was right. She was tired of chasing an acting career around the country and wanted to take my advice and use her Oscar nomination and experience to offer classes and begin teaching. Most importantly, she wanted to do this in Chicago and was willing to leave L.A. for good and move back in with me.

I was completely caught off guard. Her words felt like being hit by a truck! I was dazed, mesmerized, and in a trance. *I have to give it a shot,* I thought. But I immediately realized that there were things I loved about both women and that were good about both relationships. I was torn. The stupid pop song "Torn Between Two Lovers" by Mary MacGregor tortured me relentlessly from that moment on, entering my (theatre of the absurd) mind, often and without my permission.

So, I sat Beth down and honestly explained the situation, including how torn I felt. I loved two women in different ways. Beth handled it surprisingly well. She said she didn't like it but understood why I had to do it. I decided that Amelia would move back to Chicago and in with me. It coincided perfectly with Bob moving in with his girlfriend, who would later become his wife.

The things Amelia had in storage for years would be put out in a sidewalk sale, except for her most prized possessions. She would have those shipped and arranged to store them in a family friend's basement.

I remember picking her up at Midway airport in a van I was driving at the time. Then on to some warehouse-type facility to pick up 14 or so giant boxes of "stuff." We began to bicker and argue immediately. Then came the long trek to unload the goods.

The next day, when I got home from work, we argued and bickered the entire time. By day three, it was like waking up from a really good dream to a wide-awake nightmare. Reality set in, and just like that, it was over. I realized I was no longer in love with her. My "eyes" had been "bigger than my stomach," and I couldn't stand being with her for another day. These feelings were magnified by the fact that I also missed Beth.

I dreaded it, but I knew I had to tell Amelia right away, and as soon as I got home from work, I did. She was obviously hurt and angry. In tears, she yelled, "What am I supposed to do now?!"

I suggested she stay with her mother, and I would pay for her airfare back to LA, between profuse apologies and trying to find a way to explain that I was just as shocked as she was.

The next day, I came home from work to find a long, nasty message on my answering machine. No, it wasn't Amelia. It was one of her celebrity friends from LA who shall remain nameless.

Amelia stuck around Chicago for a while, but she again got the acting itch and bounced around the country before ending up back in New York, where she remains to this day. Outside of a few "cameo appearances" (not worth mentioning) the story of our relationship was officially over.

Amelia was one of the most important relationships I've ever had. Her contribution to my personal growth and development can't be overstated, and I will always be grateful for it.

As I said earlier, Beth and I would also be over by 1996. But before our relationship ended, we would go on a few very important trips together. The first was to Northern California to visit the places of mine and Frank's great adventures there. We stayed at the "haunted" Leger Hotel and toured the town.

During the visit, I reunited with a few old bandmates: keyboard player Ron and bass player "Catfish Bob." They, along with Joe Marino, had formed a new band called Chicken Feet. They told me that Miles had moved to the San Francisco area and had become a well-known artist and sculptor. Dusty never returned to the area and was never heard from again by anyone, including her good friend Anita.

The second trip Beth and I made was to New Orleans. We went during Mardi Gras, which was a bit too much of a "drunk fest" for my tastes, but it didn't keep me from falling in love with the city.

The last "nail would be driven into the coffin" for Beth and me upon meeting my soulmate, the woman who would eventually become my wife, Shelley. She was assigned to "shadow" me as an intern at Interventions, and I admit, I may have given a whole new meaning to the term "taking her under my wing."

Shelley was a unique blend of all the great qualities of my previous relationships since being in recovery. I was attracted to her immediately the first time I saw her at work at the table with several other staff members. This did not go unnoticed by one of my colleagues whose eyes followed me from the time I set foot in the room, to the back to hang up my coat. He smirked knowingly after observing how I looked at her. He followed me to the back room and warned, "Stevie, I saw that look in your eye."

I tried to play it off. "What?" pretending I had no idea what he meant.

He continued, "Stevie, she'll chew you up and spit you out!"
I appropriately responded, "Yeah, but what a way to go!"

Shelley and I felt that our meeting was engineered by God. Even if it would have amounted to nothing else, our attraction to each other helped us both end long-term relationships that were difficult to end but desperately needed to. We didn't know where our relationship would go, but we knew we "more than liked" each other. "More than like" would eventually turn into love.

It turned out that Shelley had been to an annual event in New Orleans several times that was a bit more in our wheelhouse—The Jazz and Heritage Festival, or Jazz Fest, as it's better known. The food (there's nothing like a basket of fresh, warm crayfish), the sights, the sounds, and the people became some of our favorite things in life, but at the top of that list was—the music! From local acts like The Neville Brothers and Zachary Richard to major acts like the Eagles, George Clinton and P-Funk, and Paul Simon, we saw some of the best live music ever. We returned almost every year, and it felt like home.

As Beth and I faded away, another extremely important relationship also started to wither and die. A relationship that had been essential to my recovery. It began dying what I can only describe as a "natural death"—my reliance upon and relationship with the 12-step programs.

As my life continued to expand and flourish into more and more of what it was meant to be, I found it demanding more and more of my time, energy, and attention. I was clean for almost nine years, and the desire to use drugs was dead and buried. Also, because of what I did for a living, I could no longer work with addicts and talk about recovery all day, then go home, continue to work with addicts, and continue talking about recovery. I stopped sponsoring people after my last sponsee "left the nest."

It was an unexpected result of my growth and evolution, but I found I no longer had problems that required me to share in meetings and get support or guidance for them. Life problems no longer overwhelmed me. The AA promise: *We will intuitively know how to handle situations which used to baffle us* had become my reality. My life became much more manageable, and I was *restored to sanity* in the sense that I could now trust my judgment. Bad decisions were fewer and farther between, and I accepted and could handle the results either way. I've always said if I didn't do this for a living, I would still be going to meetings and sponsoring people. It was scary to "cut the apron strings" of the program, and I remember running back to meetings during several life crises that occurred back then. However, once the storms passed, I found myself sinking back into the realization that I had outgrown the need to talk about my problems or my life, in rooms full of other recovering people.

Make no mistake: the program is part of me, and I continued applying the principles that got me where I am today. Every morning, I still read the *Twenty-Four Hours a Day* book. I pray, meditate (talk and listen to God), continue to work the steps and apply the slogans and philosophies that changed my life—even some from my treatment days at Gateway. I still occasionally carry the coin Pete gave me in my pocket (at the urging of my wife) to remind me to "Shut the fuck up" and listen, and I never forget where I came from. How could I? I deal with clients who constantly remind me of who I was, where I used to be, and what my life was like.

As I said earlier, everyone's path in recovery starts out similarly, and there are some basic essential ingredients. But as recovery continues, our paths become more individualized and our "recipe" more unique. Some may need to go to meetings for the rest of their lives; some may do so because they want to and have no reason to stop. For me, this was the path my recovery led me to.

During a brief period of returning to meetings after my breakup with Beth, one meeting I attended was the Independence Park meeting I took my brother Paul to before he died. As I sat there waiting for the meeting to start, I saw some familiar faces sitting around the tables. These people helped me through crucial times simply by sharing their recovery. There was no other deep bond or friendship needed other than that.

They probably didn't recognize me due to my appearance being drastically different from when I attended the meeting on a regular basis. The clean-shaven guy with short hair, now had shoulder length hair and a full beard. I felt like a spy incognito.

One of those faces stood out. It was a woman around my age named Suzanne. I had been seeing her in meetings for my entire recovery. Though we were never close in the typical sense, whenever we talked, there was always a sense of deep respect we had for each other's recovery, especially as we witnessed each other celebrate multiple years clean. Often, my comments followed hers or vice versa because our words would often inspire each other. There was always this subtle healthy competition between us like we were trying to "out-comment" each other. It wasn't so much a "pissing contest" as it was us trying to understand and articulate the whys and wherefores of recovery on a deeper, more meaningful level.

I remember my comment at that meeting like it was yesterday: "I know that you probably don't recognize me because my appearance is a lot different from when I used to attend this meeting. I haven't been here in years, but I'm looking around the room, and I'm seeing your faces, thinking to myself, God, if these people only knew how important they were to my recovery. I wouldn't be here if it wasn't for you people."

Just like the old days, Suzanne commented next.

She shared an insightful, wise comment, which ended with… "and of course we recognize you Steve. No matter how long your hair gets or how thick your beard is, we'll always recognize you." We all laughed, and I felt like I was home again, just like I had in Jim and Jeff's basement while coming down from acid as a teenager, only this time, without the drug-induced foreboding and sadness. These connections will be a positive part of me forever.

Before I could move forward into the next phase of my recovery and my life, I still had a loose end that needed to be tied up. I had to drop some guilt. Unfortunately, by the time I had gotten around to doing it, she was gone. Sheila Jackson had passed away. So, I did the next right thing.

While at one of my last meetings at the Mustard Seed, I noticed Counselor Jeff K. was there. After the meeting ended, I went to him, and after initial greetings and "how've ya been" check-in was out of the way, I informed him that I had some guilt I needed to drop. This immediately wiped the smile from his face, which was replaced by a serious look of concern.

I dropped it "like it was hot" (an old Gateway saying). I proceeded to tell him how Sheila caught me on the payphone upstairs and how I lied to her about it, not just once, but every time she saw me thereafter. Jeff laughed and exclaimed, "That's it!?"

"Yep. After I heard Sheila died, it bugged me even more," I confessed.

Still laughing, Jeff made the sign of the cross and assured me, "You're officially absolved Steve."

In the back of my mind, I felt Sheila laughing too, and I was free from the last of my treatment guilt.

The next chapter of my life, again, brought an abundance of blessings. The "terminal bachelor" had finally met his match. Shelley and I were married on October 10, 1999, in a small, intimate outdoor ceremony, followed by a breakfast reception. It took place on a beautiful Autumn morning at one of our favorite breakfast nooks, the Mill Race Inn in Geneva, Illinois.

Our invitations summed it up...

We, Steven Fiorito and Shelley Simmons, invite you to join us during our favorite season, at our favorite restaurant, for our favorite meal, to celebrate our exchange of marriage vows with our favorite person...each other!

It was a unique, unconventional, eclectic wedding with just the right blend of simplicity, funkiness, and a touch of elegance. The event beautifully represented who we were as individuals and as a couple. My recording partner Dave played piano when the mixtape we made of our favorite songs wasn't playing. Then, some of our other musical friends came up and joined me in playing several songs I selected to honor my bride, including "We're All the Way" by Eric Clapton and "Love Letters" by Boz Scaggs. It was a beautiful day. I do have more guilt to drop, though...During breakfast, I admit listening on a single earbud to the Chicago Bears beat the Minnesota Vikings on a transistor radio I had stashed under our table. Bearrrrzzzzzz!!

The next day, we departed for our honeymoon to Niagara Falls, Salem Massachusetts, and Bar Harbor Maine, where we basked in the beauty of a breathtaking east coast autumn and took in tours of the Salem Witch Trials. In Maine, we stayed at a beautiful bed and breakfast, where we ate fresh lobster at reasonable prices and homemade muffins for two glorious weeks. We saw the most beautiful autumn colors we've ever seen while hiking through the Acadia National Forest. It would be one of the last times we would ever get that much time off, due to significant changes to our daily lives that lie ahead.

As for the other gifts and blessings, the list is too long, but here are some of the ones that stand out: When Shelley and I bought our first "big boy home," I felt it was validation to my family that I really had recovered from addiction, and I was a functional, productive member of society. It wasn't a fluke. I especially wanted Albie to be proud of me. But it was bittersweet when we brought her to see our new house. When she got there, she commented on how beautiful it was, followed by, "Whose house is this?"

"It's mine Mom. Mine and Shelley's."

"Steven, this is so beautiful," she replied.

Then, 30 minutes later: "Who did you say lives here?"

Unfortunately, by this time, her dementia was starting to take hold, so I had to settle for a "Ground Hog Day" of sorts— her being proud of me for brief periods, followed by forgetting what we had just talked about.

This was the beginning of a period where my sisters and I had to return the favor for the years she had so willingly given to us. It was time to take care of Albie and see her through to the end of her life. I'm proud of being there to fulfill my role as her son, especially with my brother Paul being gone. Recovery had changed my perception about aging and death, and I accepted them as a natural part of life and not a tragic catastrophe.

I had a similar experience when I walked my daughter Jessica down the aisle on her wedding day. I was acutely aware during the father/daughter dance that I could have easily been a ghost, dancing unseen alongside her and whatever stepparent had taken my place. Due to Laura's husband Dan being good to Jess and in her life for some years, Dan walked her halfway, then handed her off to me to take her the rest of the way down the aisle to the altar.

Recently, at our family Christmas party, Jessica gave me the best gift I've ever gotten. As I opened the flat package, I saw a copy of her birth certificate. I had, of course, seen her birth certificate before and thought to myself: *Why is she giving me a copy of her birth certi....* Then, I saw it—in the space where the name of the "father" goes, which had always been blank. It now had my name in it. She had me legally added to her birth certificate as her father! I didn't even know you could do that. I was caught off guard and so choked up I had to leave the room. There wasn't a dry eye amongst my family.

It's not that I needed an award, but it was one of the few times my struggles to be a father were ever acknowledged or appreciated since her grandma Rhoda acknowledged my efforts years ago. Looking back, I have to give some credit to that 19-year-old junkie for stepping up and taking on a responsibility that he certainly wasn't ready for or equipped to handle. Love is what gave me power that I didn't have and sustained us through the good times and bad. The love from and for my kids, ultimately helped to save my life.

As these meaningful gifts and rewards of my recovery continued, the creative side of my life also continued to flourish and grow. My creative energy would eventually "shapeshift" and redirect itself into various creative endeavors.

I continued to write music and record with Dave. Once I had enough original material, it was time to put my own band together. Elsie's Porch was like putting my toe in the water, but now it was time to dive in. In me late 30's, I felt the pressure of the proverbial clock ticking, and I decided it was now or never to put a band together. I ran ads in local musician publications, and after auditioning people for the better part of a year, I finally had the right personnel. I named the band Soul Miners. We rehearsed, played a few "warmup shows" at a few local dives, and were finally ready to start booking shows at serious venues in Chicago.

Our first legit gig was booked at U.S. Beer Company on the corner of Clybourn and Sheffield avenues. We took out an ad in the *Illinois Entertainer* magazine to advertise the band's debut. We called our music "New Classic Rock."

Then, out of nowhere, lightning struck. Not the good kind, but the kind that splits mighty trees in half and burns them to the ground. One mishap after another made what had taken almost a year to put together, unravel, and fall apart in a matter of weeks. I had to cancel the U.S. Beer Company gig, but unfortunately, it was too late to cancel the ad in the *Illinois Entertainer*. To this day I refer to the ad as "the gig that never happened" and pasted in a scrapbook.

Was it all possibly a message from God that I still wasn't quite ready to hear yet? I was devastated and musically frustrated, until Shelley and I attended a street fair in Chicago to see her good friend Patty perform as… Patty Elvis…female Elvis Presley impersonator extraordinaire! She was great, and I couldn't help but notice that she was having a gas on stage! Right after her performance, I made my decision. I would put together a Doors tribute band.

I always *got* Jim Morrison and could reasonably mimic his singing voice. Inspired by Patty Elvis, and the sudden collapse of Soul Miners, I set out to put together a band that would bring back The Doors music to a whole new audience. Unlike my purpose for Soul Miners of becoming a recording artist, I just wanted to have some fun, make a few bucks, and play some good music.

Within a few months, a lead guitarist and a drummer answered an ad I placed. We added a keyboard and a bass player (We were The Doors *with* a bass player) and started rehearsing. I named the band The Crystal Ship—one of my favorite songs from their debut album, and I booked our first gig, ironically at… U.S. Beer Company.

Our guitarist was a phenom; the problem was, he was only 20 years old. I had a knot in my gut when we arrived at the club and prayed that they wouldn't card him. I breathed a sigh of relief once we got him through the door.

I took the stage donned in my black leather pants, Concho belt, and white pirate shirt. We played to a packed house and the show was a success.

Sadly, it would be the only show performed by The Crystal Ship. No, we didn't break up, but we did change the name based on some bogus intel from Freddy. After I told him the name of the band, he warned, "Kid, you've got to change that name. There's already a band out there called The Crystal Ship." I took his word for it without properly investigating his claim. I informed the rest of the band, and we changed the name to Strange Days. I later found out that Fred had gotten most of it wrong. The other Crystal Ship was out of Milwaukee, and they had been broken up and had not been playing for well over a year. It was too late; we had already changed all the promo material.

We started getting booked every weekend. This first incarnation of the band would be pioneers who would design the blueprint for the band's unique approach to shows. It started with our knack for spontaneous improvisation, as we weaved in and out of sounding like The Doors and using the music as a vehicle to indulge in our own individual styles. I ventured off into caricatures of what I'd describe as "Morrisonesque" poetry, antics, and tirades in the middle of songs. When we weren't creating complete original bits, we were focused on bringing The Door's music back to life.

I'd be chugging my fifth of "Jack Daniels" (iced tea mixed with green Gatorade) and getting progressively more "drunk" and confrontational with the audience in an attempt to duplicate the infamous Miami rant that led to Morrison's arrest. We were having a gas!

There were a lot of great shows and stories that I can tell, and although that's not what this story is about, I hope you'll bear with me as I indulge in one of them.

It was at a club called The Edge in south suburban Midlothian. We were doing the song "The End" near the end of our show when this beautiful girl with long silky brown hair to the middle of her back spontaneously joined me on stage and picked up one of my tambourines. She started dancing with me as I performed the song, but a better description than dancing would be a sensual, sexual tantric movement of our bodies in rhythm with the music. At one point, she was lying on the stage on her back, between my legs, looking up at me as I sang to her. She gently shook her tambourine in front of my crotch as I played my tambourine just above hers…

Lost in a Roman, wilderness of pain,
And all the children, are insane,
All the children, are insane,
Waiting for the summer rain, yeah!

She then snaked up my legs, and somehow, I accommodated her by dropping to my knees as she slid up my back with hers. She was now lying on me back-to-back with her long brown hair draped over my shoulders. To accentuate the scene, someone wisely cut all the stage lights off, and all that remained was the red spotlight that was trained on the two of us. It was very erotic and spontaneous…

There's danger on the edge of town,
Ride the King's highway baby,
Weird scenes inside the goldmine,
Ride the highway west baby,

Ride the snake, ride the snake,
To the lake, the ancient lake baby...

We were so in sync, it's hard to describe. The audience, realizing that they were witnessing one of those special, spontaneous, Strange Days moments, started whistling and cheering. In 1981, Frank and I walked into the infamous Whiskey a Go Go on Sunset Strip, and I imagined what it was like to be Morrison on that stage. Well, now I knew exactly what it was like! At times, I was so in the "Morrison zone," I felt possessed by his spirit while on stage, and I felt what it must have been like to be performing that music to a live audience. Talk about a natural high. I had one almost every time we performed.

A typical show also included a psychedelic light show, T-shirt sales, occasional Silly String fights with each other and the audience, and an autographed can of Spam giveaway (borrowed from Firetruck days). It would usually be rounded off with either a trance-producing rendition of the song "The End," or a rowdy, rousing, raunchy rendition of "Roadhouse Blues"!

After the band's third year, big changes to the lineup occurred when two original members were replaced by an older, seasoned veteran on guitar, who was also a violinist for a North Shore orchestra, and a young Doors-loving hot shot on drums, and the band carried on.

We enjoyed continued success, getting booked into all the local clubs as a headliner or opening act. We were usually paired with acts like Axis, a Jimi Hendrix tribute, and Hot Rocks, a Rolling Stones tribute.

Some of the highlights included doing a few cable TV shows, outdoor festivals, and our biggest gig, at the House of Blues, when we were invited onto the Jonathan Brandmeier ("Johnny B.") radio show.

One of my personal highlights was an article written in a local newspaper about local tribute bands, Strange Days being one of them. The opening paragraph in the article focused on me...

At night, the singer cinches up his black leather pants and concho belt, writhing before a microphone in a hallucinogenic haze.

By day, Steve Fiorito counsels drug addicts and alcoholics. But, when the sun dips, he morphs into his anarchic alter ego, Jim Morrison, in The Doors tribute band, Strange Days."

The band had an amazing eight-year run. All the goals that I had for putting it together had been achieved, and then some.

The importance of sharing my experiences about Strange Days is to illustrate that when one is truly anchored in recovery, the sky's the limit! We can engage in almost any creative endeavor, even some that may be considered off-limits or high-risk for those who are too early in their recovery.

Luckily, the band's demise coincided with my rekindled interest in theater, when Shelley suggested that I audition for a play she saw advertised in a local paper. I needed a British accent for the role, which luckily always came easy to me. I guess watching *Monty Python's Flying Circus* every Sunday at Matt's paid off.

I was once again bitten by the acting bug and continued to land roles in local plays with several local theater companies. During one of the shows, a fellow actor encouraged me to audition for a British comedy at The Riverfront Playhouse—a community not-for-profit theater that had been started by a group of local actor friends in the 1970s. Upon my arrival for my audition, I instantly fell in love with the quirky, funky, 80-seat theater.

The play was an absolute gem. Written in England by two Britts, the show would be making its American debut on the Riverfront stage. The premise? Two British businessmen attempt to sell their failing business to two unsuspecting Euro-playboy tycoon types, one (Kurt) from Germany, and the other (Sven) from Sweden. Their plan is to distract them with liquor and prostitutes and get them to "sign zee papers" by the end of the evening. A wrench gets thrown in their plan when the hookers cancel, just before their wives show up to look in on things and ensure that their husbands don't screw up dumping their financial burden. When the wives run into Kurt and Sven, they soon realize that they are being mistaken for the deal-sweetening hookers. The wives decide to play along in an effort to "seal the deal." Things get even more complex and hysterical when the real hookers show up unexpectantly.

I had my eye on one of the British business owner roles when, out of the blue, the director asked me to read the next few scenes as Kurt. I pulled my best bastardized Colonel Klink-like German accent out of my ass and read the next few pages.

Two days later I got the call: "We'd like to offer you the role of Kurt." After snapping out of a brief period of shock, I accepted the role. I remember thinking: *Wow, my British accent was impeccable, and they want me to play the German guy?!* So, I worked on my German accent and got it down. As it turned out, the role of Kurt was much more fun than the role I had my eye on.

I wound up doing many shows at the Riverfront, most of which were British farces, but I have to say that to date, *Business Affairs* was one of the best shows I've ever been a part of. Well-written, clever, funny, and almost perfectly cast, with plenty of room for improvisation that my seasoned fellow actors and I took full advantage of. It got rave reviews in the local *Aurora Beacon-News*!

Two of my fellow cast members who portrayed a husband and wife in the show, actually *were* husband and wife in real life. Jack and Sherry met while doing a play in the early days of the Riverfront. I soon found out that Jack

Schultz was not only one of the founders, but one of the "behind the scenes" driving creative forces. He had written original shows with original musical scores that had become annual fan favorites.

I discovered that Jack had his fingers in a variety of creative endeavors, including as a writer for *The Chicago Reader* and *Suburban Nightlife* newspapers. He published a regular column in both, as none other than; "Fubar the Adequate," a tongue-in-cheek, sarcastic, edgy "astronomer" whose weekly horoscopes would either have you wishing you'd never been born, or laughing your ass off, and quite often, both. A typical line from one of Fubar's horoscopes might go something like this: "Oh, poor arrogant Sagittarius. You're about to have your parade rained on big-time, so don't even bother leaving the house today because some of that 'rain' will be of the bird poop variety."

My ex, Beth, was a huge fan and never missed his horoscopes. If she could've started a Fubar fan club, she would have. I was tempted to call her and say: "Hey. You'll never guess who I'm in a play with…Fubar the Adequate!" Unfortunately, in those days, Beth and I were not on speaking terms.

The best was yet to come with Jack in 2009 when he unveiled his most recent and (in my opinion) best masterpiece, *Night of the Living Dead: The Musical*, a spoof based on George Romero's 1960s cult classic. I landed the role of Harry Cooper, who was attempting to escape the ensuing zombie apocalypse with wife Helen and young daughter Karen.

Once again, the original musical score would be written by Jack with much collaboration musically from Kathleen Dooley, an excellent musician and composer and the musical backbone of The Riverfront for years. It's the only show I know of at The Riverfront that recorded and sold CDs of the soundtrack, done by the original cast members.

When audience members started showing up dressed as zombies, it had all the earmarks of becoming another annual Riverfront staple and fan favorite with an almost cult-like following. The show was a hit and was critically acclaimed. I believe we were reviewed in an Australian newspaper. The title of the article was "Chicago steals the show" and compared the Windy City's local theater scene with New York City's. Quite an accomplishment in my book…and…it *is* my book.

But my revived love affair with the theater wouldn't last. By 2010 the other side of the theater world started to rear its ugly head, in the form of cliquishness, back-stabbing, competition for roles, favoritism, and the like. It started to leave a bad taste in my mouth and disillusionment started to set in.

Not long after things soured, God dangled a "carrot" in front of my face that offered me an unexpected, unlikely alternative. He literally put my old goalie equipment bag in my path in my basement and I all but tripped over it. I pulled out the badly antiquated, obsolete equipment, and out of nowhere, I felt a small fire ignite deep inside me. I remember thinking, *I don't want to play on skates anymore, but I wonder if there's anybody playing a serious brand of adult floor hockey out there.*

I decided to check into it. That spark may have been magnified by my rekindled interest in the Chicago Blackhawks who had just brought the Stanley Cup back to Chicago after an almost 50-year drought. As I walked away from my equipment, that could have easily been the end of that part of the story, but it wasn't. After I came out of the basement and got on with my day, the fire was still there...and it grew.

At the same time, I could feel another fire in me slowly dying. The creative musical explosion that I experienced was an important part of my recovery and my life, but at some point, I had to accept that my recording-artist "ship had sailed." I was heading into my late forties. I feel it was one of the casualties of my 12 years of addiction. I was grateful that I escaped with my life, and I was proud of what I had accomplished musically, but at that time, I finally surrendered to the fact that I would probably never make a living playing music. Apparently, God had other plans, and I had come to accept that this was His will for me.

I could feel the creative energy begin to "shape-shift" once again. I felt it reignite the life-long passion I once had for a sport that I thought I'd never play again. However, that fire was almost extinguished as my inquiries into playing seemed to go nowhere.

I was just about to give up the idea of ever playing again when I came across a website called Sportsvite that connected players with teams. I created my profile as a goaltender, specifically stating that I was looking for floor hockey, and didn't want to be on skates. Within a week I had a hit from a team in the western suburb of Carol Stream that needed a goalie for a Tuesday night league. The league was technically co-ed, and the captain was a woman. She explained that the puck was a hollow plastic ball, and the sport was better known as "ball hockey." Then, I got another offer from a team that played on Friday evenings in the south suburbs.

I wasn't sure what night I'd be playing, so when Jack was getting ready for the third year of NOTLD, I declined to do the show. Jack had lost his Harry Cooper to, of all things, hockey, or as Jack called it with his East Coast accent, "hawkey."

I informed him that I couldn't be in the show because there was a chance I'd be playing hockey on Friday's. He looked at me a bit in shock...

"Are you telling me you don't want to be in the show because you're...playing hawkey?"

"Yep. I've been wanting to get back into playing for a while now. I've got a chance to play, and if it winds up being on Fridays, I won't be able to commit to the show."

"Okay, if that's what you really want to do."

He tried to be supportive, but I could tell he was not pleased. He was probably even less pleased when I came in on a Friday night to see the show a few weeks into the run due to finally settling on Tuesday over the Friday league.

Once again, Jack had that shocked look on his face when I walked into the box office to buy my ticket.

"I thought you were playing…hawkey."

I explained to him that, as it turned out, I wound up not playing on Fridays after all.

"Okay, well, enjoy the show," he said somewhat sarcastically.

He tried to hide his discontentment, but Jack was never good at hiding anger or even mild discontentment.

I did enjoy the show, well, except for the performance of the guy who stepped in to play the role of Harry Cooper. The late Thom Dickens was a mainstay at The Riverfront and one of the original members. I always had the utmost respect for him as a great actor. His ability to improvise if he forgot his lines (which started happening more often) was unmatched. But, in all objectivity, his performance as Harry was subpar, especially the singing.

Harry had a great song that ended the first act. It was a poignant and unexpected exclamation point on Act I, which showed Harry's vulnerability and humanness. Singing was not Thom's strength, so the song sort of quivered and sputtered us into the intermission instead.

His performance triggered some mixed feelings. On the one hand, I felt bad because it confirmed that Jack was likely not thrilled with me because my decision forced him to settle for Thom and that the performance was lacking in spots. On the other hand, I felt that after taking a break, I would likely rejoin the show. In time, I figured I'd get my appetite back for doing more theater. But…it wasn't to be.

On September 12, 2012, the world lost Jack Schultz. I believe he died suddenly of a heart attack. One of the things Jack and I had in common was our love for New Orleans. His family honored his love of the city with a traditional New Orleans-style "jazz funeral." Friends, fellow theater performers, patrons, and family, made up a procession that marched its way through the streets of Aurora with musical accompaniment, from the funeral home to the cemetery, and ending at The Riverfront Playhouse.

I wasn't able to attend the procession, but I made it to The Riverfront gathering. It seemed every person who ever set foot in that playhouse since its inception in 1978 was there to send Jack off. It was a memorable event with people getting up, reminiscing, and sharing numerous stories about Jack. To date, NOTLD has not been done by The Riverfront and seems to have been laid to rest with Jack.

I continued to do local theater, although my appearances became few and far between as hockey took over as my new passion. I'd like to tell you that my transition to playing hockey was a smooth one, but it was anything but. My very first game in the Tuesday league stunned me and showed that I was ill-prepared to play at that level. I don't remember the score, but we got killed. Maybe it's because of being one of the last remaining co-ed teams in the league. Or maybe I just sucked!

Games were played in a grade school gym and the league played two grueling 25-minute periods, not to mention it was summer, so it got hot in that tiny gym. Because of the size of the court, I also took a lot more shots than I would have on a normal-sized playing surface. Not only was I physically in no shape to play, but my antiquated equipment was also a problem and resulted in some colorful bruises. My street hockey glove was too thin and left my hand stinging in pain when I did get it in front of the 70 to 80-mph slapshots some of these guys could deliver. Finally, my Mylec street hockey pads were plastic-covered, which meant after making a pad save, there was no telling where the rebound was going, and often wound up going all the way to midcourt.

I thought I was going to keel over and die by the end of the game. I promptly told team captain Carolyn, "I can't do this. If I die playing hockey, my wife will kill me!" I fully expected her response to be "That's okay. Well, thanks for coming out and giving it a shot." but she totally surprised me and said: "You'll be fine. Just keep showing up and playing, you'll get it back. You made some good saves out there."

Then she gave me the most important encouragement to keep playing, "The guys we played against tonight are some of the most talented players in this entire area."

I thought she was blowing a bit of smoke up my ass to make me feel better, but as it turned out, she was not exaggerating. As I continued to show up every week and play, I learned that there was a group of 40 or 50 guys who had been playing together for some time. They truly were some of the most talented ball hockey players in the area. For some of them, that "area" might even include the entire Midwest. Both teams continued to kick our asses for the remainder of the season, but my play did continue to improve. I found the nearest Play It Again Sports store and upgraded my equipment.

To make the mountain I had before me even more treacherous, I found out that I was also facing top-tier goaltending. One of those goaltenders was Eric Geraghty. Eric started a more informal "club" (as opposed to an organized league) on Sunday mornings in the western suburb of Woodridge at an outdoor rink. He named the club Hockey Monsters. Out of the blue, he asked me if I wanted to play. I know one of the reasons was that the club was still relatively small and had a shortage of goaltenders. At the time, he and Greg Frer, the guy I played my first "beat-down" .... ah...game against in Carol Stream, were the only goalies. So, I think the invitation was more out of necessity than anything, but I also think Eric saw potential in me that hadn't been realized yet.

If you recall, I never got formal training on how to play the position and approached goaltending much like I approached music and acting— by instinct and natural ability. I became Eric and Greg's "project." They were going to turn me into a "quality goaltender" or at least a serviceable one.

So, in order to spare you the story of my development as a goalie, fast-forward to 12 years later. I wound up taking over the team when Captain Carolyn and her husband decided to have a family. As the new manager of the team, the first order of business was to change the team's name! We became The Killer Bees (made sense considering the team color was yellow). My nephew Gary, now an international business owner with a graphic artist background, designed our logo. We went on to win several championships.

Since getting killed in that first game, I've had my share of achievements. But my greatest accomplishment in the sport to date is merely to be able to show up and be on the same courts with some of the most skilled, talented, hockey players I've ever known. Just because we're not on skates, it doesn't diminish the intensity of the sport, nor the skill level of the athletes playing it. As it turned out, there is a whole ball hockey world out there. The National Ball Hockey League continues growing in Canada as well as the USA.

Please don't misunderstand my point about these endeavors I've shared. I don't mean to brag, especially where hockey is concerned. In comparison to most of the talent I'm up against, I'm adequate, and that's on a good day. My point is simply that since my recovery began, all my childhood dreams and desires have been realized in one form or another.

Reinvesting in my dreams and aspirations became an important part of my recovery, my emotional health, and my well-being. I'm certain that none of the cool experiences I shared in this book would have been possible if it wasn't for staying clean and maintaining my recovery. I believe that one of the essential keys to recovery is eventually replacing chemical highs and the related lifestyle with real, natural highs. Your "highs" don't have to be like mine. They could be cooking, knitting, gardening, or swimming—it doesn't matter. It could be things you bring back into your life, or new things that you never did before.

My adolescent client's question from years ago comes to mind: *How else could you see your friend's head melt?* My answer was spot-on: *"Why do you need to see your friend's head melt?"*

Well, now I have a more complete answer: You need to see your friend's head melt when you haven't created enough natural life adventures, and "highs," and brought enough magic into your life through natural means and your consistent efforts. Only then does it become important to see your friend's head melt.

As my life continued to blossom, the future held more blessings, successes, gifts, and rewards—though rarely in a material sense.

The most rewarding of these gave me a sense of coming "full circle" on my journey from addiction to recovery. Two of these experiences were related to me being asked to be the lead speaker at a meeting. Yes, I had been the lead speaker at many meetings, but these two stood out and were very special to me.

In 1994, I was asked to give a lead at my old Methadone clinic, which now also housed Intervention's outpatient treatment program. I was hit with a flood of memories as I walked through the door and down the hall for the first time in nine years. As I passed the office once occupied by my counselor Jason, I heard his famous words of wisdom echoing in my mind: *"Steve, it's hard to contemplate hunger on a full stomach."* as he tried to get me to slow down my detox off Methadone. I remember being hardheaded and insisting I was ready.

From there, I walked to the back of the clinic where the meeting was being held. I sat at a table next to the chairperson, facing the people attending the meeting and the window, now steel-gated after hours, that I stood in line at, and drank my daily dose of Methadone. I couldn't help but flashback to downing the awful-tasting orange liquid that would relieve the discomfort of withdrawal and get me "right with the world" again.

As I started my talk, I pulled my ID from my pocket, from when I was a patient at the clinic and passed it around. All were able to see the face of who I once was: skinny, and drawn, my pallor complexion, with red blemishes covering my cheeks caused by the toxins I put into my body daily. Then there were those damn sunglasses that were always too big for my face. I sat there now weighing 45 additional pounds, my skin glowing and healthy, and my eyes and mind clear—no longer needing the orange liquid to feel a sense of well-being. I gave an inspired talk that was full of hope that they too could recover!

After the meeting, many of them came to me and thanked me. "That was a great lead! We've had good speakers at this meeting before, but you're the first person that's ever been in our shoes and knows what it's like to stand at that window every day." I felt honored and heard God's voice in the back of my mind: *See how far I have taken you?* All I can say is, I never thought a day like that was possible for me. It's one of those rare moments when you become fully aware of what a miracle you are. There's no price you can put on it.

Then, years later, in 2003, I celebrated 16 years clean. Willie asked me to give a lead at Kedzie House where he had been chairing a meeting for some time. From the moment I walked in the door to "relate in" at the front desk, to the moment I took my seat in the rear of the dining room, the memories came flooding back. I of course peeked into the laundry room before taking my seat to see if it was still there. It wasn't, but for a second, I thought I may have heard the faint echo of The Oreos rehearsing some acapella doo-wop in there. My mural was gone, and the room had been remodeled. It made me a little sad at first, but I remembered what the program had taught me 16 years ago: *There's nothing constant but change*. The mural had served its purpose for me.

I studied all the new faces, some with hope in their eyes as if waiting for some magic I brought with me that would save them. Other faces reflected hopelessness, sadness, anger, and remorse. I glanced over at Willie, then back at the residents and I remember thinking; *Those were our faces at one time* as a wave of gratitude came over me.

I don't remember exactly what I said that night except for one thing...I remember saying to them that I loved coming to Kedzie House now more than ever ... because... I could leave! I got a big laugh for that one.

My basic message to them was based on the wisdom I had acquired from my treatment and getting caught up in "the treatment game." I encouraged them not to fear treatment or being honest, but instead, fear what will happen after treatment if they don't get honest and change.

At the end of the meeting, we made them laugh even more as Willie recalled some of our antics, trials, and tribulations—some of which occurred in that very room. It was the room that I danced in for the first time in my adult life. You could see some of the gloom disappear from many of their faces.

Then, Willie informed me that he had a surprise for me, and he pulled from his pocket a piece of pewter that was worth much more than 100 times its weight in gold. He presented me with a 16-year medallion that he ordered specially for me. The entire dining room burst into applause. It brought back warm memories of my treatment families and past applause in that room, from our efforts to support and encourage each other. I left with a prayer whispering through my mind that I had reached some of them and made a difference.

Yet another full-circle blessing was being able to reconnect with my brother-in-law and early mentor, Gerhardt. He had moved back to Herbster, Wisconsin, from Texas, which allowed my niece and nephews (Gary, Amy, and Jamie) to reestablish a relationship with him, though not without some serious reservations from oldest son Gary, who probably had the worst emotional wounds from his father's alcoholism. I was able to re-establish a connection not only with him but with the entire area, including others like Elma, Iva, and Louie—all of whom were also now permanent residents after retiring from Texas.

My niece Amy helped Gerhardt buy a house on 30 acres of beautiful land. We spent many Fourth of July and other summer get-togethers there with family, pets, and friends. Gerhardt was finally placed on the right medication to deal with PTSD from his Vietnam experiences, and we got to see, some of the old Gerhardt come back to us. I was able to express my gratitude to him for his efforts to save me from self-destruction and share with him how those efforts helped me survive my addiction. Our conversations, watching him interact with family (including grandchildren), watching him on his riding mower, tending his garden, and petting his dog "Suzy" (a little shot at my sister?) —all warmed my heart and made me grateful for the gift of our reunion.

Unfortunately, one thing he couldn't get back was his physical health, which we watched deteriorate over the next several years. All that hard living, combined with alcohol and drug abuse, had taken its toll and finally caught up with him. He died of congestive heart failure in 2019. I wrote a eulogy for him that I read at his services. Here are some of the highlights from it …

<u>Testimony to One of My Heroes: Gerhardt Glass by Steve Fiorito</u>

On April 11th, 2019, I hobbled down the stairs and poured a cup of coffee as I do every morning. I was hobbling from the injury that, so far, had kept me from doing one of the things I love to do the most in life – play hockey. I'm a goaltender, and I've been playing in earnest again since 2010. I'm one of the oldest guys in the leagues I play in but have managed to win five or six championships in that time. I've been sidelined for just over a month with a lower back injury. As I wandered into the den where I keep some of my equipment, I looked at my bag on the floor and wondered if I may have played my last game. Just then, my phone alerted me that I had a text message. The text was from my sister Sue, letting me know that "Gerhardt passed away last night." As tears filled my eyes, the irony of the previous moments before receiving the message did not escape me, and I immediately flashed back to a day in 1975. At that time, I was a troubled teen who my parents had lost control of. My sister Sue and Gerhardt had agreed to take me in, in an attempt to "right the ship."

I told the story that you read earlier in this book—of Gerhardt and my sister taking me in and signing me up for hockey. Gary was my first mentor in life, and that was just one example of many of how he tried to instill in me the things I'd need to be a productive person. But his greatest gift to me was his child spirit! He never lost it, right to the end of his life.

Matthew 18:3 *Verily I say unto you, except ye be converted and become as little children, ye shall not enter the Kingdom of Heaven.*

I went on to give some examples of the things he did that kept the child in him alive and his diehard love of Chicago sports teams.

Not only did the seeds he planted in me finally take root and grow, but before he passed away, he got to see the results. What a great gift from God to both of us.

Next came one of the most unlikely full-circle events of all. I reconnected with my first love and high school sweetheart, Carol. I don't remember the details, but one of us saw the other's profile on the website Classmates.com. Reconnecting with her brought up a plethora of mixed bittersweet emotions and old wounds that were buried deeply. Though it brought back some old pain, I was glad to be able to communicate with her again and recognized that it was a rare opportunity for healing. We exchanged email addresses and began writing.

We dropped our initial bombshells on each other, mine being that I was clean and sober for over 16 years, and hers being that she was an officer in the U.S. Air Force! I admit that I had difficulty picturing that cute little blonde flying jet aircraft through the skies, as I'm sure she did imagining me being clean and sober for one day, let alone 16 years.

In the conversations that followed, she told me she still had family in the area—all of whom she still had strong relationships with. She was trying to get them to move to Georgia, where she now lived. She also confided that she was in the middle of a divorce. She said she'd be in the area later that month, so we set up a meeting, ironically, on her birthday. I explained to my wife that I thought it would be a good thing to do, and Shelley, knowing the story, agreed and gave her blessing.

We met for dinner at Goose Island, a local brewery in Chicago that served food. After getting over the initial shock that she was sitting right across from me, we began to share our stories and review our lives after we broke up. I admitted that my heart was broken and that my addiction escalated after our breakup, but I was careful not to blame her or make her feel responsible. I explained that the real problem was me. She put her hand on my arm as her eyes welled with tears. "I had no idea that it hurt you that badly. I'm so sorry."

I confessed that after getting clean, I discovered that part of my pain was related to my ego and that as my life deteriorated and I imagined her life progressing, my pride was hurt almost as badly as my heart was.

Now it was her turn, and she wasted no time clearing up some major misconceptions I had by dropping a few more bombshells and confessions of her own.

"Well, I didn't do so well after we broke up either. I developed a bit of a drug problem myself. My thing was speed and alcohol. It's one of the reasons I joined the military. That was my treatment, and thank God, it worked."

Then, the real shocker…

"I missed you too, and I thought about you a lot. No one made me feel loved quite the way you did."

I almost fell out of my chair, but I maintained my composure and just took it all in. I was shocked as I came to the realization that I had it all wrong about her.

Then we talked about her marriage, and she described how they met and how his neglect and lack of attention soon set in. She said that the pursuit of their military careers was partially to blame, and I can't recall for sure, but his drinking may have also contributed.

When the meal was over, I picked up the check as part of her birthday present. I also bought her a gift, but I can't remember what it was. I do remember that there were flowers and a small decorative handmade box. After she opened it, I joked that there were two tickets to see Led Zeppelin hidden in there. We both laughed. She brought me a gift too, Italian "worry beads," a necklace made of big, hand-crafted, wooden beads. We walked out the door, I drove her back to her sister's, and we hugged and said our goodbyes at the door. I told her how good it was to see her, and that was it—mission accomplished.

Meeting with Carol face-to-face was very healing and brought about more "closure" than I could have ever imagined. Part of that closure was an important realization: When we're emotionally wounded and in a state of extremely low self-esteem, our distortions and assumptions tend to conjure up scenarios that don't really exist, making us feel even worse. All the hurtful things I thought to be true were just figments of an imagination driven by low self-esteem, guilt, and other unrelated failures in my life. We still keep in touch via email and wish each other happy birthday every year. I hung the "worry beads" from the rearview mirror in my truck, where they remain to this day.

So, I was able to have closure and make peace with two of the three things that I refer to as "The Traumatic Trifecta." Unfortunately, to date, I have not been in contact with Jim or Jeff Decino. I did make some half-assed attempts to find them and noted that neither have obituaries online nor are they on any typical social media sites. Years ago, rumor had it that they had become priests or were heavily involved in some role related to their Christian faith. The fact that both are nowhere to be found supports the possibility that, at the very least, they are on some type of unusual path. Maybe they're CIA operatives or Monks. If I'm being honest, part of me is more than okay with never speaking to them again in this life, while another part of me wants to see the shock on their faces (or at least hear the shock in their voices) when they discover how things have turned out for me.

I have little tolerance for people who call themselves "Christians" but who never made one attempt to reach out for their friend who, to the best of their knowledge, was self-destructing. Maybe they were some of the people who prayed for me.

Next, one of my biggest full-circle moments happened in 2003 when I was hired by Gateway as an assistant director of their Sheridan Program. The program occupied an entire prison designed specifically to treat about 1,000 male inmates with histories of substance abuse.

Seeing the plaque on my door that read, "Steve Fiorito, Gateway Assistant Director," I couldn't help but flashback to sitting on the prospect chair, slightly buzzed from downing a pint of Peppermint Schnapps, as I descended into opioid withdrawal 18 years earlier. I was a mere "possibility" back then, and now, that possibility had been all but fully realized. I was again reminded of God's miraculous power.

Unfortunately (or fortunately, depending on how you look at it), my stint as assistant director at Sheridan was relatively short-lived. I would discover the many barriers and challenges of delivering quality treatment services in a prison setting.

Shelley and I had grown tired of working for agencies that we considered to be dysfunctional and that weren't delivering quality treatment. This would become the catalyst and part of the "blessing in disguise" that would lead to us opening our own agency. After getting licensed by the Department of Human Services, and a false start or two, we finally opened the agency we currently operate at the time of this writing. We've always referred to it as "God's program," not ours. There are perks that come with owning an agency, but we haven't had a full nine-day vacation since we opened and have had to settle mostly for long weekends.

Our agency had its grand opening on May 14, 2005. I wouldn't realize the significance of that date for years. May 14, 1978, was the day my friend Warren overdosed and died. I view the symbolic date as a nod of approval from above, just as I had with my clean date being February 2nd. The date Ricky ended his life was, in essence, the date mine began again.

I always thought I was Ricky's guardian angel, but maybe it's the other way around, and he is mine. Have you met my sister Alice, Ricky? I didn't realize the significance of that date until Beth and I went to visit his grave one Sunday just before our relationship ended. As we stood in prayerful silence, the realization about the date hit me, and the remaining grief was free to find its way to the surface. I began to sob while my words echoed through the still silence of the cemetery: "We used to watch cartoons together. I'm so sorry I couldn't be there for you!"

Beth held me as I continued to cry until all the remaining grief, guilt, and remorse were finally released. As we walked back to the car, an inexplicable sense of peace came over me and a feeling of being forgiven.

I've had to do a lot of forgiving myself as an essential part of my recovery. I could have been swallowed up by the guilt and "what ifs." *What if I hadn't ripped Ricky off? What if I'd been available for him during his time of need? Would he still be alive today?"*

That's just a few of many "what ifs". The list is long, but I chose recovery, and in doing so, I had to find a way to forgive myself and heal the guilt and shame from the past. It's part of my responsibility to make peace with my past so that I can be available for the present.

Last on the list of full-circle events involved my experience with Blue Man Group. When they opened in Chicago at the Briar Street Theater in 1997, I remember the joy of taking friends and family to share that experience with. I was very proud to have seen the original performances in New York.

While at one of their shows in 2006, I started up a conversation through one of the "tubes" hanging in the lobby. The crew member I spoke to, happened to be a bit higher up the food chain in the Blue Man hierarchy, and when I told him about my history with the show, he was fascinated and impressed with my recovery, and that I was a counselor who owned my own agency. I explained how I wanted all recovering people to experience the natural high that I did. He asked if I had any proof that I had seen the original show at the La MaMa. I did, and I told him about the program I still had that was printed on one sheet of 8.5 by 11 paper. He said if I gave him a copy of the original program, he would give me 10 tickets so I could bring my clients to see the show.

This would be the beginning of a long relationship with the show, and we would get 10 tickets, twice per year, to bring our clients to see it. As I had "foreshadowed" after experiencing my first show, I got to witness many of our client's natural highs while seeing the show.

For today, I still try to live my life by The Serenity Prayer...

God, grant me the serenity to accept the things I cannot change,
the courage to change the things I can,
and the wisdom to know the difference.

I've learned that the humility that one experiences from applying The Serenity Prayer to daily life makes everything "right sized." This resulted in a more realistic view of myself and the world, which, in turn, led to me having more realistic expectations of myself, others, and situations in life. When things are "right sized", we're better able to handle them.

I have some simple rules I live my life by today, the first being, "No one is allowed to make me miserable," especially within the walls of my home. If you consistently make me miserable, I'm showing you the door, and I don't care whose blood you have coursing through your veins. I've worked too hard to be successful and happy to allow anyone to sabotage it with their personal bullshit.

Coming back from the depths of Hell was God's gift, but I was required to do the footwork, which was no easy task. Some view this rule as me being selfish and cold. They're entitled to their opinion, but I call it being emotionally healthy and having good boundaries. It's normal that people have occasional discourse and disagreement. I accept and even welcome it at times, but when you cross that line on a regular basis, it's time to part ways. Like my counselor Ron Orlando once said to me, "*If my mother got in the way of my recovery, I'd cut her loose.*" I completely understand what he meant now.

I have little tolerance for attitudes of "entitlement." No one owes us anything, or as we used to say in treatment: *You got nothing coming.* We alone are responsible for our lives and our happiness. Taking *personal responsibility* is the key to our happiness and success. I have little tolerance for excuse makers or the blame game: "My life sucks because of what you did to me (or didn't do for me)!" I understand the effects of traumatic events in life, especially those maliciously inflicted by others. I empathize with people who have been victimized (whether real or perceived) however, we are still ultimately responsible for our own healing. No one else can do it but us.

Unfortunately, this wound up being the case with my daughter Melissa. As a teen, Melissa was a female version of me, only without the substance abuse. I had very little patience for her "My life sucks because of what you did to me (or didn't do for me)!" attitude. We tried to go to counseling, but it didn't work out. I never said I didn't want her in my life, though. She made that decision, and except for a few appearances at family get-togethers, it remained that way for years.

I realized that it wasn't really about any incident that may have occurred between us. The issues with Melissa run deeper, and most have nothing to do with me. Melissa has problems with all her relationships. She needs therapy to get more emotionally and spiritually healthy, but I have no control over that. I recognized that I couldn't help her, and I stopped trying to "put a square peg in a round hole" years ago. For me, any hurt and anger that may have once been there is gone, and I completely accept that this is just who she is, and her life choices led her away from mine.

Recently, she has tried to reconnect, and I am hopeful that we can salvage a relationship. We can't get back the time we lost, but I hope that we can start from today to heal and have a new relationship. I've never stopped loving her.

While writing this book, I got in touch with and was able to relive a lot of memories that were buried and forgotten. One of these was how special and almost magical mine and Franko's adventure in Northern California was. I decided to try to connect on Facebook with our bandmate from 1982, Miles. Unfortunately, I couldn't remember his last name. I had no luck searching, so I prayed and asked God for help. Immediately after that, on a whim, I put these words into a Google search: Miles/Sculptor/Soapstone/Northern Ca. Boom, there he was, a bit down the page, Miles Metzger!

It turned out that Miles had become a very successful artist and sculptor. One of his sculptures, called "Guardians at the Gate," is at

Fisherman's Wharf in San Francisco. It had become the most photographed sculpture in the USA. I was so excited to have found him. I immediately went to his Facebook page and shot him this note on Facebook Messenger…

"Hi Miles,
I'm sure you wouldn't remember me by name, but you may if I remind you of how I know you. We played music together in a band in Moke Hill and the surrounding area around 1982 called Dusty Rhodes and the Rainbow Boogie Band! I'm currently writing my story (mostly about recovery from heroin/cocaine addiction. Clean for over 30 years), and I'm writing about mine and my friend Frank's adventures in that area at that time. Frank unfortunately didn't make it and passed away in 1998. Do you know what happened to Dusty? I went back in 1994 and stayed at the Leger and ran into Ron and Catfish Bob! So happy that you have had continued success with your art. It was such a fluke that I found you on the Internet. I couldn't remember your last name, so I just searched: Miles/Sculptor/Soapstone/Northern Ca. and I saw one sentence with your last name in it! I will try to scan and post the only photos I have with you in it at a gig we did. I will send you a copy of the book when it's complete (may be a while yet). That part of my life was a small but important part of my story. Hopefully, the story will inspire others trapped in addiction to find a way out. You and the others from Moke Hill may not realize it, but the good times we had played a role in saving my life. Drop a quick response and let me know how it's going.
… Steve"

    I excitedly awaited his reply.

    Finding Miles was like finding "a needle in a haystack." But it occurred to me after I got off his Facebook page that there had been no recent activity on it. I went back and checked again, which confirmed that the last post was several years ago. Then, a sinking feeling came over me, and I Googled "Miles Metzger Obituary," and there it was. Miles passed away several years before, in 2013, at the age of just 63. This made me very sad due to how young he was and the letdown I experienced after being so excited at the prospect of reconnecting with an important part of my past. Being age 62 at the time, the sad news about Miles also got me in touch with my own mortality.

    Our time seems long when we're young, but as we get older, every tick of the clock brings us closer to that inevitable day. Since I started this story with lyrics from Pink Floyd's *The Dark Side of the Moon* LP, it's only fitting that I should end this way…

Tired of lying in the sunshine, staying home to watch the rain.
You are young, and life is long, and there is time to kill today.
And then one day you find, ten years have got behind you.
No one told you when to run, you missed the starting gun.

More like 30 years have got behind you!

Every year is getting shorter, never seem to find the time.
Plans that either come to naught, or half a page of scribbled lines.
Hanging on in quiet desperation is the English way,
The time is gone, the song is over, thought I'd something more to say.

      When I come to my last twenty-four hours on the planet, after I take my last breath, I hope that I will have been worthy of God's saving grace and the divine intervention I received that day in 1984. I hope I hear the words that all God-fearing Christians want to hear…

Well done, thou good and faithful servant. "Enter into the joy of thy Lord."
These words are for many people, including those we would too easily pass by.
There are many quiet followers who serve God unobtrusively and faithfully,
who bear their crosses bravely and put a smiling face to the world. "Enter into
the joy of thy Lord." Pass into that fuller spiritual life, which is a life of joy and
peace. - Twenty-Four Hours a Day, November 17

And remember…

"There is no dark side in the moon really.
Matter of fact, it's all dark."

Thump thump, thump thump, *thump thump, thump thump, thump thump, thump thump, thump thump …*

Book Club Discussion Questions

1. Out of Steve's early "addictions" to Sugar, Play, and Laughter, which do you think was the worst and why? What could have/should have been done differently about them?

2. What other things in Steve's early childhood may have contributed to his becoming addicted. Were there things that also may have prevented it?

3. What are your recommendations for ways that Steve could have dealt with "The Traumatic Trifecta" without turning to drugs?

4. Almost all addicts have enablers that unwittingly support their addiction and enable it to continue. Who were Steve's enablers? What was their impact? Who were the people that did not enable his addiction? What was their impact?

5. What are 3 typical characteristics of addicts that aren't directly related to their substance abuse? How could they sabotage recovery efforts if not eliminated or reduced significantly?

6. What were the 3 most important aspects of Steve's treatment at Gateway that you feel had the most beneficial impact on him?

7. Medication Assisted Therapy (Methadone, Suboxone, etc.) is used frequently today to treat opioid addiction. What do you feel are the pros and cons of using this approach?

8. In your opinion, what made the "Open Report" exercise in Grant Hospital so effective and such a big turning point in Steve's recovery?

9. In your opinion, what are 4 of the most important ingredients in being successful at recovering from addiction?

10. On the day that Steve was fired from his first job and wanted to use but instead went to the Desplaines Alano Club, what was the most important thing he did that day that saved his life? Was there anything else that happened before that day that may have helped him?

11. What were some subtle things, not directly related to recovery, that were important to Steve's success. How did they contribute to it?

www.ingramcontent.com/pod-product-compliance
Lightning Source LLC
Chambersburg PA
CBHW052006070526
44584CB00016B/1637